The Household Cavalry at War

The Story of the Second
Household Cavalry Regiment

Roden Orde

With Illustrations By Eric Meade-King

Pen & Sword
MILITARY

First published in 1953 by Gale & Polden Ltd
This edition published in Great Britain in 2023 by
Pen & Sword Military
An imprint of
Pen & Sword Books Ltd
Yorkshire – Philadelphia

Copyright © The Household Cavalry Foundation, 2023

ISBN 978 1 39907 335 6

Typeset by Mac Style
Printed in the UK by CPI Group (UK) Ltd, Croydon, CR0 4YY.

Pen & Sword Books Limited incorporates the imprints of Atlas,
Archaeology, Aviation, Discovery, Family History, Fiction, History,
Maritime, Military, Military Classics, Politics, Select, Transport,
True Crime, Air World, Frontline Publishing, Leo Cooper,
Remember When, Seaforth Publishing, The Praetorian Press,
Wharncliffe Local History, Wharncliffe Transport, Wharncliffe
True Crime and White Owl.

For a complete list of Pen & Sword titles please contact

PEN & SWORD BOOKS LIMITED
47 Church Street, Barnsley, South Yorkshire, S70 2AS, England
E-mail: enquiries@pen-and-sword.co.uk
Website: www.pen-and-sword.co.uk

Or

PEN AND SWORD BOOKS
1950 Lawrence Rd, Havertown, PA 19083, USA
E-mail: Uspen-and-sword@casematepublishers.com
Website: www.penandswordbooks.com

Dedicated to our Comrades
who gave the lives for their
King and Country

Contents

APPENDICES

List of Illustrations

List of Maps

Foreword
To the First Edition, 1953

by
Lieutenant-General Sir Brian Horrocks,
KCB, KBE, DSO, MC

I am delighted to have this opportunity of paying a tribute to the 2nd Household Cavalry Regiment, and I can say unreservedly that there was no other Regiment in the British Army which I got to know so well, or for which I had a greater regard. An Armoured Car Regiment occupies an especial position in a Corps because there is (or at least there should be) the closest possible link between it and the Corps Commander. It follows, therefore, that Squadron and even Troop Commanders are often far more in the picture of the general situation on the Corps front than are even Brigade Commanders in Infantry or Armoured Divisions. During mobile operations the Corps Commander is always seeking for information on which to base his plans, and this flows in from two directions, the air and the ground—the two are complementary, and it is the duty of the armoured cars probing on a wide front, or on an exposed flank, to provide the latter. It would not be an exaggeration to say that the whole Corps plan can be influenced by the action of a single Troop of armoured cars.

The 2nd Household Cavalry Regiment first came under my command at the end of August, 1944—a fortunate moment for us both, because 30 Corps had just broken out of the bridgehead over the Seine and was about to set out on that long advance which ended in the bitter and confused fighting at Arnhem. At long last, after months of frustration in the bocage country, mobile operations were about to start and the armoured cars were to get their chance. I have always counted myself a lucky man that during this historic thrust across the Somme into Belgium, our advance was preceded by two such fine Armoured Car

Regiments as the 2nd Household Cavalry Regiment on the right and the Inns of Court on the left.

This was the moment for which the Household Cavalry had been waiting, and the results of many months of hard training in the United Kingdom were about to bear fruit. That the Regiment was very successful nobody is likely to deny, and this was due primarily to one basic cause— their high standard of training. While others might complain that they were out of touch with their leading cars, I do not remember a single occasion when the wireless communications of the Regiment failed, even when faced with the enormous distances over which the Troops had to operate during the fighting in the Ardennes. From dawn to dusk there was a steady stream of information pouring into my Headquarters.

In a foreword like this it is quite impossible to do justice to their many exploits; I can only take some examples to show the spirit which animated the whole Regiment.

It is probable that the battle honours most prized by the 2nd Household Cavalry Regiment are "Faith", "Hope" and "Charity", the code names given to the three Somme bridges which they captured so successfully on the 31st August 1944. We had definite information that the Germans were striving to establish defences on the line of the river and it was imperative to take every possible risk in the hope of being able to seize the Somme bridges before the Germans had time to organize their defensive arrangements in detail. The orders to advance were only received by the Squadrons at 0100 hours, when they were settling down to a well-earned night's rest. The ensuing advance must have been a nightmare; the men were already tired before they started, it was pouring with rain, and the roads were blocked by every form of traffic, including German tanks.

Nevertheless, the leading Troops, commanded by Groeninx van Zoelen, Buchanan-Jardine and Hanbury on the right and Peake on the left, pushed on relentlessly and the seemingly impossible was achieved—the bridges were all captured intact. But what was even more important, having enlisted and armed members of the French Resistance Movement whom they collected on the spot, the Regiment succeeded in holding these bridges for four hours until the Grenadiers arrived—a most memorable night's work which could only have been achieved by well-trained, determined men whose morale was high.

Another stirring example of the same sort was the capture of the bridge at Louvain by Lieutenant Hanbury's Troop. Corporal-of-Horse Thompson gave a remarkable exhibition of initiative and bravery when he found an alternative way across the Dyle river, although this entailed getting out of his car and bridging the gap in the road with broken-down doors under intense small-arms fire.

Both these examples show that the Regiment were always ready to fight in order to attain their objective, and this was one of the reasons why they were so successful in obtaining information. Not even their worst enemies could say that the Household Cavalry lacked the offensive spirit.

As an example of initiative in obtaining information which had a vital effect on the Corps plan, it would be difficult to beat the action of Lieutenant Creswell's Troop when approaching the Meuse—Escaut canal. Creswell had been ordered to carry out a reconnaissance of the one remaining bridge over this canal and had successfully worked his way round behind the German lines in order to do so, but he was still some way from his objective. Realizing that it would be impossible to go farther without being observed by the Germans, he left his cars hidden in a wood while he and his Corporal-of-Horse, Cutler, set off on bicycles. After numerous adventures they succeeded in getting on to the flat roof of a factory from where they could study at their leisure all the defensive arrangements which the Germans had made for the protection of this vital bridge, which was their only remaining escape route. Thanks entirely to the accurate information supplied by Creswell, the Irish Guards were subsequently able to put in a surprise attack and to capture the bridge intact in spite of the elaborate defences with which it was surrounded.

I realize that this foreword is already getting too long, but I cannot possibly conclude without mentioning the epic dash made by Lieutenant Buchanan-Jardine and two scout cars to Valkenswaard in Holland. I had been rash enough to ask the Household Cavalry Regiment whether they could find out the depth of the German defences on the Meuse—Escaut canal. This was a most difficult task, because we were in close contact with the enemy and there was no way round his flanks. The Household Cavalry, however, were not to be defeated. Buchanan-Jardine, to whom this task was allotted, decided that the only possibility of getting through the German positions was to drive down the main road which ran through the centre of their line, trusting to surprise to get him through. It seems incredible now, but this daring manoeuvre succeeded. The two scout cars drove straight through the German line, then sent back valuable reports of the situation in the rear, and subsequently returned the way they had come. In the words of the author, "By the time they got back everything on the outside of the cars was punctured and broken by small-arms fire".

I always consider this to be the most daring reconnaissance that was carried out in the last war. This last episode brings out another quality which is vital for successful armoured car work—i.e., the capacity to think quickly.

Many successful operations were only made possible by the lightning decision of the corporal or corporal-of-horse in the leading scout car—the men who must surely have had the highest life insurance premium of all in the war. It requires strong nerves to be the leading man in the leading car, day after day, always anxiously scanning the hedgerows for that hidden anti-tank gun which must sooner or later be encountered.

I should like to congratulate Major Orde on the great care which he has so obviously taken in the preparation of this history. It is not only factually correct, but he has managed to convey to a remarkable extent the atmosphere of the different battles in which the Regiment took part. I have enjoyed reading this history immensely, not only because it revives memories of a happy partnership between the Household Cavalry Regiment and 30 Corps, but also because it is well that we should be reminded from time to time that present-day soldiers are just as capable of carrying out the most gallant actions as were their forefathers before them.

The men who have made this story possible are now scattered far and wide in civilian life. To all of them I would say: "You certainly did your share, and more than your share, towards any success which we as a Corps may have achieved. Thank you".

B. G. Horrocks
Lt Gen

Foreword
To the Second Edition, 2023

by
Lieutenant-General Sir Barney White-Spunner, KCB, CBE

It is now nearly 80 years since Second Household Cavalry Regiment's (2 HCR's) remarkably successful deployment in North West Europe from landing in France after D Day until the German surrender in May 1945. The regiment was formed specifically for the invasion of Nazi occupied Europe. After the war it was disbanded as Household Cavalrymen returned to their parent regiments. This accurate, complete, and very readable history is therefore the entire story of the regiment – and it is quite a story. Lieutenant General Sir Brian Horrocks, who commanded 30 Corps under whom the regiment served from late August 1944, says in his original foreword that there was no other regiment in the British Army that he knew so well nor for which he had a greater regard. That is high praise and there can be but few regiments who contributed so directly to the operational success of the 21st Army Group.

The regiment's influence on the Household Cavalry after its disbandment has been almost as powerful. There were two reasons for this. First, the organisation of the post war armoured reconnaissance regiments was largely based on the orbats and tactics developed by 2 HCR and their sister armoured car regiments during that campaign in North West Europe. In many ways they still are. Secondly, those of us who served in Windsor in the decades after World War Two got to know the 2 HCR veterans very well. Their experience was particularly relevant to our training, and to our frequent operational deployments, and I can recall many fascinating trips to France with old comrades as they talked us through their war. The vehicles and equipment may change but the principles of reconnaissance are timeless. Some of the best training we could give young officers and NCOs was to put them in a car with a 2 HCR armoured car commander and drive his route from the Normandy Beaches to the Rhine. We also came to know them as old friends and the 2 HCR reunion dinners were a highlight of Windsor life.

General Horrocks picks out several examples of the regiment's operational achievements. One he neglects, because 2 HCR was not under his command at the time but arguably their most important, was the capture of an undefended bridge over the Souleuvre by Lieutenant Dickie Powle's troop on 31st July 1945. Five miles behind the German lines, the bridge was on a German formation boundary. Powle's action allowed the 11th Armoured Division to breakout and to the success of Operation Bluecoat which led to the subsequent German surrender at Falaise. It was a classic example of what resolute armoured reconnaissance can achieve.

2 HCR's story is also one of exceptional personal courage. Day after day, for almost a year, the young officers and NCOs, most of whom were wartime volunteers, led the allied advance in the face of determined German resistance. They demonstrated the bravery, spirit and resourcefulness that is so necessary to successful armoured reconnaissance, prepared to fight for information when they had to but never out of communication with their parent headquarters. Many of them did not come home and we should always remember the 78 who gave their lives and the 142 who were wounded, many seriously. They, and the lucky ones who did come home, still sitting in their crews at dinner in the Combermere mess in the 1990s, are the spirit of the Household Cavalry.

Barney White-Spunner

Introduction

When war broke out in 1939, the Household Cavalry, as befitted their state ceremonial duties, were still horsed. The Composite Regiment (The Life Guards and Royal Horse Guards), eventually to become the 1st Household Cavalry Regiment, sailed for Palestine with the Cavalry Division in February, 1940. They remained mounted (with the exception of one Squadron which had been mechanized some months previously) until March 1941, were then issued at a moment's notice with an assortment of battered trucks, and within a week were taking part in the Iraq and Syrian campaign. The leading part which they played in that important but little publicized theatre of operations, and their subsequent fighting in the Middle East, Italy, and North-West Europe, has been recorded by Colonel the Hon. E. H. Wyndham in "The Story of the 1st Household Cavalry Regiment." The Training Regiment, also composite in character and from which sprang the 2nd Household Cavalry Regiment, did not lose their horses until September 1940. They stood-to during the tense days following the fall of France, prepared to defend the vital reservoirs of Staines and Laleham, then considered German parachutists' objectives, and Langley aerodrome (where the Hawker fighter aircraft were manufactured), armed with their personal weapons and half a dozen old Hotchkiss machine guns without butts! After a period of training as a Motor Battalion, in which role it was known as the 2nd Household Cavalry Motor Battalion, the Regiment was reorganized as an armoured car regiment to become the 2nd Household Cavalry Regiment. It is with their story that we are concerned.

When Colonel Sir Henry Abel Smith first asked—or should I say detailed?—me to write the history of the Regiment, I was both pleased and honoured. The pitfalls awaiting the enthusiastic but amateur military historian were as yet unknown to me, and I looked forward in somewhat over-confident anticipation to the task of recording the doings of those Household Cavalrymen with whom I had served as a war-time soldier. Preliminary researches soon convinced me that there are a bewildering number of approaches to the subject and that history shows nearly every battle to have been fought in a different manner from that intended by those who originally planned it. This disturbing fact, it seems, is an essential condition governing the combat of nations down to the smallest Troop section. An infinite number of uncontrollable forces—for never is man more uncontrollable than in action when it is a matter of life and death—and an infinite number of independent forces influence the outcome of the struggle. These forces are often obscure and difficult to trace once the smoke and noise of battle have abated, even for the trained research worker, which I certainly lay no claim to be.

Sir Ian Hamilton once wrote, "On the actual day of battle naked truths may be picked up for the asking; by the following morning they have begun to get into their uniforms." Like all generalizations, however, these words are but partially true. The Americans, in their enthusiasm, tried the experiment of allowing historians to follow front-line companies into action, only to realize when correlating their documents at a later date that, although one sector of the battle had been under the microscope, it was but a minute part of the whole—the general perspective had shrunk.

Immersed in our problems of survival at the front or routine behind the line, it was all too easy to forget that war consists of the same sort of thing happening over and over again. Each campaign is made up of a series of attacks and retreats. The same situations constantly recur, and before he has covered many pages, the would-be historian realizes to his dismay that his regiment shares a characteristic in common with every other unit in the British Army, inasmuch as it can only do one of three things: (a) advance, (b) withdraw, (c) stay where it is. Faced with the problem of providing variety to his narrative, the desperate writer is tempted to have recourse to certain well-worn dodges. I have tried to avoid the more obvious ones and have borne in mind that I am recording actions and describing scenes primarily for the benefit of members of "2 H.C.R". Whatever the recurrence of situation, there is assuredly no lack of diversity in the deeds and actions of the Regiment and the exploits of individual and collective gallantry speak for themselves.

Although I have drawn plentifully on documents and histories at Corps and Divisional level for the general situation and as an aid to appreciation of our senior commanders' problems and intentions, I have tried to keep the general narrative within the confines of the individual Squadron and its Troops because it was here that the feel of battle was most sensitive. Needless to say, the War Diary has been my bible and mentor throughout—no one could have wished for a better-kept document from which to cull the relevant facts which, if they are not recorded therein, can so easily be lost forever.

An armoured car regiment is not the easiest subject to deal with in an historical sense, if a well-knit story is to result. Being the eyes and ears of the Corps Commander, as we have read in the foreword, it has an enormous battle front (normally Divisional, sometimes Corps) to cover and therefore many times the length of that covered either by the infantry or tank battalion. Patrols are liable to find themselves combing the countryside in search of information at a moment's notice and under a variety of local commands and attachments. Even in Europe, isolated Troop encounters frequently took place separated by a range of anything up to thirty miles—sometimes even more. The fighting in Holland in the autumn of 1944 will make this abundantly clear.

When dealing with the Troop actions, collectively the most important part of the Regiment's history, I have tried, wherever possible, to obtain details of the story from the Troop Leader, his corporal-of-horse, and at least one other soldier, preferably one of the men in the leading scout car. The disclosure of interesting and hitherto unknown facts arising from this method has often been remarkable, not due to any wish on the part of officer or man to make a good "story" out of an episode, for in nearly every case I have had to drag their own part in the battle out of them, but because it is apparent that in the heat of action there may well be different "truths" as seen from different angles—that desideratum, "everyone in the picture," is a counsel of perfection rarely achieved in war. If my conclusions are sometimes at variance with facts, I ask forgiveness of the person concerned and accept full responsibility.

The 2nd Household Cavalry Regiment, campaigning in the van of a victorious army, lacking none of the essentials of war and therefore not suffering from the crippling shortages of manpower and equipment which beset the British troops in Dunkirk days and other theatres of war before "the end of the beginning," were never once involved in that most difficult and heart breaking military operation—a retreat. Apart from the fortnight's fighting in the Normandy Bocage, as tough fighting as any in the war, and the check before Arnhem, their story is one of almost continuous advance – often slow and grinding, at other times exhilarating in its speed, but continuous forward movement, nevertheless. With their long period of intensive training in England—a training which from the early war years was intended to fit them for the eventual assault on Europe—and with their knowledge gathered from other formations who, less fortunate, had had to learn their lesson in the stern school of battle, it followed naturally that the Regiment, with its past traditions to look up to, would give a good account of itself. But it is the manner in which it rose above the demands made upon it which will remain to its eternal credit and serve as an example for future generations of Household Cavalrymen. "I can honestly say," wrote General Sir Richard O'Connor, "that I have never met a unit which so wholeheartedly carries out the spirit of instructions that are given to them. Whether you are chasing the enemy through France and Belgium; watching the line of the Meuse, digging trenches, or acting as infantrymen in defence, you always do it 100 per cent."

★   ★   ★

The illustrations throughout the text are the work of Mr. Eric Meade-King (Corporal "Speed" King to his comrades in the Regiment with whom he served during the war). They are of special interest because, with the exception of one of the colour plates and the line drawings which form the tailpieces to the chapters, they were all executed during operations. Many saw the light of day under adverse circumstances, to say the least of it, and were not drawn with a view to reproduction. They then travelled under the grimy cushion of his three-tonner lorry seat until the cessation of hostilities. The design for the dust jacket [for the first edition] is the same artist's work, and I can hear Trooper Mundy's triumphant shout, "I knew he'd get his beloved horse in somewhere." It is a great relief to feel that the inadequacies of my writing will shelter behind the protective screen of these illustrations, and I am indeed grateful for all his help and co-operation.

The hand of Major A. J. R. Collins will be recognized in many parts of the book. To him also I owe a deep debt of gratitude for his help and advice. He has read the proofs over and over again and, by his suggestions and knowledge of the regimental "picture," saved me from making innumerable blunders and false assumptions. Major Collins's secretary, Miss M. Fairhurst, typed the first draft of the book in her spare time as well as carrying out countless other tasks. I realize the debt I owe to her.

All members of the Regiment will be delighted to see that Lieutenant-General Sir Brian Horrocks has spared the time from his many duties as Black Rod, military correspondent and reviewer for the Sunday Times, and lecturer, to write the foreword. Few commanders can have had greater confidence reposed in them by officers and men alike. We were proud to serve under him.

The references quoted upon the following pages will serve to indicate the number of authorities consulted and how much I am indebted to them for their help.

I have in the first place to thank all those members of the Regiment, both officers and men, who have lent me their private papers and diaries. Also for their photographs, many of which are reproduced herein. Most appreciated has been the help given to me by Corporal-Major J. Oxberry, who, although he did not serve with the 2nd Regiment, checked my lists with painstaking thoroughness.

I also wish to take this opportunity of expressing my obligation to the many outside people who have assisted me. To French, Belgian, and Dutch nationals, especially the town and village Mayors and Burgomasters who responded to requests for information about battle incidents where the local Resistance were involved. Of seventy-two letters written to them, only one remained unanswered. To Colonel T. M. Penney, of the Cabinet Office, for his kindly undertaking to "vet" first drawings and produce fair copies of the maps, and to Mr. R. W. Bliss, of Messrs. Edward Stanford Ltd., for stepping into the breach at short notice and completing the major portion of them when Colonel Penney, through pressure of official work, had to give up the task. To Colonel A. E. Warhurst, also of the Cabinet Office, Army Historian for North-West Europe, who allowed me to pick his brains and occupy much of his time seeking information—his phenomenal memory and accuracy of work are something to which I can only faintly aspire. Should he happen to glance at this book, I hope he will not be too hard on its faults.

Nor must I fail to mention the infinite pains taken by Miss A. M. Durrant and Miss K. M. Forsyth, of Messrs. Vivian of Hereford, in the preparation of the photographic section. The plate of the Brussels Standard is from their coloured photograph done at Combermere Barracks, Windsor.

Lastly, because to me it is by far the most important, the invaluable aid which my wife has given to me throughout, reading and checking every word written, correcting my erratic spelling, and arranging the composite photographs—the last a nightmare of a task. She also designed and drew the first drafts of all the maps.

★   ★   ★

Regimental histories, by reason of their subject matter, are destined to be read chiefly by those who served within the ranks of the unit in question. The story of the 2nd Household Cavalry Regiment is no exception to the rule, and it has been written for those whose life it was for six long and eventful years. It lays no claim to literary merit, but if the verdict is that, within the limits of human fallibility, it is an accurate record of gallant deeds and duty faithfully accomplished, I shall be well pleased.

Seven years have elapsed since the "2 H.C.R." that we knew was disbanded and the Life Guards and Blues returned to their parent Regiments. Once again, in a world starved of pageantry, the British Empire rejoices to see that the Sovereign's escort in full panoply is no longer a rarity and that the Queen's Life Guard at Whitehall is strictly true to its title. It is fitting that this should be so because the Household Cavalry, bodyguard of the reigning monarch, are rightly jealous of the dignities conferred upon them by the Sovereign and yield to none their valued privileges. Ceremonial duties, however, must perforce take their place alongside the stern realities of the age. An uneasy peace broods over the nations. Even at the time of writing these words, Household Cavalry armoured cars across the North Sea stand watch with other British troops in occupied Germany, while behind the Iron Curtain a force as menacing as Hitler's millions darkens the horizon. Should a third and even more frightful conflict burst upon mankind, which God forbid, these Household Cavalrymen will be ready, as were their comrades before them, to rise to this highest plane of merit, confidently upborne in the knowledge that from those who are greatly trusted, great things are due.

R. P. G. Orde
August 1952

Acknowledgments

Grateful acknowledgment is made to the authors and publishers for the quotations taken from *Normandy to the Baltic*, by Field-Marshal the Viscount Montgomery of Alamein, K.G., G.C.B., D.S.O. (Messrs. Hutchinson & Co. (Publishers) Ltd., London); *Eclipse*, by Alan Moorehead (Messrs. Hamish Hamilton Ltd., London); *Our Armoured Forces*, by Lieutenant-General Sir Giffard Le Q. Martel, K.C.B., K.B.E., D.S.O., M.C. (Messrs. Faber & Faber Ltd., London); *Operation Victory*, by Major-General Sir Francis De Guingand, K.B.E., C.B., D.S.O. (Messrs. Hodder & Stoughton Ltd., Publishers, London); to General Sir Miles Dempsey, K.C.B., K.B.E., D.S.O., M.C., for permission to include his orders to the Regiment during the German counter-offensive in the Ardennes and for his letter on the same subject; to General Sir Richard O'Connor, G.C.B., D.S.O., M.C., for similarly permitting me to include his letter to the Regiment when under his command on the line of the River Maas in Holland; to Commander M. G. Saunders, R.N., of the Foreign Documents Section of the Admiralty, for his information about the war appointments of Konteradmiral a.D. Siegfried Engel; and to Major the Hon. F. F. G. Hennessy, M.B.E., for allowing me to quote from his several articles about Guards Armoured Division which appeared in *The Household Brigade Magazine*.

For photographs and details of equipment relating to armoured cars and other vehicles, I am indebted to Mr. J. Rowland-Rouse, of Messrs. Rootes Motors Ltd., to Messrs. Associated Equipment Company of Southall, and the Imperial War Museum. Mr. P. E. Janisch, of the Cinematograph Section of the War Office, kindly arranged for private viewings of countless films of the North-West European campaign in which the Regiment featured.

Finally, to officers, men, and friends of the Regiment, without whose generous backing in the shape of guarantees and subscriptions, the maps, drawings, and photographs could never have been included on such an ample scale. A list of their names appears at the end of the book.

R. P. G. O.
August 1952

Editors' Notes

Roden Orde wrote a wonderful book over 70 years ago, and there was really little that the current editors needed to do to produce this second edition. Thankfully digital publishing has made our task considerably easier, a factor that defeated Roden Orde back in 1970 when he attempted to get the book republished. The original printer's plates had been destroyed and so the cost of republishing had become prohibitive. Roden wrote to many publishers in the late autumn of 1970, however the quotes he obtained for such a large book, with colour plates and pull-out maps, was not commercially viable.

The one compromise we have made was on the maps, which are all here, including those in colour, however those that originally were in a pull-out format have now been reduced to the size of the book. For this reason, we will publish a folder, with the original maps overlaid onto current mapping, which will be available to purchase separately.

Nearly all the original photographs have been reproduced in this second edition, although some of the 'cut and paste' montages have been difficult to replicate without the original images. To compensate, we have added a number of hitherto unseen photographs from the Household Cavalry Archive at Windsor, including images from the long period of training in England prior to deploying to Normandy in July 1944 and also other photographs from the author's personal archive.

Eric Meade-King's drawings and plates are a real gem, as the Windsor Archive reveals, since all of the originals used in the book, and many more, still exist. The two colour pictures from the first edition are here, along with another that has not seen the light of day for many years. His wartime pictures, drawn hurriedly in a sketchpad or painted on the back of wooden ammunition boxes, using army-issue paints, capture moments in time; they are the essence of the war artist's talent. A commercial artist before and after the war, with a similar style to his acquaintance, Lionel Edwards, Eric Meade-King was clearly a 'gentleman cavalryman' if ever there was one, gently chided in a post-war note by Roden Orde for never bothering to apply for a commission. His work, from the pre-war Knightsbridge era to the 1970s, deserves to be seen by a new generation.

This book is a rare example of a regimental history published in the 1950s that sought to tell the whole story of a regiment, and all its ranks, from commanding officer to the most junior trooper. It is not just anecdotal in places, nor is it merely an 'officer's book' like some of those post war films that portray the war as being won on the playing fields of numerous public schools. Winston Churchill was clear on that when he described this book as the finest regimental history ever written. Lieutenant General Sir Brian Horrocks, who wrote the Foreword to the first edition, never changed his view about 2 HCR. In 1978, in a letter to Rupert Buchanan-Jardine MC, former member of the regiment, he wrote:

'I have always felt the 2 HCR were the finest Armoured Cars Regiment that any country produced during the last War. You were extraordinarily well trained by Henry Abel Smith, but your Corporals of Horse in the leading armoured cars and scout cars were magnificent .... When walking down Whitehall I always look at the two Household Cavalry sentries in full dress, on horseback, outside London District H.Q. and I feel like taking my hat off to them, because they belong to the finest and most efficient regiment that served in 30 Corps during the war.'

Acknowledgements

Our thanks go, first and foremost, to the author Roden Orde, whose wartime regimental history has stood the test of time. Roden's first (and late) wife, Cicely, drew the early drafts of the maps, helped with the photos and proof reading, and supported Roden in many other ways during the three years of researching and writing the book. Cicely, formerly married to Captain Adrian Bethell, 2nd Life Guards, was the mother of Lieutenant Tony Bethell who served with Roden in 2 HCR during the war.

Roden's second wife Antonia not only generously gave her permission for the Household Cavalry to republish the book for the benefit of the Household Cavalry but, with their son Gavin, has donated, to the Household Cavalry Museum, Roden's meticulous records including his extensive archive of photographs, papers, letters, his wartime diary, and his library of post-war film in which he followed 2 HCR's advance across NW Europe. They have also been generous in their support for the overall project.

Roger Field, formerly The Blues and Royals and an accomplished author himself, for acting as our literary agent, and steering us through the minefield of modern publishing.

Lieutenant General Sir Barney White-Spunner, formerly The Blues and Royals, for writing the Foreword to the second edition, and emphasising so eloquently why this book remains both interesting and relevant to Household Cavalrymen of the 21st century.

Stanfords, the bookseller and mapmaker, for their permission to reproduce their original hand-drawn maps from the first edition; these detailed maps have also stood the test of time, from an era long before digital map-making.

Catharina Groeninx van Zoelen, daughter of Lieutenant Jonkheer Groeninx van Zoelen MC ('Pico'), who generously supported the project to republish this wartime history.

Brigadier Henry Wilson, formerly Irish Guards, and now a commissioning editor at Pen & Sword, has been immensely helpful in guiding us to re-publication. Matt Jones, who has skilfully overseen the typesetting, not an easy task given the size and shape of the original book published in 1953. Matt has met all our demands in this respect; the result is as near to the original as we could make it, and with very few compromises.

Pete Storer, the former Curator of the Household Cavalry Museum, Windsor, and his successor, Ted Heath, have given us access to their extensive archive. The museum is also the custodian of the Brussels Standard which deserves to be prominently displayed as a tribute to 2 HCR and all who served in the regiment.

The Household Cavalry Foundation (HCF), under its Director, Lieutenant Colonel Giles Stibbe, formerly The Life Guards, has been a stalwart supporter of this project from the outset. We also thank the many benefactors who have given generously to the HCF to enable this book to be published, and hope that the book will inspire a new generation of Household Cavalrymen as they face a future which is as uncertain as it has ever been in the Household Cavalry's long history.

Finally, a word about those who served in 2 HCR during its five year wartime existence. Sadly they are all dead now, but their names live on in this book including, in the appendices, those who were killed or wounded, and the many (of all ranks) who are mentioned in the text. This book is dedicated to all these Household Cavalrymen who served King and Country, and indeed, to their families at home.

W.S.G.D. and J.J.H.
November, 2022

Part One

Training in England

Chapter I

Windsor and Knightsbridge

*War declared—Mobilization—Composite Regiment formed—Invasion threat—
Training Regiment given operational tasks—Lack of equipment—"Cromwell"—
Horses given up for duration—1st and 2nd Household Cavalry Motor Battalions
formed—Increased establishment of motor battalions—Exercises under 20th and
30th Guards Brigades—Guards Armoured Division formed—2nd Household
Cavalry Motor Battalion becomes 2nd Household Cavalry Regiment (armoured
cars)—Bulford*

At a quarter past eleven on the morning of Sunday the 3rd of
September, 1939, the inhabitants of Great Britain switched on
their wireless sets and learnt from Mr. Chamberlain, the Prime
Minister, that the nation was once again at war with Germany. To all
but a few confirmed optimists the Munich autumn settlement of 1938
had been but a postponement of the inevitable, and as he spoke to the
hushed millions, Mr. Chamberlain's firm but sad voice seemed to echo
the mood throughout the land. Outside the sun was blazing down from
a clear blue sky which, in spite of an air raid warning, was to remain void
of enemy planes for many days to come.

Mobilization schemes have always been the bane of peace-time
adjutants and orderly room staffs, but when at the end of August 1939,
the order had been given to mobilize, although one might have thought
it would have been organized chaos, things really went extraordinarily
smoothly.

The Life Guards were in London and the Blues at Windsor. The
plan envisaged the immediate formation of three composite regiments
made up from regulars and reservists. One regiment was to take its
place in the Cavalry Division and was to mobilize at Windsor. There
was to be a Reserve Regiment in London, and a Training Regiment at
Windsor. Initially, however, the Life Guards mobilized at Knightsbridge
and the Blues at Windsor, and it was some days before the Life Guards'
portion of Regimental Headquarters and of Headquarter Squadron and
the Life Guards Sabre Squadrons moved to Windsor. The Life Guards
Sabre Squadrons were billeted at the Royal Ascot Hotel and at the Eton
Country Club. The stabling used was the Ascot and Windsor race
stables, respectively.

Meanwhile, horses had been arriving at Windsor from all parts of the country and those men not looking after horses were fully occupied building sandbag walls and blast protection in barracks and at the Castle.

The Composite Regiment was commanded by Colonel E. J. L. Speed, M.C., the Life Guards, the Reserve Regiment by Lieutenant-Colonel R. Fenwick Palmer, the Life Guards, and the Training Regiment by Lieutenant-Colonel the Lord Forester, Royal Horse Guards.

The Composite Regiment mobilized as a regiment of cavalry (horsed as opposed to armoured) and did a certain amount of training, but, of course, most of the time was taken up in conditioning and September training remounts. In September it moved to the Newark area. The manner in which the Composite Regiment was mobilized meant that the Blues Regimental Headquarters, composed of active and fit personnel, was left behind with the Training Regiment, while the rest of that Regiment was made up for the most part of reservists, and recruits.

The winter of 1939–40 was for the Training Regiment at Windsor a dull and somewhat tedious time, as indeed it was elsewhere during the "phoney war." Nothing much could be done except steady training of recruits and remounts; equipment, practice ammunition and stores were very short and transport was practically non-existent. It is questionable whether, apart from rifles, the Regiment had any effective weapons. The Hotchkiss and Vickers machine guns were certainly "DP" models, and there were no Brens. Recruits were still being taught dummy-thrusting, and their bible remained "Cavalry Training (Horsed)." Little tactical training, even of the simplest kind, could be attempted because of the pressing need for individual training.

At the beginning of February 1940, the Composite Regiment, having been brought up to strength by drafts of all available trained men from Windsor and London, left with the Cavalry Division for Palestine.

In March and April 1940, came the quickening of the war when the Germans invaded Norway and Denmark. However, owing to the lack of equipment and to purely training duties, the Training Regiment did not have an operational role. It was still thought that horse cavalry drafts would be required, and it was not until the fall of France that any change in this attitude was made.

After the invasion of Holland, when it was seen that the Germans were making great use of parachutists, the possibility of invasion by air was considered. The Training Regiment was given operational tasks immediately and some small amount of equipment was issued.

At Windsor, the Regiment's regular jobs were to form a mounted Troop with a twenty-four-hour tour of duty at Cumberland Lodge, with the Troop patrolling the Great Park at dawn and dusk; and there were also dismounted positions to man at the vital Metropolitan Water Board reservoirs at Staines and Laleham, where it was thought that the enemy might land in seaplanes. For the latter job, a few Hotchkiss guns (without butts) were issued from Woolwich!

The Regiment was also issued with six motor coaches with civilian drivers subject to no order or military discipline whatsoever. Should the need arise, these coaches were to be used to move what fighting troops the Regiment could muster to defend Langley aerodrome, where the Hawker fighter aircraft were manufactured.

From this time onwards little real interest was taken in horses or horse training and the Regiment had bi-weekly schemes on foot with long route marches. Colonel Robert Laycock, Royal Horse Guards who had returned from France, where he had been Gas Officer at G.H.Q., became responsible for dismounted training until the formation of the first Commandos in July 1940, when several of his Troops formed initially at Windsor.[1] A Household Cavalry platoon was formed in the Commandos under the command of Lord Sudeley[2], who had been Adjutant of the Training Regiment up to this time, when he was succeeded by Captain A. J. R. Collins.

Throughout the late summer and early autumn of 1940, during the Battle of Britain period, the Training Regiment carried on with the operational roles which have already been mentioned, but it would have been desperately badly armed had an invasion taken place. Although it could have mustered some 350 men, there were between them but six automatic weapons!

It was on the 7th of September, 1940, that Home Forces issued the code word "Cromwell," which meant that invasion was imminent, and Captain Collins returned to Combermere Barracks to find that the Grenadier Guards Duty Officer from Victoria Barracks had come to find out what the word meant as his code was locked up in the safe. The Duty Squadron was turned out and moved with all speed to Langley airfield, where the only incident of note was that a Troop Leader, Lieutenant Bowes Daly, an officer of some seniority, who had seen service in the First World War, after failing to get an answer to his challenge to some dim form that grunted in the darkness, fired his revolver and found that he had shot a cart horse.

---

1. Robert Laycock later succeeded Vice-Admiral Lord Louis Mountbatten as Chief of Combined Operations, 1943-1947.
2. Lord Sudeley died at sea, 26th August, 1941.

Throughout the autumn, infantry training went on hard and the Regiment received great help from the Grenadier Guards, who lent them every sort of instructor. To even the most loyal and biased cavalryman, it had now become apparent that there was no room in the present shape of things for a horsed cavalry regiment. One detects a note almost of desperation in Lieutenant-Colonel the Lord Forester's appeal to Field-Marshal the Lord Birdwood that the Regiment might surely be used as a "Cavalry Machine-Gun Regiment (Vickers guns) on the lines of the old M.G. Squadrons of the last war." "The Regiment," he continues, "could be used in France in marshy country where mechanized vehicles could not be used." However, in spite of a sympathetic reply, it was not to be, for although the C.I.G.S. seemed "entirely in favour of the proposal, it is not feasible because we have not at present the necessary guns, equipment, etc., to carry this out." The fate of the "blacks" was therefore sealed, and in September and October they were sent away for the duration of the war to Melton Mowbray, to which place, certain sections of the daily Press seemed convinced, the rest of the Regiment had followed, also for the duration.

The anti-parachute patrol of the Great Park was hereafter carried out unglamorously on bicycles, and the Troop Officer was allotted an Austin "7" for the performance of his duties. The Regiment was now entirely occupied in its operational roles and in dismounted training.

On the 19th of November 1940, orders were received that a change of role was to take place. The Composite Regiment in Palestine was to become the 1st Household Cavalry Motor Battalion; the Training Regiment, the 2nd Household Cavalry Motor Battalion; and the Reserve Regiment, a Motor Training Battalion. Like so many other orders, before these could be carried out they were cancelled, but they were renewed, very little altered, on the 12th of December. This meant that all fit officers and men in the Reserve Regiment were moved immediately to Windsor.

The plan was that the 1st Household Cavalry Motor Battalion should have a Life Guards Headquarters with two Life Guards and two Blues Companies and that the 2nd Household Cavalry Motor Battalion should have a Blues Headquarters, equally with two Blues and two Life Guards Companies. It was envisaged that as soon as shipping became available, the 2nd Household Cavalry Motor Battalion would be moved to the Middle East and that the Regiments would then re-form as Life Guards and Blues. In England these orders, which were only regularizing what had practically been the case for the last six months, were put into force immediately. In Palestine they were not received until the end of the following January. The 1st Regiment there did not lose its horses until March,1941 and although one Squadron had been mechanized in the autumn of 1940, the remainder were not to be issued with trucks until a week before being thrown into the Iraq and Syrian campaign at the end of April and beginning of May.

★ ★ ★

In England, the formal change-over to the new War Establishment was a great blessing. It meant that long-delayed promotions among officers and men could now be made. In addition, the Regiment was almost made up to the new increased strength of a motor battalion by drafts from 3rd and 5th Horse Cavalry Training Regiments at Welbeck and Shorncliffe, which were then being disbanded.

As usually happens in the Army when a War Establishment is granted, more equipment and transport flowed in than could be absorbed. Particularly was this the case with regard to 15-cwt. trucks, Bren carriers and Bren guns. Naturally, although all this equipment was disgorged for training purposes, it had to be instantly available for the anti-invasion operational roles allotted to the Regiment.

Up to this time all schemes (and since the fall of France there had always been two regimental schemes per week) were carried out on foot, and officers and men were undoubtedly fitter than they had been at any other time in the war when either horses or, later, cars were available to carry them. Of course, the area in which training could take place had been necessarily restricted because of lack of transport, but there was no part of the Windsor area, Burnham Beeches, or Chobham ridges with which everyone did not become thoroughly familiar. The Copper Horse, well-known landmark in the Park, came in for more than its share of rough handling, being the focal point of innumerable assaults by both the Household Cavalry and the Grenadier Guards by night and by day.

It has been said that the Training Regiment was not quick enough to give up its trained men for the Composite Regiment, but it must be remembered that the invasion scare was a real one, and the fact that it was recognized that the Training Regiment would turn itself into a motor battalion was a clear sign that the War Office was prepared to admit that the Household Cavalry could form two active-service regiments at an early date.

The change-over enabled the difficult problem of provision of officers to be tackled more firmly since the officer War Establishment of a motor battalion was considerably larger than that of a horsed cavalry regiment.

Boys of school-leaving age who were not prepared to take up the dying prospects of the cavalry were more prepared to come forward to join a motor battalion. Apart from the understandable reluctance of boys to join the cavalry, there were two other important factors governing the problem. Firstly, the Household Cavalry had in peace time no organization in force to deal with the officer problem and was therefore at a disadvantage when competing with the Foot Guards, the Rifle Brigade and the K.R.R.C. (60th). Secondly, the more so at this time of the struggle, the glamour of the Royal Air Force and its achievements, as opposed to the (to date) somewhat drab results of the Army, was a great attraction to the Public-School boy. Not until 1943 at the earliest did the problem of officer reinforcements begin to sort itself out. At the next change-over from motor battalion to armoured car regiment in September 1941, the question was to become acute.

The original War Office plan envisaged that the 2nd Household Cavalry Motor Battalion should be moved to the Middle East as soon as shipping space became available. But in spite of the strongest representations, this move never materialized, and in the early spring of 1941 the question of placing the unit in a field formation arose. It had already been inspected by the then Director of the Royal Armoured Corps, Lieutenant-General Sir G. Le Q. Martel, and the G.O.C., London District, Major-General Sir Bertram Sergison-Brooke, but so far no collective training had taken place. Every exercise, apart from a few anti-invasion ones in conjunction with the Grenadier Guards Training Battalion, stationed in Victoria Barracks, had been on a purely regimental footing. The overhanging threat of invasion also meant that the Regiment, like so many other units at that tense period, was obliged to undertake regimental exercises long before individual training was anything like complete. We were trying to run before we could walk.

On a wider front, the Motor Battalion now formed part of London District Mobile Reserve; the primary duty being that of a counterattack role in the defence of Fighter Command Headquarters, located in Bentley Priory, Stanmore. There were also counter-attack plans in force for possible enemy raids on aerodromes to the north and west of London.

In March 1941, the Regiment moved to Pirbright Camp (Stony Castle) under canvas. Both for training and operational purposes it was placed under command of 20th Guards Brigade (Brigadier W. A. L. Fox-Pitt), with headquarters at Woking. One motor company, as these were now called, was to be changed every fortnight and left at Windsor to form part of the Windsor garrison. Ground forces in 1941 were far more air conscious than they were towards the latter part of the war. Bitter memories of the Dunkirk beaches were still fresh in many instructors' minds, and so all tents were pitched under the cover of pine trees in the darkest, dampest and most insect-infested parts of the Stony Castle area. The tents were sunless and miserable and we had still a lot to learn about making ourselves relatively comfortable out of doors. The camp, however, was close to barracks, and an extremely good half-hourly train service to London was some sort of solace to the Windsor regulars, who rather viewed the sojourn at Pirbright as their exile in the wilderness. Proximity to barracks also enabled attached personnel, such as Captain Brown, R.A.M.C., who liked his creature comforts, to give the men the benefit of his medical knowledge and yet sleep in the luxury of his Combermere bedroom.

Driving instruction and route marches now came to the forefront, and officers and men were introduced to the still unfamiliar No. 11 wireless set by Lieutenant the Lord Maitland[3], who had succeeded Captain T. Clyde as Signals Officer.

Captain Gerald Balding ran the Carrier Company, a much-coveted job, for only he and his immediate entourage escaped with any degree of certainty from the route marches which were daily radiating from the camp in ever-lengthening numbers of miles.

In May two and three-day exercises were carried out under command of 20th and 30th Guards Brigades. A significant fact was at once apparent. Although the Regiment was as yet only partially equipped and trained as a motor battalion, the tendency was to use it in the role of reconnaissance. Possibly this tendency was encouraged because of the then great lack of Bren carriers in the infantry battalions of both brigades and the fact that the Regiment could muster two fully equipped platoons of twelve carriers apiece. Whatever the reason, the return to the employment of the Regiment in its old cavalry role in a new shape was foreshadowed.

During May rumours that the 2nd Household Cavalry Motor Battalion was likely to revert to a cavalry role as the armoured car regiment of a new Guards Division about to be formed were translated into fact. On the 29th of the month, Lieutenant-Colonel the Lord Forester attended a conference at London District Headquarters at which the impending formation of a Guards Armoured Division was formally announced. The 2nd Household Cavalry Motor Battalion was to become the new division's armoured car regiment. Simultaneously came the announcement that in future the establishment of an armoured

---

3. Lord Maitland was later killed in action in North Africa after he had transferred from the Blues to the Lothians and Border Horse.

car regiment was to be increased to a headquarter squadron and four sabre squadrons.

War Office approval was not immediately forthcoming for this change; nevertheless training on the new lines started at once. A considerable number of officers, non-commissioned officers and troopers were sent off on courses all over the country. Cross attachments were arranged between the 2nd Household Cavalry Motor Battalion and the armoured car regiment of the 1st Armoured Division, the 12th Lancers. Potential tradesmen[4] were dispatched not only to military training centres but also to civilian firms, such as courses at the Humber works at Birmingham and the Daimler works at Coventry. These were very popular, as were the rarer courses in London. Lecturers and instructors were assembled, and from the beginning of June onwards, until the end of the year, the Regiment was greatly reduced in strength owing to so many key persons being engaged on courses.

The Royal Armoured Corps Wing at Sandhurst Royal Military College arranged a series of two months' officers' courses. These embodied general principles of wireless (the first sight of the No. 19 wireless set), driving and maintenance, and gunnery (the 2-pdr. anti-tank gun, the 7.92-mm. and 15-mm. Besa machine guns). The course was primarily intended for officers of the future tank battalions of the new armoured division and therefore did not really cater for the armoured car Troop leader. In fact few instructors had ever seen an armoured car—one even going so far as to introduce his lecture by saying that "Lawrence might have liked to play about with them in Arabia, but they are not made to blend with the complexities of a modern armoured division." This remarkable statement nevertheless summed up a view widely prevalent at the time, because it must be emphasized that in spite of the magnificent work of the 12th Lancers in France during the 1940 campaign, and later on in the North African desert of the Royals and the 11th Hussars, the idea that armoured cars were a somewhat unorthodox and expensive luxury was to die slowly.

At Bovington, spiritual home of the tank, the instructors at the Armoured Fighting Vehicles School responded nobly to the new calls made upon them and in due course a steady stream of Household Cavalrymen was to pass through their hands, although here again it should be stressed that the armoured car part of training was still almost a closed book and no specific provisions for training such personnel had yet been provided.

---

4. Tradesmen: an army term denoting specialists—e.g., wireless operators, vehicle mechanics, etc.; they receive extra pay.

The general plan for the Guards Armoured Division, before its actual formation, was to dispatch to the various training units as many officers and senior non-commissioned officers as could be spared. These would in time develop into unit instructors. The division was to form in September 1941, by which date, it was hoped, individual training could begin. As events proved, because of there being no specialized trainers for armoured car work, the time forecast was a trifle optimistic. In the meantime, until unit instructors should become available, such progress as was possible with limited resources of men and equipment at once began.

In order to facilitate this object, the 2nd Household Cavalry Motor Battalion returned from Pirbright to Windsor on the 12th of July.

The 12th Lancers obligingly lent two officers and four non-commissioned officers, and classes started for driving instruction and the general principles of the internal-combustion engine. Two old Guy armoured cars were dug out, and by the time these vehicles had passed through several hundred pairs of hands, more accustomed to bridles than to steering wheels, they had undergone their fair share of collisions and ditchings.[5] The quantity of other transport now flowing into barracks was proving, in view of general inexperience, to be an *embarras de richesse*.

On the 11th of July 1941, Colonel the Lord Forester was due to finish his term of command of the Blues, and Major Henry Abel Smith, then with the 1st Regiment, had been ordered to return and take over. However, when he landed on the 23rd of July his Middle East news was already out of date. Fully expecting to command a motor battalion, to his great surprise he found an armoured car regiment already established at Combermere Barracks.

Almost his first action on assuming command was to "lay on" a Maintenance Parade, due to take place on the day after his arrival. The term "Maintenance" and what it portended was as yet imperfectly understood at Combermere Barracks and the chief victim of this parade turned out to be Captain Hubert Duggan, Conservative Member of Parliament for Acton, who, still attired in service dress instead of the newly issued denim overalls, found himself at pains to explain the meaning of a large cobweb linking the back axle of the office truck to the stable wall. Thenceforth Maintenance Parades were to become a stern daily chore, with an especially rigorous inspection at week-ends; while Captain Duggan, wisely bowing to the inevitable, decided in the national

---

5. Major M. A. Little, later killed in action in France, was not endowed by nature with a mechanical turn of mind. He never managed to negotiate the entrance gates of Combermere Barracks and they bear marks to this day.

interest to attend as many secret sessions of the House of Commons as military duties permitted.

★ ★ ★

On the 15th of September 1941—the same day as the official formation of the Guards Armoured Division—the Regiment, reinforced by four more Guy armoured cars, moved off to a hutted camp at Bulford Fields on the edge of Salisbury Plain. The new camp was on the site so often occupied in peace time by the Regiment of the Household Cavalry when on manoeuvres. Thus ended, after an existence of ten months, the 2nd Household Cavalry Motor Battalion.

With a copy of the Special Order of the Day dated the 22nd of September 1941, and signed by Major-General Sir Oliver Leese, this chapter, giving briefly and barely the story of the nucleus from which sprang the 2nd Household Cavalry Regiment, may fittingly be ended.

SPECIAL ORDER OF THE DAY
By MAJOR-GENERAL SIR OLIVER LEESE, BART., C.B.E., D.S.O.,
Commander, Guards Armoured Division

The following message has been received from His Majesty The King:

BUCKINGHAM PALACE.

The General Officer Commanding
Guards Armoured Division.
The formation of the Guards Armoured Division is a landmark in the history of the Household Brigade, and I am proud to think that my Household Troops are to take their place among the most powerful units of modern warfare.

I am sure that it will not be long before they have acquired in their new role the fame which they have rightly enjoyed as Infantry for centuries past, and I send to all ranks my best wishes for success in the tasks which lie ahead.

GEORGE R.I.

19th September 1941.

The following reply has been sent to His Majesty The King on behalf of all ranks by the General Officer Commanding Guards Armoured Division:

His Majesty The King,
Buckingham Palace.
All ranks of the Guards Armoured Division present their humble duty and wish to thank His Majesty for the gracious message received on the formation of the Guards Armoured Division.

It will be the endeavour of all ranks to carry out the tasks which lie before them in a manner worthy of His Majesty's trust and of the high traditions of the past.

O. W. H. LEESE, Major-General,
Commander, Guards Armoured Division

22nd September 1941.

(*Signed*) DEREK SCHREIBER, Lieutenant-Colonel,
General Staff, Guards Armoured Division.

Chapter II

Bulford and Trowbridge

Problems of armoured training—Shortage of instructors—General war background—
"Bumper"—Individual and Troop training—Inspections—Changes in command
within the Regiment—"Rommel"—Linney Head ranges—Trowbridge—H.M.
The King inspects Guards Armoured Division—Armoured cars to become Corps
troops—Further changes in command within the Regiment

Retrospect shows the move to Bulford to have been a complete
break from the old to the new—an exchange from the
permanency and comfort of Combermere Barracks and
London weekends to the dreariness of wind-swept Nissen huts on the
Plain. It was to be a new division and another role—a role which, let it
be said, was frequently criticized adversely. Many affirmed that it was
too bold an experiment, doomed to failure from its inception. Infantry-
trained Guardsmen would not fit into turrets, nor could Household
Cavalrymen accustomed to horses be expected to imbibe the necessary
mechanical knowledge to fit them to take their place in a modern
armoured division.

There were others, however, who viewed the problem free from
unreasonable professional prejudice. Lieutenant-General Sir G. Le Q.
Martel, during a distinguished career, had always been closely associated
with armoured warfare. As far back as 1916 he was consulting with
Major-General Sir Ernest Swinton about tanks before their use in France.
Subsequently, he was mainly responsible for producing the models which
led to the development of the Cromwell tank and the heavier Matilda and
Churchill models. When the 2nd Household Cavalry Regiment became
an armoured car regiment he was Commander, Royal Armoured Corps.
This is what he wrote in after years when discussing the formation of the
Guards Armoured Division:

> "In April we began to consider our future expansion. Our five armoured
> divisions and three army tank brigades (21st, 25th and 31st) were well
> launched and we could now expand further. The first problem that arose
> was whether we should form these new formations *ab initio* on cadres
> supplied by existing Royal Armoured Corps units, or whether we should
> take existing infantry formations and convert them into Royal Armoured

Corps formations. We pressed for the latter, because we did not consider that the existing Royal Armoured Corps units could spare any personnel suitable to send as cadres.

"This principle was adopted. The first decision arrived at was to form a Guards armoured division, but it was not reached without a good deal of trouble. The War Office wanted to insist that the Guardsmen should leave the Guards and join the Royal Armoured Corps. We could see no necessity for this. We all agreed that the Guards go to extremes in these matters. Men belonging to the Grenadier Guards cannot go into the Coldstream Guards, etc. etc. In this way they handicap themselves unnecessarily. But there was no reason why the Brigade of Guards should not supply Guardsmen to form Guards armoured regiments. The War Office, however, remained completely opposed to forming a new armoured division from the Guards unless they became part and parcel of the Royal Armoured Corps. They would obviously make a magnificent armoured division and that was all that really mattered, but we had considerable difficulty before we obtained War Office sanction for a Guards armoured division which would always be supplied and manned by Guardsmen. As soon as this had been settled, the Guards went to work with their usual enthusiasm and efficiency. Major-General Sir Oliver Leese was selected to command them. There was great competition to be in the Armoured Division and they got their pick. They started going to our training regiments in June. It was quite exhilarating to see the intense keenness with which they attended these classes. The Guards were, of course, determined to have the best armoured division. Anyone who did not seem to be grasping the work was changed, and they had plenty of excellent material to pick from. In this they had, of course, a great advantage. There was never any doubt as to the future success of this division. When they had found their feet, the Guards formed their own training centre for their recruits. This relieved the pressure on our own training centres. The logical course would then have been to form a holding unit of Guardsmen trained in Royal Armoured Corps work who could flow to any Guards armoured regiment, but this was resisted. The *esprit de corps* of the regiment was greater than that of the Brigade of Guards."[1]

This was the carefully considered opinion of the Commander, Royal Armoured Corps.

★   ★   ★

---

1. *Our Armoured Forces* by Lieutenant-General Sir Giffard Le Q. Martel. (Faber & Faber Ltd., p. 106 *et seq.*)

The new establishment of officers was a considerable increase in numbers, jumping from 33 to 48; the establishment of other ranks remained constant in the region of 800. Senior officers on arrival at Bulford were:

Commanding Officer	Lieutenant-Colonel Henry Abel Smith RHG
Second-in-Command	Major T. Philipson MC, LG

A Squadron

Squadron Leader	Major M. A. A. Little RHG
Second-in-Command	Captain D. Bowes Daly RHG

B Squadron

Squadron Leader	Major E. J. S. Ward RHG
Second-in-Command	Captain the Duke of Beaufort RHG

C Squadron

Squadron Leader	Major B. R. Williams LG
Second-in-Command	Captain T. Clyde RHG

D Squadron

Squadron Leader	Major T. A. Fairhurst LG
Second-in-Command	Captain H. J. Duggan LG

HQ Squadron

Squadron Leader	Major the Hon. M. E. Dillon RHG
Second-in-Command	Captain G. Balding LG
Adjutant	Captain A. J. R. Collins RHG
Regimental Corporal-Major	Regimental Corporal-Major A. Jobson RHG

★   ★   ★

It was soon discovered that, with the limited number of instructors upon whom to call, a serious blunder had been made over the question of the Regiment's driving and maintenance instructors. An assurance had been given that as the unit had been a motor battalion its non-commissioned officers would be immediately available in a teaching capacity; in fact, the Regiment had not obtained enough vacancies on courses to make this even remotely possible. The calculations of London District and Headquarters, Royal Armoured Corps, were based upon this supposition, and the 2nd Household Cavalry Motor Battalion (as it was then) was, therefore, never allotted such courses in the original planned distribution. Notwithstanding the most strenuous efforts on the part of Colonel Abel Smith—for the weakness of the original calculations was only too well realized by him—he never succeeded in getting it entirely corrected.

★   ★   ★

At this stage, a glance at the general war situation will not be out of place. Compared with the corresponding period in the 1914-1918 struggle, the plight of the British Empire was infinitely worse and although the United States, with all her war potential, was veering more and more towards open friendliness, we were nevertheless alone in the fight; nor had Russia, deeply embroiled in the folds of her treacherous treaty with Hitler, yet fallen out with her Nazi ally. It is still barely possible to hazard a guess at what must have been the secret torments tearing at our Prime Minister's indomitable heart.

The naval burden in the Mediterranean was crushing. British forces in North Africa, weakened through having to dispatch an expeditionary group to the aid of Greece, were savagely man-handled by Rommel and driven back from Benghazi to the Egyptian frontier. An anti-British revolution broke out in Iraq[2], and in April Germany, disgusted at the ineffectiveness of her Italian ally, launched herself at Greece and a divided Yugoslavia. When Athens fell on the 27th one more melancholy evacuation had to be completed with the help of the Royal Navy, though not without considerable loss in military personnel and ships.

Grim looking as was the horizon, all was not wholly black. July saw the closure of the Syrian (Vichy) campaign, and in August Mr. Churchill and President Roosevelt, meeting in the closest secrecy out at sea, published the "Atlantic Charter."

But in the meantime an event had occurred which was to prove to be one of the turning points in our island's struggle for survival. At dawn on the 22nd of June, Germany leapt at the throat of her erstwhile Russian friend on a front of over a thousand miles. Who of those millions who heard him will ever forget the Prime Minister's broadcast that night? It rallied the Empire and the occupied countries as never before and steered the United States into all but open warfare on the side of the Allies.

---

2. In the quelling of which the 1st Household Cavalry Regiment was to play a prominent part.

It was hinted darkly by the knowledgeable within the Division that "the Russians will only last six weeks," and when after a series of lightning thrusts the Germans had attained the banks of the Dneiper by the beginning of July and, following swiftly in a series of gigantic battles, had torn away vast slices of territory up to the gates of Leningrad and Moscow, it certainly appeared as if those irrepressible prophets might for once be right.

Against this momentous world background, the Regiment prepared to wrestle with the problems of internal-combustion engines and electrical circuits, which latter, Bovington assured us, now flowed from *left to right* and not from *right to left*. Lieutenant van Cutsem still wearing riding breeches started a muttering campaign against the wearing of the new beret, while, to the great disappointment of newly joined officers, the Adjutant announced that only those of field rank and *himself* would be permitted to wear embroidered badges on that same debatable headgear. Meanwhile, intent on playing his full part in the new mechanical age, Major the Hon. M. Dillon threatened to put a man in the book for reporting that "the big end" of his motor-bicycle "had gone."[3]

★   ★   ★

It is now common knowledge that at the time of the Dunkirk evacuation not more than one fully trained infantry division was available for the defence of the British Isles. Yet somehow, by early autumn of 1941, four armoured divisions as well as other troops were standing by prepared to take part in "Bumper," the largest military exercise in the country to date. "Bumper" roamed over the southern and Midland counties for ten days. The weather was fearful and the Regiment's small part consisted of providing twelve officers on motorcycles, suitably equipped with notebooks and a sense of direction. They were to act as umpires and follow the moves of the 2nd Derbyshire Yeomanry (armoured cars). The exercise brought out the decisive influence of armoured formations on the field of battle. Returning enthusiasts stated that the tanks could almost be handled like a pack of hounds, "but," said the authorities, "there was serious lack of reconnaissance and observation at times." There were cases of tanks charging home against unlocated guns and without artillery support.

---

3. The dialogue ran on these lines: "Sir, the big end on my motor-cycle has gone." "Oh, has it? Then I shall give you a quarter of an hour to find it." Which conversation about summed up our then mechanical knowledge.

Some armoured cars had overturned in the course of the exercise, and an order came out that car commanders would henceforth keep all but head and shoulders inside the turret—no mean feat with the attendant clutter of map boards, Slidex code cards, and the monstrous Lakeman mounting of the turret ack-ack Bren gun.[4]

Captain Collins used to shout warnings from the steps of the Orderly Room as troops went out on their training runs, but not until the day that Regimental Headquarters *in toto* decided to explore the countryside from their own turrets was the regulation relaxed.

Those who had imagined that individual training would leave the Regiment on a peaceful island of self-sufficiency, for a few months at least, were soon disillusioned. Officers and non-commissioned officers who had been sent off early in summer on Armoured Conversion Courses began to trickle back from Yorkshire, the Midlands, and the Home Counties by the beginning of October. Another batch of some 350 junior non-commissioned officers and troopers was sent off to Bovington and up to Catterick in Yorkshire.

Already, Lieutenant J. H. D. Ward had taken part with his Troop in a demonstration in the area of Spettisbury Rings in connection with the Divisional Commander's "Study week." The month of October went by in a spate of inspections because everyone wished to see for himself the War Office's latest venture in armoured warfare, the Guards Armoured Division.

On the same day that His Majesty The King approved of the new name, "2nd Household Cavalry Regiment," Her Majesty Queen Mary graciously visited the camp, watched training and honoured the Regiment by staying to lunch in the Officers' Mess. Further visits from the Major-General commanding London District, Lieutenant-General Sir Bertram Sergison-Brooke, and from the Secretary of State for War, the Right Hon. David Margesson, followed. The latter was shown an example of armoured car Troop drill, of which up till then no set form was known to exist, and the Minister was presented with a curiously complex mixture of Caterham and Weedon, plus echoes of the D. and M. Wing[5] at Bovington, which strangely enough worked.

---

4. Slidex: a system of encoding map references and words for security in wireless transmission. Lakeman mounting: a murderous contraption intended to serve as a mounting for the ack-ack Bren gun on the turrets of the armoured cars. It was based on counterpoise weights and strong springs and had a habit of turning itself inside out without warning and either throttling the car commander or causing him to fire the weapon in some totally unexpected direction. Wisely, this Heath Robinson device was put on the scrap-heap.

5. D&M Wing—Driving and Maintenance Wing.

One show piece deservedly never failed to impress the casual or official visitor. It was the mechanical model room. Collected together by Captain W. Writer, temporary Technical Adjutant, who had been lent to the Regiment by the Royal Gloucestershire Hussars, it was the result of numerous skirmishings amidst the surrounding W.D. and civilian car dumps. Embodying a comprehensive assortment of broken-down parts, this catalogued scrap iron was instrumental in forming a solid groundwork of knowledge for the drivers and future fitter mechanics upon whom, as time progressed, more and more vital work was to devolve.

The arrival of twenty armoured cars, both Daimlers and Humbers Mark I, foreshadowed the day when exercises would be staged on the Plain. Already divisional weekly signal schemes down to and including Squadron rear links had taken place in skeleton form, and exercise "Hotspur," a Southern Command performance covering the counties of Wiltshire, Somerset and Dorset, gave the embryo operators on the No. 19 wireless sets a taste of just how tiring three days' continuous operating could be. Great was the excitement when someone in camp reported receiving a faint message from the top of Beacon Hill, less than three miles away! We were not yet very good, but we were learning and there was plenty of enthusiasm.

Up to the present an acute shortage of "B" vehicles[6] under the new establishment had been staved off by using the old Motor Battalion lorries, but when the new Fords and Bedfords materialized it was found that they had spent several days at the bottom of the River Mersey, from which place they had been recovered from the holds of a bombed ship. They appeared, however, to have come to little harm as the result of their immersion.

★ ★ ★

There had been several changes of command within the Regiment during the past twelve months. Major T. Philipson had left to become Officer Commanding Guards Divisional Training School at Weston-Super-Mare, and temporarily, until the arrival of Major Walter Sale from the Middle East on 22nd December, the post of Second-in-Command was to be held by Major A. W. Stanley. Major M. A. Little left to take up a Staff appointment, and he was succeeded in "A" Squadron by Major D. Bowes Daly. Captain the Earl of Lewes was soon to join him as his Second-in-Command.

---

6. Armoured vehicles were known as "A" vehicles; lorries, etc., as "B" vehicles.

The Medical Officer, Captain J. Brown, R.A.M.C., had remained behind at Windsor, and his place had been taken by Surgeon-Lieutenant R. U. F. Kynaston, R.H.G. He was, he admitted, very new to Army life and routine.

> "I joined on a Saturday afternoon at Windsor in September 1941. There was not a soul about and I was astonishingly frightened, the more so because a War Office Medical Brigadier had told me that it was a plum job in the Army. At last I found the anteroom and with growing confidence I inquired from a solitary figure behind *The Times* how I might find my room. *The Times* lowered. 'I should press the bell,' said Archie Little, with obvious irritation. Up went *The Times* again and I retired to my room so shattered that I dare not emerge till dinner."

Roger Kynaston was a most conscientious officer, particularly so where the men's medical welfare was concerned, which was to result, soon after he had joined the Regiment at Bulford, in an unforeseen encounter with the Second-in-Command.

> "I had a number of 'problem men' and so formed up to the Colonel to do what I could for them (the Colonel and Walter Sale shared an office in the orderly room at that time). One was a trooper who had grown restive, for he had been in charge of some 150 Wall's ice-cream barrowmen before the war and now found himself permanent barrack road sweeper! I suggested to the Colonel that perhaps he might be given the chance in some more responsible position, whereupon Walter jumped up in a fury and inquired how it was that I was so grossly abusing my position as to suggest to the Colonel how he should run the Regiment. Shaking at the knees, I replied that I conceived my duty to lie not only in the physical but also in the mental welfare of the Regiment. I saluted and retired. Walter appeared at my M.I. Room the next day and apologized, and we were the greatest friends thereafter."

Roger Kynaston soon became very much part of the Regiment in every way. Life to him, especially the war part of it, was a perpetual surprise, which attitude frequently earned him a leg-pull, but he was always where he was most needed in a crisis, calm and efficient and very understanding. Most popular with fellow officers and men alike, all came to know his sympathetic greeting in moments of stress and action, "My poor friend, and how is the world treating you?" He was the best and most painless jabber of the hypodermic needle in the British Army.

★　★　★

Although the United States of America had entered the war on our side in December 1941, following the treacherous attack on her fleet in Pearl Harbour by the Japanese, the New Year was to open in the full gloom of Far Eastern disaster. Hong Kong had fallen on Christmas Day. Singapore was shortly to follow suit. The entire Indian subcontinent was in peril and the Americans were about to experience another heavy naval defeat in the battle of the Java Seas. Even if Russia's absorbent immensity kept swallowing up entire German armies, there were but few rays of light to brighten the Home front. Yet we still grumbled at the cuts in railway transport and the curtailment of forty-eight hours' leave passes, for, after all, everything is relative.

The weather was arctic—January 1942 was the coldest for fifty years—and in the middle of the worst spell, exercise "Rommel" took place. We always blamed Colonel Laycock for "Rommel." In the latter part of 1941 his Commandos, raiding the North African coast behind the German lines, had nearly cost Field-Marshal Rommel his freedom, if not his life. It was a daring incursion resulting in the gallant death of Colonel Keyes. For his part in the operation, Colonel Keyes, son of Admiral of the Fleet Sir Roger Keyes, the leader of the Zeebrugge raid in 1918, was posthumously awarded the Victoria Cross.

Some restless spirit at home believed that a German reprisal on similar lines and directed at an important British Headquarters was a distinct possibility. Hence exercise "Rommel." All headquarters in the district were warned that they might be attacked by men masquerading as friends. All outsiders were suspect and store sheds and magazines enfolded in coils of Dannert wire. With the thermometer well below zero and a blizzard raging over the Plain, the entire Regiment patrolled and guarded, listened, and shivered. Around Bulford, posses of cavalrymen, led by Major Bowes Daly with a "cosh," sought out dark corners of woods for possible enemy concentration areas. No person slept or lived in his normal abode. Colonel Abel Smith moved from hut to hut heavily guarded, while a disguised Orderly Room, next to the cookhouse, grappled with urgent or suspect telegrams. To fox the enemy someone had the bright idea of turning night into day, and at every corner of the camp armoured cars, their turrets humming in the vibrant cold, waited for the call to action. The climax came on the second night. Through some unguarded chink, enemy disguised as friends slipped into the camp. When dawn came it was found that Captain Collins had been "shot dead" at his adjutantal post, blaming with his dying breath lax security precautions of the Intelligence Officer, Lieutenant Haskard. The echelon subalterns, who it was thought had come off best by having been ordered to guard dumps of vulnerable stores in the centre of the camp, were also liquidated, and, as corpses, were sleeping in comfort amidst piles of spare blankets. The person responsible for the outrages had penetrated the camp posing as organizer of the scheme. It seemed unfair, but cautious inquiries at other centres elicited the information that the Foot Guards had suffered even worse chaos. As the result of "lessons learnt at the post mortem," the fate of officers' wives, until then permitted to be domiciled locally, once more trembled in the balance for security reasons.

In spring, after nearly six months of classroom work on the 2-pdr. anti-tank gun and the Besa machine gun, the Regiment prepared to test theories and marksmanship on the Linney Head Ranges in Pembrokeshire. Now up to full strength both in armoured cars and scout cars, there would be no shortage of ammunition, nor of guns—a welcome change. One half of the Regiment made the two days' journey by road, staying the night at the Royal Welsh Infantry Training Centre in Cardiff. The other half travelled by train to Pembroke non-stop, Major Williams contributing to military history and shaking Movement Control to the core by refusing to sign for safe receipt of the locomotive and carriages!

Before departure, Captain Cyril Falls, *The Times* Military Correspondent, visited Bulford, and a few days later came the news which revealed to the general public that Guards Armoured Division was in existence.

Linney Head was a great success. Stacpoole Court, a rambling and ugly house, accommodated the Regiment with ease, although its bare, unheated rooms had not the comfort of the near-by modern Belisha Camp at Merrion which was to harbour the Regiment on its next visit. The time spent here, away from the boredom of routine training, was a great mental rest for officers and men alike. The town of Pembroke was near and for those who had the energy to make the journey, Tenby, an attractive little coastal town, was a few miles farther in the opposite direction. The ranges engaged everyone for most of the day, however, and, if any form of training is tiring, range firing with its continual noise and demands on alertness is so in the highest degree. Most people after breathing the strong sea air all day were only fit for bed.

The tanks, whose range this primarily was, had all been put through a Troop run towards the end of their stay. In conjunction with the Gunnery Officer, Captain Profumo, and the Range Officer, Colonel Abel Smith devised a variation for armoured cars. The run of some three miles long produced a variety of targets. These were by no means easy to pick out, especially, as so frequently happened, with a sea fret haloing the late afternoon sun in the car commander's eyes. One innovation brought in was a loop intended to test the Troop Leader's control of the rear half of his Troop.

If successfully negotiated, the loop brought the Troop together again near a derelict farmhouse filled with Hun effigies, at which Besa machine-gun fire, Sten guns, pistols and hand grenades were directed in quick succession. It proved to be good practice for the close country which was to be met in Normandy; it was also fun to meet foes with so little idea of taking cover.

The finale came with the order to gather the Troop in extended line for a cavalry charge over a Pembrokeshire stone wall, at the other side of which popped up yet more targets lining the cliffs. The successful tackling of the wall was a magnificent advertisement for the Daimler suspension, which took the shuddering impact without a murmur.

The Signals Officer, Lieutenant C. H. Waterhouse, had erected a cruel contraption enabling Colonel Abel Smith to tune in to the participating Troop Leader's car on a loud speaker. With this set-up the commanding officer listened-in with unconcealed glee to the tortured accents of his officers attempting to deal with two wireless sets, the driver's "intercom", the controlling of the corporal-of-horse's loop, the spotting of targets and the loading and fire orders for the 2-pdr. gun, all while trying to avoid the weapon's violent recoil mechanism. Never was war half as bad!

The run was on a competition basis, and a point-to-point atmosphere reigned throughout. Inevitably, Major Fairhurst made a book on the back of old bits of paper, while Lieutenant van Cutsem glided shrewdly from target to target assessing current form from the range personnel. Lieutenant Hanbury's Troop, with orders cut to the basic minimum, carried the day.

Plans were now afoot to move the Regiment to a new location, for Bulford, with its unusually good gliding and dropping zones, was required by Major-General Browning's new Airborne Division, the same one which was later to make the first landing of Allied troops to capture the Orne bridgehead in the early hours of D Day, 1944. We were therefore not to see Bulford again, and the Regiment moved direct to a new camp at Trowbridge after a night spent in Cardiff on the way. On the second day the route lay past Badminton, where Her Majesty Queen Mary was staying as guest of Captain the Duke of Beaufort. On hearing that the Regiment was to pass, Her Majesty expressed a wish to see the armoured cars. The arrangement was entirely spontaneous and the first of its kind since turning over to armoured cars. Her Majesty took the salute on the march past with Lieutenant-Colonel Abel Smith and Major Ward in attendance.

★   ★   ★

To retail all the exercises and milestones in training which followed would be boring and serve no useful purpose. Suffice it to say that slowly but surely, often imperceptibly to those concerned, the building up of an armoured car regiment progressed. Month by month, wireless distances increased. Map reading improved noticeably and drivers began to get the feel of their engines, and mechanical failure due to the ill-usage of inexperience became rarer.

There were night drives through the pretty but narrow lanes of north Wiltshire, where a misread map spelt chaos and wasted hours of disentangling vehicles by the light of a torch and much cursing. There were days when, to produce versatility, jobs were reversed. Car commanders became for a time operators, and drivers found themselves with the responsibility of a leading scout car corporal. These occasions were frequently amusing in retrospect. "Never," wrote Captain N. Ford, "shall I forget Harry Stavordale and Mick Dillon on an officers' exercise, as driver and operator in a leading scout car. The former did not know how to turn on the wireless set and the latter how the engine switched off. It took some beating and was a good start to the day!"[7] But what really mattered was that we were making progress all the time.

★   ★   ★

In May, Guards Armoured Division was considered ready to be inspected for the first time by His Majesty The King, accompanied by Her Majesty The Queen. The Regiment was commanded to provide a Captain's Escort composed of Captain's car (Captain T. Clyde) and two Troops each of two armoured cars and two scout cars, commanded by Lieutenants the Hon. M. Eden and R. Wrottesley. The escort was drawn up outside Gillingham Station and escorted Their Majesties to East Knoyle. Parties of Household Cavalrymen lined the route, while the Regimental Aid Post, commanded by Surgeon-Captain R. U. F. Kynaston, was on parade at the Divisional Administration demonstration.

There now arose the question of forming a second Guards Armoured Division and, arising therefrom, a second Armoured Car Regiment. Both the Divisional Commander, Major-General Sir Oliver Leese, and Lieutenant-Colonel Abel Smith were anxious that the 1st Household Cavalry Regiment should return from the Middle East for this job, as with resources then available (particularly in officers) in the country

---

7. Captain the Lord Stavordale, Headquarter Squadron M.T. Officer, and Major the Hon. M. Dillon, O.C. Headquarter Squadron. Neither, to date, had received much instruction in either the No. 19 wireless set or the Daimler scout car.

it did not appear feasible to form another completely new regiment in England. However, the whole project fell through in its infancy because it was decided that two Guards Armoured Divisions were, owing to the manpower problem, out of the question.

June, 1942, found the Regiment moving for the first time as a complete armoured car regiment (exercise "Savoy"), and in July the first complete divisional scheme (exercise "Cheddar") took place, with the Regiment harbouring in the picturesque country outside Cheddar and at Fonthill. In the latter place Lieutenant the Hon. E. Carson (future M.P. for the Isle of Thanet), mistaking his way in the dark and inadvertently treading on the slumbering form of his Squadron Leader, Major T. A. Fairhurst, learnt in no uncertain fashion of the value of careful movement in harbour.

Following almost immediately came the ambitious Southern Command exercise ("Sarum"). It started in Devonshire and finished in a welter of slaughter by the umpires on the Regiment's own doorstep. Petrol shortage and lack of tyres had diminished its scope, and made it peter out prematurely. Throughout, the armoured cars had been in great demand for reconnaissance purposes.

One day that summer, Major Ward, in temporary command of the Regiment during Colonel Abel Smith's absence, received an order to send immediately to London docks a mixed column of Daimler and Humber armoured cars, scout cars, a water-cart, a "Gin Palace," and some three-ton lorries, twenty vehicles in all—the move to be in the greatest secrecy. It later transpired that these were required for loading tests about to be made on various types of vessels intended for the forthcoming invasion of French North Africa. I was ordered to take charge of the convoy. For some reason, no specific route had been given, which was strange, for London District was very jealous of its London thoroughfares, and I decided to travel the direct way, which was heresy, passing through the centre of London. Many of the men had never been in the capital before and were delighted at the chance of seeing the sights. The convoy passed round Hyde Park Corner, Buckingham Palace, down the Mall, under Admiralty Arch and moved somewhat jerkily to negotiate the one-way traffic of Trafalgar Square (most of the men were from Headquarter Squadron and unfamiliar with the vehicles they were driving). For some unaccountable reason, the B wireless sets chose to work perfectly, and the troopers were just being warned to stand by for a Cook's tour description of the Houses of Parliament when a War Office conference chose at that moment to debouch its Generals into the middle of Whitehall. Their expressions repaid study as they leaped back to avoid the cavalcade, one obviously making a mental note of the convoy's serial number. However, we gave a succession of magnificent salutes from the turret, and passed safely on to Woolwich, where the night was spent with the Gunners in hospitable comfort. Next morning the cars were driven to the King George V Docks to be loaded and unloaded from ship to ship by dock labourers, whose lunch-time breaks were the envy of all the soldiers. Apart from the water-truck which was dropped forty feet into one of the holds with a concussion which burst all tyres and shot the steering wheel through the roof, all went well.[8]

The completion of the trials happened to coincide with the early morning news of the Dieppe raid carried out by the Canadians. To a public starved of recent military successes and weary of a long series of evacuations, the chance was too good to be missed, and as the cars, dirty and battered after their handling by the dockers, passed through the East End on the return journey to Trowbridge, the citizens of London placed their own interpretation on the meaning of the scene. Wild cheering broke out which steadily grew in volume until, by the time Blackfriars Bridge was reached, a crowd five deep lined the pavements, shouting themselves hoarse. The troopers waved a disclaiming "No," but this was only taken to be the deprecatory gesture of modest returning heroes and the crowd redoubled their cheers, delighting the men beyond measure. The West End was less credulous, but when the convoy reached Trowbridge the crews were greeted with surprise, so sure were their comrades in camp that they had been sent to Dieppe as reinforcements.

In September, the Division heard with regret that Major-General Sir Oliver Leese had suddenly been called away to assume command of 30 Corps in North Africa.[9] The battle of Alamein, turning point in the Middle East campaign, was but a month away. Shortly afterwards it was decided that armoured cars were no longer to form an integral part of the armoured division but were to be Corps troops in future. Although this turned out to be but a temporary separation from Guards Armoured Division, the split was a sad one for the Regiment, and for the time being we were nobody's child.[10]

Autumn came round once more, and the Regiment paid a second visit to the ranges at Linney Head. Again a great amount of shooting took

8. The driver, liking the idea of being swung aloft by the crane, had asked permission to sit at the wheel of the vehicle. Fortunately for him, permission was not granted.
9. Leese was succeeded by Major-General Allan Adair, who was to command Guards Armoured Division throughout the North-West European campaign.
10. With the return of the 11th Hussars, the operationally inexperienced 2nd Household Cavalry Regiment might well have been disbanded, for there were now more armoured car regiments than there were Corps to employ them.

place and it was found that marksmanship had improved noticeably. This time we were housed in the comfortable Belisha Camp at Merrion. The famous Troop run was revived and it was again won by "D" Squadron, this time by Lieutenant R. A. Bethell's Troop.

A very sad accident unfortunately marred the atmosphere of the runs. Corporal-of-Horse Ives, a most popular and efficient non-commissioned officer, and Trooper Hammond, both of "B" Squadron, lost their lives when a stray ricochet shot from a 2-pdr. gun pierced the turret of their car—they were killed instantaneously.

★　★　★

The spectre of invasion had now faded away and, symptomatic of the easier state of affairs reigning, the Regiment was released from all home operational commitments in December.

As another year drew to its close, further changes in command took place. Captain F. E. B. Wignall, recently returned from the Middle East, after a long period of sickness out there, assumed command of Headquarter Squadron from Major the Hon. M. E. Dillon, who now became second-in-command to Major B. R. Williams in "C" Squadron. However, as Major W. M. Sale was due to leave shortly afterwards to become A.A. & Q.M.G., Guards Armoured Division, Major Wignall, after a few weeks, became Second-in-Command of the Regiment, while Captain A. W. P. P. Herbert, also newly returned from the Middle East, took over Headquarter Squadron. So frequent were Major Dillon's changes of Squadron and rank that it was said the morning greeting from his soldier servant soon became, "Is it crowns or stars on the battledress today, sir?" After a brief stay in "C" Squadron, he again returned to Headquarter Squadron when Major Williams went off temporarily to the Household Cavalry Training Regiment at Windsor in January 1943.

★　★　★

The months passed by and, together with the rest of Guards Armoured Division, we began to wonder if we should ever go to war. One scheme easing the routine boredom of training had a great success. Someone had the idea of chartering an old "Dragon" plane to fly the men over their camouflaged vehicles to see what they could detect. Two demonstrations were arranged. At one, cars were to be parked and camouflaged as badly and obviously as possible; at the other they were to be carefully hidden. The flights were greatly enjoyed by the men, but a seal was set on the trip when it was noticed that the "carefully camouflaged cars" were easily visible while the "badly parked vehicles" blended so well with the grey Wiltshire stone villages as to be almost indistinguishable from the cottages. Only one car, however, avoided discovery completely, that of Trooper Mundy, who with sublime logic had parked his Humber inside the local blacksmith's shop, where it remained undetected throughout the day!

Regimental wireless had improved out of all recognition, and in a scheme in conjunction with 170 Air Corps Squadron, R.A.F., distances exceeding twenty miles through the interference of the heavily built-up Birmingham area were attained with ease. Contact was made and held with aeroplanes circling overhead in spite of bad weather conditions, while attempts on the part of Captain Profumo's rear link officer to erect an enormous aerial in the middle of Birmingham in order to maintain touch with Regimental Headquarters caused a sensation.[11]

Armoured Car Commander

---

11. Regimental Headquarters had slipped away early and were installed in great comfort at Willey Park, home of Lieutenant-Colonel the Lord Forester, the late Commanding Officer. Captain Profumo's party, on the other hand, was in the middle of Birmingham, in a snowstorm, at one o'clock in the morning, and armed with only a quarter-inch map and faced with one of the most complex and futile one-way traffic systems in the country. The idea at R.H.Q. had been that a loop should be made round Birmingham further to test wireless capabilities. Tempers were slightly on edge when eventually, at half-past four in the morning, the gates of Willey Park hove into sight. The last dregs of brandy had been polished off by the Mess President, Lord Stavordale, who greeted us sleepily with a leaky thermos of cold, sweet tea! *Author*

Chapter III

Norfolk and Yorkshire

"Spartan"—Norfolk—Move to Yorkshire—The "Staghound" as the H.Q. armoured car for R.H.Q. and all Sabre Squadrons—Organization of the armoured car regiment finally settled—Wading trials at Weymouth—2 H.C.R. hears General Montgomery for first time—"Eagle"—Last months in Yorkshire

In November 1942, a letter was received by Headquarters, 8 Corps, then in the south-western defence area, from the Commander-in-Chief, Home Forces, General Sir Bernard Paget. He wrote: "It is my intention to form an armoured corps in this country, and I have selected 8 Corps to be the Headquarters commanding it." On the 20th of January 1943, Lieutenant-General Sir Herbert Lumsden arrived straight from commanding 10 Corps in the Western Desert, to take over 8 Corps. He was experienced in armoured fighting and was himself an old armoured car man, for he had commanded the 12th Lancers in France. That his views would be stimulating is instanced by his final words when addressing the Staff College on the battle of Alamein: "Well, gentlemen, the race to Benghazi may not have been a classic, nor was it run entirely as we had hoped, but at least it was a record for the course—by either side—either way." His appointment augured well for armoured cars, but before we were to join 8 Corps as their reconnaissance regiment we were to endure a bad moment of suspense.

Exercise "Spartan" was planned to take place at the end of February 1943. It was designed at high levels "to test the system of command and supply evolved to date and to find out whether our forces would be able to maintain a high rate of advance after a fast withdrawing enemy in a situation such as might be anticipated on the Continent once a break-through had been achieved." To us it meant a crucial test of our training to date.

For weeks we had been hearing about "Spartan" and preparing for the exercise. Then, some ten days before it was due to start, there was a rumour that we were not to be employed. Colonel Abel Smith got to work without delay and registered protest "at the highest levels." What exactly happened many of us will never know, but those familiar with the Commanding Officer's methods can hazard a shrewd guess. The 2nd Household Cavalry Regiment did take part in "Spartan."

"Spartan" was to be a dress rehearsal on a grand scale. On one side the Canadian Army, commanded by Lieutenant-General A. G. L. McNaughton and composed of 1 and 2 Canadian Corps and 12 Corps (British), was to play the part of the invading force; the occupation force, made up of 11 Corps (Infantry) and 8 Corps (Armour), that of the Germans. The latter force's task was to withdraw after initial contact and retreat with all speed northwards. The Regiment was to form part of 2 Canadian Corps, commanded by Lieutenant-General E. W. Sansom, which with its two armoured divisions, Guards Armoured Division and 5th Canadian Division, was to be the spearhead of the attack.

The operational area encompassed the whole of the south of England, the Midlands, and the North Midlands, although troops moved up to battle from as far afield as Land's End and John o' Groats'.

On the 27th of February 1943, the Regiment bade good-bye to Trowbridge, moving in column through the night past endless lines of guns and transport, to harbour at dawn near Fordingbridge in Hampshire. Nothing happened for several days. The cars were dispersed in woods hiding from aerial observation. The generals, sensing, like us, that they were on trial for their existence, were extremely air conscious and not even inter-squadron games of football were permitted. There was complete wireless silence and a fever of spying and counter-spying. Civilians wandering too near a vehicle were pounced on and sent for grilling to keen young officers newly returned from Buxton Intelligence Courses. Visits to shops and farms of any kind were strictly forbidden owing to the disorganization which hordes of hungry soldiers would cause to existing food supplies. But the country-bred troopers soon found the spare eggs, and their city cousins were quick to learn. Umpires also played their part nobly.

Breaking all honourable pacts, the enemy crossed the agreed-upon frontier at half past twelve (noon) on the 4th of March, and the Regiment, already split by "A" and "D" Squadrons having been moved to guard an open flank on a line extending from Wylye to Blandford, found itself rushed off at less than half an hour's notice to make contact with the enemy and screen the advance of two armoured divisions. Because of security orders, all wireless sets had been netted by wavemeter, and so, for a time, there was chaos on the air.[1]

---

1. Like ordinary civilian sets, the No. 19 wireless was normally tuned in (netted) to a master station (the control set). But the enemy can hear this taking place and is thus able to pin-point positions. In times when security is vital, sets can be netted to an apparatus giving off a very faint signal and known as a wavemeter. In theory this works if all sets can be switched on and warmed up at the same time. In war this is a counsel of perfection.

By nightfall the Regiment, advancing on the line Tilshead—Wootton Bassett—Cricklade—Cirencester, reached Broad Hinton with patrols of "B" Squadron held up on the River Kennet. Contact had been made with the Inns of Court Regiment (armoured cars), who, on orders, had retreated. At breakfast next morning it was learnt that Regimental Headquarters had spent a perilous night, surrounded (although their foes did not themselves know it) by enemy armoured cars and infantry. At one critical point, patrols led by Surgeon-Captain Kynaston, Lieutenant the Hon. M. Eden and the Regimental, Mr. Jobson, had groped forward into the night to search for a way out. But the scare died down and Regimental Headquarters lived to fight another day, while everyone else had an unkind laugh at their expense.

Next day the regimental front, which had been stretched at one time to fifty miles, shrank to twenty-five, while the advance pushed on northwards to the River Evenlode. Slow advances continued to be made, prodding for the armour of an elusive enemy who refused to be drawn into battle. Suddenly, after several days of search, the Corps plan changed to a swing west of Swindon and a night approach march to an area north of Cirencester. As in war, this came with no warning. Half the Regiment was asleep in an orchard on a hot afternoon, having been informed that there would be no move for at least a day. After a tiring regimental night drive ably led by Lieutenant Haskard, the Intelligence Officer, "D" Squadron discovered a way over the River Windrush, pushing forward to the Cherwell—Oxford Canal. There were signs that a major clash was imminent. Divisional artillery was located at Slapton, many infantry prisoners captured and, curiously prophetic of the later exploit of another "C" Squadron Troop in Normandy, Lieutenant C. Petherick's Troop made a deep penetration of the enemy's defensive screen and, lying up in Evenly Park, sent back a stream of reports on the movements of 42nd Division around Brackley.

Soon it became clear that the enemy's main armoured forces were concentrated in the area of Towcester—Buckingham—Brackley—and now began a slaughter unique in the history of any exercise.[2] Troop after Troop was sent to its destruction. Lieutenant Ainsworth, ordered to move round to the north of Northampton, ran into strongly entrenched Polish infantry, who with infinite zest smashed up his wirelesses and left all his cars, minus their wheels, sitting in the middle of the town. Prisoners were bundled off to a realistic "cage," where, among many

---

2. Prisoners taken on "Spartan" were on a lavish scale. "If", wrote Colonel Abel Smith, "I had not made an arrangement privately with Bertie (Lieutenant-Colonel Bingley, commanding Inns of Court Regiment) to release each other's prisoners, I should have ended up with the greater part of his regiment and he with a large portion of mine!"

others, languished Lieutenant Mitchell of "A" Squadron, looking like a concentration camp inmate with three days' growth of beard on his face, having had even his shaving kit confiscated. "A" Squadron ceased to exist apart from a few Headquarter cars, but a depleted "C" Squadron found an unblown bridge by a mill on the 11th of March and moved over before the enemy knew they were among them. The Troops hid up (two were never discovered} and reported on concentrations of armour preparing to move southwest. Unfortunately, the Higher Command's appreciation that the armour would retreat along a certain line proved to be incorrect and both "C" Squadron and the remains of "A" Squadron incurred further heavy casualties.

On the right, Guards Armoured Division, having still made no contact with the enemy armour, cut adrift with a vengeance and ran headlong into infantry strong points heavily backed by anti-tank guns four miles east of Towcester. They suffered heavily. This really was the end of the battle and next day "Cease fire" was called.

Regimental Headquarters and Squadrons grouped themselves around Mears Ashby and there spent three pleasant days resting and generally cleaning up. "B" Squadron, which had left the Regiment early on to work directly under command of 5th Canadian Division on the right, once more came under regimental command on the 11th of March. The Squadron had spent the last days of the scheme in the more or less uneventful role of Corps H.Q. protection troops.

It was said afterwards that "Spartan" had proved to be rather too ambitious an exercise, because many useful deductions could not be made. But this was a high-level verdict. Except for the weather, which though bitterly cold every night could not have been finer in daytime, "Spartan" certainly fulfilled all expectations at regimental levels. It proved a great test both for men and their equipment and brought out the lesson of husbanding strength for the supreme moment. For those who had not yet learnt this art of conserving energy and of living as comfortably as circumstances permit, it produced exhaustion of the kind which is generally avoidable in war. No soldier was ever again to be as tired in North-West Europe as he had been at times during "Spartan." Driver's fatigue at night, inducing a tendency to wander off the road, was a problem, nor were the spare drivers all the answer, for only rarely could these be made available at the time most required. In addition, it was a praiseworthy fact that drivers showed strong disinclination to let strange hands look after their cars, on whose proper care and maintenance their lives would depend in battle.[3]

---

3. In operations there proved to be no case, other than due to casualties, when a spare driver replaced the first string in action.

Regimental mechanical casualties were light, and starting the battle with fifty-one armoured cars and forty-nine scout cars, only two armoured cars and three scout cars failed to stay the course—tribute indeed to Captain Victor Myall, R.E.M.E., and his L.A.D. staff.[4] Owing to the enormous frontages which had to be covered, the withdrawal of Squadrons at any time during the exercise for maintenance and rest was out of the question. Had the scheme gone on much longer, the problem would have become acute, although, again, in actual warfare, the question rarely arose, because Colonel Abel Smith nearly always managed to have one Squadron at rest.

On paper, questions of supply such as petrol and rations appeared likely to be tricky. There were two reasons for this. In the first place, 2nd Canadian Corps was known to be short of R.A.S.C. transport. Secondly, the armoured cars, as already stated, were working on a long frontage and by nightfall always well ahead of the main body. Nevertheless, thanks in a large measure to the regimental commissariat under the Quartermaster, Captain Charles Firth, rations were plentiful throughout. A large reserve of petrol was always made available and held in readiness by Squadron echelons for any possible dash forward. But in this connection Squadrons did experience great difficulty in getting up their echelons at night because of the harassing activities of the opposing armoured cars, and troops which could with difficulty be spared had to be detached to protect the "soft vehicles."

Wireless communications, apart from the first day, were excellent and no case occurred of a message failing to get through due to breakdown in communications. There was one instance of the enemy trying to break down security by copying voices and mannerisms over the air. But the Corps of Signals expert was misguided enough to start off by trying to simulate Captain Collins on the control set at Regimental Headquarters. "The voice," at suspiciously close range and of great amplitude, asked for a map reference of a certain Squadron's location, while at the same time, but twenty miles away, the Adjutant was also passing a message. The stratagem failed completely, for no man living could hope to succeed in shouldering the Adjutant off the air when he really wished to make himself heard.

At the conclusion of the exercise, Colonel Abel Smith received the following letter of thanks from Lieutenant-General Sansom:

---

4. L.A.D: Light Aid Detachment.

"MY DEAR ABEL SMITH,

"This is just a note to tell you how very much I appreciated all your hard work and that of your fine Regiment throughout the course of the 'Spartan' Exercise.

"My previous experience with armoured cars had been disappointing in that failure of communications generally prevented information reaching the Commander.

"By your high standard of training you have most effectively overcome that difficulty and I was always kept in the Armoured Car picture.

"Your Liaison Officer, Captain Ford, I found of the utmost value in keeping me and my Staff constantly informed of the happenings as they occurred.

"Also your nightly reports were invaluable to me in planning the next day's operations.

"My association with you and your fine Regiment has given me a standard of efficiency towards which my own Armoured Car Regiment will now have to work and I am very grateful.

"Please accept my congratulations on a good show.

"Yours sincerely,

"ERNEST W. SANSOM."

★   ★   ★

Squadrons converged upon Mears Ashby from the adjoining villages of Wilby, Ecton, Pitsford and Great Doddington, prepared for a day's drive which would take them to their new camp at Wolterton, in Norfolk. The advance party had already reported that for the men the new location was not as well situated as Trowbridge. It was more than six miles from the nearest large village, Aylsham, and, apart from a few bedrooms for officers in Wolterton Hall and Nissen huts, everyone slept under canvas.

Soon after arrival, General Lumsden came over to see his new regiment, for we had now officially come under command of 8 Corps. A fortnight later most officers and many non-commissioned officers attended his lecture in Newmarket, which tactfully finished early enough to enable the audience to attend the races after a long walk from the town to the July Course.

Exercises followed thick and fast, and "A" Squadron took part in exercise "Spring," the first occasion on which armoured cars had worked with the new Sherman tanks of Guards Armoured Division.

Practice ammunition for the first time was really plentiful, and as the route to the ranges near Brancaster meant passing through the village of Stiffkey, the troopers were granted a never-ending excuse for ribald merriment as the lorries drove past the vicarage of its notorious ex-rector.

★   ★   ★

In June Major Sir Peter Grant Lawson, who had sailed from England with the 1st Regiment in 1940 and subsequently been employed on Staff duties with the Eighth Army, returned to become Second-in-Command. Squadron Commanders and their seconds-in-command were now:

A Squadron	Major D. Bowes Daly; Captain P. Profumo
B Squadron	Major F. E. B. Wignall; Captain J. H. D. Ward
C Squadron	Major A. W. P. P. Herbert; Captain T. Clyde
D Squadron	Major T. A. Fairhurst; Captain C. H. Waterhouse
H.Q. Squadron	Major B. R. Williams; Captain G. Balding

Major E. J. S. Ward left to assume temporary command of the Training Squadron at Windsor, with Captain D. J. Sandford Shone as his second-in-command. The latter had until then been second-in-command of "A" Squadron.

Although Norfolk, with its old flint churches and abundant bird life, was an attractive county in summer time, its possibilities as a training ground for armour were limited, and the next move, destined to be to the edge of the Yorkshire Wolds, gave promise of greater scope for armoured cars.

The Regiment left Wolterton at the end of June for a new area, first travelling up to Cumberland to fire over the newly opened ranges at Warcop. A night was spent *en route* at Welbeck Abbey in the Dukeries. After a week's field firing at Warcop in the heart of the Pennines, Squadrons concentrated in the area of Pocklington in Yorkshire, Regimental Headquarters, H.Q. Squadron and "A" Squadron at Kilnwick Percy Hall and "B" and "D" Squadrons in Pocklington village, where the little Feathers Hotel was immediately commandeered by the married officers and their wives, as was all its available drink. "C" Squadron were some miles away in splendid isolation and comfort at Bolton Hall.

Distances were not too far for administrative purposes, but it was a new experience for Squadrons to find themselves on their own instead of living on top of one another, and it was greatly appreciated.

The move to Yorkshire marked the end of an argument which before it was to be settled had reached Cabinet level. This land of rich soil and

EXERCISE "SPARTAN"

"Cease fire" at Great Doddington, March 1943. The Humber armoured cars here form part of Squadron Headquarters but are shortly to be replaced by the larger and more heavily armed Chevrolet Staghounds.

undulating wolds produces some of the finest crops in England. It is also ideal for tank training, and the needs of the latter just won the day.

8 Corps had started to move north at the beginning of June, establishing Headquarters at Sandhutton. By mid-July it had assumed its final shape, Guards Armoured Division—11th Armoured Division—15th (Scottish) Division—6th Guards Tank Brigade—2nd Household Cavalry Regiment.

At the end of July General Lumsden left 8 Corps to command 2 Corps District for a short time. He was soon to leave on an important mission to the Far East, and his untimely death on the bridge of an American battleship attacked by the Japanese was a sad loss to the nation. In the short time that he had been with 8 Corps we had realized that he thoroughly understood and appreciated the problems of armoured car work. He it was who taught the Regiment the value of the indirect approach to the objective, and Colonel Abel Smith's oft-repeated enjoinder on a sticky front, "Try tapping in," owed much to Lumsden's inspiration. He was succeeded by Lieutenant-General Sir Richard McCreery, who had been Chief of Staff to General Alexander during his North African Campaign, but he only stayed three weeks before flying out to take over 10 Corps for the Salerno landings in Italy. His successor, Lieutenant-General A. F. Harding, did not arrive for several months and then, before he had time to settle down, was in his turn whisked away to go as Chief of Staff to General Alexander at 15 Army Group Headquarters in Italy.

★   ★   ★

During July, the Regiment mobilized. All equipment except a full complement of scout cars was forthcoming. The Regiment was now for the first time up to strength in officers, including reinforcements, and some extra officers were attached over and above strength—a remarkable change from the unsatisfactory position of a year ago.

Following mobilization, a new type of armoured car made its appearance, and so did Mr. King, a cheerfully efficient American with a picturesque vocabulary whose job it was to demonstrate to us how the vehicle worked. The American Staghound was intended to replace the Humber in Regimental and Squadron Headquarters. Built originally to British order when an armoured fighting vehicle to counter the Germans in the Western Desert was urgently needed, it was nevertheless a true product of the New World. It was well finished and lavishly equipped, full of gadgets, from telescopes and built-in compasses to watches and torches (which never got beyond Ordnance), and it was powered by a double bank of Chevrolet engines of ample horsepower. As a vehicle, it did not make a good Troop Leader's car because it was too unwieldy for manoeuvre in confined spaces and, due to its great weight, was apt to bog down in soft going. But as a Headquarter car it was ideal. It carried a crew of five instead of the three of the Humber. This meant a good reserve of operators and spare drivers. Armament consisted of a 37-mm. gun firing both armour-piercing shot and high-explosive shells. There were three Browning .300 machine guns, one mounted co-axially with the 37-mm. in the turret, another in front of the spare driver, and a third mounted on the turret top for use against aircraft.[5]

Jeeps, which had been issued once before at Trowbridge but withdrawn almost immediately during the North African crisis, were now reissued to the Support Troops, and were an invaluable addition in the transport line. Originally, the Support Troop, of which there was now one in each Squadron, had been split up among the Reconnaissance Troops, a small section travelling behind the armoured cars. But the two motor-cycle combinations which carried them had proved quite inadequate to the task of transporting three hefty troopers apiece, plus the 2-inch mortar and ammunition, demolition charges, grenades and all the personal weapons. They invariably broke down, leaving the disconsolate "Blitz men," as they were nicknamed, far in the rear of their parent Troop and out of touch with the battle.

For various reasons the Support Troop had tended to become the poor relation in the Squadron, and on the arrival of the jeeps a new organization was worked out and brought into effect immediately. Ten jeeps were to carry three sections and a Troop Headquarters. Armament consisted of rifles, Sten guns, Bren guns (one per section), and a 2-inch mortar.

The Support Troop's likely role in battle was also reconsidered. It was decided that it would involve patrolling on foot by day to obtain detailed information about the enemy when the size of the armoured car would make it too easily visible; the protection of Squadron harbours by night, ensuring rest for the Reconnaissance Troops which had been out all day; the lifting of mines and booby traps and their laying and setting; the moving of enemy road-blocks covered by fire; and in general being conversant with infantry tactics when the need for dismounted action arose. Lastly, personnel was, within limits, to be trained to replace armoured car and scout car casualties.

However, as the jeeps suffered from the disadvantage of affording no protection to the crews in battle, they were eventually replaced by the White scout car, which, if more cumbersome to manoeuvre, at least possessed armour capable of resisting small-arms fire.

★   ★   ★

---

5. With a hair trigger which tended to go off in harbours on little provocation.

There was still controversy in high quarters about the organization of the armoured car regiment, but after a conference at 21 Army Group, attended by Colonel Abel Smith, it was decided to retain a Headquarter Squadron and four Sabre Squadrons, each composed of a Headquarters and five Reconnaissance Troops, one Support Troop and a Heavy Troop. The Daimler armoured car was to be used for reconnaissance both by the Troop Leader and his corporal-of-horse, the Staghound for Headquarters. The aim was that the Coventry, a more up-to-date type of armoured car, would eventually replace the Daimler, but as it turned out, both the Daimler and Staghound were to finish the war together, each in its sphere having rendered yeoman service.

★   ★   ★

Major the Earl of Lewes, who had left in Bulford days to become Brigade Major to 6th Guards Tank Brigade, now returned for a short spell of regimental soldiering and assumed command of "D" Squadron, in place of Major T. A. Fairhurst, who had commanded it almost from the days of its formation and now had to leave because of a breakdown in health. Tom Fairhurst was a great loss and a character much missed by all. Possessing a rooted aversion to all forms of paper work, he carried Squadron details in his head or else on the backs of old envelopes. His unorthodox conferences, conducted with shrewdness and an ingrained sense of absolute fairness, were unique, although to newcomers, not yet accustomed to his methods, at times startling. The toss of a coin used to decide a forty-eight hours' leave, including his own, and a chuckle emerging from behind a barrage of cigarette smoke would announce that once again "Mr. T." (Lieutenant Hanbury, his senior Troop Leader) had failed to work out a "V.T.M." sum.[6] As a map reader he was unsurpassed, moving from one featureless set of contours to another with an accuracy bordering on the uncanny.

★   ★   ★

A further change, this time of a temporary nature, resulted in Major Williams leaving to command the Training Squadron at Windsor,

---

6. V.T.M. stood for vehicles to the mile; thus 30 V.T.M. would mean an interval in a road convoy of approximately 60 yards between cars. Major Fairhurst's question would be varied, but it was always on the mathematical side issue of the ten minutes' halt at the odd hour that Tom Hanbury's arithmetic broke down under the strain. The latter would then burst into laughter of such an infectious nature that it was not long before the entire squadron office had joined in. *Author.*

changing places with Major Ward, who returned to Headquarter Squadron.

★ ★ ★

After exercise "Blackcock"—a combined Corps effort in which the Regiment took part at the end of September, and which envisaged with great precision future developments in Normandy—a further move was made to a thoroughly featureless part of Yorkshire, near Selby. Regimental Headquarters, H.Q. Squadron and "B" and "D" Squadrons were stationed in a hutted camp at Pollington, a mile and a half from the village of Snaith; "A" and "C" Squadrons, the former in huts and the latter in billets, in Selby itself.

Winter set in on preparations for the invasion which everyone felt could not now be long delayed. There were thorough wading trials at Weymouth, where Captain Balding and other officers experimented for weeks on the waterproofing of armoured cars. Over at Harrogate the transport officers wrestled with similar problems with the "B" vehicles. Here a certain amount of difficulty was experienced in getting the Ford 3-tonner to go through water. It was first thought that the sudden immersion in cold water affected the electrical circuit of the ignition system, which was at the front of the engine. However, when it was discovered that it was only the sudden rush and pressure of water which tore off the waterproofing from round the coil, a metal guard was fitted and all was well.

On top of the waterproofing demands, there were further calls on manpower in the shape of firing on the Midhope Ranges near Barnsley, and an Infantry Tactics Course at No. 59 Training Regiment at Barnard Castle, which all but emptied the camp. The Support Troops disappeared for weeks on end to learn to crawl through waterlogged drain-pipes, be blinded by the acrid fumes of artificial fog, and suffer Chinese firecrackers to be thrown at them as they wove through lines of tracer machine-gun fire. Back at Pollington, parades consisted of the sanitary man, the odd cook who felt strongly that he should never have been detailed, and a junior officer trapped into "giving an A.B.C.A." Lecture.[7]

Senior appointments on 31st December were as follows:

---

7. A.B.C.A. stood for Army Bureau of Current Affairs. This was a favourite hobbyhorse of the Army Educational authorities. The object was doubtless praiseworthy in its intentions, but it invariably ended with the lecturer (usually the newest joined subaltern) being asked by the barrack room lawyer, complete with copy of *Daily Mirror*, whether the Russian soldiers were "compelled by their officers to blanco their kit?". *Author.*

Commanding Officer	Lieutenant-Colonel H. Abel Smith RHG
Second-in-Command	Major Sir Peter Grant Lawson, Bart. RHG
A Squadron	Major D. Bowes Daly RHG
	Captain P. Profumo LG
B Squadron	Major F. E. B. Wignall LG
	Captain J. H. D. Ward RHG
C Squadron	Major A. W. P. P. Herbert LG
	Captain T. Clyde RHG
D Squadron	Major the Earl of Lewes LG
	Captain C. H. Waterhouse LG
HQ Squadron	Major E. J. S. Ward RHG
	Captain G. Balding LG
Adjutant	Captain A. J. R. Collins RHG
Regimental Corporal Major	R.C.M. A. Jobson RHG

In January 1944, Major the Earl of Lewes was posted to the Staff of 30 Corps, as G.2. His place in "D" Squadron was taken by Major E. J. S. Ward, and the change-round completed by Major B. R. Williams returning from Windsor to command H.Q. Squadron, which in the course of three years had had many masters. Captain the Lord Stavordale, H.Q. Squadron Transport Officer, left to become A.D.C. to Major-General R. E. Laycock, then Chief of Combined Operations. At the end of January the Regiment remobilized with a hundred fewer men.

Lieutenant-General Harding was succeeded as 8 Corps Commander by Lieutenant-General Sir R. N. O'Connor, a Cameron Highlander, well known for his brilliant defeat of the Italians under Marshal Graziani in Cyrenaica in the winter campaign of 1940. This, it is frequently forgotten, was the first important British victory after the sombre days of Dunkirk. He had been captured in the Western Desert in April 1941, but after several efforts had succeeded in escaping from Italy and was back in England by December 1943. Under him, 8 Corps prospered and was happy. He was to lead us into battle.

★   ★   ★

We had yet to experience the mass fervour which members of the Eighth Army assured us a visit from "Monty" would inspire in our breasts, and so it was with a sense of anticipation that we heard that he was coming to address the Corps in February. Would he give the slightest pointer as to future invasion plans? The Regiment's only part so far in the planning for "Overlord" had been the daily dispatch of Lieutenant le Poer Trench and a little sealed box from Yorkshire to London. He was so heavily guarded that he "had never once been able to slip away even to the '400'".[8]

When the day arrived, five hundred Household Cavalrymen, forming part of 8 Corps troops, assembled to hear what General Montgomery, as Commander of 21 Army Group, had to say to them. Outwardly simple in character, the parade was really the result of the most detailed instructions which had come direct to Corps Headquarters from the General's personal staff. Everything, including the "spontaneous surge forward," was laid on by the hand of a master of publicity.

The Rolls-Royce arrived flying an outsize Union Jack, and the men were drawn up in the form of three sides of a square. The boundaries of the square consisted of rows of soldiers facing each other. There were in all six thousand men waiting. The General, a surprisingly small figure, walked slowly up and down the rows. After a long time in the desert his skin looked rather yellow, as if from malaria, and the glance he threw out from keen blue eyes was quick and almost ferrety. "What have we here?" were his opening words to Colonel Abel Smith, as he prepared to scrutinize "A" Squadron, headed by the inexorable bulk of Major Bowes Daly. "The Household Cavalry, sir." Those nearest gained the impression that he already knew the answer, but for some reason had been determined to ask the question. It was a curious introduction.

The inspection being concluded, the men were told to break ranks and gather round the General's jeep and sit down. A surging khaki maelstrom bubbled and eddied and finally subsided on the grass after many cries of "Sit down" from the rear. "Monty" spoke from the bonnet of a jeep with microphone attached. It spluttered once or twice and after adjustments he asked whether everyone could hear him.

One suspected that this had also happened before, but it served the purpose of focusing attention on the speaker. "Yes, sir," shouted the audience and he began.

He said that he had come to 8 Corps because he wanted to get to know them, adding that he felt that we might also wish to "take a look" at him. Summing up past events in which he had played a prominent part, he recalled how he had "been knocked into the sea in 1940" and that he did not like it at all, and that at present he was looking for a good sea into which to knock the Germans. This crack went with a swing, as it had always done in the past, and he and the men were on good terms thereafter.

---

8. Unaware of the true contents of the precious box, he was actually carrying orders and secret codes between Sandhutton (8 Corps Headquarters) and Second Army Headquarters near Victoria Station.

Dealing with future developments, he enthralled the troops with what he was going to do"together, you and I will knock the enemy for six." He told how he never started a battle until he had first won the air fight. This was going on at the present time, and when he had won it, as win it he would, the Allies would invade—not before"; the last said with such ringing and sudden vitality that we knew it must be so.

The talk had none of the fire of the Napoleonic address, nor could one imagine that this metaphorical handing out of cigarettes to "the lads" would ever produce the kind of following which a Marlborough inspired, but it was ruthlessly twentieth century. The Press and public lapped it up. And although at times almost embarrassing, so different was it to anything we had experienced before, we felt nevertheless that here was a captain who would not even let us out of the pavilion until he had morally won the match. In the words of the War Diary, "this was an inspiring parade of an unconventional character."

Revitalized by the "Monty" talk, we plunged into exercise "Eagle". It was "laid down" that living was to be in the open, whatever the weather, and the elements proved to be as merciless as anything we were ever to encounter. Two men from the Monmouthshire Regiment died of exposure. Our umpires, Middle East experts who cheerfully retired to the warmth of country pubs every night, informed us blandly that they never sheltered in houses in the Western Desert. For most of the time we humped shells with frozen fingers while the vehicles sank deeper and deeper into the mud and the wind howled across the wolds. Finally a great battle took place at Octon cross-roads, traffic jammed to a standstill, and with chains and towropes and much effort in the gluey mud, the Regiment returned to camp.

The last months in Yorkshire were busy, for apart from waterproofing, firing on the ranges still continued, new cars of operational mileage kept arriving, and there were many inspections.

On the 23rd of March the Regiment found a Captain's Escort composed of one armoured car (Captain Profumo) and two armoured car Troops (Lieutenants Ainsworth and Tabor) as escort for His Majesty The King who was visiting 8 Corps with Her Majesty The Queen and Her Royal Highness The Princess Elizabeth.

The preparations for the royal visit brought up the escorting armoured cars to a standard of spit and polish never before equalled. There was no precedent to follow in the history of armoured cars and the event produced the greatest rivalry between the two Troops. The men entered into the spirit of the occasion with enthusiasm and determined that the Regiment in war time with its armoured cars should certainly not lag

PREPARING FOR THE RANGE

Testing the recoil mechanism of a new 2-pdr. gun on Daimler armoured car.

behind its peace-time splendour. Every inch of metal gleamed in the sun—even the muzzles of the 2-pdrs. were burnished, and the tyres blackleaded until they shone.

The escort was inspected at Bridlington station and a comprehensive tour of the area was then made, passing through Great Driffield, the Wolds area (11th Armoured Division), Malton and Helmsley (Guards Armoured Division). The tour continued next day among troops quartered near Otley and Corps troops at Sandhutton were inspected. The Royal Party then left for London from York station, where 500 officers and men of the Regiment were drawn up lining the main departure platform and approaches. His Majesty spent fifteen minutes inspecting the Regiment before the train left.

A few days later, while still in its burnished trappings, Lieutenant Tabor's Troop escorted Mr. Winston Churchill on yet another visit to 8 Corps. In addition, a party of 100 men under Captain Ford were also inspected by the Prime Minister. All these visits could have but one meaning.

In April the Regiment carried out what was to prove to be the last big shoot in England, and Midhope Ranges, situated high up on the Yorkshire moors whose blackened surface it was difficult to believe had once sheltered grouse, echoed to salvo after salvo. It was as if all realized that this was the last chance of improving faulty aim or doubtful technique. Troop Leaders practised indirect control of fire, using the 75-mm. gun of the Heavy Troop as artillery. Even the sedate Staghounds seemed infected with the spirit of the occasion and trundled backwards and forwards over the concrete firing points belching flame and shell to a running flow of exhortation and advice from Corporal-Major Ring. The last four Humbers left in the Regiment, and grouped together to form an Ack-Ack Protection Troop under Captain Wrottesley, who led in a car named "Death,"[9] then lurched over the peaty turf to fire their 15-mm. Besas at slowly rising balloons—a form of amusement distinctly flattering to marksmanship. To conclude the day's meeting someone even found enough spare ammunition to enable officers and corporals-of-horse to fire off a few practice rounds with their revolvers[10], and the sounds of these enthusiasts potting at tins continued

9. This car had arrived from another unit and was already in possession of its name. Trooper Grimsley, the driver, rather naturally objecting to going to war in a vehicle of so macabre an appellation, formed up to his Squadron Leader and respectfully asked that it might be changed. It was thereupon rechristened "Destruction".

10. Although the revolver was the personal weapon of all officers and corporals-of-horse, practice ammunition was traditionally limited to the barest and most inadequate amount.

long after the last car had been closed down for the day. Gradually even these echoes died away in the mists of Langsett Moor, and lorries rolled back to a camp soon to be vacated on the last stage of the journey to Normandy.

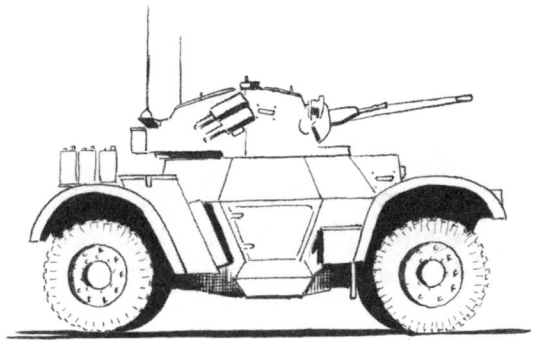

Daimler Armoured Car

Chapter IV

Brighton

Brighton—Final preparations—D Day—Regiment moves to Gosport for embarkation

The 2nd Household Cavalry Regiment concentrated in Selby and on the 20th of April 1944, moved off at full war strength secretly bound for Brighton. The weather was fine, and the atmosphere one of excited suspense. The first night's halt was made at Stevenage after a run down the Great North Road devoid of either incident or breakdown.

Shepherded with great efficiency and a minimum of fuss by Metropolitan Police who had joined the convoy at the Barnet By-pass, the column drove straight through the heart of London in fine style. There was something heartening in the thought of striking a blow at the enemy with the good wishes of the Empire's capital ringing in our ears. Traffic lights flashed in our favour as we sped past Hyde Park Corner and Vauxhall Bridge and so, by way of Walton-on-the-Hill, over the Sussex downs and on to Brighton. The completed run was remarkable in that out of a full number of 240 vehicles, plus training cars, only one had fallen by the wayside after a journey of nearly 300 miles—a great tribute to the work of Captain David Crewdson, the Technical Adjutant, and Lieutenant T. R. Hudson, R.E.M.E., and his staff.[1]

The advance party had reported favourably on the billets in the Preston Park area, although, due to the hard standings being in some cases nearly a mile from billets, a great deal of time was to be spent marching to and from parades. Half of Guards Armoured Division was in Brighton and the remainder in the Eastbourne area. 8 Corps Headquarters was in Worth Priory, about two miles outside Crawley; it had formerly been the property of Lady Cowdray, but latterly had become a Catholic private school. 11th Armoured Division were some distance away in the Aldershot area, while there were some 15th (Scottish) Division troops near Brighton, the rest being at Worthing.

It was difficult, after all these years of training and waiting, to realize that the forthcoming invasion could not be long delayed. Tasks which

---

1. Captain V. Myall, R.E.M.E., had been promoted and gone to 15th (Scottish) Division.

previously had been performed as part of daily routine, suddenly assumed an added importance and urgency as the fateful hour drew near.

These were days of hectic last-minute waterproofing when "Bostic Balding" reigned at the Savoy Garage.[2] Cricket matches in the sun at Preston Park and ten o'clock morning coffee in Brighton if Maintenance Parade was dismissed in time to enable officers to catch the only bus. In the evening young staff officers discoursed at length in the bar of the Norfolk Hotel trying to appear as if only they knew the D Day date and were being frightfully "secure" about it. The "Norfolk" shareholders must surely have been in receipt of handsome dividends after the departure of Guards Armoured Division, to judge by the numbers who daily frequented its bar and dining-rooms. Concerning their welfare, Mr. Bloom, the manager, was touchingly solicitous, "liking," as he put it while scrutinizing the backs of cheques to confirm addresses, "to see the young people enjoying themselves during their last few days in England."

It was very secret that the Regiment was in Sussex at all, but as everybody wore the Corps sign as well as unit flashes, and the electric trains to Victoria ran every half-hour and were filled with soldiers, an enemy agent had no need to look far for his information.

In spite of a nominal ban, many officers' and other ranks' wives still found their way through the cordon to Brighton, and in this illegal traffic the Household Cavalry proved itself more than a match for the Foot Guards.

The three divisions composing 8 Corps were all unblooded, but General O'Connor could not have been more reassuring on that score. It was his opinion, which he gave out to Household Cavalrymen at Guards Armoured Division Headquarters at Eastbourne, that in the battles which lay ahead, the more fresh troops available the better. Men with long years of fighting behind them frequently grew too canny and knowing—a somewhat understandable tendency. What he required above all else in the forthcoming trial was dash. We had the training and the best available equipment, now was the time to put it to the test.

Toward the end of May, Captain Clyde and I were ordered to report forthwith to Second Army Headquarters. We were told no more than that it was "for some sort of very secret wireless job." Colonel Abel Smith bade us good-bye rather as if we were about to join a frog-

---

2. Captain G. Balding, nicknamed thus because he now rarely appeared at H.Q. Squadron, being invariably busy affixing strips of waterproof sheeting stuck on with Bostic solution to the cars. "I have no second-in-command now," used to complain Major Williams mournfully. Some idea of the work involved in waterproofing may be gathered from the fact that each Matador car required 240 man-hours' work on it. *Author.*

man enterprise—we did not expect to see him again. No maps were permitted, but we got to our destination easily enough by watching the main flow of military traffic into Portsmouth.

We found Second Army Headquarters situated in an old Napoleonic era fort high up above the town. Here, after an interview with an officer at the bottom of a moat, we were informed that we were to man the forward wireless net from Second Army Headquarters to its "two assaulting Corps" (1 Corps and 30 Corps). We exchanged rapid glances—2 H.C.R. was therefore to have another wait. How long, we wondered?

After being "Bigoted," which curious expression meant among other things that we were given passes allowing us the run of the Operations Room, we descended an interminable number of concrete stairs into a deep underground honeycomb of rooms and corridors. Soldiers and sailors, liaison officers, both American and British, and Waafs, Ats and Wrens scurried about in all directions with papers under their arms—all looked unnaturally wan under the blue glare of neon lights.

We slid through the jostling throng to knock timidly on a door marked "Operations Room—NO ENTRY." Clutching our passes, we entered and the door was carefully closed behind us. On one wall and covering its entire space was a large black curtain hanging from ceiling to floor. The G.1, a young-looking Rifle Brigade Colonel who had taken part in the planning of the invasion of Italy, greeted us. He said that we should be working for him and that, firstly, we should have to make ourselves familiar with the names of all the units and formations within Second Army. Quietly, as if announcing the date of the local flower show, he said, "The invasion will be taking place on the 5th of June." Saying which, he pulled aside the black curtain and there revealed lay a huge map of the forthcoming invasion beach-head —NORMANDY. Caen jumped to the eyes, and far away to the west we noted that Cherbourg was scheduled for assault by the Americans. Slowly we read across the coastline dotted with peace-time holiday resorts the names of countless little villages destined to be pulverized within a few weeks by shell fire and bombing. All D Day objectives down to battalion and even company levels were carefully shaded and marked in chinagraph. Caen and Bayeux were scheduled to fall on the first day of the assault, their cathedrals, we noted, marked as historic monuments to be spared (if possible). The 6th Airborne Division, which had taken over our Bulford Camp, was to capture Troarn east of the River Orne to ensure the safety of the British left flank. German radar stations and strong points were singled out for special attention and marked accordingly. There were lists of enemy equipment to be captured intact if possible and other lists containing further objects of historic interest to be spared. The assault beaches were labelled and docketed: *OMAHA, GOLD, JUNO*, and *SWORD*. The naval sea lanes and deviations across the Channel were as meticulously traced as if they had been cross-country paths on dry land. Another large map showed the latest enemy situation and was being continuously altered to conform with Intelligence reports as they came in. I remember a minor "flap" because a panzer division had disappeared and aerial reconnaissance had not yet been able to pick it up again. The over-all impression was one of planning down to the last split-second detail. We gazed at all we saw for a long time. At last Tommy Clyde broke the silence. "I hope," he said, "that neither of us talks in his sleep."

The work which followed proved to be of absorbing interest in a three weeks packed with incident. On the wireless net, besides 30 Corps and 1 Corps, there were to be various Naval and Air Force Commands, among others H.M.S. *Hilary*, Admiral Vian's flagship—he was in command of the Naval Task Forces for the assault—and H.M.S. *Bulolo*, in which was to be Brigadier Tarleton, the British Liaison Officer with the American V Corps on the right of the British.[3]

As the Royal Air Force co-operating formations were also represented on the Second Army wireless net, and as each of the three Services talked a different wireless language, and in addition some talked in the old wireless jargon used in the desert while the remainder employed the new method brought in to conform with the Americans (and in which we too were now trained), the state of the air when things were to "hot up" during the invasion can well be imagined.

On the 31st of May came the presentation of plans down to Corps level, and from the back row we listened in rapt attention. The Chief of Staff explained the problems of the staggered assault. The Intelligence Officer dealt with the German formations likely to be met and what was being done to hamper possible reinforcements to the threatened zone. The Air Force was faced with the difficult question of knowing how much to bomb without risking giving away future intentions to the enemy. Except for sleep and a brief meal, we lived underground like moles in a hot, stuffy atmosphere fraught with expectancy.

Two days before the invasion was due to take place, Colonel "Bertie" Bingley breezed into the Operations Room. He was in tremendous form and surprised at seeing us there. His Regiment, the Inns of Court,

---

3. The assault was to be on a four-corps front: VII U.S. Corps, V U.S. Corps, 30 Corps, 1 Corps; the Americans based on Plymouth, the British on Portsmouth.

was sending over a specially picked squadron of armoured cars on D Day to try to blow up bridges on the Orne (the left flank of 1 Corps), and thus delay enemy counter-attacks from the east. It was a daring operation and he was rightly proud that his armoured cars were to carry it out. He was furious at not being allowed to go himself. He had come in because it had been discovered at the last moment that a certain bridge marked on the Operations Room's map did not exist on his! After a hurried consultation with the G.1 the query was settled to his satisfaction and he departed, stopping for a moment to speak to us. "Well, I suppose we shall be seeing you sometime later; give my regards to your Colonel." He passed on down the dark concrete corridor, grinning mischievously, and delighted at having stolen a march on 2 H.C.R.

On the morning of the 4th of June, General Eisenhower and his sub ordinates met to consider the meteorological forecast for the following day, which had been chosen as best suited for the invasion. The forecast was unpropitious and it was decided to postpone the operation for twenty-four hours, but by the time this decision had been taken, part of the American assault force had already put to sea. There was, of course, complete wireless silence, and I believe a destroyer was actually sent after them to bring them back. In any case, so heavy were the seas that many of the craft had already been compelled to turn about and seek shelter. On the morning of the 5th there was little improvement in the weather, but as the forecast for the 6th showed a gleam of hope, with a return to high winds during the evening, the Supreme Commander made his decision. The invasion of Normandy would take place on the 6th of June.

The news reached Second Army Headquarters by special courier. The two assaulting Corps and the two follow-up Corps were to be informed likewise by word of mouth and the G.1 sent for Captain Clyde. In recollecting the scene afterwards he wrote, "The only time I felt of any importance was when we were on that wireless job together! I was sent for by whoever the most senior officer was with whom we came into contact and told that I was to take a message, so secret, to the Commanders of 8 and 12 Corps (the follow-up Corps) that I was to memorize it on the spot by word of mouth and repeat it to them personally. On no account was there to be anyone else present when I gave the message. The message was simply that the invasion had been postponed twenty-four hours. I was put in a huge Staff car with an armed M.P. in front, a huge flag, and a D.R. as outrider. We drove to the area of Tunbridge Wells, firstly to 8 Corps H.Q. There, Henry Garnett was waiting.[4] He had had a signal that an officer was on his

---

4. Captain H. C. L. Garnett, RHG, ADC to Lieutenant-General Sir Richard O'Connor.

way from 21 Army Group Headquarters, with a top priority message for the Corps Commander. You can imagine his face when I stepped out! He took me to General O'Connor and I explained that I could not give my message until we were alone. Henry gave me a look that would kill. O'Connor, seeing that we were of the same Regiment, took the precaution of seeing me back into the Staff car after our session was over (he asked a great many questions which only Winston or Monty could have known the answers to!). He knew what he was doing because Henry was hanging about so very obviously—he was so mad keen to know what it was all about. The same procedure took place at 12 Corps."

Tommy Clyde returned towards evening and as the light faded we climbed the battlements of the old fort and looked down at the fleet of waiting vessels of various sizes at anchor in Portsmouth Harbour. Then silently we descended to our subterranean hide-out to take our place by the wireless sets at a little table rather like a post office booth. Cunningly we each tried to manoeuvre that the other should go to bed and snatch a few hours' rest, but neither would give way on this historic occasion. Judge our consternation when from the set a high-pitched wireless whistle started to vibrate through our eardrums. It grew in intensity, stopped for a moment, then started off again. Although at the time there was still complete wireless silence this interference would surely swamp all conversation when the battle started. "I knew that the German bastards over in France would start their jamming tricks sooner or later," said the operator from the Corps of Signals at the dials of the new Canadian set. A so-called expert was called in and, after fiddling about with the set for ten minutes, announced himself baffled. He left shortly to return in triumph. Apparently a workman had been drilling a hole through a steel girder in an adjoining cubicle and his electric machine had been the cause of all the trouble. After that the invasion, as far as we were concerned, went according to plan!

With Second Army Tactical Headquarters moving over to Normandy some days later, our job finished and we returned to Brighton.

★   ★   ★

Apart from Captain Garnett, the Corps Commander's A.D.C., the first members of the Regiment to go abroad were those in 1 Troop, "A" Squadron, commanded by Lieutenant J. N. Creswell. This Troop had joined 8 Corps at Worth Priory in May and sailed for Normandy on the

12th of June, acting as Corps Commander's Protection Troop. It was not to rejoin the Regiment until the beginning of September.[5]

Seven days after D Day a curious-looking object with squat wings and a red-hot backside passed rapidly over the Brighton roof-tops belching exhaust flames and making a noise like an oversize motor bicycle. Hitler's V1, expected for some time, from Intelligence reports, had arrived. The British called them "buzz bombs" and the Americans "doodle bugs." Both said that it was just the kind of weapon the German mentality would think up.

Regimental reinforcements under the command of Captain G. D. Cooper at Eastbourne took pot-shots at the first comers from high buildings and Corporal-of-Horse Jenkins claimed to have brought one down outside the town, but thereafter indiscriminate shooting was officially discouraged. Soon London's anti-aircraft defences and the Royal Air Force brought in joint arrangements for dealing with the menace in open belts of country outside the Metropolitan area, where their destruction and subsequent explosion would cause least damage. Nevertheless, the civilian population was to suffer greatly from this robot and impersonal form of attack.

Now came a trying period of waiting for the Regiment. The enclosed type of fighting taking place within the bridgehead made it clear that there was yet no role for armoured cars, but we felt as we moved out of Brighton to the concentration area near East Grinstead that a happier choice of name than "Corps Residue" might have been given us!

The Regiment was harboured in Paddockhurst Woods. The weather was generally fine, although towards the end it deteriorated, hindering the final waterproofing of vehicles and wireless sets, for we were under canvas. Continental type maps and the pronunciation of French place names were studied. The R.A.O.C. dumps were visited for unofficial extra kit, resulting in a haul of dual-burner stoves for many cars, a great advantage for the quick brew-up on the roadside because the issue model, fitted with an ineffective little single burner, was far too slow even

---

5. Although the Troop at first consisted of a normal armoured car set-up—i.e., two Daimler armoured cars and two Daimler scout cars—it was soon realized that such a formation was impracticable in the still-overcrowded beachhead. Therefore it was decided that only two scout cars should accompany the Corps Commander on his visits to lower formation headquarters. When the Corps was putting in an armoured attack, the General decided that he would like to be completely "in the picture" and able to move with his Brigadiers if he so wished. For this purpose, Lieutenant Creswell was given five Cromwell tanks. The armoured car crews transferred themselves to these with Royal Armoured Corps drivers attached. Having had a certain amount of tank training at Sandhurst, Creswell was not completely at sea with his new command. At one period he was in charge of a detachment of forty men, including Royal Corps of Signals personnel, and some sixteen vehicles, five of which were tanks.

when it did choose to work properly. For the last time that gallant and distinguished old warrior, Field-Marshal the Lord Birdwood, Colonel of the Blues, came down to bid us God-speed, but as Colonel Abel Smith, the Commanding Officer, was away sick with a bad attack of shingles, Major Sir Peter Grant Lawson took the parade, while the afternoon was devoted to a sports meeting, with the rain coming down in torrents.[6]

On the 9th of July, the Regiment was placed at six hours' notice July to move and the Colonel returned from sick leave. While the Adjutant perforce sat at the end of a telephone line, Major Sir Peter Grant Lawson stalked from tent to tent with a spring balance, carefully testing officers' bed-rolls and valises for overweight. He only caught one person, Lieutenant Hughes, who happened, more by chance than design, to have submitted the genuine article. It was a pound overweight![7]

At a trestle table with an Army blanket spread out before him, Captain Firth counted out French francs (Allied issue) and warned troopers of the penalties for taking more than ten shillings in English money out of the country. For most people this was their first insight into the mysteries of continental currency and the rackets attached thereto.

Next to the money-changing tent R.Q.M.S. Goody was filling a wholly unaccustomed role, and actually entreating Household Cavalrymen to help themselves to kit from mountainous piles of greatcoats and gas capes which no lorry could hope to carry.

A note of grimness crept into proceedings when the padre, the Rev. S. F. Moore, lectured in detail to an attentive audience on the necessarily depressing subject of disposing of the dead on the field of battle. With the sunshine now again streaming through the beech trees we returned to the shade of our tents thinking on this July day that never had England looked more beautiful.

Then, on the morning of the 11th July an order came through to move to Marshalling Area, Camp Al. There were few opportunities for farewells and the Regiment slid off unobtrusively in a warm drizzling rain, bound for Gosport.

---

6. In spite of his age (he was born in 1865) Field-Marshal Lord Birdwood always followed the fortunes of 2 H.C.R. with the greatest interest. He had visited us at Trowbridge, and again at Pollington, where not only did he command the Regiment on church parade, but also inspected the armoured cars, witnessed a demonstration by the Support Troop, and wound up his tour by lecturing on his Gallipoli Campaign to all officers. He then insisted on inviting both the Army and Corps Commanders to dinner on consecutive nights before returning to London.

7. All the others had presented suspiciously limp valises because the rest of their kit was secreted in the bracken by the tents. Lieutenant van Cutsem had even managed to hide a loaded "C" Squadron 3-tonner lorry in the undergrowth until all danger had passed. Thus do the cunning prosper in war.

ORGANIZATION OF 2ND HOUSEHOLD CAVALRY REGIMENT ON SAILING TO NORMANDY, 13TH JULY, 1944.

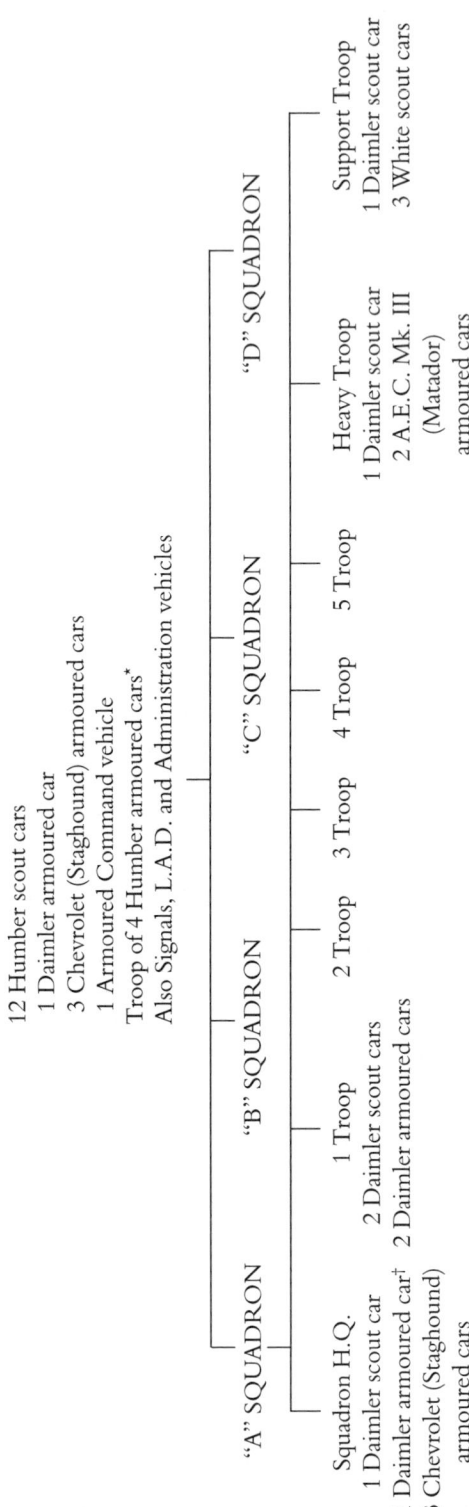

R.H.Q. and H.Q. Squadron

1 Daimler scout car
12 Humber scout cars
1 Daimler armoured car
3 Chevrolet (Staghound) armoured cars
1 Armoured Command vehicle
Troop of 4 Humber armoured cars*
Also Signals, L.A.D. and Administration vehicles

"A" SQUADRON

Squadron H.Q.
1 Daimler scout car
1 Daimler armoured car†
3 Chevrolet (Staghound) armoured cars
and Administration vehicles

"B" SQUADRON

1 Troop
2 Daimler scout cars
2 Daimler armoured cars

2 Troop   3 Troop

"C" SQUADRON

4 Troop   5 Troop

"D" SQUADRON

Heavy Troop
1 Daimler scout car
2 A.E.C. Mk. III (Matador) armoured cars

Support Troop
1 Daimler scout car
3 White scout cars

Notes.—The armament of the Daimler armoured car consisted of one 2-pdr. gun and a 7.92mm. Besa machine gun. The Troop Leader's 2-pdr. gun being fitted with the Littlejohn apparatus, a form of "squeeze" gun to give added muzzle velocity and therefore greater penetrative power, could only fire A.P. shot. The corporal-of-horse's car could fire either A.P. shot or H.E. shell.

The Staghound armoured car was armed with one 75mm. gun, also capable of firing either A.P. or H.E., and one 7.92mm. Besa machine gun.

The scout cars, both Daimler and Humber, carried a Bren gun. Each White scout car carried a section of the Support Troop with Bren gun and 2in. mortar.

Total number of Armoured and "Soft" vehicles, 240.
Total number of Officers, 55. Total number of O.R.s., 778.

* This troop was intended for use in an ack-ack capacity, but was disbanded early on in the campaign when the virtual extinction (over Normandy) of the German Air Force rendered its continued existence a waste of valuable manpower. Its armament consisted of dual-mounted Besa heavy machine guns.

† Squadron Corporal-Major's car and replaced during winter of 1944 by a fourth Staghound.

Part Two

Normandy

Chapter I

The Crossing

Move to Gosport—Uneventful crossing—First night at Brécy—Warning of Operation "Goodwood"

APART from a certain amount of overheating trouble from the 3-tonners caused by the waterproofing, the journey to the marshalling area was uneventful. The Regiment on arrival was split up into four shiploads irrespective of squadrons, and personnel was entirely looked after by the "Hotel Service" provided on the spot. This idea was a stroke of genius because it released everyone from last-minute routine duties, and the apparent chaos due to lack of "organization" soon sorted itself out when the men got into the habit of being on their own, only having to put in an appearance for meals, which they did, of course, with unfailing regularity.

The reinforcements under Captain Cooper had already left 153 Delivery Squadron, Eastbourne, ahead of the main body, on the 9th July and travelled to their marshalling area via London.

"We passed through the West End in the early hours of the morning, after an all-night run. People were still leaving the '400'. Our marshalling area was in a park in North London. Flying bombs were coming over every quarter of an hour or so. We started off again at 7.45 in the morning of the 11th, and journeyed in convoy through the East End, cheering crowds touchingly waving and flinging cigarettes at the men, although they must have been seeing such scenes since before D Day. Our ship was loaded in 2 hours 40 minutes and broke all records.[1] During the loading four 'Doodle' bombs fell on to the Docks, but we left Victoria Docks prompt at 1.30 p.m. to stand off Southend in one huge convoy. Ours was an American ship and the food was excellent. There were pork chops, sauerkraut, pineapple, ices, and even fresh cherries! All the men in tremendous form. The ship sailed at 9.15 at night; it was fairly calm. 'Slit' Trench[2], by an oversight, arrived very late for boat drill and caused the greatest amusement when he asked to be shown to the 'officers' raft. He intended to fight the war as comfortably as circumstances would permit,

---

1. The Navy were both tactful and encouraging, for they were to say the same to the main body of the Regiment at Gosport, and, one suspects, to all other units.
2. Lieutenant D. le Poer Trench.

and one of his last letters to England had been an order for the *Tatler* to be sent out to him regularly. Passed through the English Channel during the 13th of July and only five miles out from Calais. The German guns did not fire a shot. By 8.15 a.m. we were off Beachy Head and could see the Grand Hotel clearly. Joined a second enormous convoy off Portsmouth. In it was 2 H.C.R.!"

★   ★   ★

There was a slight hitch with the main body at Gosport. Just before dawn on the 12th, two shiploads, those commanded by Colonel Abel Smith and Major Sir Peter Grant Lawson, moved down to the embarkation point. Then, after further spasmodic moves and halts lasting four hours in all, the tedium of which was relieved by the local inhabitants who dispensed refreshments with great generosity, the parties were returned to another marshalling camp at Roche Court without even having seen the sea. Something had delayed the ships and it was not until ten o'clock at night that these parties again started off for the hard standings. Meanwhile, Major Wignall's party had already embarked, followed by Major Ward's. The remainder spent most of the night on the shingle waiting for the tide and the L.S.Ts.[3] All felt convinced that this move, as on schemes, would take place at first light.

The dozing men were jolted to their feet at half past three in the morning by the sound of a rattling anchor chain, rending metal and hearty naval oaths. Two vessels had bumped one another in the half light. Eventually quiet reigned again. The dim forms of sailors could be seen leaning over the rails of their ships, spitting tobacco on to the sands. Then a rumour started that the ship's captain "was a devil for speed." He liked his gin, it was also said, and had frequently broken records for the D Day cross-Channel run, leaving the rest of the convoy to come along in its own time. One hoped that on this occasion he might desist from such hazardous-sounding tactics.

As dawn was breaking Captain Collins arrived with a sackful of luggage labels on which Household Cavalrymen were to inscribe their name, rank, and number. The War Office required yet further proof that the sleepy shivering forms gathered in knots about the shingle were at last leaving the shores of England.

Suddenly the steel doors of an L.S.T. opened with a crash and a petty officer shouted, "Take her away."

---

3. L.S.T.—Landing Ship Tanks.

No one was quite sure what this meant, but clearly loading was about to begin. A scout car started up and drove slowly towards the cavernous stomach of the vessel. One month before leaving Pollington, the hand signals so laboriously learnt had been arbitrarily swept away and we had been taught a new series to fit in with Navy procedure, for it was said that the sailors would insist on loading our cars themselves. Nothing of the sort happened and as the Navy wisely left us to it, each Troop Leader guided his own cars into their allotted space in the hold. The normal embarkation point practice was for vehicles to drive on to L.S.Ts. backwards, and land on the other side of the Channel forwards. However, Colonel Abel Smith, who feared that he might miss a favourable tide, ordered all vehicles to drive on forwards and risk landing with their rear to the enemy! "You are a keen lot," commented a grinning A.B., but the plan worked and in a remarkably short time both decks, capable of holding forty vehicles apiece, were filled. Now with some truth the Captain might acknowledge that loading time records had been broken! An encouraging beginning.

So smoothly did the L.S.T. slip away from the shore that before we knew where we were we were miles out at sea. It was a fine sunny day and dead calm. Not an enemy submarine or aircraft was to be sighted the whole way over. The smell and closeness below decks, where the cars were lashed down, were unpleasant, but fortunately everyone was allowed on deck. The sailors were friendly and communicative; there were hot showers and plenty to eat. There was also ample opportunity to make good the lost hours of rest, a chance which Captain Firth, the Quartermaster, was not slow to seize upon, for he slept like a log most of the way over.

Surprisingly, although the bridgehead was still small, the beaches were not under enemy shell fire.[4]

To landward, floating serenely overhead, was a huge balloon barrage, each silver shape beginning to glow red in the setting sun. The immediate landing front was almost clear of debris, but westward it was possible to see the flotsam of war between high and low water lines. There were amphibious tanks, carriers, lorries and all that variety of machines which a war of perpetual movement and adaptability produces. Lying where they had been hit, all were rusting and salt encrusted.

Out at sea, myriads of red and green lights were beginning to wink and signal to one another from a vast semi-circle of vessels at anchor.

---

4. Caen had fallen on the 10th of July. It was, however, but that part of the town lying north of the River Orne. The task was only to be completed when the Canadians cleared the Faubourg de Vaucelles in heavy fighting, between 18th and 21st July.

DUKWs[5] were plying to and fro from the ships to a spot on the shore lost in the darkness, where they were presumably unloading supplies. Darting in and out of the traffic, which appeared to consist of everything from liners to Thames river tugs, were squat little naval launches, throwing up lanes of frothy spray far out at sea. One launch bumped an L.S.T., was sworn at, and careered off in a sweeping arc, with its puce-faced R.N.V.R. commander trying to appear unconcerned; while far out at sea a battleship steamed majestically up-Channel, accompanied by its retinue of destroyers.

The tide was unfavourable for landing that night, although one party, Major Sir Peter Grant Lawson's, just scraped in. The remainder stayed aboard, passed a comfortable night, many between sheets, and awoke fit and fresh. One cabin group was even awakened with an early morning cup of tea and biscuits.[6] Hardly had the steward closed the door when a tremor, followed by a slight grating noise, announced that the L.S.T. was aground. The moment the ship let down her bows, it was obvious that the waterproofing would not be put to the test, and, following one another in quick succession, the cars rolled backwards down the ramps, turned in shallow pools of water, and roared off over the wet sands. As sacred as the Hindu juggernaut. Squadron Leaders' staff cars rolled ashore dry shod.

Two soldiers were kicking a football about the beach, waiting in desultory fashion for a launch to come in. The sands looked so peaceful that one almost expected to see children paddling in the pools. Along a taped route indicated by a yellow windsock floating over the dunes, signs pointed to the village of Graye-sur-Mer, beyond which lay the transit area where we were to dewaterproof cars and sample for the first and last time the contents of our cardboard box called the twenty-four-hour pack.[7] Under the shadow of another notice marked "The Penalty for Looting is Death" three soldiers were lifting potatoes. In the village itself the few remaining civilians were dressed in their Sunday best, for it was the 14th of July, France's great annual holiday—the celebration of the fall of the Bastille.

The transit area was soon reached, and while theories were propounded on how to deal with snipers, Captain Kynaston's medical crew basked in the sunshine counting scalpels and rolls of bandages. Apart from a few

---

5. DUKW (colloquially known as Duck) – an amphibious load-carrying vehicle.
6. Captain Clyde, Captain Waterhouse, Surgeon-Captain Kynaston, and the author.
7. It contained, among other things, sweets, dehydrated food, and a tiny metal stove using solidified methylated spirits. The food, unless thoroughly watered down and cooked, tended, with disastrous results, to go on swelling during digestion.

crumps from the direction of Caen and a brief aerial combat overhead, in which a dozen Allied fighters chased off a solitary enemy reconnaissance plane, all was quiet. The entire Regiment had reported present and in fighting trim, with the exception of Lieutenant Smallwood, whose Matador had caught fire on the journey to Gosport. He was to catch up within forty-eight hours, beaming with retrospective delight at the series of minor disasters caused by the conflagration. Very keen and mechanically minded, Lieutenant Smallwood was persistently dogged by engineering mishaps which never seemed to touch ordinary mortals.

The afternoon was spent in pulling off the waterproofing and repacking kit. The three issue "bags, vomit" allotted to each person, and thankfully unused, came in useful for shaving kit. Likewise, for heavier stuff, the wireless waterproof bags. The metal chutes fitted to the Staghounds' exhaust system for the crossing (part of their waterproofing system) were only partially removed, and the bases as conveyors of hot air later proved invaluable for drying damp clothes.

As the day wore on, orders flooded into Regimental Headquarters. "All officers must understand that their object is to get to the CONC Area as soon as possible"— "Troops must be warned of the potency of all types of wine" (there was little wine left, but a great deal of calvados, deadly stuff but excellent for lighting fires)— "Money found on bodies will be handed to Fd Cashier and a receipt obtnd"! —"Washing—Until the arrival of a MU or BU, each man must fend for himself. Once in CONC Area they are responsible for own admn incl hyg." Regarding the latter, most of the Regiment were already "incl hyg"-ing as hard as they could go—the British soldier requires no urging to wash his face at the slightest provocation.

When the Regiment moved off to the assembly area, which lay some miles away in the village of Brécy, it was already dark. The road led through the village of Creully, dominated by its picturesque twelfth-century castle, still sign-posted by the French Office of Works as a historic monument to be preserved! Just as the convoy was passing beneath its high walls, an enemy plane droned overhead. This was the signal for all the ack-ack guns in the bridgehead to open up. Multi-coloured trace streaked across the skies in a wonderful firework display. Then one by one the searchlights switched on and started to grope about, tentatively waving their beams across the sky. Now and again one of the more aimless shafts of light would shine through the dust which had been disturbed by the cars and momentarily illuminate the castle ramparts, imparting to them an atmosphere of gossamer-like beauty strangely out of keeping with the grimmer background of war.

As suddenly as it had started, the barrage died down, and the searchlights, following suit, switched off one by one. The scene vanished and the convoy, still swallowed up in a cloud of gritty dust, bumped off down a side lane to Brécy.

★   ★   ★

Many villages in this part of the bridgehead had been terribly scarred by the preliminary bombardment—in some places almost blotted out—but there were still a few, with their protecting châteaux and air of gentle decay, which had avoided annihilation. One hoped that when the tide of destruction had finally swept over for good, the markets and the farmers' gatherings, the blue-clad peasants and the contented "hey-diddle-diddle" cows would all resume the tenor of their ways. This country of Maupassant, with its prolific cider orchards and waving cornfields, was the last place in the world to be created for war, and the draped coils of signal wire wrapped round the telegraph poles, the discarded petrol tins and empty shell cases all struck a note of horrible incongruity.

Although Brécy had been a D Day brigade objective, the tide of battle had in the main avoided the village. It consisted of a few houses, a small church, and the usual cemetery with its rows of wrought iron crosses, metal flowers in baby greenhouses and sun-bleached photographs of the departed. There was also a small château, now turned farm, but which still retained its somewhat consequential little gateway, and an overgrown avenue of beeches leading up to it. Behind was a rather mysterious garden, terraced in Caen stone. We were informed by the inhabitants that the château had recently belonged to an actress from the Comedie Francaise, but that since her boyfriend, a wealthy soap manufacturer, had been locked up by the Nazis, it had been unoccupied. This story added vicarious glamour to the "D" Squadron Officers' Mess, which settled down close at hand.

The farm, with its courtyard and tumbledown barns, had also seen better days. Nearby was a wooden cross made out of a ration box which marked the spot where a Canadian officer and two men had fallen, and a German helmet was already in use by the village pump as a bucket. But there were obviously worse assembly areas. The orchards would afford shade from the sun, and the farm the possibility of butter and fresh eggs. It was late, and as nobody was yet quite sure of the form, before turning in for the night slit trenches were dug with due solemnity.

Dawn confirmed the impressions of the previous night. Brécy was a pleasant little spot, and Lieutenant Bethell lolloped over to the farm

NORMANDY – 13TH JULY 1944

View of "Juno" beach near Graye-sur-Mer, where the Regiment landed. The sea was calm and the L.S.Ts. here shown were able to ground well inshore on an ebbing tide, and not one vehicle was called upon to put its elaborate waterproofing to the test.

entrance ostensibly to engage three children in conversation. But they did not understand his French and he soon returned, having been told that he spoke their language "comme une vache Espagnol."[8] There were many stories of sniping from the cornfields, but the men were too busy penning their first letters home to worry. "The officers," wrote a corporal-of-horse in his diary, "although suffering the worst they have yet suffered, as far as rough living is concerned, still manage to look pretty comfortable!"

★   ★   ★

On Sunday, Colonel Abel Smith was summoned to 8 Corps Head-quarters to hear from the B.G.S. about "Goodwood Meeting," the forthcoming operation. This was to be a drive employing three armoured divisions (11th Armoured, Guards Armoured, and 7th Armoured), with the intention of breaking out south of Caen to a line overlooking Falaise. After softening up of enemy defences by bombers employed on a lavish scale, the corps was to cross the River Orne by the now famous Pegasus Bridge[9] at Benouville (and other pontoon bridges built for the operation) and force its way out of the airborne bridgehead by weight of armour and aerial bombardment. Guarding the eastern flank would be 3rd Division along the Bois de Bavent, while on the right 3rd Canadian Division was to have the thankless task of driving up the eastern bank of the River Orne and clearing the suburbs of Caen known as the Faubourg de Vaucelles and Cormelles. Two squadrons of the Regiment were to be ready to co-operate with Guards Armoured Division on the following day, a Monday.

"A" Squadron (Major Bowes Daly) and "B" Squadron (Major Wignall) were therefore ordered to move off almost immediately to the divisional concentration area near Bayeux. In addition, a scout car traffic control net of wireless stations manned by officers from "C" Squadron was required to assist in the move to the assembly area at Anguerny, a few miles west of Pegasus bridge. These were to be commanded by Captain Balding.

Greatly to Colonel Abel Smith's chagrin, and in spite of all his attempts to have the decision altered, Regimental Headquarters as it stood was definitely forbidden to take part.

---

8. His brother officers averred that he was, even at this early stage of the campaign, assessing his chances of obtaining a French car for his own use!

9. Pegasus Bridge, Benouville, so named after the sign of the 6th Airborne Division, which captured it on D Day.

Chapter II

Operation "Goodwood"

Operation "Goodwood"—"A" and "B" Squadrons only engaged—First casualties—Premature end of operation mainly due to enemy 88s and bad weather

The rolling cornlands of the Plain of Caen over which operation "Goodwood" was to unfold itself were, as far as a study of maps could make it, well known to the Regiment. Wisely, when still in England, various exercises had been set, using continental maps, to familiarize people with the different scales used, the topography, and the strangeness to British ears of French place names.

One of the immediate problems which arose was whether the Squadrons should operate separately on the Guards Armoured Divisional Command wireless net or whether a skeleton co-ordinating headquarters should take part. It was decided that Major Sir Peter Grant Lawson assisted by Lieutenant Haskard, the Intelligence Officer, should co-ordinate the work of the two Squadrons.

The move on the night of 17th/18th July to the forming-up area south of Anguerny went smoothly, although the well-nigh insuperable difficulties attendant on moving three armoured divisions on narrow roads across the run of traffic feeding the main front resulted in some units dropping behind schedule. The attack, it was hoped, would be a complete surprise to the enemy, although even at night the immense column of dust caused by the wheels and tracks on the crumbling roads must have been visible for many miles. We were told that enemy spotting planes had been chased out of the sky.

It was a beautiful morning without a cloud in the sky when, at a quarter to six, the first heavy bombers flew in from the sea. They passed over in a steady stream, 1,100 planes of Bomber Command and 600 of Eighth United States Army, together with 400 medium bombers of Ninth United States Air Force, and the suburbs of Caen and the little villages to the south were drenched in an avalanche of noise and destruction. Powdered rubble was still rising heavenwards as the leading ground troops began their advance at a quarter to eight.

We were told, and fully believed it, that we were on the threshold of great events. "We are ready to break out of the bridgehead … we still firmly retain the initiative … we have punished the enemy severely."

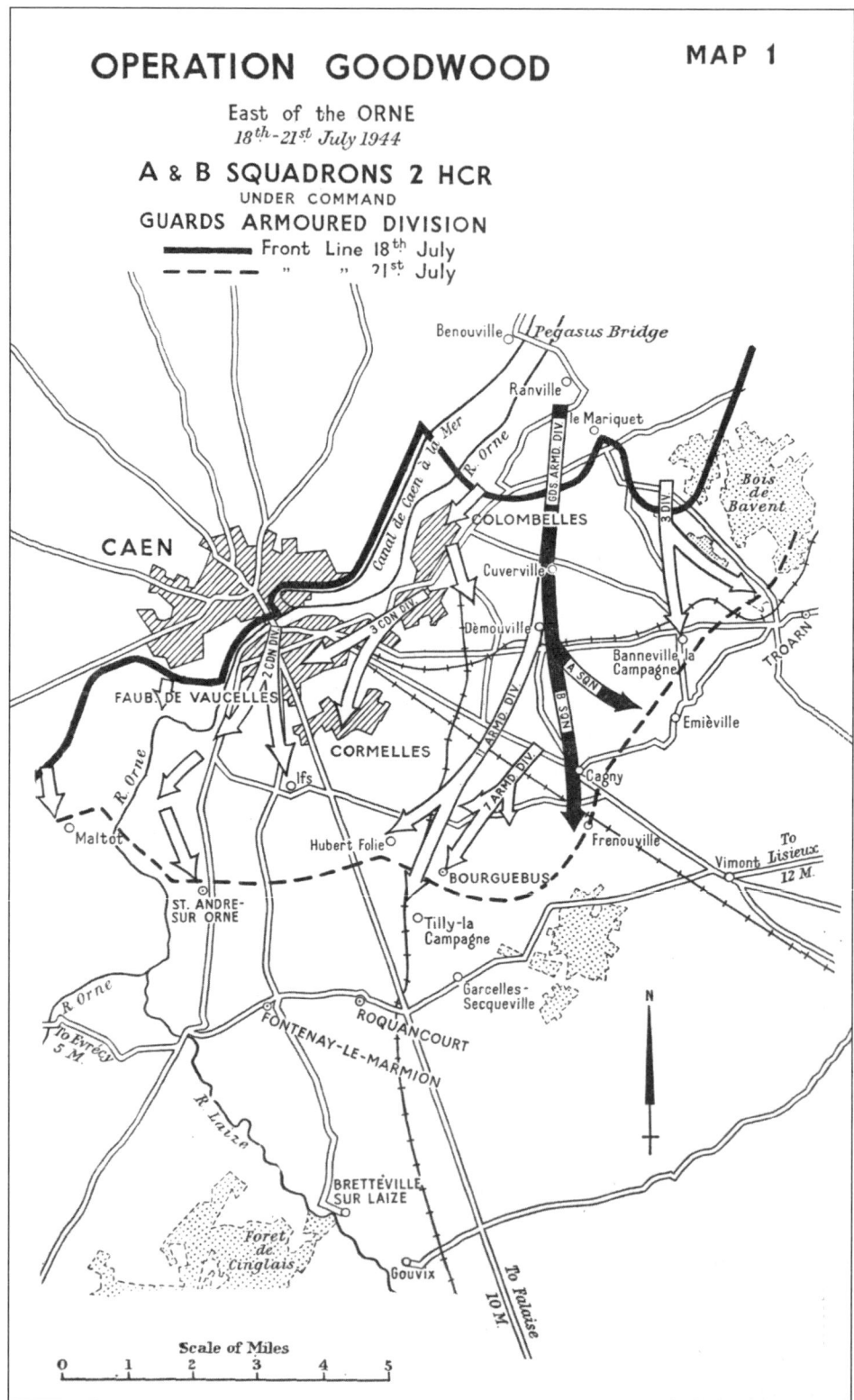

OPERATION GOODWOOD

MAP 1

East of the ORNE
18th-21st July 1944

A & B SQUADRONS 2 HCR

UNDER COMMAND

GUARDS ARMOURED DIVISION

——————— Front Line 18th July
    "   " 21st July

Benouville   Pegasus Bridge

Ranville

le Mariquet

R. Orne

GDS ARMD DIV

Bois de Bavent

3 DIV

COLOMBELLES

Canal de Caen à la Mer

CAEN

Cuverville

Dèmouville

3 CDN DIV

Banneville la Campagne

A SQN

TROARN

2 CDN DIV

FAUB. DE VAUCELLES

B SQN

Emièville

CORMELLES

1 ARMD DIV

R. Orne

Ifs

Cagny

Maltot

Hubert Folie

Frenouville

To Lisieux
Vimont 12 M.

ST. ANDRE-SUR ORNE

BOURGUEBUS

Tilly-la-Campagne

R. Orne

Garcelles-Secqueville

N

To Evrecy 5 M.

ROQUANCOURT

FONTENAY-LE-MARMION

R. Laize

BRETTÉVILLE-SUR LAIZE

Foret de Cinglais

Gouvix

To Falaise 10 M.

Scale of Miles
0   1   2   3   4   5

Nothing could now stop us, and the next move, it was confidently felt, was designed to force the Germans into what Montgomery called "wet hen tactics"—rushing about trying to stem our repeated thrusts and frantically trying to plug the growing numbers of holes in their line.

But in the meantime things were not going too well. The 11th Armoured Division, which was leading, and now across the Orne Canal, found the gaps through the minefields dangerously narrow. Tanks went up on mines, making it difficult for the others to pass them. The Germans, recovering from the aerial bombardment more quickly than had been anticipated, came out of their trenches relatively unharmed and, quickly stepping back a thousand yards, manned a line of anti-tank guns with devastating effect. What had been hoped might be a break-through to the Falaise Plain petered out after a few hours into a series of local engagements. 11th Armoured Division veered off south-west of Cagny and was halted dead on its tracks by the main German body. Guards Armoured Division became heavily engaged in the area of Cagny and was badly shot up by a well-sited line of 88-mms. barring the Paris road. And 7th Armoured Division, last to cross the river, never really got going at all.

For this reason, the two Squadrons of the Regiment were never able to operate in their true reconnaissance role. A few troops did move forward, got in the way of the tanks, and were then shot at by the invisible guns of an enemy who was able to enjoy to the full the obvious British discomfiture. There was some talk of sending armoured car patrols eastward to the low-lying country around Troarn to blow up bridges in the event of enemy counter-attacks, but it came to nothing.

However, as "Goodwood" was the Regiment's baptism of fire, it is worthwhile following the story of the two Squadrons over the Orne.

The Squadrons followed down 5th Brigade centre line in the rear of the 2nd Welsh Guards (Cromwell tanks), the armoured reconnaissance battalion of Guards Armoured Division. Both Squadrons moved over the Orne in the early morning of the 18th of July. Around the bridge at Benouville soldiers could be seen comfortably housed in the old shells of the 6th Airborne Division's discarded gliders—washing hung out on lines stretched between crashed planes, and the now returning French peasants gleaned among the heaps of twisted aluminium to see what was left of their possessions.

One Troop Leader described the crossing of the Orne:

"We had driven all night in the direction of Caen, having slept for some time in an orchard with the shrapnel from the thousands of ack-ack guns falling down through the half-dead apple trees, sometimes cutting off a branch. All around were scattered pamphlets in German that the R.A.F. had dropped on D Day, asking the Germans to give up the struggle. Some hope! The whole sky last night was one stream of tracer shells. I wish I could describe it to you, with planes threading their way like bats through these branches. When the planes flew low all the guns fired low and some of the shells were bursting in the next-door field. I slept half underneath my car, and I saw one chap wearing his tin hat in bed.... No breakfast until we move, though no one seems to know exactly where we are going—somewhere beyond Caen, I believe.

"... We have driven for some time; dust everywhere so that one can see nothing. I have just been following the car in front of me for the last three hours. I heard the nightingales singing for the first time. Overhead now an endless humming went on; it was bright morning, and I could see thousands upon thousands of big four-engined bombers. They dipped as they passed over Caen. We could watch the dust rising from the bombs on the low hills on the other side of the valley, and yet I lay back on my sleeping-bag contentedly, and watched this battle starting. Soon it was six o'clock and we were off, clutching some biscuits and a mug of tea. Tanks were passing us on a taped track over the downs as we drove alongside on the road. We drove down and over a canal bridge and up the steep side beyond. Notices everywhere. 'Dust brings shells'—it did. Others, 'Tracks Left,' Bridge Class 40,' etc. Up the hill, the ominous notice saying simply, 'Mines.' We went into the tapes as though we were to start a hundred-yards race; already the Welsh Guards had been through in the morning mists. In fact, we soon learnt that the Armoured Divisions 'were through already,' and we must catch up as soon as we could. Instead, we were held up by the dense traffic and spent an hour sitting on the skyline in a minefield being shelled. I read a detective novel sitting inside my car, munching more biscuits. From the top of one's car one could see quite a bit of the battle. The tanks were milling around and I remember criticizing their tactics! Red Cross half-tracks with their huge flags plied backwards and forwards carrying a continuous stream of casualties. At last we went off again in a convoy line, pausing occasionally in the thick dust. We had been actually issued with compasses in case the dust became too bad to see at all. That day the battle was too tight for us to 'debouch,' although we saw some of the Inns of Court cars returning with various trophies."[1]

At night both Squadrons moved back to harbour with Tactical Headquarters of Guards Armoured Division, a thousand yards south of

---

1. The Inns of Court Regiment, armoured cars to 11th Armoured Division.

the village of Demouville, their echelons some little distance back at Le Mariquet. Taking advantage of the bright night, the enemy made a sharp bombing attack on the divisional area, and Lance-Corporal Kenneth Barnes, one of the "A" Squadron despatch riders, was killed.

There had also been bad news from Captain Balding, who had arrived back at Regimental Headquarters with his scout car and van riddled with shell splinters.[2] One of his road traffic control parties at Biéville had received a direct hit from a parcel of anti-personnel bombs. Lieutenant Anthony Potter suffered severe wounds, dying almost immediately, as did Captain Balding's officer's servant, Trooper Edward Ariss, also Lance-Corporal Richard Dooley and Driver Philip Jackson of the Royal Corps of Signals. Corporal-of-Horse Geoffrey Reynolds, terribly injured in the head and abdomen, was evacuated to the casualty clearing station at Douvres-la-Délivrande and thence to England, where he died a fortnight later. The wounded included Corporal J. R. Guy, of Headquarter Squadron, and Corporal A. F. Emery, Royal Corps of Signals. Guy, who was Captain Balding's Humber scout car driver, received shrapnel wounds through his right thigh and backside and remembered little of the journey to the first aid post. There he was placed on the top bunk of an ambulance. "The driver was in a hurry and he hit a hole in the road. I left the bunk, hit the roof with a crash and cut my head open on a wing nut on the roof. Up till then I had not felt any pain, but I felt that!"

★ ★ ★

On the 19th, heavy rain started to fall. It laid the dust, which was some relief, but brought out mosquitoes in their millions. Worse, the armoured cars now found it impossible to keep up with the tanks, whose tracks had churned up the roads into a quagmire. Fields proved a veritable morass for slithering vehicles, and an unpleasant day was spent under steady mortar fire.

Slight hope of forward movement arose next day, but it was short-lived. Given tasks in the morning of patrolling ("A" Squadron to the east towards the Troarn—Argences—Vimont road and "B" Squadron southwards beyond the Caen—Vimont road), both Squadrons were withdrawn in the late afternoon. Little headway had been made against the enemy tanks and anti-tank guns, whose crews with the light behind them picked out turrets in that flat country from a great distance with unerring accuracy.

---

2. Regimental Headquarters had moved from Brécy to an area farther east at Amblie on 16th July (afternoon).

This is how Lieutenant Franklin's Troop prepared for action:

"I took down my first orders in feverish detail; then they were cancelled. Instead of having to 'seize and hold' a bridge behind the enemy lines at St. Pierre du Jonquet (five miles south-east of Troarn), I was ordered to get into the hills above Troarn on the boundary of 1 and 8 Corps. The main attack had now moved due south on Cagny through Demouville. Emieville harboured a few Tiger tanks and it was unfortunately on my route. Our own tanks had had trouble there and we had watched them the day before being knocked out. All one sees when a tank is knocked out is a coil of black smoke spiralling up through the open turret. Sometimes a man or two jumps out if they are lucky. I led off in one of the scout cars, with another following, and left the larger armoured cars, which showed up so plainly above the corn, to follow a mile or so behind, when I had found good cover. We travelled in this manner for a mile and then found some tanks of the Welsh Guards. They were hunting a Tiger tank and going very cautiously—which surprised me at the time—we were very green then."

Meanwhile, owing to the dust, the rest of the Troop under Corporal-of-Horse Booth had missed the way. The armoured cars turned off at a side road and continued the advance, hoping to make contact with the rest of the Troop farther on. They went too far and on turning a bend ran straight into a Tiger tank. It gave no sign of having recognized them and after a time spent in observation Booth took it to be deserted. An old German coat was hanging over its side and so Corporal Thompson got out and went through the pockets. All contents, including the pay book, were extracted. Then someone started machine gunning from a copse, and as Trooper Baxendale was reversing the car to manoeuvre into a better position, a second Tiger tank opened up from the edge of a wood. Trooper Evans fired back though without much hope of success against the monster's armour, and the two armoured cars beat a hurried retreat. They had by chance stumbled upon the very Tiger tank which was holding up the advance in that sector and had removed the enemy's documents as he was having his morning "brew up"! The troop experienced its share of luck that day, for already an 88-mm. shell had landed underneath Corporal-of-Horse Booth's Daimler, failing to explode "but spoiling the tea."

"The mess around the battlefield," wrote a Household Cavalryman, "is now frightful. The infantry are digging in along a bank where they joined us. The smell is awful, a mixture of slaughterhouse, cheap soap, and oil. There is an old self-propelled gun knocked out in our cornfield, rubbish blowing about around it, and a dead British soldier with a bayonet through his neck. The main street of Cagny is still in enemy hands and blocked by heaps of rubble, and they have hung a camouflage net over the road so that we cannot see what goes on beyond. Our tanks and S.Ps.[3] are firing from every conceivable angle, some of the hidden enemy guns being behind us. I haven't seen many dead Germans. They mostly seem to have got away, though a very smart German Medical Officer and his batman strolled into our lines a moment ago. No one here can see the German guns firing as the Jerries seem to be using a completely smokeless powder. Occasionally a Sherman that is burning blows up and the turret flies off."

Later, on the 21st of July, the Squadrons were ordered to withdraw to a harbour about a mile behind the infantry and were there subjected to a certain amount of shelling and mortaring. One shell, suspected of being a short from our own side, landed in the middle of "A" Squadron, killing Trooper John McGuiness outright and wounding Corporal Francis Reynolds so seriously that he died some hours later. Also wounded were Lieutenant G. L. M. Murray, the Heavy Troop Leader, and his driver, Trooper J. Baird, and Trooper A. Cottrell. "It was a horrible scene— one moment everyone talking and standing around, the next shambles. Burning earth and cordite, and bodies all over the place. It is always hard on troops untried as yet for such scenes. My driver was sick at the sight and I have had a glass of whisky. Peter[4] was absolutely first class."

After an evening thunderstorm had turned the tank-churned soil into a complete gluepot, it became obvious that the attack had completely fizzled out. The battle had been accompanied by abnormally heavy tank casualties, although the proportion of casualties in personnel eventually turned out to be not as great as had been feared. It was surprising how often a Sherman tank would be seen to receive one or more direct hits, burst into flames, and then the crew emerge unhurt.

Major Bowes Daly had insisted on taking into action a large marquee, which he now erected to dry the sopping clothes of his men. Stoves appeared from nowhere, and in a short time clouds of steam announced that they were fulfilling their purpose. This "A" Squadron marquee was of proportions such as had not been seen in these parts since the Field of the Cloth of Gold. It caused a great stir in Guards Armoured Division, but as it contained beer and calvados it soon became popular with the

---

3. S.Ps.—self-propelled guns, the nearest German equivalent being their 75-mm. gun mounted on a Mark III Tank chassis.

4. Major Sir Peter Grant Lawson, Bt., commanding the two-squadron group.

local staff officers, who flocked over to "fill in their picture" on the situation map.

On the 21st of July, when the infantry were ordered to relieve the armour, "Goodwood" was officially over. Military historians are wont to write up the operation as having achieved its full purpose because the enemy had successfully resisted the attack only by switching many crack Panzer divisions from another front. This may have been so, but there was no hiding the disappointment of all those taking part, who had been led to expect far greater results for such a lavish use of armour. Nor can any number of post-mortem apologies ever make the participants believe that commanders had foreseen those lines of 88s which were, as the Americans truly said, to "stop us cold."

It is also now known that the Germans had got wind of the attack beforehand and they were therefore able partially to anticipate the effects of the Allied bombing. The difficulties of secretly concentrating three armoured divisions were enormous, and the resultant, if unavoidable, traffic congestion must have played its part in helping the enemy to gain time in the deployment of his defensive troops. In addition, the bombing programme had caused many of the village objectives to be blocked with fallen masonry, thus hindering the rapid follow-up of our tanks.

After the battle was over it was said that the true reason for the Germans' advance knowledge of "Goodwood" was a simple Redskin trick of the commander of the 1st S.S. Panzer Corps, General Sepp Dietrich. This soldier, from all accounts a genial rogue who had started life as a butcher, ignoring the Intelligence Summaries of his staff, simply put his ear to the ground and said, "I hear the rumble of British Panzers crossing the Orne."

★   ★   ★

A last picture of "Goodwood" is worth recalling.

During the early thrusts, General O'Connor, coming forward to see for himself what was holding things up, jumped on to a tank containing one of the tank battalion's commanders in the process of ordering forward his Squadrons. On the back of this tank was also the Brigade Commander and behind him the Divisional Commander, Major-General Adair, all urgently ordering one another on in descending order of seniority, the final version doubtless reaching (in wireless form) some harassed subaltern as he struggled through Cagny. A Household Cavalry trooper, witness of this unusual party, turned aside to his companion, "Well, I thought that when I had the Colonel and two other b——s giving advice on the back of my Daimler at Linney Head it was bad enough, but three Generals is b——y murder!"

Chapter III

Waiting for the Next Move

Awaiting further developments on the Normandy bridgehead

Meanwhile, after two nights spent at Brécy, Regimental Headquarters and "D" Squadron had moved a few miles east to a small sloping field on the outskirts of another little village called Amblie. "C" Squadron, apart from supplying the men necessary for the traffic control posts, had departed on the 16th of July to St. Aubin-sur-Mer, where they were to prepare a seaside corps rest camp.

Amblie was also virtually untouched by the fighting, and it was here, after Lieutenant Turnbull, the Signals Officer, had rigged up his wireless masts and a loud-speaker, that those of the Regiment not engaged in "Goodwood" had listened in to the doings of their comrades over the Orne. "D" Squadron also found time for some cricket, while the village children begged for chocolate and entertained the men by trying out on them their already extensive vocabulary of rude English words.

The enforced inactivity at Regimental Headquarters was too much for Colonel Abel Smith. He decided to go and see the battle for himself, taking with him in a jeep Lieutenant Turnbull and Trooper Shaw. The Colonel came back beaming. Not so Lieutenant Turnbull or Trooper Shaw, the latter lying uncomfortably face downwards bent like a croquet hoop on top of a mountainous pile of kit, field glasses and maps, nursing a slightly punctured behind. The party had run in rather too close to the enemy's positions and been chased back down the road by "Moaning Minnies."[1] Poor Shaw, looking very sorry for himself in his undignified position, was soon surrounded by laughing companions, while Lieutenant Turnbull muttered fiercely under his breath, "Never again"!

The next to undergo the ordeal was Surgeon-Captain Kynaston, who drove to meet his fate wearing an expression of infinite resignation.

"The Colonel and I set off in his jeep, myself as map reader. The Colonel said, 'Avoid this wood' (pointing generally to the map) 'for they are shelling it.' Five minutes later I was hopelessly lost. Ten minutes later we were within a hundred yards of the wood. The Colonel was very angry.

"Soon he spied a covey of partridges alighting gracefully a hundred yards

---

1. "Moaning Minnies"--German multiple-barrelled mortars.

from the road. The Colonel was delighted, stopped the jeep, and said, 'Roger, we'll walk these birds up—you go this way, I'll go that.' We soon came to notices marked 'Achtung Minen,' but in true Household Cavalry spirit pushed on. Thank God, the birds got up well out of shot and we returned."

★   ★   ★

The congestion of troops throughout the bridgehead was growing daily and the fitting of men and vehicles into fields, roads, and even narrow lanes was proving a veritable Staff nightmare. As part of a general reshuffle, the Regiment moved off again, this time to Camilly, where on the 23rd of July "A" and "B" Squadron were to rejoin it. They came back through Caen, whose southern suburbs had only just been cleared by the Canadians, and they saw (and smelt) the devastation of this martyred town. Thousands of civilians, forbidden by the Germans to leave, had been trapped by the Allied air bombardment and still lay buried beneath the rubble. Rescue squads were badly hindered by the plague of flies, and there was no drinking water. Food was desperately short and Household Cavalrymen never forgot the sights of horror they witnessed there in passing.

The men had soon grown accustomed to the noisy nights of aerial barrage and the activity of the relatively few German reconnaissance planes. Fragments of our own ack-ack shells fell like rain, but no one seemed to get hit. Corporal-Major ("Snatch") Ring, true to form, produced an ugly-looking piece of hot metal and a complicated theory on speed of impact and penetration as affecting canvas tents. The splinter had pierced his bivouac. He and I discussed the theory long into the night, but the fragments, undeterred, still pattered down.

Meanwhile, troopers continued to milk the herds of untended cattle in the fields, for "it's a pity to let it get sour, sir." There was a sudden unaccountable outburst of shorn heads. Lieutenant Hopkinson's Support Troop took to the style almost to a man, its members appearing to have trained for battle at Dartmoor. The habit soon died a natural death.

Compulsory P.T. reared its ugly head at last, but there were compensations. A well-organized run round Camilly brought in good dividends of butter, eggs, Camembert cheese and cider, for the farmers would always barter for cigarettes.

Generally speaking, however, the peasants were not very forthcoming, and there were even stories of pro-Vichy sympathizers refusing to hand over their châteaux for use as headquarters. But most of the taller stories could be discounted. Perhaps it was that the Englishman, brought up to expect the excitable type of Frenchman, failed to understand the taciturn Norman. Stories of German-sympathizing Frenchmen in the role of snipers were also ridiculously exaggerated and obviously enemy inspired.

True peasant, the Norman distrusted anything new, and he certainly failed to give the impression that he enjoyed all aspects of liberation. There were reasons for this. The people of France in this part had in the main been treated well by the German occupation troops, who were mostly composed of middle-aged category men and only too pleased to live and let live. They did not interfere with the farming and marketing arrangements of the natives and, his immediate necessities of life being thus safeguarded, the Norman farmer suffered with mixed feelings the sudden influx of Allied soldiers with all the attendant holocaust of death and destruction. He viewed the Allied liberation francs with suspicion, nor could he understand our bombing, especially at Caen, where he reiterated that when the worst raid came there were no German soldiers in the place. Understandably, the civilian frequently failed to appreciate the difference between friendly and enemy shells. Both killed his cattle. Alan Moorehead truly wrote, "Our soldiers did not behave like angels. They seldom do, nor can you expect them to be gentle creatures if you are to pitchfork them into war. Vegetables and fruit were stolen. There were other misdemeanours." It was all part of the misery of war.

★ ★ ★

While waiting for the break-through, Troop Leaders took their men on daily map-reading runs to visit the neighbouring town of Bayeux, which, unlike Caen, was not in ruins, having been captured relatively unharmed on the second day of the invasion. The Cathedral, with its beautiful twin spires, was intact, but within its shadow hundreds of homeless refugees from Caen slept on the stone cobbles in exhaustion and despair.

The old streets and alleyways seethed with military activity, and the Press appeared to be in firm occupation of the only sizeable hotel in the place, the Lion d'Or. Nevertheless, there were still a few tables vacant and Lieutenant van Zoelen was able to write after a luncheon of steak (from war slaughtered cattle) and fried potatoes and salad that "this charming little town has an atmosphere of its very own which not even the mass of soldiery can dispel entirely."

The arrival of a mobile bath unit at Pierrepont was a great relief, and following its warm showers, the Keating's powder, which so far had not been used, was packed away.

The Inns of Court Regiment was close at hand and Colonel Abel Smith wasted no time in paying a visit to its Commanding Officer, Colonel Bingley. The latter had produced a revolutionary theory on the use of armoured cars under the present conditions of fighting. He believed that the Germans fired at the turrets of the Daimler armoured cars, mistaking them for tanks, and frequently let the scout cars through. He argued that as the turret was much more visible silhouetted above the standing corn, why not take off the Daimler armoured car turret and use the vehicle as an additional scout car? This scheme would have the added advantage of giving extra space for a spare driver. On hearing of this, General O'Connor suggested that the Regiment might like to follow suit but pressed it no farther. In a matter so closely related to the safety and efficacy of the Reconnaissance Troop, Colonel Abel Smith decided to leave the final decision to individual Troop Leaders. They unanimously agreed to leave the cars as they were. It was a wise decision. With their turrets rusting in some Normandy dump there would have been many an occasion later on in the campaign when their loss must have been keenly felt. But the conclusion was reached that where possible two scout cars leading was the best drill to be used in close country; and it was anticipated, correctly as things turned out, that when the corn was cut, in the more open country to be met farther east, turrets would again prove very necessary. The Inns of Court Daimlers without their turrets, which we were to meet frequently at later stages of the campaign, came to be known as "Sods"—sawn-off Daimlers.

Colonel Bingley was also the originator of another dashing plan—that of brigading 2nd Household Cavalry Regiment and the Inns of Court Regiment under his command, to form a sort of roving guerrilla party of armoured cars, aimed to create havoc behind the enemy lines, when the break-through should occur. The proposition, had it materialized or been feasible, would have found both regiments milling about the American sector bound for the Loire at the time of the German counter-attack at Mortain, and the full force of five Panzer divisions would have swept over their fragile structure. By good fortune, when the subject was first broached, the Americans flatly refused to have anything to do with a scheme which visualized planting two armoured car regiments into their lines of communication, and for this long-sightedness the 2nd Household Cavalry is eternally grateful.

As beginners we learnt much from the Inns of Court Regiment, who, like us, were waiting to know what was to be their next job. Their officers came over for a drink and were subjected to a battery of questions. One fact of paramount importance stood out. It was never the enemy's light reconnaissance units which they had first encountered, but invariably either the tank or the anti-tank gun, and unless the leading scout car saw these first its chance of survival was much reduced. Once spotted, the scout car had to act like lightning, put down smoke and reverse as hard as it could go. And the German 88-mms. were deadly up to a thousand yards.

Having heard all this, it was with interest that Troop Leaders inspected the first batch of electrically fired smoke generators which had just arrived. Previously smoke canisters had only been fired from two short barrels at the side of the turret of the armoured car, using a ballistite charge. The system was unreliable, the smoke frequently failing to go off. In addition, the whole turret had to be aimed, and there was a time lag of several seconds before the smoke canister hit the ground and began to screen the threatened vehicle. The new electrically fired smoke was attached to the front of both the armoured cars and the scout cars and could be instantaneously fired by the driver flicking on his side-lamp switch. The vehicle under fire would then make its own screen in the manner of a destroyer, retreating behind a dense cloud of smoke. Lieutenant Kavanagh was the first to give a demonstration of this new gadget and got badly choked in the process, but it worked, and was to save many lives in the future.

★   ★   ★

Close on a million men were now packed into the Normandy bridgehead, an area but half the size of Dorset county, while, unknown to us as yet, the first moves for the big push aimed at forcing a breakthrough at the junction of the Anglo-American line were already under way.

Undeterred by the experience of "Goodwood," a further heavy Allied aerial bombardment was rained down on the enemy on the 25th of July. Then the American ground forces on our right went over to the offensive in the sector lying between Perriers and St. Lô. The British, in conformity, were themselves mounting their own main thrust which was due to be launched five days later. The battle of the Falaise Pocket, which was to culminate in the virtual annihilation of the German Seventh Army, had begun.

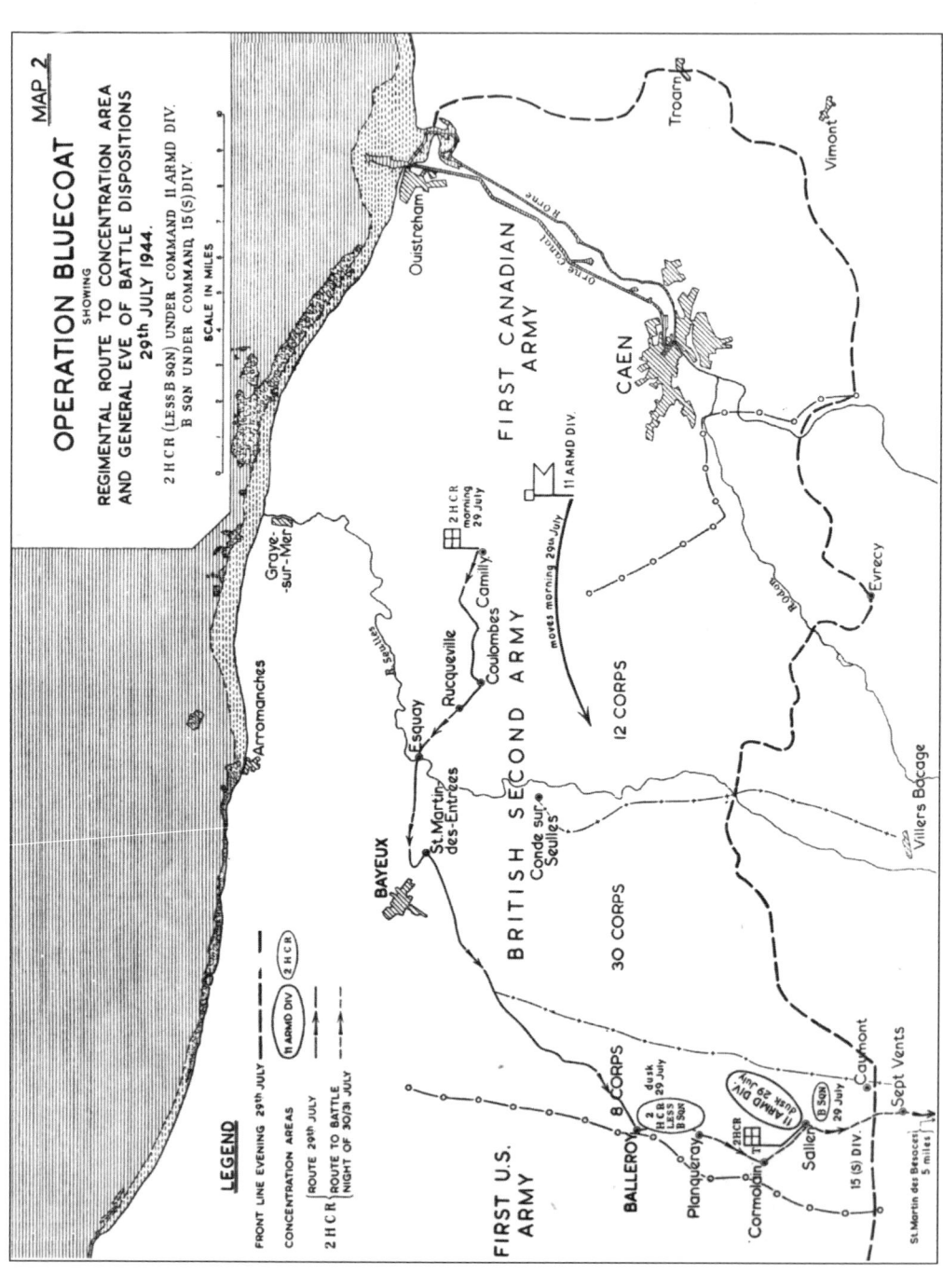

OPERATION BLUECOAT

MAP 2

SHOWING

REGIMENTAL ROUTE TO CONCENTRATION AREA
AND GENERAL EVE OF BATTLE DISPOSITIONS
29th JULY 1944.

2 H C R (LESS B SQN) UNDER COMMAND 11 ARMD DIV.
B SQN UNDER COMMAND 15 (S) DIV.

SCALE IN MILES

LEGEND

FRONT LINE EVENING 29th JULY

CONCENTRATION AREAS

2 H C R { ROUTE 29th JULY
{ ROUTE TO BATTLE
{ NIGHT OF 30/31 JULY

11 ARMD DIV   2 H C R

Chapter IV

Cavalry Bridge

Situation before Operation "Bluecoat" (the break-through)—Initial stages—The British part—The Regiment is briefed under 8 Corps—Move to Balleroy—The Bocage—"B" Squadron under 15th (Scottish) Division—Lieutenant Kavanagh's Troop operates at night—"C" and "D" Squadrons move forward at night—Traffic congestion—Advance through Caumont Towards St. Martin des Bésaces—Major-General Roberts (11th Armoured Division) decides to exploit salient—Situation at dawn, 31st July—Respective exploits of Lieutenants Tabor's, Cody's and Lord Burghersh's Troops—Corporal-of-Horse Johnson's narrative—"C" and "D" Squadrons exploit salient—Lieutenant Petherick's Troop held up, but Lieutenant Powle's Troop meets with success—"D" Squadron in front of St. Martin des Bésaces—Difficulties of close country—Corporal Bugby's narrative—Lieutenant Powle's half-Troop reaches vital bridge behind enemy lines—Corporal Bland's story—"Cavalry Bridge"—Lieutenant Bethell's Troop ambushed—Fall of St. Martin des Bésaces—Another night march for "D" Squadron

When at the end of July the Allies were preparing to break out of the Normandy bridgehead, they were in fact well behind the basic conception schedule, for it had been visualized that their armies by then should have advanced to a line roughly extending from Nantes, at the mouth of the River Loire, eastwards to Tours, and thence up to the River Seine estuary below Le Havre. And yet by mid-September, on the eve of Arnhem, the Allies were so far ahead of planned schedule that they had already reached the German and Dutch frontiers and were in possession of a sizeable bridgehead across the Moselle.

What brought about this remarkable change of situation? To a major extent, the stern battles which were to rage in the heart of the Normandy Bocage during the first two weeks in August. These hammer blows produced an enemy debacle beyond even the most sanguine expectations, for few could have reasonably anticipated that the stubborn dictates of a maddened Hitler, flying in the face of all his Generals and against the demands of military necessity, would order an entire army to stand to and bleed to death west of the Seine.

As originally planned, the outcome of the Anglo-American operations envisaged three possibilities. Firstly, given fine weather and a normal measure of success, the elimination of German units west of Vire—in other words, the creation of an open flank, making it unnecessary to detail large forces for the conquest of Brittany. Secondly, that the enemy might be able to establish a line running from Caen to Avranches, in which case the reduction of Brittany would require another heavily mounted attack on the right flank. Thirdly, if the enemy could manage to hold up the Allied advance beyond a line Caen—Avranches, a special amphibious-airborne operation was in readiness to seize Brittany in the enemy's rear. Thus it will be seen that the all-important aim in July was to capture Brittany's ports. So crushing a defeat of the Germans and the culminating collapse of the entire Normandy Front had not at this stage been visualized.

The American offensive was originally scheduled for the 19th of July, one day after the beginning of "Goodwood," and likewise it intended to use an overwhelming air bombardment as prerequisite to success. However, the weather, as we know, broke on the same day, and caused a temporary cancellation in the plans and the attack did not eventually start until the 25th of July, six days later.

On the morning of 25th July, after what General Eisenhower has described as six of the most miserable days ever spent by the Americans, huddled in fox-holes under dripping hedgerows and overlooked by an enemy constantly on the alert, 5,000 tons of bombs were unloaded less than a hundred yards in front of the leading G.Is., patterning an area five miles in depth and one mile long to the west of St. Lô.

This air blow produced disappointingly few casualties but caused immense confusion immediately behind the German front line. Communications broke down and supplies from the rear were cut off. Dazed troops staggered towards the wrong lines. It is even recorded that four Tigers were captured intact, their crews waving white flags, unable to realize that the ground attack had not yet come in. This time the lesson of the quick follow-up had been learnt and the American success was immediate.

Coincident with the American thrust, 2 Canadian Corps attacked across the flat plains south-east of Caen towards Falaise—a thankless task which, though meeting with little success, was to engage a large force of enemy armour, thus keeping it away from the main Allied objective.

By the 27th of July, the Germans facing the Americans had started to withdraw, though not without heavy fighting. The following day, American armoured columns had reached Coutances; then, leaving behind the infantry to take care of the pockets of resistance, the tanks gathered momentum and surged forward. Avranches fell on the last day of July.

By 31st July, opposition west of the River Vire had collapsed. Documents captured later give a vivid picture of the German Generals vying with one another in the dispatch of agonized SOSs for help which could never come. From his underground shelters in St. Germain, near Paris, von Kluge could with truth say, "The whole Western Front has been ripped open." There was now no effective barrier between the Allies and the ports of Brittany, and the most optimistic expectations of an open flank had been more than fulfilled. Chaos reigned behind the barriers with which the enemy vainly tried to stem the pounding armour. Fighter bombers roamed at will, shooting up the jammed columns of transport to such good purpose that the American spearheads began to complain bitterly that their own advance was being held up by the jumble of knocked-out German transport!

But the battle had only just begun. Reacting desperately, the enemy now attempted to form a hinge in the Percy—Tessy area with two armoured divisions; a forlorn hope of preventing the entire collapse of the Normandy front, but he hoped to hold out long enough there to enable him to scrape together reinforcements from farther east, and Allied Intelligence had already noticed signs of westward-bound traffic crossing the Seine.

The Supreme Commander, however, had no intention of allowing a reeling foe to regain his equilibrium. In the words of General Eisenhower, "Our policy must be to indulge in an all-out offensive and, if necessary, throw caution to the winds." Side by side with the First U.S. Army, two Corps, the British 8th and 30th, were to concentrate on a thrust towards Caumont and beyond. Then, the moment that road space became available, a new Army, the Third U.S. (now arriving under General Patton) would take up the chase and dash for the ports of Brittany and beyond.

The proposed British thrust was intended to be a powerful two-corps drive on a narrow front; 30 Corps attacking south-west to the line Villers Bocage—Aunay sur Odon, with Mont Pincon as its main objective, while our own 8 Corps, in a wider sweep just entering the then American sector, was to head through Caumont in the direction of Vire and thus protect the right flank of 30 Corps. Within 8 Corps the initial assault was to be made by 15th (Scottish) Division with 11th Armoured Division moving up on the right flank as protection because, initially, the Americans (V Corps) were to be echeloned back, catching up as the battle developed. Guards Armoured Division were to be held in reserve, ready to pass through and exploit at the first favourable opportunity.

ROCKET-FIRING TYPHOONS IN ACTION NEAR CAMILLY, 27TH JULY 1944.

The complicated regrouping entailed secretly swinging a large part of 30 Corps and the whole of 8 Corps to the western flank. But such was the Allied domination of the air, denying all chance of enemy reconnaissance, that this preparatory move was to achieve a degree of tactical surprise never before deemed possible.[1]

---

1. There was to be an interesting sequel later on which showed how secret had been the move of 8 Corps. Trooper Allen, a member of Lieutenant R. A. Bethell's Troop which was to be ambushed

On the 28th of July, Major Wignall, "B" Squadron, was asked to dine at Regimental Headquarters to meet Brigadier Joe Kingston, an old friend of the 1st Regiment which had served under him in the Iraq campaign. Towards the end of the meal, Colonel Abel Smith received an urgent message to send one Squadron of armoured cars to be prepared to operate under 15th (Scottish) Division in the forthcoming operation. Major Wignall was warned to prepare his cars for an immediate move to the area of Caumont, while the Squadron Leader himself had to interrupt his dinner and dash off in his staff car ahead of the main party.

The roads were jammed with traffic and he did not reach his rendezvous, Major-General McMillan's Headquarters, until dawn on the 29th, after an all-night journey. This lay a few miles short of Caumont, which was then the front line. Here he learnt what was to be the Squadron's role. Later that day, Captain Ward brought up "B" Squadron, which harboured nearby.

By now the Regiment (less "B" Squadron) had been notified that it would be operating under command of 11th Armoured Division and was to move to concentrate south of Balleroy on the same day. It was very hot and cars were packed under a blazing sun. Goggles were donned with great care for the dust was bad. Dead on time at 1400 hours the first vehicle passed over the Caen road and bade good-bye to Camilly. For security reasons all corps signs had been obliterated. The route avoided main roads and wandered cross-country through many villages until, after passing Coulombes and Rucqueville, and over a dried-up rivulet called the Seulles which trickled past the château of Esquay, the main thoroughfare into Bayeux was reached by the church of St. Vigor Le Grand. Here the convoy swung almost back on its tracks to avoid the town and make use of a bulldozered highway which ran from St. Martin des Entrées south-west to link up with the Balleroy road a few kilometres south of Bayeux.

The journey dragged on in interminable halts with every sort of vehicle packed nose to tail for miles ahead. Mercifully, there was wireless silence and so we were spared the irritating questions asking us to explain why we were not moving faster.

---

and destroyed on the 31st of July, was wounded and taken prisoner. He was brought before a senior German interrogating officer. Again and again he was asked to explain why the Regiment was fighting with the Americans. "We know perfectly well that your Regiment, commanded by Colonel Abel Smith, formed part of 8 Corps—we have listened in on our wireless to many of his conversations, so you might as well tell us what we already know." But Allen gave away nothing. Had the Germans but realised it and chosen to scrape away the fresh paint from one of the captured scout cars, they would have seen the White Knight of 8 Corps come to life underneath.

Shortly after leaving Bayeux the landscape changed noticeably. Tight little fields and orchards surrounded by high banks overtopped with hedges and trees now restricted the view. The flatness of the Caen plain had given way to thickly wooded hills, and it was plain to see that the country into which we were penetrating would be a menace to the handling of armour. The line of advance was also barred by countless small streams which frequently could only be crossed by fragile wooden bridges too weak to support a tank or armoured car.

This then was the Bocage, a picturesque and gentle countryside in peace time, but whose sombre, leafy lanes we now felt were entirely in favour of the defending enemy.

Ordinarily, the journey from Bayeux to Balleroy by one of the hooded gigs so common in this part of the country would take half an hour, but it was dusk when the last vehicle reached harbour south of Balleroy, after six and a half hours on the roads.[2]

The village of Balleroy was approached by one long street, built it seemed entirely as a drive to the château belonging to the Marquis de Balleroy. By the château gates the road turned left, where at his forge a blacksmith was still at work mending, of all things, the butt of a soldier's Sten gun. There was a post-office-cum-general-stores and here Lieutenant Hughes had time to enjoy a last pre-battle steak, "beautifully cooked."

Squadrons harboured in orchards beyond the village and a ceaseless flow of traffic rumbled past them along the road to forward units. Despatch riders, bearing their quota of last-minute enjoinders which even the most careful planning never entirely succeeds in eliminating, tore past in both directions. We took careful mental note of the number of ambulances moving up to the front and wondered how soon they would be returning laden. Jeeps labelled "Press" flashed back to Bayeux and the snug comfort of the Lion d'Or.

In harbour stoves hummed away merrily cooking the evening suppers. Soon it grew dark, and drivers made a final check-up to assure themselves that tanks were full of petrol, that oil levels showed no unaccountable drop and that stowage of kit permitted unrestricted traverse of the turret. I watched Corporal Harrison, "Rev' up Harry," indefatigably touring his Squadron area with his water-cart of chlorinated ditch water for drinking and washing purposes. All familiar sights no doubt, but on that

---

2. When the head of 8 Corps was launching its attack in the area of Caumont, the tail element was still east of the River Orne over fifty miles away. The strain on tank crews was very great." (Extract from "Operations Eighth Corps—Normandy to the River Rhine," by Lieutenant-Colonel G. S. Jackson; St. Clement's Press Ltd., Portugal Street, Kingsway, London, W.C.2.)

day every detail seemed to have special significance and remain sharply engraved on the mind.

One by one the bivouac lights were extinguished. A torch flashed on, groping for a mislaid article. A scout car lid closed with a metallic crash. In a far corner of the orchard which harboured "A" and "D" Squadrons a constellation of glowing cigarette ends smouldered, and men in half-tones discussed the respective merits of their home towns. Soon even that fruitful source of debate died, and by midnight all slept save the American "Mediums" and "Heavies" which thundered away to the west.

★   ★   ★

Meanwhile, Regimental Tactical Headquarters had moved forward to the hamlet of Sallen and joined 11th Armoured Division Headquarters. They were grouped round a farm, which, noted Captain Collins, was "the very image of many of the farms on the Yorkshire Wolds."

★   ★   ★

In the early hours of the 30th of July, at about three o'clock in the morning, 15th (Scottish) Division, supported by the 6th Guards Tank Brigade (Churchill tanks), went over to the attack on the axis Caumont—St. Martin des Bésaces. "B" Squadron waited at their disposal for reconnaissance when required. Preceding the infantry by some few minutes; medium and heavy planes showered down fragmentation bombs upon the enemy emplacements.

Seven roads and a railway line radiate from Caumont, and it was felt that the Germans would resist strongly to any threatened advance into their defences through this centre. The British attack did not progress as quickly as had been anticipated, due in the main to mines and thorough demolition. 11th Armoured Division, starting their attack four hours later, reported similar difficulties. Every wood contained snipers. Every detour and lane was found to be mined.

Throughout the day "B" Squadron moved forward in fits and starts, awaiting the word to go, whilst the artillery support pounded around them. It was not until late afternoon that they passed through Caumont.

"We reached Lutain Wood (just south of Caumont) about dusk, only to find the infantry still dealing with snipers by burning them out of the undergrowth with wasp flame-throwers. After a short halt we were ordered to continue the advance, leaving our centre line because it was not yet clear and following a complicated cross-country route on to the

Caumont—St. Martin des Bésaces road, from whence it was intended that we should push on through St. Martin des Bésaces and the country to the south-east of Quarry Hill. Mont Kavanagh[3] was the leading Troop and we duly set off in the darkness, relieved only by the flames from burning houses." Thus wrote Lieutenant Tabor.

His route proved to be extremely difficult due to countless small streams and was further complicated by pockets of German infantry which still existed in the area. However, the main road was hit somewhere in the region of Hervieux at about three o'clock on the morning of the 31st of July. Lieutenant Kavanagh's Troop was still in the lead threading its way through several knocked-out Churchill tanks belonging to the Coldstream Guards, and contact was made with outposts of the Rifle Brigade from 11th Armoured Division working to the west. Lieutenant Kavanagh's Troop was the first to encounter trouble.

"It is difficult to remember many particular actions, but this one I recall quite clearly, it being one of our earliest and at night. St. Martin des Bésaces was a small village about a mile or two in front of our forward positions, and the road approached it through a deep cutting about 800 yards long. Boy told me to take two scout cars and find out if there were any Germans in the village.[4] Someone was in a hurry for news, so my orders were to drive through it—if we succeeded, then presumably it was empty. A large patrol of some Recce Regiment was to back us up, but it did not materialize. It was completely dark so we drove somewhat cautiously through the cutting and into the village without seeing any sign of life. In the middle of the place, however, a grenade exploded on Corporal Tutt's car and something, I think a bazooka,[5] blew the front wheels off my car. My driver and I climbed on to Tutt's car and we reversed out of the place at speed, being shot at by many assorted weapons, including a few rounds of H.E. I reported it to be held and quite a strong attack was laid on next morning which cleared it after about six hours." (Lieutenant M. Kavanagh).

★ ★ ★

It is now necessary to return to the Regiment near Balleroy and the situation as it had developed throughout the preceding day, the 30th of July.

---

3. Lieutenant M. Kavanagh, 4 Troop, "B" Squadron.
4. 'Boy' – Major F. E. B. Wignall, "B" Squadron.
5. The German infantryman's anti-tank weapon, the Panzerfaust. Based on similar principles to the British PIAT mortar or American bazooka, it also came to be called bazooka by all soldiers.

THE BOCAGE COUNTRY

"C" Squadron: moving through the hamlet of Planquery towards the front in the late afternoon of 30th July 1944.

At Sallen, Tactical Headquarters had spent a quiet Sunday. Colonel Abel Smith was in some pain with a boil, and it was indeed lucky for R.H.Q. that they did not have to operate that day. News of the battle kept passing back, but it was not of great progress on any front and the remaining Squadrons kept wondering when they would be called forward. Captain Waterhouse had departed early that morning to 29th Brigade Headquarters that he might report the moment there appeared to be a chance of slipping through Squadrons, but from the news he sent back over the air it was clear that the tanks were finding the going sticky.

It had been another day of blazing sunshine, scorching the last drops of moisture from the soil, and the shimmering heat sent spirals of battle dust high into the air. Chinagraph pencils were melting, making a coloured blur upon the talc of maps. Out on the road beyond the harbours, ambulances were threading their way back against the long columns feeding the front. Intermingled with the stream of two-way traffic, batches of weary-looking prisoners were trudging towards Balleroy, escorted by a solitary despatch rider on a motor-bicycle in bottom gear. All looked haggard and unshaved.

They talked of Rommel's death from wounds but knew nothing of the plot on Hitler's life on the 20th of July.[6] It was the first time that we heard the cry, "Hitler kaput, only the S.S. wish to fight!"

Groups of Household Cavalrymen clustered round the Rear Link cars for news. No sooner had one set of maps been marked up than a liaison officer would call up and half the stuff had to be rubbed out again. Sometimes their dust covered Humbers would arrive from a forward unit and out would jump a familiar figure. I remember welcoming the sight of Derek Cooper, with his quiet grin. He invariably had the information that mattered to Squadrons, and in addition imparted those little touches, amusing or macabre, which helped to give us the feel of things. He had just come back from the American sector, where he had been given two wrong map references, thereby nearly having been put in the bag. The Germans had dug slit trenches along the roads of their retreat and lined them with French pillows and sheets taken from the houses. At one place he had come upon a dug-out containing five dead Germans, a woman and several bottles of Cognac, obviously a "party" which had been abruptly terminated by one of our shells. At another, in a deserted and smouldering farmhouse, he had nearly been caught by a booby-trapped Bible. He had released the cattle from their stalls and

---

6. Like most soldiers' rumours, this was only half correct. Rommel had been gravely wounded on the 17th of July near Lisieux when his car had been attacked by an Allied plane, little realizing whom it was strafing. He died mysteriously in Germany a few months later.

milked some of them, while in the parlour a dead goat sat bolt upright in an armchair! He was soon off again, bound for Headquarters, 11th Armoured Division, and we wondered what would be his next graphic news bulletin.

It grew dark. There would surely be no move until dawn on the 31st. Squadron Leaders had gone to Tactical Headquarters to be at hand for orders and to obtain large-scale maps. Bed rolls came out and everybody "got down to it."

High-level despatches tend to suggest an almost supernatural preordination of tabulated events often far removed from reality. Even written at regimental level, history can rarely achieve that impression of day-to-day uncertainty dogging the simple soldier's steps to victory or defeat. How familiar is every serving man with that "no move for a week" which, changing on the dread beat of a motor-cycle engine to "ready to move in ten minutes," puts all plans at naught. This night was to be no exception.

At about a quarter to midnight, a despatch rider brushed through the laden apple trees with a hoarsely whispered message. "We're moving, sir," and if the impressions of the next few hours are mine, they are surely also those of most Household Cavalrymen who were torn from their sleep that night to grope forward into their first battle.

"C" Squadron, who were farther down the road than "A" and "D" Squadrons, had already received the news and were in a fair way to moving. With the remainder it was different. An agonized and penetrating "Say again ..." came floating over from an adjoining field and told me that Peter Grant Lawson, who had remained here with the rear part of Regimental Headquarters, was grappling with the intricacies of Slidexed orders from Sallen.[7] Within ten minutes an urgent summons to his blacked-out tent suggested that he had successfully decoded the message. Gathering my map, in obedience to the call, I stumbled through a tank-torn gap in the hedge, cursing my issue torch which had failed and wondering how, after nearly five years of war, the British Army still failed to produce a decent model on American standards. My map board had lost its clips in the scramble through the hedge, and when I arrived a dozen people were already breathing hard over the one marked map. Summed up, the gist of the orders were that we ought to have been moving ten minutes ago. So far, the form was as on schemes.

---

7. Slidex. The special form of code used on the wireless to fox the enemy. It frequently used to fox us as well.

"D" Squadron were to lead, followed by "A" Squadron, who were to be in reserve; then that part of Regimental Headquarters re-joining Tactical Headquarters at Sallen. The Squadrons would pick up their respective Squadron Leaders by the church at Sallen as they passed. Further detailed orders would then be issued.

The middle of the night is a bad time to awaken slumbering soldiers and obtain sense quickly. Nor would Lieutenant Ainsworth, who was to lead the way, find the route easy in the dark. There was no moon. The large-scale maps were still at Sallen and following a main axis in England was not the same as here, where entire divisions were moving along footpaths so narrow that even a Devonshire lane seemed like the Kingston By-pass.

On scrambling back to grope among my kit for a new torch, I met Captain Profumo, very much in control of the situation. He had sensed that this might happen, and from the overtones of familiar noises it was plain that "A" Squadron were at least ten minutes and a "brew up" ahead of "D" Squadron.

Rapidly the maps were marked up and Lieutenant Hanbury, who was now in temporary command of the Squadron, for Captain Waterhouse was still with 29th Brigade, gave out his traditionally brief orders. We had been given some sort of road priority, but this was merely a Staff gesture, for there was little that could be done should other units be blocking the way (as they were).

There was also anxiety as to whether the single narrow entrance to the field might not itself cause a blockage should a vehicle break down, and Corporal-Major Ring went off to enlarge another exit which facilitated the manoeuvring of the larger cars.[8] These would have to negotiate a sharp left, then an acute right-angled bend, before reaching the road. From somewhere in the darkness a voice shouted "Good luck," and one by one the Daimler armoured cars and the little scout cars nosed their way forward. The order was, "No lights." Occasionally the purr of Daimlers would give way to the throb of the twin-engined Staghound, and then, like a labouring London motorbus, a Matador clanked past the exit. Corporal-of-Horse Cawte, a keen rugby footballer in civilian life and now almost unrecognizable amidst the ferocious assortment of rifles and Sten guns which formed his panoply, had just steered his fitter's jeep, groaning under the weight of tools and saucepans, on to the road when an armoured car driver chose this moment to inadvertently touch

---

8. It must be remembered that even the tanks were frequently baffled by the high earthen banks which surrounded all fields. To an armoured car they were impassable.

his side lights switch —up went the electric smoke apparatus. The move until then had been one of naval precision. I had just time to catch a glimpse of the first three-tonner driver's agonized face before the entire field was obscured in dense clouds of choking fumes.

We were already late, and this contretemps did not improve matters, but by the time that "A" Squadron were in position to move through, "D" Squadron lungs had absorbed most of the smoke and the air was comparatively fresh again.

It seemed to take an unconscionably long time to reach Sallen and I cannot remember the hour of arrival. The way twisted past a small hamlet called Planqueray and then over a stream to Cormolain, where another acute left-handed turn compelled all the large cars to take a double bite to get round the corner—a further delay of twenty minutes per squadron.

Beyond Cormolain the road forked to the right; it was here so narrow that the wider-tracked vehicles could only just push through. To help matters, two identical lanes led off at almost the same angle into the inky blackness. Only one was marked on our map, and there was further delay while a scout car reconnoitred the more likely lane in low gear. It returned ten minutes later to report that the lane led up the side of a "young mountain" and petered out in a wood. Fortunately, the alternative one, in spite of a signpost which pointed in the opposite direction, eventually took us to Sallen, where Major Ward, laden with maps, was waiting patiently by the church. In front lay a dense block of Sherman tanks, carriers and columns of vehicles, their drivers half stupefied by sleep and petrol fumes.

Major Ward wisely decided to give out further orders at daybreak and we moved on without delay. Hitherto the slow progress had been caused in the main by the narrow, winding tracks; now, as we advanced, more and more units joined the throng from side turnings—all were feeling their way to the front and the congestion was unbelievable.

We eventually passed burning Caumont, leaving this sadly battered little village on the hill to our left, and entered a taped track. This was not yet the battle proper, but we were in its immediate wake and the aftermath of a successful advance is never a pleasant sight, however generally uplifting to morale.

Only those who have taken part in a night drive into country but recently fought over can recapture the starkness of the picture. Little hamlets, existing in a world of their own and toned by the years to tranquil somnolence and peace, lay torn wide open, desecrated and burning. What had been but a few hours ago inhabited farms and cottages now crackled fiercely, casting eerie shadows across the path of the advancing cars as they lurched over the debris.

The route led by yet more taped detours across country where only with the greatest difficulty could the wheeled transport negotiate the deep ruts made by the previous passage of tanks. Reaching the bed of a stream, we suddenly found ourselves squelching through mud. Two cars stuck and had to be dug out. At other times, the column would scrape past the glowing carcass of a Sherman tank or have to avoid a burning truck whose stinking rubber tyres were a reminder that the battle had not long receded. A German tank, a Panther, had been hit and was still burning in the corner of a barn. Helmets, mess tins, mattresses, sheets, and even a large oaken dresser lay scattered about the fields. Countless rifles had been flung aside, and belts of ammunition, strewn across our path, crunched beneath the wheels of the vehicles.

The villages were deserted and what remained of livestock roamed terror-stricken about the wreckage. Two goats, still tethered to a burning outhouse, their horned shadows dancing against a whitewashed wall like a pair of bearded satyrs, were bleating piteously. A trooper ran across and cut them adrift.

At long last the first rays of dawn appeared and with them Major Ward called a halt to give out further orders.

We had come out on to a minor road running into the village of St. Jean des Essartiers; two kilometres to our west lay Dampierre; to our front, St. Martin des Bésaces.

At this juncture, let us consider the reason for this unexpected night move.

★   ★   ★

During the late afternoon of the previous day (30th July), the leading troops of 11th Armoured Division were still but a mile to the south-west of the village of Dampierre, having skirted Sept Vents to the west. On the right, 159th Brigade had been experiencing heavy fighting in the vicinity of Haye, three miles due west of Caumont. Here resistance was finally overcome by six o'clock at night, though not without considerable loss in tanks and infantry, one company of the Herefords being severely mauled in the process.

Farther afield, on the right, the Americans, finding the going heavy, had advanced no farther than Biéville.

However, largely due to the initiative of a battalion of the 6th Guards Tank Brigade (Brigadier G. L. Verney), which was attached to 15th

(Scottish) Division, tanks were in partial occupation of the high ground dominating St. Martin des Bésaces from the north-east. By seven o'clock at night the 4th Coldstream Guards with their Churchills had obtained a foothold on Point 309, an eminence a thousand feet high.[9]

There were now signs that the Germans were breaking under the pressure and also, thought Major-General Roberts, the commander of 11th Armoured Division, the makings of an exploitable salient. With both his brigades in contact with the enemy at last light, he suddenly decided on the by no means easy manoeuvre of pushing them on through the hours of darkness, to aid the Scotsmen to capture St. Martin des Bésaces. It was a bold move. Somehow, he told Colonel Abel Smith, the Household Cavalry would have to force their way through the inevitable traffic jam in order to be ready to operate in the lead next morning.

★   ★   ★

Thus at dawn on the 31st of July the situation following the night march was broadly as follows.

On the right "C" Squadron was to operate in front of 159th Brigade, which was already astride the main road west of St. Martin des Bésaces and preparing to move in to the village from that direction. In the centre was 29th Brigade, in a holding role ahead of which "D" Squadron would be operating. To the left was 15th (Scottish) Division (with "B" Squadron still under command), preparing to attack St. Martin des Bésaces from the north, and 6th Guards Tank Brigade, the latter busy repelling heavy German counter-attacks on Point 309, which were to continue during the next twenty-four hours.

It must be emphasized that although the three operating squadrons were situated as mentioned above, their orders were that they were in no way to allow themselves to become involved in the close fighting about St. Martin des Bésaces, but independently "C" and "D" under 11th Armoured Division and "B" Squadron under 15th (Scottish) Division were to reconnoitre for gaps in the enemy line to the south.

This was to be the first and last time that a Squadron was ever to work under direct command of an infantry division, as "B" Squadron was doing. It proved to be an unsatisfactory form of co-operation, for the different tempos of the armoured car and infantryman could not be fitted in to the same sector of the battle. Armoured cars are wasted if used as tanks, nor are they suitable for use as static pillboxes. The infantry

9. Also known as Quarry Hill.

company sees the battlefield in terms of a few fields to be cleared by slow, hard-fought slogging matches. The armoured car Squadron, with its speed and adaptability for swift darting thrusts, views it in terms of the limits of its wireless range. Moreover, on the 31st of July there was to be bad overlapping with "B" Squadron continuously being ordered to reconnoitre country already adequately patrolled by "D" Squadron, and vice versa. Little could be done about it for, being under different formations, there was no direct wireless interchange of information, although Regimental Headquarters, who had a wireless set listening on the "B" Squadron net, was only too well aware of what was happening.

It was thought at Division that until St. Martin des Bésaces fell there could be no question of advance to Le Bény Bocage, for the village controlled both the direct route through the Forêt de l'Évêque and the longer easterly one via Le Tourneur. Events were to prove otherwise.

Before seven o'clock in the morning the majority of the Reconnaissance Troops had passed through the tanks and infantry and were beginning to fan out beyond. Fierce fighting was taking place in the northern outskirts of Saint-Martin-des-Bésaces, which locality, as far as possible, was avoided. The main road running east and west was found to be covered by several 88-mm. anti-tank guns, and 11th Armoured Division's tanks were being knocked out with clockwork regularity as they approached it.

With the advantage of having already started operations on the night of 30th July, "B" Squadron were the first to make any progress from a position about a thousand yards short of St. Martin des Bésaces. It was an unpleasant spot due "to the near proximity of many dead horses and considerable German mortar fire. "Moreover, it was clear that, due to enemy fire from the village, a direct approach was impracticable. Therefore 1 Troop (Lieutenant Cody) and 3 Troop (Lieutenant Tabor) decided to try to find a way across country to the east and round Quarry Hill. They turned up a track off the main road. About half a mile off the road they passed a German mortar crew, busily firing in the direction of Caumont, apparently quite unaware that they had been spotted or that the Coldstream tanks had been holding their hill for several hours! Due to their preoccupation, the mortar crew and attendant infantry failed to see the two scout cars, which continued unmolested. Farther on, the road was blocked with tree trunks, but the two Troop Leaders and their scout car crews were able to move them aside without too much difficulty. At the time, the air was completely blocked with messages, and so Lieutenant Tabor decided to motor back to bring up the remainder of the two Troops (the armoured cars), which had been left behind until a route could be found.

"I told the armoured cars," wrote Tabor, "to start up and follow me up the track. Corporal-of-Horse Munn must have had difficulty in starting up, and must also have misunderstood my instructions, as the next thing we saw was his car travelling at high speed straight down the main road into St. Martin! I could not get him on the air to warn him of the danger because of other traffic. I merely had to wait for the inevitable. When the car was about 400 yards from the railway crossing, a Panther tank hidden in some houses opened fire. He was hit three times, one shot passing between the driver's legs, one removing the front suspension, and one travelling clean through the whole length of the car, engine, and all. The crew then bailed out and escaped with injuries."[10]

In the meantime, Lieutenant Tabor had returned to where he had left Lieutenant Cody, only to find that the latter had continued with his task. Tabor therefore took his Troop round under the railway and up to the St. Martin des Bésaces road, where it ran east past the Bois du Homme and on to St. Pierre du Fresne, at which place he made contact with some of the infantry holding Quarry Hill. He was later joined by 2 Troop (Lieutenant the Lord Burghersh) and both continued with their tasks, broadly speaking that of reconnoitring the crossings over a stream in the area of Le Brun—La Mancellière, some two miles due south of St. Martin des Bésaces. This stream eventually runs into the River Souleuvre, which was destined to feature prominently in the day's operations. Lieutenant Tabor's Troop passed through the hamlet of Galet, which had obviously only recently been evacuated by the enemy, but met no opposition, although no suitable crossing could be found over the stream. Then while in the area of La Mancellière, our own artillery farther back opened up with a heavy barrage which forced the Troop to make a hurried move.

In the meantime Lieutenant the Lord Burghersh on his route had driven into a field, which he soon discovered he was sharing with half a dozen German half-tracks loaded with infantry. He successfully extricated himself out of this difficulty after a brief interchange of fire and much letting off of smoke and grenades.

During this time Lieutenant Cody had succeeded in getting part of his Troop, two scout cars, across the stream farther west, but then was unlucky to find himself badly bogged in the middle of a field with the Germans around him. The vehicles were evacuated and the Troop became infantry, playing a game of hide-and-seek with the enemy. When on the

---

10. The lucky members of 1 Troop, "B" Squadron, were, Corporal-of-Horse L. J. Munn, wounded by fragments of metal; Trooper R. T. Housden, the driver, badly burnt; and Trooper Foster, the gunner-operator, untouched.

point of reaching their own lines they were surrounded. Hoping that the Germans might fail to find them, the party hid up behind an earthen bank. Eventually, all appearing quiet, Lieutenant Cody peered cautiously over the top of the bank, saw no movement, and decided to push on. Unfortunately, some grazing cattle, seeing four cavalrymen crawling about on all fours in their own pasturage, took fright and stampeded straight for the enemy, whose suspicions were aroused. There followed a brief scuffle, shots were exchanged, and Corporal A. J. Blowers and Trooper J. Bambrough were captured, the latter wounded. Trooper Austin was also wounded and missing for some time, but both he and Lieutenant Cody succeeded in escaping to rejoin their Squadron the next day.

★ ★ ★

Corporal-of-Horse Johnson, temporarily on his own since Lieutenant Kavanagh's car had been knocked out during the night, was ordered to join up with Lord Burghersh's Troop, which was also short of an armoured car. He eventually found the Troop on Quarry Hill, preparing, along with the infantry who were dug in on a forward slope, to repel a German counter-attack. No sooner had he arrived than a battery of "Moaning Minnies" opened up from the direction of the Bois du Homme. One bomb landed on the turret of Johnson's car and Trooper Tyrer was seriously wounded in the back. Corporal-of-Horse Johnson was then ordered back to La Morichesse les Mares, which was by this time harbouring most of "B" Squadron Headquarters, and ordered to patrol a stretch of road which had been recently reported as sheltering German stragglers shooting up soft vehicles. He wrote:

"I took my armoured car and one scout car with Corporal Britton as its commander. After going for nearly two miles I halted to see whether that part of the road was O.K. and ordered Corporal Britton to advance to a certain cross-roads. As he approached the crossroads I saw him standing up and firing his Bren gun. Then all of a sudden, round the corner, at a mad gallop, came a German field kitchen drawn by two enormous horses with an N.C.O. and two men aboard. They turned and came straight for my armoured car. So put my car across the road to stop them and the occupants were real scared. Anyhow, the car stopped them, and while my gunner kept them covered, I dismounted and searched them thoroughly. I found quite a lot of good information and material in the field kitchen, which I reported. So, after handing the field kitchen over to the French villagers, who I may say stripped it of everything in five minutes, I put the three prisoners on the back of my car and soon after returned to harbour."

Three years later that field kitchen, now transformed into a cart, and the two horses were still rendering good service to the village of La Morichesse les Mares.

★   ★   ★

The activities of "C" and "D" Squadrons must now be taken together, for throughout the 31st of July their patrols inevitably overlapped.

At dawn "C" Squadron got away to a good start, hoping to cross the main east—west St. Martin des Bésaces road about two miles west of the railway station. This would avoid the main body of 159 Brigade's leading battalion, preparing to engage the enemy on the outskirts of the village. Troops moved south from Dampierre and La Fouquerie; the road used was no more than a narrow lane and bordered by high banks—it was impossible to see more than fifty yards ahead. The order of march was as follows: 1 Troop (Lieutenant Powle), 4 Troop (Lieutenant Corbett) and 5 Troop (Lieutenant Petherick)—all, to begin with, following the same route. After a short while Lieutenant Powle's Troop turned left, followed by Lieutenant Corbett's Troop, Lieutenant Petherick's Troop carried straight on. He relates:

"I thought Rory Corbett had gone wrong and continued straight on, taking the lead. Perhaps he had been given a last-minute change of centre line and I did not know it. Almost immediately Rory Corbett's Troop turned about and came after me. Some way on, we came up to a Northamptonshire Yeomanry tank camouflaged on the right of the road and the crew told us that there were enemy a short way ahead. I must have reported this and we were told by the Squadron Leader to push on. This we did. Just before reaching some farm buildings about a mile from the main St. Martin road which lay ahead we saw at least two parties of rather uninterested enemy and shortly after, by now moving rather cautiously, we reached the farm and I remember seeing a German standing in the farmyard with a rifle in his hands. Corporal Hindle, in my leading scout car, a few moments later reached the main St. Martin road beyond the railway line. After a pause, I signalled him on and moved up myself in the Daimler armoured car across the level crossing in order to cover him as he started off along a long stretch of straight main road westwards. By this time we all had our eyes very much about us, but after a look through my binoculars I could see nothing ahead of the scout car and moved off after him."

Then things began to happen suddenly. Less than a mile down the road, which was lined on the left by a ditch and a thick hedge, Corporal Hindle was fired on by an anti-tank gun. He stopped, threw out smoke, and reversed back. To help him get back, Lieutenant Petherick ordered his driver, Trooper Jones, to fire smoke likewise.

At the same time enemy infantry began to fire at the backing cars from the side of the road.

"I shall never forget that awful electric smoke—the whole car enveloped in a choking fog and apparently no possibility of escape until of course we were blown out on to the road! Just as my car was beginning to reverse, the scout car, itself reversing, ran into us. I think I had time to give one shout of rage and then there was a very loud bang indeed and flames flew out of my turret. We jumped out, the operator, Trooper High, and myself, and then between us dragged out the driver, Jones 924, who had managed to open the door of the armoured car himself. We were then faced by one very heavily armed German, who took fright and ran away! We then retreated along the ditch to some buildings where Corporal-of-Horse Cridland was positioned. He was, as ordered, busily turning round, after having closed down the turret. We yelled at him at the top of our voices and managed to scramble on to the back of his car. In turning the car promptly ran into the ditch and along it in the direction from which we had originally come. I think that Jones had not managed to get properly on to the car, for I remember seeing him clinging to the wing nearest the hedge. By this time we were being steadily fired on and I suppose that he must have fallen off without us realizing it. I remember seeing a German run out into the road and fire a bazooka at us, and seeing the missile sail through the air and land just short of the car, wounding High (who was already hurt) seriously and myself not so seriously.[11] Then the car got out of the ditch and round the corner, joining Rory Corbett's car which had stuck in a ditch itself just off the main road."

It must be explained that many of the narrow lanes had a deep ditch on both sides, or else such high banks that when the cars tried to get through they stuck fast and had to be towed or dug out.

Corporal Hindle and his driver, Trooper Conry-Candler, after being held up by another 88-mm., managed to rejoin their Squadron later in the day.

Meanwhile, Lieutenant Corbett's Troop came in for its share of shooting. Lieutenant Petherick had in fact set a fast pace past numerous

---

11. Both had been badly burnt when their car was first hit.

German posts, which were by now thoroughly roused, and they started to retaliate on 4 Troop. There was about half a company hidden up in a group of buildings near the St. Martin road, and when the Troop Leader's car ditched itself, these were presented with a sitting target. However, with great presence of mind, Corporal-of-Horse Jenkins manoeuvred his car to where his gunner, Trooper Chennel, could keep the Germans' heads down with Besa fire and at the same time protect the stranded Daimler from being stalked by bazooka-men. Seeing, however, that it would not be able to get itself on to the road without further help, he drove up to it, and under fire calmly dismounted and helped Lieutenant Corbett to hitch a tow rope to the vehicle, when it was then dragged back on to the road.

On being informed of what had happened to Lieutenant Petherick's Troop, Major Herbert ordered Lieutenant Corbett to try another loop farther west, but this met with no better success than the first one. Small groups of enemy were by-passed, but then the tracks deteriorated to such an extent that further progress became impossible. The Troop retraced its steps to try another route and had reached a village two miles west of where Lieutenant Petherick had first encountered trouble when one of the scout cars, commanded by Corporal Wilby, was knocked out by another 88-mm. gun. Both Wilby and his driver, Trooper Beckett, escaped unharmed, but any further advance westwards was out of the question.

★ ★ ★

In so far as they were unable to obtain a clear break-through at any part of the enemy line, the experience of Major Ward's Squadron was the same. But being in the centre of operations "D" Squadron had relatively less room for deployment and all Troops found themselves under the direct fire of the guns in St. Martin des Bésaces before being able to cross the main road.

The first to get away to a dawn start was 1 Troop (Lieutenant Jonkheer Groeninx van Zoelen). It advanced up the road from St. Jean des Essartiers "as on a scheme in England, for we bowled along merrily until my scout car in the lead was passing up a slope between high banks. It passed some fellows in field grey uniform, was fired on, and duly fired back."[12]

---

12. Lance-Corporal-of-Horse S. R. Wilson (commander), and Trooper Osborne (driver).

Enemy infantry were fairly thick on the ground here, and with the bazookas "describing graceful parabolas over the hedgerows behind which the Germans were relatively safe from machine-gun fire," the Troop Leader decided to alter his route and try farther west. Both cars let off smoke, the Germans behind the banks threw grenades, and once again an armoured car ditched itself.

The theory of the armoured car reversing procedure was all very well, but in practice it was not so simple. It entailed the commander himself turning about in the confined space of the turret, then kneeling, and grabbing with one hand a second steering wheel fitted to the back of the fighting compartment while holding the "intercom" microphone mouthpiece, by which the driver was directed, with the other. Add to this the entanglements of wireless leads, the limited vision, and the fact that when on the turret floor the commander had to leave his gunner without a loader, and it will be seen that it was an operation to be carried out only in direst emergency. Those first few weeks in the dense undergrowth and narrow lanes of the Normandy Bocage were to be trying times for armoured car commanders, and Lieutenant van Zoelen's summing-up of his first action, "The scout car let off smoke, I let off smoke, then he got ditched, then I got ditched, but luckily the Hun failed to take advantage of our predicament," might well serve as ending for half the Troop sagas for the 31st of July.

In the meantime another "D" Squadron Troop, that of Lieutenant Ainsworth, had been ordered to try the direct route to St. Martin des Bésaces, eventually to reconnoitre southwards in "B" Squadron's area. The crews heard several loud bangs and were just in time to see Corporal-of-Horse Munn's car hit and burst into flames, as already described. Duly warned, they continued with caution. Shortly afterwards, it being obvious that St. Martin was strongly held, Major Ward ordered Lieutenant Ainsworth to try a loop to the east before striking south. The latter thereupon decided, in view of the country, to put his two scout cars in the lead, himself commanding from the second vehicle. The rest of the Troop were left some way back with the infantry, in charge of Corporal-of-Horse Royston. It was a wise decision. Once beyond the main St. Martin road the route ran down the side of a steep hill, from which a perfect view could be obtained of the valley and high ground beyond, which led to the village of St. Denis Maisoncelles. Ainsworth now decided to avoid even the lanes and concentrated on hugging the hedges and fields. Progress was necessarily slow, but much enemy movement was observed. Two Tigers were shadowed as they sullenly retired towards Le Tourneur, which village in enemy hands blocked one of the three possible roads to the Souleuvre. Soon a section of infantry was observed to follow the tanks in single file. No sooner had a report been sent back than a Hurricane bomber flew over the woods and dived on to the enemy, dropping a bomb in their very centre. It was a first-rate shot and no further movement was seen from this quarter.

The patrol continued under cover until picking up a small road leading to the hamlet of Houdan. Here let Corporal Bugby tell his story.

"The village appeared lifeless as we gingerly approached it, and although nothing stirred, I had a feeling we were being watched. How I envied my driver, Rose, his complete disregard of all danger! I myself felt jittery and was glad when at last I was ordered to report back to Mr. Ainsworth for further orders. These were to go to, and report upon, the river bridge and strength of enemy if held. Heading east, we soon came upon definite signs of enemy in the area. An orchard to our right had a number of dug outs with washing suspended between the apple trees. Rose and I dismounted and went into the orchard for closer inspection and found ammunition dumped around, and also long yellow canisters which we casually inspected and threw carelessly down (shortly after we found these were bazookas!).[13] Everything pointed to a retreat and yet we somehow felt this to be unlikely. Mr. Ainsworth ordered us to remount and we proceeded until we reached a small T road on our left. Our Troop Leader wisely decided to remain covering this place while Rose and I 'recce-ed' the bridge which lay now less than 200 yards away. The turning right and then south was in visual distance of the scout car 'Dingo' (Troop Leader's vehicle), with Trooper Young at the wheel, and we had the satisfaction of knowing that our rear was in good hands. Very carefully we turned the corner and halted with our nose just showing. We were amazed to see about fifty or more of the enemy standing on the bridge about eighty yards from us, either on parade or getting company orders. What a target at eighty yards, and slap in the centre of a straight road! I fired three or four Bren magazines at them without stopping and with chaotic results. As I was finishing, I heard Lieutenant Ainsworth shouting over the wireless, 'Retire at once. Enemy tank advancing on you. Have laid down smoke.' We retired like scalded cats and were very pleased to see a huge cloud of smoke a few yards up the road. Rose and I retired up the hill at full speed and re-joined Mr. Ainsworth and the rest of the Troop. After he had sent in his report, Mr. Ainsworth told us how lucky we had been to have passed the T road just before the tank which was directly behind the smoke he had laid. After this incident we realized

---

13. It must be remembered that at this stage of the campaign, most of the damage to British armour had been done by the 88-mm. The bazooka was just beginning to put in an appearance.

how careless the enemy had been to have no guard or lookout on their positions, and why were they not capable of returning one round to the hundreds we had fired? This gave us confidence that the enemy were not the super soldiers we had been led to believe."

★   ★   ★

At about a quarter to ten in the morning, in the crisis of the battle, with troops committed east, west, and south, there was to occur a sudden tremendous "flap." An urgent message arrived that all the country east of the road St. Martin des Bésaces—Le Tourneur was shortly to be pattern bombed to aid the advance of 15th (Scottish) Division and 30 Corps on our left, whose progress to date had been slower, "All armoured cars must get out of the area immediately." This was easier said than done, nor was the situation improved by 30 Corps' artillery proceeding to smoke out part of our zone of operations, thus rendering armoured car movement extremely difficult.

The order principally affected "B" and "D" Squadron Troops, but before it could be acted upon many groups of map references had to be encoded and then decoded again, by which time the bombing was due to start. However, after Lieutenant Ainsworth's Troop had returned in haste to Squadron Headquarters for further orders and Lieutenant Buchanan-Jardine's Troop had realized that they had been stalking a dummy wooden Tiger tank for the last half hour,[14] the bombing was abruptly cancelled!

★   ★   ★

At this stage it was clear that even if broken and withdrawing, the enemy had every intention of denying to us the main east—west St. Martin road for as long as possible. One of the Troops south of the village had reported three Panther tanks as showing no signs of leaving, and no British tanks had yet succeeded in penetrating into the village proper. Over to the west "C" Squadron found that St. Symphorien les Buttes Groucy was still in German hands, and that the Americans were echeloned some way back.

Then, at about 1030 in the morning, just as the tanks and infantry could be seen forming up for the attack which was to result in the capture of St. Martin des Bésaces half an hour later, a message came

---

14. "D" Squadron Headquarters discovered a large dump of dummy wooden tanks stored at St. Jean des Essartiers.

through from "C" Squadron having a vital bearing on the outcome of the battle. Badly distorted by being sandwiched in between a routine location check and an inordinately lengthy situation report from "One Eight Able,"[15] it was difficult to decipher, but its implications were of the utmost importance. So much so that Colonel Abel Smith grabbed the mouthpiece of his wireless set and demanded of Lieutenant Armes, the Rear Link, an immediate re-check. Within a minute it came back from Major Herbert, who tended to "take to the air" in person at moments of high drama!

The message, definite and unaltered, ran thus: "I say again, at 1035 hours, the bridge at 637436 is clear of enemy and still intact."

This meant that Lieutenant Powle had found a way clean through the enemy lines and was at this moment a good six miles behind them. With one armoured car and one scout car, he had slipped through west of St. Martin des Bésaces, somehow dodged the 88-mm. guns covering this sector, and, travelling through the Forêt l'Evêque, had reached the River Souleuvre by the bridge carrying the main road into Le Bény Bocage and Vire beyond. This was wonderful news.

It could be seen, so ran the report, that the bridge was being used for two-way German traffic. There were no signs, as yet, that the enemy were preparing to demolish it. Lieutenant Powle was ordered to keep on watching it and to report any further developments.

At all costs help had to be rushed southwards to back up the solitary half-Troop, for should its hide-out be discovered, not only would the position be untenable, but the probability was that the enemy would destroy the bridge.

Meanwhile, as the half-Troop watched, waited and reported, Major Ward to the east ordered his then only available Troop, Lieutenant R. A. Bethell's, to move towards the Souleuvre by whatever way and means were possible.

Divisional Headquarters had reacted immediately and wasted no time in organizing a relief party of tanks, but the enemy had by now been thoroughly alerted, and it was to be some time before they were able to get through and then not without casualties.

Of the occasion, the *History of 11th Armoured Division* says:

> "Meanwhile, on the left, 8th Rifle Brigade encountered more resistance, but with admirable perseverance they pushed onwards astride the Caumont—St. Martin road throughout the night, and by morning had

---

15. Captain N. Ford, Liaison Officer at 8 Corps. "One Eight Able" was his wireless code sign.

succeeded in establishing themselves on the northern side of the railway immediately north and east of the village. An attack on St. Martin thus became possible from two directions, with the 29th [Brigade] holding from the north and 159th [Brigade] moving against the place from the west. The village was entered by 1100 hours; but the importance of its capture was soon forgotten for, half an hour earlier, there had been received the report of a single local and unheralded exploit which was destined to shift the whole impulse of the battle and give to its further stages a new significance.

"Patrolling and probing in front of 159th Brigade Group, the Household Cavalry had discovered a track through the Forêt l'Evêque which was neither blocked by mines nor defended by Germans. This track evidently formed the boundary between two enemy divisions, 2nd Parachute and 326 Infantry, and apparently the enemy had omitted to make it inclusive to either formation or the formation responsible had failed to guard it. This theory was confirmed subsequently by a radio intercept which presented the route in question as a subject of dispute between the two Army Commanders concerned; but for the moment it mattered only that the way was clear.

"Down this track therefore had gone a Troop of armoured cars.[16] Emerging from the trees, they discovered that the bridge over the River Souleuvre on the main road from St. Lô to Le Bény Bocage was also unprotected, and promptly seized it. Two hours later they were joined by a Troop of tanks from 2nd Northants Yeomanry. These had made their way through the forest only after overcoming the opposition of two German self-propelled guns which had made a belated and ineffective appearance. This force held the vital bridge for the next six hours, by which time it had been decided to push the entire division over it and the leading tanks of 29th Brigade Group had already arrived on this mission.

"The capture of the bridge and the advance southward which it made possible was unquestionably a turning point in the campaign in France. The battle beyond Caen had obstructed the collection of a counter-attack force sufficient to halt the American drive farther west. This advance prevented the immediate reinforcement of that force. In order that the stroke might be exploited the Army plan was changed and its most westerly troops became recognized as the main striking component. The commanding heights around Le Bény Bocage, originally the objective not even of 15th Scottish but of 30 Corps on their left, now lay within our grasp; and we were ordered after securing them to push on with all speed to Étouvy".

16. In actual fact, only half a Troop. *Author.*

It is indeed an astonishing thought that in modern war, because of the speed of wireless communication, an entire Army plan can be altered in so short a space of time, on receipt of a faint message from five men by a bridge, six miles behind the enemy line.

★   ★   ★

We can now see that with the Americans temporarily held up to the west and with 15th (Scottish) Division meeting strong opposition to the east of St. Martin des Bésaces, 11th Armoured Division was venturing its head into a salient with long and vulnerable flanks and very liable to counter-attack. This was exactly what was to happen. The main body of the German 21st Panzer Division was probably hiding on the high ground between Le Tourneur and Vaumartin, and with 15th (Scottish) Division committed to an easterly flank guard because of the slower advance of 30 Corps on the left, Guards Armoured Division prepared to pass through them and take up the running. But by nightfall the latter's 5th Brigade was to be halted in heavy action with enemy armour around Point 238, southeast of St. Martin des Bésaces—the same spot where Lieutenant Cody's half-Troop had come to grief earlier in the day.

Before continuing the narrative, let us take a closer glance firstly at the means whereby Lieutenant Powle's Troop reached the Souleuvre, and, secondly, at what befell Lieutenant Bethell's Troop, which also tried to reach the same spot to help hold the bridge.

When Lieutenant Powle first branched left from the main body of "C" Squadron after leaving Dampierre at dawn, he soon lost both his rear vehicles. Corporal-of-Horse Brown's armoured car became hopelessly jammed between high banks, suffering from accelerator trouble, and the rear scout car commanded by Corporal Ray was thus unable to follow. When these vehicles eventually extricated themselves, their route had been covered by two enemy guns. Their Troop Leader, who had decided to go on, said later that this proved eventually to have been a good thing, because he did not think that a whole Troop would have made it.

Of the actual run, in the first vehicle, a scout car, were Corporal G. B. Bland, of Epping, a printer by trade, and his driver, Trooper H. G. P. Read, later to be killed north of Nijmegen in a gallant attempt to reach the airborne troops at Arnhem. In the armoured car were Lieutenant Powle, his gunner-operator, Corporal P. Staples, and the driver, Trooper Clarke. Both Lieutenant Powle and Corporal Bland have written down some of their impressions. They are worth recording.

Bland, whose job it was to lead, starts his story at the time of leaving harbour in the morning:

"Forgive me, please, if I have forgotten certain dates and times. The first four miles being rather nerve-racking for us as this was our first real taste of leading into the unknown, so to speak. Early on we found ourselves with only two cars left. Lieutenant Powle decided to go on without them. Shortly afterwards, I spotted a German look-out guard; he ran, but luckily a grenade I threw accounted for him. The idea of the grenade was better than using our guns as it was harder for the Germans to determine what it was; this served us lucky. We quickly came upon a couple of 88-mms. and a number of smaller calibre jobs, but fortunately they were without warning, and although they tried hard they missed us. Unfortunately, they hit another of our Troops very badly; this I believe was Lieutenant Petherick's. We pushed on rapidly now, in order to get past this sticky spot, and got through safely.[17] I remember Lieutenant Powle shouting a remark to me, 'We may as well try what's in front—it can't be worse than trying to neck it back through that lot!' After taking a number of enemy posts by surprise, I had occasion to look at the map and realized that we were getting close to the bridge and also a rather long radio range away from Headquarters.[18] This came as a bit of a shock. We tried to get a message through but could not at the time make contact. It was decided that I should have a crack at crossing the bridge, covered by the other armoured car. It worked, and after quickly dismounting we (myself and Trooper Read) slipped up behind a German sentry and quietly finished him off. We had to dispose of any such visitors, otherwise we were sunk as there was not a hope of holding any numbers off with only two cars if the warning went off.

"I think that it was sheer luck that we were never spotted as we later learnt that a number of Panthers had the bridge covered. We had decided to dismount to hold the bridge; this kept us out of sight. The cars we covered in bushes. Only Corporal Staples remained mounted to try to make contact, which he did after some brilliant operating. Anyhow the message was received that tanks would be arriving to consolidate the old bridge. They hit the same bad patch as we did on the way, but five arrived and between us we held the bridge with hardly a breath until some more arrived in the evening after nearly shooting us up."

---

17. The Troop was now passing across the main St. Martin des Bésaces road, where Lieutenant Powle's narrative begins.
18. Major Herbert's Squadron Headquarters near Dampierre. The wireless interference was then probably as bad as it was ever to be because there were so many British and American formations in abnormally close contact.

Lieutenant Powle's letter:

"As the rear half of my Troop had become immobilized in a narrow lane as we crossed the main road we had to move quickly. I had to rip across speedily because it was dominated by an anti-tank gun which had not yet spotted us. The rear half stayed quiet and re-joined me the next day. I can remember rushing madly through the Forêt l'Evêque after a German four-wheeled armoured car. We followed it for two miles, then it disappeared round a corner. Odd people, etc., who hadn't the vaguest idea who we were until I shouted at them. The appallingly bad interference on the wireless. Then preparing to do a 'seize and hold' according to 2nd Household Cavalry Standing Orders, and then realizing that the Germans were mostly coming from behind me! Losing my temper with my Troop individually and finally en masse. Coming across a dummy wooden tank which was so well camouflaged that I didn't see it until I was only twenty yards away, so that it entirely lost its purpose. We reached the bridge at ten-thirty in the morning … if you could harness the amount of nervous energy which we used in these metallic man-traps, the armoured cars, the miners could take a year's holiday. However, when I look back, I find I remember only the pleasant parts of military service. I remember the Camembert of Normandy rather than the dust. In fact, the picture which I have in mind is pleasant and hazy, and therefore perhaps essentially false".

★   ★   ★

Near this same bridge, which 8 Corps immediately named "Cavalry Bridge," but which to the Regiment was to remain for all time "Dickie's Bridge," lies half hidden, in the trees two hundred yards distant, a farm. To this place the Regiment were to withdraw to rest some weeks later before resuming the advance to the Seine. Passing the spot three years later, my wife and I had halted at the bridge when a swarthy middle-aged peasant harvesting in a near-by field waved frantically. He introduced himself with a broad toothless grin as Monsieur Desire Papillon and said that he was the owner of the farm. We talked. I drew him on to the last days of July and early August 1944. Instead of the usual "What I did to the Boche," Monsieur Papillon, who surely because of his powers of observation would have made a good scout car commander, proceeded to give a most accurate résumé of the 31st of July 1944.

He had temporarily abandoned his farm as he not unreasonably expected trouble that morning. The Germans were in a state of evil-tempered panic. Hiding in the woods which line the banks of the

Souleuvre, he had watched and noted the numbers of the enemy crossing the bridge in both directions. Then, continued Papillon, "Just after ten o'clock in the morning, I saw one little *chenillette avec roues* and *un espèce de char*, also on wheels … they cautiously crossed the bridge and hid in the woods." Here he pointed to the exact spot at the south-west corner of the bridge where Powle had placed his cars, adding with a chuckle, "Oh yes, I knew where they were hiding, but the Boches didn't, although I shall never know why they were not discovered." We asked him how he knew that the two cars were British, and he said that civilian messages had already filtered through from St. Martin that the English tanks were close at hand. "Some hours later," he continued, "a few more tanks came along from La Ferrière, but they were big ones this time; then I felt it was safe to go back to my farm. In the evening others arrived, and I was beginning to think of going to work in my fields when the Boche dropped a heavy shell into my farmyard." At this stage of the narrative we had to go and look at the still carefully preserved crater.

The civilians could never differentiate between tanks and armoured cars, calling them all *chars* (tanks). Sometimes they got as far as calling the scout car *une chenillette*, meaning "small tracked vehicle." Hence Papillon's contradictory description, *chenillette avec roues*, which, although it actually meant "baby tracked vehicle with wheels," did at least show that he recognized the difference.

Only then did I tell him the name of the regiment whose troops he had seen holding the bridge. Monsieur Papillon gave utterance to a long drawn out "Vous l'avez dit," the Norman's "Says you," and insisted on us meeting the rest of his family. Further effusive handshakes; then cider in quantity, and politics. Monsieur Papillon was healthily reactionary in sentiment. His children and labourers sat around grinning and mopping their brows, for it was very hot. Then after we had been compelled to down a further glass of cider, followed by coffee laced with calvados, in honour of the occasion, we were taken to see the old parking places of every armoured car. Some of the slit trench marks were still visible and I suspect that Papillon had sentimentally avoided ploughing over them. The bottom half of an old petrol "flimsy", marked with squadron signs, and several mildewed packets of English cigarettes were reverently handed round for inspection. Finally, at Monsieur Papillon's insistence, the procession walked slowly down to the place where the watercarts had filled up. Papillon gazed in silence, then awakening from his reverie, exclaimed, "And how is Corporal Harrison?[19]. That soldier certainly liked my cider!"

---

19. Corporal ("Rev' up") Harrison, "D" Squadron.

Monsieur Papillon then posed for his photograph in grim Napoleonic stance by the shell crater, and after hearing that his ambition was to come to England to buy a tractor, we bade each other farewell, though not before I had been made to promise that every Household Cavalryman revisiting the battlefield should be asked to pass by his farm to toast the Regiment in cider. "Yes," he chuckled, as he waved good-bye to the car, "I knew that the English were there in the woods, but the Boches didn't."

★   ★   ★

Just before noon, with a scorching sun beating down on turret tops, unbearable to the naked hand, the Regiment was to suffer its greatest blow of the day. An entire "D" Squadron Troop, that commanded by Lieutenant Bethell, disappeared, leaving as only clue to the disaster a burnt-out armoured car and scout car, found on the road to St. Lô the next morning. Nor until many months later was it possible to piece the full story together, after Lieutenant Bethell, badly wounded, had been flown back to England from a German hospital in Paris, following the liberation of the French capital during the American advance in late August.

Ordered to the aid of Lieutenant Powle's Troop and precluded from advancing south-east of St. Martin des Bésaces to seek another approach to the bridge, he had crossed the main road west of the village to plunge through the sombre closeness of the Forêt l'Evêque. He was taking almost the same route as had the "C" Squadron Troop earlier on. There is no doubt that the enemy had been fully alerted by the first patrol, and subsequently by the Northamptonshire Yeomanry Troop of tanks dispatched to the bridge and which had just preceded him. These latter he met, after emerging from the forest, halted in the village of La Ferrière.

The tanks told him that there was enemy resistance to their front on the direct route to the bridge, and that they were temporarily held up. But there were several tracks leading in a north-westerly direction on to the St. Lô road, running roughly parallel to the St. Lô—Vire railway line. If he could only get his Troop up to the main road, Lieutenant Bethell would be in a fair way to the bridge by a route which had not yet been tried.[20] The first track attempted proved impassable and the cars ripped off half their wings. The second one tried proved better and eventually led the Troop on to the St. Lô road about a mile south of Point Aunay. From there, as usual bounded by high banks and hedges on both sides, the way

---

20. In fact, this road from Point Aunay southwards was to remain partially in German hands until the next day.

led directly to the bridge, but after having travelled some few hundred yards the Troop encountered trouble. One of the scout cars had already made contact to the west with enemy infantry on bicycles. These had been dispersed by fire by Corporal Watkins. The Troop Leader's own car had had to engage enemy to its front and to the rear, in the direction of the Point Aunay cross-roads, while further groups of infantry had also been seen filtering down the sides of the banks.

Ahead, the impenetrable leafiness of the hedges made it almost impossible to see the German infantry who crawled about at close range.

Then "something" hit the leading scout car, which after a loud report burst into flames. Corporal Watkins, its commander, found himself with the débris of the wireless set in his lap, but was otherwise unhurt, and with his driver tried to regain Lieutenant Bethell's car. The latter was endeavouring to cover Corporal-of-Horse Soper's armoured car, which had been ordered to turn to cover the rear, for this was obviously an ambush. At this moment, the Troop Leader's car was also hit by what was probably a bazooka. Lieutenant Bethell, who had been standing in the turret, had his right leg severed, but did not realize this until he tried to abandon the now blazing car by placing his foot on the seat. He managed, however, to crawl out and drag himself to the ditch. Trooper Allen, the driver, had been badly wounded about the head and was blinded with blood, while the gunner-operator, Trooper Cable, although also wounded, tried to give first aid to his now helpless officer. The remainder of the Troop, caught in the act of turning, were surrounded and overpowered by the Germans, who swarmed over the trapped vehicles.

Then followed a grim journey. The Germans placed the wounded prisoners on the back of the captured scout car and drove to what must have been an enemy rallying point somewhere near Le Tourneur. Lieutenant Bethell, who probably owes his life to an unexpectedly tough constitution and to the small care which his men were able to give him (they still had a little whisky salvaged from one of the cars, which they poured down his throat), naturally remembered little of the route taken, but there was a faint chance that the Germans might run into British patrols. However, it was not to be. Lieutenant Powle, who was on what might easily have turned out to be the Germans' route, saw nothing, so the enemy party evidently struck eastwards before reaching the Souleuvre. Even so they cannot have missed the troop of Northamptonshire Yeomanry tanks which passed down that road on its way to the bridge from La Ferrière by more than a few minutes.

Thereafter, for the Household Cavalrymen, it was to be a story of a disorganized enemy lacking anaesthetics, pain-deadening drugs and even the most elementary surgical necessaries. Their bandages were made of paper. A German doctor spoke to Lieutenant Bethell in English and did his best for him but said that he would have to clean up the wound with nothing more than a local anaesthetic—explaining it was the same for his own men. There was a terrible succession of journeys in jolting ambulances and cattle trucks, packed nose to tail in columns, all fleeing from the Allied aerial strafing. The Germans were not too particular as to what vehicles were draped with the Red Cross flag, and when the planes came in to bomb or machine-gun the columns, the wounded of both sides were left while the orderlies sheltered in the ditch until the attack was over. This performance would be repeated over and over again.

When halts for rest or change of transport were made, wounded Americans and British and Germans found themselves dumped together on to the hard floors of makeshift hospitals. Lieutenant Bethell, whose wound had received no treatment apart from the superficial dressing from the original Wehrmacht doctor, was to continue in this state until he finally reached Paris. He will always remember the good offices of a badly wounded American soldier on an adjoining stretcher who shared with him a bottle of wine which he had acquired on the journey at some halt—it saved his life. Without it he could not have reached Paris.

Once in the French capital, daily rumours of the Allied progress trickled through to the wounded prisoners in the hospital, but although most encouraging to morale, these reports had to be treated with reserve, for it was never certain whether they originated from genuine Resistance sources or from planted agents. Food was inadequate, but Red Cross parcels began to arrive almost immediately and their contents helped to eke out the meagre rations.[21]

Two days before the Americans arrived, the German hospital staff fled, and for several days the more badly wounded who could not be moved had to look after each other as best they could. Trooper Allen, who was in the same hospital, attempted to stay behind by pretending that his head wound had broken down again, but it was unavailing and he was removed to Germany with the less severely wounded. He thus missed being repatriated until the end of hostilities, as did the rest of the Troop. (See Corporal-of-Horse Soper's letter, Appendix A.)

★ ★ ★

21. The experience of Household Cavalry prisoners, as far as the receipt of Red Cross parcels was concerned, varied greatly.

Back at St. Martin des Bésaces the hot day wore on, and with the fall of the village at midday, the question of the disposal of prisoners at Squadron Headquarters became acute. We had not yet learnt the simple art of doubling them off to the rear with threats that they would be shot if they ever stopped running. These, our first prisoners, were a most dishevelled and frightened lot, with little of the vaunted superman about them. They watched us search their kit apprehensively, cringingly anxious to please and co-operate. We asked to see their pay books, glanced at the rest of their papers knowingly, refused them a cigarette and a drink (except to the wounded), and ordered a three-tonner driver to stalk up and down their lines guarding them—all strictly according to the book. In time a lorry would arrive from the echelon and they would be bundled back to Lieutenant Haskard, the Intelligence Officer, who must have had a busy day, swamped with sweaty Teutons and great bundles of mostly worthless documents and private letters.

With memories of the previous night's traffic jam, Colonel Abel Smith had earlier anticipated further congestion on the single forest track leading to Powle's bridge. He had accordingly moved up Regimental Headquarters during the day from Fierreville to La Fouquerie, where by nightfall he felt well situated should the threatened breakthrough result in another jockeying match with the tanks for position. It was to be a vain hope.

Of the four Squadrons, "D" felt as rightly confident as any that they would not be used again that night. In any case, only in the direst emergencies did armour fight in the dark. They were soon to be disillusioned.

By sunset, the van of 29th Armoured Brigade was moving towards the bridge. The last two "D" Squadron Troops were about to be withdrawn from the area of La Ferrière to a new Squadron harbour south of Dampierre, and "A" Squadron, which had been in reserve, was preparing to take over. Then, just as it was getting dark, Major Ward was called to the Rear Link set. "Sunray"[22] was coming to him in person— he would be arriving any moment—the Squadron was to stand by for orders—no one was to move.

---

22. Within the Regiment, the term "Sunray," applying to any commanding rank, soon achieved a series of delicately shaded gradations. Thus the Squadron Leader would be the Troop Leader's "Sunray." Colonel Abel Smith was the Squadron Leader's "Sunray," and so on up the scale. To the Regiment, General Adair, commanding Guards Armoured Division, became "Very Senior Sunray"; General O'Connor and later General Horrocks, 30 Corps Commander, were always known as "Super Sunray"; Field-Marshal Montgomery was "Enormous Sunray." Fittingly, when Mr. Churchill came to be escorted to the preparations for the Rhine crossing by Lieutenant the Lord Burghersh's Troop, he was referred to by one Household Cavalry wireless operator as "The Sun Itself"

The men were all very tired after being nearly twenty-four hours in operation and hoping for a rest. In one corner of the lush little field which was "D" Squadron's harbour near Dampierre, so refreshingly cool and green after the dust and clamour of the day's fighting, someone was carrying on an interminable wireless discussion with the echelon about a water-truck which could not get through the traffic. The echelons were then in the vicinity of Caumont, and Caumont might have been Cambodia for all the hope there was of driving past the tightly wedged columns.

The harbour was alive with the sounds familiar to all armoured car leaguers. Clusters of dusty troopers were sharing out their evening rations while recounting the day's adventures. Stoves were boiling away at the sunset "brew up," odd shots still rang out from near-by woods, and the inevitable captive German stragglers wearily wended their way northwards. The fitters to a man had their noses buried in the works of a temperamental scout car, while from the back of a lorry a civilian wireless set droned out the current hit, "It's Love, Love, Love." "I hope" said Captain Waterhouse to a Corps of Signals electrician, "that you are not wasting our spare batteries; we may need them tonight." "No, sir," answered the signaller, a stocky little Scotsman, "and if you need more battery juice tonight, I'll step up the charger engine and just bash it thru' them, sir."

Then, just as the last Daimler was being filled with petrol and a late-arrival Matador was elbowing its solemn way down a line of munching crews, Colonel Abel Smith arrived in a cloud of dust and avalanche of maps, from under which Lieutenant Haskard slowly unwound himself. The Colonel exuded an almost diabolic optimism. We, the Regiment, had "done extremely well"; the Corps Commander was "delighted," and he himself was "delighted." Then, turning his gaze full on to Major Ward, at the same time seizing a huge map board from Lieutenant Haskard, he announced that we were about to have the chance of doing even better within the next twelve hours. "D" Squadron, whose turn for rest it was, would have to continue operating because "A" Squadron was still inextricably held up by traffic north of St. Martin des Bésaces. Given luck, "D" might be in Vire, and certainly Étouvy, by eight o'clock the following morning—a prophecy which, had the subsequent congestion in the Forêt l'Evêque been less, might well have come to pass.

There are some born by nature pessimists, and to me, Vire, even on the smallest scale map, looked very far away, especially at night. I turned to Lieutenant Haskard for a gleam of more human and personally

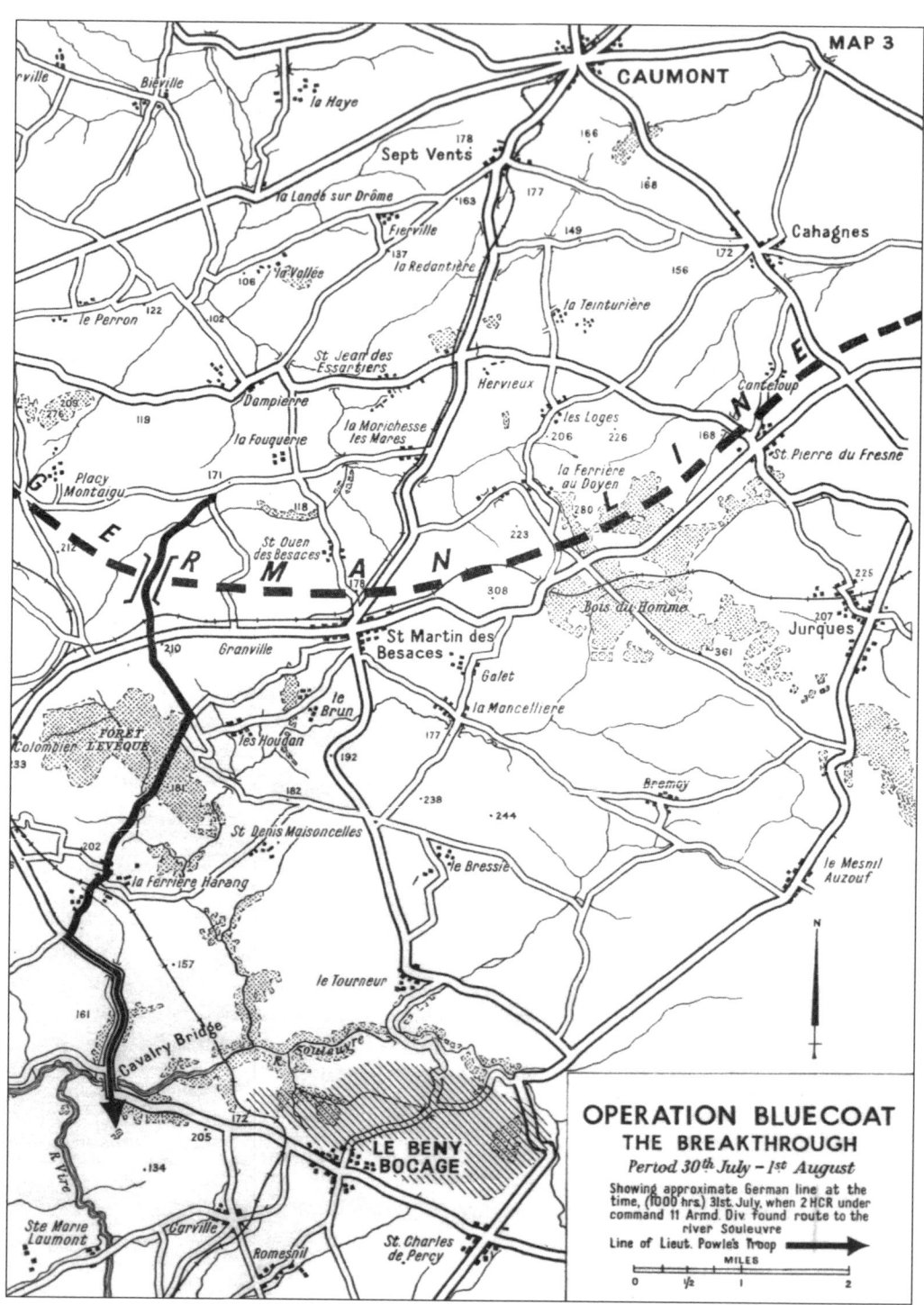

MAP 3

OPERATION BLUECOAT
THE BREAKTHROUGH

Period 30th July – 1st August

Showing approximate German line at the time, (1000 hrs.) 31st July, when 2 HCR under command 11 Armd. Div. found route to the river Souleuvre

Line of Lieut. Powle's Troop ➤

MILES

0   ½   1   2

encouraging information—of the kind which high-level "I" could normally be relied upon to supply about the enemy's wilting morale. But all Lieutenant Haskard said to me that evening was, "I don't envy you all," which, as the Colonel was still within earshot, was even more muttered than usual.

The orders were plain—over the bridge, on to the heights of Le Bény Bocage; Étouvy by breakfast, possibly Vire; and the greatest obstacle to success, our own traffic ahead.

Chapter V

Beyond the Souleuvre

"D" Squadron advance to the Souleuvre—Americans and British in bad traffic jam—Adventure of Captain Waterhouse and Trooper Strange—Exploitation by armoured cars south-east of Le Bény Bocage—Battle at Le Reculey cross-roads—More night work for Squadrons—Trouble at Étouvy for Lieutenant Metcalfe's Support Troop—Further trouble on main road to Vire—Deep penetration of enemy lines by Lieutenant Everard's Troop—Lieutenant Tabor knocks out enemy S.P. gun in unorthodox fashion—Corporal Kendrick plays leading part in shooting up twenty-one German vehicles—Lieutenant Powle's boots—Corporal Bland loses his cooker in collision with Tiger tank!—A day in Captain Cooper's liaison job

It was quite dark when "D" Squadron moved off with all lights out. There had been last-minute rumours that the Americans on the right had moved up and captured another crossing on the Souleuvre. But we were wary of this because, if correct, it would mean that they had advanced much more rapidly than our liaison officer's reports had stated. To the east, the left flank was known to be meeting strong German counter-attacks and had not got beyond Point 238 and Vaumartin, two miles south-east of St. Martin des Bésaces.

Our route—the only one practicable, for the main road from St. Lô was still in enemy hands and in any case reserved for the Americans— was through St. Martin and the Forêt l'Evêque. The village had paid cruelly for its capture and was still burning fiercely. Glass and other debris littered the road, and as we turned off south at the cross-roads the upturned barrel of a knocked-out dual-purpose 88-mm. – which must surely be one of the most efficient pieces of ordnance ever turned out— was momentarily silhouetted by a burning hayrick close to the railway line. Every now and then a charred rafter would collapse in a blaze of sparks. Smoke and dust, mingling with the acrid fumes of smouldering feather beds, choked our throats. The previous night's tableau was repeating itself in every detail as we found ourselves threading our way through personal belongings and the pathetic frameworks of human habitation. St. Martin was a village of the dead.

The emptiness and the absence of civilians was eerie, and the crackle of burning timber and the throbbing of our car engines somehow accentuated the feeling. We turned right at a church and this brought us on the road to the forest. Suddenly a hot gust of wind blew up from the west and set all the curtains mournfully flapping from the splintered casements. A dead dog lay on a heap of bedclothes in the middle of the road. We turned past the last dwelling, and then came the smell—an unmistakable, all-pervading, evil smell of death, like damp stone floors in a haunted house. Floating over the pastures and through the trees and mingling with the hot odours of the grease and petrol and half-burnt oils, it drifted over everything until one even smelt it in one's hair and battledress and shaving kit. A trooper said, "It's the smell of Germans, sir."[1]

At the edge of the forest, the soil suddenly turned a curious brick red. Days of sunshine had dried it to a fine ochre dust. The dead cattle, the grass and the trees were all thickly coated with it, and within minutes so were the vehicles and the goggled faces of the crews as they tried to pierce the gloom of the way ahead. Every time a burning house collapsed in St. Martin, the sparks lit up the overhanging branches, which reminded one of an Arthur Rackham drawing as they groped and clutched at our faces and wireless aerials like demons out of a satanic foundry.

The head of the column moved forward in fits and starts, its speed governed by the tanks in front. After what appeared to be an interminably long drive through the forest, the head of the squadron column halted by an empty cottage on the outskirts of the village of La Ferrière, where two of the Troops were awaiting our arrival. A now faint "Report my signals" from Captain Collins was the sole link with the world we had left behind; inconsequently I found myself wondering whether he had managed to obtain a new bed-roll to replace the one which had been destroyed by a shell landing in his slit trench at Sallen.[2]

The earthen banks at La Ferrière were as high as the tops of the turrets and it was inky black. Corporal-of-Horse Strowbridge, who had been bent over the mouthpiece of the Squadron Leader's wireless set non-stop for nearly twenty-four hours, was absolutely dead-beat, but still kept sending out calls to "Able Victor Roger 5," thinking that one of

---

1. This was no figment of the imagination. Perhaps it was the German oil used in cleaning their weapons, or the synthetic petrol or even food? Kit found in their tanks was particularly tainted. Whatever it was, many a scout car commander is convinced that he owes his life to his sense of smell, halting his driver with the whispered warning, "I smell Germans." The enemy said that we had our own characteristic aroma, which doubtless on occasions must also have been true!

2. Captain Collins, manning the regimental forward wireless net, was on the point of retiring for a few hours' rest when a "Say again" from Major Sir Peter Grant Lawson brought him back to repeat the message. The Adjutant was not in the best of moods, for the message had been a long one, and in code. Just before he finished for the second time, a shell landed in the middle of his slit trench, demolishing his bed-roll. "If the orders had gone through more quickly I should no doubt have been in the bed-roll as well!"

Lieutenant Bethell's cars might yet answer. Time and again we thought we heard a faint reply, but it was only the crackling ether mocking our hopes. Major Ward had recently fallen off his Staghound, cutting his elbow to the bone, and was in great pain, but stubbornly refused to admit it. He tried to rearrange the Troops' order of march for easier deployment at dawn, but it was impossible. No one could move either forwards or backwards. One car in attempting to manoeuvre hit its neighbour with a crash and became wedged between it and the bank. I swung my torch in the direction of the rending metal and its rays alighted on a pair of bloodshot eyes and a black moustache projecting from under an ochre background of dust —they belonged to Lieutenant Ainsworth. Pointing to the mangled wings, he announced with a characteristic high-pitched chuckle that at that moment he was probably blocking the whole of the Second Army's axis of advance. The joke was hardly appreciated by Captain Waterhouse, who with myself was clambering from turret to turret trying to keep the tired operators awake long enough to obtain a satisfactory "net."[3]

Lieutenant Ainsworth's remarks were cut short by a sudden fusillade from behind, and drivers, resting their cramped limbs on the engine covers, jumped back into the cars, and started up. The lane filled with petrol fumes. Realizing that only one vehicle in ten could fire without hitting a comrade, car commanders grabbed a grenade. Then tracer bullets spattered down the lane, pinging off the cars and into the banks with a thud. With a further rending of metal and much swearing, the interlocked Daimlers were torn asunder. We waited tense and expectant for the attack to come in, while an operator, in the middle of the column, oblivious of what was going on around him, kept calling persistently for a report of signal strength. At last, preceded by another fusillade, the strangest of cavalcades appeared out of the darkness. The "enemy" were Americans. When last heard of these had been at Placy Montaigu, well to our north and on our right flank. We had been informed that they were making for the bridge west of "Cavalry Bridge" and that the main St. Lô road, which was to be their route, had not yet been cleared. How had they got so far east? Perhaps some order of which we were as yet unaware had switched them over to the British sector? Possibly it was a misunderstanding such as will arise in the best-planned operation, or it may simply have been what we suspected, that they just reckoned ours was a better route.

We watched them pass with curiosity. It was our first meeting with our Allies under active service conditions. They were infantry moving in

---

3. Sending out a call to tune in all the troops under Major Ward's command.

single file and, being also dog tired, they did not take the slightest notice of us. If British faces have a reputation for stolidity, then surely those of the Americans are graven. Quite expressionless, sallow with fatigue, one and all masticating gum and silent in their rubber-studded top boots, they padded by in their tight-bottomed trousers.

They were about a company strong. In the middle of their column and sitting like Buddha on a mound of kit in the back of a jeep was an officer chewing a large cigar and studying by its glowing ash a crumpled map folded to the size of a small pocket-book. The jeep, finding it difficult to pass our vehicles and adjust its pace to the infantry, was groaning in bottom gear. Its occupant nodded to me as he passed and, casually glancing from his map to the shadowy outline of a tree, as if identifying a landmark, sprayed its topmost branches with a Tommy gun. "Snipers," he grunted. When he ran out of ammunition someone else took up the running; the amount of small-arms ammunition carried by these Americans must have been prodigious, for long after they had scraped by our cars we could still hear them firing at the tree-tops.

Two hours before dawn the Squadron moved off again but was soon halted by more transport ahead—this time American lorries. Obviously, something must have gone seriously wrong with the "tie-up," because 11th Armoured Division and the American 19th Division appeared to be using the same road.

Regimental Headquarters began to chafe and ask what was holding us up. Captain Waterhouse was dispatched with Trooper Strange as driver to liaise with the Americans and see what could be done to ease the traffic problem. We were assured that 19th U.S. Division were now in firm possession of the bridge to the west, and also well over the river.

It was past eight o'clock in the morning before Lieutenants Ainsworth's and Groeninx van Zoelen's Troops, with Lieutenant Metcalfe's Support Troop close at hand, were over "Cavalry Bridge." Their role was to deploy as quickly as possible to the south-east, leaving 29th Armoured Brigade's tanks and infantry to tackle the village of Le Bény Bocage which lay on the heights south of the river. But the long climb up to Le Bény Bocage was already blocked with traffic and the first available road forked nearly a mile and a half ahead. Two Tiger tanks and some infantry were holding up proceedings mainly because of the difficulty which 29th Armoured Brigade was experiencing in getting off the road.

This was our first close view of the cruel disparity between the armour and hitting power of the German tanks and that of our own Shermans. Nor could inspired propaganda ever convince the British soldier to the contrary, for he knew well enough that both the German Tiger and

Panther could knock out his tank at well over a thousand yards range, while his own shots bounced off harmlessly unless he could close to less than half that distance.

Major Ward had established his temporary headquarters on some high ground to the north of the Souleuvre from where a view across the valley might be obtained when the mists had cleared. From here also a few of 29th Brigade's tanks were firing in desultory fashion across the valley into Le Bény Bocage. Wild strawberries were growing in profusion by the side of the road, and magpies, disturbed by the firing, chattered ceaselessly in the trees overhead. It was a good spot, and while waiting to move farther forward, breakfasts were cooked. Resting in the ditches were our American friends of the previous night and, sad to relate, they admitted they were lost. "It's those hell goddam Normandy bridges," said their commander in explanation; "they're kinda difficult to locate and I've got my orientations all balled up."

Meanwhile, Captain Waterhouse, who had just reached the place where these Americans should have been, called up in some agitation. He pointed out forcibly that the bridge was NOT in Allied hands. Ten minutes later, breathing rather hard, he was back with his story.

In accordance with orders, he had taken the road along the northern bank of the Souleuvre. It ran through a rocky defile reminiscent of the Cheddar Gorge. On nearing the bridge, he had ordered his driver, Trooper Strange, to slow down while he looked about for a headquarters. Two things surprised him. Firstly, there were no Americans in sight, and, secondly, it was strange that the German prisoners should all have been permitted to retain their arms. However, feeling that Americans were notoriously casual in some ways, he pushed on. Disinterested stares from countless unshaven Huns met him from all sides. Telling Strange to halt, he was about to dismount when the full meaning of the situation suddenly smote him. These Germans were still free, fully armed, and the Americans had definitely not arrived.

In reverse, the Daimler scout car is unrivalled for a quick getaway. But today, in the confusion, poor Strange stalled the engine and it took several pulls at the self-starter to get it going again. The feelings of the two Household Cavalrymen can be imagined as they waited amidst the groups of Germans for the machine to come to life. After an apparent eternity of time, the engine fired, and, by a miracle which can only have been occasioned by complete surprise on the part of the enemy, they got away before a shot was fired.

On his return, Captain Waterhouse voiced his opinion of inaccurate Intelligence information in no uncertain terms, but as he ate his breakfast

EXPLOITING THE BREAK-THROUGH

Near St. Martin des Bésaces, 1st August 1944: 11th Armoured Division tanks bound for Le Bény Bocage. At this stage of the campaign the only crossing over the River Souleuvre available to 8 Corps was the bridge seized by the Regiment.

of baked beans and biscuits he began to feel better and was further cheered by the thought that his meal might well have been one of black bread and cabbage soup behind the barbed wire of a prisoners' cage.

This personal contretemps in no way deflected the general development of the greater plan. By ten o'clock patrols had got clear of Le Bény Bocage and advanced some miles to Carville. Here the cross-roads were found to be held, but the enemy were soon dealt with, although Corporal-of-Horse Royston in 4 Troop was forced to finish his part of the battle by lying full length under fire alongside the engine cover of his car, working the carburettor controls by hand —the accelerator linkage having fallen into the bottom of the engine compartment and the driver having found that otherwise he could move neither backwards nor forwards. From Carville, Lieutenants Buchanan-Jardine and Ainsworth were then switched to guard the right flank along the River Vire, and their troops were soon engaged in some very close fighting amidst typical Bocage country and the high ground overlooking the village of Ste Marie Laumont, which was found to be held by the enemy.

3 Troop (Lieutenant Hanbury) and 1 Troop (Lieutenant Groeninx van Zoelen) made good progress eastwards, then cut across the main Caen—Vire highway and continued towards Presles in a south-easterly direction. It was found that the enemy were in a state of great confusion and had there been more road space available for our tanks and infantry there is little doubt that Vire would have been in British hands by nightfall. As it was, 11th Armoured Division could only occupy the heights north-west of Le Bény Bocage with its 29th Brigade by midday, while 159th Brigade, having turned off south of Le Bény Bocage ridge, came level on the right.

"A" Squadron (Major Bowes Daly) arrived in the area at noon and set up headquarters north of the River Souleuvre, near La Ferrière. "D" Squadron were by then well established, with three Troops overlooking the River Vire, and a fourth, Lieutenant Hanbury's, across the Vire—Caen high road heading south-east. Many prisoners were being captured, and their various identifications demonstrated all too clearly the uncoordinated character of the resistance. Indeed, the enemy's reaction to the breaching of their line was not only unprecedentedly slow, but when their counter-attacks did come in during the late afternoon they showed a curious predilection for throwing their weight against the Americans on the right and Guards Armoured Division on the left. When recalled to harbour at dusk, Lieutenant Hanbury's Troop, almost up to the railway north of Vire, was reporting that "those little men in field grey are all coming back as we retire." The question of moving up infantry reinforcements after an armoured break-through will ever be a difficult problem, and in this case the appalling road congestion made the task impossible. It was all rather disappointing.

In "A" Squadron Major Bowes Daly had lost no time in pushing out his troops eastwards in the direction of St. Charles de Percy and south-east to make contact with "D" Squadron. A group commanded by Captain Profumo encountered opposition at the cross-roads at Le Reculey, where a stubborn party composed of paratroopers and soldiers from 9th S.S. Panzer Division disputed the way.

Supported by the Heavy Troops commanded by Lieutenant I. M. Clark ("A" Squadron) and Lieutenant Smallwood ("D" Squadron), Lieutenant Wordsworth attacked with his Support Troop infantry.

After a sharp struggle in which Lance-Corporal-of-Horse Lewis Evans[4] and Trooper G. Copage were badly wounded, the former by machine-gun fire and the latter by a grenade, the Germans retired, leaving several prisoners and wounded behind. Later, after a warning from a civilian that a near-by cottage contained more of the enemy, one of the Heavy Troop Matadors gave it a purging with its Besa. The Germans, belonging to the 9th S.S. Panzer Division, soon withdrew. "The cottage," wrote Lieutenant Clark, "was such a clean little place that I had not the heart to put a shell into it, merely contenting myself with a couple into the garden and calling it a day ... we then occupied the road junction."

The day was full of minor incidents. Lieutenant Wordsworth, hot from the battle at Le Reculey cross-roads and after an enormous expenditure of energy and ammunition, celebrated his return to harbour by blowing off his Squadron Leader's Staghound tyre. This accident failed to amuse Major Bowes Daly at the time.

Neither the Royal Air Force nor the American Air Force were too sure of our ground recognition signals, and Lieutenant Buchanan-Jardine's Troop ("D" Squadron) was resolutely attacked towards evening by three Lockheed Lightnings. The most furious and indignant appeals for redress came back over the air from La Maubandière, north of Étouvy, and quantities of yellow smoke were put up, all to no avail.

Fortunately, an armoured car is a small target to hit with a bomb, although the planes showed no lack of perseverance. One machine dropped its load a few yards from Corporal-of-Horse Clarke's car just as he was diving into his turret and blew the car across the road into a ditch, knocking him out. He remembered nothing further until he got to the

---

4. Corporal-of-Horse Evans died of his wounds two days later.

first-aid post with a lump the size of an ostrich egg on his forehead, but fortunately he was only concussed and he was back with the Troop in a few days.

Lieutenant Jonkheer Groeninx van Zoelen collected many prisoners, explored a deserted farmhouse, turned through a wood and found himself face to face with an anti-tank gun. Having effectively dealt with that situation, the Troop rounded another bend and saw "some blue-grey shapes, sunbathing of all things. They were most surprised when tickled up with the Besa."

159th Brigade had mined their outposts at dusk and there was therefore considerable delay before the returning troops were able to get through. The last car did not reach harbour until after midnight.

Regimental Tactical Headquarters had by now moved to Carville, where close at hand were "C" and "D" Squadrons, and also "B" Squadron (at Mauger), who on reverting to regimental command had spent all day motoring from the area of St. Martin des Bésaces.

With the sudden expansion of 11th Armoured Division's front due to the break-through, their southern flank was now virtually open to all corners. In addition, because of the frightful traffic jam at the only available bridge over the River Souleuvre, there was still a desperate shortage of infantry to fill the widening gaps. But this was the price of bold exploitation and a risk worth taking. In fact, had the enemy chosen to counter-attack this sector during the night of 1st/2nd August, Regimental Tactical Headquarters must have borne the first shock!

The situation on the northern flank was equally insecure, with Guards Armoured Division still echeloned some way back. There were confused reports of enemy tanks at Le Tourneur, north of the Souleuvre, while isolated pockets of Germans were still on the wooded heights south-west of "Cavalry Bridge." "To add to the confusion," wrote a "B" Squadron Troop Leader, "Julian Ward[5] accidentally trod on the firing gear of his 37-mm. gun coming into harbour and very nearly scored a direct hit on his Squadron Leader!"

★ ★ ★

Due to "D" Squadron's relatively unopposed advances towards Vire during the afternoon of 1st August, the official view was that the enemy was now on the run. Based on this assumption, General O'Connor

---

5. Captain J. H. D. Ward, second-in-command, "B" Squadron.

personally ordered the advance to be pressed home throughout the night. "2 Household Cavalry will tonight patrol south with the utmost vigour in the direction of Vire. This task is essential to the Allied plan."[6]

Immediately on receipt of orders to exploit boldly throughout the night, Colonel Abel Smith had attempted to move "A" Squadron from La Ferrière, but Divisional Headquarters still could not allow the necessary road space. The echelon of 29th Armoured Brigade had to come up to refuel the tanks, and the Regiment had been left to come on with what it had in front at the time. In fact, Regimental Headquarters themselves had had a mad dash in the late evening to get on to the road before the tank echelon arrived. Only by the skin of their teeth did they so reach Carville. "Thus," says the War Diary, "once again, only 'D' Squadron was initially available for this unenviable job."

On arrival at Carville, Colonel Abel Smith and the Adjutant, Captain Collins, had gone to Le Bény Bocage (which had been occupied about midday) to see Brigadier Roscoe Harvey of 29th Brigade to arrange for "D" and "C" Squadrons to go through the mined outposts, and it was getting on for two o'clock in the morning when the Squadron Leaders eventually received their orders, Major Ward in his own harbour field, and Majors Wignall and Bowes Daly in the small White scout car at Tactical Headquarters which served as the Regimental A.C.V. "I can well remember," wrote the Adjutant, "how absolutely dead-beat was everyone in 'D' Squadron. Personally, I had a cracking row with the second-in-command at Tactical Headquarters about the amount of light we were alleged to be showing on an exposed slope!"

To attempt to describe and disentangle the complications of the next day's fighting at any level is difficult if confusion is to be avoided. For the Regiment, the battle is best viewed from the Troop angle, with certain salient features borne in mind.

Dispositions were by no means ideal. We were strung out thinly, and across the line of our advance south-eastwards to the Vire—Vassy road lay three ridges, the last two notably forming between them a deep and thickly wooded valley on the slopes of which much bitter fighting was to occur. These came to be known as the Burcy, Presles, and Perrier ridges, although in the case of the first named the actual village of Burcy was at the bottom of the valley.

In addition to Étouvy, it was then thought that the advance might be developed south-westwards to include Vire, which was an important centre of communications, therefore the Regiment had been ordered to probe hard in that direction.

---

6. *History of 8 Corps*, p.135 (privately printed).

Haggard eyes gazed at Major Ward when he returned to his tent and announced to his assembled Troop Leaders that the advance was to continue without delay, for this was the third night with no sleep. His orders were brief, for nobody could really have taken in more than the absolute minimum necessary to get on to the road, head in the right direction, and push on.

Dimly one could see the flashing of shaded torches in corners of the field, as commanders pointed out the route and in their turn gave out orders to the weary semi-circles of kneeling men sharing the maps spread out on the grass.

"D" Squadron moved off shortly before three o'clock in the morning, the main body making for Le Reculey and the Vire—Caen road beyond. Lieutenant Metcalfe's Support Troop was to branch off at the village of Romesnil, having been given the task of seizing the bridge over the River Vire at Étouvy. The Squadron wended its way in pitch darkness along the lanes for a few miles with no untoward incident. Someone reported an enemy tank at Le Reculey. To the right, a sharp ear detected the sound of German half-tracks. Apart from this not a sign of life. Again it was a question of one long line ahead, and of only the first vehicle being able to fire. In the lead, Lieutenant Buchanan-Jardine's Troop, headed by Lance-Corporal Jones and Trooper Lee, turned south at the Vire road, but on the far side of the village of La Bistière ran into an enemy self-propelled gun which opened fire at close range and knocked out the scout car. Both men were seriously wounded. They were, however, extricated with the aid of covering fire from the Troop Leader's car, while the prompt arrival of Captain Waterhouse in his Staghound, firing rapid from his 37-mm. gun, caused the enemy vehicle to withdraw.[7] The Germans were found to be in fair strength in La Bistière and were not finally ejected for some time.

Dawn was breaking when a wireless message from Lieutenant Metcalfe informed Major Ward that the Support Troop had also bumped trouble on the outskirts of Étouvy. They had travelled by side roads to avoid, as far as possible, the enemy outposts on the outskirts of the village. On the way, because of the darkness, one of the White scout cars had slid into a deep ditch and had to be towed out. By then, the Troop had already by-passed a sizeable body of Germans without being challenged, so Lieutenant Metcalfe decided to go on. Corporal-

---

7. The German self-propelled gun was normally of 75-mm. calibre, mounted on a Mark III tank chassis with non-traversing turret. The gun had a limited angle of fire but was heavily armoured. Our 2-pdr. and 37-mm. guns could not penetrate head-on unless close up, but with the Littlejohn apparatus (an attachment making the weapon into a sort of squeeze gun with added muzzle velocity) the former could do so.

of-Horse Allenby was in the lead, accompanied by Trooper Sutton. Just before entering Étouvy this scout car came to a sharp bend in the road. Some houses blocked the view beyond, but in any case vision was limited to a few yards because of the dark. Suddenly the scout car stopped dead and Lieutenant Metcalfe went forward on foot to find out what was wrong. He discovered the vehicle actually underneath the gun muzzle of a German tank which was preparing to move off. There were several more tanks guarding the direct approach to the bridge. Fortunately, the Germans were not on their toes, and Sutton switched off the engine of his scout car, which was then quietly pushed to safety round the corner before the alarm was given and the enemy started firing wildly into the dawn.

The Troop retired back about a quarter of a mile, set up a roadblock controlling the entrance to Étouvy from the north, and was ordered to remain there until the light had improved sufficiently for Lieutenant Metcalfe to form some estimate of the opposition in the village.

Half an hour later Corporal-of-Horse Allenby again approached the village, this time from a new angle, to see if the bridge was still held. Unfortunately, instead of taking a previously reconnoitred track he missed the turning and swung into the village. This time the Germans were prepared. Lieutenant Metcalfe, who was approaching Étouvy on foot down another track, heard the sounds of gun fire, followed by a burst of Bren and the explosion of grenades. Then there was silence.

Fearing that something was amiss, he took a patrol, composed of Lance-Corporal Clarkson and Troopers Webb and Canny, across some intervening fields to see what had happened. This patrol ran into an enemy party of mechanized infantry and three tanks which appeared to be preparing to move off. Unfortunately, the Germans spotted the patrol, which had to beat a hurried retreat. Shortly afterwards the enemy were heard to be moving off and another patrol saw them retiring southwards. The village proper was then found to be still held in some strength, so Lieutenant Metcalfe was ordered to remain in observation and await the arrival of the Northamptonshire Yeomanry tanks. These, about a squadron strong, arrived shortly after daybreak and from positions overlooking Étouvy proceeded to shell the village.

After an interval Lieutenant Metcalfe took a further patrol down the road, supported by the tanks. The northern outskirts were now found to be clear. Several houses were burning and the Support Troop scout car was discovered blazing opposite the village church. Later, the bodies of Corporal-of-Horse Frank Allenby and Trooper Raymond Sutton were found lying in a shop window. "We covered them up," wrote Metcalfe, "feeling very sad at losing two of the very best of men and returned past the tanks on being ordered back to rejoin the Squadron."[8]

Meanwhile the rest of "D" Squadron had crossed over the Vire—Caen road, and for the remainder of the day encouraging progress to the south-east was made both by the armoured cars and the tanks. Although harassed from the east, deep penetrations by three Troops —those of Lieutenants Groeninx van Zoelen (1 Troop), Hanbury (3 Troop) and Ainsworth (4 Troop)—brought them, along with the tanks of the 23rd Hussars supported by the 8th Rifle Brigade, to the area of Chênedollé. Mortar fire, at which the German is past-master, was now becoming heavy.

From Sourdevalle, a village which was later to become only too well known, a Troop infiltrated south-west, crossed under the railway line a mile above Viessoix and was able to send in full reports on enemy movement along the Vire—Vassy road. This was to be the last day for a long time to come that the armoured cars were able to move with such impunity behind the enemy lines. Lieutenant Groeninx van Zoelen records his Troop's day thus:

"Off again in the dark. All very, very tired. Feet very sore.[9] We intend going to Vire and Étouvy. Enemy tank reported at Le Reculey. Whole of Squadron halted between high banks for an hour. Horrible feeling. My orders to go to Étouvy cancelled, thank God! Rupert Jardine ran into anti-tank gun on the Vire road. Lost scout car. Sat near cross-roads for a long time, then went on with the tanks. We all went straight to Presles and then towards Chênedollé. There, leading tank was knocked out on the cross-roads and the rest held up by infantry. Suddenly the cry 'Five Panthers,' and a commotion ensued and the long column that wound all the way over two hills started deploying where it could. Tanks suddenly disappeared in a sheet of flame. I retired slightly and got sniped at. Sniper later killed by my Bren gunner. He was an ugly brute. The next night was to be spent out where we were, with Michael Ainsworth, for our respective Troops were to lead the advance the following morning."

★   ★   ★

---

8. The Étouvy flank was to remain most uncomfortable for several days. After nightfall 2nd / 3rd August, German infantry penetrated the Northamptonshire Yeomanry positions at Étouvy and knocked out several of their tanks with bazookas. So short of infantry were 11th Armoured Division that a squadron of Sappers was dispatched to assist the tanks.

9. The result of standing in the turret for nearly three days without a break.

Although "D" Squadron had provided the patrol to Étouvy, this was because of the original difficulties of deployment within the Regiment. By dawn, most overlapping had sorted itself out and "B" Squadron was then able to operate on the right flank for the rest of the day.

In some trepidation, for he remembered the difficulties of the first night before St. Martin des Bésaces, Major Wignall had dispatched two Troops before dawn—those commanded by Lieutenant the Lord Burghersh (2 Troop) and Lieutenant Everard (5 Troop). The air, needless to say, was frightful, and the Troops, due solely to wireless interference, were soon out of touch. Lord Burghersh initially lost touch with part of his Troop and then bumped enemy at Le Reculey cross-roads. Of Lieutenant Everard there was at first no news. In view of the dreadful wireless situation, the rest of "B" Squadron moved off, with Lieutenant Tabor's Troop leading Squadron Headquarters. Progress was slow and dawn found the Troop Leader on the main Le Bény Bocage—Vire road, where he met part of "D" Squadron and Lieutenant Hoare's Troop from "A" Squadron.[10]

From the Le Reculey cross-roads the "B" Squadron centre line ran roughly through the villages of Le Queillet—Le Brien—Forgues—Burcy—Viessoix. Lieutenant Tabor's Troop was still leading at this stage, followed, to begin with, by Lieutenant Hoare's Troop. The latter had a good shoot at some enemy half-tracks in an orchard near Le Queillet. Soon afterwards the Troops parted company.

There being numerous bodies of enemy in the area, Lieutenant Tabor decided to by-pass the villages as far as practicable. He made reasonably rapid progress and reached Burcy by eleven o'clock in the morning. Here he met Corporal-of-Horse Johnson (Lieutenant Kavanagh's Troop), who was temporarily on his own in his armoured car, "Brocklesby." The Troop had split up, Lieutenant Kavanagh being on reconnaissance farther west.

Burcy itself lies in a deep, narrow valley. The road leading southward towards Viessoix climbs a steep ridge out of the village and then drops just as steeply into another valley. Lieutenant Tabor and Corporal-of-Horse Johnson drove on together out of Burcy and on to the next ridge. Here they halted in order to establish wireless touch with Squadron Headquarters, as communications were still bad. While the operators

---

10. This is to the best of Lieutenant Tabor's recollection, but I am inclined to believe that it must have been on the road Carville—Le Reculey that the meeting took place, because "D" Squadron travelled that way. I remember that suddenly, just after an enemy scare, the form of David Tabor loomed up from behind a hedge as he went to speak to Jackie Ward. One of my crew very nearly lobbed a grenade at him—the pin was out! *Author.*

were waiting for a netting call, Tabor and Johnson walked up to the crest of the hill and saw through their glasses an enemy self-propelled gun on a Mark IV chassis standing at the bottom of the far hill.

As the gun was pointing in the direction of the armoured cars, the two discussed taking it on with the 2-pdr. This, however, seemed impracticable at the range, and so the vehicles were driven off the road into a field and hidden as best could be. Then Tabor and Johnson, having armed themselves with "77" phosphorous grenades, stationed themselves in the hedge at the top of the hill so that they could look down into the valley. In a minute or so the German S.P. started up its engines and began to move very cautiously up the hill towards them. As the vehicle breasted the crest, it could be seen that the turret hatch was open and that no commander was standing up in it, and at the moment that it drew level both threw their grenades. Lieutenant Tabor's hit the lid of the hatch and dropped inside. For about three seconds nothing happened and the S.P. continued on its way undisturbed. Then there was a muffled explosion and it stopped. Clouds of smoke shot out of the turret, and with a yell two Germans leapt out and made off down the road as fast as they could go. "I was so surprised at the results of the grenade that I did nothing about them," related the Troop Leader. "Then after a second or two a third man, presumably the driver, appeared out of the hatch. I shouted at him to stop, but he jumped off the back of the S.P. and started to run off down the road. I pointed my pistol vaguely in his direction and fired. Much to my surprise, he went over like a shot rabbit. Within a few seconds there was a rumbling sound and a squadron of British tanks appeared round the corner from the direction of Burcy. The leading tank took one look at the abandoned S.P. and opened rapid fire with its 75-mm. It narrowly missed us and completely missed the S.P.! After two or three more shots he ceased firing and we liaised together."

While Lieutenant Tabor was talking to the commander of the leading tank, an Auster aircraft flew low over their heads, then dived and dropped a message. The contents were disturbing. It said that the next ridge to the south, Chênedollé—Sourdevalle, was strongly held by enemy armour. In addition, Lieutenant Everard's Troop was now reporting Tiger tanks to the east.[11] On receipt of this news the squadron of tanks was ordered to withdraw slightly, while Major Wignall ordered Lieutenant Tabor and Corporal-of-Horse Johnson with his half-Troop to advance no farther, but to remain in observation.

---

11. The same as were being encountered by "D" Squadron and the 23rd Hussars and mentioned in the "D" Squadron narrative earlier on.

On examination Tabor found that the German S.P. was relatively undamaged. The fire had gone out and there was only slight charring in the fighting compartment. Identification from photographs and papers were sent back over the wireless. Further investigation revealed two more German S.Ps. in the valley, both abandoned intact with their engines still running, and the driver of the original S.P. in a farm nursing a bullet in his ankle. The Troop Leader later learned that the disabled S.P. had been towed back to the British lines and claimed by the tanks as a knock-out to them!

Not far distant another "B" Squadron patrol, Lieutenant Kavanagh's Troop, about to move through a small deserted-looking village, was halted by a Frenchman, the Mayor, who rushed out of his house shouting, "Attention, attention, MINES!" On closer examination, the road was found to be dotted with small pieces of paper marking the exact spot where each mine lay buried. It appeared that before evacuating the place the hidden villagers had watched the Germans laying them. The Germans in turn were now hiding in the woods and started to fire on the Troop as ropes were being affixed to drag out the possibly booby-trapped mines. The four cars thereupon turned their machine guns on to the corner of the wood from where the fire was coming and soon a stream of prisoners emerged with hands upraised. After being searched they were doubled back down the road, to the delight of "Monsieur Le Maire", whose best heifers had been stolen by them that very morning.

As already mentioned, 5 Troop (Lieutenant Everard) had been one of the first "B" Squadron Troops to operate at dawn. This patrol had been sent out on a special mission with the object of reaching the Vire—Vassy road south of the railway line in the vicinity of the high ground Point 237, a mile and a half west of Viessoix. If successful, the Troop was to lie up during the hours of darkness and then continue on towards Vassy, to observe from a suitable position on the outskirts what the enemy was doing in the town itself.

Without incident (for it had been ordered to avoid Étouvy, which was Lieutenant Metcalfe's responsibility), the patrol reached the Y roads two miles south of La Papillonnière, at which place, when almost in Vire, the leading scout car, commanded by Corporal Kendrick and driven by Trooper Taylor, halted. The unmistakable sounds of German voices could be heard, followed by the noise of moving tracks. A minute later two half-tracks moved southwards into Vire. They were not pursued for there was no point in giving the game away at this stage. Moreover it was still quite dark. The Troop, wishing as far as possible to avoid main roads, retraced its steps for about a mile and then struck off east along narrow tracks until it reached the hamlet of La Blanquaire. There was no sign of enemy here, so it moved on eastwards. Shortly afterwards the patrol bumped a lorry-load of infantry, preceded by a despatch rider. The lorry was set alight and, in the words of the report, "the personnel therein entirely liquidated by Corporal Kendrick".

Following this coup, the Troop continued by small tracks and without further adventure to a spot north-west of the village of Burcy. Here, six miles behind the enemy lines, two more half-tracks loomed up in the semi-light. The leading armoured car could now see enough to take a hand in the proceedings, and both enemy vehicles were knocked out before they could fire a shot.

Leaving the wrecked half-tracks burning in the lane, the patrol now turned towards the cross-roads north-east of Forgues, where it was hoped a suitable way might be found across the valley and so to Viessoix. A short way on, however, two Panther tanks were encountered. Hiding up in a farmyard until this threat had rumbled past, Lieutenant Everard realized that the Troop would soon be operating in daylight and that the scout cars would have a better chance of remaining undetected working on their own. He therefore ordered Kendrick to make a preliminary investigation of a narrow track which led east of the village of Presles and thence southwards to a small wooden bridge over a stream. This was reported clear of enemy. It now appeared possible that the patrol, by following this route, might be able to approach Vassy avoiding the main road altogether. Kendrick was therefore ordered to continue up towards Chênedollé, which lay over the brow of the Perrier ridge on a forward slope to the south, two miles away. Meanwhile Lieutenant Everard brought up the remainder of his Troop, the two Daimler armoured cars, and the rear scout car.

Unfortunately, the track east of Presles was found to be too narrow for the armoured cars and they could make no further headway, added to which the enemy could now be seen moving in behind them and also along the main road from Estry towards Vire. Because of this threat, Lieutenant Everard ordered the rear scout car (Corporal Harmsworth and Trooper Upton) to reinforce Kendrick at Chênedollé, which he had by now successfully reached. The Troop, in two halves, was now in a position to keep the Regiment continually informed of the developing counter-attack which was coming in from the east by what proved to be 9th S.S. Panzer Division.[12]

---

12. This was the counter-attack which developed in the afternoon of the 2nd of August against originally the 23rd Hussars (tanks) and 8th Rifle Brigade (infantry), with whom "D" Squadron were operating. The British eventually withdrew from Chênedollé in the evening to take up firm positions on the Bas Perrier ridge just north of the village of that name. With both flanks completely exposed, the Burcy—Presles valley offered a standing invitation to the Germans to cut off the forward troops. This they were not slow to accept.

In the case of Kendrick's half-Troop, the Germans were actually passing their infantry, tanks and S.P. guns through the village of Chênedollé within fifty yards of him and he was to remain thus isolated, sending back a continual stream of information, until the arrival of British tanks in the late afternoon. Lieutenant Everard's half held the Presles crossing until similarly relieved, and between them, when recalled, they had knocked out a total of twenty-one German vehicles, including an armoured car, two armoured half-tracks and seven staff cars, as well as a number of infantry. They had been behind the German lines for sixteen hours.

★   ★   ★

"C" Squadron and, when they were able to get through later on, "A" Squadron[13] moved east across the Vire—Caen road with the object of reconnoitring towards Estry and at the same time keeping a look-out towards the left northern flank of the salient. They were therefore initially echeloned back from "D" Squadron on their right. But later in the day, on receiving news of the progress of Guards Armoured Division from the direction of Le Tourneur, Colonel Abel Smith ordered the two Squadrons to veer southwards, where the threat from 9th S.S. Panzer Division was becoming serious, and information was urgently required by the commander of 11th Armoured Division.

"C" Squadron moved off from their harbour west of Le Bény Bocage shortly before four o'clock in the morning, as Major Herbert hoped to reach a line of observation posts east of Estry. The route lay via St. Charles de Percy and Montchamp.[14]

Lieutenant Powle, whose Troop had been ordered to patrol the left flank of the Squadron advance, made steady progress, reporting isolated groups of enemy infantry to be in a general state of disorder and confusion. By midday he was approaching Presles. It was deserted. Then, according to Corporal-of-Horse Brown:

> "Having passed through Presles without making contact, we were only using two scout cars with a 'Blitz'[15] section under Corporal-of-Horse Bradbury attached. We approached a very sharp bend in the road when a vehicle I took to be an American armoured car came round the corner.

---

13. Although "A" Squadron had had difficulty in moving up through the traffic, they had managed early on to slip one or two Troops forward. Lieutenant Hoare's Troop, mentioned in "B" Squadron's narrative, was one of them.
14. Guards Armoured Division subsequently incurred heavy fighting in all these areas.
15. Blitz section. Another name for Support Troop Section.

We halted about thirty yards apart, then to my surprise I saw the black
and white cross of the Hun on his turret. We had nothing heavier than a
Bren gun with us so we threw out smoke and, giving him a few bursts of
Bren gun fire, we retired. (It was a Jerry six-wheeler with a 40-mm. gun,
but he did not manage to hit us.)

"We then returned through Presles and tried a new route about a mile
to the east in the direction of Estry[16], near where we halted to check our
bearings. Meanwhile a whole mass of orders in 'Slidex' were coming over
to Mr. Powle on the blower, altering our direction of advance, so while
Corporal Bland and I were taking them down and trying to make sense
of them, Mr. Powle went for a stroll in the direction of the enemy. He
was soon back to report that he had spotted a Tiger tank with its track off
on the main road a little way to the east. So seizing a captured Jerry rifle
off my car he went back alone to snipe the crew.

"As he did not return for a long time I sent a further patrol (Corporal-
of-Horse Bradbury and Corporal Bland) to look for him."

Bradbury and Bland moved cautiously down the lane taken by Lieutenant
Powle until they had reached cover. They then halted, for in front of
them, standing in solitary splendour, was a pair of British Army boots!
Of their Troop Leader—not a sign. The incident, said Bland, "shook us
rather at the time, because it had all been carried out so silently."

What had happened eventually transpired some days later when it was
learnt that Lieutenant Powle had been treated for wounds at a first aid
post and evacuated to England. He had gone down the lane with his rifle,
intent on sniping the Tiger crew as they emerged from the turret. But he
had not reckoned on being himself stalked. The German commander of
this tank happened to be stretching his legs while his crew were repairing
the broken track. Angered at seeing his 50-ton monster the object of
what he considered presumptuous attention by a lone British officer
armed with nothing more lethal than a rifle, he had let fly with his Luger
automatic, hitting Powle in the arm and spinning him over.

The rest of the story follows the best Conrad Veidt film tradition.
Powle was taken prisoner by the tank crew. The German officer came
up and introduced himself. He had lived in England and knew Torquay.
While the Troop Leader's wound was being dressed, he talked to him

---

16. Later in the afternoon leading elements of the Guards Armoured Division were
attacked after passing through St. Charles de Percy. The 2nd Welsh Guards
(Cromwell tanks) got to within 2,000 yards of Estry but were then halted. The
village, by then strongly reinforced by the Germans, was to be the scene of much
fighting until finally taken by 15th (Scottish) Division over a week later.

in perfect English. "Yes, I was at Winchester; where were you?" They passed the next quarter of an hour in the courtesies of a slightly guarded conversation—neither wishing to give anything away. At last the Tiger was ready to move. The Germans had no wish for a prisoner on their tank who would be nothing but an encumbrance. "As a matter of fact we are rather pushed," said the tank commander. "Your chaps, as far as I can make out, should be advancing towards this spot, and we have been ordered to retire. I trust you not to look where we are going. When we are out of earshot you can make your way back to your lines, I hope? However, as a formality, I shall have to ask you to leave your boots behind." Saying which, he ordered his tank to move off, leaving Powle to trudge back to his own lines in stockinged feet.

Having lost their Troop Leader, the remainder of the Troop continued, plus the boots, towards Burcy and then southwards to the Vire—Vassy road. Corporal-of-Horse Brown, who was now in command, soon made contact with the tanks of the Fife and Forfar Yeomanry and informed them that he would be advancing on their centre line across the valley and up towards Sourdevalle. The Troop motored carefully through the deserted village. Then, on turning a corner when approaching the village of La Teinturerie, where a track runs down to the Vire—Vassy road, Corporal Bland and Trooper Read ran into another Tiger tank. The scout car reversed in a flash and was back up the hill before Corporal-of-Horse Brown knew what had happened. "I've bumped a b--- Tiger," said Bland breathlessly. "How far off?" inquired Corporal-of-Horse Brown. "Look at my front tool-box," replied Bland, offering no further evidence. It was completely crumpled, and "by far the worst thing," commented Brown in recounting the episode, "was that this accident had put paid to the cooker!"

The Tiger tank then began to advance up the lane, which was the inauspicious moment chosen by the White scout car to break down, thus blocking the line of retreat of the other two vehicles. Corporal-of-Horse Brown ordered the crews to dismount, and they retired to some high ground from where they could watch the Tiger and, if it advanced any farther, try to lob grenades into the top of its turret from the high bank. It could now be seen that there were several more tanks, two of them Mark IVs, but none made any further sign of forward movement. At this juncture some Fife and Forfar Yeomanry tanks came over the brow of the next hill, and Corporal-of-Horse Brown recognized their commander as being his old instructor on his Equitation Course at Weedon. The latter, wasting no time, put in a strong flank attack and the German tanks retired towards the Vire—Vassy road, leaving one of their number burning with a hole through its engine. All three armoured cars were then recovered intact with the help of Lieutenant Corbett's Troop, which had since arrived on the scene to tow away the disabled White scout car.

★   ★   ★

In such times of confused fighting, much depends on the liaison officers for the rapid dissemination and corroboration of information. Captain Balding was working with the Americans on the right flank who were driving towards Vire. Captain Cooper's task was to pass back to the Inns of Court Regiment and Guards Armoured Division (then echeloned back) the information which the Household Cavalry troops in front were obtaining, and, in particular, warn them of the direction of the enemy counter-attacks. He kept a full record of his day's operations:

"August 2nd.—American Combat Troops taken out of the line so I report back to Regiment at Le Bény Bocage to give the Colonel information. French girl gave me an enormous bunch of flowers and some cider on the way up. More prisoners pouring back—two old ladies with white flag bringing one down the main road, very funny sight! Have got new job. Have to get into touch with Guards Armoured Division and Inns of Court Regiment, who are just beginning to advance on the Caen—Vire road. Contact with 'A.,''B' and 'C' Squadrons of our Regiment around La Ferrière. The 'C' Squadron leading troops are already moving on to the road to Estry. Glass of cider with Bowes Daly ('A' Squadron)—a very hot day. Came under machine-gun fire at Pont D'Eloy and met an 11th Armoured Division patrol.[17] Shortly afterwards met leading Coldstream carriers with the 'Micks' [Irish Guards] armour moving up the hill. Contact Micky O'Cock's[18] tank and also Arthur Cole's and tried to get some information from them. Hell of a battle started and had to take cover behind Micky's tank—heavy small-arms fire from a wood and odd mortars. Told Micky about some Tiger tanks up the road, and then met Giles Vandeleur[19] and Colonel Kim. Germans start shelling road in earnest and we lie in the ditch for a while—shells bursting up and down the road and a 3-tonner lorry behind my scout car goes up. Went back to cross-roads at St. Charles de Percy, and Inns of Court leading scout car hit by 88-mm. as I arrived. Irish Guards tank ten feet away had a near miss and a Guardsman on the back wounded. Inns of Court crew got out safely—car

17. North-east of St. Charles de Percy.
18. Captain M. O'Cock, Irish Guards.
19. Major G. A. M. Vandeleur, Irish Guards.

brewed up. Four German horse-drawn artillery trucks blocking the road with eight dead horses. Had to make a detour round by field—no mines, thank goodness! Got back eventually to R.H.Q. and hear poor Allenby has been killed. Ordered to relieve Tommy[20] at Corps H.Q., where I shall be working with General O'Connor. On way passed Tony Bethell's cars—both burnt out. No sign of him; hope he is a prisoner. His cap has been found. Farther back the road I saw Corporal-of-Horse Munn's armoured car knocked out, also a 'B' Squadron scout car. Several dead on the road—we have been advancing so fast there has been no time to bury the dead. St. Martin des Bésaces has been completely flattened. Met Jack Creswell at Corps, also Nickie Paget and 'Happy' Younghusband. Had my first real shave and wash since the battle started five days ago. Drink with Brigadier Glyn Hughes (R.A.M.C.), Phipps-Hornby and Colonel Tommy Wilson and many others I knew. Henry Garnett in good form. A really good night's sleep at last—sent for my kit and mail. Carroll, my servant, arrived from 257 Corps Delivery Squadron. Dickie Powle is missing tonight. Fired some three magazines at some Germans in a wood today, but I don't know if I hit any—the Bren fitting on the Humber scout car is not much good for use against ground troops, although O.K. against aeroplanes, but the German air force seems non-existent."

★   ★   ★

By the evening of the 2nd of August it was clear that the German resistance had hardened along the entire front. There were to be no more break-throughs for many days, and the Regiment settled down to some stern and unpleasant patrolling in this close country, which in so many ways favoured the defenders.

Chevrolet Armoured Car (Staghound)

---

20. Captain T. Clyde, second-in-command, "C" Squadron, who had been temporarily at 8 Corps H.Q. manning General O'Connor's wireless.

Chapter VI

Hide-And-Seek in the Bocage

German infiltration tactics—The Sourdevalle ridge—Bad wireless interference—Tigers and Panthers hold up proceedings—"D" Squadron temporarily surrounded—Lieutenant Smallwood and Trooper Noakes vanish—Their story—Phantom work by "D" Squadron for 159th Brigade—"B" Squadron on the Vire-Estry line—"A" Squadron on the Burcy salient—Mortaring near Viessoix—More Panther tanks—Lieutenant Jonkheer Groeninx van Zoelen's diary—Corporal-of-Horse Brown's narrative—Lieutenant Franklin's recollection of the Sourdevalle-Burcy positions—Americans make good progress towards Vire—Enemy lines formed in strength, Vire-Viessoix-Estry—Trooper Niven's battle picture

Although there had been slight withdrawals from the area of Chênedollé, General Roberts, commanding 11th Armoured Division, ordered his two brigade groups to hold on to the Perrier Ridge at all costs. "Had the enemy been able to reoccupy this ridge," wrote the author of 8 Corps History, "then there is little doubt that the whole area back to the River Souleuvre would have been untenable." This is no overstatement.

The morning of the 3rd of August therefore saw the Regiment patrolling southwards from the Burcy—Presles valley; while several Troops had spent the night with the infantry outposts, a fact which from the point of view of obtaining information proved to be a great advantage. As early as five o'clock in the morning one Troop had penetrated across the Vassy road by the railway east of Viessoix. It was noted, however, that the Germans were equally inquisitive and aggressively minded.

The Bocage might be described as a country specially designed for hide-and-seek, and the Germans were quick to seize on the fact that, with our tanks and infantry working in more or less isolated bodies, there was no firm front.

In the meantime, Presles had been counter-attacked and recaptured by a strong enemy force of tanks and infantry, and for the next twenty-four hours several of the Regiment's Troops were to be cut off with the 23rd Hussars and 8th Rifle Brigade.

Emboldened by their success at Presles, the enemy infiltrated groups of approximately two or three tanks and a company of infantry on to the main Caen—Vire road, which created considerable alarm and dislocation of traffic. On one occasion a party of four Tigers and thirty infantry cut the main divisional supply road near La Bistière and nearly intercepted a long column of ammunition trucks, which were only saved at the last moment by having fortuitously taken a wrong turning.

In fact, 9th S.S. Panzer Division's reconnaissance regiment accomplished a fine performance in plotting our positions with great accuracy[1], and it was all the more remarkable that when 10th S.S. Panzer Division eventually attacked the British salient in force on the 6th of August it should have been directed at its apex and by then strongest defended sector.

★ ★ ★

"C" Squadron Headquarters moved off at half past five in the morning, crossed the Vire—Caen road and harboured in a field about two miles to the south of Le Reculey, expecting to advance at a "sedate" pace when their forward Troops had reported the route clear. "Instead of which," wrote Captain Clyde, "just as the usual automatic 'brew-up' was taking place, there was a horrible shout of 'Tigers down the road and coming this way!'" The effect of two or three Tigers on Major Herbert's three-ton lorries was fearful to contemplate and he rather wisely decided to increase the wireless range of his forward troops by retiring northwards at speed to finish his breakfast near the village of Beaulieu.

Meanwhile, as 3 Troop (Lieutenant Halliday) had been held up by mortar fire and accurate shelling on the outskirts of Presles, Corporal-of-Horse Brown's Troop turned off to try a loop to the right and soon reached the village of Burcy. Here they found that 1 Troop (Lieutenant Groeninx van Zoelen), "D" Squadron, which had spent the night in the area, had already tried all routes south to the main Vire —Vassy road, but that these were now blocked by enemy tanks and S.P. guns. The 23rd Hussars (tanks) could advance no farther than the Sourdevalle Ridge and the main enemy armour could be plainly seen forming up on the Vire road beyond. Both Troops remained on the ridge all day and, being cut off by the enemy infiltration to their rear, were compelled to spend the ensuing night with the Monmouths (infantry), who were also isolated. "It was," noted Lieutenant Groeninx van Zoelen, "a lively night, with the enemy infiltrating everywhere." The Monmouths' commanding officer, with a large unexploded shell sticking out of his dug-out roof,

---

1. A captured map showed that the Germans had located all but one R.H.Q. or Battalion H.Q. in 11th Armoured Division and many Squadron and Company H.Qs.

was pleased to welcome the Household Cavalry cars, whose fire-power added to the strength of his already hard-pressed infantry.[2]

Lieutenant Corbett's Troop, advancing on the left to beyond Chênedollé, fared better than Lieutenant Halliday's, but as the cars were approaching the Vire—Vassy road they ran into a S.P. gun which forced them to withdraw slightly. Before doing so, however, they knocked out a laden German staff car, killing the driver with a round of 2-pdr., "all our Besa ammunition having already run out in the course of the morning's fighting."

Participants in that area on the afternoon of the 3rd of August witnessed what was perhaps as confused a day's fighting as was ever to occur in North-West Europe. Every officer at the command end of a wireless set was clamouring for information. The infantry, as usual having to bear the brunt of the fighting, were being heavily shelled and mortared whenever they moved, and knew nothing of what was happening on their flanks. The echelons were equally in the dark and when sent forward to reprovision their forward units were promptly hunted all over the place by Tigers. Regimental Headquarters (it was another day of frightful wireless interference) moved up from Carville to Le Reculey, which had just been vacated by "D" Squadron Headquarters and taken over by 11th Armoured Division. When the Corps Commander came forward to give orders to General Roberts he was promptly and heavily shelled.[3] He personally ordered back Regimental Headquarters. No sooner had the latter got back at their new headquarters than they were subjected to one of those disturbing attacks from American Thunderbolts, fortunately without anyone being hurt.

Major Herbert, at Beaulieu, just across the Vire—Caen road, was still emphatically reporting Tigers and Panthers to his immediate front (east); and Major Ward, moving "D" Squadron Headquarters across the same road but farther south, in order to maintain wireless touch with Lieutenant Buchanan-Jardine[4] and Lieutenant Groeninx van Zoelen's isolated Troop, was immediately bottled up in Le Brien by tanks which had cut the main road near La Bistière.

---

2. Lieutenant Groeninx van Zoelen had only two scout cars with him.

3. "My wireless aerial was blown away. We got the Corps Commander, General O'Connor, into a slit trench—he just will not put on his steel helmet and it's simply maddening, for then neither can we!" (Captain G. D. Cooper, who was escorting him.)

4. Lieutenant Buchanan-Jardine had moved his Troop into an excellent position overlooking the Vire—Vassy road. He was able to report on enemy concentrations of tanks and also, in conjunction with a Gunner F.O.O. at "D" Squadron Headquarters, was by remote wireless fire control wreaking havoc on enemy transport with the 25-pdrs.

From Le Reculey to Chênedollé and from Chênedollé back to La Papillonnière nothing faintly approximating to a line now existed, and to state that the Tiger tank dominated the battlefield during those days is to cast no aspersion on the fighting qualities of the British soldier. But the fact remains that if the warning "Tiger" passed round, all transport, including most of our tanks, halted cautiously until the menace had been located. Tank crews said bitterly, and not without truth, that to have been armed with bazookas might have been preferable in the circumstances. They could then at least have dismounted and stalked the brutes!

One boldly confident Tiger used to emerge from its lair near La Bistière, amble up the road, take pot-shots at three-tonners and then withdraw to its hide-out. It did this all afternoon until, running out of petrol fifty yards from the Le Reculey cross-roads, it was abandoned. Two more Tigers tried the game but were knocked out in successive shots by a Firefly[5] which had hidden up at the side of the road in some flanking trees.

★   ★   ★

Major Ward's task with "D" Squadron was not made easier by having, at the time, only two reconnaissance Troops at his disposal. He had lost, as we have read, Lieutenant Bethell's Troop, and two others were still temporarily cut off beyond the Perrier Ridge. But he dispatched Lieutenants Hanbury and Ainsworth to see whether they could make contact with the forward patrols of "C" Squadron on the left. In addition, he ordered Lieutenant Smallwood to liaise with 159th Brigade Group, whose headquarters were situated near the village of Le Queillet. The latter move was not a success. Brigadier Churcher would neither accept any of the reports passed to him by the Regiment nor admit that the situation was fluid. Some Maquis man had informed him earlier on that Vire was clear, "and he simply would not believe a word to the contrary and so I spent the day with him being given hell for all my 'Sitreps'."[6]

In spite of this, the enemy encountered by "D" Squadron's patrols were very real. No contact could be made with "C" Squadron, and every lane was found to be covered either by an enemy tank or, what was really much more of a problem to deal with, infantry patrols with bazookas, lying up in the hedges and behind the banks. Presles, another village which Brigadier Churcher insisted was in British hands, was confirmed

---

5. Sherman tank armed with 17-pdr. gun.
6. Lieutenant Smallwood, "D" Squadron (Letter). "Sitreps" = Situation reports.

as being now occupied by a force of German tanks and infantry, and both Lieutenants Hanbury's and Ainsworth's Troops were machine-gunned and mortared with accuracy when crossing the Vire—Estry road.

Nevertheless, by half past four in the afternoon, a fairly clear picture had been obtained of a large concentration of enemy tanks and S.P. guns and infantry moving to their positions along the Vire—Vassy road. Twenty-two Tigers and Panthers, one of the largest concentrations we were to see at one time in that country of limited vision, were pinpointed by Lieutenant Buchanan-Jardine's Troop, and he and Lieutenant Groeninx van Zoelen were warned to stand by for an artillery "stonk" from Corps. This would have made a wonderful shoot to observe, for the two Troops could plainly see the German armour in harbour with their crews dismounted. Unfortunately, a heat haze descended over the valley and the shoot was called off.

If doubt still existed that heavy infiltration was taking place, numbers of civilian refugees streaming westwards was clear evidence to the contrary. One group forced its way into "D" Squadron Headquarters at Le Brien, begging for food and water. They implored to be taken to the Allied lines and it was impossible not to sympathize with these poor people in their distress, but at the same time it was realized that it would have been only too easy for the Germans to slip in an agent or two disguised as peasants. They were accordingly bundled off, generously supplied by the men with chocolate and bully beef and told to walk west until they found "les Anglais"; but, added Corporal Jenkins, my operator, who fancied his French, "Méfiez vous des chars Boches." They needed no urging on this score.

The party had no sooner left the orchard harbour than more reports from scout car patrols confirmed that the line of withdrawal to Le Reculey was still cut by tanks. Major Ward thereupon ordered Lieutenant Smallwood, who had now returned from 159th Brigade, to take a scout car and reconnoitre for an alternative route out. He set off with Corporal Noakes at dusk, but after one report was received that he had safely advanced three miles, nothing more was heard. We were not to learn what had happened until after his release from a prisoners-of-war hospital in Paris in September.

Soon after leaving harbour he had made contact with a Troop of Northamptonshire Yeomanry tanks. He told them where he was going and they said that they had some more tanks on the main Vire cross-roads and would warn these by wireless that the scout car was approaching. As it was getting dark, Lieutenant Smallwood pushed on fast.

About half a mile from the cross-roads he came to a few houses which appeared deserted—one was burning quietly. From the map it seemed that there was a fairly sharp corner just before the crossroads. From there the road was dead straight either way.

As Panther tanks were known to be on this road, Smallwood decided that if there was no sign of the Northamptonshire Yeomanry tanks when he rounded the corner he would go over the cross-roads at speed, and then have a good look round.

Noakes drove round the corner slowly—it was a very acute bend and bounded by high banks—and then ran slap into a tank at ten yards range. It took Smallwood a moment to realize that it was not the Cromwell he had been looking for, but a Tiger; then he found himself looking down the barrel of an 88-mm. pointing straight at the car. "It seemed a very long time before Noakes began to reverse!"

There were three Germans on their feet by the Tiger and they seemed as surprised as their foes. Smallwood got off two or three rounds from the Bren, which then jammed. The car, which had gone back fairly fast, unfortunately ran into a ditch at the acute corner, but far enough away to be out of sight of the tank, which was now about twenty yards distant. Smallwood hurled a grenade which failed to explode, and as the car was stuck fast with wheel spin, both he and Noakes jumped out, one going to each side of the lane. Smallwood ran back about a hundred yards and then cut across into a garden, intending to work round to the main road and try to find the British tanks. He was rounding the corner of a house when he received a burst of machine-gun fire in the legs at point-blank range from behind and a couple of Germans pounced on him.

Thinking about it afterwards, the Troop Leader came to the conclusion that most of the houses must have been occupied by the enemy when he had first passed them. The Germans in this locality seemed quite careless of their front, and it later transpired that in the dark the scout car had gone straight through their infantry outposts into some sort of tank leaguer. Noakes had run into this same leaguer and was also taken prisoner.

After the initial shock of the wound, Smallwood was able to hobble with assistance and was taken into a house outside which were three more Tigers, one of them (noted the mechanically minded Smallwood) with a track off, on which the crew were doing maintenance.

The German party was commanded by a Major, who, true to form, "spoke perfect English," and appeared to have worked on the Manchester Cotton Exchange. At this stage Smallwood's narrative becomes "a trifle vague about the sequence of events."

"I was fixed up with some rough crutches and, escorted by an infantryman, went, together with a D.R. from another unit who had been captured, to an aid post. I got a shot of anti-tetanus and a paper bandage on my leg. So far as I remember, the orderly, who spoke some English, left my boot on, as one foot was fairly chewed up at the top and he seemed to think that if he started to try to clean it up, he might not be able to stop the bleeding.

"I then went back to the original house. I think I saw Noakes there, unhurt, and at one stage of the proceedings the German Major asked me to take the wireless set out of the scout car. I was glad of the chance, as I had forgotten to put it off net. I therefore unscrewed the locking nuts[7] completely and put everything right off and then said that I could not get the set out.

"My legs seemed to have calmed down, and as they seemed a pretty casual crowd, I thought I might get away during the night.

"The Major was very chatty—I managed to get a look at all his maps and a fair idea of the set-up. They had recently come from Russia and their morale was very high. I remember being very certain of some identifications—Panzer Lehr Division, I think.

"I must say that I was very well treated by them—after a long harangue about Bolshevism and the true 'Democracy' to be found in the German Army—and he told me that another scout car had been knocked out down the road and the crew killed, and asked me if I'd like to superintend their burial and see if I could make a note of their names for next of kin. I wasn't quite happy about the last bit, but agreed to bury them; however, when I got to my feet again, I had a sharpish twinge, and after a few yards passed clean out."[8]

★   ★   ★

At this stage, the "D" Squadron wireless log makes interesting reading, and the following extracts show that the Regimental command net was certainly fully occupied:

"EVENING. 3 AUGUST

"*Three minutes to eight* (Major Herbert to Captain Collins, Adjutant)
     'My sub unit is being sniped at from church at Presles.'

"*Eight o'clock* (Major Herbert, 'C' Squadron, to Colonel Abel Smith)
     'My sub unit stationed a mile north of Le Reculey has shot up enemy infantry—also two of our tanks (Gds Armd Div) have been knocked out in same area by SP gun.'

---

7. The locking nuts kept the set tuned on to one frequency, which in this case was "D" Squadron Headquarters.
8. The remainder of Lieutenant Smallwood's narrative is included in the appendix dealing with prisoners-of-war experiences.

"*Three minutes past eight* (Lieutenant Orde, 'D' Squadron, to Captain
    Collins)
    'There are three Mark IV tanks at La Barbière, a patrol is shadowing
    them as they move west towards Le Reculey.'
"*Seven minutes past eight* (Major Ward, 'D' Squadron, to Colonel Abel
    Smith)
    'My sub unit at Burcy has patrolled south and reports approx one coy of
    enemy infantry at La Teinturerie—enemy mortar at hill three hundred
    yards west of them, also infantry. Panther tank fired at him from railway
    embankment near Viessoix.'
"*Nine minutes past eight* (Captain Balding with Americans south-east of
    Étouvy, to Captain Collins)
    'Four enemy tanks at La Papillonnière Y roads.'"

And so it went on during the gathering gloom.

At dusk Major Ward decided to vacate his farm orchard headquarters,
which was so enclosed that vehicles could have been easily stalked by
bazooka parties. The new choice of position, which was only a quarter
of a mile away, was in the middle of a cornfield on top of a hill and,
being a certain distance back from the surrounding banks, was out of
bazooka range.

On one side of the field a small track ran down towards Le Queillet,
part of which was held by the Germans—those forming part of the force
which was making such a nuisance of itself to transport on the main road.
Two Cromwell tanks and their crews were halted here "brewing up"
their evening meal. They told us that they felt "rather lonely" and we
offered them the hospitality of our "covered wagon" leaguer, but they
politely declined the invitation, preferring to remain in the lane. We
therefore made our dispositions without them, and as the three-tonner
lorries carrying the petrol, oil and ammunition lurched into the centre
of the cornfield we thought of the harbouring demonstration given by
Captain Julian Ward on that bleak day on the Yorkshire Wolds during
exercise "Eagle".

Dannert wire encircled the perimeter, and the crews of the soft
vehicles dug themselves slit trenches, while in each turret a man kept
watch. Slightly ahead and facing down the slope towards the Vire—
Vassy road, two Troops, those of Lieutenant Ainsworth and Lieutenant
Hanbury, covered the obvious tank approaches.

At half past nine at night the Rear Link officer called up Regimental
Headquarters and said, "My Sunray may be late for tonight's conference—
all roads to you are blocked." And the Colonel answered "I agree and

understand—our other reports also show that the enemy is about you—put out skirting patrols, keep in touch with your patrols to the south by wireless,[9] and we hope to relieve you with 'B' Squadron by first light tomorrow morning". Nothing could be heard but the penetrating crackle of the wireless sets and at intervals the crump of a shell or the distant explosion of a tank "brewing up".

The German bazooka patrols were busy that night. Several tanks were knocked out, and to our immediate south the infantry suffered heavily from mortar fire. Then at about half past two in the morning there were two dull explosions in the adjoining field, followed by more explosions, a vivid sheet of flame, and for the next half hour the crackle of burning ammunition. When the heat had died down and it was possible to approach the scene of the trouble we saw that our friends the Cromwell tanks were no more than glowing hulks of red-hot metal. The crews had disappeared and nothing but a few articles of kit lay strewn about the charred grass. As there were no bodies visible we hoped that they had only been taken prisoner. The German patrol must have infiltrated through with great skill, aided by the dark night, for no one had heard a sound.

★   ★   ★

The situation was still very confused when Captain Waterhouse motored over at eight o'clock next morning to see Brigadier Churcher in the area of La Barbière. He returned spluttering with rage. Apparently Brigade Headquarters were now complaining that our patrols were finding the enemy all right, but when, as the result of these reports, the infantry were sent after them, the Germans were no longer there, having moved off into the next village. This, of course, was exactly what was happening, and we realized it only too well; but until further reinforcements could arrive, the situation was unlikely to improve. Somewhat tartly, it was pointed out that the remedy was for Brigade to allocate infantry to move forward with the armoured cars and see for themselves, instead of expecting the cars to continue their circular tours of the villages. However, this suggestion, made in the heat of the moment, was out of the question, for 159th Brigade was already extended to its limit pending the further advance of Guards Armoured Division on the left. After breakfasts, hard feelings were soon forgotten, and by midday we were again the firmest of friends with 159th Brigade, the Brigadier in person acknowledging in handsome terms the work performed by the armoured cars on his front.

---

9. Lieutenant Buchanan-Jardine's Troop (2 Troop) was able to return to Carville that night at dusk.

By ten o'clock in the morning, the Vire road was cleared to a distance of one mile north and south of Le Reculey. This freed the main divisional centre line and traffic began to flow once more towards the Vire—Vassy road.

The situation on the flanks was also beginning to improve. On the right, the Americans pushed southwards through Étouvy and made for Vire, which was now to become their responsibility. On the left, Major Herbert reported that Guards Armoured Division had made small advances, although the German-held village of Estry was still resisting obstinately. But with several of their units still isolated and the German tactics continuing to be in the form of sharp local counter-attacks delivered by small battle groups consisting of three or four tanks and a company of infantry, the policy of 11th Armoured Division was to sit tight and hunt the infiltrators, until the position could be improved. Within the scope of this plan the Regiment was now called upon to play the part of Phantoms[10]—a role which it was to carry out for the next six days.

With the advance of Guards Armoured Division on the left flank, "C" Squadron patrolling came to an end, and they were withdrawn to harbour in the Carville field near Le Bény Bocage. "B" Squadron duly relieved "D" Squadron, and "A" Squadron under Major Daly moved out during the morning with orders to patrol for 29th Brigade in the Burcy area.

"B" Squadron, from headquarters near La Barbière, immediately pushed forward patrols towards Presles and the Vire—Estry road. They also probed south-east through Montisanger to the Vire—Caen road and made contact with the Americans on the right who were advancing towards Vire.

Severe fighting was taking place along the line from Vire to Estry, and the infantry were incurring heavy casualties from German mortar fire, which fortunately, unless a direct hit, was relatively harmless against the armour plating of our cars. The only casualties sustained during the day in "B" Squadron were Lieutenants the Lord Burghersh and P. A. W. B. Everard, both when dismounted from their cars being wounded by mortar fire, and Trooper Henry, driver of the former's leading scout car, by shell fire.

In the case of Henry, who recalled the incident later, he was wounded when trying with Corporal Loving to remove a string of mines stretched

---

10. A term derived from the original organization known as "Phantoms," which maintained patrols at divisional and higher headquarters. These transmitted direct to Army Headquarters latest reports of the situation in the fighting line, thus by-passing the "usual channels" and saving much time.

across the road. The Germans saw what was happening and ranged their guns on the pair. "There was a blinding flash, a deafening crash, and a cloud of black smoke. I next saw Corporal Loving standing in the car with the branch of a tree wrapped round his neck and swearing like only a trooper can. I could not help laughing. Then I sat down and said, 'I have been hit.' 'Where?' said Corporal Loving, to my mind, anyway, the best scout car commander in action. 'In my arm,' I said. 'Can you drive back?' said he. 'Yes, I think I can,' and using my left arm, which was a fairly easy thing in these cars, I reversed back to a farm, where we dismounted. What an infuriating end to what I had thought might have been an exploit for others to talk about, for Lord Burghersh had decided that we were going to dash at full speed past the enemy outposts and then hide up to see what we could spot. I felt very sad and lonely when I left his Troop to go back to the dressing station."

★   ★   ★

Several "A" Squadron Troops were able to reach the Burcy salient by independent routes, but whenever they tried to move forward to the railway line near Viessoix they were violently mortared; Lieutenant Hoare and Troopers Holder and Flood, all of 5 Troop, were thus wounded while with the 23rd Hussars at Sourdevalle.

In "C" Squadron, Corporal-of-Horse Brown was to remain in the area until the 5th of August, as was Lieutenant Jonkheer Groeninx van Zoelen's Troop in "D" Squadron. The latter had gone forward at first light to observe for the artillery and was then cut off again.

Later on, Lieutenant Clarke's Troop in "A" Squadron was able to attain the high ground at La Botrie south-west of Sourdevalle with two scout cars, when it encountered a Panther tank at eight yards range, and it was here that Corporal Boon was to save his officer's life in circumstances of extreme gallantry. The tank fired at point-blank range and the armour-piercing shot tore away the complete side of the scout car. The combined effect of the concussion and blast from the barrel of the 88-mm. gun knocked out Lieutenant Clarke, leaving him otherwise uninjured but quite helpless. Then the German tank, which had moved closer, hoping to crush the vehicle beneath its tracks, started to fire its machine gun. The driver of the scout car had nothing but his pistol, because the Bren gun had been carried away with the side of the car at the first shot. Nor could the scout car be reversed, for the steering had been damaged. Fortunately, the very closeness of the German tank prevented its guns from firing effectively, for these could not be depressed sufficiently.

Seeing the predicament of Lieutenant Clarke and driver in the first car, Boon ordered his own driver to advance at full speed while firing his Bren gun at the tank cupola to keep at least the enemy commander's head down. Boon was then able to crawl up to the crippled vehicle and under continuous machine-gun fire eventually extricate both driver and Troop Leader to a place of safety.

Several Household Cavalrymen recorded their impressions of this ill-omened area where so many of the Monmouths and later men of Guards Armoured Division were to die.

Lieutenant Jonkheer Groeninx van Zoelen's diary:

> "*4th August, Friday.*—Started out again at dawn to observe for 29 Brigade. Heavily shelled and mortared from direction of Chênedollé. Tried forward in another direction and contacted a gang of Frenchmen. Found Viessoix to be an anti-tank stronghold and Chênedollé village to be strongly held. Went back to Brigade H.Q. later to obtain fresh orders and on a hairpin bend on the road down to Burcy came under very accurate mortar fire. The enemy was infiltrating everywhere. 'A' Squadron had come up and so I was ordered to return to Regiment in the afternoon, but could not get back, and in trying nearly got the cars bogged in a shallow stream. Two other Troops joined me. Everybody manning their Bren guns at night. Very heavy shelling and mortaring on the poor Monmouths, who are suffering a number of casualties. I heard that the rest of 'D' Squadron had had a sticky night at Le Brien area. We managed to make a dash for it the next morning (the 5th August) and got back to Le Bény Bocage area, where I found heaps of letters and parcels awaiting me. Coming back I had to drive one of the cars myself. The enemy fire came pretty close but I came much closer to overturning the car!"

Corporal-of-Horse Brown's narrative:

> "First thing at morning I was informed that Lieutenant Franklin would be relieving me at nine o'clock. Unfortunately, we did not get relieved till sometime later. Meanwhile things were happening in our rear. Corporal-of-Horse Sallis ('C' Squadron) of our 3rd Troop reported that three Tigers were to be seen retreating from the direction of Vire and making for Burcy. Then another message informed us that Presles had been occupied by a couple of Panthers and some infantry and that about a company of Panzer Grenadiers had moved into a village between these two places. Therefore we and the infantry were cut off again. We moved into an orchard with Battalion Headquarters of the sadly depleted Monmouths.

"We began to think that some of the enemy who were infiltrating through us had been driven southwards by the Guards Armoured Division to the north, but at least they were making things warm for us and it was not safe to keep one's head up above ground level for very long. We were being continually shelled from the south as well—the 'Moaning Minnies' were bad and there were many more casualties among the Monmouths. I put our chaps with their Brens to help the infantry with their guards and many shells were falling close to our right.

"On the following morning [Saturday 5th August] we were again shelled badly and things began to look serious, for the numbers of wounded were increasing and of course no ambulances could get through. The Monmouths, whose Echelon should have arrived on Thursday, were almost out of food and water and ammunition, but at last, at about two o'clock in the afternoon, I heard a Troop of 'B' Squadron, whose frequency I was locked up on, report Burcy clear of enemy. I shall always remember that the code word for Burcy was 'Retriever.' A couple of Bren carriers went out to confirm this and came back to say that this was so. We then started for home because Mr. Franklin's Troop had by then joined us."

Lieutenant Franklin's record was written sometime later. He was to remain out for two days, returning to his Squadron on the 6th of August. The narrative therefore outstrips the main thread of the history, which is still at the 4th of August, but it is best included at this stage.

"I was cut off with the Monmouths on my way back to the Squadron. It was on a small hill called Sourdevalle and we got mortared by those infamous 'Moaning Minnies' until everyone was 'writing home to Momma,' as the Americans say. I was foolishly on a forward slope observing the enemy when the balloon went up and we came away so fast that one of the cars got ditched. We had to leave it and take cover. Our tanks were brewing up under our noses and I sat in our car and listened and put my microphone over the side so that those at Squadron Headquarters would be able to hear the shindy! The noise 'eugh, eugh, eugh' as the things go up, while the smoke trails far away show you that you are the target; then a pause of silence; then, 'roum, roum, roum' all around and you look up and see a pall of brown dust drifting through the farm buildings close to where you are. At lunch and tea the Jerries gave you a half-hour's rest. The commanding officer of the Monmouths, with whom we found ourselves, had a shell sticking in the roof of his dug-out-unexploded. Others less lucky in their slit trenches had severe casualties. I continually tried to find out on the air what was happening to the village that the Jerries had retaken behind us, but it appeared from one of our other Troops in that area that some S.S. formation had now occupied it. We were longing to hit back with the 3-inch mortars, but there were no targets to engage. We felt rather like a golf green on to which everyone was playing their approach shot.[11]

"We had run out of water and I remember having a conference as to whether the water in an old well was fit to drink. The infantry Captain seemed to think that it did not matter terribly whether it was or not. Other things seemed more dangerous! We had a long talk with the infantry, who rather surprisingly preferred their way of fighting to ours—sitting in a tin box, as they put it. The Bren guns kept firing through the night and German attacks came to within fifty yards, then were driven back. I slept part of the time in straw in an old barn after having placed the cars in fire positions. The infantry naturally preferred to do things their own way. At dawn, and it was cold and grey, the Jerries started their first big attack. We drove one car into a field and started firing at nothing much in particular. Mortaring started after breakfast and the infantry dug deeper. It was very hot during the day and we drank the brackish warm water and ate dry biscuits. No one really knew what was happening behind us. Actually the enemy were now beginning to retreat through the little village of Burcy, and one could see the church burning and the smoke coming from the houses there. I had a talk with the Colonel of the Battle Group here and he asked me to help him. If I got back in reasonable comfort when things cleared up a bit, would I send up the ambulances. They had run out of morphia and the doctor was almost out on his feet. I knew what all that meant—that the casualties I had watched yesterday streaming in might not last another day of this. There were two bays in the improvised dressing station, in a barn, one for those who were hit, and another for those who were 'bomb happy.' Men were rolling in like drunkards without a scratch on them—just from the concussion of shells. Others were not so pretty. We could do no patrolling here and now was a chance to do something useful instead of sitting around in our cars. I agreed to his plan, which was to send a dismounted patrol down the lane on foot. If clear we would make a dash through the village and get clear. I collected my chaps together —I found them in a barn with a very green German prisoner who hated his own side's shelling more than did ourselves. A sound hit on the head had quietened him. We started down the hill after waiting some time for the report of the infantry patrol. They appeared to have got lost. As the dust rose from our movement (we were going down the hill at maximum speed) I looked

---

11. The weakness of the Sourdevalle—Burcy position was that most of the British were on a reverse slope with poor observation. If they moved forward the Germans on the superior heights of Viessoix still dominated them. *Author*

round and saw the mortar bombs landing where we had just left. We went through the village like smoke, and then round the corner and up the road were coming our friends—the Warwicks and with them a car of [David Tabor's] with him on the turret, tin hat on the back of his head. I felt a complete ass at going so fast. I halted and he said how interesting it had been watching me come down the hill followed by the shells! We then found Headquarters and called for ambulances on the air. The last I saw of the scene was the armoured ambulances going forward, and on their way picking up some civilians who had been hit and were lying on their beds beside the road."

★   ★   ★

By the evening of the 4th of August the over-all situation had improved. Although there were still many enemy groups in the reoccupied villages of the Vire—Vassy road, and "B" Squadron could report by nightfall that three Panthers were again patrolling the route along which "D" Squadron had moved back to harbour during the afternoon, the wholesale infiltration had ceased.

On the right, the Americans were making good progress towards Vire and relieving 11th Armoured Division of anxiety on that flank. To the south-east the Warwicks were preparing to retake Presles, thus greatly easing the strain on the 23rd Hussars and 8th Rifle Brigade, and the cry for more infantry had been answered by the arrival of 185th Brigade of 3rd (Br.) Division.

The situation remained much the same on the following day, the 5th of August. There were still no indications of large-scale enemy withdrawals. "A" Squadron (less Lieutenant Franklin's Troop) were withdrawn to rest, while "B" Squadron continued to patrol to the right, now making contact with the Americans.

At midday, on an appreciation of the Commander, 29th Brigade (Brigadier Roscoe Harvey), that the enemy might be pulling out, Major Herbert was ordered to patrol south-east towards Vassy. "C" Squadron soon encountered opposition, however, and there appeared little evidence that the Commander's appreciation was correct.

Lieutenant Hopkinson's Support Troop had an eventful day removing many mines and road-blocks for the armoured cars and then meeting three Panther tanks. His Troop scout car was closely missed three times running, and the armoured car on which he was himself riding, four times—three accompanying Cromwell tanks were then hit in rapid succession. To finish off, Thunderbolts started dive-bombing the survivors, but after the Troop had let off yellow recognition smoke, the planes turned for home.

* * *

"B" Squadron, with 159th Brigade, noticed during the afternoon that there were signs of the enemy pulling back to the south of the stream running past Burcy westward into the River Vire. The bridge at Vaudry which carried the Estry road into Vire had been blown and in addition refugees had been returning to Montisanger and many of the adjoining villages. One Frenchman told of thirty German soldiers, a motley collection from many disintegrated units, wandering through his village commandeering all available male clothing. Perhaps it was these reports which helped to strengthen the official view that at last the enemy were pulling out. They were, on the contrary, forming a strong line running from north-east of Vire, through Viessoix, past Chênedollé and on to Estry, and repeated attacks were to be made before they finally withdrew.

* * *

On the 6th of August, while "C" Squadron continued with their phantom work on the left flank towards Estry, "B" Squadron were withdrawn to rest. 3rd (Br.) Division, which had arrived during the evening to take over part of the line and at the same time put in an attack south-east beyond the Perrier Ridge, was to be screened by "A" Squadron. However, the attack never got going, for the enemy chose to launch one of their own at the same time, thus denying to 3rd (Br.) Division even their start line. As it transpired, the clashing of attacks was fortunate, because the enemy, 10th S.S. Panzer Division, who might otherwise have succeeded in breaking through a weakened 11th Armoured Division, was faced by an extra Infantry Brigade (185th Brigade) on an otherwise thin sector of the front.

With 3rd (Br.) Division's attack indefinitely postponed, "A" Squadron, who would normally have been in the van of the advance as a screen, were withdrawn. Instead, they were ordered to carry out liaison patrols with the Americans driving towards Vire.

It was while on one of these patrols down the long straight Vire road that Lieutenant P. L. Peake's Troop of two scout cars ran into an enemy ambush, an event epitomized in newspaper reporter's best staccato style by Trooper Niven, driver of the leading scout car.

"France—Recceing down long wide road—Stop—Having a look—Jerry infantry pop up either side—throw grenades and open up with L.M.Gs.—then anti-tank guns open up, but misses. Reverse back, but still not sure of anti-tank exact position. Brave Commander says, 'Let's go back and see.' O.K. round the corner again—Bang! Rotten shots these Jerries, but we had this position taped and a big chalk from the General."[12]

★ ★ ★

For the next few days, the situation at Sourdevalle and Chênedollé was to remain extremely precarious. In the latter place the balance of the hard-pressed Warwicks cannot have been improved by yet another Thunderbolt sortie in which their Battalion Headquarters was bombed. Deepest German infiltration took place in the region of Bas Perrier, where, assaulting time and again, the Panzer Grenadier Regiments were to attain the crest of the ridge and begin, aided by the thickly wooded approaches via Chênedollé, to pick off the 23rd Hussars' tanks one by one with bazookas. By forming a tight leaguer, however, the defending force managed to hold its own in the darkness. Gradually the German losses mounted, the fury of the attack died down and the British infantry regained their old positions.

On the 7th of August "D" Squadron relieved "C" Squadron on the left in the area of Beaulieu. They then came under the direct command of 11th Armoured Division and carried out patrols to the east and southeast. The Regiment (less "D" Squadron) reverted to 8 Corps command and moved to an area two miles west of Le Bény Bocage.

---

12. The commander of that scout car was Lance-Corporal-of-Horse B. E. Pulford. Niven and Pulford went right through the North-West European campaign as crew of the leading scout car to Lieutenant Peake's Troop. They saw much fighting together.

Chapter VII

Further Close Patrolling

The Mortain counter-offensive and its implications on the regimental front—2nd Household Cavalry Regiment under several divisions—The Monmouths' heavy casualties at Burcy—Corporal-of-Horse Thompson's narrative—Lieutenant Tabor's successful shoot—Operation "Grouse"—R.H.Q. moves to Montisanger

The attack carried out by 10th S.S. Panzer Division was really the implementation of a very much larger scheme. This limited counterattack, we now know, had as its object the safeguarding of the northern flank of a powerful Panzer drive aimed at Avranches, past which town the lengthy but vulnerable lines of communication of General Patton's Third U.S. Army were now streaming. If successful, the German counter-offensive would cut off the American spearheads directed at the ports of Brittany from their supplies.

To understand the implications of this move, it is necessary to turn back to the 31st of July, when, wheeling westwards from out of the Cherbourg peninsula, Patton's soldiers, with no effective barrier between them and the sea, apart from the port garrisons, drove at speed towards the Atlantic seaboard. "The Airborne operation which we had prepared to assist in turning the corner into Brittany," wrote General Eisenhower, "was rendered unnecessary by the unimpeded rapidity of the ground force advance." Rennes fell on the 4th of August; from there, while the British were struggling in the closeness of the Bocage, one long straggling column of armour raced for Nantes and the River Loire while another American division hammered at the gates of Brest. Two days later the Brittany peninsula had been sealed off.

To achieve this truly amazing feat of mobility, Patton had had to force his columns through the narrow corridor of land to our west barely twenty miles wide. Only two roads were available for his supplies until the fall of Vire could relieve the bottle-neck, and it was on to these vital highways that German strategy was now directed.

A formidable array of armour hitherto kept to the east of the Orne had been collected in the area of Mortain and was unleashed on the Third U.S. Army's left flank on the 7th of August. The German High Command knew that the critical moment in the battle of Normandy had arrived. Even the German long-range bombers were diverted from their nightly tasks of laying mines off the invasion beach-heads in support of this desperate thrust. General Hausser, Commander of the German Seventh Army, in an order to his troops implied that the Fuehrer himself considered the fate of the Battle of the West to depend on the successful outcome of this operation. The German field commanders were under no illusion about the terrifying risks involved. It is now known that Sepp Dietrich, who personally took charge of the 5th Panzer Army for the effort, protested vehemently to his superior, von Kluge. There was not enough petrol, and there was no air cover. To concentrate five Panzer divisions in these circumstances courted disaster. But the answer was always the same, "It is a Fuehrer-befehl (Hitler's order)."

The brunt of the German attack was borne by one U.S. Infantry Division, which held up the onslaught long enough to allow two other divisions, passing south, to be switched over to help stem the tide.

By great good fortune, the weather was fine and the Allied Tactical Air Forces were able to play a decisive part. The packed German columns were mercilessly strafed. Bombers held their loads waiting for the cross-roads to jam up with soft transport while the rocket and cannon-firing planes dealt with the hard core of the Panzers. By these and other means, what had been a dangerous threat to the entire Allied forces in Normandy was turned into a resounding American victory; and although the fighting amidst the picturesque hills between Vire and Mortain was to continue, heavy and confused, for several more days, the issue had really been settled on the first day. It may well have been here that the German soldier, fighting as ever with undeniable courage, first saw the writing on the wall. As he gazed from the Normandy hills towards Avranches and the sea which he was destined never to attain, he must have become aware that this was failure on a gigantic scale. Worse was yet to come.

★   ★   ★

On the Eastern sector of the front the Canadians and the Poles, fighting every inch of the way, were driving from Caen to Falaise. 30 Corps had recently captured the dominating heights of Mont Pincon (south of Aunay-sur-Odon), while close at hand, to our immediate left, Guards Armoured Division had improved their position slightly in the region of Estry. With the Americans already pressing up towards Argentan from the south, the outlines of the Falaise Pocket were clearly beginning to show.

★   ★   ★

The regimental lull under 8 Corps did not last long. 15th (S.) Division were mounting an attack on Estry. This began on the 8th of August and, though unsuccessful in capturing the village, the infantry gained enough ground to enable Guards Armoured Division to sidestep southwards into part of the line which had previously been 11th Armoured Division's responsibility. And so "D" Squadron, continuing to operate from Beaulieu, now found themselves operating under Guards Armoured Division.

On the right flank, 3rd (Br.) Division had taken over the sector of the line between the Americans in the Vire area and the right flank of 11th Armoured Division.

The intention was to withdraw the last named for rest and refitment and to prepare for a new phase in the campaign, while at the same time 3rd (Br.) Division were to put in an assault on the Vire—Vassy road and southwards towards Tinchebray. Guards Armoured Division were to take part in this attack on the left.

This entailed an exchange of positions between Guards Armoured Division and 11th Armoured Division, but as the Germans were now mainly concentrating on defence, for which their positions on the heights to the south were well suited, the operation was carried out without incident and was completed by the morning of the 10th of August.

Meanwhile the Regiment (less "D" Squadron still with Guards Armoured Division) had come back under command of 3rd (Br.) Division for their forthcoming attack. R.H.Q. moved west of the River Vire to Ste Marie Laumont on the 8th of August, and at the same time "B" Squadron was ordered to move forward to the area of Le Pont de Vaudry and to patrol once more up to the now heartily detested Vire—Vassy road.

Major Wignall's Troops were no strangers to the district lying between the Burcy stream (which had now been spanned by a Bailey bridge at Vaudry) and Viessoix. Over and above the normal day patrolling, the Squadron had been given the task of manning a line of night outposts between 3rd (Br.) Division and Guards Armoured Division while the change-over of fronts was taking place; for this task the Squadron was reinforced by two Support Troops, those of Lieutenants Wordsworth and Hopkinson ("A" and "C" Squadrons), and the "C" Squadron Heavy Troop commanded by Lieutenant van Cutsem.

Enemy reaction to probing patrols on both divisional fronts was immediate, particularly on the front of Guards Armoured Division, where Lieutenants Hanbury's and Buchanan-Jardine's Troops were heavily mortared all day (9th August). "The winding road out of Burcy was the biggest strain of all," wrote Lieutenant Jonkheer Groeninx van Zoelen, "and the sight on reaching the Monmouths' positions was appalling. A hurricane seemed to have hit the place.[1] All their transport was gone, the farm burnt, and dead lying in rows awaiting burial. I tried to get on to the ridge, but immediately got shelled, and so it went on all day."

Corporal-of-Horse Thompson, of 3 Troop, "D" Squadron, wrote of this day:

"Our Troop had a rather hot time near Burcy. We had been given our orders and had to reconnoitre the Vire road. To do this we had to shoot our way over a bridge and push on to another road. The few French peasants were very quiet, which made us a bit wary. About a hundred yards from the road, Lieutenant Hanbury decided to pull off the lane and camouflage the cars. Patrols were then sent out on foot while those left behind got some food cooked. The patrols returned with good information and we soon saw Germans moving about the houses on the main road. Shortly afterwards a French peasant came along, shouting at the very top of his voice, 'Vive la France!' This was all very well, but it made our position rather obvious, so we soon got rid of him and moved off as quickly as possible to another position. As the leading car got on to the main road once more, about thirty Germans were seen coming towards it on foot; they were about a hundred yards away. Lance-Corporal-of-Horse Hyde immediately opened fire with his Bren and scattered them. Several Germans came running forward, intending to give themselves up; others kept on firing at the Troop. One of the supposed prisoners had a badly shattered leg and I got out of my car to give him a shot of morphia, only to be greeted by a burst of fire from a machine-gun. This taught me a lesson, and, covered by Lance-Corporals-of-Horse Hyde and Brook, I made a quick getaway and got back into the turret. On arrival at the bridge we found that it was held by the Germans, but as they only appeared to be infantry, with the two scout cars between the two armoured cars, we dashed over. On reaching the other side my engine cut out, but luckily the ground sloped away from the bridge and my driver, Trooper Cudmore, had the presence of mind to put his foot on the selector pedal and so put the car into neutral, which allowed the car to go on running downhill to safety."[2]

---

1. This was the result of the German counter-attack by the 10th S.S. Panzer Division of the 6th of August.
2. The Daimler armoured car engines, like their civilian counterparts, were fitted with pre-selector gear mechanism and fluid fly-wheels.

Further Close Patrolling   161

This Troop under the command of Lieutenant Hanbury was to remain behind the enemy lines for the rest of the day. It finally returned at dusk with a large haul of prisoners, the broken-down Daimler having been towed back three miles through the enemy lines by the Troop Leader's car, driven by Trooper Parris. 3 Troop was already well known for its unorthodox tactics and formations, but the "Hanbury sandwich formation" was a new one for the book of armoured car practice. Nevertheless, it worked well that day!

Before the big attack across the Vassy road was due to take place on the 10th of August, our artillery undertook a heavy strafing programme, both with the idea of harassing the German troop concentrations along the Vire—Vassy road and of knocking out the numerous "Moaning Minnies" whose favourite emplacements lay along the railway embankment where the permanent way crossed the Vassy road. Lieutenant Tabor was to carry out a particularly successful shoot in this area. He wrote:

"During the period 9th/10th August, 'B' Squadron were under command of 3rd Division Recce Regiment and were working on the 9th Infantry Brigade front. The Ulster Rifles had reached the main road Vire—Vassy at one place and were holding the village of Vaudry. 'B' Squadron and some elements of 3rd Recce Regiment were then holding a line of O.Ps. facing east.

"My troop (3 Troop) was ordered on the morning of the 10th of August to take over an O.P. about 500 yards east of Vaudry from No. 1 Troop. At this time we had been allotted a Gunner O.P. from one of the Field Regiments of 3rd Division. He was travelling with Squadron Headquarters and answering our forward Troops' requests for fire support. Troop Leaders passed back targets and corrections to Squadron Headquarters, where they were passed to the Gunner O.P., who in turn transmitted them to the gun positions. This was found to be a very rapid and effective way of obtaining fire support.

"On arrival at No. 1 Troop (Lieutenant Cody) position I found that they were having a sticky time and had just had casualties from mortar fire.[3] Julian Ward came up shortly afterwards with the ambulance and removed the casualties. Thereupon 1 Troop was withdrawn. For about two hours we suffered from spasmodic but rather accurate mortar fire. Luckily, we escaped without further casualties. About eleven o'clock in the morning all fell quiet, and as our existing O.P. had practically no field of fire due to the high hedges, I began to search the map for an alternative. The obvious one which stood out a mile was Point 237, about a mile to

---

3. Trooper Robert Gamble was mortally wounded and Corporal-of-Horse L. J. Munn and Trooper C. H. Foster slightly wounded.

the east along the Vire—Vassy road (a mile and a half west of Viessoix). I drove up to it in a scout car and discovered that it had a wonderful field of view over Viessoix and about two miles up the Vire—Vassy road. There was considerable enemy activity on the main road and near the railway crossing at Viessoix. For the next two hours I amused myself calling down fire on the numerous targets which presented themselves. These varied from half-tracks on the main road to parties of infantry laying mines. Eventually all movement ceased with the exception of two or three mortars firing from behind the railway embankment at Viessoix. About two o'clock in the afternoon a Gunner O.P. from 4th Armoured Brigade in a Sherman tank joined me at Point 237. We spent two more hours bringing the combined fire of two Field Regiments on any reasonable targets. This obviously made things uncomfortable for the Germans and they went to ground again. We had, however, still failed to silence the mortars behind the railway embankment because it was impossible to observe them accurately. In view of this, I decided to go forward to see if I could pin-point them more accurately. My driver[4] and I set off along the hedge. When we were a short distance along the embankment there was a terrific explosion from the direction of our O.P., followed by a column of black smoke. Fearing the worst, we hurried back towards the O.P. A short distance from it we found one of the crew of the Sherman lying in the hedge, badly shocked and quite incoherent. We found that the Sherman had been stalked by German infantry and bazooka-ed and that only two of the crew had survived. By luck, the Germans had not bothered about the scout car. This I ordered the driver to move to a position of safety under cover of smoke, whilst I assisted the wounded. On the strength of my report I was ordered to withdraw to my original O.P.

"The next night was spent in the original O.P. in a very exposed and uncomfortable position. Foot patrols to our left flank revealed no signs of friendly troops.

"Next morning as we were having breakfast a terrific artillery concentration from our guns began, with many of the shells dropping very close. This concentration was closely followed by infantry from 3 (Br.) Division with fixed bayonets, supported by tanks from the Greys. From these troops we gathered that an attack was in progress and that our O.P. was some 200 yards in front of the start line!

"The attack met little opposition and we later reoccupied the O.P. on Point 237 in time to witness the tank attack on 3rd Parachute Division troops in Viessoix by the Grenadier Group."

★   ★   ★

---

4. Trooper C. J. A. Jones.

The joint Anglo-American attack on the western perimeter of what was generally becoming known as the Falaise Pocket was called operation "Grouse." It started on the 11th of August. A variety of complicated reasons were given as to why it had to take place, but to us it seemed that this was simply another general heave forward on a sector of the front which had so far proved to be extremely costly and stubbornly defended by the enemy.

The plan was that U.S. V Corps should advance on the right, clearing Vire. Conforming on the left would be 8 Corps with 3rd (Br.) Division on the right and Guards Armoured Division on the left. 3rd (Br.) Division were to advance along the road to Tinchebray and Guards Armoured Division to the Vire—Vassy road and thence towards the ultimate objective, the Mont de Cerisi, an imposing feature a few miles north-west of the town of Flers. The Regiment (less "D" Squadron, still with Guards Armoured Division) was to move through 3rd (Br.) Division, fanning out in a reconnaissance role on a centre line Vire—Tinchebray—Flers. With this in view, "A" and "C" Squadron, which had been resting in the Carville fields, joined up with Regimental Rear Headquarters and concentrated in some orchards near a collection of farm buildings called Montisanger.

From the beginning the attack went badly, and although they could be ill afforded, the enemy kept pouring yet more troops into the western side of the pocket. The hinge of the position, as expected, proved to be Viessoix and Chênedollé, and Guards Armoured Division suffered many casualties, particularly the Grenadiers and the Irish Guards, who became engaged in ferocious hand-to-hand fighting with elements of 5th Parachute Division and 9th S.S. Panzer Division on the Sourdevalle ridge. Many of the wounded Irish Guardsmen lay in the middle of a burning cornfield set alight by tracer bullets and perished in the flames before they could be rescued.

On the right, 3rd (Br.) Division fared better and made slow but steady progress along the Tinchebray road, greatly hindered by mines and booby traps. But as the attack never really got going there was no question of the Regiment being able to pass through to exploit. "D" Squadron, which had moved from Beaulieu to near Presles, carried out flanking patrols to the east for Guards Armoured Division, but here the enemy were generally quiet behind their minefields. One scout car was lost while clearing a road-block made up of trees and a dead and booby-trapped cow tied to a string of mines. Corporal F. F. Conway was wounded and his driver, Trooper Albert Jones, mortally wounded.

ENEMY ROAD-BLOCK AHEAD

Despatch rider bringing news of an obstruction on main centre line.

Throughout a hot and sultry day, commanders at varying levels kept imagining that the enemy was about to pull out, but nothing of the sort happened. The Estry—Chênedollé line gave slightly, and the Grenadiers entered the outskirts of Viessoix. Then, after incurring further heavy casualties, the attack creaked to a standstill for good. The assault was not renewed next morning and consolidation was the order of the day. Regimental Tactical Headquarters came down to join "A" and "C" Squadrons at Montisanger on the 12th of August. Then, and it came as a complete surprise, word went round that the Regiment was to take over a sector of the line as infantry.

Chapter VIII

The Regiment as Infantry

The Regiment to become infantry as temporary measure—The Falaise Pocket and even wider American encircling movements—8 Corps pinched out in the general advance—The desolation at Sourdevalle—Lieutenant I. M. Clark's narrative—Lieutenant Peake talks to General Montgomery—The Regiment (less "B" and "D" Squadrons) returns to refit near "Cavalry Bridge"

There were gloomy faces in all Squadrons when the first news reached Montisanger orchards that they were to abandon their armoured cars and become infantry. Our armoured cars had become very much part of our way of life in war. The two-man bivouacs, the car cooking, the bulky bed-rolls (so disliked for reasons of austerity by Major Sir Peter Grant Lawson), the bottle of whisky, and the extra water-cans that one could carry for washing or filled with cider, all made a great difference to comfort at the front. However, most of the forebodings proved to be groundless, and although somewhat more than half the Regiment were to forsake their armoured cars for the role of infantrymen in trenches, the change was only to be a temporary one, and of short duration. The reason for the change-over was not far to seek.

Although the shrinking of the Falaise Pocket had yet to make itself felt on our sector of the front, farther afield events were unfolding themselves with rapidity. Perhaps we were in danger of overlooking them.

Even as the Americans were dealing with the death struggles of the Mortain thrust, a wider enveloping sweep of our Allies had already moved through Mayenne and Laval as early as the 6th of August. Continuing east towards the Orleans Gap and Paris, the U.S. Third Army had swung round a Corps at Le Mans to run a north-bound spearhead towards Argentan. This was to reach the outskirts of the town on the 9th of August. The thrust achieved a two-fold purpose. Firstly, it formed the southern shoulder of the Falaise Pocket; and secondly, it finally sealed the fate of the German Panzers struggling to disengage at Mortain.

Meanwhile, 30 Corps had continued to make good progress south of Aunay-sur-Odon and Mont Pincon. 11th Armoured Division, as we have seen, had been withdrawn from most of its commitments to rest and refit, but had left 159th Brigade as left-flank guard to shield the advance of Guards Armoured Division on the 11th of August. This brigade was about to be withdrawn to return to its parent formation, which was due to come under command of 30 Corps.

The convergence of 30 Corps on the left and the Americans on our right meant that our own 8 Corps was being pinched out. However, the immediate result of the withdrawal of 159th Brigade was that Guards Armoured Division were compelled to feel out to the left to take over the village of Le Busq, and they were short of infantry. We were to make good that deficiency and take over a sector of the line vacated by the Irish Guards near Sourdevalle.

On the 13th of August, "D" Squadron, still under command Guards Armoured Division, continued their armoured car patrols along the Vire—Vassy road, but their Headquarters moved from Presles to Montisanger to be with the other two Squadrons, to act if required as infantry later on. "B" Squadron made no advance but encountered yet more mines. The remainder of the Regiment, with the Heavy and Support Troops of all four Squadrons, took over the Sourdevalle sector on their feet.

In passing it is interesting to note that in spite of the British tendency to write up the battle of the Falaise Pocket as the logical outcome of planning which at times, to the ordinary onlooker at least, appears to have bordered on the prophetically miraculous, this was not the case. The Falaise encirclement had not been foreseen at any level and the Supreme Commander, General Eisenhower, leaves us in no doubt that it was mainly the fanatical tenacity of the Nazi leaders themselves, and the ingrained toughness of the men they led, which doomed so many of Germany's soldiers to die where they stood when all military wisdom dictated an earlier retreat to beyond the line of the Seine. And it should be remembered that not until the 10th of August, as a result of "a conference at General Bradley's Headquarters, was it decided to seize the opportunity for encirclement offered by the enemy tactics."[1]

★   ★   ★

The desolation at Sourdevalle was appalling. As far as Guards Armoured Division were concerned, this was to prove to have been the scene of some of the severest fighting in North-West Europe. The Monmouths and Norfolks four days before had also suffered terribly in the very same place. Our patrolling casualties in this area had, however, been negligible.

---

1. Report by the Supreme Commander to the Combined Chiefs of Staff on the Operations in Europe of the Allied Expeditionary Force (p. 54). (H.M. Stationery Office)

Colonel Abel Smith had his Headquarters in the same dug-out as the Monmouths' commanding officer. Numbers of burnt-out Shermans belonging to the 23rd Hussars and the Irish Guards littered the forward slopes and orchards. Many had not yet been cleaned out, and there were still some corpses in them. We counted over fifty knocked-out transport, mostly belonging to the Monmouths and Norfolks. There were a few German tanks, but theirs were mostly farther south. German dead were piled in groups and lay all over the forward slopes, black and swollen and covered with flies. Cattle and sheep and human remains and filthy bandages littered the hillside. The barns were blackened and roofless. The apples, shaken by shell blast from the trees, lay in their hundreds among the scorched grass together with half-empty bottles of calvados and pieces of blood-soaked blankets. Lieutenant Franklin walked over to a cross at one corner of a field and recognized the name of the young Captain who had made the remark about the brackish water. An insupportable smell of decay and death clung in heavy vapour over the valley; it permeated clothing and hair, and even the strongest were overcome with nausea.

The Welsh Guards were on the left and a unit of 3rd (Br.) Division was on the right. The line was now quiet, with little shelling and some desultory patrolling on foot. By far the worst job was that of Padre Moore and Lieutenant the Hon. M. F. Eden; the latter had just re-joined the Regiment from sick leave in England. These two had to organize the burial parties and try to decipher the identification discs buried deep in the swollen flesh of the corpses.

A sanitary unit arrived and started chemically disposing of many rotting cattle carcasses, which improved matters. In other cases the men used petrol and set fire to them.

As the line was thinly held, Colonel Abel Smith was allotted considerable weight of supporting arms, which made up for the loss of the fire power of the armoured cars. These were one squadron 2nd (Armoured) Irish Guards (Sherman tanks), one troop of 17-pdr. anti-tank guns, one platoon of Vickers machine guns, with, in support, a squadron of 3rd Scots Guards (Churchill tanks).

In consequence of the strength of this battle group, Captain Collins, the Adjutant, to the great delight of Sir Peter Grant Lawson, issued for the first and last time, until the Regiment next had an infantry role in Holland, a written operational order.

Lieutenant I. M. Clark, who was in command of the "D" Squadron Heavy Troop, gives an account of his first experience as an infantryman, with his two Matadors still close at hand to give fire support if needed.

"My job was to hold a most unattractive village called Burcy, which lay in the valley behind Chênedollé. It was quite a small place with a little church which harboured hundreds of jackdaws. The jackdaws had a habit of suddenly flying out of the tower with a great commotion for no obvious reason; this always made us imagine that a patrol was creeping up and was generally disturbing. After I took up my position I found it necessary to tow several bloated carcasses out of the immediate vicinity. The next job was to destroy a goose with one leg blown off and a most pathetic calf with a terrible wound in its hindquarters. This gave me a most distressing minute or two as it would not die when I shot it in the head with my revolver. Luckily, I had a rifle handy, which dispatched it first shot.

"We had to man several small machine-gun posts which I had placed round the village. The nights were not long as it was about midsummer, but as there was very little relief for the men, the strain was rather heavy.

"The first night in Burcy we were shelled for about half an hour. I was doing a tour of the various posts when it started and, like a fool, I refused to lie up till it was over. Of course, I was very green as an infantryman and had some perverted idea of setting an example! In point of fact, I set an extremely bad one by walking about without a steel helmet and only ducking for cover when the whistle got really close! Of course, the inevitable happened and I played the trick once too often. I jumped for a slit trench which was already occupied. The shell dropped about twelve yards away and I got hit on the head by a piece of shrapnel which tore my beret and scalp, but which was too light to penetrate my skull. The luck was undeserved, but it did teach me a lesson.

"After a visit to Roger Kynaston at R.H.Q. to be patched up, I returned to Burcy and enjoyed a roaring headache for several hours. Then another of the shells landed five yards from one of my posts, but as it was properly dug in nobody was hurt.

"We spent three days and nights in this depressing place, then returned to 'D' Squadron at Montisanger."

All next day, the 14th of August, the enemy remained quiet on the regimental front, while 3rd (Br.) Division pushed on towards Tinchebray. From the north, "B" Squadron (in their cars) had moved their Headquarters to La Salette, south-east of Vire, and reported practically no enemy but mines at every turn. There was one sad casualty. Major Ward had been ordered by the Commander of 3rd (Br.) Division to send out a patrol on a certain narrow front towards Tinchebray, but actually on the Vire—Vassy road. There was a possibility that it might not be so heavily mined as was the direct approach. Lieutenant Jonkheer Groeninx van Zoelen's Troop was given the task, supported by Lieutenant Metcalfe and his dismounted men to probe for mines. The Troop got some way beyond the outposts and was then held up. Major Ward decided to have a look at the situation himself, and Trooper Hill, his staff car driver, volunteered to go with him as "he wanted a chance to see a bit of the war"—the usual scout car driver was for some reason unavailable. To get to the Troop, Major Ward had to by-pass a road-block by driving through an orchard. The route taken by the armoured cars was obvious and the scout car soon caught up with the Troop, where the Squadron Leader watched Lieutenant Metcalfe's Troop carry out a dismounted advance with some success. He then retraced his steps, after having issued further orders, returning by exactly the same route, and promptly got blown up at the corner of the orchard, the scout car being thrown bodily up on to a bank. Major Ward was wounded in the left forearm and head and badly concussed. Hill was mortally wounded, although he did not die until next day in hospital near St. Martin des Bésaces.

Meanwhile Corporal Hart and Trooper Gee had arrived from 1 Troop to help, and Major Ward, still dazed, directed Gee to drive up to the wrecked car, then suddenly realized to his horror that Gee's vehicle was in the middle of the minefield, too! A mine detector patrol then arrived and dug up twelve mines from between the wheels of Gee's car. Amazingly enough, Lieutenant Jonkheer Groeninx van Zoelen's entire Troop and Lieutenant Metcalfe's Support Troop had also driven over this very spot in the morning, sustaining no casualties.

Back at Sourdevalle, at about nine o'clock in the evening, as was invariably their custom before pulling out, the Germans hurled over a fair-sized barrage. Shells and mortar bombs crashed into positions which had been overlooked by the enemy all day, but the greater portion fell into the trenches of the Welsh Guards to the east and the Regiment came off without a single serious casualty.

The following morning our dawn patrols, who throughout the night 15th Aug. had made no contact with the enemy, were able to confirm that the Germans had withdrawn. Their salvoes of shells had been but a parting gesture. The enemy was now in full retreat.

On the 16th of August, the Secretary of State for War, Sir James Grigg, and General Montgomery came to look over the Sourdevalle position. As luck would have it, there had been a heavy thunderstorm during the night and arrangements for the visit had been made at about one in the morning over line telephones, which continually broke down and which only gave the people who operated them electric shocks. Wireless was also most unsatisfactory. However, the party turned up.

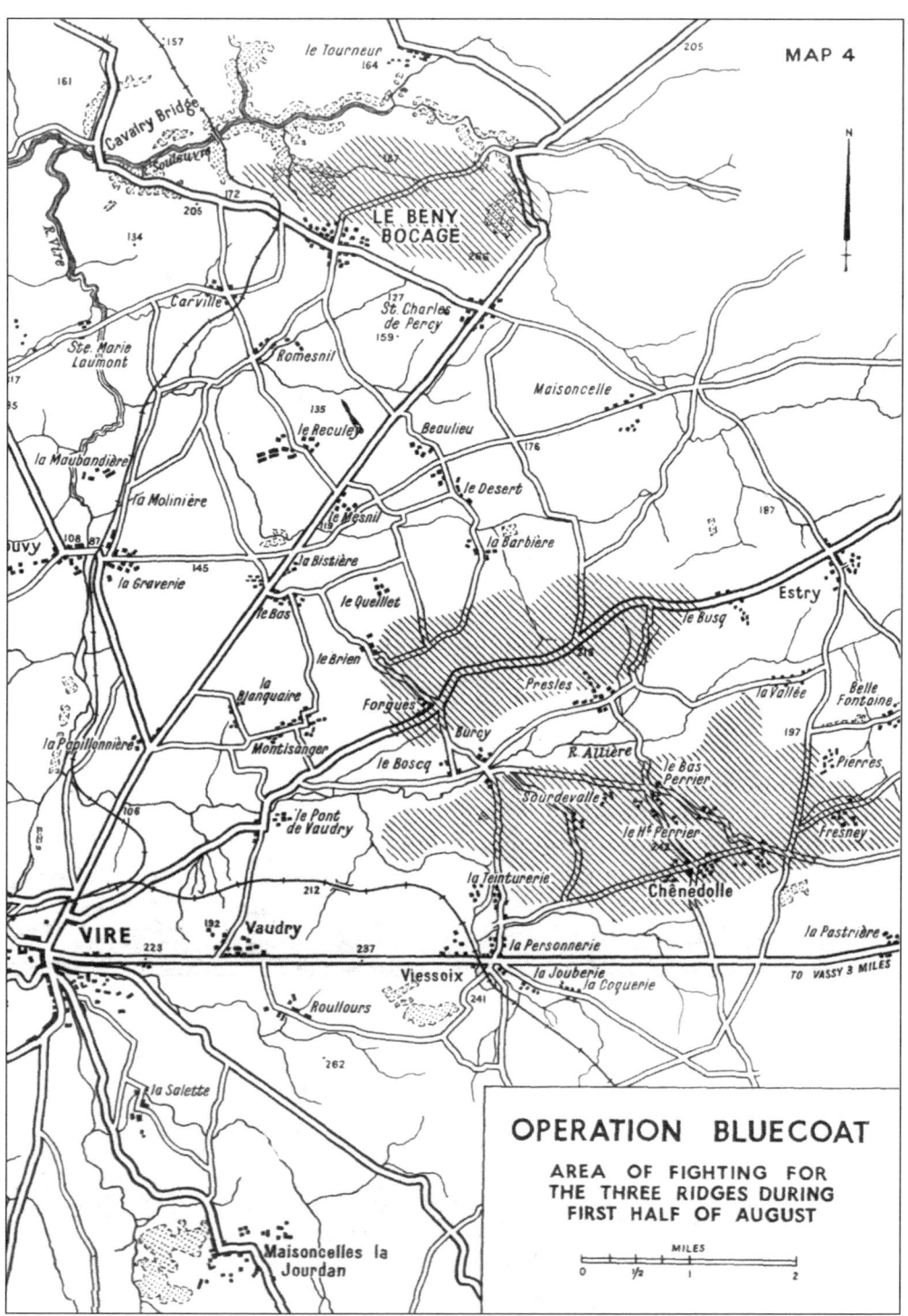

MAP 4

OPERATION BLUECOAT

AREA OF FIGHTING FOR
THE THREE RIDGES DURING
FIRST HALF OF AUGUST

One of the first persons to meet General Montgomery was Lieutenant Peake, who had been in occupation of an old Irish Guards trench for the past three days.

"How do you like being infantry?" inquired the Commander of 21 Army Group, doubtless expecting a reply according to the book.

"I hate it, sir, and the sooner I am allowed to get back to my armoured cars, for which we have been trained, the better," was the unexpected rejoinder. From that day Lieutenant Peake became known as "the Field-Marshal."

Colonel Abel Smith had arranged a most extensive programme for looking at burnt-out tanks and the forward positions. Fortunately, instead of staying for ten minutes, which had been the original schedule, the party stayed for one and a half hours because of a move of the next unit to which they were going. General Montgomery was therefore able to address a group of officers and men at Regimental Headquarters. As usual, he exuded complete confidence and was most sanguine about the outcome of the Falaise Pocket. (The British doggedly referred to the "Falaise Pocket," while the Americans equally stubbornly insisted on calling it the "Argentan Gap.") He said that surely and inexorably the German Seventh Army and an appreciable part of the German Fifth Panzer Army were being forced into a narrowing appendix (about to be sealed completely at Chambois). Those Germans who did escape, said the General, would be run up against the Lower Seine by a wider right hook by the Americans.

This hook was one being carried out by the American Third Army and due to reach the Seine at Mantes Gassicourt three days later. To carry out this feat, Eisenhower had, in his own words, "decided to turn his back on Brittany, where only one Corps invested the still resisting ports." Considering their enormous lines of communication, radiating southwards and eastwards, the American feat of transportation was little short of miraculous.

★ ★ ★

8 Corps, which had now been completely pinched out in the general convergence of the British advance, was withdrawn into Army reserve, and after Major Herbert's "C" Squadron had been mounted once more to occupy for a short while the heavily mined and booby-trapped village of Viessoix, the Regiment (less "B" and "D" Squadrons) was relieved of further responsibilities and returned, once more armoured cars, to Montisanger in the afternoon of the 16th of August.

Next morning they moved back to harbour near the village of Loraille, north of the Souleuvre and close to "Cavalry Bridge."

Chapter IX

Chanu and the Headwaters
of the Noireau

*"B" Squadron advance to the headwaters of the Noireau—Lieutenant Tabor's
Troop saves the bridge at Mont Secret—Lieutenant Cody's dismounted patrol
taken prisoner—Many mines encountered by "B" Squadron—Captain Ward's
Staghound blown up, but four dozen eggs in the vehicle have a miraculous escape!—
"D" Squadron liberate Chanu in spite of 'the unwanted attentions of hundreds
of Mongolians—More mines—Contact made with the Americans—Regiment
concentrated on the Souleuvre by 19th August*

Having left Regimental Headquarters and two Squadrons to sun
themselves in well-earned rest in the meadows above the River
Souleuvre, we must return to follow the moves of "B" and
"D" Squadrons, whose work was not yet finished.

Two days previously, on the 15th of August, working under the
command of the 3rd Reconnaissance Regiment of 3rd (Br.) Division
in their drive toward Tinchebray, "B" Squadron had advanced rapidly
against negligible opposition up to the headwaters of the River Noireau.
By evening troops were patrolling on a broad front in the area of the
river and railway crossings north-east of Tinchebray at Clairefougère,
Mont Secret and St. Pierre d'Entremont. Only on the natural and
well-defined obstacles was there any attempt by the enemy at defence,
and this was to melt away at night when the rearguard tasks had been
accomplished.

But the Germans knew well that the pursuit in this type of country
would be forced to conform to the roads, and they laid their plans
accordingly. They blew bridges and culverts and felled trees to cause
maximum by-passing and consequent delay. They sowed mines in great
numbers and booby-trapped the villages with cunning. In some places
the enemy continued to resist with an odd anti-tank gun and a few
dispirited infantry, but in most cases, on the principle of saving their best
troops, the S.S. and the Panzers were in full retreat.

We have said that only on the well-defined obstacles was any attempt
made at defence. Such an obstacle was the River Noireau, over whose
bridges the remnants of the German troops were converging towards the
narrowing gap between Falaise and Argentan.

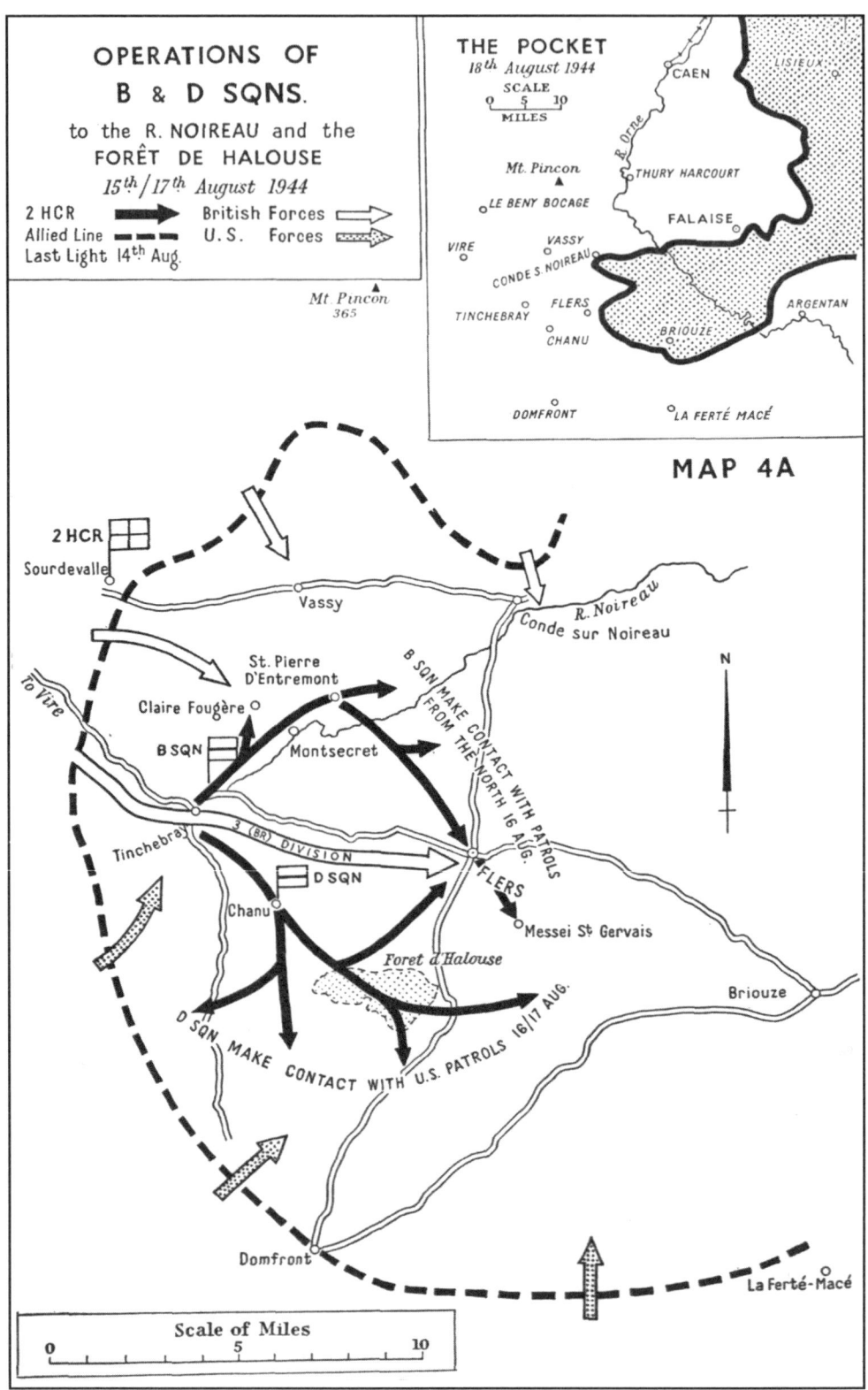

OPERATIONS OF
B & D SQNS.

to the R. NOIREAU and the
FORÊT DE HALOUSE
15th/17th August 1944

2 HCR   British Forces
Allied Line   U.S. Forces
Last Light 14th Aug.

Mt. Pincon
365

THE POCKET
18th August 1944
SCALE
0   5   10
MILES

CAEN   LISIEUX

R. Orne

Mt. Pincon   THURY HARCOURT

LE BENY BOCAGE

FALAISE

VIRE   VASSY
CONDE S. NOIREAU

FLERS

TINCHEBRAY   FLERS   ARGENTAN
     CHANU   BRIOUZE

DOMFRONT   LA FERTÉ MACÉ

MAP 4A

2 HCR
Sourdevalle

Vassy

R. Noireau
Conde sur Noireau

To Vire

St. Pierre
D'Entremont

Claire Fougère

B SQN

Montsecret

B SQN MAKE CONTACT WITH PATROLS FROM THE NORTH 16 AUG.

N

3 (BR) DIVISION

Tinchebray

D SQN

FLERS

Chanu

Messei St Gervais

Foret d'Halouse

Briouze

D SQN MAKE CONTACT WITH U.S. PATROLS 16/17 AUG.

Domfront

La Ferté-Macé

Scale of Miles
0   5   10

The headwaters of the Noireau, small streams in themselves but barriers nevertheless if the bridges were blown, run in a north-easterly direction to join the parent river at Condé, whence in turn, still flowing east, the latter empties itself into the Orne at St. Marc d'Ouilly, eight miles farther on. The Vaulige is one of those tributary streams and it flows through the attractively named village of Mont Secret. Across the Vaulige to the north-east can be seen the neighbouring village of St. Pierre d'Entremont, situated at an altitude to dominate the surrounding countryside. South of it, the Mont de Cerisi, a thousand feet high, helps to form the valley through which the Vaulige courses. All bridges from Clairefougère to well beyond Mont Secret, both over the railway and river, can be overlooked by an enemy on these heights.

Through these hills, Major Wignall had ordered his Troops to reconnoitre and try if possible to prevent the German rear-guard from blowing the bridges.

Lieutenant Tabor's Troop was to save the bridge at Mont Secret from destruction. The route lay along the Vire—Tinchebray road as far as St. Quentin les Chardonnets, thence almost due east to Mont Secret. The Troop Leader had been ordered to include among his tasks reports on crossings in Mont Secret and a further one to the east. On the left, Lieutenant Cody's Troop was to report on two bridges to the east of Mont Secret.

The main road to Tinchebray had already been cleared, except for mines, by the Americans sweeping round on the right flank of 3rd (Br.) Division, and therefore good time was made to St. Quentin les Chardonnets. From there the road ran due east initially through close country, then about two miles from Mont Secret along an exposed ridge into the river valley and on to the village itself. The Troop mopped up a few German stragglers on the way, and on approaching Mont Secret the cars were slowed down to a crawl to avoid raising the dust, which would certainly have given the alarm to the enemy, who were overlooking the entire village.

Lieutenant Tabor halted outside the village and hid the two scout cars in a lane. Then he and Lance-Corporal-of-Horse Sparrow started off to make a reconnaissance on foot. Everything was deadly still and there was nobody visible in the main street. As they reached the turning off the main street, Tabor glanced round the corner and saw two armed Germans approaching. These were promptly and silently collared as they came past. Lance-Corporal-of-Horse Sparrow then went back for the two scout cars, brought them up and parked them well away from the bridge. Other Germans must have observed this manoeuvre because as soon as the dismounted patrol started off again, a very heavy and accurate concentration of shell fire came down, which pinned them to the ground for about five minutes. When the fire had slackened, Tabor and Sparrow made a dash for the bridge, which was found to be prepared for demolition with four large charges, one at each corner. A cable to the exploder disappeared up the road on the other side. Still under observed enemy fire, they crawled up to the corners, removed the detonators and then tipped the charges into the river.

As they withdrew they noticed more Germans in some near-by houses, and so Tabor ordered up the scout cars, which took up positions to cover the bridge. Meanwhile Trooper Jones, one of the drivers, kept a further half a dozen prisoners quiet behind the church wall by ominously dangling a "36" grenade, with the pin half out, in front of them!

A call for reinforcements to hold the bridge did not get through, so one of the scout cars went back to seek aid and returned with one of Lieutenant Cody's armoured cars, which effectively covered the bridge while the remainder of the patrol prepared to move on to the next objective.

Enemy shelling had by now almost ceased, but as the patrol drove up the street a squadron of the 3rd Reconnaissance Regiment came down the hill, unfortunately raising a cloud of dust, and an accurate concentration from the German guns hit them fairly in the middle. They sustained several casualties, including their Squadron Leader killed, and withdrew again out of range when they had confirmed that the Household Cavalry cars were already in occupation.

Lieutenant Tabor's patrol continued eastwards, but the Germans were not caught napping a second time, and they blew the next bridge; the patrol once again coming under accurate and observed fire. Continuing eastwards, the party next made contact with Corporal Hewitt and Trooper Kapper (Lieutenant Cody's Troop). Hewitt informed Tabor that the road bridge was blown, but that Lieutenant Cody had gone off to reconnoitre a near-by railway bridge.

As Cody was somewhat overdue, Tabor and Hewitt went off to look for him. They worked along a sunken lane which was obviously under observation because they were shelled as they progressed forward. At the end of the lane was a farm, which was approached carefully and found to contain a large party of Germans. They were all talking hard and the Troop Leader reluctantly concluded that his brother officer must have walked into an ambush and been put in the bag.

Ordering the remainder of Cody's Troop to wait a stipulated time, and then, if there was still no sign of the missing Troop Leader, to return to base, Tabor retraced his steps. When his party reached the Mont Secret bridge again, the Daimler armoured car was discovered burnt out, a large calibre shell having passed clean through the petrol tank. There was no sign of the crew, but they were subsequently found to be safe, having returned to Squadron Headquarters with a 3rd Reconnaissance Regiment car which had given them a lift.

The rest of the day was described as "uneventful," although the patrol captured several more prisoners, suffered periodic heavy shelling, and found every house by the bridge to be booby-trapped, of which fact the infantry were duly warned when they arrived to take over at dusk.

★   ★   ★

Lieutenant Cody's Troop had started the day in much the same manner. On approaching their bridge, the cars were shelled. The crews heard bridges being blown to the east and one behind them. Groups of straggling enemy were encountered and, with the object of achieving some measure of surprise, the Troop halted and the cars were concealed. Lieutenant Cody and Corporal Collins then went forward on foot, but on passing the farmhouse already mentioned, they were pounced on by a party of the enemy and taken prisoner.

★   ★   ★

Next day "B" Squadron carried out limited patrols to the southeast of Flers and were ordered to take up positions of observation pending the arrival of the infantry. Generally speaking, nothing but stragglers were met and these were mostly only too anxious to give themselves up. Mines were still a great hindrance to operations, and four vehicles were blown up, including the Scammel recovery vehicle.

One of the victims in Lieutenant Kavanagh's Troop was reconnoitring the road towards Messei St. Gervais, south-east of Flers. The Troop had picked up a brace of Germans asleep by their machine gun and were hunting more enemy down a rough track leading to a farm, when the scout car commanded by Corporal Tutt and driven by Trooper Price ran over a Teller mine. The explosion (there were probably two or more mines on top of each other) caused the scout car to turn a complete somersault, and it landed wheels uppermost with the crew trapped underneath. Kavanagh and Corporal-of-Horse Johnson ran forward to see if they were still alive. "They were," reported Johnson, "but Tutt's arm was trapped by the sharp edge of the vehicle. However, with the aid of some farmers, we managed to raise the scout car sufficiently to push the arm in and then inject morphia. Then after a terrific struggle we got them both out, with Trooper Price cursing the Germans in real Army lingo. Corporal Tutt's arm looked an awful mess, but Trooper Price was O.K."

Meanwhile Captain Ward, who had arrived in his Staghound, jumped out and started to back his vehicle down the road, only to see it suffer the same fate, the huge wheel soaring over the turret and across a field, followed by wings, nuts and bolts. In one of the bins of the wrecked car, Captain Ward's servant, Trooper Taylor, had packed four dozen eggs with loving care—not one was broken!

Since landing in Normandy, over forty Household Cavalry vehicles, including twenty-five scout cars, had gone up on mines, but the protection of the floors with sandbags had proved to be an excellent safety precaution and, although uncomfortable and cramping for the long-legged drivers, had prevented many casualties. This was no innovation, however, for it had long been the recognized practice in the Western Desert.

With 11th Armoured Division now under 30 Corps swinging due east at speed along the road to Landigou, the infantry was left behind and eventually pinched out altogether as the British armour from the north veered across their path. 3rd (Br.) Division had therefore no further need of an armoured car screen and "B" Squadron rejoined the Regiment on the 17th of August.

★   ★   ★

"D" Squadron had been given a similar role, also working under command of 3rd (Br.) Division, but their task developed on different lines. In parts it became sheer comic opera, in other strangely touching, as troops liberated little villages whose inhabitants had been waiting five years for this great day.

In the early morning of the 16th of August, "D" Squadron left their orchard at Montisanger with orders to patrol to the southeast of Tinchebray. The object was, firstly, to make contact with the Americans, whose sweepingly rapid movements were already setting the Corps map markers a problem, and, secondly, to investigate the extensive Forêt de Halouse area, in which there were reputedly large dumps of enemy equipment.[1] Departure was delayed by an unfortunate accident to Staff-

---

1. Lieutenant Hanbury's Troop, with the aid of the French, discovered a large dump of enemy equipment hidden in the disused workings of an iron ore mine. An unaccountable half-hour's wireless breakdown at the height of the liberation celebrations was ingeniously put down by Corporal-of-Horse Brook to the magnetic effect of this ore on the No.19 set!

Sergeant Camfield of the R.E.M.E., who was badly burnt when trying to put out flames caused by a faulty primer in a phosphorous grenade in one of Lieutenant Jonkheer Groeninx van Zoelen's scout cars. As Camfield was bravely attempting to approach the blazing vehicle to affix a tow rope to drag it clear of other cars, its tank exploded, drenching him in flaming petrol. He was carried away in great agony, not expected to live, but we later learnt that he had made a remarkable recovery in England. Apart from being a tower of strength to the regimental L.A.D., Camfield was an extremely good N.C.O. Colonel Abel Smith later made repeated efforts to get him back to the Regiment, but others had also realized his worth, and so it was to no avail.

For the first few miles "D" Squadron drove through the usual welter of knocked-out transport and burnt-out dwellings. Thereafter, the country showed fewer signs of the ravages of war. Breakfast was eaten in a field beyond Tinchebray, where a liaison officer from the 3rd Reconnaissance Regiment was waiting with orders. Tinchebray was the first undamaged town we had seen since Bayeux. The Squadron then forked right by the putrefying and swollen carcass of a horse—by common consent, the worst smell yet encountered. First contact with the enemy was of an unexpected sort, Lieutenant Buchanan-Jardine reporting back that he had captured some Japanese, but that he was "a little doubtful of their identification as they are rather curiously dressed." Major Ward sternly wirelessed back not to give facetious identifications over the air. There was a pause, until from the same Troop came another message. "I'm sorry, but there *really* are many more of those queer fellows—perhaps they are Chinamen. At any rate they are a rum lot, certainly not European, and coming in from all sides."

To this last message Major Ward could give no more than a brief acknowledgment, for the next moment he had turned a corner and was himself in the thick of them.

They came in their hundreds. Either Russia had changed fronts or we had taken the wrong road. Great bearded ruffians from the Caucasian foothills scrambled for right of way with slant-eyed Mongols and Turkomen. Two grinning characters (wearing top hats) would have looked much more at home gnawing frozen fish on the banks of the Yenesei than in the Normandy Bocage on a summer's day.

They laughed and gibbered, they gesticulated. Some ran across the road to shake hands like ambling bears, others half fearful raised their arms in token of surrender. Some carried sticks, many had shot-guns. A man with a butcher's knife dangling at his side trundled a dripping wheelbarrow-load of horseflesh in front of him. Yet another was hauling a small go-cart on which were piled an armchair, some pumpkins and a crate of chickens.

Many came across to pat the great rubber tyres of the Staghounds, which seemed to fascinate them. They looked at the guns, shook hands with the drivers through the visors, and made a variety of curious signs indicating that they had finished with their German masters for good, ending by passing a finger across their throats and roaring with laughter, shouting, "Hitler kaput—kaput—kaput!"

One Chinaman trotted by wearing a farmer's blue smock and an oversize bowler hat, oblivious of the fact that underneath could be seen his German uniform, including top boots. Over his shoulders he carried a pair of roller skates!

A single dominant idea seemed to permeate this motley cavalcade: to possess a hat, whatever shape or size or style—anything so long as it was not the German helmet.

Helplessly, Major Ward waved the throng of destitutes westwards towards Tinchebray. For once we sent in no report of identifications to Lieutenant Haskard, for he would not have believed us. Neither did we appreciate at this stage that we were witnessing, at first hand, one of the migratory phases of the tragically unwanted "Displaced persons."

As the war dragged on we were to see many thousands more liberated but homeless outcasts, but never again anything quite like this. An explanation was later forthcoming. These people, mostly Mongolian, had been roped in by the Russians for duty on the Eastern front, then captured by the Germans, to be subsequently put into low-grade jobs in their armies. By 1944 Hitler considered it safer to move them to the Western Front rather than risk them nearer Russia. They deserted when the Normandy retreat began.

The first village to be reached after this episode was Chanu, where every man, woman and child turned out to welcome our arrival. Unfortunately, Lieutenant Ainsworth's Troop took a wrong turning when half-way through the village and halted. This was fatal, for in a matter of seconds his cars were surrounded by a seething mob. It was useless threatening to shoot if they did not move out of the way, for they were determined that we should listen to their welcoming speeches and see how happy they were to be liberated. The children were in their Sunday best and carried posies of flowers. Everybody talked at once, offering information about the enemy's latest moves which, had they been credited, showed that Chanu was surrounded by half the German army. However, as not a car could move, and not a German was in sight, it could not have mattered less.

The troops eventually forced their way out of the village, and after running over a few toes, fanned out southwards towards Domfront and the Forêt de Halouse. All cross-roads were found to be mined and Lieutenant Younghusband's Troop lost a scout car, the Troop Leader and his driver, Trooper Allen, escaping with no worse than a shaking, thanks to the sandbagging on the floor. Then the Americans, coming up from the south in their Greyhounds[2], signalized the event by shooting up the cars in mistake for the enemy. Fortunately their aim was on the erratic side and no damage was done. After effusive hand-shaking all round, our Allies rushed off eastwards, although not before exchanging the major portion of their rations for two Luger automatics.

The Forêt de Halouse proved to contain much equipment and ammunition and two abandoned Panther tanks. Firm contact with "B" Squadron and butter was made in the outskirts of Flers.

Back at Squadron Headquarters Lieutenant Clark, stationed at the gate of the harbour field with his Matador car, ostensibly to prevent the mob from entering, only succeeded in getting himself drenched in calvados and smothered in flowers and kisses. The echelon lorries arrived and took away bedraggled batches of Germans, while Lieutenant Ainsworth argued through the afternoon with a German officer as to how long Hitler would last, until Major Ward in desperation sent him off to buy more eggs.

Time passed quickly, but the Squadron wanted to get back to the Souleuvre to refit—the warning order "bottom plates off" meant a lot to the fitters, and there would surely be little time to spare before resuming the advance to the Seine.

It was therefore with slight feelings of misgiving that Major Ward heard that 3rd Reconnaissance Regiment wished his Squadron to remain with them for the next few days—the right flank, they said, was a possible danger spot. As the right flank was now seething with cheerful G.Is. it was felt that there was little justification for this apprehension. Further, not only were 11th Armoured Division now well beyond Briouze to the east, but so were the Americans, who in addition firmly maintained that the main road to Argentan was their right of way. But it was to take two more days of argument and high-level persuasion before "D" Squadron obtained their release.

The 18th of August was spent in rounding up stragglers and investigating the facts of what promised to be (for the Squadron) the first authentic case of rape. A French farmer's wife had rushed wild eyed

2. Greyhound—the American six-wheeled armoured car.

to the Rear Link officer with a story of "many German soldiers —all *méchants* —taking all she valued most in life." Accordingly a patrol under the auspices of Squadron Headquarters was dispatched to the scene of the suspected crime. The farm building was stalked and stealthily surrounded and four Russian deserters dressed in German uniform were discovered playing cards in the kitchen. Apart from having helped themselves to the contents of her larder, there had never been any question of a "fate worse than death" for the good woman. When apprehended, the Russians accepted their fate with cheerful insouciance and before they left insisted on kissing each of her thirteen children good-bye.

On the 19th of August, the Squadron returned to Monsieur Papillon's farm on the Souleuvre. Some made the return journey by motoring through the Forêt de Halouse and round into Flers. The town had been an important railway and road centre through which passed the main line Paris—Cherbourg. The railway sidings and the houses adjoining had been badly bombed and nothing but twisted steel rails remained to show what had once been the permanent way. The inhabitants told of how the main body of retreating Germans had wreaked their vengeance on the town as they had passed through a day before the British. There was evidence of great wanton damage. In now peaceful Chanu there was but one sign of damage, and that caused by a stray shell—a large slice taken out of the church tower and a ruined Presbytery. In the debris had died, two hours before the arrival of "D" Squadron, an old village priest whose dream it had been, since the days of Dunkirk, to be the first Frenchman to welcome the British in Chanu.[3]

---

3. I later ascertained that the large concourse which had greeted the Squadron at Chanu had been swollen by no fewer than 15,000 refugees from the adjoining communes, Chanu having been the only place in the district to disobey the German order to evacuate on the 15th of August. (Information and figures supplied by the Mayor of Chanu.). *Author*

Chapter X

Rest and a Hurried Move

Rest and refitting by the River Souleuvre and general reflections on the Regiment's part in the campaign to date—Change of Corps and preparations for a hurried move

The ensuing days of warm sunshine by the banks of the Souleuvre passed rapidly, and until the weather broke on the 21st of August those who wished it were able to bathe in the stream, which at any rate looked clean. A few volunteers who were prepared to brave a long and bumpy journey in the back of a lorry for a sight of the sea were sent off to the Rest Camp at St. Aubin-sur-Mer, which "C" Squadron had helped to construct in the early days of landing, and they thoroughly enjoyed the change.

For those who hankered after Lancashire, George Formby and a banjo visited the area in pouring rain and catered to their tastes. "He has," sighed a homesick trooper, "brought Lancashire to my tent."

As several days' rest appeared probable, Colonel Abel Smith ordered a complete overhaul of all Squadron vehicles, and the fitters set to work with a will. That they were unable to finish their task in time was to be no fault of theirs.

For the remainder of the Regiment the welcome absence of hurry and flap, the visits to and from each other's Squadrons, conversation with friends, many of whom we had not seen since Brighton days, the journeys, tight packed in the staff car, along leafy and now friendly lanes to the nearest mobile bath unit at Le Tourneur; and, above all, the warm caress of an August sun, were decidedly conducive to a mood of lazily retrospective and agreeable reverie.

How restful to recline outside one's tent and allow the eye to dwell upon the peaceful lush water-meadows, to alight casually upon those innumerable scenes which go to make up a regiment taking its ease. Even the muttered oaths of the hard-working fitters as they wrestled with the oily innards of the cars (fitters never seemed to stop working) appeared to float away on the breeze in friendly unison with the drone of the numerous dragonflies and midges!

Now and again the dull reverberation of an explosion could be felt and we marvelled that the sounds of distant battle could carry so far. It later transpired that Colonel Abel Smith had taken a few hours off to go fishing in the waters of the Vire, while above him, in his own style, Captain Cooper was also poaching with a handful of grenades and an old umbrella.

It has been said that "the thread of an armoured division's advance winds forward through the ever-extending pattern of armoured car reconnaissances," and in their hazardous role of seeing without being seen and stalking without being stalked, perhaps the heaviest burden had fallen upon the leading scout car crews.

Yet, as one studied the faces of the men making up the Troops, one was struck by how quickly the signs of fatigue disappeared after a few hours' rest; particularly the armoured car drivers, whose long periods of cramped confinement hauling away at a heavy wheel, shouted at through the "intercom"—the dust and darkness of narrow lanes before dawn, the eternal stopping and starting with but the vaguest inkling of what was happening—was all a considerable physical strain. Perhaps only the Troop Leaders themselves really knew what they owed to their drivers whose part in battle could so easily be taken for granted.

Experience to date had shown that operations were largely influenced by the sheer physical problems which the Bocage country invariably presented to the advancing troops. It therefore followed that reconnaissance had been slow and hard and information painfully won. Once the front around Vire had become static, there was no longer any question of a sudden break-through as at St. Martin des Bésaces, and the Troops gradually found themselves playing the role of Phantom for the division under which they were working. Troop Leaders had therefore normally elected to go into battle with their two scout cars leading, themselves in the second vehicle, and with the corporal-of-horse in the armoured car within supporting distance should opposition be met. The handiness of the scout car with its great manoeuvrability, coupled with the fact that it had no turret to be shot at, had been the answer in the Bocage as far as an Armoured Car Regiment was concerned. And, most important, the scout car could penetrate down lanes and over bridges where no armoured car or tank could hope to follow.

Lest it might be thought that the armoured cars had been eclipsed by their smaller brethren, it must be remembered that as soon as the country was to open out, they were immediately to resume their rightful place in the normal Troop set-up. And then not an officer or man was to regret the decision of the "Camilly Conference of Troop Leaders," that in no circumstances should the turrets be removed, for to do so was to degrade a fine fighting vehicle to the status of a box on wheels.

Some of the most successful patrols and harassing of the enemy had been accomplished in close liaison with the Gunners. It had originally been feared that there might be difficulty in relaying back our calls for fire support to the 25-pdr. batteries in terms relating to their special requirements, but it was not so. The Royal Regiment of Artillery from the beginning seemed to understand and be able to respond to our calls with remarkably little insistence on any private trade jargon of their own or closed shop policy. They always appeared to have the guns at the right place, and at the right time, in spite of their other commitments ranging all over the field of battle. A six-figure map reference, and reasonable observation on our part, was all they ever asked for. Certain Troop Leaders became expert at guiding the 25-pdrs. on to the target with a minimum of corrections, and the feeling that an isolated Troop behind the enemy lines could call upon this support almost at will was a tremendous aid to morale.

The Heavy Troops were rather touchy on the score of the 25-pdrs., feeling with rightful pride that their 75-mm. guns could accomplish the same feats of indirect fire from all sorts of curious angles. Indeed, the Matadors were excellent at close-range work, and their shelling was to send many a German soldier to his grave or at least scuttling for cover. But it was sometimes admitted that when in forward observation, Troop Leaders did prefer to take cover themselves when the first sighting shots came over!

Being rather heavy for their four wheels, the cars, which weighed nearly thirteen tons, had a propensity for sliding into ditches and sticking there, and so for this reason were normally put at the back of the Squadron column when on the move. Which fact, bemoaned Lieutenant Clark, "meant that we were always destined to guard the Squadron harbours and shook off too inquisitive civilians."

The Support Troops were the "Jacks-of-all-trades." They were infantrymen, sometimes fighting actions on their own, as at Étouvy, or else lending their aid to Reconnaissance Troops when the dense Bocage made it necessary to send out protective patrols on foot to deal with stalking bazooka-men. They guarded harbours at night and de-mined road-blocks and verges during the day. They certainly earned their keep.

In training there had been a fear that the echelons would have great difficulty in reprovisioning their forward Squadrons, principally because of lack of road space. To a certain extent this had proved to be the case, especially during a break-through, as after St. Martin des Bésaces. The job of the echelon commanders was no sinecure during operations. Theirs was a continual struggle to force their way past traffic jams and that curse of the battlefield, the "I'm-priority-get-out-of-the-way" man of some seniority. But the Regiment was well equipped to deal with this menace. In his own hesitant manner Lieutenant Hughes was a past-master at dealing with what he called "the keenies," while Lieutenant Oliver, another echelon commander, simply talked all obstruction off the roads, blasting his way forward to "B" Squadron by verbal strafing, as if jet-propelled. Never, for one day, did any of the Squadrons have to go short of ammunition or food.

Normally, one lorry, known as the Mixed Load, travelled with Squadron Headquarters. It was filled with petrol and ammunition and sundry other high explosive material, and carried out a shuttle service with a second lorry similarly loaded to and from the front under the command of a N.C.O. When Sabre Squadrons were operating, the other lorries, including the cook's lorry, normally remained brigaded under Major Williams at H.Q. Squadron. When the front became static, the respective Transport Officers (or Echelon Commanders, by which title they were more usually known) brought them up to Squadrons, often at dead of night, and frequently to be greeted after a gruelling journey with cries such as, "Have you brought up the N.A.A.F.I. cigarette ration?" or "Where are the 'A' packs this time?"[1]

The echelons were individualists to a man, and when once in harbour, whatever the conditions of campaigning, they could always be relied upon to supply a fearsome array of epistolary warriors to keep the censoring officers quiet.

When in harbour for any length of time, Squadrons cooked centrally, but in fact the men really preferred their car cooking. The corporals-of-horse, those autocratic Boulestins of the armoured car world, supervised the Troop cooking pots with a rod of iron, and woe betide the man responsible for the "fry-up" if his dish failed to come up to the required standard. Cider, in gallons, found its place in every spare water can or bottle, but "hot sweet tea" in a thick, chipped enamel mug flavoured with chlorine and powdered milk was the panacea for all battle ills, and, strange as it may now seem, tasted very good indeed.

Nor were the officers' messes when in harbour any less well served. Captain Balding, ranging far and wide among the Americans with tins

---

1. The "A" pack was a much-sought-after luxury in the armoured car world. There were several different A.F.V. ration packs, but this one contained steak-and-kidney pudding and tinned peaches, which made a welcome change from the eternal M. & V. (Meat and Vegetable) or the quite repulsive so-called Ox-Tail, a concoction of crushed bones and weak meat juice worthy of the worst governmental bulk buying. The "A" pack rarely got far forward, being, so ran the generally discredited story, "reserved" for hospitals!

of bully beef, dealt faithfully with Regimental Headquarters, bringing back brandy and rough red wine in such quantities that it frequently kept the "Acorns" and the "Love Oboes" and even "Halo" talking far into the night.[2]

As a blessed relief, and for the first time since landing in Normandy, the wireless sets were at last switched off, and people such as Corporals-of-Horse ("Ding-Dong") Bell and Strowbridge and Millege were at last able to regain their voices. Squadrons always insisted that Regimental Headquarters were "Mush-Happy" and never permitted switching off until all Squadron Leaders were within speaking distance of each other. This as a jest may have been a trifle unkind, but assuredly the relief and quiet in harbours seemed to symbolize the end of an important phase.

On the whole, the wireless had worked extremely well. But mainly because of the great concentration of troops within the bridgehead, the frequency bands were badly overloaded. This was noticed especially on the Squadron Command nets at dawn and dusk, during which time commanders would experience the greatest difficulty in maintaining touch with their forward troops because of interference.

In the early days there was another snag—the interference of the high-power stations working from the beach-heads, particularly the Americans. Wireless sets were frequently swamped by an individual calling himself "Blackboid," whom all H.Q. operators could have cheerfully murdered. Another working from Cherbourg prefaced and signed off every call with a reiterated "I can hear you now fine and dandy." Certainly, for long-winded messages, American stations had little to learn from even the most verbose British signaller.

Colonel Abel Smith's firm principle of always having a representative at Corps level—and whenever possible, with flanking formations, at Divisional level—worked well, and the more or less permanent trio, of Captains Ford, Balding and Cooper, developed an information service second to none. Little escaped their roving Humber scout cars.

Even when at rest, as on the Souleuvre, the duty of keeping the Regiment in social contact with the rest of the world continued to devolve on that genial colossus, Neville Ford, who, striding from Regimental Headquarters to 8 Corps and back again, in a never-ending succession of journeys, might be heard by all within a two-mile radius of the command tent booming out a General's latest *bon mot*, or the current gossip of the remoter military hierarchy. From the beginning

2. Acorn – Intelligence Officer. Love Oboes – Liaison Officers. Halo – The Padre (all wireless jargon).

of operations, "Foghorn Ford"—or just plain "Foggers," as he came to be known by General Horrocks later on—had found his natural *milieu* at Corps; to have removed him elsewhere would have savoured of vandalism, and at Corps he was to remain throughout the campaign.

His wireless call sign, "One Eight Able," must have been as familiar to the German intercept stations as the chimes of Big Ben.[3] At a later stage of the campaign, I remember, it was a near thing as to who managed to get in his daily bulletin first, General Ditmar from Berlin or Captain Ford from Neerbosch on the Maas, each with a style peculiarly his own. Indeed, on one occasion in Holland, due to a misunderstanding and an over-zealous newspaper reporter, both were to be quoted simultaneously by the Press—Ditmar on "Eventual Victory for the Reich," Ford on "Hitler's Great Blunder"!

Captain Balding became with the Americans what Captain Ford was at Corps. His pre-war residence in the United States, where his magnificent record on the polo field alone would have assured him of a ready acceptance among the games-worshipping Americans, made him eminently fitted for the job. But he was one of those rarities, an Englishman born and bred who in many ways saw life through American eyes. When excited, even his intonation and expressions became New World. However, his friends said that he had been chosen liaison officer by Colonel Abel Smith, not for those qualities alone, but also on the strength of his graphic descriptions in the mess of Hollywood night life!

A few words are perhaps necessary to explain how Regimental Headquarters worked.

Colonel Abel Smith commanded the Regiment from Tactical Headquarters, and he had with him his Adjutant, Captain Collins, his Intelligence Officer, Lieutenant Haskard, and his Signals Officer, Lieutenant Turnbull. Tactical Headquarters usually moved with the Tactical Headquarters of the division under command of which, or in conjunction with which, the Regiment was operating, or with the leading brigade of this division when the latter was very strung out.

Main Regimental Headquarters, under the command of the Regimental Second-in-Command, Major Sir Peter Grant Lawson, only moved with Tactical Headquarters when that Headquarters was with Main Divisional Headquarters, as Tactical and Main Headquarters of the Regiment were then fused; this always happened during more static operations. Otherwise Regiment's Main Headquarters was separated

---

3. "One Eight Able" was the wireless code sign for Captain N. Ford, Liaison Officer at 8 Corps.

from its Tactical Headquarters and would probably move with Main Divisional Headquarters.

The Regimental wireless net was operated by high power 19 sets, the Regimental Rear Link being a still higher-powered set. Liaison officers with flanking formations and the liaison officer at Corps Headquarters were always on the Command net, with their alternate frequency on either that of the formation with which they (the Regiment) were working, or that of the Command net to which the Regimental Rear Link was netted.

The Regiment, as we have read, always had a liaison officer at Corps Headquarters, and when operations were to be more stretched, as in the advance to the Somme and to Brussels, he was to be provided with a super-high-power wireless set by Royal Corps of Signals.

The period which the Regiment had spent under the command of 11th Armoured Division, dating from the beginning of the offensive at the end of July, had been in experience a profitable one. It was felt, not without justification, that we had fulfilled all and more than had been asked of us as armoured cars. We had encountered as good German troops as we were ever likely to meet and had more than matched them in guile and cunning and general "inquisitiveness," which latter quality in particular is the role of the armoured car. Moreover, bearing in mind the severity of the fighting, the variety of tasks, and the type of country totally unsuited to armour, our casualties had been remarkably few.

Although most of the Regiment's work had been for 11th Armoured Division, it had yet to operate its four Sabre Squadrons as a single unit. In fact at one time, for a short period, the Regiment had been so split up that it had found itself patrolling simultaneously for Guards Armoured Division, 11th Armoured Division and 3rd (Br.) Division, with Squadrons each under separate command. Undoubtedly, from the point of view of co-ordinating reconnaissance, this had proved to have been a serious disadvantage, particularly when working with an infantry division. Somewhat understandably, the infantry at battalion levels could never depart from the fixed idea that the armoured cars were either a new type of tank or else a sudden addition to their machine-gun strength; the result being that reconnaissance frequently bogged down into a series of small isolated actions.

It was infinitely preferable that Colonel Abel Smith should be able to command all four Squadrons working on a corps or divisional frontage, preferably the former. If this was not done, sooner or later reconnaissance got hopelessly intermixed; the resultant overlapping causing an unnecessary drain on available liaison officers, far too many wireless sets at Regimental Headquarters and Squadron Headquarters, and consequently greatly overtired operators.

These were all lessons we had learnt in the course of operations during the last month, and they were not to be forgotten in the forthcoming battles.

★   ★   ★

On the 21st of August we heard that the Falaise Gap had been closed. The fine weather, which had been such an advantage for the great developments taking place to the east, broke without warning into a day of heavy rain. However, to our relief, it showed signs of recovering at dusk, and for no particular reason beyond that of wishful thinking we looked forward to a few more days of leisure. As there appeared to be no immediate place on the packed battlefield for 8 Corps, we were not to quarrel with the decision to leave us in relative idleness for a while. Then, just before midnight, a sudden order arrived that we were to be ready to move in the early hours of the morning. We were to be transferred to another Corps, and, although we did not yet know it, were shortly to join in the speed of the chase which so far had been almost entirely the preserve of General Patton's flying columns of Americans.

A.E.C. Armoured Car Gunner

Part Three

The Pursuit

Chapter I

Transfer to 30 Corps

Regiment transfers to 30 Corps under command of Lieutenant-General B. G. Horrocks—Écouché—Last days of the Falaise Pocket—Argentan-L'Aigle— St. Symphorien des Bruyères—30 Corps prepares assault crossing of the Seine— Regiment's task on the flank.

While the trapped Germans within the sealed Falaise Pocket were being eliminated amid scenes of indescribable carnage, the Anglo-American forces were advancing eastwards in increasing numbers to force the crossings of the Seine. Already the Americans had crossed the river at Mantes Gassicourt on the 19th of August and, with this important communication centre in Allied hands, the roads from Paris to Normandy were severed. Below this point no bridge remained intact and, to escape, the enemy would be compelled to rely on boats and ferries, and these were under the continuous attention of our Air Force. The French 2nd Armoured Division entered Paris amidst scenes of wild enthusiasm on the 24th of August, and on the following day their commander, General Leclerc, received the surrender of the German commander.

In the general surge forward 30 Corps were on the right flank of the British Army and aiming to force a crossing of the Seine at Vernon. This Corps, under the command of Lieutenant-General B. G. Horrocks, now consisted of 50th (Northumbrian) Division, 43rd (Wessex) Division, 11th Armoured Division and 8th Armoured Brigade.

The Regiment was to have the good fortune of joining 30 Corps at the time that 8 Corps were withdrawn into Army Reserve, and was thereby enabled to take a prominent part in the historic dash across the plains of Northern France and through Belgium; a dash which was only to be temporarily halted on the Dutch frontier through the Allies having outrun their lines of supply. The Inns of Court Regiment had re-joined 11th Armoured Division, which formation, it will be remembered, had transferred to 30 Corps on the 14th of August. We were to be the Corps armoured car regiment, and as such were to remain, until armoured car regiments once again in the late autumn became divisional troops, when we then became part of Guards Armoured Division.

★　★　★

On D Day, General Horrocks was still in a convalescent hospital recovering from a serious wound sustained at Bizerta in May 1943, and at one time it had been feared that he would never be strong enough to command actively again. He had but recently succeeded Lieutenant-General G. C. Bucknall, who had led 30 Corps into Normandy.

To all but a few in the Regiment, General Horrocks was still only a name. Not for long was he to remain so. In our new Corps Commander, we were soon made aware of a personality and leader who understood and exploited our possibilities as an armoured car regiment to the fullest extent. Field-Marshal Montgomery's Chief of Staff has compared him with another equally forceful character well known to the Regiment, and an ex-commander of Guards Armoured Division —General Sir Oliver Leese. "They were both great commanders possessing drive and enthusiasm—in fact, all the right qualities. Leese was more methodical and thorough, whilst Horrocks was more spectacular and colourful. I always think of him as Marshal Ney."[1]

We were destined to carry out nearly all our future war operations under General Horrocks; from the dash through the night to the Somme bridges up to those last slow and plugging days across the North German plains before the final surrender. In men and officers alike his leadership inspired the greatest confidence, and we soon learnt to trust to his judgment implicitly, hoping in our turn that our reports and actions went some way towards giving him what he called "the smell of battle."

★   ★   ★

As we had been assured of several more days' rest, the sudden order to move on the 22nd of August caught the Regiment with most of its vehicles minus their bottom plates and sumps drained of oil. However, with the fitters working throughout the night, every car was ready for the road by breakfast time next morning. Long before dawn, Colonel Abel Smith and a small party of officers were already speeding ahead of the main body along the road to Écouché in which area the Regiment was to harbour for the ensuing night.[2]

The rain had stopped and it was with a strange feeling of leaving what was by now history that we prepared to say good-bye to "Cavalry

---

1. *Operation Victory* by Major-General Sir Francis De Guingand, K.B.E., C.B., D.S.O. (Hodder & Stoughton)
2. The route taken by the Regiment to join 30 Corps was as follows: Le Bény Bocage—Vire—Tinchebray—Flers—La Ferté Macé—St. Ouen-sur-Maire-- Écouché —Argentan—Gacé—L'Aigle—St. Symphorien des Bruyères.

Bridge" and the little villages around Le Bény Bocage which we had all come in such varying circumstances to know so well.

Major Williams's echelon, finally convinced that there were no more German tanks at Le Tourneur, put away their PIATs and bade farewell to La Ferrière and the bakery and café at the cross-roads. While oblivious of the last-minute flaps engaging the attention of ordinary mortals, that inveterate letter-writer, Corporal Weald, sat in the "D" Squadron staff car, piled high with maps and codes, scribbling for dear life to catch Corporal Briggs's[3] last outward mail.

The wreckage of Lieutenant Bethell's two cars had since been removed and long lines of traffic now sped by the charred patches where the vehicles had burnt themselves out on the edge of the forest. But we hoped that at any rate some of those who had formed the old 5 Troop might still be alive.

Slowly the Regiment wound up the long hill and through Le Bény Bocage towards the Vire road for the last time. Again hard at work in their liberated fields, the peasants halted in their toil for a while to wave and watch until we were out of sight. Soon the convoy increased pace, and as we sped past the myriads of signs and slogans which spring up as fast as the *marché noire* in the wake of an advancing modern army, there came the thought that history is not always to be measured in time, but in accumulated experiences, and not a few felt the older for last month's crowded hours.

There were noticeable signs of returning stability in the countryside so recently devastated. Children were playing on the knocked-out Tiger at Le Reculey. The faded blue signpost by the cross-roads had been propped up again. Many of the gaps torn in the hedges and banks had been made good by the energetic Norman peasants with our own Dannert wire. Sheds and barns repaired with ammunition boxes filled with earth were springing up all over the place. The cattle, though depleted in numbers, were finding their way back to their pastures in twos and threes and grazed by the rusting Shermans through whose tracks the rich grass was already beginning to push.

Vire was only skirted, but close enough for us to see the chaos and desolation wrought in this once beautiful old walled Norman town. An important road junction standing high up on a hill and overlooking the river which bears its name, one realized why the Germans had held on to it with such tenacity. The greater part of the destruction had been caused on D Day by American bombers which had been required, as

---

3. Corporal Briggs – the Post Corporal.

part of the general plan, to paralyse rearward centres of communication. How efficiently they had carried out their task could be seen by the heaps of splintered coaches and jumble of twisted rails which had once carried the Paris—Cherbourg expresses. It had "sure been liberated," as an American Military policeman remarked to Captain Balding.

We crossed over the fateful Vire—Vassy road and, guided by tapes along but recently mine-cleared lanes, reached the main road to Tinchebray. Wherever one looked, the blackened hulks of tanks and other vehicles shared place with the rotting cattle, now distended to enormous dimensions. One burst with a loud hissing sound as of a punctured motor tyre, and the stench was to be our last memory of martyred Vire.

At first—and this applied to most of the villages around Vire—one wondered if order and human habitation could ever return to the heaps of rubble and mouldering death. Then imperceptibly one became aware that where the character of the fighting had changed from static resistance to hurried enemy withdrawal, so had the pattern and debris of war conformed. The roads joining village to village were relatively unencumbered, but where a route crossed a stream, or a valley had caused a bottleneck, there would be the signs of bombing and destruction once again. And while we bowled along in regimental column with our necessarily limited vision of the larger operational aspects and with but

BOIS JEROME, ST. OUEN. ON THE ROAD TO L'AIGLE

the vaguest idea as to what our future role was likely to be, the Falaise Pocket was being finally eliminated north of Argentan.

"Until the 17th of August there was a steady seep eastwards through the gap, but then came a convulsive surge to get out on the part of all ranks; and the orderliness with which the retreat had hitherto been carried out collapsed suddenly. The 12th S.S. Panzer Division, aided by other elements which had managed to escape, counter-attacked from outside the pocket to assist the remainder, but as the gap narrowed they were forced to abandon their efforts and look to their own safety as the advance of the Third Army to the Seine threatened a new trap behind them. All became chaos and confusion as the remaining forces in the pocket struggled to get out through the diminishing corridor by Trun, which was all that remained of the escape route. Road discipline among the columns fleeing towards the Seine became non-existent, and vehicles plunged madly across the open country in an effort to avoid the blocked roads. Our Air Forces swept down upon the choked masses of transport, and there was no sign of the Luftwaffe to offer any opposition. With the U.S. Third Army on the Seine, the German fighter force had been compelled to retire to airfields to the east of France, too far away for them to be able now to give any assistance to the ground troops in Normandy.

"Back inside the pocket the confusion was still greater, and the destruction assumed immense proportions as our aircraft and artillery combined in pounding the trapped Germans. Allied guns ringed the ever-shrinking 'killing ground,' and while the S.S. elements as usual fought to annihilation, the ordinary German infantry gave themselves up in ever-increasing numbers. By the 20th of August, the gap was finally closed near Chambois, and by the 22nd the pocket was eliminated. The lovely wooded countryside west of Argentan had become the graveyard of the army which, three months earlier, had confidently waited to smash the Allied invasion on the Normandy beaches. What was left of the Seventh and Fifth Panzer Armies was in headlong flight towards the Seine, and a further stand west of the river was impossible."[4]

★   ★   ★

For part of the way we shared the road, double banking with the Americans. We were on the famous *Red Ball* route, one of the main supply arteries feeding the U.S. Third Army to the Seine, and everyone was amazed at the speed at which their columns drove. For our part, we firmly retained the spacing and becoming dignity of a British column

---

4. *Report by the Supreme Commander to the Combined Chiefs of Staff on the Operations in Europe of the Allied Expeditionary Force, 6th June, 1944, to 8th May, 1945.* (H.M. Stationery Office)

on a peace march. The Americans may have been impressed at our road discipline, but as their lorries swept past us at breakneck speed we spent most of the time swallowing their dust.

Convoy after convoy of those six-wheeled lorries, endowed with magnificent acceleration and springing far surpassing that of our Fords and Bedfords, making light work of ruts and pot-holes, flashed by. Most of them were piloted by grinning negroes who had but the vaguest idea where they were going and cared less. And what was fascinating to behold was the rubber-like elasticity of their limbs as they drove, many with one leg dangling out of the cab window, the other on the accelerator pedal. No such "nonsense" as vehicle spacing and regulation halts for them. They simply raced flat out for the Seine, smoking large cigars.

★   ★   ★

At Flers the Regiment turned right in order to by-pass Briouze in a wide sweep to the south, thus avoiding for a time the congestion of American traffic flowing eastwards towards Argentan and L'Aigle. We reached St. Ouen-sur-Maire in the evening, there to harbour for the night.

The weather, which for the day had recovered to such an extent that the roads were again as dusty as ever, was now about to play false in earnest, and the break, bringing much rain, which was to last four days, came just at the wrong time. By this piece of bad luck for the Allies, the Germans were given the opportunity of shepherding what remained of their troops across the River Seine with comparatively little aerial interference.

30 Corps Headquarters was still on the move, and we did not yet know what was to be our jumping-off ground for operations. The advance was going so well that it was even impossible to forecast with accuracy when or where we should catch up. But it would certainly be a long way ahead, and with the knowledge that an early move before dawn would be the precursor of another tiring day's convoy march, the incautious were tempted to "get down to it" fully dressed. Two hours after dark the heavens opened, and these hapless people soon found themselves drenched to the skin.

Next morning, the 23rd of August, still somewhat damp and bedraggled, the Regiment pushed on to rejoin the main Paris road a few miles outside Argentan. The approaches were in a terrible state, and the town itself had sustained not only a heavy pounding from the air but also considerable damage from Allied artillery when the American and French troops had advanced to capture it from the south. Soon after leaving Argentan we met some of the latter in their Sherman tanks and American uniform, forming part of the French 2nd Armoured Division, which was being moved into position to take its place of honour in the liberation of Paris.

Since leaving Flers, the landscape had changed considerably, and the closeness of the bocage country had given way to a more rolling type of scenery, although still in parts interspersed with attractive hills and woodland. Gacé was reached in the early afternoon and the Regiment harboured in an orchard. For a brief spell, the sun came out and gave everyone the opportunity of drying their still sopping clothes and bedding.

★   ★   ★

When new orders arrived just before dusk it was clear that forward British units were losing touch with the enemy rear-guard, and, although sizeable pockets were still being mopped up along the line of advance, the main German body, aided by the weather, was obviously slipping away.

The Regiment was therefore given the task of combing the extensive area situated to the north of 30 Corps' line of advance, which was itself directed on the axis of L'Aigle—Evreux—Vernon, at which last place it was intended that 43rd Division should force a crossing of the Seine. This would take time and the plan was that, pending its execution, the Household Cavalry should fulfil the dual role of acting as flank guard to the Corps and at the same time mop up those stragglers who had failed to make their escape over the river.

The ultimate object of 30 Corps, once a crossing had been effected, was to establish two armoured divisions, Guards Armoured and 11th Armoured Divisions, in the area of Amiens—Arras. For this operation Guards Armoured Division, wisely occupied at the time in making the best of their well-earned rest, eating, and sleeping in the area of Conde-sur-Noireau many miles back, were to be brought forward.

Our own operation was to be based on L'Aigle. As it visualized what an American General aptly called "collecting real estate," three members of the French Maquis conversant with the local country were attached to each of the Sabre Squadrons. These were mostly local peasantry, claiming to be in touch with their "Intelligence," and fired by Gallic fervour for their work. They were given all our spare German hand grenades and surplus German rifles and ammunition which had begun to litter the back of every car. One member of the Maquis, a tiny little man, said that if the enemy caught him he would be shot on the spot as a *franc-tireur* because he had no uniform. He made this statement in no spirit of faint-heartedness, for strangely enough he appeared delighted at the risk. Major Ward, however, thought this hazard a trifle unnecessary and suggested that his own trio of Maquis should be given British denim overalls. But the stock sizes being for six-foot and over Household Cavalrymen, the three Maquis men were quite lost in them. To give the set-up a more authentic military touch, berets complete with badges were added. This gesture gave the Frenchmen great pleasure and their leader immediately asked to be enlisted in "La Cavalerie Royale" and be allowed to continue the war with us. They were given cigarettes and travelled for the most part in the Squadron medical cars, which was perhaps an even more flagrant breach of the Geneva Convention than Captain Kynaston's "Spartan" counter-attack. They soon made themselves at home and whenever I came across them, like true British soldiers, they were always eating. They were broken-hearted when, two days later, we had to leave them behind.

★   ★   ★

The night drive over the 23rd/24th of August to L'Aigle was a brute of a journey. The rain came down in torrential bursts, flooding through pistol ports and periscope joints and trickling down the necks of the disconsolate crews. There were no maps available, and, to cap everything, it followed that on a pitch-black night most of the column should lose itself and veer too far to the right. The town of L'Aigle had to be avoided owing to the chaos of its bombed communications, and it was past three o'clock in the morning when the last car rolled into harbour by the village of St. Symphorien des Bruyères.

As the Regiment was due to start operating at dawn, few men bothered to settle down to sleep, contenting themselves with dozing away the odd hour, crumpled up in the cab or turret. Now and again the roar of an engine starting up would mean that someone was warming himself or trying to dry clothes over the hot exhaust fumes streaming out of the Staghound's waterproofing breathers.

A.E.C. Armoured Car (MATADOR)

Chapter II

The Pheasant Drive

Disentangling formations—Large area north of L'Aigle to patrol—Rapid advance—Many prisoners—Contact made with Canadians, Americans and various Second Army formations—Lieutenant Jonkheer Groeninx van Zoelen's Troop reaches Elbeuf on the Seine—Captain Cooper's diary for the day—Return to St. Symphorien des Bruyères.

When the final collapse of the enemy on the Normandy front took place it tended, like the unexpected bursting open of a door, to precipitate the Allied formations forward in a headlong rush, and considerable sorting out was necessary.

The administrative problem alone of disentangling such numbers of formations must have been the cause of many a Staff officer's headache, for events were now moving so fast that few Headquarters even claimed to be up to date with the situation. They called it, with great presence of mind, a "Security Black-out."

Colonel Abel Smith was warned that his Regiment would be meeting not only the forward elements of 12 Corps and the Canadians on their way to the Seine farther north but also, on the right, those Americans (part of XV Corps) who were in the course of working their way downstream from Mantes Gassicourt towards Elbeuf—and across the British line of advance. To complicate matters further, there were still numerous elements of the American First Army (which had been engaged in the Argentan fighting) north of 30 Corps' line of advance, trying to redeploy and once more take up the running on the right.

A Troop Leader rightly summed up the next two days' operations over the 24th and 25th of August as "an odd mixture of Maquis, mines, collaborators, champagne, and shot-down Allied airmen."

★ ★ ★

The area to be patrolled was large. It extended in a north-easterly direction from L'Aigle to Conches, thence to Le Neuborg and westwards to Bernay; from there southwards to Broglie and back to L'Aigle. There was an obvious risk that converging Allied bodies might shoot one another up. For this reason all the available liaison officers had been already sent out: Captain Cooper to the Americans, Captain Balding to the Canadians, and Lieutenant Winterbottom, who since the return of Lieutenant the Hon. M. Eden from sick leave was spare, to 50th Division in the area of the Forêt de St. Evroult.

Two Troops of "D" Squadron, those of Lieutenants Hanbury and Younghusband, were held back at R.H.Q. in case of the need for additional liaison patrols.

Although it was a practice which he avoided whenever possible because it left him with no reserves, Colonel Abel Smith had this time, because of the area of operations, no alternative but to employ all four Sabre Squadrons simultaneously. These moved off half an hour before dawn from St. Symphorien des Bruyères. "D" were on the right, next to them "B," followed by "C," and "A" on the left.

From the outset "A" and "C" Squadrons were able to advance the more rapidly, for, naturally, what Germans still remained were fewer in numbers on the west. However, nearly all the roads were found to be obstructed by road-blocks of felled trees and mines, and these took time to clear. One report from a patrol leader read: "Am temporarily held up by a road-block in a forest ride; through my glasses I can count over thirty tree trunks down one behind the other."

★   ★   ★

"B" Squadron's route took them up the River Risles, which, because of the numerous obstructions on the way, troops were having to cross and re-cross continually. North-west of the town of Rugles, Corporal-of-Horse Johnson found himself halted by a newly blown bridge, covered in desultory fashion by a rear-guard. His crew set to work with great ingenuity to construct a new bridge of tree trunks and old planks, while the enemy discussed what they should do. Their doubts were soon put to rest, for very shortly the Troop moved over the makeshift structure, rounded up the Germans, and continued their advance northwards, cheered by the delighted French.

★   ★   ★

"C" Squadron continued to advance at speed, and after two armoured cars had been lost on mines near Beaumesnil[1], Major Herbert entered

---

1. Corporal-of-Horse Brown's armoured car (Lieutenant Paget's Troop) was trying to pass a German lorry which had blown up on one of its own mines. The Maquis thought that they had cleared a way through the minefield, but, with no proper instruments to check ground,

Bernay unopposed by one o'clock in the afternoon, there to join forces with British patrols from 12 Corps which had come in from the west.

★ ★ ★

Farther east along the line Conches—Beaumont-le-Roger, the other two Squadrons in turn met the armoured cars of the Royals (12 Corps), who informed them that they were heading for Louviers and Les Andelys.

The picture was now becoming clearer and forward troops concentrated their efforts on avoiding shooting and being shot up by their own side. There had already been some narrow squeaks. Still, we hoped that as long as the trigger-happy Typhoons were kept grounded —and thank goodness the clouds were low enough—all would be well from the air, at any rate.

★ ★ ★

Over to the west, Major Daly was in almost continuous contact with the Canadians, who initially had been most surprised to meet him there. From their reports it was clear that the main body of Germans had slipped away. Civilian stories of movement the previous night confirmed this—we were a half-day too late. The S.S. had ransacked the farms for food before escaping, and little else but the sick and the halt remained to do battle.

By midday there was a general tendency in all four Squadrons for Troops to lose their commanders on "Sunray Recces" when required at the wireless set—a sure sign that operations were not of a strenuous nature. Meanwhile the enthusiastic French dashed off on bicycles to scour the woods and lanes for prisoners. Their estimates of enemy still at large were fantastic, but they were desperately keen to do the right thing and be of help. The advance on the right flank was resumed with the sun shining fitfully between the rain clouds, and troops were thankful to find themselves moving through a country relatively untouched by war. As the day wore on, unproductive of any major occurrences, Squadrons combed the countryside in widening sweeps, and prisoners rolled in by their hundreds.

---

must have left one behind. Corporal-of-Horse Brown's car was completely wrecked, but, thanks to the heavy sandbagging, only Trooper R. F. Holman, the driver, was wounded by his knee striking the steering wheel. Captain Wrottesley's Troop then arrived on the scene, tried a lane to the right of the wreckage and also struck mines, Trooper E. J. Shanley being seriously wounded.

"D" Squadron Headquarters found an intact but overturned travelling workshop near the village of Sébécourt. Round it the civilians were clustering like flies about a honeypot, carrying off its tools and instruments. With our coffers already full of loot, slight qualms of conscience made us feel that Captain Hudson might like to have some for his L.A.D. crew, and we sent back a message to Regimental Headquarters. For once they too seemed to be badly affected by postprandial lethargy. The Colonel was away to another unit, the Adjutant was unavailable, the Intelligence Officer was resting, and Lieutenant the Hon. M. Eden answered in the majestic intonation of a Gladstonian orator that he thought it best, "after due consideration, to leave well alone." A French blacksmith was waiting inquiringly for our answer, so we said "oui", and he made off with his selection—a basket of hammers, a pair of fire-tongs and three large steel balls!

In just appreciation of the situation, the Americans encountered were patrolling with no more than one reconnaissance car out in front (the Greyhound six-wheeler), followed closely by convoys of lorries for their prisoners. They were most helpful and took all our captives as well. They were said to be aiming to make Paris that day, for, as one G.I. announced, "Our Colonel is sure bursting to sample its night life without delay."

Many Allied airmen who had been shot down by the Germans and then rescued and sheltered by the French were picked up during the course of the day. They were loud in praise of their hosts and the risks they had undergone on their behalf. In fact, one young Pilot Officer discovered by "B" Squadron was so grateful to the French family which had looked after him that he had to be almost forcibly persuaded to come before he could tear himself away from the farmer's pretty daughter who had hidden him.

★   ★   ★

Meanwhile Lieutenant Buchanan-Jardine's Troop had made contact with the Americans and Captain Cooper to the west of Sébécourt at a village called Louversey. From them it was learnt that their forward troops were well to the north and advancing towards Elbeuf along the banks of the Seine. They wished to pull out some of their troops from the Conches area, and so it was arranged that "D" Squadron should take over responsibility here. At the same time Lieutenant Jonkheer Groeninx van Zoelen's Troop was ordered to resume the advance northwards towards Elbeuf via Beaumont le Roger and effect another link up with the Americans. He moved fast, met a group of released Dutchmen ("who seemed to know all about my past life") at Beaumont le Roger, and pushed on. When nearing Elbeuf, within a mile of the Seine, he came upon American infantry and light armour engaged in a spirited battle with the largest force of Germans yet encountered in the course of the day's operations. The Americans formed part of a detachment of XV Corps and confirmed that they had come from Mantes Gassicourt. This was the first definite information received by 30 Corps that the Americans were so far north, and really completed the picture which the Regiment had set out to obtain. Shortly afterwards these same irrepressible Americans had begun to move west from Elbeuf, when they shot at, and fortunately missed, Lieutenant Palmer's Troop in the half-light at Le Neuborg.

As usual, Captain Cooper had found no shortage of material with which to fill the pages of his daily diary.

"…we are fifteen miles in front of the British front line—a few Germans holding out in a wood nearby; we fired a few shots, killing two and wounding one, and 28 more surrendered without firing a shot. They were nearly all Poles, Russians, and Czechs, and they said that the whole battalion wanted to surrender, but a few S.S. with them put a stop to that. Decided to try to find Rupert Jardine, Jackie's leading Troop, and met him near Conches with an American patrol. They had just shot up a German anti-tank gun at the cross-roads at St. Martin. The French are now rising properly and are armed to the teeth with new weapons dropped by parachute and are riding with us on the cars. We've given them a lot of grenades. I have a man with me wearing a French tin helmet, Life Guards badge, battledress trousers and a bathing-dress top with the usual French resistance armband. They beat up the woods and shoot the Germans on sight. Just heard that the enemy are holding out in a farm at Sébécourt, so attacked it with an army of about fifteen Maquis—the Germans left by the back entrance and surrendered to a party of Americans who came up on the other road. Rupert Jardine has a splendid man riding with him on his Daimler with grenades hanging all over him. Three Germans have been left in the wood where they were shot last night by the French. One died during the night, and we eventually persuaded some French women to look after the other two. It began to rain again like hell, and we had some food in a house at Louversey, where Rupert had to make a road-block. By this time all the cars have been covered with the most wonderful flowers and flags. There was a knocked-out German gun at the corner of the house and two dead horses. In spite of the rain some corn is on fire. The Americans are everywhere and great fraternization goes on with our men. The American supplies are endless and the French civilians are doing well. Back into Conches that night—the rain has stopped and the people are so thick on the streets we cannot get along.

> Much kissing and jumping on cars. Arrived back at American H.Q. at midnight. The Americans have given us endless cigarettes and chewing-gum. They are very cheerful, extremely efficient in their way, and go like hell. Very tired, very hot, large whisky and bed."

One of the last messages to come through to Regimental Headquarters as they were slipping into their bed-rolls for the night gives some indication of the chaos which must have reigned within the German formations. It was from "C" Squadron and addressed to an already harassed Intelligence Officer: "How and why do you expect us to classify three Mongols and four captured Turks? We already have over seventy prisoners of mixed breeds and colours and still no transport to send them back to you for interrogation".

Next morning Colonel Abel Smith visited his Squadrons in turn. Delighted at the way things were going, he was nevertheless convinced that there was now no need for the Regiment to be in operation, and he soon obtained permission to withdraw everybody to St. Symphorien des Bruyères.

The day's operations were to close on a rather nice note. Captain Waterhouse, ardent subscriber to the British school of thought that "abroad ought to be abolished," was lifted bodily off his feet by an enormous bearded Frenchman and rapturously kissed on both cheeks to the cry of "Vive notre brave petit liberateur!"

★   ★   ★

Two days of rest followed and maintenance of vehicles was brought up to date. Soon the scout cars were speeding over the countryside on vague official missions of a generally non-military character. Some visited L'Aigle to see if the damage was really as great as it had appeared to be when we had passed through the outskirts at night. It was a pleasant surprise to find that the destruction, although heavy, was confined to the area of the railway station and main line. The old twelfth-century church of St. Martin had been hit but not irreparably damaged. The Dauphin Hotel in the Place Halle, looking as if it might have been a German headquarters, still had a pre-war notice pinned to its doorway, faded but readable: "Specialités; Escargots de Bourgogne, Filets de Sole Normande, Escalope de veau maison—garage gratuit." It was, alas, closed for the duration.

Lieutenant Ainsworth and I drove to Conches and tried to forget the war there. We walked round the old Norman keep, and sat outside a little café, imbibing watery beer. The Germans had taken much of the food, but the children looked rosily healthy and smiled their thanks when we fed them on N.A.A.F.I. chocolate.

As we motored through the well-kept forest rides we were struck by the vast quantity of shells and mortar bombs stacked in avenues under the trees. None of it had been destroyed and its loss to the enemy must have been crippling.

The Germans and war now seemed very far away, and little disturbed our pleasant lethargy in the harbour fields. Indeed, the only untoward occurrence took place when peace was shattered by the roar of a Heavy Troop's 75-mm. gun fired off in error. This oversight, labelled "Incident near L'Aigle," resulted in the unfortunate trooper concerned retiring to England with a wrist badly shattered by the recoil and acid comments from Lieutenant Ainsworth, between whose legs (so he swore) the armour-piercing shot had ricochetted before flying off harmlessly into the blue.

There was a large lake close at hand on which the Germans had left a wooden raft. This stretch of water was surrounded by trees and covered with water lilies. It was very hot and the spot soon attracted a party from R.H.Q., who decided on the spur of the moment to indulge in the luxury of a bathe. Everyone had been badly bitten by ants and harvest bugs, and the sight of Major Sir Peter Grant Lawson, Captain Cooper and Lieutenants the Hon. M. Eden and Muir Turnbull disporting themselves in the nude like so many water sprites stricken with measles held a large mixed audience of villagers spellbound for hours.

Ford 3-Ton Lorry Driver

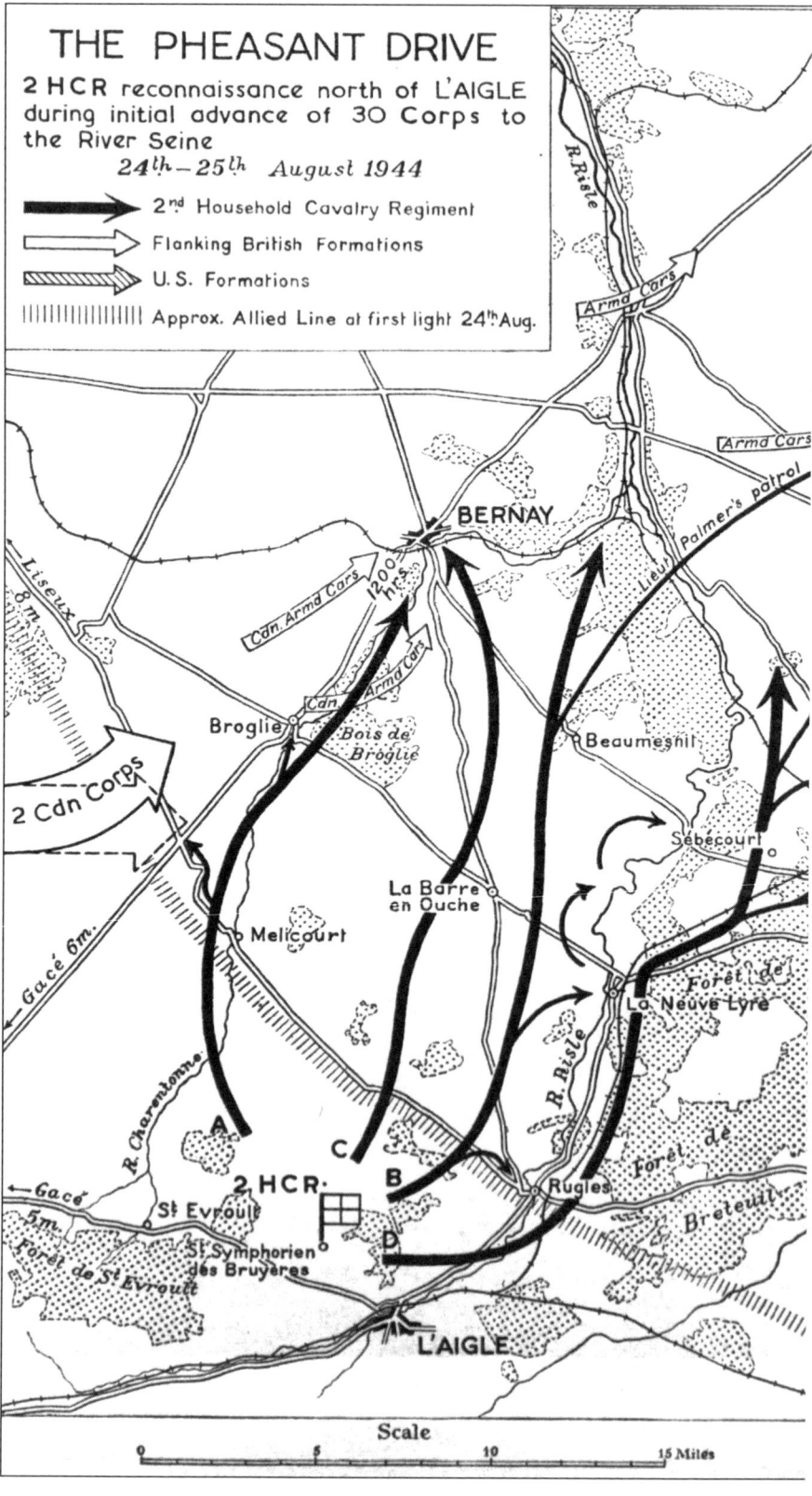

THE PHEASANT DRIVE

2 HCR reconnaissance north of L'AIGLE during initial advance of 30 Corps to the River Seine

24ᵗʰ – 25ᵗʰ August 1944

- ➤ 2ⁿᵈ Household Cavalry Regiment
- ➤ Flanking British Formations
- ➤ U.S. Formations
- ||||||||||||||| Approx. Allied Line at first light 24ᵗʰ Aug.

R. Risle

Armd Cars

Armd Cars

Lieut. Palmer's patrol

BERNAY

Liseux
8 m.

Cdn. Armd Cars

1200 hrs.

Cdn. Armd Cars

Cdn.
Broglie

Bois de
Broglie

Beaumesnil

2 Cdn Corps

Sébécourt

Gacé 6 m.

La Barre
en Ouche

Melicourt

R. Risle

Forêt de
La Neuve Lyre

R. Charentonne

A

C

B

Rugles

Forêt de

← Gacé
5 m.

2 HCR.

St Evroult

St Symphorien
des Bruyères

D

de Breteuil

Forêt de St. Evroult

L'AIGLE

Scale

0   5   10   15 Miles

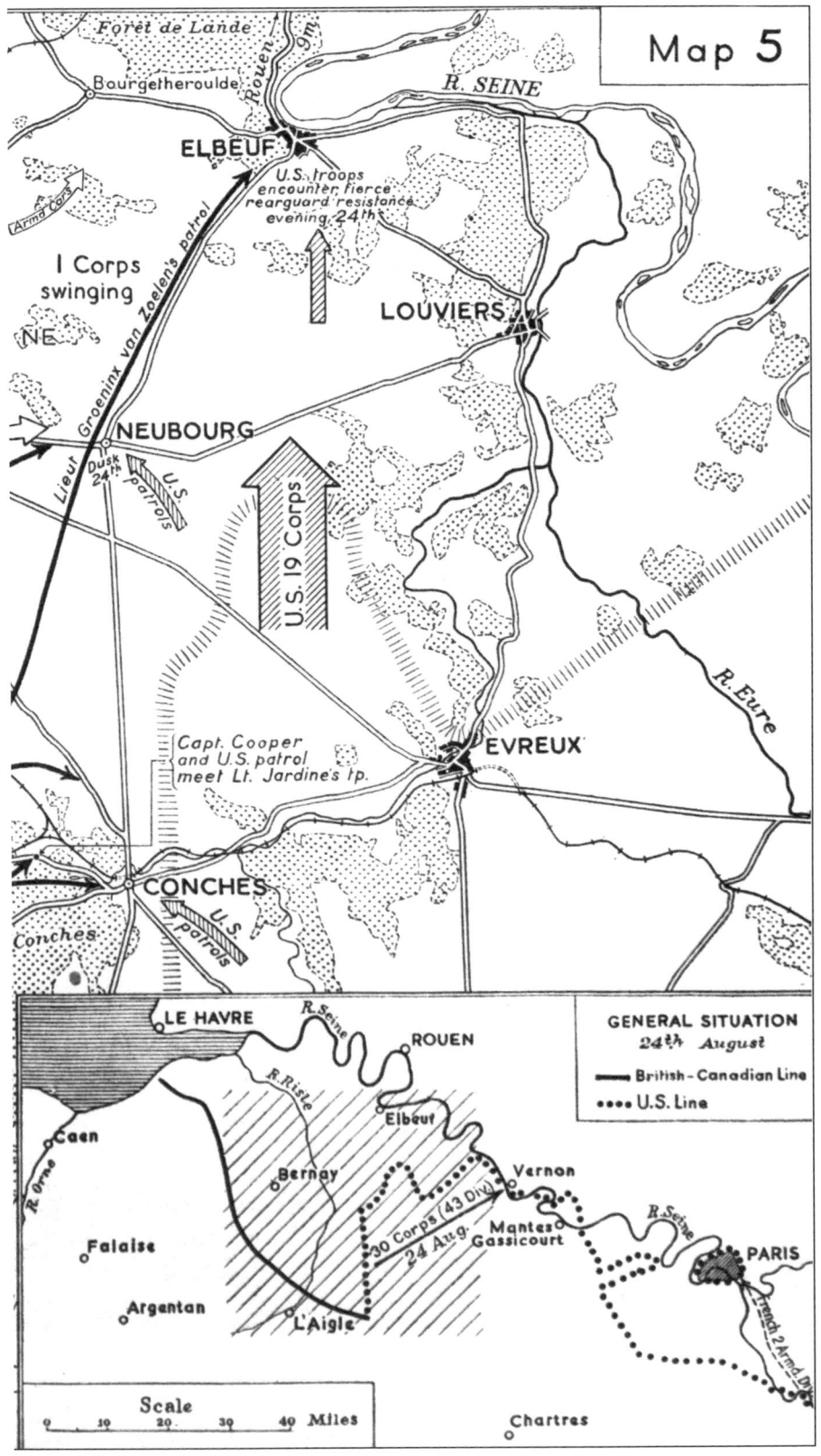

Map 5

Forêt de Lande

Bourgetheroulde

Rouen 9m.

R. SEINE

ELBEUF

U.S. troops encounter fierce rearguard resistance evening 24th

I Corps swinging

NE

Armd Corps

Lieut. Groeninx van Zoelen's patrol

LOUVIERS

NEUBOURG

Dusk 24th

U.S. patrols

U.S. 19 Corps

Capt. Cooper and U.S. patrol meet Lt. Jardine's tp.

EVREUX

R. Eure

CONCHES

U.S. patrols

Conches

GENERAL SITUATION
24th August

——— British-Canadian Line
•••• U.S. Line

LE HAVRE

R. Seine

ROUEN

R. Risle

Elbeut

Caen

R. Orne

Bernay

Vernon

30 Corps (43 Div)
24 Aug.

Mantes
Gassicourt

R. Seine

PARIS

Falaise

Argentan

L'Aigle

French 2 Armd Div

Scale
0   10   20   30   40 Miles

Chartres

Chapter III

"Faith," "Hope" and "Charity"

Move to the Seine under command of 11th Armoured Division—Across the river prepared to operate under command of Guards Armoured Division—Corps Commander's concern at danger of being hemmed in on narrow bridgehead—Reconnoitring crossings of River Epte and other operations with 8th Armoured Brigade—Good initial progress by 11th Armoured Division towards Amiens—Gisors—"A" Squadron (Lieutenant Routledge's Troop) held up by 88-mms—Regiment prepares to harbour short of Beauvais for night—Orders to seize "Faith," "Hope" and "Charity"—Night dash to the Somme—Colonel Abel Smith's problem of communications—Bad wireless reception—Lieutenant Hanbury's Troop seizes the bridge at Corbie—Grenadier Guards relieve "A" and "D" Squadrons, but Lieutenant Jonkheer Groeninx van Zoelen's Troop has to hold "Charity" for another night—Trooper Wood shoots down German from tree when in the act of blowing "Faith"—Further notes from Captain Cooper's diary for the day

The rest period was soon over, and on the 28th of August, at six o'clock in the morning, under command of 11th Armoured Division for movement only, the Regiment drove off to a concentration area at St. Vincent des Bois—three miles west of Vernon—arriving at four o'clock in the afternoon. The route[1] was a long, grinding convoy drive, with interminable halts and, noted a driver lax in his road spacing, "unfortunately the Adjutant kept turning up at unexpected places."

Meanwhile 43rd Division had established their bridgehead over the Seine at Vernon and, in conformity with the general plan, 11th Armoured Division prepared to pass through them. To aid 11th Armoured Division in their task of advancing towards Amiens, and while awaiting the arrival of Guards Armoured Division, 8th Armoured Brigade had been placed temporarily under their command.

The Regiment was now actually under command of Guards Armoured Division, for operational purposes, but as the latter were still a long way back, coming up on tank transporters, there was to be no move from the concentration area at St. Vincent des Bois until the morrow.

Next morning, after hours of steady downpour had resulted in the cars bogging themselves up to the axle hubs in the chalky soil of the harbour area, we moved into Vernon and up to the Seine bridge.

---

1. Route: St. Symphorien des Bruyères—L'Aigle—Breteuil—Damville—Pacy-sur-Eure—Vernon.

More delays caused by the traffic gave us time to study the river at close quarters. This had been by far the most difficult water obstacle for the Sappers to overcome since landing in Normandy. The road bridge lay a tangled mass of steel girders round which the waters of the Seine swirled.

The first regimental troops to cross the pontoon bridge were those of "B" Squadron. They were due to operate immediately, but there was a dense traffic jam on the far side and the leading vehicles were to take four hours to do as many miles.

Enforced halts on the pitching pontoon gave those who followed ample time to study the opposite bank. The steeply rising chalk cliffs looming out of the drizzle bore signs that the passage of 43rd Division had by no means been unopposed.

On the river one or two assault boats were stuck half-way across on submerged islands and bobbed and swung against the centre pier of the wrecked bridge, gathering the usual interesting debris of a French river on their bows.

The rain was now torrential and visibility down to fifty yards, but as the bridgehead perimeter was still very constricted there was nothing to do but to wait in patience.

In an interview given to the Press later on, General Horrocks stated that at the time he had been greatly concerned lest he should find his Corps hemmed in in a narrow bridgehead and unable to deploy. For this reason, not only had 11th Armoured Division been pushed through early on, as we have read, but it had been allotted 8th Armoured Brigade as well. The latter was to advance on the right of 11th Armoured Division to protect its right flank until the arrival of Guards Armoured Division, for ultimately the advance north-east was to be carried out two armoured divisions up. As events turned out, it was to be on the right that opposition proved most stubborn, and for a time 8th Armoured Brigade's advance was keenly contested. To this flank we now turn our attention.

While the Regiment had been moving across the Seine, Colonel Abel Smith had been back along the centre line to meet Major-General Adair, who had flown forward with his two Brigadiers to find out the situation and give out his orders. Pending the arrival of Guards Armoured Division, the Regiment was to operate with 8th Armoured Brigade and also reconnoitre the crossings of the River Epte as far north as the bridge at Dangu inclusive. The Epte flows in a southerly direction from Gournay and Gisors to enter the Seine just below Vernon.

The rain had changed to a fine mist when Major Wignall slipped his first Troops through the bridgehead. After encountering considerable resistance at Bray, which was to hold up the tanks of 8th Armoured Brigade for a time, "B" Squadron was able to push on and confirm that the enemy had blown all the bridges up to Dangu. However, these delaying tactics aided the enemy but little, for the Americans (2nd Armoured Division), who had crossed the Seine farther south, were working up the east bank of the Epte and parallel to "B" Squadron's line of march. Thus, taken in their flanks, the Germans had no choice but to withdraw as quickly as possible. Seeing what was happening, Major Wignall ordered his Troops to cross the first intact bridge and chase up the enemy tail, but his first patrol had no sooner engaged the German rear-guard than it found itself also embroiled with the American advance columns. This time the Americans were adamant about their right of way and insisted from the Divisional Commander downwards that it belonged to them. Considering that entire armies had been swinging and gyrating in one another's paths since the Falaise break-through, it was extraordinary that such a contretemps had not occurred before. The mix-up was in no way due to the troops on the spot, and in fact only a last-minute adjustment of the Anglo-American Army boundary enabled Guards Armoured Division's centre line eventually to run through Tournai and Brussels. Previous to this the projected British thrust was aimed farther north, missing out the Belgian capital entirely. What historic scenes might we thus have missed but for the stroke of a chinagraph pencil![2]

"C" Squadron had also to some extent become entangled with the Americans, and in one place Lieutenant Hopkinson was forced to halt his Troop to try to sort things out. A stream of vehicles belonging to U.S. 2nd Armoured Division was flowing at right angles to his line of advance. The Troop Leader stopped the first person he saw. "We were all talking to a little fellow with a mackintosh whom we thought to be the driver of a jeep. We were interested in his crystal-controlled wireless set and asked him how it worked. He gave us all the information in the friendliest way, plus a cup of coffee each. When the rain stopped he took off his mackintosh and we saw that he was a full Colonel commanding the tank brigade, which he was doing from his two jeeps only, with no more than the help of a couple of motorcyclists. The whole thing was most amusing to us, but he had everything absolutely taped. Later on we were to meet him again at Hasselt and Rochefort in Belgium."

By the time a new route could be sorted out and troops disentangled, it was dark and the advance had halted for the night. But although 8th

---

2. See alteration of forward boundaries mentioned in Montgomery's *Normandy to the Baltic*, page 126, para. 4. (Hutchinson & Co.)

Armoured Brigade had been held up in the area of Dangu and Vesley, the left flank of the advance had made significant progress. There was news that elements of 11th Armoured Division had been reported as far forward as the village of Longchamps. Yet more startling developments were to come from that quarter next day.

During the night, Guards Armoured Division began to cross the Seine, and by early next morning, the 30th of August, they were complete on the other side. At the same time, the Regiment was to continue its advance, covering 8th Armoured Brigade's front. On the right "B" Squadron, with a certain amount of good-natured abuse on both sides, were still laboriously contesting the right of way up the east bank of the Epte towards Gisors with the Americans.

On the left, however, along the other road, considerable progress was being made by "A" Squadron. Before ten o'clock they had stormed through the town of Gisors to thunders of applause from its joyful citizens. Here, "D" Squadron, who were following up, saw an old Frenchman in a beret and button boots chasing "collaboratrices" with a rusty cavalry sword of Franco-Prussian vintage. Swept on by the *élan* of the advance, few cars witnessed the climax of the old boy's efforts, but one of the three-tonner drivers said later that he saw him, puffing and blowing, at the corner of the street and wiping his blade on a handkerchief!

Once through Gisors, the advance forked on to two routes, that on the right leading to Beauvais along the main road, the other on the left to Lallandelle. Opposition at first was slight and the armoured cars progressed rapidly, leaving small pockets of enemy to be mopped up later on.

Things were going so smoothly that Beauvais appeared to be a certainty by mid-afternoon. Then almost simultaneously strong rearguards were bumped at Auneuil and Ossembray. At the former place, 1 Troop, "A" Squadron (Lieutenant Routledge), overtook the German tail on a long S bend winding down a steep wooded slope to the village at the bottom. The place was cunningly chosen as an ambush, and two 88-mm. guns, one fitted to an S.P. chassis, lay hidden up in the undergrowth. The first scout car saw nothing as it nosed forward over the brow of a reverse slope and was hit at point-blank range. The commander, Corporal Alistair Hoddinott, and his driver, Trooper Ronald Littler, were both killed outright and the car burst into flames.

Lieutenant Routledge, although unable to locate the gun hidden in the undergrowth, tried to manoeuvre his car to the side of the road and cover the burning scout car with his Bren gun in case either of the crew were still alive, but his own vehicle was immediately hit by the S.P. gun, and crashed into a ditch. Corporal-of-Horse Corton then brought up his armoured car, and under cover of its smoke both Lieutenant Routledge and his driver, Trooper Smith, were able to crawl back out of range. The two German guns, together with some infantry, commanded the only direct approach to Beauvais, and these subsequently engaged the 13th / 18th Hussars, who had followed up close behind, in some sharp fighting, resulting in the loss of several of their tanks and considerable delay before the enemy was finally overcome.

The hard-pressed Germans were nevertheless in no fit state to make an effective stand on more than one road at a time, and "D" Squadron, who had now taken over the running, moved north-west with the object of entering Beauvais from the west. Contact was soon made with the Inns of Court Regiment, whose leading vehicles were already well on the road to Amiens. From them it was learnt that their patrols were beyond Marseilles-en-Beauvais and going strong. Shortly afterwards, at about five o'clock in the afternoon, the tanks of 4th/7th Dragoon Guards, approaching Beauvais from the west, stormed into the town, and after a sharp bout of street fighting the place was theirs.

This was extremely good news, for the southerly entrance to the town by the main road, along which it had been planned to pass elements of 11th Armoured Division as well as, later, the Guards Armoured Division, was still denied us by the Germans holding out at Auneuil.

★   ★   ★

The incidents of the next twenty-four hours were to be as dramatic as any the Regiment was ever to experience. Individual impressions may vary, but none will forget them, and when all else has faded, three names, "Faith," "Hope" and "Charity," will surely conjure up to old 2nd Household Cavalrymen a vivid picture of a wild and blustering night, an unearthly gallop along poplar-fringed roads, waking villages and fleeing Germans, and a final panting finish to save three fragile but vital bridges from destruction.

It is perhaps best to visualize the opening scene first from the angle of the forward squadrons and then return for a while to Regimental Headquarters.

As the two Squadrons which had operated throughout the day prepared to snatch a few hours' sleep before resuming the advance, the situation was believed by them to be as follows: That the enemy who at any moment might withdraw were still definitely holding up the tanks of Guards Armoured Division on the main road.³ That to the west, 11th Armoured Division were well on their way towards Amiens, having been given orders to establish themselves north-west of Beauvais, ensuring that their tail was well clear of the town so that Guards Armoured Division, who were scheduled to pass through on the morrow, might have an unimpeded run. Furthermore, that "B" and "C" Squadrons, positioned at the western approaches to Beauvais, were well placed to lead the advance when it should be resumed.

Whatever was to be, "A" and "D" Squadrons, who had recently been operating, felt justified in the assumption that they would not be called upon to operate until morning. Armoured divisions are by their nature averse to night work. They were to learn once more the lesson that in war nothing is ever certain.

"D" Squadron were harboured on some high ground to the west of Beauvais.

> "The rain was torrential. We had jogged along sometimes in convoy, sometimes carrying out patrols, at other times had indulged in brief skirmishes with the enemy. We were very tired.
>
> "I remember passing the most lovely château, high up on a hill—a graceful white group against a background of green trees. Also a strange farm by the side of a river and another castle, turreted at the corners and containing a courtyard, quite charming. Then another lovely village with the most enormous spireless church of intricate Gothic tracery— an amazing example of medieval workmanship. Then we ran into six German tanks near Beauvais and spent the first part of the night there.
>
> "After midnight we were warned that we might have to make an emergency night drive to the Somme. We waited for what seemed hours, wet and shivering, before being called in for 'Troop Leaders' Orders.' Rupert and I were to be the leading Troops."⁴

The Heavy Troop (Lieutenant I. M. Clark's) was preparing a meal before settling down to rest.

> "We had harboured at about nine o'clock at night in a field on a piece of high ground whence it was possible to see vehicles burning and guns

---

3. 8th Armoured Brigade had by now been withdrawn into reserve.
4. Diary of Lieutenant Jonkheer Groeninx van Zoelen. He loved the continent of Europe and all that its past glories stood for, and probably suffered more mental anguish than any other member of the Regiment to see the inevitable destruction of so many of its old buildings and customs. The diary which he kept of the doings of his Troop is interspersed with architectural commentaries, mentally noted as he reconnoitred for Panthers and Tigers with his mind back in the splendours of the seventeenth and eighteenth centuries.

flashing in the outskirts of Beauvais. Everybody's temper was ragged as we had had a wearying day of indecisive movement, partly in reserve, and now it had started to rain again. It always seemed to rain on these occasions. To make matters worse, the orders we received sounded quite fantastic. 'As soon as Beauvais is sufficiently clear, "D" Squadron will pass through, march by night to the line of the Somme and seize three bridges east of Amiens by 0800 hours, 31st of August.' These orders were not received with joy!"

Major Bowes Daly's Squadron, "A" had been withdrawn slightly and was harboured near the village of La Houssoye on the main road south-west of Auneuil. His troops also hoped that they were in for a few hours' rest. Lieutenant Franklin wrote:

"We were rather tired and only too glad when the order came over the air recalling us to Squadron Headquarters. We set off for home and found the harbour by asking for 'Major Daly?' 'Oh, Major Daly's found a stud farm down the road, as you would expect, sir,' replied a trooper, and in the dark I parked the cars and went off for orders. There was nothing yet. 'Good, a day's rest tomorrow.' I had just got into my bed-roll, after we had all eaten, when came the cry of, 'Troop Leaders for orders.' Out of bed and groping for a torch and over to the Squadron Leader's tent. Major Daly was poring over a map, smoking a cigar, and beside him a large tumbler of port. 'We must push on through the night,' he said. There was no sleep."

★　★　★

Back at Regimental Headquarters there was hectic activity, and to understand exactly what had happened it is necessary to go back to the village of St. Germer, where, at five o'clock in the evening, lay the Headquarters of 11th Armoured Division. Here, General Horrocks had met his Divisional Commander, General Roberts, and ordered a night march on Amiens. The reason for this snap order was that the good progress made by the armour on the left flank suggested that the enemy had collapsed on this front and was retreating in disorder to beyond the Somme. Amiens was still, at five o'clock in the afternoon, some thirty miles away from the leading troops, and so it was a bold undertaking. The problem of supply would be difficult. March tables had to be revised; units rearranged and changed over while still in contact with the enemy, and their various echelons brought forward many hours ahead of schedule and along packed roads. Wisely, it was decided to carry out the advance as far as possible by daylight, then halt for a fill up with petrol. The plan worked well and by nightfall the leading 11th Armoured Division unit had reported that it was beyond Crévecoeur, twenty miles short of Amiens.

But the rapid advance of the armour on the left flank had in no way altered the main plan of establishing both armoured divisions north of the Somme in the general area, Amiens—Arras—Doullens. On the contrary, it had encouraged the hope that, given normal luck, the time-table might be speeded up. The difficulties confronting Guards Armoured Division were, if anything, even greater than those of 11th Armoured Division. Firstly, they were still echeloned many miles back, having marched some hundred miles in slow columns for the past twenty-four hours. Secondly, to move forward they would initially be compelled to use the narrow roads of the western loop into Beauvais. In addition, the head of their column at Auneuil and the tail of 8th Armoured Brigade, still withdrawing into reserve, would have to keep out of each other's way.

Regimental Headquarters had remained on the escarpment above Vernon awaiting the arrival of Tactical Headquarters of Guards Armoured Division. Shortly after five o'clock in the afternoon "A" and "D" Squadrons were warned to be prepared to withdraw into reserve, whilst "B" and "C" Squadrons, who had not been employed that day, were ordered to move up to join the head of 5th Brigade (Guards Armoured Division) in order to be ready to resume the advance next day.

At eight o'clock in the evening there was still no news of Tactical Headquarters of Guards Armoured Division, and wireless conditions were becoming more and more difficult. Colonel Abel Smith therefore decided to move Regimental Headquarters forward to the area of Advance Headquarters, 30 Corps, in order to ease the communications problem with the forward Squadrons and also to receive orders for the next day's advance.

It was a very dark night. Captain Ford was warned to meet Regimental Headquarters when it reached the area of Corps Headquarters near Gisors, which it did just before midnight.

Colonel Abel Smith went straight to the operations tent, where the B.G.S. gave out the following orders:

> "2nd Household Cavalry Regiment will capture three bridges over the River Somme at Sailly-Laurette, Corbie and Vecquemont by 0800 hours today [it was then past midnight and therefore 31st of August]. The bridges will be known as 'Faith', Hope' and 'Charity.' Move at once as 5th Brigade have been ordered to advance at 0200 hours."

The problem for Colonel Abel Smith to solve was a difficult one. Before their withdrawal into reserve, "A" Squadron had been involved with the enemy; "D" Squadron was well north-east of Gisors. There was no reason to believe that the enemy had withdrawn from this sector. Unless "C" and "B" Squadrons could be got on the move immediately they would be cut off by the advance of 5th Brigade before they could leave their harbour area.

Wireless reception for the Regiment at Corps Headquarters was very difficult owing to the interference of the latter's high-power sets. Regimental Headquarters were therefore moved to the nearest high ground, where even their communication was difficult and it was getting on for one o'clock in the morning before the orders eventually bellowed through by Captain Collins were finally acknowledged by Squadrons.[5]

The task in hand was so important that Colonel Abel Smith decided to insure against failure of either "C" or "B" Squadrons being able to get through 5th Brigade, by calling upon both "A" and "D" Squadrons to advance at once and to move well behind the tail of 11th Armoured Division, whose continued good progress on the left had been confirmed by Captain Cooper. When clear of the line on which the Germans had been standing at dusk they were to swing east to the bridges. As events proved, it was a wise decision. Major Herbert, whose "C" Squadron had acknowledged receipt of orders in record time, had jumped for the road, then halted to put his Troops in the picture, only to find himself hopelessly mixed up with the tanks, and "A" and "D" Squadrons, slightly better placed by circumstances, moved in, got clear of the tanks, and were to show them a clean pair of heels to the Somme.

There are many stories in existence, ranging from the factually prosaic to the higher flights of journalese, regarding the reactions of commanders to this memorable night's events, but all are agreed that the Corps Commander, quite undeterred by the appalling weather conditions, encouraged his subordinates with the same words he is said to have used to General Roberts on a similar occasion in Tunisia: "There's moonlight tonight." He omitted to add, however, that this time there would be no guiding stars and limitless African horizon, but a leaden sky filled with rain and scudding clouds. No General relishes moving his armour at night, especially when the territory to be traversed still happens to be in enemy hands, however disorganized. But, said the Corps Commander, "I could smell that it was all right. Sometimes you sniff the air and it doesn't smell right, but this time it smelt right."

★ ★ ★

---

5. This effort was rightly described as "the Adjutant's greatest shouting triumph".

And so, with nothing but the red mesmeric glow of tail lights to illumine the way, the two Squadrons set off, "D" in the lead, "A" close behind them.

The fears held at Regimental Headquarters that the armoured cars might not be able to get through were only too well founded. There were tanks and lorries head to tail practically into Beauvais. Never was there such a night of mutual cursing and bumping and boring, but at last the two Squadrons shook themselves clear. Their route until reaching Breteuil was to be the same, then "A" Squadron would deploy to the west and follow the line of the stream called the Noye, which flows into the Somme east of Amiens.

The map section at Army may perhaps have been caught on the wrong foot by the rapidity of the advance, for we were all short of large-scale maps to cover the run to the Somme, and much depended on the initiative of the Troop Leaders and the co-operation of the local inhabitants.

A night march through enemy territory is at the best of times a tense affair. The drivers peer out of their visors, intent on avoiding falling asleep or landing in the ditch. The car commanders also stare ahead, trying to penetrate the gloom for signs of the enemy and check-ups on the right route. The operators live in a strange world of their own at the bottom of the turret, tormented by crackles and demoniac wireless noises while map boards and chinagraph pencils drop on to their heads. Gunners grip the trigger mechanism as much for support as anything else, for they are almost blind at night. Over everyone the desire for sleep descends in recurrent and overpowering waves.

★ ★ ★

To begin with, No. 1 Troop (Lieutenant Jonkheer Groeninx van Zoelen) was in the lead. On the outskirts of Beauvais, two lorries burnt fiercely. The town itself appeared to be endless. The lanterns of the F.F.I. flickered on and off. The column turned into the main square and Corporal Wilson's scout car, driven by Trooper Osborne, almost collided with what in the dark "looked like the biggest tank we had ever seen." It was a deserted Panther. There were a few infantry outposts about, but I remember they could give us no idea of what was the situation ahead of them, and they disappeared into the darkness.

After a halt to check the route, the column moved off once more. Occasionally there came a break in the scudding clouds and for a brief moment the immensely high outline of Beauvais Cathedral was visible as it towered above us. Then the rain lashed across our faces and all but the shadowy bulk of the preceding vehicle was lost to sight. Soon the leading cars found themselves on the concrete runway of an abandoned Luftwaffe aerodrome. It was pitted with bomb craters and the wreckage of fighter planes. By the light of a burnt house, still glowing red like a huge Chinese lantern, the leader corrected himself, turned about and was off again. As we in turn passed the house, one saw through the windowless holes into its shell. Inside was an inferno of heat and iron bedsteads and the overpowering smell of burnt flesh.

A few miles farther on the road was blocked by a tangle of blazing vehicles pulled across our path. It smelt of the booby-trap and mine and because of the heat was difficult to approach. Eventually, by pulling and pushing, the debris was cleared sufficiently to allow the column to scrape past, which it did for the loss of Corporal-of-Horse Royston's entire kit, which was swept off into the flames.

Farther on another road-block of old farm wagons and barbed wire once more held up the column, but it was not covered by enemy fire and only the trees swayed back and forth to shower the nerve-tautened soldiers with a fine spray from their leaves. Next came a supposedly abandoned Mark IV tank at the side of the road, which later proved to be alive; the exhausted crew had fallen asleep in the ditch and had not been noticed.

Dark enemy figures flitted across the countryside. They were ignored—the objective lay ahead and time was pressing. It was strange that, for all the throbbing of the engines and the crackle of the wireless, the general silence was uncanny. Few words were spoken and everyone peered intently into the darkness.

Sometimes there would be a halt while the crew of a scout car investigated a suspicious shape which would prove to be nothing more harmful than an old cart or heap of manure. Even the trees could simulate the barrel of an 88-mm. with startling realism, and at one time a section of the Support Troop was bundled out of its White scout car prepared for an action which petered out inconclusively after three inquisitive cart horses had been nearly shot.

Slow at first, for the roads were narrow and the risk of blocking the entire Squadron by an early mishap at the front was considerable, the tempo of advance quickened, "until back at Regimental Headquarters, it seemed as if the pace became terrific."

Villages began to slip by. Most of the inhabitants realized that the British had crossed the Seine and were on their way forward, but none had imagined that they could be arriving so soon and in the middle of the night. They believed that the Germans were still passing through and not many stirred from their beds. But occasionally a keen-eared

Frenchman would detect the difference between the sound of the fleeing enemy transport and the more sustained roar of the pursuing British cars, and then he knew that it must be "Les Anglais." We saw them stir, silhouetted figures pulled back the curtains, flung open their bedroom windows and shouted their heartfelt greetings as they cheered the cars on their way. One old farmer, already downstairs, tore out from his yard and stood in the road, waving his lantern at every vehicle in turn, too happy to speak and the tears coursing down his cheeks.

Apart from stray and uninvestigated shots, there were few encounters with the enemy during the hours of darkness, but as the skies lightened things began to happen. A long open stretch led to a wood by a small hill and a light blinked in a house. A civilian rushed out to shout a warning of two German tanks and a column of infantry. They were *méchants*, he said, and meant business. Corporal Wilson halted and scanned the wood through his binoculars and saw that it contained a number of infantry. From one of the corners a Spandau machine gun opened up in sharp bursts. Lieutenant Buchanan-Jardine's Troop was about to direct its guns on to the wood when a warning came from the rear. There was a Panther a few hundred yards behind, and a small group of infantry with it. Travelling with the Troop was a section of the Support Troop under Corporal Hartley, and these put in an attack on foot. The enemy proved to be out of petrol and morale and gave in without firing a shot. The prisoners' numbers were soon swollen by the party which had manned the machine gun in the wood and these were bundled off down the road to Squadron Headquarters, who during this brief interchange of fire had been hard at work wirelessing back the latest news and cooking their breakfasts! Among the prisoners captured by Lieutenant Buchanan-Jardine was a sixteen-year-old Austrian S.S., fair-haired and blue-eyed, whose wallet was found to contain photographs of row upon row of naked Russian civilians, dangling from trees by their necks. When asked to explain the meaning of the photographs he burst into tears and inquired whether we were going to shoot him before or after breakfast. His officer had told him that "the Guards always execute their S.S. prisoners immediately."

Meanwhile, Lieutenant Clark had taken his troop of Matadors forward and started to shell the wood. "The first," complained Lieutenant Jonkheer Groeninx van Zoelen acidly over the air, "has fallen twenty feet from my car but hasn't even exploded." However, the next salvo flushed a large batch of Germans into the open and dim shapes could be seen scuttling across the fields for all they were worth. More prisoners started to give themselves up, but Major Ward, with his eye on the ball, ordered the advance to be resumed without delay. It was all too easy to lose sight of the true objective in the heat of the moment and time was pressing. We gulped a quick mug of tea, grabbed a biscuit and chunk of bully beef and were off again.

By this time Lieutenant Hanbury's Troop was in the lead. For obvious reasons, much nonsense will always be written about the thrills of pursuit in war. There is nothing elevating in the horrid business of scattering corpses and destruction along the line of advance, even if subsequently described in terms of the chase or a good day's bag on the moors. But the undeniable fact remains that the chatter of machine guns, the sudden head-on encounters and accessions of loot, the cheering populace, orders and counter-orders, all tend, when allied with fast movement, to build up a nervous exhilaration hard to define yet almost impossible to suppress.

There could be no question of tactics—the Squadrons simply went forward at the pace of the leading scout car and, apart from the advance guard Troops, very nearly nose to tail. Nor was it only the Troop in the lead which did the shooting, because so little aware of the true situation was the enemy that he would frequently blunder into the middle of the column from a side turning. At other times he would come bowling down the road, visiting farms in search of provender, straight into the sights of the advancing Besas.

The wireless enabled the two Squadron Leaders to check up on one another's progress as they sped on, but Major Bowes Daly had not yet reached his deploying point and so was still some way behind.

Meanwhile every crew and vehicle appeared to be imbued with but one common purpose—to speed flat out for the Somme. For the first time since landing in Normandy, the armoured cars felt that they had been given a job really suited to their cavalry role, and nobody in the British Army was going to catch them. The scout cars were in their element, the armoured cars were beginning to wonder whether their ammunition would last out, and even the Staghounds forgot their world of wireless and galloped on, neck and neck with the clanking Matadors. Close behind, with its inflammable cargo of ammunition and petrol, the mixed load lorry, overloaded as usual and hard put to keep up on the hills, nevertheless devoured the miles for all it was worth.

The medical orderlies, Troopers Healey and Robinson, were performing prodigies of first aid for the wounded, almost all enemy. Normally moving with Fighting Headquarters, the squadron medical cars travelled on this day at the back of the column, with orders to catch up as best they could, after halting to attend to casualties. They had no maps with them, but, deviating neither to the right nor to the left, they simply followed the signs of the chase.

For pure discomfort, the medical White scout car ranks next to Boadicea's chariot, and as a makeshift springless ambulance it was positively inhuman, and one could only hope that as few wounded as possible would have to ride in them at this pace. In fact most of the wounded, once they had been tended, had to be left at the side of the road to await the follow up.

By the time the village of Paillard was reached it was broad daylight. There was a short check at the front, and as the Squadron waited to move on the villagers burst forth into the single main street, cheering. Each had a different story and request. "There are hundreds of enemy in the woods." "The Boche took away my tractor yesterday; a great blond sergeant was driving. Will you please catch and shoot him?" "The enemy have no boots so you'll catch up with them before Chirmont." Pushing them off the turrets in relays, we moved on.

The slight delay had been caused by Lieutenant Hanbury's Troop having to pull an overturned gun limber out of the way. Four dead horses and a Russian with a purple-banded cap and British gas cape lay in a ditch beside a basket of smashed eggs. Bursts of Spandau fire from somewhere on the left, followed by cheers, told us that the Maquis were on the job. We could see them, armed with shot guns and Sten guns, combing the woods. A Frenchman in black leggings and a fireman's peak cap was guarding a dejected-looking bunch of Wehrmacht youths whose hands had been tied behind their backs one to the other.

As the Somme bridges drew nearer more and more leaderless groups of enemy appeared. Those who resisted were shot down, as were others who tried to make a race of it in stolen cars, but by far the larger proportion gave themselves up willingly, only too thankful to escape the vengeance of the Maquis. Without the help of the latter the question of prisoners would have been a most difficult one, for we could spare neither the personnel nor the time to guard them.

Such was their fear of Allied air power that the Germans had impressed labourers into digging slit trenches for them along both sides of the road at fifty-yard intervals. These were freshly dug, but the disarray of abandoned ground-sheets, rifles, mess-tins and ammunition testified to headlong flight on an unprecedented scale.

Between Moreuil and Demuin a dawn sortie of fighter planes had attacked a column of horsed transport, and some of the poor beasts were still alive and struggling in their traces. They were put out of their agony to lie with their dead companions, grim tribute to the power of the Air Force preceding us.

A Headquarters of sorts had been caught by the same sortie, and from a wrecked staff car and tractor-drawn pantechnicon streamed a river of pay-books and photographs and bundles of typewritten sheets to flutter over the countryside like a monstrous paper-chase trail.

By now "A" Squadron had branched left, and only one small obstacle, a stream called the Luce, lay between "D" Squadron and their objective. When about four miles short of Demuin, Lieutenant Jonkheer Groeninx van Zoelen's Troop ran into a large private car filled with soldiers. Trooper Scott's first burst of Besa sent it careering over a stubble field for a hundred yards with the driver dead at the wheel. It was filled with loot, cigarettes, crates of benedictine, brandy and cherry brandy.

Yet another car had been knocked out by Corporal-of-Horse Brook in the lead of Lieutenant Hanbury's Troop. This had also run off the road, to overturn in a field. All four tyres had been shot to ribbons and the windscreen and bodywork riddled. Trooper Healy ran over to see what could be done for the wounded. It was a gruesome sight. The driver, seeing the armoured car, must have tried to jump out on the move to save himself. He had somehow fallen and got dragged and was lying trapped beneath the running board, badly wounded. Another man, dead, with his face blown away, still gripped the steering wheel. A youth, who appeared to be no more than fourteen years old, had crawled away before collapsing at some distance on to his face. The lower part of his back was shot away, but he was waving feebly to show that he was still alive.

The party had obviously been returning from a foraging expedition. In the back seat, sprawled across smashed bottles of champagne, which bubbled and frothed over his blood-spattered uniform, lay a very fat officer, also dead.

Somebody tore away at the back door which, half off its hinges, was caught in the soft earth. It gave with a lurch and an avalanche of alarm clocks clattered to the floor, followed by the fat officer, who slowly rolled over to slump with his face resting on a large French ham.

Leaving the medical orderlies to tend those still living, the advance was resumed. Shortly afterwards there was a dull explosion to the rear, and for a moment Major Ward feared that the Germans had blown up the bridge at Demuin. Luckily, this proved not to be the case, but a railway bridge to the east was seen to be enveloped in black smoke and flames.

Farther on a group of cottages maliciously set alight by an enemy rear-guard burnt fiercely. Outside them, the villagers, enraged beyond endurance at such callous and wanton damage, vowed vengeance on their next batch of prisoners.

By this time Lieutenant Hanbury's Troop was nearing Villers-Bretonneux. "I remember," wrote Corporal-of-Horse Thompson, "going through a village just before it, when we saw a German tank in the trees to the right. There was no visible movement in it so we didn't bother about it. The next thing we met was a horse and cart with two Germans perched on top. The cart was full of pork, which must have been a good haul for the people following on, but we had no time to waste, so we unhitched the horse, fastened it to the wheel, and chased the Germans back down the centre line. Then came a German private car. Corporal Brook, in the leading scout car, gave him a burst and he careered off the road and stopped. Again we had no time to investigate but just kept pushing on."

★   ★   ★

Villers-Bretonneux was entered just before eleven o'clock in the morning, and here the Squadron split. Two Troops, those commanded by Lieutenants Hanbury and Buchanan-Jardine, made a dash for "Hope" at Corbie, while Lieutenant Jonkheer Groeninx van Zoelen's Troop branched right towards "Charity" at Sailly-Laurette. Between these bridges another structure was reported to exist at Vaux-sur-Somme, and a possible ferry two kilometres to the east, which Lieutenant Ainsworth's Troop was ordered to investigate. These last were found to be non-existent, however; the ferry was disused and in a sinking condition, while the bridge, an old wooden structure, had been blown up by the French in the 1940 retreat.

As Lieutenant Hanbury's Troop approached Corbie bridge, the Germans were still trying to form some vague sort of protective screen to deny its approaches, which lay through the outskirts of the village, but they were completely taken by surprise. "It was easier than shooting pigeons, with Mr. Hanbury's and Corporal Brook's cars dealing with the front and that great shot Trooper Elmore picking them off on the flanks. After we passed these people there was nothing until we reached the village, the entrance to which was a right-hand turn. After the first scout car and armoured car had got round this corner, something opened up at the rear of Mr. Hanbury's car. I noticed this from my position about fifty yards behind him, so when I turned the corner myself I had my guns ready to engage them. There was a machine-gun post and goodness knows what else, but I have never seen people move so quickly as when

Elmore got cracking with the Besa. The whole Troop arrived at the bridge, leaving the German dead *en route*. I was placed at the approaches to the bridge while Mr. Hanbury's car and the scout cars dashed over to the far side. All the bombs (there were four), 250 lbs., and electrically detonated, were laid out in readiness, but we had just beaten the enemy to it and none were actually connected up."[6]

A situation where armoured car troops, working on their own, might have to deal with the simpler type of tasks normally undertaken by the sappers had been visualized. Moreover, the Support Troops had been trained to detect and neutralize several types of enemy mines. But in this case even the section of sappers which had travelled with Lieutenant Hanbury's Troop in the last stages confessed themselves baffled by these four bombs. It was suspected that they might either be time bombs or else fitted with a trembler fuse which the slightest jar might set off. One false move could blow the vital bridge skywards, and so an urgent message was sent back to Guards Armoured Division, asking for advice. The C.R.E. replied, "On no account tamper with bombs. I shall send up an experienced officer to deal with them." [7]

In the meantime the enemy infantry, who were on both sides of the river, were showing signs of recovering from their initial surprise, and both Troops were forced to keep a wary eye open for possible infiltration to within bazooka range. They were also having to be sparing with ammunition, so much having been expended on the run up. In addition, a spur of high ground running east-north-east of Corbie afforded the Germans good observation both on to the bridge and the village, most of which lies on the northern bank of the river.

The enemy began to snipe back; then growing bolder, opened fire from several points of vantage in near-by houses. After consultation, Lieutenant Hanbury and Lieutenant Buchanan-Jardine, whose Troop had been following close behind in support, decided that as well as holding on to both sides of the bridge, it would be necessary to station look-outs in Corbie village to give adequate warning of further infiltration.

The Maquis, who had now arrived in fair numbers, proved their worth and, armed with German rifles and as much Besa ammunition as could be spared, they were posted at strategical points. Lieutenant Hanbury's

6. Extract from narrative of Corporal-of-Horse W. L. Thompson, 3 Troop, "D" Squadron, now better known as Corporal-Major Thompson, D.C.M., the Life Guards, winner of the King George VI Cup for jumping at the Royal Military Tournament, Olympia, the first and to date only N.C.O. to gain this honour.

7. According to Corporal-of-Horse Brook, the Sappers had discovered the secret of the fuse on at least one of the bombs before receipt of this message because they carried it away to a place of safety resting across two large baulks of timber. *Author*

problem was to get them to stay where they had been posted for they were prone to dash about the countryside scalp hunting.

After the approaches had been secured and prisoners handed over to the Resistance, Lieutenant Buchanan-Jardine went forward with Corporal Hartley in a scout car to reconnoitre the land to the north, for a message had come through that the Grenadier tanks and infantry were still some way back and would not be able to relieve "D" Squadron for several hours.

The scout car passed through Corbie before encountering more enemy. After which Lieutenant Buchanan-Jardine saw a large party of Germans making for the Amiens—Bapaume road. "They were pretty demoralized and I thought it would be a good scheme to give them a burst on the Bren. This hastened up their retreat considerably, but one or two took a poor view of this and started firing back."[8] Just then Corporal Hartley, who had been riding on the back of the car, caught sight of some enemy on the side of the road about to fire a bazooka. He made a dash for the ditch, got there unscathed, shot dead several Germans, but was then pinned down by machine-gun fire at close range and eventually captured. Meanwhile, after several more bazookas had narrowly missed the scout car, Lieutenant Buchanan-Jardine was forced to retire to the bridge again, where he re-joined the remainder of Lieutenant Hanbury's group still in firm control.

About an hour later the civilians who had gathered in the streets and around the bridge suddenly melted away. Flags were hurriedly withdrawn, the rumble of tracked vehicles was heard to the north, and rifle shots cracked out. "It really looked as if the two Troops were about to have to fight it out to the last." Then round a bend in the road appeared the triumphant Maquis with about two hundred German prisoners and a large haul of weapons! The civilians showed themselves again, flags fluttered once more, and at last it was felt that the "brew up could begin." Until relieved by the Grenadiers, the rest of the stay was uneventful, and the bridge remained intact.

Meanwhile Lieutenant Jonkheer Groeninx van Zoelen's Troop had been having equal success in its dash to capture "Charity."

Shortly after leaving Villers-Bretonneux the Troop Leader had been warned by the civilians at Warfussé-Abancourt, the next village on his route, that the enemy were in some strength on the river line, but "still undecided about blowing the bridge." A brief reconnaissance forward

---

8. Lieutenant Buchanan-Jardine.

confirmed that there were enemy at the bridge and long columns of transport could be seen on the far side.

At this point the River Somme is so undecided about its eventual course that, after it has been altered by artificial channellings and cuttings, it is difficult to know which part is Somme canal and which river. The road bridge is in fact a pair of lock gates as well as several other smaller structures almost running into one another and making a total of five successive crossings in all. These are approached by a run-up of several kilometres, overlooked for most of its length from the northern bank. Lieutenant Jonkheer Groeninx van Zoelen decided that his only chance of success lay in the Troop charging flat out, trusting that the Germans ordered to do the blowing would be slow or else panic. There was little time to spare—give the enemy an inkling that a Troop was in the area, and the bridge would go up forthwith.

The plan worked perfectly, although as soon as the Troop came into view it was subjected to a fair amount of small-arms fire, which did no damage but had considerable nuisance value for it forced everybody to keep their heads down inside the turrets and thus limited visibility. Machine guns were trained on the bridge itself, and, as hoped, the enemy entrusted to blow it fled on seeing the cars approaching at speed. Like the Corbie bridge, this one was found to be mined with several bombs, all of which were eventually neutralized with the help of the sappers and the French Maquis, who had actually cut some of the wires when they had seen the Troops approach.

The Germans put in an immediate counter-attack, but with the Troop able to enjoy a fair measure of manoeuvrability and a good field of fire (unlike the situation confronting the Corbie defenders), the enemy were soon driven off, leaving their casualties behind.

Possibly the Germans may have had some idea of renewing their attack later on, for as Corporal Hart took his scout car into the village of Sailly-Laurette he was able to count over a hundred infantry as well as some half-tracks forming up. These at first showed no signs of retreating, and one shot from a bazooka hit the scout car in the engine, knocking it out and forcing Hart and his driver, Trooper Gee, to bail out and dive for cover. They were both eventually able to rejoin their Troop after having nearly been run down by a carload of Germans making a last surprise bid to blow the bridge. Seeing this last threat, Corporal-of-Horse Davis, who was in the act of giving orders to some of the dismounted Support Troop, shouted a warning to Trooper Savage, his gunner, who knocked out the car with his first shot. "It pulled up like a racehorse, and the soldiers tumbled out all ways, but only one man got away and an officer

"WHOA—HOLD IT!"
Night Harbour, Winter, 1944.

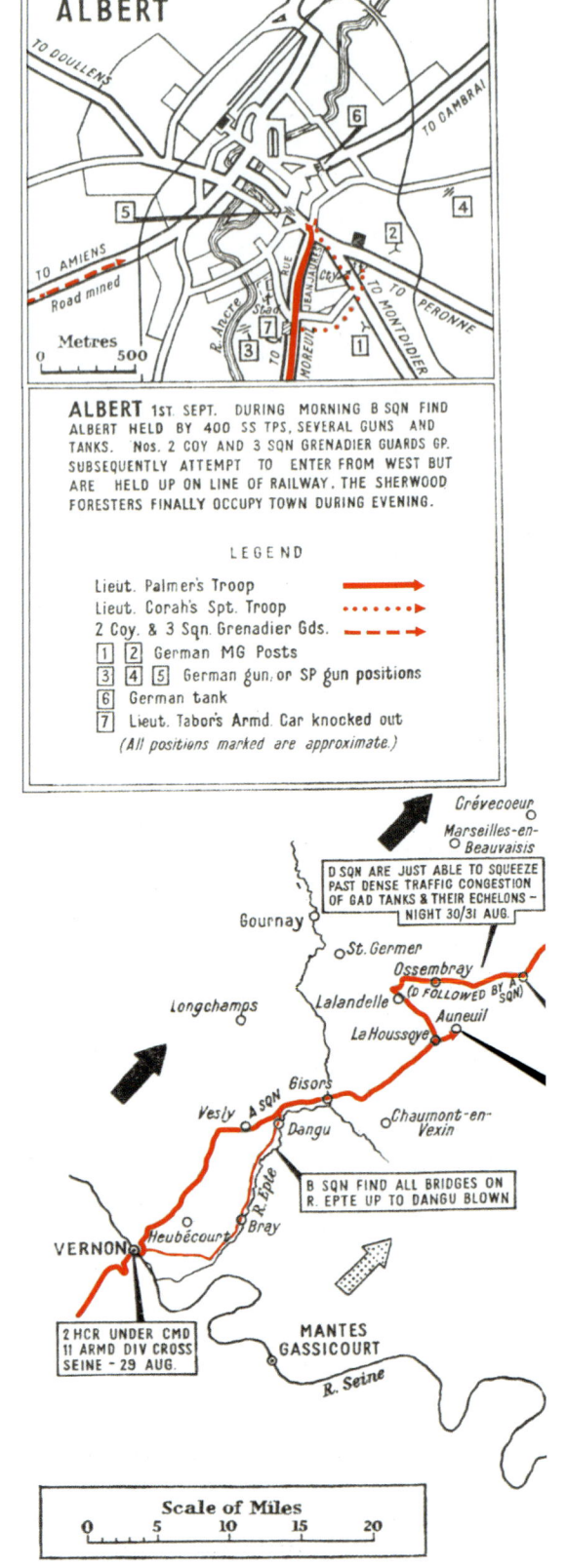

ALBERT

TO DOULLENS

TO CAMBRAI

6

TO AMIENS

Road mined

5

4

Metres

R. Ancre

Stad.

0   500

3

7

1

2

(Ct)

TO PERONNE

TO MONTDIDIER

ALBERT 1ST. SEPT. DURING MORNING B SQN FIND
ALBERT HELD BY 400 SS TPS, SEVERAL GUNS AND
TANKS. NOS. 2 COY AND 3 SQN GRENADIER GUARDS GP.
SUBSEQUENTLY ATTEMPT TO ENTER FROM WEST BUT
ARE HELD UP ON LINE OF RAILWAY. THE SHERWOOD
FORESTERS FINALLY OCCUPY TOWN DURING EVENING.

LEGEND

Lieut. Palmer's Troop
Lieut. Corah's Spt. Troop
2 Coy. & 3 Sqn. Grenadier Gds.
1 2 German MG Posts
3 4 5 German gun, or SP gun positions
6 German tank
7 Lieut. Tabor's Armd. Car knocked out
(All positions marked are approximate.)

Crévecoeur
Marseilles-en-
Beauvaisis

D SQN ARE JUST ABLE TO SQUEEZE
PAST DENSE TRAFFIC CONGESTION
OF GAD TANKS & THEIR ECHELONS –
NIGHT 30/31 AUG.

Gournay

St. Germer
Ossembray

Longchamps

Lalandelle

(D FOLLOWED BY A SQN)

Auneuil

La Houssoye

Gisors

Vesly   A SQN

Chaumont-en-
Vexin

Dangu

R. Epte

B SQN FIND ALL BRIDGES ON
R. EPTE UP TO DANGU BLOWN

Bray

VERNON

Heubécourt

R. Epte

2 HCR UNDER CMD
11 ARMD DIV CROSS
SEINE - 29 AUG.

MANTES
GASSICOURT

R. Seine

Scale of Miles
0   5   10   15   20

MAP 6

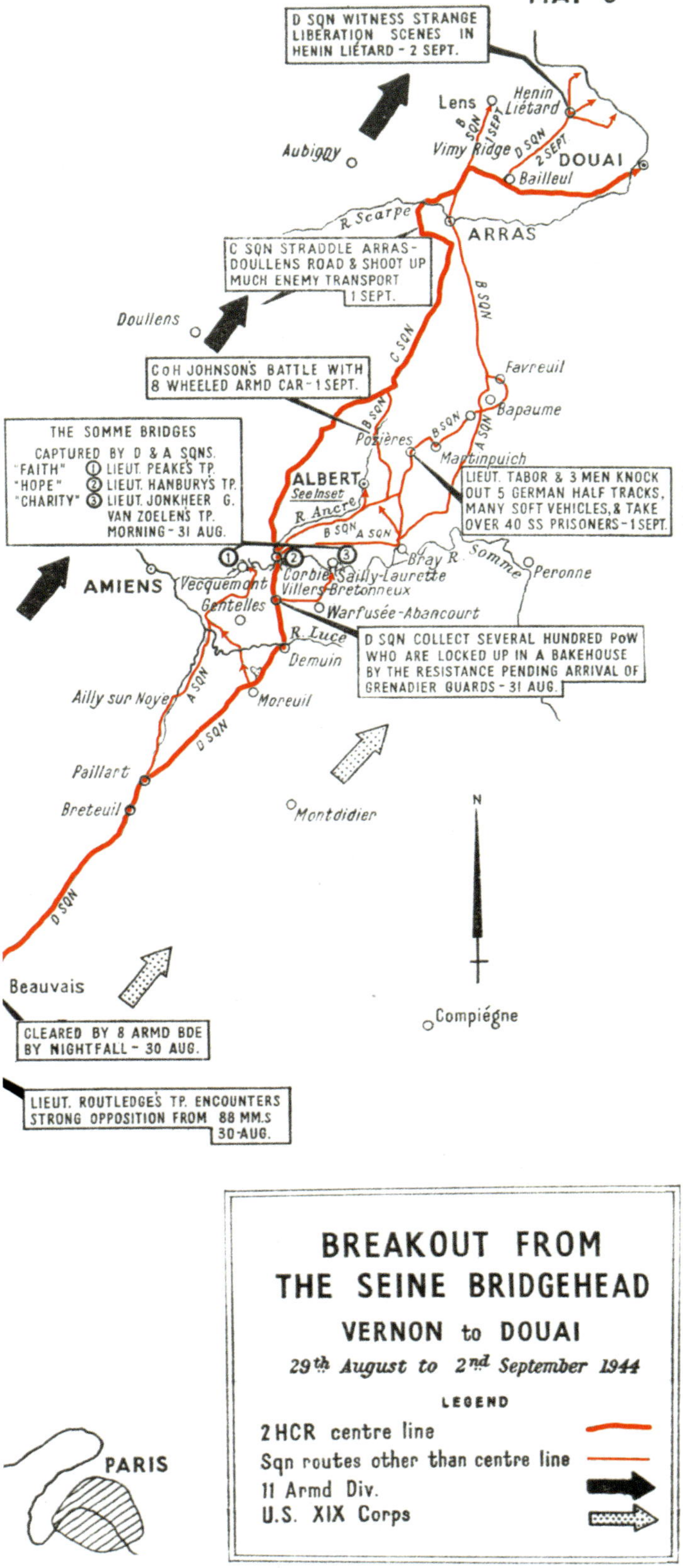

D SQN WITNESS STRANGE
LIBERATION SCENES IN
HENIN LIÉTARD - 2 SEPT.

Lens
Henin Liétard
Aubigny
Vimy Ridge
DOUAI
Bailleul

R. Scarpe
ARRAS

C SQN STRADDLE ARRAS-
DOULLENS ROAD & SHOOT UP
MUCH ENEMY TRANSPORT
1 SEPT.

Doullens
Favreuil
Bapaume
CoH JOHNSON'S BATTLE WITH
8 WHEELED ARMD CAR - 1 SEPT.

Martinpuich
Pozières
THE SOMME BRIDGES
CAPTURED BY D & A SQNS.
"FAITH"   ① LIEUT. PEAKES TP.
"HOPE"   ② LIEUT. HANBURYS TP.
"CHARITY" ③ LIEUT. JONKHEER G.
            VAN ZOELENS TP.
MORNING - 31 AUG.

LIEUT. TABOR & 3 MEN KNOCK
OUT 5 GERMAN HALF TRACKS,
MANY SOFT VEHICLES, & TAKE
OVER 40 SS PRISONERS - 1 SEPT.

ALBERT
See Inset
R. Ancre

Bray
R. Somme
Peronne
AMIENS
Vecquemont
Corbie Sailly-Laurette
Gentelles Villers-Bretonneux
Warfusée-Abancourt

R. Luce
D SQN COLLECT SEVERAL HUNDRED PoW
WHO ARE LOCKED UP IN A BAKEHOUSE
BY THE RESISTANCE PENDING ARRIVAL OF
GRENADIER GUARDS - 31 AUG.

Demuin
Ailly sur Noye
Moreuil

Paillart

Breteuil
Montdidier
N

Beauvais
Compiégne

CLEARED BY 8 ARMD BDE
BY NIGHTFALL - 30 AUG.

LIEUT. ROUTLEDGE'S TP. ENCOUNTERS
STRONG OPPOSITION FROM 88 MM.S
30-AUG.

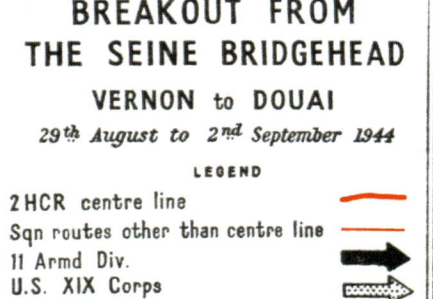

BREAKOUT FROM
THE SEINE BRIDGEHEAD

VERNON to DOUAI

29th August to 2nd September 1944

LEGEND

2 HCR centre line
Sqn routes other than centre line
11 Armd Div.
U.S. XIX Corps

PARIS

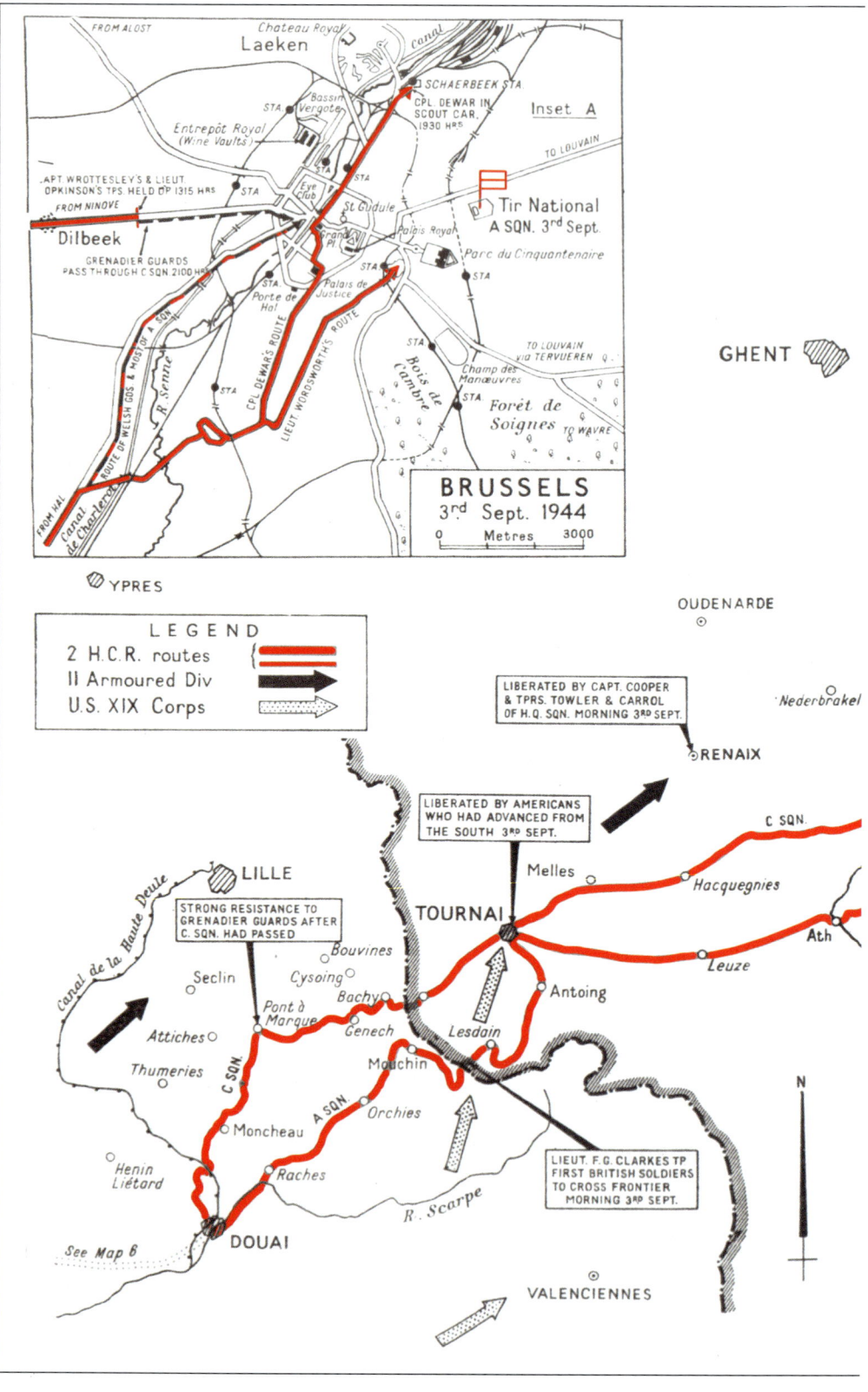

Inset A

FROM ALOST

Chateau Royal

Laeken

Bassin Vergote

SCHAERBEEK STA.

CPL. DEWAR IN SCOUT CAR. 1930 HRS

TO LOUVAIN

Entrepôt Royal (Wine Vaults)

Tir National A SQN. 3rd Sept.

CAPT. WROTTESLEY'S & LIEUT. OPKINSON'S TPS. HELD OP 1315 HRS

FROM NINOVE

Dilbeek

Eye Club

STA.

St Gudule

Palais Royal

Parc du Cinquantenaire

Grand Pl.

GRENADIER GUARDS PASS THROUGH C SQN. 2100 HRS

Porte de Hal

Palais de Justice

TO LOUVAIN via TERVUEREN

CPL. DEWAR'S ROUTE

LIEUT. WORDSWORTH'S ROUTE

R. Senne

ROUTE OF WELSH GDS. L. MOSTUI A SQN.

Canal de Charleroi

FROM HAL

STA.

Bois de Cambre

Champ des Manoeuvres

Forêt de Soignes

TO WAVRE

BRUSSELS
3rd Sept. 1944

0   Metres   3000

GHENT

YPRES

OUDENARDE

LEGEND
2 H.C.R. routes
II Armoured Div
U.S. XIX Corps

LIBERATED BY CAPT. COOPER & TPRS. TOWLER & CARROL OF H.Q. SQN. MORNING 3RD SEPT.

RENAIX

Nederbrakel

LIBERATED BY AMERICANS WHO HAD ADVANCED FROM THE SOUTH 3RD SEPT.

C SQN.

LILLE

Canal de la Haute Deule

Melles

Hacquegnies

TOURNAI

Leuze

Ath

STRONG RESISTANCE TO GRENADIER GUARDS AFTER C. SQN. HAD PASSED

Bouvines

Cysoing

Seclin

Bachy

Antoing

Pont à Marque

Genech

Lesdain

Attiches

Mouchin

Thumeries

C SQN.

A SQN.

Orchies

Moncheau

LIEUT. F.G. CLARKES TP FIRST BRITISH SOLDIERS TO CROSS FRONTIER MORNING 3RD SEPT.

Henin Liétard

Raches

R. Scarpe

N

See Map 6

DOUAI

VALENCIENNES

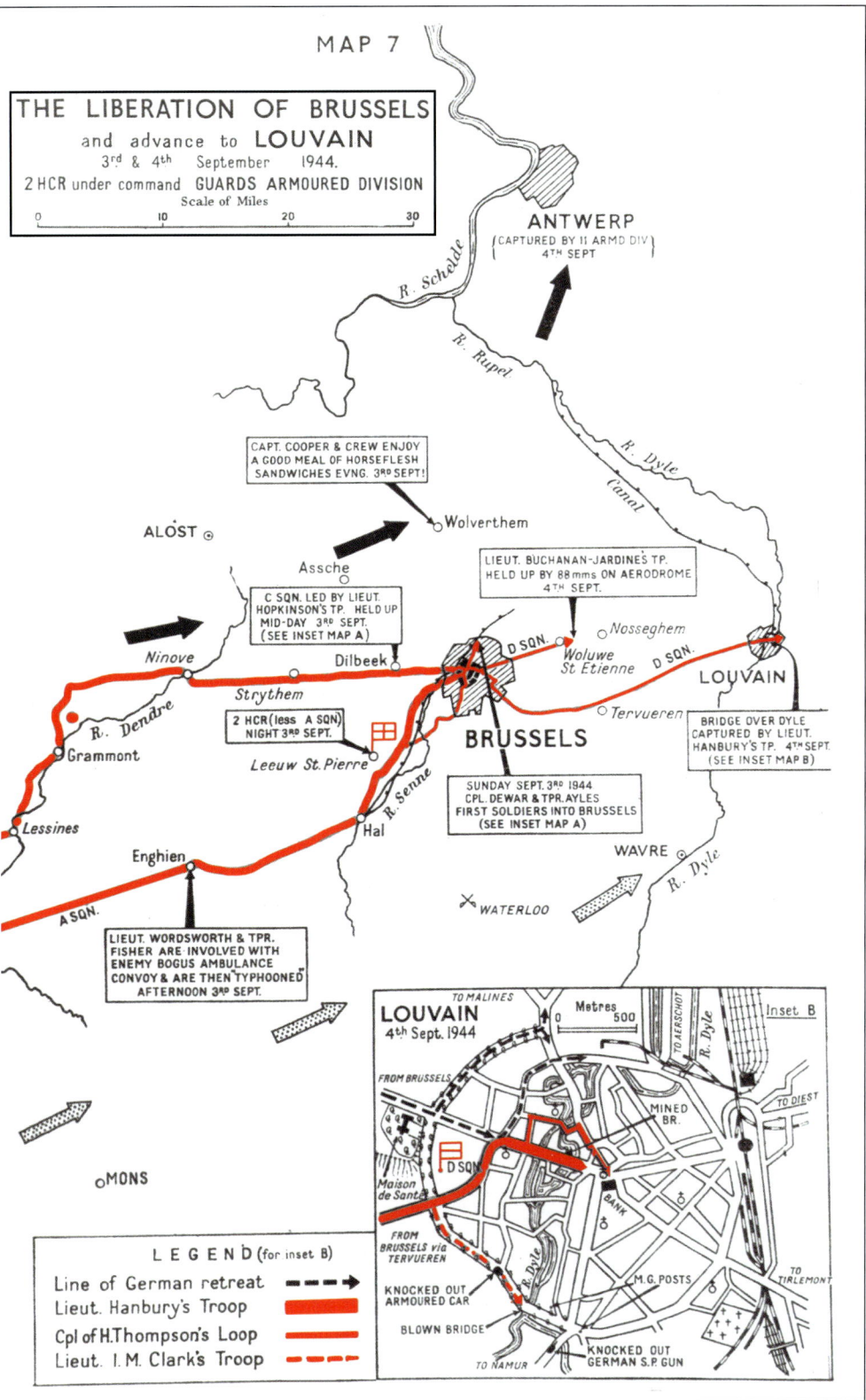

MAP 7

THE LIBERATION OF BRUSSELS
and advance to LOUVAIN
3rd & 4th September 1944.
2 HCR under command GUARDS ARMOURED DIVISION
Scale of Miles
0   10   20   30

ANTWERP
(CAPTURED BY 11 ARMD DIV)
4TH SEPT

R. Schelde

R. Rupel

R. Dyle
Canal

CAPT. COOPER & CREW ENJOY
A GOOD MEAL OF HORSEFLESH
SANDWICHES EVNG. 3RD SEPT!

ALOST

Wolverthem

Assche

LIEUT. BUCHANAN-JARDINE'S TP.
HELD UP BY 88mms ON AERODROME
4TH SEPT.

C SQN. LED BY LIEUT.
HOPKINSON'S TP. HELD UP
MID-DAY 3RD SEPT.
(SEE INSET MAP A)

Ninove

Strythem

Dilbeek

D SQN.

Nosseghem

Woluwe
St Etienne

D SQN.

LOUVAIN

R. Dendre

2 HCR(less A SQN)
NIGHT 3RD SEPT.

Grammont

Leeuw St.Pierre

BRUSSELS

R. Senne

Tervueren

BRIDGE OVER DYLE
CAPTURED BY LIEUT.
HANBURY'S TP. 4TH SEPT.
(SEE INSET MAP B)

Lessines

Hal

SUNDAY SEPT. 3RD 1944
CPL. DEWAR & TPR. AYLES
FIRST SOLDIERS INTO BRUSSELS
(SEE INSET MAP A)

WAVRE

Enghien

A SQN.

WATERLOO

R. Dyle

LIEUT. WORDSWORTH & TPR.
FISHER ARE INVOLVED WITH
ENEMY BOGUS AMBULANCE
CONVOY & ARE THEN TYPHOONED
AFTERNOON 3RD SEPT.

LOUVAIN
4th Sept. 1944

TO MALINES

Metres
0   500

TO AERSCHOT

R. Dyle

Inset B

FROM BRUSSELS

MINED
BR.

TO DIEST

MONS

D SQN.

Maison
de Santé

BANK

FROM
BRUSSELS via
TERVUEREN

KNOCKED OUT
ARMOURED CAR

BLOWN BRIDGE

R. Dyle

M.G. POSTS

TO
TIRLEMONT

TO NAMUR

KNOCKED OUT
GERMAN S.P. GUN

L E G E N D (for inset B)

Line of German retreat
Lieut. Hanbury's Troop
Cpl of H.Thompson's Loop
Lieut. I. M. Clark's Troop

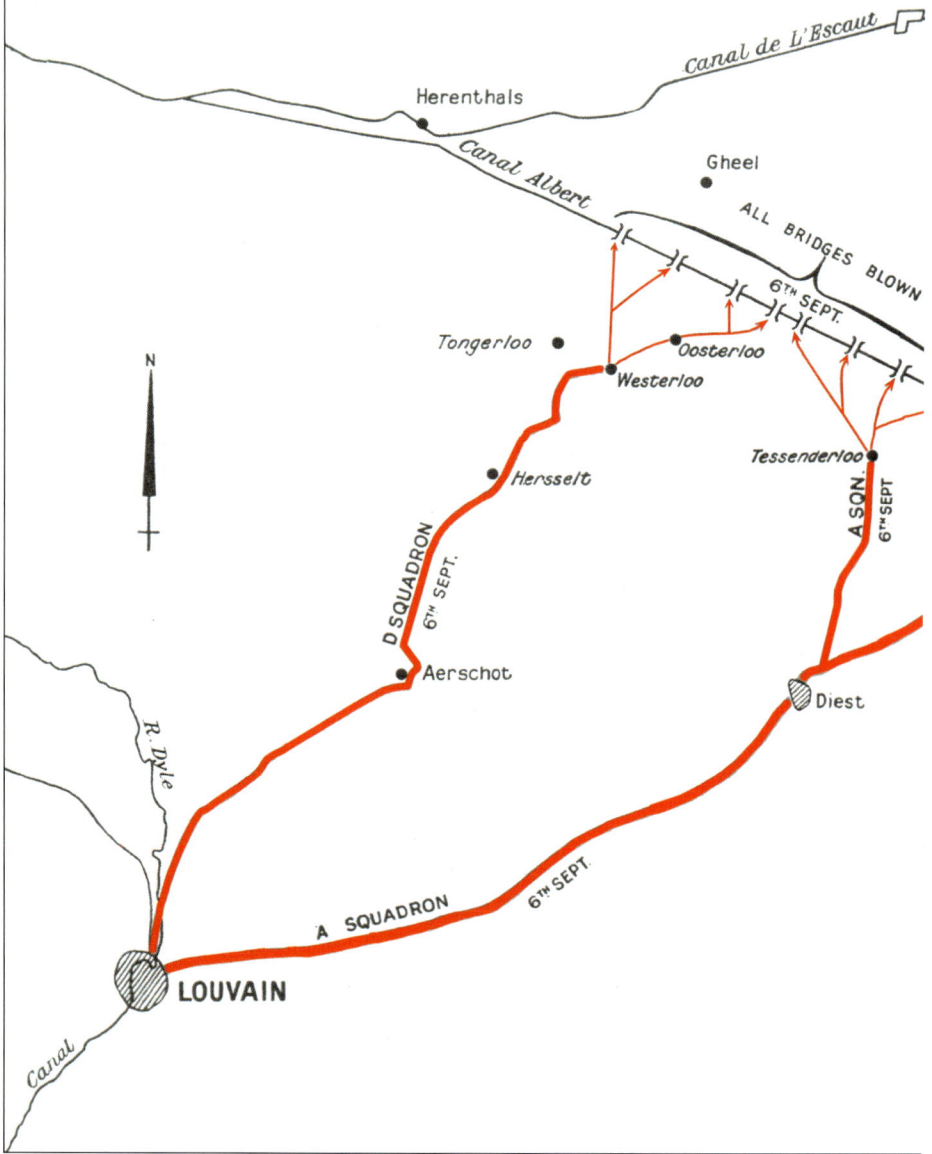

MAP 8

LEGEND

Regimental Centre Line..........

Sqn. Reconnaissance.................

Troop Patrols...........................

① Lieut. Creswell's Tp. ④ Lieut. Franklin's Tp.

② Liaison with Americans ⑤ Lieut Creswell's loop

③ Lieut. Peake's Tp. ⑥ Lieut. Buchanan-Jardine's

dash.

Canal de L'Escaut

Herenthals

Canal Albert

Gheel

ALL BRIDGES BLOWN

6TH SEPT.

Tongerloo

Oosterloo

Westerloo

Tessenderloo

A SQN.
6TH SEPT.

Hersselt

N

D SQUADRON
6TH SEPT.

Aerschot

Diest

R. Dyle

A SQUADRON 6TH SEPT.

LOUVAIN

Canal

HOLLAND

⑥

R. Dommel

● Valkenswaard

D SQN
11TH SEPT

"Joe's
Bridge"

Lommel ●

"The
Factory" ■

Lille St. Hubert

⑤

● Neerpelt

10TH SEPT

● Overpelt

④

10TH SEPT

③

10TH SEPT

"The
Blasted Heath"

● Petit Breughel

10TH SEPT.

● Exel

Bourg Leopold ●

● Hechtel

● Peer

Bree ●

A SQUADRON

BELGIUM

● Beverloo

Beeringen ●

① Peel

● Helchteren

Dorne ●

A SQN.

6TH SEPT

7TH SEPT.

Heusden

Lieut. Franklin's Tp.

BRIDGES BLOWN

6TH SEPT

● Lummen

C SQUADRON

● Zonhoven

● Asch

● Waterschei

②
▨ Hasselt

Canal   Albert

ADVANCE TO THE DUTCH FRONTIER
(SHOWING MAIN PATROLS ONLY)
6th – 11th Sept. 1944

Scale of Miles

0   2   4   6   8

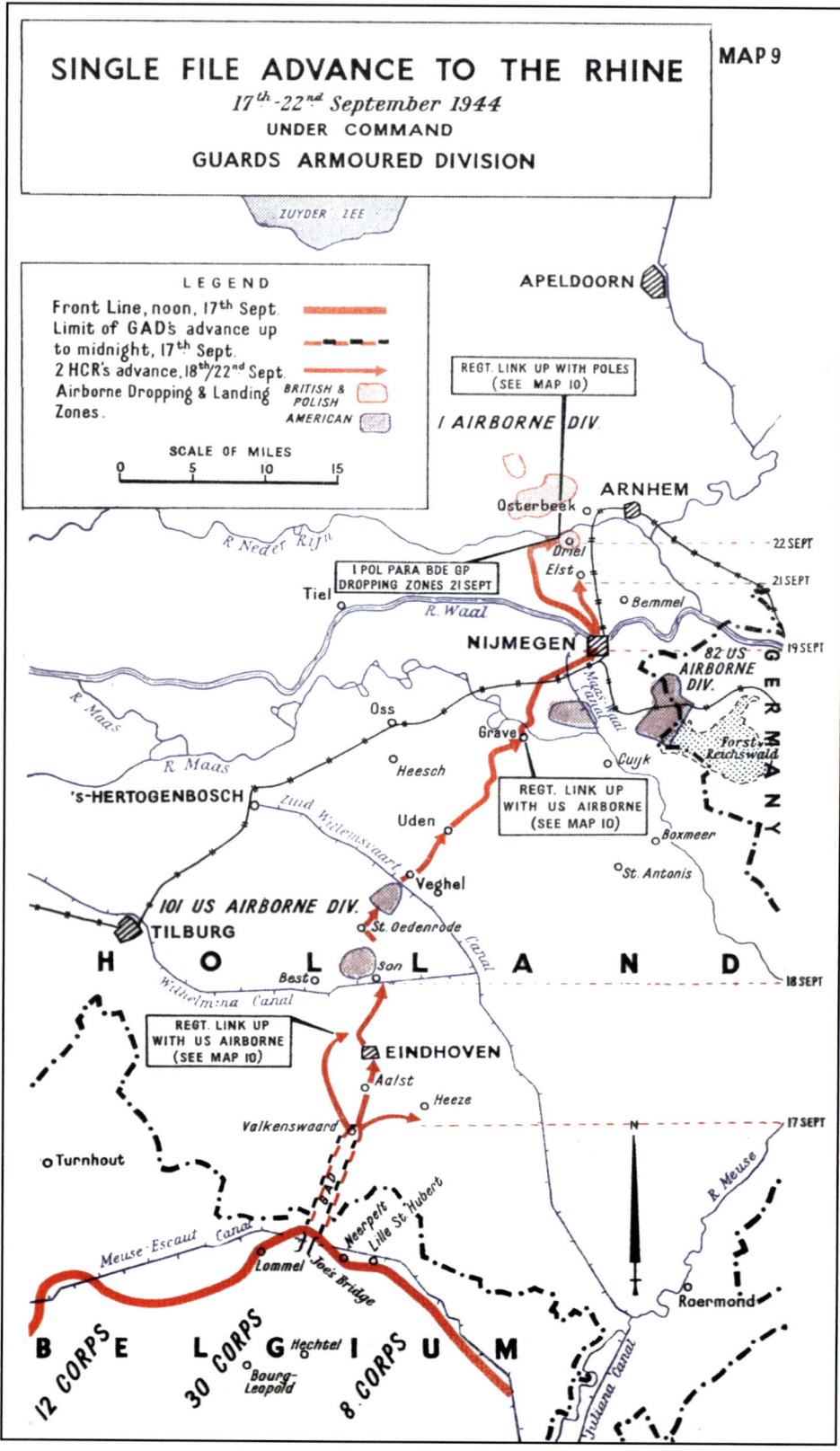

SINGLE FILE ADVANCE TO THE RHINE

17th-22nd September 1944
UNDER COMMAND
GUARDS ARMOURED DIVISION

MAP 9

ZUYDER ZEE

LEGEND

Front Line, noon, 17th Sept.
Limit of GAD's advance up
to midnight, 17th Sept.
2 HCR's advance, 18th/22nd Sept.
Airborne Dropping & Landing
Zones.

BRITISH &
POLISH
AMERICAN

SCALE OF MILES
0   5   10   15

APELDOORN

REGT. LINK UP WITH POLES
(SEE MAP 10)

I AIRBORNE DIV.

R. Neder Rijn

Osterbeek   ARNHEM

Driel   22 SEPT
Elst   21 SEPT

I POL PARA BDE GP
DROPPING ZONES 21 SEPT

Tiel

R. Waal

Bemmel

NIJMEGEN   19 SEPT

82 US
AIRBORNE
DIV.

Maas-Waal Canal

Forst.
Reichswald

R. Maas

Oss

Grave

Cuyk

G
E
R
M
A
N
Y

Heesch

's-HERTOGENBOSCH

Zuid Willemsvaart

Uden

REGT. LINK UP
WITH US AIRBORNE
(SEE MAP 10)

Boxmeer

St. Antonis

Veghel

101 US AIRBORNE DIV.

TILBURG

St. Oedenrode

H O L   Best Son L A N D   18 SEPT

Wilhelmina Canal

Canal

REGT. LINK UP
WITH US AIRBORNE
(SEE MAP 10)

EINDHOVEN

Aalst

Heeze

Valkenswaard   17 SEPT

N

R. Meuse

Turnhout

Neerpelt
Lille St. Hubert

Meuse-Escaut Canal

Lommel   Joe's Bridge

Roermond

B   E   L   G   I   U   M

12 CORPS   30 CORPS   8 CORPS

Hechtel

Bourg-
Leopold

Juliana Canal

who ran for cover into a ditch and, armed with a machine gun, refused to give himself up." A member of the underground forces volunteered to go and fetch him, and while he was carrying this out another German opened fire at the Frenchman from an upstairs window but was promptly shot dead by Trooper Savage.

It was hoped that when Guards Armoured Division arrived reinforcements would be sent to the river line, thus enabling the troops to withdraw for some rest. However, when the Grenadier group appeared four hours later (shortly after three o'clock) they were unable to undertake responsibility for this right-hand bridge. This was a blow, for Major Ward had been informed that the bridge at Sailly-Laurette was required by 30 Corps as a future supply route, and was of the utmost importance.[9] However, the arrival of the tanks and infantry meant that the two Troops at Corbie would be available to reinforce the right-hand bridge, should this be required. Meanwhile Lieutenants Ainsworth's and Clark's Heavy Troops, together with the remainder of Lieutenant Metcalfe's Support Troop, had moved across to reinforce Lieutenant Jonkheer Groeninx van Zoelen, and this battle group was to hold the Sailly-Laurette bridge throughout the following night. Apart from one rather half-hearted counterattack in the dark which fizzled out after the enemy forming-up point in a small wood had been raked by fire, no further trouble was experienced. The only casualty was Corporal-of-Horse Royston, who spent the next day with a sore tummy after his gunner had pressed the wrong trigger in the dark and the 2-pounder recoil had rudely driven him back into the works of his wireless set.

★   ★   ★

Back at "D" Squadron Headquarters there were the usual scenes attendant on the first hours of liberation, and only now was it possible to realize how many Germans had been caught on the wrong side of the Somme by the rapidity of the British advance. Spreading themselves northwards in a blind urge to escape but having no idea of our dispositions and being continually harried by the Maquis, they had run into the Troops on the bridges and given themselves up in their hundreds. The local Maquis prisoners' cage was soon overwhelmed and prisoners then overflowed into the streets. Squadron Headquarters, which had halted between Villers-Bretonneux and the river at Corbie in a field still pitted with First World War shell-holes, had also many more prisoners than could be

---

9. It was subsequently taken over and used by the Americans.

dealt with, and the advent of the Grenadier group, driving the remnants of the enemy before them, merely increased the pressure.

By now all fighting had died down on the south bank of the Somme, and not a shot was fired as the Grenadiers took over the Corbie bridge and prepared to advance northwards. Apparently the Germans from their new positions on the northern slopes could no longer see the bridge and they awoke too late to the danger. The King's Company of the Grenadiers was fired on from a churchyard close to where Corporal Hartley had been captured, but the enemy soon gave in and the tanks of the 2nd Battalion climbed the slopes beyond without difficulty. Two of their tanks were then lost to an anti-tank gun before it was destroyed, and after this the opposition melted away.

During this time remnants of the enemy caught south of the Somme, most of whom had by now hidden themselves between "D" and "A" Squadrons in the Bois de l'Abbe, started to slink out of cover and attempted to make a dash for the river by coming round the blind side of Villers-Bretonneux. The Maquis spotted this move and most of the enemy were soon rounded up.

Later in the afternoon, however, when all appeared quiet, two Spandau machine-gun posts suddenly opened up on the villagers from some farm buildings on the outskirts of Villers-Bretonneux. It transpired that stragglers under an S.S. sergeant had decided to die fighting sooner than fall into the hands of the Maquis. Major Ward thereupon dispatched a scratch force of officers' servants, backed by the Rear Link Staghound (with Corporal-of-Horse Copus to act as substitute loader to the 37-mm. gun) to drive them from their lair. The ensuing battle resulted in a large farm being reduced to ashes and a bakery severely damaged by the explosive cannon shells. Then after the officers' servants had put in a spirited flank attack, encouraged from a safe distance by the local *maire*, and after Major Ward had nearly lost for good the services of Trooper Costello, whose beret, proudly waved on high, was riddled by shots, the Germans thought better of their resolution and surrendered. Night fell with the Foot Guards holding a substantial bridgehead north of the Somme and "Battle Group Ainsworth" in firm possession of the right-hand bridge at Sailly-Laurette.

★   ★   ★

Meanwhile, although initially "A" Squadron's advance had been governed by the speed of "D" Squadron in the lead, their story following their branch-off at Breteuil had been very similar, culminating in the capture of their single objective—the bridge "Faith" at Vecquemont, which was some three miles west of the one at Corbie.

There were the same scenes of enemy disruption, punctuated by brief halts to eradicate snipers and bands of Germans. In one such battle Lieutenant Hoare, 5 Troop, was seriously wounded, being shot through the spine as he was standing in his turret directing operations.

2 Troop (Lieutenant Peake) was the first to reach the bridge and was closely followed by 4 Troop (Lieutenant Franklin).

For Lieutenant Peake's Troop the run-up until within a few miles of the river had been relatively uneventful. Contact was made in the village of Aubigny with Lieutenant Younghusband's 5 Troop, "D" Squadron, which was acting as flank guard and covering the approaches from the south. Half a mile from the bridge, Peake's Troop was fired on by a section of infantry in a cabbage field. In reply, three Germans were killed and the remainder taken prisoner. Being a very methodical person, the Troop Leader carefully entered the numbers of casualties in his notebook!

To reach the road bridge it was necessary first to cross another bridge spanning the main railway line from Albert to Amiens. As Peake's armoured car was moving over it, he saw a train disappearing into the distance just out of range of his machine gun. He cursed his luck, but it later transpired that this was the last train out of Amiens, and that it was filled with British prisoners of war. When the Troop had all but attained the objective, near enough for them to see a large cylindrical object in the middle of the bridge, a machine gun opened up from a house to the right. This was soon silenced, only to be followed by a tremendous explosion, which on closer inspection was found to be yet another bridge carrying the railway line over the river some 200 yards west of the road bridge. It had been effectively destroyed.

Fearing that the road bridge might follow suit at any moment, Peake jumped into the scout car and went forward to have a look at the cylindrical mechanism in the roadway, and as he was bending over it, Corporal-of-Horse Neill's gunner, Trooper Wood, opened up with his machine gun into a tree close by. He had spotted the leaves rustling, and sure enough a German soldier fell like a plummet to the ground, dead. The French civilians, who had watched this development with keen interest, made a concerted rush and pinched the corpse's boots. It was subsequently confirmed that this German had been responsible for blowing both the road and railway bridges, as there were found to be wires from the tree to both structures. Fortunately he had only accomplished half his task.

Meanwhile the sappers attached to the Troop had been brought forward, and a section of Lieutenant Wordsworth's Support Troop was placed in a position to defend the bridge, while over the wireless buzzed the usual questions and answers about bridge reports and the size of bombs.

By this time Lieutenant Franklin's 4 Troop had arrived on the scene of action.

"When we got out of the forest and up to the bridge, we found that four huge aircraft bombs were wired up on it. Luckily, Peake's corporal-of-horse's car had shot up the Jerry as he was in the act of blowing the bridge. There were others around the bridge, so we blazed away and cleared the road. I took some 'Gardeners'[10] up to the bridge to clear off the bombs. We greatly admired the way they did it. I sat on the end of the bridge and watched (with my head just over the turret!). They came back to me and said that they had never seen the bombs before. As they put it, 'they were not in our book of instructions.' However, they would try to lift them, but they were a little chary, as they suspected that they might be ones fitted with a mercury fuse. If you tipped them one way or another, the mercury would slide into a tube and set the mechanism off. They tossed for it and two of them went forward again. Bending down they slowly raised one bomb and carried it to the side of the road. One could hear them sighing. The rest were easy. Peter Peake led over the bridge as he had found it first and wanted the honour of crossing the Somme first! I congratulated the sappers on their fine job, and they remarked that if one had gone off the remainder would have followed suit and finished off the bridge and much of the surrounding countryside. I realized then that they included me! As we crossed over, the Germans could be seen retreating out of range on the hills, using any transport they could lay their hands on, including many old farm carts. After a false alarm (about fifty Germans in the village hall) we had a brew-up. The French dragged out two women from a near-by house by their hair and began beating and kicking them, and when I intervened I was told that it was none of my business and that they could deal with 'les collaboratrices' themselves. They cut off all their hair. We all left at dusk and, passing through the tanks on the way back to harbour, one wit shouted, 'Oy, the battle's the other way.'"

★ ★ ★

It is perhaps not too much to say that had the advance from Beauvais been postponed some two or three hours until daylight, the first soldiers

---

10. Wireless code word for the Royal Engineers.

to reach the Somme might well have found the river line securely held, with all the consequent delays and casualties of an assault crossing. As it was, the Germans were just beaten to the draw, and the Regiment had good reason to be pleased with the part it had played.

When at last there was time to assess what had happened on the left flank, it was realized that the success of our old friends, 11th Armoured Division, had been equally spectacular. Well ahead of us in time schedule, having started several hours earlier, they had kept their lead, and their first troops had entered Amiens at five o'clock in the morning, crowning the operation with final success when at twenty minutes to eleven, 23rd Hussars and a company of 8th Rifle Brigade had captured the main town bridge over the River Somme intact.

From 11th Armoured Division came two most interesting pieces of news. The first was that in a captured German staff car had been found a map showing the entire enemy dispositions in the West. In detail, it gave away the intention of the High Command to withdraw to, and consolidate, a line of the Somme as the right-hand sector of a new German defence line extending to Switzerland. The second piece of news was that the Division had surprised General Eberbach at breakfast. When asked what he commanded, he replied, not without dignity, "I commanded what used to be the Seventh German Army."

The scenes in Amiens baffled description and, as frequently happened, there were so many stragglers that those who followed had as much shooting to do as those in front. Captain Cooper, it will be remembered, was liaising with 11th Armoured Division.

"By daylight we were well into the German lines and we fired at the odd infantry positions as we moved on in column. Took many prisoners. The Germans in Amiens were taken completely by surprise at dawn and resistance collapsed after the outer defences and a few road-blocks were knocked down. After a hurried breakfast, went into Amiens with some tanks and an American liaison officer. The Commander of the Seventh German Army has this moment been captured by the Fife and Forfar Yeomanry. Everybody has had a day out shooting German transport of all descriptions. They are burning all along the road into Amiens and prisoners are coming in *en masse*. Many Mongols, Russians particularly. All the bells in Amiens are ringing, as they have been in the villages we passed through. The people are off their heads with joy and chasing the odd German sniper and racing round the houses in taxis armed to the teeth. The American and I arrived first at the town hall (he had to see the Mayor) and we were completely mobbed—most embarrassing being kissed by at least a hundred men and women. Eventually got to the

Mayor's parlour and found a French Red Cross girl interpreter. Six bottles of champagne arrived and everything imaginable was toasted. Then I saw Carroll and Towler surrounded and being given brandy and calvados by everybody at once and flowers thrown all over them. All the police and civilians appear to be firing rifles into the air at the same time, and the prisoners pass through in ever-growing numbers, being booed and spat at by the mob. Eventually got back to my car and made contact with 'C' Squadron at different places, being plied with drink, flowers, and flags. Bernard[11] had captured some champagne. Got rid of all our chocolate and cigarettes, then mobbed again in the town square, where Carroll was 'overcome' by a girl with both arms round his neck. More calvados, champagne, and hundreds of kisses. At this stage, the Germans started some desultory firing into the centre of the town, so warned the people to get indoors, but the warning was quite ineffectual. Shots, cheering, guns, church bells and an old man beating a drum incessantly. Eventually the whole of 'C' Squadron arrived in. They say that they have had a good shoot (Bernard has shot up a large ammo lorry with his Matador's 75). Met Tommy and Peter[12] and exchanged information, then back to 11th Armoured Headquarters, more champagne and kissing. Could hardly keep awake—still no shave and wash. The Regiment has been over sixty miles in last forty-eight hours, and we look like being off again at dawn."

Guards Armoured Division Headquarters, Regimental Headquarters and the reserve Squadron, "B," moved forward by dark to the outskirts of Villers-Bretonneux. "I remember," wrote the Adjutant, Captain A. J. R. Collins, "that it was one of the most bitterly cold spots ever. I was quite beat, having had no sleep for forty-eight hours and having been on the wireless for about three-quarters of the time!"

Willys Overland (Jeep)

---

11. Lieutenant Bernard van Cutsem, "C" Squadron Heavy Troop Leader. "C" Squadron had moved up in the wake of 11th Armoured Division and also mopped up the country to the immediate left of "A" Squadron.
12. Captain T. Clyde and Major A. W. P. P. Herbert, "C" Squadron.

Chapter IV

Albert, Arras and Douai

Advance to Arras—Lieutenant Winterbottom and Trooper Gregory have difficulty in delivering the maps—"C" Squadron Support Troop captures its second German General for the day—"B" Squadron run into a hornet's nest at Albert—Corporal-of-Horse Johnson's description of his battle north of Albert—Lieutenant Tabor's Troop successfully loops round Albert to the east and pushes on—"A" Squadron act as right flank guard and make contact with Americans—The story of Corporal Hartley's and Captain Ward's escapes from the S.S.—Good work for the Regiment's wounded by the civilians in Albert—Surgeon-Captain Kynaston is nearly put in the bag (his narrative)— "D" Squadron at Henin-Liétard—An unusual banquet—2 H.C.R. at Douai.

At four o'clock in the morning of the 1st of September, Guards Armoured Division moved forward over the Corbie bridge, aiming to reach Arras by nightfall. There were to be two lines of advance, that on the right led by Major Wignall's Squadron and that on the left by Major Herbert's. Major Bowes Daly's Squadron was to carry out a right flank guard and at the same time maintain contact with the Americans.

"It is the first day of the partridge shooting season," wrote a member of the Regiment wistfully, "and how far better employed we should be chasing them and not a bunch of scruffy Germans."

The day started with a chapter of accidents as, owing to a misunderstanding, new orders giving the Guards Armoured Division final objective and bounds and report lines were not received by R.H.Q. until after the advance had started. In order to save time in passing complicated messages over the air, Lieutenant Winterbottom was sent off to both "A" and "B" Squadrons with marked-up maps and revised orders, but he was shot up outside the town of Albert by American Thunderbolts firing .5 machine guns. The armour of the Humber scout car kept out most of the bullets, but one penetrated the driver's window, wounding Trooper Gregory in the head and starting an oil fire in the air filter inside the compartment of the vehicle. All bedding, maps and tyres were burnt out. Lieutenant Winterbottom then tried to reach "A" Squadron by going cross-country on a bicycle, but was forced to turn back after running into a German patrol. He then met a French baker,

Monsieur Felix Lefevre, and his daughter, driving along the road, and after consultation it was decided that it would be best to try to get to Albert, where there might be signs of "B" Squadron. He accordingly jumped into the back of his horse-drawn van, but they had not gone very far when they again ran into another enemy patrol. This time there was no hope of avoiding the Germans, so with great presence of mind Lefevre drove through the middle of them with Winterbottom hiding under "the well-filled skirts of the daughter." Thus, although necessarily incognito and in this somewhat Decameron style, the future Socialist M.P. for Central Nottingham could rightly claim to be the first Allied soldier to enter Albert. The town proved to be full of S.S. troops, and with no sign of "B" Squadron; there was therefore no alternative but to try to move out again and obtain aid for the wounded Gregory.

Before letting Winterbottom go, however, this kind French family insisted in feeding him up with an ample though mixed breakfast of brandy and three fried eggs. After a further series of hairbreadth escapes south of Albert, Winterbottom met an American patrol, then a lost British D.R. who gave him a lift part of the way, and finally he collected Gregory in a White scout car and so back to the Regiment in an amphibious Volkswagen.

★   ★   ★

"C" Squadron on the left of the advance made excellent progress during the day, and both they and the Welsh Guards group captured many prisoners, doing great execution on enemy transport when they cut the main Arras—Doullens road. "As far as 'C' Squadron were concerned it was their first really good looting run," wrote Lieutenant Hopkinson. "My troop captured their second S.S. general and we collected ten of their cars and lorries filled with clothing and drink. Unfortunately, we had to leave some of the drink lorries behind. We collected 85 prisoners and another hundred which we did not bother to pick up, but left to the Maquis. We continued to advance until we reached Vimy Ridge (north of Arras) and Lens. Corporal Camidge shot an S.S. colonel for trying to draw a pistol after he had surrendered."

The advance on this centre line was noteworthy for the variety of headgear captured and displayed by the British. Top hats were in great favour with the Welsh Guards, but Trooper Bracewell, one of the Bren gunners in "C" Squadron Support Troop, tried to go one better in the heat of the moment and sported the medals and cap of a German general when entering squadron harbour that night. However, Generals' hats and medals are very rightly protected by the conventions of war, and these were returned the same evening to their owner in captivity.

★ ★ ★

Meanwhile "B" Squadron, unaware of Lieutenant Winterbottom's episode, had run into a hornet's nest at Albert. Three Troops had set off from the harbour area south of the Somme almost simultaneously, with the intention of branching off at Albert. The order of march was—Lieutenant Palmer's Troop, followed by Lieutenant Tabor's and Lieutenant Kavanagh's. On Palmer's reaching the junction with the main road in Albert running east-west, he was confronted by an 88-mm. gun at twenty yards range, but Corporal Harmsworth and Trooper Upton in the leading scout car were too quick for the crew and dealt with them before they could fire a shot. Civilians reported, and there were other obvious signs, that the town was held in some strength, and Palmer concentrated his Troop to make a plan of action. Lieutenant Tabor's Troop had arrived on the scene by this time and confirmed enemy to the rear—a platoon of German infantry having crossed the road behind them. Accordingly, Palmer continued to remain in observation while Kavanagh tried a loop to the north, Tabor effecting a similar move to the south. After an interval, Palmer thought that the enemy might have pulled out of the centre of the town, and Corporal-of-Horse Kendrick tried once more to push forward by an alternative route with his Daimler armoured car. He immediately met heavy small-arms fire and hand grenades from the houses, which put his turret traversing gear out of action and destroyed all the outside equipment. Unable to fire, the vehicle withdrew slightly.

In the meantime Major Wignall had ordered up Lieutenant le Poer Trench's Troop as reinforcement and it tried yet another route, but was immediately fired on "by something armoured" and small-arms fire from a cemetery, where the enemy "dodging in and out of the gravestones were difficult to locate." A German tank now appeared round the corner and took a shot at Lieutenant Palmer's car, which fired back simultaneously. The tank's first shot tore away the rear wing of the armoured car and one of the tyres, making it impossible to manoeuvre in the confined built-up area, but the crew managed to extricate the vehicle without further trouble. Both Palmer's armoured cars were now out of action.

By now the fighting had become general, and Lieutenant Medlen's Heavy Troop and the infantry Support Troop commanded by Lieutenant Corah arrived on the scene of action to try to dislodge the Germans from the cemetery. Soon everybody was blazing away in a confused situation in which no one could be quite certain as to whom they were taking on.[1]

Eventually Lieutenant le Poer Trench's Troop was able to find a way round to the left, and Lieutenant Medlen was ordered to follow him, while Corah's Support Troop, using Palmer's Troop as a base, advanced towards the cemetery from opposite sides. These last two Troops now settled down to "a quiet little war on their own." Suddenly an unlocated German gun to the rear opened up on the two armoured cars belonging to Lieutenant Tabor's Troop (which had been ordered to remain in Albert pending preliminary reconnaissance by the scout cars which had gone off to the south), killing Troopers Roger Rawlence and Gordon Ebbage, in the first vehicle. The undamaged car, commanded by Corporal-of-Horse Collier, was then ordered to move forward to the aid of the Support Troop, by now nearing the cemetery but temporarily pinned down by small-arms fire. The latter, ordered by Major Wignall to withdraw, were finding some difficulty in disengaging as the road behind them was being accurately shelled by two other unlocated guns, and they had incurred several casualties, including Troopers Bolden, Hunt and Newman.

Eventually Lieutenant Corah extricated his two sections with the aid of Lieutenant Palmer's two scout cars, but in the action Corporal Smith, at a dismounted Bren-gun position, was shot through the head at close range and killed.

As three of the wounded men had not yet been located, Lieutenant Palmer obtained permission for himself, Lieutenant Corah and Corporal-of-Horse Kendrick to stay on to try to find them while waiting for Captain Ward in his Staghound and for the medical car to arrive from Squadron Headquarters. This party arrived shortly and was met by Corporal Harmsworth, who directed Captain Ward where to find Lieutenant Palmer's position. The Squadron Second-in-Command left his Staghound some way in the rear and went on in the medical car, but unfortunately took a wrong turning and ran straight into a group of S.S., and he and Trooper Dodimead were captured.

Meanwhile news having been passed back to Guards Armoured Division Headquarters that Albert was strongly held, the Grenadier Guards group were accordingly ordered to swing part of their force east from the main road and if possible try to capture the town from the west,

---

1. Lieutenant Palmer recounts how during the height of the battle, with bullets flying and ricocheting across the pavements, he was amazed to see a little old Frenchman step into the road from an adjoining building and calmly photograph both friend and foe before stepping back into his house again.

for it was known to contain a large store depot. No. 2 Company and No. 3 Squadron (tanks), Grenadier Guards, were detailed for the job. Two of their leading tanks were knocked out as soon as they entered the suburbs, and it was realized that the S.S. were determined to make a stand. One platoon of Grenadier Guards infantry was, however, able to work its way round as far as the railway level-crossing in the western half of the town, but no link-up with the armoured cars could be effected because the road here was mined and covered, and a self-propelled gun knocked out Lieutenant the Hon. C. E. Stourton's tank, wounding him and his crew. Captain the Duke of Rutland, commanding the infantry company, then attempted to pass through two of his platoons to try to cross the railway at another point. But when they reached the railway embankment they came under heavy fire and were pinned down, so a plan was made to contain the town until an infantry battalion from the 50th Division could make a concerted attack with the Grenadiers later on.

★   ★   ★

While the "B" Squadron group was having its battle in Albert, Lieutenant Kavanagh's Troop was making excellent progress to the north and eventually, after several skirmishes with the enemy, it cut the Albert—Arras road about three miles out of the town, an operation resulting in a "classic" armoured-car encounter, described with great verve by Corporal-of-Horse Johnson.

The Troop was evidently quite unexpected because German traffic was plying both ways along the Albert road. Two enemy staff cars were "brewed up" and also numerous trucks, some carrying troops into Albert, others supplies. Then came an enemy eight-wheeled armoured car.

> "Our Troop, No. 4 Troop, 'B' Squadron, had been ordered to take up position north of Albert and to drive back any Germans trying to escape by that route. So off we went. On approaching a slope leading down to our patrol point, Corporal Britton (leading scout car) reported that several Germans in cars and on cycles were all over the village, so I put my field-glasses on to the village and sure enough they seemed to be going all over the place as if they did not know what to do. So Mr. Kavanagh's car and mine opened fire and sort of made up their minds for them at 500 yards with the Besa guns. I've seen sheep scatter, but nothing like these Germans did when they heard our fire and saw from what direction it was coming. After a while, all the doors started to open and the villagers came out, waving and cheering. This told me that the

place was clear of enemy. Mr. Kavanagh then took up a vantage point where he could see the road leading from Albert to our cross-roads in the village. He then ordered Corporal Britton and myself into the village to take up a position on the crossroads, so into the village we went, with our guns pointing over the rear of the car.[2] Directly we arrived we were surrounded by mobs of French people. We were in a bad position if these people remained, for if anything had happened we could not fight our way out of them. I threatened to fire on them if they did not clear off, but it was no good.

"All of a sudden one villager came running like a madman, shouting, 'Les Boches! Les Boches!' and pointing towards Albert. They cleared like magic and shuttered all their windows. I told my gunner (Trooper Price) to train his guns on a bend in the road. For five minutes nothing happened, then around a corner came a soft vehicle loaded with equipment and infantry. It was going pretty fast, so I ordered the gunner to fire his Besa, but he pressed the wrong trigger and fired the 2-pounder. I never saw a car stop so quick. One shot and he had blown the engine clean out. Then he fired the Besa at the retiring infantry, killing plenty; but three were still running back to Albert, so I ordered my driver, Corporal Mellish-Smith, to reverse slowly to the bend in the road—the gunner, Trooper Price, still firing. Saw a couple more drop—third one got away. Decided to remain where I was on bend of road.

"Suddenly Corporal Britton says, 'Something big coming along the road,' so I ordered his scout car back to the cross-roads to wait for me. Nothing happened for a while, then we both saw each other at the same time, an eight-wheeled armoured car and myself. He fired first and missed, but advanced towards me very confident. I ordered 2-pounder to fire and Trooper Price scored a hit. Then we felt a terrible explosion and I saw flames coming through my periscope. Corporal Mellish-Smith said, 'We've had it.' O.K.,' I said; 'retire slowly,' and I was amazed when our car started to move as I thought that the engine had been hit. I reloaded the 2-pounder and gave order to fire again. Trooper Price said, 'Can't see the b.....s through these flames.' So I opened up cupola and stuck my head out and gave gun-laying directions from here. Then I was spotted by enemy gunner, who fired at my head but luckily only cut my wireless mast in half instead. I then got down, locked gun, and tapped Trooper Price. He put three rounds into the German car. Had another look over the top, but was now choked with smoke so gave order to evacuate the car. We all tumbled out and ran to scout car around the corner, jumped on the back, and said, 'Drive like hell.'

---

2. The Daimler armoured car mechanism enables it to be driven in reverse, the commander kneeling in the turret using a second steering wheel and remote control accelerator lever.

"Mr. Kavanagh was surprised to see us, as he had been firing in another direction and had heard the explosion and thought that we had had it. We then took the Troop Leader's armoured car while he carried on his part of the battle from a scout car. Then we advanced again back to the same position. On arrival we were surprised to see my armoured car standing there with the fire put out. I dare not yet get out as I did not know the fate of my enemy. He might still be waiting. So I advanced again slowly. Villagers came out and showed me how they had put out the fire. They pointed round the corner and there was the enemy armoured car with its crew of five laid out on the road, dead. The French had pulled them out and looted the car. Everything in our car was found to be intact. What had caused the explosion was some PIAT bombs I had strapped to the back of the car and which when hit had set fire to our bedding and cans of spare petrol."

The Troop continued to carry on the good work and later on in the day, while moving northwards, sighted another eight-wheeled German armoured car at long range. This time Corporal Worrall was the gunner and hit it three times until it showed no further signs of movement, but as it was some way across country, the Troop Leader was not able to spare the time to investigate, but pushed rapidly on towards Arras.

★ ★ ★

Lieutenant Tabor's Troop had been equally successful on its right-hand loop past Albert, which, since one of his Daimler armoured cars had been knocked out and the second one was reinforcing Lieutenant Palmer's Troop, was carried out by two scout cars only.

When "B" Squadron had hit trouble in Albert, Tabor had taken his two scout cars about half a mile back, then struck north-east round the outskirts of Albert. He had with him Trooper Jones as driver and, in the other car, Lance-Corporal-of-Horse Sparrow and Trooper Price (L. W.).

He made his way through the southern suburbs, and in spite of numerous stragglers, who were disregarded, and various civilian reports of mines, soon reached the outskirts of the village of Pozières, which lies on the main road from Albert to Bapaume. Here the patrol ran into five half-tracks mounting short 75-mm. guns. "Fortunately for us, the crews were mostly asleep or brewing up, but nevertheless had to be dealt with before we could carry on with our task."

The patrol eventually found itself on the main road, encumbered with about forty prisoners, nearly all of whom were tough-looking S.S. troops.

Lieutenant Tabor then blocked the main road and the cars had "some grand shoots at soft vehicles travelling in both directions." After a time, a German armoured car appeared from the direction of Bapaume, took a look at the British cars and withdrew again. The prisoners now began to get out of hand and show escaping tendencies, so they were herded out in the direction of Bapaume and dumped into an ex-Wehrmacht hut. When any man tried to get out of the door or window, Lieutenant Tabor put a burst of Bren through the roof. This warning proved most effective!

Along the main road, burnt-up motor vehicles and horse transport littered the sides, the result of previous R.A.F. strafing, while a stone cross war memorial to the last war was covered in bloodstains where some badly wounded enemy must have rested. Prisoners continued to come in from the adjoining fields, and by the time that the reserve Troop (Lieutenant le Poer Trench's) had come up to take them over they numbered over fifty.

After having got rid of their S.S. and other captives, the patrol moved on to Bapaume. On the way an old Frenchman informed Tabor that both Bapaume and the main road were clear, but luckily the scout cars went forward cautiously and soon came upon a column of German armour, including six self-propelled guns, some withdrawing to Bapaume, others halted on the road.

In view of this strong enemy force, the Troop Leader decided to by-pass Bapaume by travelling cross-country, eventually attaining the main road which runs from Bapaume to Arras. Subsequently many more German stragglers were passed, but they demonstrated no offensive intentions and, apart from these and with the "assistance of a couple of bottles of champagne," the patrol had an uneventful run into Arras.

★　★　★

In their role of right flank guard, "A" Squadron had a relatively quiet day, waiting for the Americans who had not yet come up. But due to the revised orders not reaching them until later, some of the troops became involved in the opening stages of the Albert battle and with enemy to the south.

3 Troop (Lieutenant F. G. Clarke), on appearing over the skyline on the road before it dips down into the hollow south of Albert, came under heavy artillery fire, which was watched by Lieutenant Franklin's Troop following up. "There were spurts of dust as shells fell in the fields all around him, and he did a spectacular about turn over a stubble field with all four cars firing their electrical smoke dischargers which billowed out

over the fields." Lieutenant Franklin's Troop went forward to help and see if they could locate the place where the shells were coming from, and Lieutenant Murray's Heavy Troop arrived, keen to do its share of counter-battery work. "However," wrote Franklin, "I thought that I had found a German gun and the Heavy Troop fired at it, but the shells came into the hedgerow close to me and I withdrew temporarily, not liking the sound of one's own shells any more than the enemy's!"

"A" Squadron were eventually ordered to move up to Bapaume there to await the Americans, and, if necessary, be prepared to guard the town during the night. In this task, Major Daly was to be aided by the addition of Lieutenant le Poer Trench's Troop from "B" Squadron. Among the prisoners here were two S.S. and an ambulance, captured in Bapaume town. On being searched one of them was found to be concealing a weapon in his jack-boot. However, as he was wearing the Red Cross insignia, he was given the benefit of the doubt, although it was hinted that they would both be shot on arrival at Regimental Headquarters. This threat acted like a dose of salts and they began tearing off their S.S. signs in a manner hardly worthy of the "Master race." Civilians looked on while this scene was being enacted and, for the only time in the campaign, a French woman was heard to plead for German soldiers' lives.

"Foolishly," noted Lieutenant Franklin, "I put them in their own ambulance with one of my men and sent them off. It was suggested I was taking a risk and I half agreed. I suppose I had been lulled from thoughts of war by the sunshine and brief wash we had just had, but, thinking better of it, I immediately sent off my scout car to pursue them. One of the French remarked that S.S. men are always S.S. What happened was that my Corporal asked them the way! They immediately pointed it out to him, but luckily he had the sense not to believe it and checked up. He eventually took the opposite road to our lines.

> "As a sequel to the story I learnt that the ambulance had been filled with loot, silk stockings, cigars, etc., and had been much appreciated at Regimental Headquarters. That was the first and last time that my Troop ever missed searching for a piece of booty!"

★ ★ ★

The Albert battle had in no way slowed the general impetus of the advance, which followed the route taken by "C" Squadron and the 2nd Battalion Welsh Guards; the latter, with the help of the F.F.I., having successfully mopped up the centre of Arras.

Along the entire route, even as far back as Divisional Headquarters, an enormous quantity of transport of all sorts had been shot up and pitch-forked into the ditches. Field-grey clusters of the enemy could be seen being hunted out of the woods or prodded from their trenches by the triumphant French, and long after local gaols had been filled to overflowing, they still surrendered in their hundreds, and the feeding problem, with bread running out, became acute.

Regimental Headquarters were with the Tactical Headquarters of Guards Armoured Division, and from here parties of Maquis could be seen holding miniature partridge drives in which they were flushing Germans out of every ditch. The scene was completed by a high-ranking German general who had been captured being solemnly towed in a broken-down jeep behind the Divisional A.C.V.(I.).[3]

With only a few hours of daylight left, the Irish Guards swung east for Douai, which they captured, though not without fighting, resulting in some damage to the important bridges over the canal which we were destined to cross on the morning of the 3rd of September.

★ ★ ★

As darkness fell and "D" Squadron, who had been in reserve all day, were preparing their evening meal in harbour outside Arras, a familiar voice was heard to say, "Yes, I stood on the back of that— German truck, waving my beret at the oncoming Cromwells, but the— kept firing and firing and finished by scoring a couple of —bulls right through my— beret, so I got down on to my —guts and prepared to wait until they got nearer…." We wondered what unrecorded epic had escaped the notice of Major Ward, until Lieutenant Metcalfe walked into Headquarters' tent to explain that Corporal Hartley had escaped from the Germans who had captured him beyond the Corbie bridge and was at this moment relating his adventures to the Support Troop.

After his capture he had been moved from place to place by the Germans and finally been ordered to board an escaping lorry which formed part of an S.S. convoy heading for Lille. This convoy was caught by a troop of Welsh Guards tanks. The Germans bailed out and tried to pull Hartley with them, but he sent them on their way with two well-aimed kicks full in their teeth. Fortunately, the Cromwell tanks realized in time that he was British, and the story ended happily with the Support Troop celebrating his return with their last bottle of calvados.

★ ★ ★

---

3. A.C.V.—Armoured Command Vehicle.

MORNING OUTSIDE ARRAS

2nd September 1944: After capturing the three Somme bridges east of Amiens, the Regiment advanced northwards against a disorganized enemy, reaching Arras during the afternoon of 1st September, and harbouring on the high ground to the north of the town, within sight of Vimy Ridge.

The main body of the Division, together with most of the Regiment ("A" Squadron being in Bapaume), spent the night of the 1st/2nd September within sight of Vimy Ridge and the Canadian Memorial. Pouring rain seemed to carry thoughts back to the last Great War, where so many Household Cavalrymen had fought under conditions infinitely more unpleasant and static for months on end. Only one person present— the Regimental, Mr. Jobson—had been old enough to see service then, and he remembered Arras only too well.

When next morning Guards Armoured Division concentrated at Douai, it became apparent for the first time that Brussels was to be our immediate objective.

32nd Brigade was ordered to hold the canal crossings free for the forthcoming advance, while "A" Squadron co-operated with them in their task, and the day passed uneventfully amidst a happy throng of grateful citizens and waving flags.

It was already late in the afternoon when the Regiment received their first orders to reconnoitre a route up to the Belgian frontier—an action considered advisable to ensure the minimum delay for the morrow's advance. Unfortunately, the time allowed was not enough, and "C" Squadron were compelled to turn back when the light failed, with their mission uncompleted. The local Resistance, however, proved to be most ably organized and their Intelligence Centre was able to furnish the Division with valuable data regarding which bridges were held by the enemy on the line of advance.[4]

Good news arrived at this stage about the wounded and missing in Albert, who it was feared had all been captured. Captain Ward had re-joined his squadron. He had bluffed his captors into thinking that his Blues stars were those of an army doctor. Having thus induced them to relax their vigilance, his next move was the time-honoured ruse of asking for permission to go to the lavatory, which at the second visit resulted in his escaping through a small window. Afterwards friendly civilians had hidden him in bed masquerading as a sick person, and later, disguised in the dungarees of a workman, he got safely back to the British lines, where he was picked up by a battalion of the Green Howards. He was able to report that there were in fact about 500 S.S. troops and several

---

4. On Saturday evening, the 2nd of September, a Divisional Signals officer visited the Douai exchange and asked to be connected by telephone to Brussels. To his intense surprise, he was immediately put through to the Brussels exchange, who informed him that the Germans were beginning to evacuate their heavy equipment. He asked the operator to warn the patriots that it might be possible for the Allies to reach the city on Sunday evening. Later the wires were cut.

self-propelled guns and tanks in position at the time "B" Squadron had attempted to enter Albert. The Germans had left at about midnight, many of them drunk and in an ugly mood.

The "B" Squadron wounded had been treated with great kindness by the French, who many times risked reprisals by hiding them from the enemy. An 88-mm. shell-burst had wounded three men, Troopers Hunt, Bolden, and Newman, and as they tried to crawl to cover, two of them found that, weakened by loss of blood, they would have to rest. Suddenly a door opened and Monsieur Alfred Hallot of 7 Rue Jean Jaures came out and helped in Bolden and Hunt, the latter being by this time unconscious. Another Frenchman rushed out with a bucket of water and washed off the tell-tale bloodstains from the pavement, while a next-door neighbour, member of the Resistance, took in Newman. Their wounds were dressed and they were all put into bed and given some food. When Bolden began to sit up and take notice, he chanced to look out of the window and saw Captain Ward being marched past by the Germans. Finally all three wounded troopers were found by an officer in the Green Howards, who arranged for their evacuation to hospital, taking Newman and Hunt in his own Bren carrier, and sending an ambulance for Bolden. "We were all," wrote Hunt, "treated like kings by the French and their behaviour throughout the battle had been beyond praise."

* * *

At one point it was feared that Surgeon-Captain Kynaston had also been put in the bag at Albert, but to everyone's relief he reappeared none the worse for his adventure. He had gone into Albert to tend the wounded after Captain Ward's capture but found on arrival that there was no sign of the men, for they had by then, so he rightly surmised, been taken prisoner. There being no point in waiting in Albert he pushed on with "A" Squadron to Bapaume. Towards evening he decided to return to Albert to see if there was any hope of the wounded having been recovered. "I parked some wounded F.F.I. I had treated in a nunnery. On approaching Albert, with darkness falling, I noticed a solitary Frenchman waving. I thought it was a welcome, but clearly it must have been a warning. The place was apparently deserted until I reached the main cross-roads in the middle of the town. Then Jerries sprang out on all sides. My driver stopped dead and said, 'What shall we do, sir?' and I replied, 'Drive like —.' Off we went northwards through the town, Germans continuing to pop up on all sides, but not firing, until we got stuck at the apex of a triangle, faced by a railway embankment and stream and the Germans behind us as the base of the triangle.

"There was a hurried conference, and it was decided that we were of more value to the Regiment than to the Germans, so we abandoned everything except our water-bottles and escape packs, and set off across country, guided by the stars, which Trooper Scowby, my servant (second horseman to Marchioness Camden before the war), was excellent at reading. A further six hours' marching brought us to the centre line and a petrol lorry then gave us a lift to Divisional Headquarters. Hardly a soul was awake and nobody knew where Regimental Headquarters were situated, and so after an exhaustive tramp round the harbour area I asked a sentry where the Household Cavalry was. He, of course, knew nothing. By now thoroughly fed up, we walked across the road and straight into Regimental Headquarters!"

The medical White scout car was recovered next morning minus all its medical equipment.

★   ★   ★

HENIN-LIÉTARD

While the rest of the Regiment had been moving on to Douai on the Saturday morning, "D" Squadron, ordered at first light to reconnoitre and, if intact, hold until relieved the crossings of the River Scarpe to the north-east of Arras, had soon pushed on a distance of some ten miles before encountering their first opposition in the colliery town of Henin-Liétard, on the fringe of the thickly populated Lens coalfields.

Lieutenant Buchanan-Jardine's Troop, with Corporal Jameison and Trooper Workman in the leading scout car, passed through the first part of the town, but on approaching the railway station was fired on by a self-propelled gun hidden up in some buildings. Jameison also spotted further horse-drawn guns and infantry and went back to report to his Troop Leader, who in turn went forward to see if the opposition could be by-passed. As the Troop Leader's car was turning a corner, the Germans opened fire and one shell, missing the Daimler, exploded on the wall of a house behind it, the splinters ricocheting at right angles and seriously wounding Corporal Jameison, who lost an eye. The same shell also wounded Corporal-of-Horse R. W. Clarke, who, putting his hand to his chin, felt a large piece of red-hot metal embedded there. Both men were taken to the local civilian hospital by the French, where the surgeon in charge decided to operate immediately on Jameison, and by his prompt action undoubtedly saved the sight of the other eye.

We noted that there were many more clenched fist salutes than Victory V signs in Henin-Liétard. It was the first time that this had occurred, and it was with some misgiving that one realized that the Communist virus, deadlier than even the Nazi racial theories which we were fighting, had bitten deep into these people.

But no dreary Marxian indoctrination could quell the spontaneous outburst of happiness at long-hoped-for liberation. Dense crowds swarmed over the armoured cars, offering everything they had in the way of fruit and drink and flowers.

Major Ward, who by now had had as much experience of this sort of thing as anyone, found himself surrounded by a milling throng, making all movement backward or forward impossible. For every ten people brushed off the cars, twenty took their place. The warning shout of "Char Boche" might occasionally cause a momentary panic, but the civilians only surged forward again with renewed enthusiasm.

The Frenchman's hatred of his German oppressor seemed to grow in intensity as we journeyed eastwards from Normandy, and in Henin-Liétard we found this loathing to be of a hard, merciless quality such as we had not yet experienced. In this large manufacturing area there had been much oppression and cruelty during the four years of occupation, and each fresh batch of prisoners doubled by the Maquis towards Squadron Headquarters was subjected to the crowd's rage. Clutching hands tore for victims and mouths spat as we piloted them through the mob to Corporal-of-Horse Copus's three-tonner lorry. One N.C.O., an S.S. with a bad local record, was singled out for special attention, and, cringing in terror, he was only just saved from being lynched.

Bangs and sudden shots, the meaning of which was all too plain, rang through the air, and one breathed an inward prayer for the future salvation of France that the rifles and machine pistols dealing out mob law in side streets might eventually find their way back to the safe custody of an armoury.

It said much for the men that they mostly managed to remain sober. Beer, wine, cider, and cognac were offered in lavish profusion. "Mais buvez, monsieur, buvez donc," urged the French folk, joyously. When the laughing soldiers protested good-naturedly that "this must really be the last one," unopened bottles were forced through the driving hatches and down the turret tops. Deflector bags, intended for the reception of spent shell cases, became filled with fruit and cakes which the populace must have saved up for weeks.

The profferance of flowers in this hideous smoke-laden district of colliery and slag-heap had a touching quality all its own, as wan little children shyly pushed a grubby bunch of daisies or roses into the camouflage network and even the gun muzzles of the armoured cars. "C'est jour de Gala pour nous," they cried.

Captain Waterhouse, barely recovered from the bearded Frenchman's kisses at Sébécourt, was melted by the spontaneity of the welcome. Asking me to look after his car, he was dragged off triumphantly to one corner of the seething square to be given a free shave and hair cut by the local barber. He returned immaculate, preceded by a pungent aroma of cheap scent and hair oil.

Opposite Major Ward's Headquarter cars, a cafe proprietor had thrown open his cellars to the men, while Madame, his ample spouse, as an additional contribution to the atmosphere of liberation, conferred her embraces in liberal doses upon everyone in uniform—in the intervals for breath, drinking glass for glass with the soldiers. She eventually subsided under a horse-hair sofa, sighing patriotically to the strains of "The Marseillaise" played jointly on a piano by three Maquis and a postman.

Troops by now on the banks of the Scarpe were wirelessing back similar stories of feminine adulation. Lieutenant Buchanan-Jardine, returning for a hurried conference with his Squadron Leader, remarked with an enigmatic tug at his moustache that from where he had come "one could obtain anything, absolutely anything." As first Troop into Henin-Liétard, he and his men had been invited to an impromptu banquet given in their honour in the town hall. Monsieur le Maire presided and, like Mayors the world over, he was soon speechifying at full blast. Owing to a band which was playing "Tipperary," also fortissimo, it was not easy to hear what he was saying, but it eventually transpired that he was requesting the Troop Leader and his men to honour the assembly after the banquet by attending a small shoot of his, where certain collaborators and German S.S. were to be liquidated. His invitation was politely but firmly declined.

And so, with no further signs of the enemy, and in such strange scenes of "Liberation," "D" Squadron, after having been relieved by a unit of 8th Armoured Brigade in the afternoon of the 2nd of September, re-joined the Regiment at Douai, to be informed that the advance to Brussels was to start on the morrow.

Chapter V

Liberation of Brussels

"The Division will advance and liberate Brussels" —2 H.C.R. to lead on both centre lines—Dawn, 3rd September, 1944—Opposition to the Grenadiers at Pont à Marq —Lieutenant F. G. Clarke's Troop first into Belgium—Tournai— Opposition at Leuze—Lieutenant Hopkinson's Troop reaches Brussels suburbs by half past one in afternoon—Lieutenant Hopkinson's narrative—Trooper Conry-Candler's narrative—"C" Squadron await reinforcements—"A" Squadron's race with the Welsh Guards—Trooper Ben Fisher's story—Entry into Enghien (Corporal-of-Horse Booth, Lieutenant Wordsworth, Trooper Fisher)—Corporal-Major Berrisford finds himself leading the British Army in the petrol lorry—How a Belgian town was liberated, from the civilian's viewpoint (Madame Delannoy)— Corporal Dewar and Trooper Ayles are first soldiers into Brussels—Scenes of rejoicing—The Regiment's flanking liaison, Captain Cooper with 11th Armoured Division to the north—Renaix liberated by a R.H.Q. scout car—Last shots in Brussels—Night of carnival and confusion—Major Williams and his echelon mobbed—More prisoners and rumours—The morning after.

The evening of the 2nd of September was cold, with more than a touch of winter in the air; bitter squalls were blowing across the fields where the Regiment was harboured, and for the first time as they viewed their draughty bivouacs, people really began to wish they were in warm billets.

The civilians, only too pleased to demonstrate their gratitude and friendship, had offered hospitality for the night, and the thought of a warm fire and bed in billets was tempting in the extreme. But an order from Major Sir Peter Grant Lawson soon put a stop to such extravagant ideas. "All ranks will dig slit trenches forthwith."

Resulting from higher orders received during the afternoon, Major-General Adair held a conference at Guards Armoured Division Headquarters on the western outskirts of Douai that same evening, just as darkness was falling. At the time 5th Brigade were harboured on an aerodrome about two miles farther to the west. Most of the Regiment were with 32nd Brigade, not far from Divisional Headquarters.

The General wasted few words in giving out his orders. "My intention," he said, "is to advance and liberate Brussels"; and he added, "that is a grand intention." There was a distinct twinkle in the

Divisional Commander's eyes as he watched the effect of these words on his subordinates. Brussels was a prize worth capturing, but a distance of ninety-six miles still separated it from Guards Armoured Division at Douai.

As to the method to be employed, it might be described as "Quickest the best." But there were certain important and limiting factors.

When the Corps Commander, Lieutenant-General Horrocks, had come over to confer with Major-General Adair, he had given out that an airborne operation had already been planned to precede the armoured spearhead, its main object being to seize certain vital bridges which lay ahead of the proposed line of advance, in particular those which spanned the River Escaut[1] at Tournai.

The operation formed part of an extensive project to cut off the large enemy forces now retreating from the coastal areas. The arrival of the airborne forces was to be preceded by heavy saturation bombing of all aerodrome sites up to the Belgian frontier. It was known that these aerodromes were strongly guarded "flak" positions—and "flak" positions meant the 88-mm. gun, a dual-purpose weapon equally at home in stopping ground armour as it was in knocking down our fighter planes.

The proposed bombing programme set commanders a problem— that of ensuring the safety of the divisional transport and tanks, the majority of which were packed in serried ranks carrying out much-needed maintenance on the concrete runways of Douai aerodrome. Small wonder that within the Division there had been a slit trench "flap" of the first order as far as the safety of the troops was concerned!

Few commanders relished the idea of an airborne operation at this stage of the campaign. It was felt to be unnecessary and, however carefully carried out, bound to be hard on civilian life and property. "Saturation bombing" really means that so great a number of bombs are rained over a given area that some at least will hit the intended target. But it was the thought of the overthrows which concerned us. In addition Brussels was still very far away and the plan meant that the Regiment, for we were to lead, would be unable to cross the start line until eleven o'clock in the morning—perhaps even later. Whereas if there was no airborne operation there could be a first-light start for the Household Cavalry, which, with nearly fourteen hours of daylight in hand, gave a sporting chance of attaining the Belgian capital before darkness.

---

1. Not to be confused with the Escaut Canal, which links up with it and which the Regiment was to reach a week later on the Belgian-Dutch frontier.

As commanding officers returned to their units with orders, the wind freshened. Sharp gusts whistled cheerlessly underneath the cars, lifting the flimsy bivouacs, and chilling the crews. Warning orders were issued. The hours slipped by and the gusts increased in violence. Rain began to fall and a now bitter cold increased the discomfort of the keyed-up men. Soggy earth from the freshly dug trenches clung to boots and clothing, and the thought of those friendly hearths close at hand was difficult to put out of one's mind.

To the profound relief of all, a message came through in the early hours of Sunday 3rd of September that the airborne operation was off, and corporal-majors stumbled over the trenches and recumbent men to warn the guard that "Reveille" had been put forward to half past four in the morning.

Our role that day—and in a relatively brief fighting career we had experienced many—was essentially one for armoured cars; and it is interesting to record that at this stage in the campaign started the system within the Division of allocating the tank and infantry units to formations known as Groups—a development which was closely to concern the armoured cars and ensure the speedy exploitation of successful reconnaissance. Whereas in the past it had usually been a case of working with either tanks or infantry, from now onwards co-operation normally lay with both arms. In 5th Guards Brigade the 1st (Motor) and the 2nd (Armoured) Grenadier Guards formed what came to be known as the Grenadier Group; the 1st (Armoured) and 5th Coldstream Guards, the Coldstream Group; similarly with the Irish and Welsh Guards Groups in 32nd Guards Brigade. The idea, with few changes, was to last until the end of the war, and although certain purists, undoubtedly influenced by the totally different type of fighting in the Western Desert, had been heard to murmur adverse comments, the system was to persist, and rightly so. Tanks could not operate with success in enclosed and built-up country without immediate and close infantry support. From now onwards the shortage of infantry was to make itself felt more and more and the normal armoured and infantry brigade working within the armoured division was to be a thing of the past in North-West Europe.

Quite apart from the regimental *esprit de corps* which existed within all these new groups, the liaison with our armoured cars improved out of all recognition.

Speed of advance, it was emphasized, was imperative if Brussels was to be claimed before nightfall. General Adair was determined that there should be no question of his armour being forced to fight a groping street battle after dark. Any serious opposition had, if possible, to be by-passed by our armoured cars, and for this reason, to facilitate deployment, the divisional advance was to be on two centre lines. Separate routes had been carefully worked out, graduating from single-track farm lanes and rough frontier paths in the initial stages to finish up with the wide cobbled highways which eventually run into Brussels from the west.

To lead off on the right or southerly centre line, the choice fell on Major Bowes Daly's ("A") Squadron. This ran through Raches, Orchies, Mouchin, Lesdain, then turned north towards Antoign to pass through Tournai by the southernmost bridge over the River Escaut. Thence it followed the so-called Route Nationale to Brussels by way of Leuze, Ath, Enghien and Hal.

Colonel Abel Smith decided to place Major Wignall's Squadron ("B") in the immediate wake of "A" Squadron. There was good reason for this plan, because it was anticipated that with the Americans reputedly running short of petrol, an open right flank might develop long before reaching Brussels. This appreciation proved to be correct.

Following "B" Squadron came the Welsh Guards group, commanded by Lieutenant-Colonel Windsor Lewis. They were to deal with any heavy opposition which the armoured cars were unable to tackle and brush aside.

Behind the Welsh Guards group came 32nd Guards Brigade Headquarters, with whom 2 H.C.R. Tactical Headquarters moved, then the rest of 32nd Brigade, followed by Divisional Headquarters. In their rear, and prepared for the inevitable mopping-up role, was 231st Brigade, an independent infantry formation, and, in the later stages, a brigade of the Belgian Army.

On the left centre line, Major Herbert's Squadron, "C," was in the van. Its route lay through Montcheau, Pont à Marq, Genech, Bachy, Rumes, Tournai (over the northernmost bridge), thence through Melles and Lessines. At Lessines the route struck north to Grammont and on to Ninove, where a dead straight road twenty kilometres long joined up with the other centre line in the middle of Brussels.

Behind "C" Squadron, in a similar role to that of the Welsh Guards, came the Grenadier group, followed by the remainder of 5th Brigade.

Particularly in the early stages, the selected routes were extremely tortuous, and in addition Major Bowes Daly's Squadron was to be handicapped by having to undertake initially an elaborate route reconnaissance up to the frontier.

The picture may be completed as far as the Regiment is concerned by remembering that Major Bowes Daly's Squadron would probably encounter units of the First U.S. Army (XIX Corps) up to the Tournai area, while to the north, on Major Herbert's left flank, 11th Armoured Division was bound on a similar and almost parallel advance, with Antwerp as the objective.[2]

Anticipating that rapid dissemination of information was going to be of vital importance, Colonel Abel Smith had reinforced the normal wireless channels. In addition to the old "regulars"—that is to say, Captain Ford at Corps Headquarters and Captain Cooper still on his mission with 11th Armoured Division, Captain Balding[3] was with his Americans and the forward groups (the Welsh Guards and the Grenadiers) each had a Household Cavalry representative with them, tuned in to the command net of the leading armoured car squadrons. This meant that their tanks and infantry could be notified immediately the enemy were encountered—an invaluable saving of time as opposed to the normal routine whereby squadron passed information to regiment and regiment to division, whence news had to be then passed down again to lower formations, with all the consequent delays and misunderstandings that such a system entailed. To make communications to Division doubly certain, Major Sir Peter Grant Lawson, the Second-in-Command, rode with General Adair's Headquarters, also tuned in to the leading Squadrons.

Critics have averred that the Guards Armoured Division were too "Infantry minded." This was said after "Spartan" and on other occasions. It was never mentioned again after the liberation of Brussels—for the advance, against opposition, of nearly a hundred miles, in little over fourteen hours' daylight, created a record for any division under any circumstances in all theatres of operation.

The war-time picture of the British soldier imploring his commander to "Let me get at them, sir!" is usually the fiction of some reporter, pressed for his daily quota of copy. Yet today the rivalry between the two leading Squadrons was intense. One sensed Major Herbert marshalling his men, sniffing the air, and scheming hard as to how he could outwit "A" Squadron with a "hot one." For the first and only time, Major Bowes Daly allowed his Troop Leaders to draw lots as to who should lead. This took place in a small wooden shack. Lieutenant F. G. Clarke (3 Troop) won and was to remain in that position without challenge for well over half the journey until he ran out of ammunition. The war correspondents were not slow to seize upon the possibilities of the situation, and even

2. Actually many of 11th Armoured Division's troops passed through Tournai and for a time there was quite a bottle-neck in the town.
3. Captain Balding and his driver, Trooper Chandler, were cut off by the enemy throughout the night of 3rd/4th September when operating between the Regiment and the Americans echeloned back on the right.

staid old "Auntie Times" later so far forgot herself as to allude to the race in terms almost skittish, talking of the "Cavalry Spirit," "Motor Chargers" and a race for Brussels between "an M.F.H. (Major Bowes Daly) and an amateur steeplechase rider (Major Herbert)"!

Everything was now set for the dawn advance.

At ten minutes to seven, its crew still chilled by the cold night, the first "C" Squadron scout car crossed the start line, some miles east of Douai. Ten minutes later Lieutenant Clarke's Troop followed suit for "A" Squadron on the other road, heading warily but rapidly on its first lap to Raches.

The task of screening the advance of the Division was not going to be too easy. The armoured cars had been given the additional task of guarding every important bridge along the line of advance until the infantry could take over. This was to result, as the day wore on, in both Squadrons becoming progressively weaker in strength. Major Herbert's Squadron was to suffer most in this respect, and had it possessed anything more than two depleted Troops when on the outskirts of Brussels in the early afternoon, it is morally certain that it could have overcome the opposition then encountered and entered the capital, winner of the race by several hours.

"C" Squadron, with the easier of the two routes, had started off at a cracking pace, and was soon leading "A" Squadron by several miles. The first substantial enemy opposition was encountered at Pont à Marq, on the Lille—Douai road, a strong-point consisting of six anti-tank guns and some infantry. After a brief exchange of fire, mostly small arms, Lieutenant Paget's Troop found a way round to the right, and wirelessing back the presumed German strength, pushed on eastwards, followed by the remainder of the Squadron. However, this enemy group stuck to its ground, and when the Grenadier Guards came up they became heavily involved, were considerably delayed, and finally, after a tough struggle, captured 125 prisoners, killed 25 Germans, and wounded an equal number. They themselves lost 22 killed and 31 wounded. Many of the local inhabitants were killed and injured in the battle, which turned out to be by far the most serious engagement of the day. It was subsequently ascertained that Pont à Marq was a strongly held hedgehog position, part of the defences to the approach to Lille.[4]

Shortly after by-passing Pont à Marq, Lieutenant Paget's Troop ran into further opposition in the shape of an anti-tank gun, a half-track mounting a heavy mortar, and about two dozen infantry. With admirable

---

4. The King's Company and No. 2 Squadron of the Grenadiers were engaged. The remainder were ordered to resume the advance, by-passing Pont à Marq as "C" Squadron had done.

DOUAI AERODROME

By dusk, 2nd September 1944, most of Guards Armoured Division were concentrated on the concrete runways of Douai aerodrome. Next morning, a Sunday, the historic advance to the Belgian capital began. It was to be led, throughout its ninety-six miles, by the armoured cars of the 2nd Household Cavalry Regiment.

presence of mind, Corporal Bland, in the lead, ordered his scout car driver, Trooper Read, to accelerate and charge the surprised gun crew before they could fire, spraying them in the meantime with his Bren. Three of the gun's crew were killed with the first burst before they could fire back, and another wounded, after which Lieutenant Paget's car (gunner, Corporal Staples) wrecked both anti-tank gun and half-track with four rounds from the 2-pounder. As there were more infantry, however, sniping from a farmhouse at the side of the road, Corporal Bland decided to force them to surrender before advancing again because the enemy were within bazooka range of the main line of traffic. He and Read dismounted and were immediately attacked by Germans armed with automatic pistols and grenades, which latter fortunately exploded into the bank, doing no damage. This compelled Bland to give up ideas of taking prisoners and the farm was raked with bullets from top to bottom. About ten Germans eventually came out and surrendered, many more having been killed and wounded. Squadron Headquarters "coming up later on were quite put off their lunch by the shambles which greeted them when they chanced to halt at the scene of action."

The delay at Pont à Marq had enabled "A" Squadron to catch up again, and Lieutenant Clarke's Troop moved rapidly on towards the Belgian frontier. Then there came a bad moment. Nobody could find a certain small bridge into Belgium. Three of the Troops "swanned" up and down the border looking for it, while Major Bowes Daly kept wirelessing that they must hurry up, for the Welsh Guards, on whom the Squadron had been given a twenty-minute start, were clamouring at the back to get on. At last the tiny bridge was found; Lieutenant Clarke's Troop, with Corporal Boon's scout car in the lead, resumed its advance past some old forts, and over the air came a special message from General Horrocks—Congratulations to the first Allied soldiers to re-enter Belgium.[5]

Some minutes later "C" Squadron entered Tournai, having themselves crossed the border at Bachy amidst scenes of the greatest jubilation. The Americans, as anticipated, had moved up from St. Amand and farther south, across the line of advance, and were in occupation of most of the bridges in this area. They were passed, sitting disconsolately on top of their "Greyhounds," bemoaning the fact that they had run out of petrol and could advance no farther.

In the meantime "A" Squadron reported having reached Antoing, some five kilometres south of Tournai, which latter place they, like "C"

---

5. It was not then known that the Americans, coming up from the south on the inside of the bend, had beaten us to it by several hours. Lieutenant Clarke's Troop could nevertheless still claim to be the first British soldiers into Belgium.

Squadron, would have to pass through before turning due east over the River Escaut.

Once the Americans had been left behind at Tournai, the race began in earnest, with "C" Squadron gradually increasing their lead against the sporadic resistance of an enemy still prepared at times to fight, although devoid of any centralized control. But already Major Herbert was beginning to be anxious about the continued drain on his Reconnaissance Troops. At each bridge passed he was obliged to drop off a half-Troop to guard it, and the Grenadiers were now many miles behind, still engaged at Pont à Marq . Nevertheless, Lessines, well over two-thirds of the way to Brussels, was reached before midday. "There were rather too many snipers here for my liking," said one Troop Leader (Lieutenant Hopkinson), "but we took quite a few prisoners, handing them over to the tender mercies of the Armée Blanche or the Maquis.... I shot up some Medical S.S. officers in a Volkswagen by mistake and we then captured a complete hospital on the move."

★   ★   ★

In the meantime "A" Squadron had been slowed up by encountering about a company of infantry and two S.P. guns on the outskirts of Leuze. The Welsh Guards were soon on the spot and started to deal with the main opposition, while after some delay the armoured cars were able to find a way round the town and pressed on to Ath, which they reached an hour later, only to have to begin the same sort of operation over again, this time without the support of the Welsh Guards group.

But now Major Wignall ("B" Squadron), whose cars had been occupied shooting up the stragglers on the flanks of "A" Squadron, was close at hand. Coming up fast and with the drill worked out to a nicety, he immediately ordered his uncommitted Troops to make a southerly loop with the object of coming in behind the enemy. The plan worked admirably and Lieutenant Palmer's Troop did great execution on the enemy, who, having lost a half-track and a considerable amount of transport and finding themselves harried from the front and shot up on the flanks, beat a hasty retreat, leaving their dead and wounded behind.

The photographs on pages 10 and 11 of the mono section, kindly sent to me by Doctor Vangraefschepe, late Burgomaster of Ath, and Madame P. Delannoy of Enghien, were taken on the day by a local photographer at great personal risk, for the Germans were now shooting out of hand all such recorders of their debacle. The first photograph shows the main street of Ath as the last Germans move out. There are no welcoming flags yet and those civilians visible are apparently taking no notice of the enemy—a wise precaution. The second photograph, taken two minutes later, shows the entry of the first "A" Squadron scout car. Civilians, police, and Resistance men crowd round the liberating Household Cavalrymen. The clock hands point to half past one in the afternoon.

★   ★   ★

To the north, the advance of "C" Squadron continued to be phenomenally rapid. It is perhaps best summarized by what befell Lieutenant Hopkinson. This officer had started off at dawn, "very early, after much popping of corks and drinking cognac with the civilians—there being no time for breakfast." Initially he had worked as liaison officer with the Grenadier group, but subsequently had taken over Lieutenant Paget's Troop after the latter had been wounded by shell splinters some way beyond Ninove. "It was a busy time for we were continually having to drop off troops and loop round opposition. The Troop (No. 1 Troop) by then consisted of only one armoured car and a scout car, the scout car being commanded by Corporal Bland. As we continued the advance we did plenty of shooting-up of German infantry and transport. In fact during that day my gunner, Corporal Staples, knocked out many half-tracks, etc., and kept a careful log of it all!"[6]

Such good progress did this half-Troop make that, "moving along the Ninove—Brussels road, we entered the Brussels suburbs at half past one in the afternoon—the very same time that 'A' Squadron's first scout car was being photographed in Ath, twenty-five miles back along the other road." Everything pointed at this stage to a clear run into Brussels for "C" Squadron, but now, so near the final goal, disaster was to overtake the leading Troop.

"We were fired on," continues Lieutenant Hopkinson, "by something from a copse on the right of the road. Corporal Bland and his driver, Trooper Read, managed to gate-crash the ambush and get in among some houses, and they eventually found a way back through the German defences, with their tool-box riddled and all four tyres shot away, but my armoured car was bazooka-ed in the nearside wheel and we hit first a telegraph pole and then ran into a ditch. At this juncture all the wrath of God was let loose at us, but, miraculously, the bazookas and grenades and everything else blew up outside and we had nothing touch us but a few

6. The Troop on that day accounted for five armoured vehicles and twenty-two soft vehicles.

steel splinters from inside our turret. Dickie Wrottesley[7] (5 Troop) then arrived on the scene and tried to get us out, but the firing was too hot and his scout car driver, Trooper Conry-Candler, was badly wounded in the head (the scout car was knocked out) and so he had to retire. Then the Germans started to stalk us. Incidentally, we were helpless, as the turret ring of our armoured car had jammed in the crash, and as soon as one of us popped his head out the Spandau machine guns opened up. Some stalking 'Krauts' then threw a grenade into the turret; luckily it failed to go off."

Eventually Lieutenant Hopkinson, with Corporal Staples and Trooper Clarke, had to surrender, and as they climbed out of the battered turret of the Daimler, somebody fired at them from a distance, while another German close at hand took shots at Corporal Staples as a warning to him to behave himself! Their captors were found to be S.S. troops and were "pretty annoyed at us as we had shot quite a few of their people in the mêlée. After being pushed around quite a bit, during which time they (the enemy) brought up a 10.5-cm. and an 88-mm. gun, we offered to give their wounded some of our morphia. This eased the situation somewhat, and later on, at a quarter past two in the afternoon, we were taken in an open car to the infantry barracks close at hand in the centre of Brussels."[8] Here we must leave Lieutenant Hopkinson's party in Brussels.

Having failed to extricate the crew of the knocked-out Daimler, Captain Wrottesley swung his two cars in a left-hand sweep to try to get out of the ambush by the same route taken by Corporal Bland in 1 Troop. His armoured car was successful, but Corporal-of-Horse Cridland in the scout car lost track of him in the ensuing fracas and took a different road. His driver, Trooper Conry-Candler, describes what followed when his vehicle was knocked out by an anti-tank gun.

"We were going down a hill at full speed when something hit the engine, which stopped. I managed to roll on a little farther, where we saw a turning to the right and which I hoped would shelter us from the enemy fire, which was still fairly hot, when out of the blue, it seemed, something hit me and I went totally blind for a few minutes but which to me seemed hours. When my sight came back again I managed to get out of the scout car and into a small cafe which was on a corner, and where the good lady of the house gave me a good stiff drink and then hid me in the loft, while

7. Captain Wrottesley, "C" Squadron.
8. Lieutenant Hopkinson and the two other Household Cavalrymen had been nearly put up against the wall and shot out of hand when the Germans discovered a pair of high power, 88-mm. gun type binoculars in the armoured car. Luckily, Hopkinson spotted that one of the enemy had a Sten gun, so he argued his way out of a tricky situation.

> Corporal-of-Horse Cridland, who had not been hit, went to look for a
> way out and the other armoured car."

After this Conry-Candler, who had received a bullet in his skull and
innumerable lumps of shrapnel in his body, must have fainted, for the next
thing that he remembers was finding himself in hospital in Brussels with
two good-looking blond German nurses holding his hands imploringly
and asking him in perfect English, "What will happen to us now?"

★　★　★

So far "C" Squadron, twenty-five miles ahead of their nearest rivals, on
the other road, had got four men into Brussels, but it was a somewhat
hollow triumph for these were all prisoners, one being in addition
seriously wounded. Major Herbert in the suburbs now found himself
in the invidious position of having no troops left with which to try to
force an entry into the capital. The 88-mms. which had knocked out
part of 1 Troop and the scout car in Captain Wrottesley's Troop (it was
subsequently confirmed that there were four 88s, two S.Ps. and several
half-tracks and infantry) proved to have formed part of a ring of defences
intended to cover the approaches into Brussels until nightfall; and
weakened as he was by his strung-out lines—the nearest supporting tanks
and infantry nearly forty miles back—unable to loop or break through
the enemy screen, Major Herbert was ordered to hold his ground and
await the arrival of the Grenadiers, which was not to be until some four
hours later.[9]

Leaving a skeleton "C" Squadron held up four miles from the centre
of Brussels, we again return to "A" Squadron now some miles east of Ath,
where the Germans were finding it increasingly difficult to keep their
lengthening tail clear of trouble. Targets began to present themselves to
the armoured cars in profusion, and the problem of feeding the Besas
and Brens with ammunition became acute. For this reason Lieutenant
Clarke's Troop had been compelled to drop back and the lead had passed
in turn to Lieutenant Peake's and Lieutenant Franklin's Troops. Any
strict adherence to Troop formation was now out of the question and
the race to Brussels was resolving itself into a series of contests between

---

9. Some idea of the problems confronting Major Herbert may be gathered from the fact that
at about this time 5th Brigade had sent out a special flying column (possibly with the idea of
reaching Brussels first) and this column, travelling along the same route, was to capture, kill
or wound about 300 enemy to the rear of "C" Squadron. (Information extracted from Guards
Armoured Division Report.)

available cars, while pressing hard on their heels, and frequently double banking, came the remainder of "A" Squadron Headquarters and the Welsh Guards in their speedy Cromwell tanks.

Somewhere between Ath and Enghien, Lieutenant Wordsworth's scout car challenged and took the lead. Lieutenant Wordsworth, it will be remembered, normally commanded the Support Troop, but he had chafed at the thought of guarding bridges all day and had asked Major Bowes Daly to let him "have a go at the enemy." Lieutenant Franklin's Troop was short of a scout car and so Wordsworth had stepped into the breach. And now let Trooper Ben Fisher, his driver, take up the story.

"We proceeded cautiously for a while; the targets had been many; then, gradually increasing speed, we by-passed several small groups of German infantry, who offered only slight resistance. Enghien loomed ahead. A straight length of approximately 500 yards had to be traversed before entering the outskirts of the town—sporadic rifle and machine-gun fire buzzed over our heads, apparently coming from a building on our left. A short burst from our Bren gun and the firing stopped abruptly. Deciding that it was more or less a parting gesture, we approached the edge of the town. Silence reigned. I noticed a disconsolate-looking horse harnessed to a cart, which eyed us as we passed. We turned left into the town, rounding the bend slowly, and drew up on to the pavement, scanning the street in front. Not a movement greeted our eyes. Deathly silence pervaded, a silence of expectancy often experienced before. We continued for a moment to observe the street and houses.

"The silence was broken dramatically and unexpectedly. An urgent tapping upon a window averted my eyes from the road ahead. I looked across the road; a woman's face was visible, warning us of danger from behind. Twisting round in my seat, I peered through the vision slit and immediately slammed the car into reverse. We shot round the bend, almost grazing the front wheel of the first vehicle in a convoy of German lorries! The drivers were frantically climbing into their cabs and starting up. These lorries had been drawn up along a road which was more or less hidden from our view. I reversed sufficiently for our Bren to be brought to bear upon the leading vehicle. We did not fire. They were ambulances, although I doubted the authenticity of the Red Crosses displayed on their sides.

"Mr. Wordsworth, suspecting that they were bogus, called up Squadron Headquarters. 'Shall we detain this convoy?' Major Daly replied in the negative; ambulances were not to be delayed. We waited, Bren still trained warily upon the vehicles. The convoy moved off; two despatch riders attached to it rode past, ten yards from the muzzle of our Bren; one of them looked at us and waved a gauntleted hand. We did not wave back! Several tough-looking customers peered out at us from between the canvas cover at the back. I am almost certain that these were pseudo ambulances, evacuating fit men—perhaps S.S.

"We didn't see them again.

"Lieutenant Wordsworth again called up Squadron Headquarters, 'Preparing to advance into the town.' We entered slowly in the middle of the street; again not a movement, not a sound, and so round another bend over the bridge. There was movement to the left, running figures disappeared into a clump of trees; we didn't bother about them. Still the silence persisted.

"I increased speed slightly. A figure leapt out at us; one of the Resistance men, determined to give us a welcome, darted over to us and dropped a bottle of Scotch whisky into the car! (I still retain the label which was attached to the neck.) He stayed with us until we reached the long concrete road stretch outside the town. I thanked him for the whisky on a subsequent visit to Enghien. His name is Monsieur Omer Michiels, 60 Rue Marechal Montgomery, Enghien.

"By now a few more exuberant spirits had ventured into the street and shouted greetings to us, but it was not until our car had advanced through the town that the full realization of liberation was borne to them.

"Our Resistance men (two were accompanying us by that time) dropped off when we turned into the long white concrete road, dead straight for almost a mile—the anti-tank gunner's dream and the recce man's nightmare. However, increasing speed, we proceeded down this interminable road, observing plenty of movement on our right which we deduced was caused by the fleeing enemy. Warning our rear S/C., we pushed on. A lone house 100 yards ahead held our attention, a track joined the road from behind the far side; its direction behind a house was indicated by a high hedge, which ended at the end of a wood 150 yards from the main road. We approached slowly, 50 yards—40 yards, and still no movement. Thirty yards distance separated us from the house when, leisurely and unconcernedly, out stepped a German soldier in full marching order, rifle slung over his shoulder. He walked into the middle of the road, turned to face us, and stared. Momentarily taken aback by this strange behaviour, we stared also. Our surprise was short-lived. 'Hey, that's a b.......y German! ' I shouted. The Bren opened fire. With one mighty bound he leapt for cover, rifle clattering to the ground. Our tracer zipped between his legs, past his head and under his armpits, but he somehow escaped and disappeared behind the house. What a miraculous escape! The sound of our firing had barely died away when from the wood on our right issued the sound of revving diesels.

"Vehicles, camouflaged to a ridiculous degree, careered crazily out of their hiding places and sped down another track running almost parallel with the road. A high earthen bank prevented our using the Bren with any effectiveness. Only the tops of the vehicles were visible. We drew forward, sending as we did so an urgent call to the two Daimlers. They roared up the road as the German convoy emerged approx. 300 yards ahead. What a target! We closed in on them until half that distance separated us; then suddenly the action was taken completely out of our hands. Our ears were assailed by an ear-splitting reverberating snarl, punctuated by the crisp crackling of synchronized cannon. Huge chunks of flaking concrete spewed up from the surface of the road, showering us with a white hail. The red tiles on the roof ahead disintegrated with a clatter. We stopped. Messerschmitts — Focke-Wulfs? Our relief was great when we recognized them as American Thunderbolts. They roared around and prepared for a second run-in. We retired slightly, judiciously making a more distinguishing gap between ourselves and the enemy. Guns silent, we watched the drama being enacted ahead. The Thunderbolts dived again. No mistake this time. Streams of red tracer shells hurtled viciously down into the convoy. A pathetically ineffective Spandau spat back at them and then was silent. A black greasy pall of smoke writhed heavenwards, the funeral pyre marking the end. Their mission completed, the planes disappeared, flying low over the trees. The road ahead was impassable, it was a blazing inferno. A loop was indicated. This was carried out successfully round to the right, re-joining the road beyond the burning vehicles."

At this stage, the advance broke up into a series of isolated engagements, punctuated by fighter aircraft swoops, almost as feared by the armoured cars as by the Germans. Lieutenant Peake's Troop had looped to the right, shot up some infantry and knocked out an armoured half-track. Coming back on to the main road again, he had then overtaken some enemy lorries and shot up six of them; then was in turn strafed by a Hurricane which, as well as finishing off the German vehicles, punctured all the tyres of his leading scout car, giving Corporal Ford-Nairn and Trooper Williams a most uncomfortable half-minute. Fortunately, the tyres being "run-flats," they were able to continue at reduced speed.

Corporal-of-Horse Booth (Lieutenant Franklin's Troop), who had been closely following Lieutenant Wordsworth, had been similarly suspicious of many Red Cross markings. He had, however, refrained from firing upon them. He was now beginning to lose patience at the manifest signs that the Germans were up to their old tricks.

"I noticed a villainous-looking thug armed with a machine gun peering out from behind an awning of the last of nine ambulances which sped past me. I had been behind Lieutenant Wordsworth's car, but he had temporarily gone out of sight round a bend in the road.

"Nearest to me was Corporal-of-Horse Neil's armoured car from Lieutenant Peake's Troop—one of the many cars at this time running short of small-arms ammunition. Suddenly a flight of Thunderbolts came in from the blue, opening fire on all and sundry, and literally tearing the German 'ambulances' to bits. Tiles from near-by houses clattered all over the roadway, earth spouted up all around, and then I saw that burning vehicles completely blocked the main road. Because of this I attempted to loop southwards across two small fields, and in doing so ran into a group of about 150 Germans! Fortunately, most of them showed no desire to resist, and the minority who did were soon overruled by the threat of our guns and their own comrades!

"Near at hand two enemy vehicles were blazing fiercely, and a farm cart laden with shouting Germans ran straight into my armoured car, jamming itself up against the rear wheel. The Germans redoubled their shouting and I shouted back at them, ordering them to get themselves and their wagons disentangled in double quick time.[10] The confusion in front of me was almost as bad as that which I had recently left, and I saw little prospect of being able to make a satisfactory loop. To make matters worse, Major Bowes Daly was calling up for more information. All rather frustrating at the time!"[11]

At this stage, the Air Force's close strafing was continuous, but in view of Corporal Ford-Nairn's experience and many other narrow escapes, Colonel Abel Smith had reported the situation to Corps Headquarters and they immediately stopped all close air support. Friend and foe were by now so inextricably mixed up at the front of the column that to expect pilots to be able to differentiate targets was asking the impossible.

Having by now got through the tangle of Germans, Corporal-of-Horse Booth regained the main road, where he found that the Welsh Guards had arrived and were busy pushing and crushing the burning debris of lorries out of the way in magnificent style; most of "A" Squadron and the Welsh Guards' tanks were now running neck and neck, and at one period even the refuelling squadron petrol lorry, with Corporal-Major Berrisford in charge, momentarily took the lead. Lieutenant Franklin's crew, who had dropped back slightly because of being held up by the same burning wreckage which had caused Booth to by-pass,

10. Booth spoke no German—it must have been a most interesting scene. *Author*
11. Corporal-of-Horse Booth's narrative was given to me during an afternoon's talk at a later date and taken down by me in long hand. I am entirely responsible for any inaccuracies which may occur in the story. *Author*

described how two German lorries attached themselves to the column. "We saw all the tank turrets turn on to them at the same time. Then a full broadside from half a dozen Cromwells went into them and they simply disappeared in a cloud of black smoke."

On writing to the Burgomaster of Enghien in the course of checking details of the Brussels advance, I was put in touch with Madame Delannoy, of 12 Avenue Albert, Enghien. She had volunteered to nurse wounded British prisoners of war in occupied Belgium from 1940 onwards, and for her services to the Allied cause had been awarded the M.B.E. Her son, Monsieur Yves Delannoy, had been a prominent member of the Resistance (Mouvement National Beige). To these two persons, together with Monsieur Maurice Weverbergts[12], I am indebted for a narrative which throws a most interesting light not only on the fateful hours preceding liberation, but also on the actual moment of entry into the town of the first liberating cars. The story is as follows:

"The College of St. Augustin at Enghien had recently been requisitioned by the Germans and in a few days had become a huge hospital for their wounded. Surgical instruments and all medical accessories were soon forthcoming and were installed there with a speed and organization that was quite remarkable, bearing in mind the chaotic state of the enemy troops.

"In the main, the retreating enemy columns came from the direction of Tournai. They belonged to an amazing variety of units and formations, and all day and night of September 2nd /3rd kept passing through in interminable relays. Many were from the Todt organization … there were infantry, artillery dragging their heavy guns, and many soldiers from the Luftwaffe. They rode in farm-wagons, beer lorries, broken-down cars dragged by horses, and a variety of other vehicles still moving along under their own power. But even all this cavalcade was quite inadequate, for the majority of the troops struggled along on foot.

"Resistance in Enghien comprised three forces—l'Armée Secrète (A.S), le Mouvement Nationale Beige (M.N.B.), and les Partisans Armés (P.A.). The first-named occupied itself especially with sabotage; the second, Intelligence; and the third with minor sabotage and purging. Theoretically there existed no link between the three, but in reality the chiefs of the A.S. and the M.N.B. met to confer at frequent intervals and worked closely together. The Geheimpolizei had one of their main

---

12. Maurice Weverbergts was seriously wounded in the course of an engagement with the enemy in the early afternoon of the 3rd of September. He was picked up "dying" by Yves Delannoy outside the little café named "Le Patriote," past which sped the 2 H.C.R. advance. He made a miraculous recovery and is now in fairly good health.

stations at Lessines, which was linked to Enghien by special telephone. In addition, there were important lines linking the Geheimpolizei, the Feldgendarmerie and the Gestapo of Brussels with that of Tournai. This was the general situation.

"Late in the evening of 2nd September an order was passed round to the A.S. to reverse the signposts and to cut all the German telephone wires. This latter act was not without danger, for the enemy kept constant patrols along the lines, but by 0200 hours 3rd September these were all cut. Then having spent the night *à la belle étoile*, the Belgian patrols returned after the lifting of the curfew, to hear that the British had crossed the frontier.

"During the morning of the 3rd a strong contingent of S.S., also in all sorts of transport, entered the town. Harried by the Allied Air Force, in continual fear of a Resistance ambush, these were in the last stages of exhaustion. Enraged at the manifest signs of joy which could be read in the faces of the spectators, their bad humour was so evident that those of us who watched them pass took good care not to annoy them. For having tried to take photographs, several of the inhabitants had already nearly paid with their lives. The S.S. installed themselves in both the 'Petit' and the 'Grand' Parcs,' while a continuous stream of other soldiers, in a generally pitiable state, continued to struggle through.

"At 1015 hours the Burgomaster, imposed upon us by the Germans in 1941, sheepishly handed over the seals of office to his successor—the very same whom he had himself supplanted.

"As for the English, who were now the sole topic of conversation, rumour placed them now at Tournai, now at Ath. Popular imagination, which one so often says is in advance of fact, was this time outstripped by reality. As we were wondering what was to happen, the last German infantry, escorted by tanks, passed by, and simultaneously we heard the prolonged and dull roar of an explosion signifying that the enemy were blowing up their last dump of ammunition, stored in the Bois Strihou. This was succeeded by a strange uncanny calm, to be broken suddenly by the soft purring of three *petites autos blindées*.[13] They halted, carefully scanned the road ahead, and cautiously resumed their journey. Thus it was on the 3rd of September at 1500 hours that the first of these little *autos blindées* reached the centre of Enghien, to be accorded the greatest and most sincerely enthusiastic welcome our little town had ever known.

"At long last the British were back again."

There follows a description of how, hot on the heels of the armoured cars, came the tanks of the Welsh Guards. How they were forced to slow

---

13. Lieutenant Wordsworth and Trooper Fisher; (2) Corporal-of-Horse Booth and driver; (3) Lance-Corporal-of-Horse Dewar and Trooper Ayles.

down to a crawl to avoid injuring the enraptured population, and how flowers and fruit and drink and *des baisers* were showered on every soldier.

The population was continually appealing to the crews of the cars as they passed by to go and help them to round up the remaining Boches. But nothing could then be done, for to make a detour at the request of every civilian was out of the question. This, it was explained, was the task of the follow-up troops. The Regiment's lay in pushing on relentlessly.

As was so often to happen in liberated places, the joy of Enghien was clouded by last-minute tragedy. The main road to Brussels taken by the armoured cars cut directly through the centre of the town, but this meant that a considerable pocket of enemy had to be left to the north, where they had fled along the road that followed the old ramparts, and also to the south in a belt of trees known locally as the Grand' Parc. An unlucky Resistance patrol of over twenty men ran into the northern pocket and was subsequently surrounded by the enemy and met a gallant and tragic end, only two of its members surviving. Even worse, to the south, corpses of a number of civilians were later found in the Parc, horribly mutilated, done to death by blows from rifle butts.

★ ★ ★

Lieutenant Wordsworth and Trooper Fisher, continuing their advance from Enghien, shortly came upon "a group of fifty or more German cavalrymen, standing dejectedly by the side of the road. Their horses were grazing peacefully in a near-by field. They (the enemy) were handed over to a very un–Germanic-looking individual who spoke with a Texas drawl. His plane had been brought down near Enghien some days previously and the locals had sheltered him. He was mounted on a fine-looking horse and appeared to be enjoying the situation immensely."

From Enghien onwards the advance was to be comparatively uneventful. More prisoners were handed over to the Belgians; there were delays caused by half-hearted rear-guards, and of course innumerable false alarms, but nothing in the way of a serious check. Both Lieutenant Franklin's and Lieutenant Peake's Troops passed through Hal shortly after five o'clock in the evening, with no untoward happening, although, as they subsequently learnt, there was opposition to the remainder of "A" Squadron and the Welsh Guards which was to hold up their progress for some time.[14]

---

14. "The next serious hold-up was at Hal in the middle of the afternoon, and it came at a time when the battle group was beginning to think in serious terms about Brussels looming nearer and nearer with every minute and every kilometre that flashed by." *Welsh Guards at War,* by Major L. F. Ellis, C.V.O., C.B.E., D.S.O., M.C. Gale & Polden Ltd., Aldershot.

Major Bowes Daly was now ordered to switch his forward troops with all speed across the southern part of Brussels to occupy the area of Schaerbeek and down to the Champ des Manoeuvres. This move had as its object the protection of the north-eastern exits from the city.

The order entailed the cars branching off the original centre line at a cross-roads in the suburbs of Zuen, where momentary delay was caused while an enemy tank's intentions were investigated. It proved to have been abandoned and was flying a white flag.

"Again," wrote Trooper Fisher, "upon entering the outskirts of Brussels, that peculiar silence persisted. Curtains were drawn aside, to be hurriedly dropped back when we glanced round. A priest crossed the road quickly, looking neither to the right nor to the left. He entered a house and slammed a door with a crash.

"Soon, however, they realized that we were British—and pandemonium broke loose. Map reading became impossible and our scout car contained at one time eleven people, about five of them in my driving compartment."

Which of the Household Cavalry cars could with justification stake a claim to have reached the centre of the capital first? Three crews had remained in front, unchallenged since leaving Enghien. And of these three, both Corporal-of-Horse Booth's and Lieutenant Wordsworth's crews confirmed that they were passed when still in the suburbs by Lieutenant Franklin's leading scout car. The evidence appears clear, therefore, that the honour of being the first soldiers to enter into and pass through the very centre of Brussels rightly belongs to Lance-Corporal-of-Horse I. W. Dewar, a Scotsman from 22 Elm Place, Aberdeen, and his driver, Trooper D. Ayles, a Londoner from 225 Walworth Road, Walworth—both members of No. 4 Troop "A" Squadron.

It was a fitting climax that a scout car from the Regiment, which had always been in the van of 30 Corps' advance since crossing the Seine, and which had led Guards Armoured Division up to the Somme and on both centre lines to Brussels, should be the first to enter the Belgian capital, and every Household Cavalryman felt proud of his share in the achievement.[15]

Let us follow Dewar's route to its ultimate destination.

---

15. At this time armoured car regiments were still Corps troops. Therefore on the run to Brussels, 2nd Household Cavalry Regiment did not actually form part of Guards Armoured Division but was under command for the operation. Although "A" Squadron cars were first into Brussels, the Welsh Guards provided the first entire battalion to enter the city because the remainder of 2nd Household Cavalry Regiment, with a view to future commitments, was deliberately held back on higher orders.—*Author*

After having passed the road junction where he was to turn right and which contained the knocked-out tank, Dewar called up his Troop Leader, Lieutenant Franklin, but was unable to obtain an immediate reply. However, Major Bowes Daly intercepted the message and ordered the crew to push on irrespective of any other considerations. The streets were still quite deserted, for the inhabitants took the scout car to be German. Dewar brought out a tiny Union Jack and propped it up at the front. This did the trick and people appeared from everywhere. Behind, the other cars in the Troop soon found it almost impossible to move, but being just that much in front, Dewar managed to keep going. The two men eventually reached a small square which, since they had been making good speed, was once again deserted. "As I could speak a bit of French, I asked the way, and a civilian mockingly told me to get a move on, as 'les Anglais' were known to be in the suburbs! I informed him that we were English, and gosh! I wish I hadn't. The Belgians made one mighty rush at us and we were completely swamped out. I tried to get a message over my 'A' set, but the aerials had already been whisked off as 'souvenirs.' So had our bedding, all our rations, the cooker, and everything else. We had 'visitors' inside the car and on its back—in fact, we could not budge an inch. Our photographs were taken and afterwards published in the Brussels newspapers as 'the first British soldiers to enter Brussels.'[16]

"To return to the scene in the square. The police had now arrived and tried to push the crowd back. I got into conversation with one of them and he told me that the Germans were still in a large building in front [Palais de Justice]. It was smoking when we arrived and there were people carrying out furniture and papers, but we did not pay much attention at the time as we had to push on.

"With the assistance of the police we cleared a way and reached our railway station at Schaerbeek, only to be surrounded by another wild crowd howling for souvenirs. We had now nothing left—not even a headphone. They then proceeded to remove our wheels, but once again the police saved us and we were spared their loss.

"We were getting a trifle worried because, having no wireless now and out on our own amidst a delirious mob, there was not much one could do. However, we backed our scout car up a lane and set up the Bren gun. It seemed all rather hopeless and silly because, surrounded by the screaming population who refused to move back and only wanted our photographs and to shake hands, there was not much one could do. The

---

16. Lieutenant Franklin, who was close behind in his Daimler armoured car, also figured in the Brussels newspapers as "The first British tank to enter Brussels"!

police told us that the Germans had just left the station, a trainload of them, half an hour ago, and there was all sorts of kit lying about. A few hours later we joined up with Mr. Wordsworth, who eventually got us back to Squadron Headquarters."

★   ★   ★

Lieutenant Wordsworth and Trooper Fisher had taken a different route, which was to lead them to another railway station farther east, close to the junction of the two roads out to Louvain. "Such chaos was taking place, that when I reached the station I found that I had one section of my own Support Troop, besides two vehicles belonging to Michael Franklin's Troop, as well as two or three other vehicles—all belonging to other Troops. Wireless, as usually happened in built-up areas, was not working too well and the Squadron was all over the place, and I was some time re-establishing communications and generally controlling the crowds. At long last, after the crews had stuffed themselves silly with ice-creams and signed numberless autographs between even more numerous bouts of kissing, we all eventually met up in the dark and harboured that night at the Tir National near Edith Cavell's Memorial."

But before the hours of darkness fall upon a further series of scenes, each more fantastic than the other, it is best to return to the main body of the Regiment.

"B" Squadron in their role of "Mrs. Mop" had been shooting up stragglers and had encountered part of the opposition which the Welsh Guards had dealt with in Ath. In addition, many Germans instead of retreating eastwards were also heading north for Antwerp and the coast and were therefore continually passing across the front.

There was a little Air O.P. flying backwards and forwards above the columns, and the sights which surely met the pilot's gaze must have been full of interest. He must have seen the long, straggling columns of the enemy converging towards the capital. He also would have seen the desperate confusion of the Germans debouching from the side roads and the forward surge of the British armour cutting in on them. It was the same story on both centre lines—a succession of burning trucks, bullet-riddled cars, smashed limbers, and derelict tanks.

Hundreds of prisoners were standing in dejected bunches by the roadside waiting to be claimed. Fearing reprisals, many clamoured to be taken aboard by the Regiment. All were handed over to the Belgian Resistance, who, like the French, provided with Sten guns but recently parachuted to them, were quite equal to the occasion.

A Colonel of the Wehrmacht was brought in on the back of a baker's tri-car with his intended loot, wrist watches and rubber hot water bottles, crammed in its lockers. In another place a soldier surrendered on a motor scooter which he admitted had been his form of transport since Amiens. His Belgian captor was armed with a scythe. Even the designer of our Boys anti-tank rifle might have been comforted to see that someone still had faith in this useless relic of Dunkirk days, when a Belgian thus armed halted a taxi-load of German officers on the outskirts of Ath.

The abundance of food showered upon us seemed rich and incredible, and a glance through personal records reads more like a shopping expedition to Fortnum and Mason's than the triumphant advance of an army. Carefully hoarded delicacies from the family store cupboard saw the light of day for the first time since the country had been overrun. Soldiers were literally bombarded with fruit. One trooper was knocked out by a pear and carried his black eye with him to the frontiers of Holland. Blankets were being unrolled to protect bottles of champagne, and tool-boxes stuffed with flagons of Burgundy. In return we gave them most of our cigarettes and chocolates and sticky boiled sweets.

Yet in spite of all these proffered treasures which had been carefully hidden from the Germans, the underlying hunger of the people was plain to see, as they descended in droves upon the still warm carcasses of dead horses lying by the roadside.

With their camouflage netting the cars lent themselves well to decoration, and they soon became festooned with flowers. In the case of the lorries and other soft vehicles, the commanders were expected by the population (and often solemnly complied) to carry bouquets in their hands. On the left-hand road a "C" Squadron Corporal-of-Horse, with his car loaded with cheering civilians and bedecked like an entrant in *La Bataille des Fleurs* (on each wing had been strapped a pot of geraniums draped in the Belgian national colours!), was seen chasing a German bus at full speed. "It was impossible in the general clamour and noise to hear whether my guns were firing, but I knew that they were from the rhythmical waving of a bunch of dahlias draping the barrels up to the muzzles!"

★   ★   ★

On the road to Antwerp, the story of 11th Armoured Division's advance was the same, although it is to be suspected that Captain Cooper's route took him much farther forward than a strict interpretation of Colonel Abel Smith's orders for liaison officers warranted.

"Up at 0615 hours and advance over start line with main H.Q. Move up the column and join Inns of Court Regiment just outside Lens. Route Henin-Liétard—Courriere—Thumeries—Attiches—Seclin—Bouvines—Cysoing, over the Belgium frontier at Wannehain—Tournai—Renaix—Ninove Strythem—Assche—Wolverthem.

"At Attiches we had some black coffee and a glass of wine and ate some pears which the people had given us. We shortly caught up with the leading Inns of Court Troop at Seclin and had a good shoot at some German infantry *en route*. At Cysoing had a report of a German tank, but when I went to have a look it had gone. The Franco-Belgian frontier was studded with forts and strong-points but was not held by the enemy. Tremendous welcome in Belgium—flags come out as we enter each town and village. I remain with leading Inns of Court Troop and send all information back to Regiment through them. Soon into Tournai with first few tanks—reports of Germans in the town and went off on our own but met some Americans. They joined in the hunt for the enemy in the streets, having nearly shot us at first.

"Suddenly two lorries filled with Germans appear round a corner of the main street—they would not stop so we shot them up. Killed nine and wounded another seven. This was pretty unpleasant and they were lying all over the street, some in a pretty bad state. An American doctor was very handy with the morphia needle, but one slightly wounded German tried to throw a grenade at me and was promptly set on by about five civilians, who, incidentally, try to rob the bodies straight away. We had to chase them off.

"Thought it time to push on so said good-bye to my American friends and started to catch up with the leading troops, who are pushing on fast, leaving the mopping up to their infantry.

"Guards Armoured Division had joined the centre line for a time at Tournai, and I went along with them as far as Hacquegnies; met Charles Rutland and had a 'crack.' Rejoined my own centre line at road junction near Renaix, when I met another U.S. patrol. Civilians are wild with joy as we are first British car. They told us of a few Germans in the area, so hid my car under some trees; saw a German half-track through my field-glasses and went round with my Tommy gun, but it moved on.

"Moved on to Renaix, hoping to meet leading troops, but discovered we were first car in and actually 'liberated' the town! Flags appeared suddenly from all over the place and the people began to cheer and sing. I was not at all happy at being so far ahead. Went to the station and was told that 150 Germans had left twenty minutes before. Suddenly there was an enormous explosion in the middle of the town, windows were smashed everywhere; apparently an ammunition dump blown up by time fuse.

But nobody minds and we are literally mobbed by thousands of people. More photographs, flowers and wine, food, etc. At least ten people are riding on our car! Decide to look over the town and clear street with greatest difficulty and the help of police. More and more people appear, bringing bunches of flowers and presents. Halted at northern entrance of town, hoping the leading chaps would come along at any minute. Told of two Germans leaving in a car but cannot go on a wild goose chase. Again hundreds of people on and around the car and I cannot keep the guns free.

"Suddenly somebody shouted, 'Boche tank,' and everyone scattered in all directions. We were left alone to face it. Carroll jumped into the seat and began turning round, and as we turned I emptied a magazine from the Bren into the leading German vehicle, which turned out to be a car, and stopped it. (We found afterwards from the civilians where it halted that we'd killed and/or wounded two of them.) The second car, a lorry, halted some way behind it. By the grace of God, we met the Inns of Court armoured cars coming into the place. I lined up with the leading Daimler and nosed round the street corner. Along came a 'combination' and some infantry. We started up a terrific barrage. Shop windows flying in all directions and ricochets off the pavement. The population disappeared like magic.

"Eventually we all pushed on. I fired on three Germans at Nederbrakel, who soon chucked it and surrendered. I had interpreter on car with me now.

"Arrived at Ninove with the first three tanks and the Inns of Court. Heard of a German general in the town and went off with civilian to find him but found he had left ten minutes before—simply maddening. So went off round the town looking for stray Germans but mobbed by hundreds of civilians. We are now literally two feet deep in flowers all-round the car. Orchids of every known variety and at least £50 worth of other flowers. More wine and endless embracing. Two girls in Belgian dress in road with bouquets and a tray of champagne to which are attached cards marked 'a present from Ninove.' Eventually broke away. (Carroll gets so very embarrassed!).[17]

"Round the corner in time to get a shoot in on three German transports. One of our tanks blazing away down main street at twenty yards range. Seven Germans killed; the remainder scatter and surrender, while civilians cheer from their doorways.

"Moved on once more with the tanks. An unfortunate German with both legs off lying in the road vaguely trying to move. It's no good me

17. Trooper Carroll, Captain Cooper's Irish servant.

stopping as we are still under heavy fire—the medical chaps are coming up. This part of war is very bloody."

Mentioning that he got to Wolverthem at dusk, very tired and sleepy, Captain Cooper concludes the day with this nice touch:

"Whenever a horse is killed the people cut it up and take it away immediately to eat, leaving only its head and insides piled in an untidy heap by the side of the road," adding unsuspectingly:
"We got some *very* good sandwiches from the civilians here!"

★   ★   ★

To return to Brussels. When later the remainder of "A" Squadron, double banking with the Welsh Guards, burst through the main thoroughfares of the city, it seemed as if a million inhabitants had of one accord gone mad. Brussels received its liberators that night as no other city had done before. In the case of Paris, General Eisenhower had arranged for the American troops to be held back to allow the French 2nd Armoured Division to enter first into the city. The French response to this gesture was to ring the approaches to their capital and to allow no one (not even American liaison officers) but a member of their own armoured division to pass. No such curious Gallic complexes guided the Belgian emotions. Spontaneously they lined the streets and pavements twenty deep and cheered and cheered and cheered. Last war veterans saluted, wives cried and laughed alternately, young women leapt on to the vehicles embracing the dusty soldiers, and youths fired rifles into the air.

British, American, and Russian flags, waving this once in closest unison, fluttered from every house. People crowded the balconies and filled the window spaces, raining streamers on to the travel-stained berets below.

For a time, because of the large white stars painted for recognition purposes on the cars, the Belgians thought that we were Americans, but having foreseen this the crews brought out Union Jacks which now fluttered from the aerials. Some had even unofficially painted them over the front armour plating.

Nobody bothered about the few odd Germans still at large in Brussels. Lieutenant Franklin, whose car had been trying to fight a battle while an old woman sat astride the 2-pounder gun, knocked out a couple of German staff cars travelling behind one another with one burst of machine-gun fire which also riddled the food tins of his colleague in front—an unpopular effort for the tins were part of an "A" pack.

As at Chanu, the Staghound tyres exerted a curious fascination on the male civilians, who would exclaim as they patted them, "Ah, mais quel beau materiel! "

Advancing slowly towards the Tir National, it seemed to "A" Squadron as if the cars were floating on a sea of upturned faces. Women chalked their names and addresses on the tyres and the turrets and every square inch of space. Children were held up to receive a kiss from "Tommy." Mothers even tried to thrust their babies through the driving visors lest their offspring should miss this friendly benediction, while those with no children obligingly held up their own faces and the crowd roared its approval as the man at the helm responded with alacrity—Brussels seemed to be filled with pretty women and fresh cotton frocks and dancing lights.

At intervals there would occur a momentary lull in the general babel of voices as a lorry-load of Germans, guarded by the Armée Blanche, hove into view. Then the cries of joy would change to the roar of a mob in anger—terrible to hear in its insistent clamour and thirst for blood.

Every so often, to add to the confusion, smooth-looking limousines of American vintage and filled to bursting with gangs of youths, armed to the teeth, would tear round a corner with a screech of tyres to make off through the scattering throng, Boche hunting. Not all these sleek-looking cars had belonged to "Collaborators" by any means, nor were their present occupants inevitably "patriots," but the process of cashing in on chaos had already begun.

Night fell and still the crowds stayed on, determined that every Allied vehicle entering the city should receive its full share of welcome. Wisely, albeit sadly, Divisional Headquarters had reached the conclusion that they would not yet be able to function in the centre of Brussels. Of the Regiment, all except "A" Squadron had been halted short of the city. "B" and "D" Squadrons together with R.H.Q. were drawn into the village of Leeuw St. Pierre, ten kilometres out, and were given the task of guarding Divisional Headquarters. "C" Squadron, whose fine effort had come so near to complete success during the afternoon, had been ordered by Colonel Abel Smith to await the arrival of the Grenadiers, who (minus a company of infantry and a squadron of tanks) had passed through them to enter the city shortly after nine o'clock. The Grenadiers reported meeting nothing more lethal in Brussels than a German motor-cyclist who ended up in the ditch, "a mutilated wreck," and four fat German quartermasters who, having joined the Grenadiers' column by mistake, when discovered shot at the Adjutant of the 2nd Battalion, luckily with little effect, and were pounced upon together with all their loot. Like us, the Grenadiers experienced the greatest difficulty in advancing to their destination through the crowds and kisses, but eventually found themselves at the Palace of Laeken.

"C" Squadron were ordered to harbour just outside Brussels, but Captain Clyde and Lieutenant van Cutsem nevertheless managed to "lose" themselves and, to "their intense surprise," they found themselves in the centre of the rejoicing city.

★ ★ ★

There was little sleep that night. The darkness only seemed to accentuate the mad carnival spirit of the occasion as to the cry of "Ah, Monsieur, comme nous avons souffert," the price of champagne rocketed from 350 to 1,500 francs per bottle within the hour. The resiliency and equilibrium of the *marché noir* was fascinating to behold. To the Belgians, the Black Market was not only profitable, it was logical as a means of withholding goods from an enemy who had purposefully flooded their country with worthless paper currency. Adjusted to rob the Germans of their money and morale, it was already adapting itself with unqualified success to its new mode of life under the "Liberators."

Four years of occupation appeared to have left the city materially undamaged, and the shops were filled with goods which we had not seen for a long time in England; but the Bruxellois for all that hated the Germans bitterly, and the people knew no limits to the excesses of passion and hate that night.

The Palais de Justice, one of the largest buildings in Europe, stands beautifully situated at the top of a hill, overlooking the centre of Brussels. It had been used to house the fearful archives of the Gestapo. When Corporal-of-Horse Dewar had first come upon it it was only smouldering. Now its flaming dome was casting a deep red glow visible for miles around and to its light the mobs danced on into the early hours.

Over by the Tir National, the Belgians, had they been allowed, would have dragged off every Household Cavalryman to their homes in triumph; as it was, "A" Squadron had no sleep at all, and after forty-eight hours Major Daly had to plead to be withdrawn to obtain some measure of rest for his exhausted men.

A similar call for help had come from the Regimental Echelon parked in a football field in the suburbs. Unused to such concentrated adulation, Major Williams had reported that he "couldn't answer for the consequences." There could, in fact, be no better way of summing up the Brussels Sunday of Liberation than in the words of Colonel Abel Smith's terse report for official use: "When liberating territory the attentions of civilians very much impede operations."

★   ★   ★

In spite of missing the entry into Brussels, those at Leeuw St. Pierre had plenty to occupy their attention. Divisional Headquarters required protection because the roads were by no means clear and the woods were still full of German stragglers wishing to give themselves up.

What promised to be the most unusual surrender of the campaign took place in a wood when Trooper Payne of Lieutenant Ainsworth's Troop was forced, in somewhat delicate circumstances, to ask his would-be captive to "wait a few minutes." The German clicked his heels, unslung his loaded rifle and bandolier, and stood discreetly with his back turned before giving himself up.

In the small hours of the morning, Corporal Meade-King and Trooper Munday, on guard duty by the main road with no more than their rifles to hand, thought they recognized the sounds of clanking tracks approaching their post. Knowing that all British tanks had been travelling in the opposite direction, they prepared for the worst, when to their surprise, instead of an enemy tank, round the bend came a Belgian tram at full speed with all its lights blazing. This phenomenon, never satisfactorily explained, was put down as another of war's unfathomable mysteries.

Not so happy was the ending to another incident in which Lieutenant Kavanagh's Troop was involved. The Troop had been posted at a Y-roads on the main road to Brussels with orders to check traffic during the night moving into the city. One scout car had been placed off the road about 800 yards in the other direction with instructions to signal if anything unusual should approach, but otherwise to take no action—this because it was a very dark night and impossible to see more than a few yards. During the night various units of Guards Armoured Division passed through at intervals, most of the tanks carrying infantry. At about two o'clock in the morning a three-tonner lorry, followed by two tanks with some troops aboard, came along the road. Called upon to halt, the lorry stopped on the far side of the road, about thirty feet away, but both tanks swung past and continued on their course—it was too dark to identify them, and possibly they had not heard. However, when the driver of the lorry, an Irish Guardsman, was questioned, he knew nothing about them, except that they had been following him for about ten miles. This made Lieutenant Kavanagh suspicious and he gave chase in his scout car, passing through the Heavy Troop which, having failed to receive a warning message, had therefore not challenged the vehicles in the dark.

Continuing the chase, Kavanagh caught up in about half a mile and saw two vague shapes halted on the road. Unable to identify them and hearing nothing, he dismounted to approach closer on foot, at the same time telling his driver, Trooper Mitchell, to reverse the car back hound a corner out of sight. Instead of reversing, Mitchell tried to turn in the road and must have been heard, for the rear tank—they both turned out to be German—opened fire and a round hit the road beside the Troop Leader, ricochetted and passed through the engine of the scout car which was then broadside on. The car burst into flames and the whole scene became illuminated with exploding ammunition and burning petrol. Kavanagh was spotted and fired on, but he managed to throw down a couple of phosphorous grenades and under cover of these got back to the burning car, where he was able to pull out Mitchell, who had been badly wounded and was helpless, and carry him to the ditch. Then the German infantry, who had already dismounted from the tanks, tried to attack, but the arrival of a corporal and two men from the Support Troop discouraged them, and they soon lost interest. A warning was sent down the road and the two tanks were eventually caught in the eastern suburbs of Brussels the next morning. The Irish Guardsman, when told of the incident, "was rather shocked at learning who it was he had convoyed through most of Guards Armoured Rear Echelon for ten miles![18]

★   ★   ★

By next morning, the 4th of September, it was found that the number of prisoners had been greatly swelled by those who had walked into the harbours and surrendered during the night, but this proved no embarrassment because the Belgians were only too happy to deal with the problem. Their organization was working most efficiently and, apart from taking off our hands all captives, they provided countless guides and interpreters and, incidentally, as Captain Collins recorded with feeling, "masses of rumours."

★   ★   ★

Gradually those men and vehicles which had become separated from each other in the turmoil of Sunday night began to reassemble. Lieutenant Franklin, whose Troop had been so completely split up, recollected that:

> "After breakfast Trooper Marsh and I walked off towards the house where we had left Corporal Evans,'[19] past the Gestapo Headquarters, now being

---

18. Letter from Lieutenant Kavanagh.
19. Corporal Evans had been wounded in the streets of Brussels during Sunday evening.

ransacked by the Belgians, with all its windows smashed. A man showed us the way to Avenue des Nations. At one time we were comforted by seeing a squadron car come roaring along the road. We waved to it to stop, but they did not recognize us and went on waving back.... We found the house and were welcomed by the family. They had sent Evans to the local hospital. So we borrowed the children's bicycles and a boy showed us the way to the hospital.

"Cycling through Brussels on a sunny morning with people streaming through the streets and dancing in the squares was a most thrilling sight. The people were still searching out German deserters or snipers, and I saw a coffin being shouldered through the streets with a German helmet on top. We arrived eventually at the hospital. The whole place came to see 'Les Anglais,' but we escaped at last and found Evans in an upstairs room. On one side of his bed was a bowl of roses and a plate of grapes, on the other a bottle of champagne on ice. Through his room came innumerable other patients as if he were holding a levee. Some were on crutches, some in bath chairs, and we had to listen to some youths who called themselves 'Terrorists' describe in execrable English how they had raided the local gaol and freed their friends! Evans seemed to be in some pain, although he managed to eat a peach or two.... We made our way out of the hospital after we had talked to most of the patients and the man whose house we had stayed in had arrived and promised to be responsible for Evans until he was taken to the military hospital.

"In the garage when we returned, the cars were ready to move, although we could yet get nothing on the wireless. We drove out with the cameras whirring and the people cheering. Eventually we found the rest of the Squadron by the Tir National, surrounded, of course, by an immense crowd. It was all rather like a race meeting. I reported to my Squadron Leader, whom I found having a glass of port with an old Belgian Count at one side of the green. I had to sign my autograph hundreds of times. One car only was now missing in the Squadron, but it turned up later, with Trooper Pickles, who had been shot in the neck—a graze. I asked him if it were true that the war was over, and he replied that they could get nobody on the wireless, so had tuned in to the B.B.C."

Throughout the rest of the day "A" Squadron sat under a long avenue of trees. Little boys cut off souvenirs from uniforms when their owners were not looking. Private wirelesses blazed away. The rumour of peace grew. Some said Hitler was dead. The Brussels radio station announced that the Germans had sued for an armistice. An odd shell fell into the city as if to deny the hoped-for good news, while in a café across the road Britons and Belgians linked arms and drank perdition to the Nazis.

"C" Squadron in another part of the city welcomed back their lost Support Troop Leader, Lieutenant Hopkinson, and his two men. They had not long remained captive. Having, as we have read, eased a rather tense situation by offering their S.S. captors what available supplies of morphia there were in the knocked-out Daimler car, they had been bundled into an open staff car together with the wounded Germans and driven rapidly into the centre of Brussels, Corporal Staples and Trooper Clarke being forced to sit on the wings and hold on as best they could. "If any Belgians got in the way, they were ruthlessly shot down by the Germans with Schmeisser automatics." The civilians were looking most despondent and stood about in small groups, seemingly astonished to see the British at this stage—it was then shortly after two o'clock in the afternoon. When his guards were not looking, Hopkinson managed to slip the Belgians a few boxes of "V" matches and "it was wonderful to see their faces instantly light up with joy."

After dropping their own wounded at a large hospital, the Germans took the Household Cavalrymen to the infantry barracks close to the Gare du Nord, where numerous S.S. were loading lorries and preparing for a hurried evacuation. "We stood around for hours and watched the Town Major and other German officers and police officials come in and do the 'Heil Hitler' and generally strut around. Some of the police, I regret to say, were collaborating Belgians, and it was a disagreeable and rather shaming sight.

"As darkness fell, we were marched out with the German column and on going up some narrow streets, the Belgian Armée Blanche started firing and dropping grenades from the windows. We did a bunk in the confusion but got caught! Next time this happened we took one of our guards with us; he came from Alsace, and we nipped up into a flat until the search parties had given up looking for us. We then joined up with the Armée Blanche and were taken into the liberated part of Brussels. The rest can be left to the imagination."

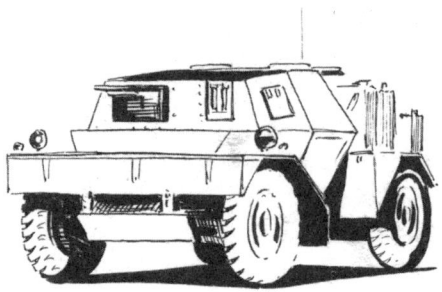

Daimler Scout Car

Chapter VI

From Brussels to
"The Blasted Heath"

Ceremonial Entry into Brussels—"D" Squadron and Grenadier group renew the advance—Capture of Louvain bridge—Corporal-of-Horse Thompson wins D.C.M.—Lieutenant I. M. Clark's diary; his Troop nearly captures a second bridge—Evening at Louvain—Probing towards Aerschott: Corporal-of-Horse Royston's narrative—Lieutenant Hughes collects wine and cigars from Entrepôt Royal—General situation before the resumption of advance to Albert Canal— Lieutenant Creswell's Troop first to Albert Canal at Beeringen—Surgeon-Captain Kynaston takes a turn at leading 30 Corps' advance—Lieutenant Franklin's recollections of the Albert Canal area—Lieutenant Ainsworth's Troop nearly saves another bridge from being blown—Albert Canal crossed and advance resumed eastwards—Helchteren—Heavy fighting for Foot Guards at Hechtel and Bourg Leopold—Liaison with Americans at Hasselt—Hechtel by-passed—Lieutenant Peake's Troop advances towards Escaut Canal, but is held up—To Escaut Canal on a bicycle!—A vital message got through to Division—Irish Guards capture "Joe's Bridge"—Major Ward and crew engage enemy tank at close range—Lieutenant Buchanan-Jardine, Corporal-of-Horse Brook, and Troopers Bateman and Buckley first soldiers into Holland—"C" Squadron mop up stragglers from the battle of Hechtel—Welsh Guards' heavy casualties—"The Blasted Heath"

By the 4th of September, pending a further advance, it was anticipated that at least two of the Squadrons would be able to obtain twenty-four hours' rest and clean up, but it was not to be. The Americans had not yet drawn level on the southern flank and our own infantry were some way behind, there being still considerable pockets of enemy to mop up. Lorries were arriving in Brussels with stories of having been chased by Panthers. To cap everything, the Corps Commander, General Horrocks, had been shot at by a tank when motoring along the centre line into the city. Therefore, both "B" and "C" Squadrons were ordered to retrace their steps and carry out protective patrolling and convoy escorts; "B" Squadron moved as far back as Ath.

But in spite of the majority of the Guards Armoured Division being committed to guarding communication centres and suchlike tasks, General Adair was determined that the citizens of Brussels should be granted a ceremonial entry representative of those troops which had liberated them. Accordingly, on the Monday (4th September) all vehicles that could be spared were collected together, cleaned, and burnished and drawn up for a really triumphant entry. Greatly appreciated by the Belgians was the inclusion of their own Brigade Piron, whose soldiers took their place alongside the British contingent. In this Belgian brigade was the same squadron of armoured cars with which we had co-operated in training when they had been stationed at Chippenham in Wiltshire.

In spite of the country's still paralysed transport system, multitudes came in from outlying districts, including even through the German lines, and the ceremonial entry was to result in Sunday's scenes of enthusiasm being repeated.

General Adair, as commanding the Division, rode in his Cromwell tank, escorted by Colonel Abel Smith, Captain Collins and Corporal-of-Horse Wilcox in a Staghound, while one Troop each from "B" and "C" Squadrons, and commanded respectively by Lieutenant Palmer and Captain Wrottesley, brought up the rear of Divisional Tactical Headquarters.

At one time during the procession there was a justifiable anxiety lest the Germans might launch a daylight air attack, as they had done in Paris before leaving. The results on the packed multitudes did not bear thinking about. However, all went well, although halfway through the procession the enemy, still in occupation of the city aerodrome, fired a salvo of shells into the area of the Palace Gardens, fortunately doing little damage.

The march led past the Tomb of Belgium's Unknown Soldier, and at the Hotel de Ville General Adair handed back the city to the Burgomaster. Thenceforth Brussels, delightful capital of a friendly and hospitable little country, occupied a special place in the hearts of all the Division.

★   ★   ★

Meanwhile, as the crowds roared and the Armée Blanche discharged its rifles into the air in joyous abandon, "D" Squadron, leading the Grenadier group, were bowling along the eastern exists past Tervueren and towards Louvain and its bridges over the River Dyle. This was to be the next lap in the advance.

★   ★   ★

Warned that his Squadron at Leeuw St. Pierre would be required to take part in an early resumption of the advance, Major Ward had gone forward at first light to a rendezvous with the Grenadier group's commander, Lieutenant-Colonel E. H. Goulburn. I was to remain with the group as temporary liaison officer and had therefore accompanied him.

The Grenadiers were still located in the grounds of the Château Royal at Laeken, which was the Royal summer residence and not to be confused with the Palais Royal in the centre of Brussels.

To reach Laeken we had to travel through the centre of the city, and we were led by a Belgian who sat on the front tool box of the scout car. It was an extraordinary journey: stale drunks still sitting on pavements where they had passed into oblivion the previous night, mysterious shots in the half-light, occasional German prisoners being doubled through the streets by the Belgians, and the most fantastic rumours and false alarms. Nor was there a single British soldier to be seen anywhere.

On passing through a long and prosperous-looking street which we subsequently found to have been the Boulevard Anspach which runs into the Place Broukère near the Metropole Hotel, we were stopped by a man with an Alsatian dog and his girlfriend in hair curlers, who told us that the Germans were still at bay in a near-by side street. The man said that he had seen a German's face at a window and that it was "horrible à voir." The woman in hair curlers added that the German had thrown a hand grenade into the street. Our "chars," said other Bruxellois, who had by now appeared from all corners like magic, were the very thing for the job of routing out the enemy.

We had been caught by this unsatisfactory kind of battle before, and Major Ward informed the gathering that he must press on at once, but that shortly the infantry would be arriving to clean up what my operator, Corporal Jenkins, used to call these "Poches de Boches." Eventually, however, he was persuaded to help, intimating as a great concession that he could allow them no more than five minutes of the Staghound's time.

Down a dark and disreputable-looking street, therefore, went the two vehicles, followed by a cheering crowd. Nothing was to be seen but a very much closed and empty-looking shop; however, the man with the dog insisted that the top floor was in the hands of desperate enemy. So Corporal Thompson, the gunner, elevated his 37-mm. to its maximum point and fired three or four rounds through a window. The frame splintered and fell apart, glass tinkled into the roadway. Civilian faith in the death-dealing efficiency of our weapons was touching, and the Belgians renewed their cheers. "Maintenant les Boches sont foutus," rhapsodized a little man astride a racing bicycle. Another, dressed *en sportsman* with ankle-length plus-fours, white socks, and patch-pocket jacket, took photographs. Everyone shook hands, the Germans were forgotten, and before the crowd could think up any other wild scheme we made off.

Major Ward and I looked for that shop weeks later when on leave, as we wished to apologize to the owner. We never found it.

★   ★   ★

The Grenadiers were centred round what appeared to be an abandoned "flak" tower or radar station. Preparations were in full swing for the forthcoming advance and the men were busy packing up and brewing mugs of tea.

Three major water obstacles lay ahead of us before reaching the Dutch border: the first, the River Dyle, with which we were to be immediately concerned; secondly, the Albert Canal; and, thirdly, the Meuse—Escaut Canal. Louvain on the Dyle held special interest for the Grenadiers, for it was here that they had held part of the British Expeditionary Force line in 1940.

It was well past noon when the advance was resumed. There are two roads leading out of Brussels to Louvain, both cobbled the entire length; and, although there is little to choose between them in distance, militarily the northern road was the better of the two and had been provisionally chosen by the Grenadier group.

The plan was for Major Ward's Squadron to advance from Leeuw St. Pierre to Louvain along both roads while the Grenadier group, starting some time later from Laeken, would remain uncommitted in Brussels until they had received preliminary reports from the armoured cars as to which was the best route. Both roads to Louvain are approached by way of the Rue de la Loi, leading directly to the Parc du Cinquantenaire, where a left or right fork then gives a choice of routes.

The Squadron moved towards battle through cheering throngs. Lieutenant Buchanan-Jardine's Troop, followed by Lieutenant van Zoelen's, was soon held up by infantry and 88-mm. guns on the old aerodrome near Woluwe St. Etienne, but on the southern road Lieutenant Hanbury's Troop made good progress and, reporting no opposition, motored fast up to the outskirts of Louvain without a shot being fired at them.

On hearing this news, the Grenadiers obtained permission to switch to the southern road, although a certain amount of delay was caused, partly by having to turn round most of the tanks when in the middle of the city, and partly by the antics of the civilians. The Grenadiers can surely never have assembled to an Order Group in stranger circumstances or at such a disadvantage as they did that day in the middle of the Avenue des Arts. Hordes of women fought to embrace Colonel Goulburn, whose officers were still battling their way through the mob to get within earshot of what he was trying to tell them to do. A little Belgian who had fought in the 1914-18 war and joined the party insisted on translating every sentence (incorrectly) for the benefit of the enraptured civilians, adding a descriptive paragraph of his own which invariably ended with, "maintenant vous allez voir, le Colonel va lancer ses chars a la tête des Boches." Unfortunately for the "chars," Major Gregory-Hood's Squadron was still (due to the change of plan) facing the wrong way, and it was a miracle that they were able to turn at all in the dense throng without causing casualties. At last, with an almost superhuman effort, Colonel Goulburn tore himself free of his adorers, and, grabbing his map board from another well-meaning Belgian anxious to show him the route, escaped at the double to regain his half-track command vehicle.

Eventually, with a grinding of tracks and much backing and pushing, the column faced the right way again and the tanks rattled off through the attractive residential suburbs, dotted with lakes and fringed by the shady beech trees of the Forêt de Soignes.

By this time great news had come through that a Troop of "D" Squadron had captured the main bridge over the River Dyle at Louvain.

★   ★   ★

Louvain, a university town and famous for its beautiful library, destroyed by the Germans in 1914 and subsequently rebuilt with American aid between wars, is ringed by a circular road from which radiate thoroughfares not only to Brussels but also to Malines, Diest, Tirlemont and Namur. The River Dyle, flowing in a series of twists and turns, passes through the middle of the town in two parts. Over these streams runs the Brussels road, and it was to these bridges that Lieutenant Hanbury's Troop had been directed.

On reaching the circular road, Lieutenant Hanbury halted to question some civilians. He was told that German tanks had recently passed through and that the main bridge was held and prepared for demolition. He was also told that "it is suicide to go on." The Troop prepared to advance into the town, undeterred by this news, "which," said Hanbury, "seemed a trifle pessimistic."

Although the advance to the circular road had been without incident, it was soon to be a different story. As had so often happened in the past, the main German garrison had fled, but a strong nucleus of S.S. troops had been left behind with the object of ensuring that all demolitions were carried out and the maximum delay imposed on the pursuers. Stragglers were gathered in at the point of a gun and made to man defensive blocks.

The centre streets of Louvain, which are very narrow[1], compelled the armoured cars to manoeuvre in a confined space most unsuitable for their type of fighting. There was no alternative but to engage the enemy in single file.

At about five minutes to three the first vehicle, a scout car commanded by Lance-Corporal-of-Horse Brook and driven by Trooper Bateman, crossed the circular road. Within the Squadron it was openly said that this efficient partnership had advanced the entire way from Normandy with no further aid to navigation than that of an old *Daily Express* war map and an occasional glance at the sun. Brook was immediately fired on from some houses, but—closely followed by Lieutenant Hanbury's car, whose gunner, Trooper Dean, was firing over the top of the scout car and to the flanks into the houses—he continued to push forward with great gallantry. Firing the Bren as he advanced, Brook surprised and scattered a party of Germans who appeared to be laying a string of mines across his path. These, however, on closer examination, proved to be nothing more deadly than a collection of old gas masks tied together with string.

This dash carried the Troop to the first and main bridge, which was found to be defended by infantry and another party of Germans who were hurriedly trying to affix wires to some firing mechanism. Underneath the single arch of the structure, which was of stone, there were several 500-lb. aerial bombs. The Germans on the bridge were exterminated, and although hand-to-hand fighting is hardly the correct description when armour fights infantry at close range, "We were," writes Lieutenant Hanbury, "down to pistols at one stage." The firing by this time had become intense, chiefly from Germans sheltering in top storeys of buildings beyond the bridge, and as Major Ward had wirelessed that sappers were arriving in an armoured half-track to help defuse the bombs, Lieutenant Hanbury decided to hold on to the main bridge himself, while sending the two scout cars forward to watch the flanks, from the Grand' Place, which lay beyond the second and subsidiary bridge, with several roads converging on to it.[2]

---

1. Within a week of its liberation the British military authorities had managed to transform Louvain streets into one of the most unnecessary, complex and delaying one-way traffic control systems in North-West Europe.

2. The crew of the second scout car supporting Lance-Corporal-of-Horse Brook consisted of Corporal Wilson and Trooper Powell.

No sooner had the scout cars reached the square than both vehicles again came under sustained small-arms fire from buildings in the street leading to the railway station east of the square. In addition, the Germans had established themselves on the north side street, which the scout cars could not cover. Seeing this, Lieutenant Hanbury ordered Corporal-of-Horse Thompson to go to their assistance and at the same time try to dislodge the enemy from the northern side of the square.

Now, in addition to his concern for his immediate front, Lieutenant Hanbury had to contend with enemy infiltrating from the rear. These came from groups which, all day, had been retreating from Brussels along the northern of the two exit roads, which, it will be remembered, was still held.[3]

Meanwhile Corporal-of-Horse Thompson had noticed, lying slightly back from the main bridge, a small alleyway barely wide enough to permit of the passage of an armoured car, but it was worth trying, for it led along the river and, from the map, appeared to end in some sort of footbridge. If the car could be got over this there would be the means of helping the two scout cars, and at the same time of preventing the Germans from crossing the Dyle from the Brussels direction. Corporal-of-Horse Thompson was therefore ordered to make the attempt by this route.

He had travelled about 150 yards of his loop along the side of the river when he was halted by a crater, only partially filled in by the Resistance, and which he gathered had been intended by the enemy to hold some electrically detonated bombs. The driver of the armoured car, Trooper Cudmore, accelerated and tried to rush the obstacle but the vehicle stuck fast, embedding its front wheels up to the axle. However, he managed to reverse out safely, but by now the Germans had seen what was happening and had started shooting at the vehicle from some old bombed buildings. Undeterred, Corporal-of-Horse Thompson leapt out of the turret and ran across to a house where he had noticed some broken window shutters. Dragging these back to the crater under heavy fire the whole of the time, he eventually succeeded in bridging the gap and directing his car to the other side. Then, crossing the Dyle by way of a concrete bridge which, partially blown, was undefended, he was soon able to rejoin the two scout cars in the square. For his gallantry and resource in this action Corporal-of-Horse Thompson was awarded the D.C.M.

---

3. Apart from Lieutenant Ainsworth's Troop, which had not yet arrived, there were no other armoured cars available, Lieutenant Buchanan-Jardine's Troop and Lieutenant van Zoelen's Troop having just disengaged from the enemy on the northern road and being therefore still in the process of moving up.

Now began a battle-royal. The Germans, having no heavy armament available, were unable to knock out the cars, nor could they get to close enough quarters to use their bazookas; but the armoured cars, without infantry support, were equally unable to dislodge the enemy from their buildings, and the crews were submitted to continuous sniping whenever they put their heads up.

Then, perhaps with the idea of some desperate last-minute effort at blowing up the bridge, a large German staff car, machine-gun mounted on the bonnet and blazing away, made straight for the Troop from the direction of Louvain railway station. Trooper Elmore put a burst of Besa into it and it stopped dead. The crew bailed out and all except the driver were shot, then Elmore's Besa jammed and another pistol duel started as the German tried to escape, taking pot shots over his shoulder, but he was quickly brought down, both Thompson and Elmore modestly claiming that the other had been the marksman! On examining the corpse later it was found that he was wearing a curious chain of office marked "Burgomaster" in some kind of luminous paint.

Meanwhile the Belgian Resistance had joined in the battle and one of their number, knowing where the wires were situated, ran up to Corporal Brook, saying, "Take my coat; I will defuse the bombs on the bridge. If I don't return you will find all my particulars in the coat pocket." Suiting his action to the words, he made for the main bridge and cut off all wires leading to the bomb.[4] This act of gallantry apart, the Belgian Resistance in Louvain "were magnificent, not only helping the Troop by acting as infantry and clearing the surrounding houses, but also in the close protection of the bridge itself."

At about this time Lieutenant Ainsworth's Troop arrived on the scene with a section of sappers, and his Troop then became responsible for guarding the rear of the bridge, whence Lieutenant Hanbury's car had already shot several infiltrating enemy.

The most serious sniping now appeared to be coming from the direction of the Banque Nationale, a building several storeys high which formed one corner of the Grand' Place. Corporal-of-Horse Thompson had several narrow escapes, and a sapper was killed while helping to check the work of the unknown Belgian on the bridge. Trooper Elmore,

---

4. Monsieur Michel Harboort, Reader in Administrative Law at Louvain University, kindly wrote to me concerning the liberation of Louvain. A citizen of Louvain claims to have cut the wires leading to the bridge prepared for demolition, shortly before the advent of Lieutenant Hanbury's Troop. This, if correct, might explain the feverish work of the S.S., who may have been disturbed in their repair work in the nick of time. Whatever the truth of the story be, it in no way detracts from the gallantry of the second Belgian, whose name is also unknown to the Regiment.

who by now had got the Besa working again, therefore started to rake the building systematically from top to bottom. Tracer set it alight and it was eventually completely gutted, although the majority of the enemy were able to escape by a back entrance.[5] All opposition close to the bridge then died down. The Resistance continued their house-to-house search with German weapons borrowed from the Troop, and a number of prisoners were collected. By this time, the remainder of "D" Squadron and the Grenadier group had arrived and the tanks took over the bridge shortly after four o'clock in the afternoon, one hour after its capture.

★ ★ ★

Barely had the Grenadiers established their headquarters on the cross-roads outside Louvain, adjoining those of "D" Squadron, than a carload of Germans drove straight out of the town towards Brussels. It saw the assembled vehicles and in a flash half turned and raced off along the circular road towards another crossing of the Dyle which was still in German hands to the south.

Corporal-Major Ring, who was nearest at hand, jumped into his Daimler and gave chase, unable to open fire for a time because of a bend in the road. He had travelled about three hundred yards when his vehicle received a direct hit through the driving visor, from what was probably either an anti-tank gun or a bazooka. Trooper William Robins, the driver, was killed instantly and the pilotless car crashed into a ditch, burning furiously. Trooper Lothian was taken prisoner, but Corporal-Major Ring, who had been thrown out by the force of the impact, was able to regain his lines after a chase in which he had to leap a high wall to escape from his pursuers.

As the Grenadiers were for the time being fully engaged in fighting in the centre of the town, and the other Reconnaissance Troops had not yet arrived, Lieutenant Clark's Heavy Troop (Matadors) was ordered to move over to this open right flank. In so doing, the Troop narrowly missed saving the bridge leading to the Porte de Namur from being blown.

"When we arrived at the cross-roads where Jackie had made his headquarters, I chugged up from the rear with my Matadors and was at once ordered to find out into what sort of a jam poor Ring was in. When we reached the long avenue leading up to the other bridge I nosed

---

5. Harboort also states that the engagement between Lieutenant Hanbury's Troop and the Germans barricaded in the Banque Nationale, which was burnt down, resulted in many casualties, whose corpses were found later in the debris.

round the corner and saw 'Dolphin' burning fiercely about 150 yards away. Corporal-of-Horse Connor, who was just behind me, then saw a sprinting figure behind the trees and traversed his gunner, Trooper Mayer, on to it, ordering him to fire. Fortunately, Mayer showed great perception and recognized the Corporal-Major through his telescope!

"Next, covering Corporal Bow (in the scout car) with the Matador's guns, I sent him to the end of the road to have a look at the bridge. To my horror I saw him and Trooper Buckley dismount and creep out of sight after firing a few bursts of Bren. A minute later there was a heavy explosion as the bridge went up. Bow and Buckley scuttled back amidst a shower of flying rubble and sought cover behind their scout car. Their efforts were not utterly in vain as they had shot the man who was setting off the bombs (500 lb.) dug into the bridge, before he had pulled the plugs on more than two of them. Thus half the bridge remained and the engineers were able to patch it with Bailey equipment very easily.

"I next moved up with all my Troop to cover the bridge, which was still quite crossable, and whilst I was doing a 'recce' out of my car I heard the 75-mm. gun go off. On my hurried return I was told that Trooper Long had just scored a direct hit on a German creeping up with a bazooka. I continued my investigations and the gun went off again! This time Long had scored three direct hits in very quick succession on a self-propelled gun which had appeared at the crossroads a hundred yards or so beyond the bridge. As he shouted at Trooper Naisby to put an armour-piercing shot into the breech, the self-propelled gun retired out of sight and did not reappear.[6] We stayed there for about a couple of hours until a platoon of Grenadiers, who had been engaged elsewhere, arrived. We gave them fire support and they unsuccessfully tried to establish themselves on the other side against machine-gun fire. That night we were all withdrawn and the damaged bridge, owing to other commitments, was left unguarded, but no further harm befell it."

★ ★ ★

The Grenadier group which had passed across Hanbury's bridge into the town lost no time in getting to close grips with the enemy, and were soon engaged in hard fighting for the rest of the evening; one platoon in particular inflicting severe casualties on a large group of Germans at the railway station who were apparently waiting for the next train home. The

---

6. Unknown to Lieutenant Clark's Troop at the time, the German S.P. gun had received mortal injury at their hands, and it was discovered next morning with its gun mantlet damaged and two of the crew dead inside, fifty yards back from where it had first appeared. It had been stripped of everything of value by the Belgians.

town was not completely cleared by the Grenadiers until the following morning.

It had been a wonderful day for the group and we felt that 3 Troop's fine achievement had more than made up for their having to leave the fleshpots of Brussels before the rest of the Division. A further and most important obstacle on the road to Germany had been overcome with very small casualties. In the evening, the Squadron collected together under some plane trees lining the side of the circular road. Below lay the town of Louvain, safe in Grenadier hands, the bank and other buildings still burning fiercely. Monks from an adjoining hospital came over to offer baths to the officers—an offer gratefully accepted, but which proved to be a somewhat unnerving performance, for the hospital was a lunatic asylum and some of the inmates in the corridors had been over-excited by the battle.

Lieutenant Hughes had brought up the echelon from Brussels and also the latest news of the general situation, including the still pervading rumour that Hitler was dead and Germany had sued for peace. Antwerp had fallen during the day to 11th Armoured Division. The moon came out, as did Corporal Meade-King's accordion. A little café at the corner of the Brussels road offered open house to all the soldiers. Under the trees where the cars were parked, people danced and talked in happy groups. One Troop in particular appeared to have attracted a large civilian audience. From the centre of this group came the strains of a song, punctuated by prolonged cheering. I walked across. Seated at the entrance to his bivouac, each arm round the waist of a Belgian girl, his own men forming a grinning and admiring semicircle, was Lieutenant Hanbury. He was singing, as if without a care in the world, "The Big Rock Candy Mountains."

★　★　★

On the following day, the 5th of September, "D" Squadron continued to carry out reconnaissance patrols in a north-easterly direction while the Grenadiers remained in and around Louvain for the next twenty-four hours, systematically clearing each street and sending patrols backwards and forwards across the surrounding fields and woods to round up a number of enemy who had hoped to avoid capture.

Lieutenant Ainsworth's Troop was ordered to patrol to the outskirts of Aerschott, while a Squadron of Grenadier tanks was held in readiness to exploit should any opportunity present itself. The first excitement took place when civilians reported that a German general was defying all attempts of the Armée Blanche to dislodge him. He had locked himself, together with a few supporters, in the local brewery with a defiant cry of "Come and get me"; but principally owing to the Belgian crowds, the Troop was unable to accept his challenge. Corporal-of-Horse Royston records the day:

> "We headed north-east for Aerschott, on the outskirts of which we were met with a tremendous reception. The Germans had pulled out just before our arrival and the town was packed tight with an excited crowd awaiting our arrival. On the outskirts we picked up the Belgian Police Chief, who had been expelled by the Germans four years previously and whose wish it was to ride back on the first Allied car. So Corporal-of-Horse Bugby and Trooper Rose ploughed through the crowds for about two miles, and still had about a mile to go to deliver the Chief when they had to give it up as hopeless.... Bugby retired about a mile to the outskirts of the town again. Civilians gathered around and once again our vehicles were draped with flowers and bouquets. It was only possible to see the head and shoulders of the crew above the decorations. In the evening we were recalled to Louvain, and we must have looked more like some carnival of flowers than machines of a great and grim war."

★ ★ ★

No record of the liberation of Brussels would be complete without reference to the huge store of wine and other goods left behind by the Germans in their precipitate flight. News of the discovery spread from unit to unit like wildfire and for forty-eight glorious hours N.A.A.F.I.'s wolfish representatives never had a look in. Some units sent their toughest representatives to deal with the threatened menace of officialdom; others trusted to the more delicate thrusts of the connoisseur. "D" Squadron chose the latter course.

Thanks to the Grenadiers, who had been one of the first to hear of the good news and pass it on, Major Ward got away to a good start.[7] He ordered Lieutenant Hughes to return to Brussels post-haste.

> "We started off from Louvain cross-roads with a three-tonner lorry, the 'Gin Palace' and a water-cart. With me were Corporal Harrison, Corporal Hussey, and others. Corporal Harrison, I feared, might be a

---

7. The Adjutant of the 2nd Battalion Grenadier Guards, Captain A. G. Heywood, drew aside the writer, who was liaising at the time with them north of Louvain, and said words to the effect that "you're wasting your time here on this front, which is quiet; tell your Squadron Leader that in Brussels are wine vaults filled beyond the wildest dreams."

bit out of his depth, but there were no flies on Hussey; he had served in the peace-time Officers' Mess. In Brussels we heard further rumours that the war had finished, which only made our desire to reach the wine vaults the keener. They were difficult to find and, as ever in Brussels, all traffic directions inevitably ended up with 'Tout droit, Monsieur, tout droit, suivez la ligne du tram.' We eventually fetched up at the Entrepôt Royal, Bassin Vergotte, in the dockland part of Brussels by the canals. The top half of the warehouse was filled with ersatz soap, 'Willem' Twe cigars and other brands (mostly brown paper), etc. The cellars were full of champagne, Heidsieck '37, Red Top (Gout Americain), and goodness knows what else. There was also some burgundy, including some most drinkable Pommard, and crate upon crate of doubtful cognac, all marked ominously, 'Reservé pour la Wehrmacht.'

"The place as far as the eye could see was crammed with drink. Corporal Hussey's eyes were bulging out of his head. I was shown through to a man at the end of the cellars, who greeted me and inquired, 'How many officers?' I replied without hesitation, 'Sixty.' [The Squadron's strength being eleven. *Author*]. Practically everybody was drunk and the little man acquiesced to my request without batting an eyelid. I pointed out certain crates which I thought would do. 'Ah, Monsieur,' replied the Belgian, 'avant de choisir it faut gouter.' So we all set to, tasting and sampling— most of those present just drank hard.

"The drive back to Louvain, loaded with crates, was memorable, but we made it. However, as the advance had by now been resumed, we had to keep the stuff several days before it could be distributed. When we did eventually make firm contact with the Squadron again, nobody had told me that Hechtel had not yet fallen, and I therefore nearly drove into it.[8] Bullets were flying about all over the place, and just ahead a lorry load of Charles Rutland's private cache of champagne (from the same source, no doubt!) went up in smoke. On arrival at 'The Blasted Heath,' I suddenly found that I had made an extraordinary number of friends because 'C' Squadron had already drunk all their stock, and Regimental Headquarters hadn't even heard of the depot."

★   ★   ★

It is now the time to glance at the general situation and see what the plans were for a resumption in the advance.

Namur had fallen to the Americans on the 4th of September, but they were still in the process of encircling a force of Germans trapped many

---

8. This happened several days later after the crossing of the Albert Canal at Beeringen—see succeeding pages.

miles back between two large prongs encompassing the area of the Forêt de Compiègne—Mons, where more than twenty-five thousand of the enemy were captured. Therefore, to our right, friendly troops were still a little thin on the ground.

On our left, 11th Armoured Division were in possession of the main part of Antwerp (captured on the 4th of September), but were still engaged in some heavy fighting where the Germans were trying to retain their hold in the dock area.

On the Sunday of the liberation of Brussels, General Montgomery had issued fresh instructions to his 21 Army Group for the development of operations. The Second Army was to drive to the River Rhine with minimum delay, while on the left the Canadians were to clear the coastal belt up to Bruges and subsequently develop operations for the clearance of the Scheldt estuary in order to give access to Antwerp from the North Sea.

As was then envisaged, the plan was to employ 30 Corps as the spearhead of the British Army's advance and to establish Guards Armoured Division in the Eindhoven area and the 11th Armoured Division in the area of Turnhout—Tilberg.

As far as the Regiment were concerned, nothing of much military significance was to occur on the 5th of September. "D" Squadron, as we know, were operating with the Grenadiers in carrying out reconnaissance towards Aerschott, while "B" and "C" Squadrons were still on their task of guarding lines of communication until the evening when, after being relieved, they were brought into reserve at Leeuw St. Pierre. "A" Squadron remained in Brussels, still being fêted by the inhabitants.

Divisional Headquarters had moved from Leeuw St. Pierre, and on the evening of the 5th were encamped behind the railings of the Royal Palace. It was already dark when General Adair prepared to give out his orders.

A group of officers, which included Colonel Abel Smith, was gathered round the situation maps, which were sheltered by a large tent pitched between two armoured command vehicles. Just as the General was beginning his orders, a paraffin lamp, placed too near the protective talc covering the maps, set them alight. Within seconds there was a first-class blaze and the nerve centre of Guards Armoured Division was temporarily paralysed.

However, apart from giving the hard-worked Staff officers a lot of extra work, no vital damage was done, and the Sappeurs pompiers quickly extinguished the conflagration. That night a British newspaper reporter began his despatch to London thus: "As I write by the light of the great bonfire which the populace have lit in the Palace Gardens to celebrate…".

Next morning, the 6th of September, the Division prepared to resume the advance eastwards with the intention of forcing the next main water obstacle, the Albert Canal; 32nd Brigade via Diest to Beeringen and 5th Brigade farther north via Aerschott to the area of Bourg Leopold.

"A" and "D" Squadrons were to lead the advance; behind them would be the Welsh Guards group and the Grenadier Guards group, respectively. The advance to the Albert Canal and the one that followed—to the Escaut Canal—were to be conducted under very different circumstances from those to which we had grown accustomed during the past two weeks. Considering the losses they had incurred, the Germans had made a remarkable recovery, and from being a disordered rabble, they were once again conducting organized withdrawals and delaying actions from water obstacle to water obstacle with all their usual efficiency.

Five miles beyond Louvain, "A" Squadron ran into slight opposition, but this was soon cleared up and Lieutenant Creswell's Troop[9] pushed straight on for Beeringen, with other Troops branching right and left after passing through Diest, which had been freed by the Belgian Resistance.

Before Creswell could reach the Beeringen bridge, however, the Germans blew it. On arrival it was found that, although the wooden bridge had fallen into the canal, the stone abutments of the original structure were still standing.[10] This information was wirelessed back to Divisional Headquarters and General Adair decided to order an assault crossing at this point, for the news from "D" Squadron farther north was that so far all their bridges had been found demolished.

Pending the arrival of the Welsh Guards, who were to force the crossing, Lieutenant Creswell's task was to ensure that the Germans on the far side should cause no further damage to the abutments. He was subjected to a certain amount of sniping and mortar fire from the far bank, but the unhealthiness of the place in no way deterred the local inhabitants from surrounding the cars with all the usual signs of friendliness. This form of welcome was at times an embarrassment, if not a positive danger, for a good position of observation was thus frequently given away. In this case, an attractive Belgian girl stepped forward from the crowd and shyly offered Creswell a glass of brandy. As he leant out of the turret to accept

---

9. Lieutenant Creswell's Troop had just re-joined the Regiment after acting as Protection Troop to Lieutenant-General Sir Richard O'Connor, commanding 8 Corps. The job had finished when 8 Corps was pinched out of the advance in Normandy.

10. The stone bridge had been blown in 1940 by the Belgians and a temporary wooden bridge had been erected by the Germans on the original abutments.

the gift, an enemy sniper took aim from the opposite bank, but the shot meant for Creswell hit the girl in the shoulder. "Luckily," relates the Troop Leader, "the wound was not serious, proving to be no more than a graze, and as at the moment of the shot I had already a firm grip on the glass of brandy, all ended well! "

Although Creswell had reached this important bridge and had started his first patrol with the Regiment so auspiciously, his lead had not remained unchallenged. In fact, for a short period Surgeon-Captain Kynaston had bid fair to be the first to reach the Albert Canal in his medical car.

"I was ordered to go with 'A' Squadron from Louvain up to the Albert Canal and to meet Bowes at a bridge on the north-east side of Louvain at eight o'clock in the morning. This was the start line. I started off from Brussels at first light and got to Louvain without mishap. I waited half an hour for Bowes on the start line, but not a sign of him. So I got on the wireless to Dickie Brayne-Nicholls[11] and asked him where the deuce was 'A' Squadron. He replied with hauteur, 'At "Nelson," of course.' I was not completely in the picture about report lines and code names that morning, so that was useless. Spent some time deciding whether to push on or not; eventually did, and was already leading vehicle in the British Army, but did not know it, when my operator got acute diarrhoea, and while he was relieving himself, 'A' Squadron swung into view, Bowes being purposely late with Headquarters because he wisely thought it would be more comfortable to have the Welsh Guards' tanks a little closer behind!"

★   ★   ★

Lieutenant Franklin's Troop was one of those operating on the right flank, for it was anticipated that if the Beeringen crossing proved unfeasible, there were three other bridges, including one at Hasselt, worth trying.

"I was sent off to the south to find a crossing of the canal after the leading Troop had reported the main bridge held and blown. What had happened was easy to see. The Jerries had made their main line of withdrawal on the parallel road to us, the one leading to Hasselt. I had not gone very far with another Troop when we ran into enemy holding the little village of Lummen as a flank protection to the main crossing at Hasselt. Luckily, some tanks from the Welsh Guards came in from the other side, and

---

11. Rear Link Officer, "A" Squadron.

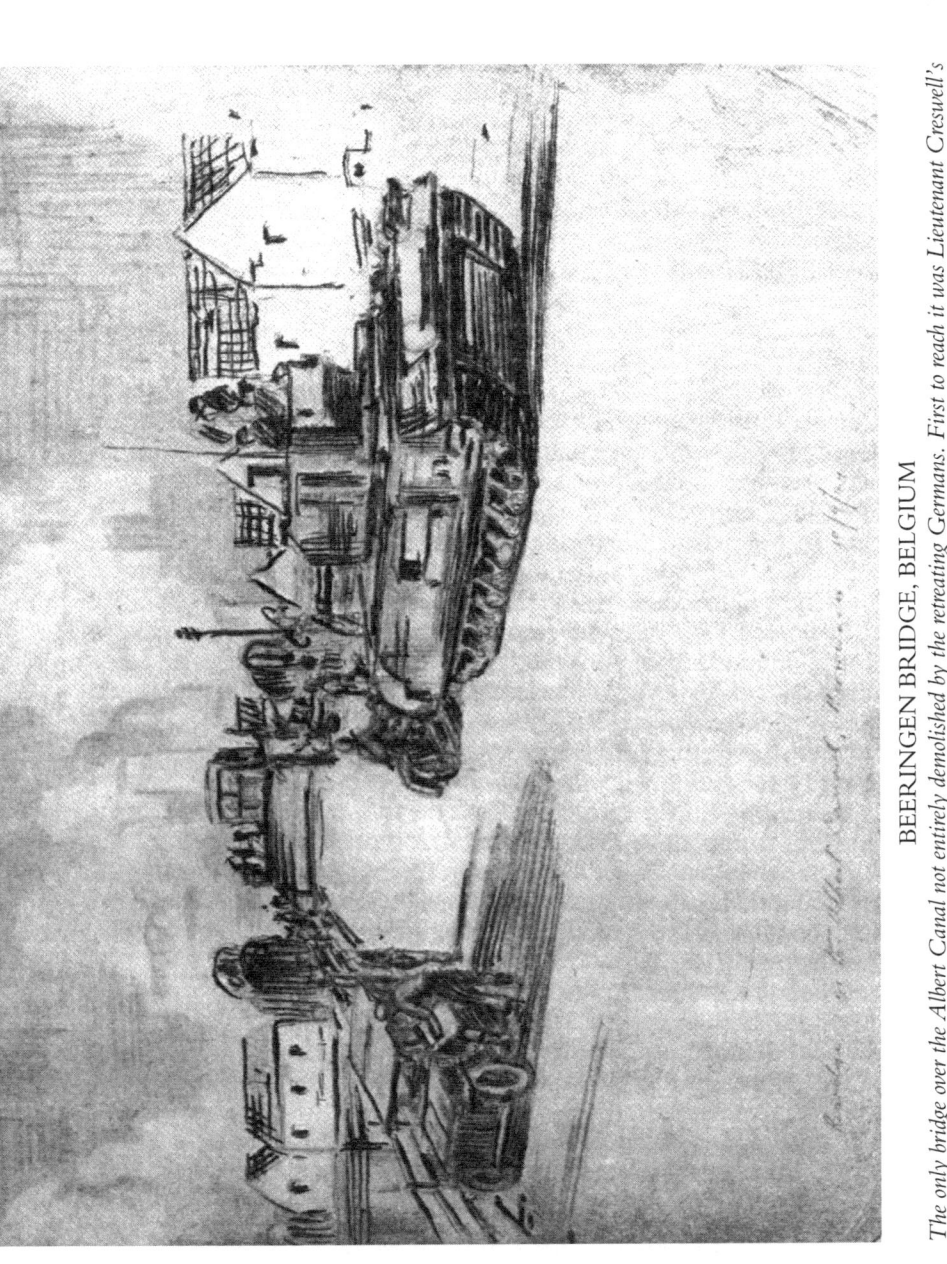

BEERINGEN BRIDGE, BELGIUM

The only bridge over the Albert Canal not entirely demolished by the retreating Germans. First to reach it was Lieutenant Creswell's Troop, "A" Squadron, on 6th September. It was found to be only partially destroyed. Pending repairs by the Sappers, the Welsh Guards made an assault crossing under fire to enable the advance to be resumed towards the Escaut Canal.

while we were having a noisy battle they literally charged the village.... We were being quietly 'stonked' from over the river by mortars, and on all sides the thatched roofs of the houses were catching fire. The Cromwell tanks went in firing into each hedge and ditch, with us following behind and on their flanks. A thick column of black smoke drifted up the hill towards the village church at the top. On arriving at the village I found their Squadron Leader, and in the corner of the square were about fifty prisoners sitting there with their boots off and looking very dazed and unhappy. They proved to be Engineer battalions used perforce as combat troops. I met the Belgian chief of the underground movement in the town, and he invited me to go to his H.Q. down the road which I was to reconnoitre. I went in a little two-seater sports car that he had taken from the Germans. On entering his office, his lieutenants stood to attention and shook hands with me. I asked for the German positions of anti-tank guns and was horrified to see that two miles down my route they had marked a 75-mm. gun. Yes, they had all seen it; there were in fact two there, and they even showed me the way in which they were pointing. I had a glass of sherry with them and they told me their story.

"The R.A.F. had promised to drop them arms, to 5,000 of them who had waited in the woods on the other side of the river near Hasselt. Unfortunately, these had not come; if they had, they would have been able to capture the town of Hasselt. I was driven back to my Troop and noticed that there were men posted every 200 metres or so in the ditches.

"I tossed with the other Troop Leader as to who should lead, and I won as usual, so he led with me in his corporal's position; and at the end of the column we had a couple of friendly looking Cromwells who had been given to us in support. Looking back on that trip, I think if we had gone fast enough we should have got that bridge, but things always look different at the time. As it was it blew up just before the Americans on the right flank got to it. The next bridge we 'recced,' too, was blown, and on inquiry we found that it had been blown in 1940 by our own troops in retreat.... During one bit of shooting I was amused to see a fight between an old woman and a young boy over a Belgian flag he wanted to put up. The old woman was not having any as there was still a German section hiding behind the cottage; I think she was wise. I once had an argument with a local parson who wanted to put up a flag on his church which I was using as an O.P.

"It was now getting late in the day, and as we came nearer to the town, which was now two kilometres south, we could hear the movement of transport hurrying east. Eventually we came to the position where the guns were supposed to be, and in the distance we could see the Jerry transport careering down the road making for the home side of the river. Just at that moment we were ordered to return home.

"That should have been the end of this episode, but it doesn't always work out that way. One of the Cromwells went into the ditch. I sent the others home and kept two of my cars as protection for the chap ditched. It was getting dark, and for other reasons than mere superstition we armoured people hated being out after closing time. The tank's track was off and they had to send for their recovery vehicle. It took some time to come. In the meantime we had to keep a weather eye open on the country, for the Underground had just discovered the Germans crossing the river behind us in rubber boats. However, the recovery eventually got the tank out and with the lights off we turned up the road, the tank leading the party. We next came to a road-block in the shape of a dead horse and broken cart which the tank could get round, but we got stuck on our lonesome for some time, searching with torches for a way round. We at last got round and, although we went pretty fast, didn't catch up with our 'heavy friends.' This made me begin to think that I was lost, the worse crime a Troop Leader can commit, when to my right I saw the broken bridge at Beeringen, and from there it did not take long to find the Squadron bogied up for the night in a little farm a few hundred yards from the road."

★ ★ ★

"D" Squadron on the left had advanced with speed to the many small bridges spanning the Albert Canal in the vicinity of Gheel, but in every case these were blown in the face of the advancing Troops. The Germans were waiting on the far bank, and as soon as the sound of an armoured car was heard, the detonating plunger was pressed. Lieutenant Ainsworth's Troop came nearest to success when Lance-Corporal-of-Horse Bugby's scout car got to within fifty yards of the bridge at Eynthout. The defenders, who were sitting sunning themselves on the near side of the bridge, were taken by surprise, and as the Bren fire spattered into the group there was a mad scramble to get to the other side. Fortunately for him, Bugby noticed that mines had been laid across his path and he was forced to come to an abrupt halt. Meanwhile the two armoured cars had arrived and joined in the firing, hoping that the enemy might be forced to keep their heads down long enough to enable the Troop to lift the mines and get across before the bridge went up. "Apart from a speeded-up film, I had never seen men run so quickly as did those Germans," wrote Corporal-of-Horse Royston, "but they were just too quick for the Troop and the structure went up with a roar, showering everyone with falling masonry and pieces of timber".

That this hardening of resistance was no localized affair was confirmed by the Inns of Court Regiment on the left of "D" Squadron, who reported that they also had found all bridges from Herenthals to Antwerp destroyed.

Meanwhile the Welsh Guards group, who within the next few days were to be engaged in some of the heaviest fighting of the whole campaign, were making valiant efforts to get over Lieutenant Creswell's partially blown bridge in single file, but the approaches were too well covered by the enemy and the attempt had to be abandoned. Just as plans were under way for an assault in boats, a civilian ran up to report that the enemy were withdrawing and, wasting no time, the infantry battalion stormed over to take up positions covering the main exits from the town. But the fighting at Beeringen was only just beginning.

Pending the construction of a bridge by the sappers, the Welsh Guards, aided by civilians, moved up nine barges, side by side, until they spanned the canal, "but while timber was being brought up to strengthen the 'deck,' a heavy burst of shell fire came down and the civilians fled." The enemy were now infiltrating back into the town.

In pouring rain the sappers worked through the night to bridge the canal, but, mainly because of the atrocious weather and mortar fire, their work was not completed until half past two next morning, the 7th of September.

Then at dawn the Welsh Guards' tanks moved over, to be met immediately by strong opposition from snipers and mobile guns hidden among the houses. These delaying tactics were to hold up the advance for a good time, and it was almost midday before Major Wignall's Squadron ("B") were able to cross in their wake.

In the meantime Major Bowes Daly's Squadron ("A"), which was waiting in a field close to the bridge, was subjected to a certain amount of mortar fire, and Corporal-of-Horse Wileman, in Lieutenant Creswell's Troop, was killed standing by his armoured car.

In the expectation that the hold-up was only temporary, Regimental Headquarters moved forward in the early morning with Headquarters of 32nd Brigade to cross the canal; but as they were also subjected to shelling, and the bridgehead was already tightly packed with troops, they were ordered back to their original harbour, close to the village of Pael.

Eventually the Welsh Guards cleared Beeringen of all bar a few obstinate snipers and pushed eastwards towards the Helchteren crossroads, leaving part of their force here and swinging north at right angles to attack Hechtel. Here they were brought to a full stop and the succeeding days were to witness some exceedingly bitter fighting in the triangle Helchteren—Hechtel—Bourg Leopold.

The divisional plan was that, while the Welsh Guards cleared Hechtel, the Coldstream group should attack in the direction of Bourg Leopold, but as the day wore on the news coming back from these two centres of resistance became increasingly pessimistic; Beeringen itself being under observation and mortar fire from a tall slag-heap to the north of the town. To complicate matters further, the Germans started to recross the canal from the area of Gheel and were later to reoccupy Tessenderloo and several other villages on the near side. There were also rumours that the enemy was threatening to cut the Louvain road behind us, "fifty tanks being reported at Liége and about to move north-west." The effect of all this was to prevent the Grenadiers crossing for about forty-eight hours, and "C" Squadron were ordered to patrol south to confirm or deny the presence of German tanks.

Meanwhile "B" Squadron had followed the Welsh Guards group to Helchteren, and as the rear of their column was crossing Beeringen bridge, a self-propelled gun opened up on Lieutenant Corah's Support Troop. All the armoured cars had passed out of sight, and as the tanks were also too far forward to be able to give help, the two defenceless White scout cars were knocked out in quick succession. Trooper Clifford Higham was killed and Lieutenant Corah had his left arm carried away by the first shell. Corporal C. R. Rudd and several others were also wounded. Having accomplished its work, the German vehicle remained in close observation until Surgeon-Captain Kynaston arrived to tend to the wounded. It then withdrew, having deliberately refrained from firing again when it could see that the badly wounded were lying helpless in the road.

"D" Squadron next passed over the canal in the late afternoon and re-joined "B" Squadron by the Helchteren cross-roads, which it helped to hold with the Irish Guards group, which had come up to relieve part of the Welsh Guards.

The advance had now taken on a distinctly lopsided appearance. The southern flank was unprotected because the Americans had not yet arrived. Although Helchteren village was in our hands, German parachute troops were strongly entrenched only half a mile to the east and also blocking the Zonhoven—Hasselt road. The Welsh Guards were only just beginning their battle for Hechtel to the north and had been compelled to advance across sand dunes and through pine woods because the road was not yet clear; while on the other flank the Coldstream group were equally held up, having encountered much stronger opposition than had been anticipated as soon as they had turned north at Beeringen.

Clearly the Division would have to be reinforced before it could push on the Escaut Canal with any hope of success, and equally clearly, from the closeness of the fighting, there was little chance of the armoured cars being able to carry out much reconnaissance.

Attempts to exploit southwards soon came to a halt as "D" Squadron met with heavy mortaring when short of Zonhoven, where the enemy had imprisoned a number of the Belgian Resistance in the underground galleries of a colliery.

The next day, 8th of September, saw the Regiment strengthened by the arrival of Major Herbert's Squadron ("C"), which came over to protect 32nd Brigade Headquarters in the Heusden area, where Regimental Headquarters were also now situated. Armoured car patrols were now able to penetrate southwards to Hasselt and liaison was effected with the Americans who had now moved up. Corporal Knight thought he would celebrate the occasion by nipping into a chemist's shop to buy his wife a bottle of scent. He was welcomed by the owner of the establishment, who presented him with a sixteenth-century Calvary, which the Belgian had cherished throughout the occupation to give to the first Allied soldier to enter the shop. The gift could hardly have been more appropriate for Corporal Knight's wife was a Catholic.

In addition to "C" Squadron, "A" Squadron had also been ordered into the bridgehead to guard the guns of the 55th Field Regiment, R.A., who were in an isolated position north of Helchteren; but apart from such moves there was little change in the general situation.

★   ★   ★

We were beginning to wonder whether the continued resistance at Hechtel and Bourg Leopold might not mean that the Division would be faced with having to spend some considerable time among the sand dunes and slag-heaps of this rather bleak part of the country. It was therefore welcome news to hear that 8th Armoured Brigade had crossed Beeringen bridge in the afternoon and that the Royal Netherlands Brigade group had taken over the immediate defence of the bridge from the Irish Guards. It was the intention of 8th Armoured Brigade to advance if possible in the direction of the village of Oostham to support the troops of 50th (Northumbrian) Division, who had also formed a small bridgehead over the Albert Canal to the north-west and were being hard pressed to maintain it. Every sign pointed to the fact that the Germans had intended to hold on to the line of the Albert Canal at all costs and were desperately trying to seal off our present penetration.

On the following day, the 9th of September, after having been reinforced during the night, the Germans launched a series of unsuccessful counter-attacks both against the Coldstream group south of Bourg Leopold and the Welsh group at Hechtel, but, apart from some mortaring, the Regiment was hardly affected by them.

However, an ambitious and desperate party of the enemy attempted to get through to the bridge itself by approaching along the canal bank from the north-west. They got to within a hundred yards of it before they ran into the harbour of the echelon of 8th Armoured Brigade, who suffered severe casualties both to men and vehicles before they drove the enemy out.

Captain Cooper had been liaising with the Coldstream group close at hand when the attack came in. He had spent a large part of the night being shelled on Beeringen football field.

> "Much mortaring from the slag-heap area. We have stand-to at six o'clock. An enthusiastic Belgian (or a German spy?) is playing a concertina and bugle on the roof of a near-by house. At about 8.15 the Germans attack Headquarters. Tanks open up with their Brownings and we divide up into groups and get behind walls with hand grenades. The Germans bring up some Spandaus and bullets begin to whistle. We emptied three Tommy-gun magazines into a near-by wood where the enemy are moving about. Many of our lorries knocked out, but after about an hour, and quite a few shells from the enemy, the attack was beaten off. A lot of German prisoners and a good few killed. Sniper got two Coldstream Guardsmen before being located and shot. Bourg Leopold and Hechtel are still holding out, although the Germans have now lost many tanks and transport. The Germans threw twenty political prisoners into a pond near here and machine-gunned the lot."

★   ★   ★

As it had become apparent that Guards Armoured Division was not strong enough to carry on the advance to the Escaut Canal unless some of its commitments were taken over, 11th Armoured Division was hurriedly brought up from Antwerp after being relieved by 51st (H.) Division. Its arrival on the 9th of September at once improved the situation on the right flank, particularly at Helchteren, where many prisoners were taken.

General Adair now decided that in order to resume the drive to the north, Hechtel would have to be by-passed, and as Bourg Leopold was still holding out obstinately to the west, there was no alternative but to advance part of the way across country between these two centres of resistance. The obvious threat to communications was considered to be outweighed by the chance of the surprise capture of a bridge over the Escaut Canal. The plan of action was as follows. While 32nd Brigade pinned down the S.S. and paratroops in Hechtel and Bourg Leopold, 5th Brigade would advance over the Hechtel—Bourg Leopold road, swing east at the first opportunity and cut the main road running north out of Hechtel, then continue up to the Escaut. As this road was bounded by woods, a comprehensive smoke and artillery programme was arranged to harass and blind the enemy, who were known to have their anti-tank guns sited in this area. The Regiment was ordered to hold two Squadrons in readiness for the advance, "A" Squadron to lead initially, with "D" Squadron close behind, prepared to loop to the east and then northwards as soon as "A" Squadron could get clear.

The morning of 10th September dawned misty and cold, but a hot sun soon cleared the atmosphere and the first armoured cars and tanks crossed the Bourg Leopold—Hechtel road shortly after ten o'clock.

Thereafter progress was slow. The Grenadiers lost several tanks and others were soon bogged in the sand dunes, as were our armoured cars. A large German gun straddling the road from the direction of Bourg Leopold contributed to the delay.

"A" Squadron were unable to deploy until after midday, and when they did so immediately encountered anti-tank guns and were fired upon by a self-propelled gun hidden up in some trees. Major Bowes Daly attempted to swing part of his Troops to the west, but they quickly sank up to their axles in the sand; the tanks, although more natural cross-country performers, fared no better.

Progress up the main road was neither fast nor spectacular. A Troop would advance some way on the flanks, then bog itself, or move down the road and draw fire. As soon as an enemy gun was located it would withdraw slightly under cover of the trees and the whole process start again. It was a laborious and nerve-racking day for the armour.

Some way north of Hechtel Lieutenant Peake's Troop was ordered to locate a gun which had been holding up the Grenadiers and had already knocked out several of their tanks. At this point the road ran dead straight until it reached a railway line, crossing it at right angles about two miles short of the Escaut Canal. Being bounded by trees and sand, there was no alternative but to advance along it in tactical bounds.

The Troop had travelled about 600 yards when there was a loud bang and a shell went whistling over the heads of Corporal Ford-Nairn and Trooper Williams in the leading scout car. They found themselves actually under the muzzle of an 88-mm. S.P., which was cleverly camouflaged in some trees at the side of the road. Obviously, the shot had been intended for Lieutenant Peake's car farther back. Williams, the driver, swerving round the German gun in a wide sweep through the undergrowth, then ran into another enemy group lining the road and at that moment the engine cut out dead and the car came to a halt in their midst and both were taken prisoner. Meanwhile more infantry had attacked the other scout car commanded by Lance-Corporal-of-Horse Pulford, and a shot from a bazooka fired at point-blank range scored a direct hit but failed to explode, and under cover of smoke and Bren-gun fire Trooper Niven was able to reverse out of range.

By this time, the 88-mm. S.P. had fired several more shots at Lieutenant Peake, who with great coolness had been able to observe the flashes and had also spotted a Mark IV tank hidden up among the pines. The 88-mm. continued to fire down the road, but it failed to hit anything, for by this time nearly all the vehicles had been able to pull in to the verge. "As it fired tracer shot, we could see them bouncing along the roadway like cricket balls, and George Murray, the Heavy Troop Leader, who was at that time some way to the rear of the Squadron, reported that they were still going strong past him."

In the meantime Major Bowes Daly had tried to obtain a "Lime-juice," the code word used when support was required from the rocket-firing Typhoons, but for some reason this was unavailable, and for several hours more the enemy continued to hold on to the area of the railway crossing and cross-roads beyond. Eventually the King's Company and No. 2 Squadron of the Grenadier Guards managed to work round to the right flank in a wide sweep, although greatly hampered by the difficult going and by anti-tank guns. After a sharp engagement they overcame the opposition, knocking out in the course of the battle seven anti-tank guns (mostly 88-mms.), three tanks, one S.P. gun, and a 20-mm. machine gun, as well as all the towing and ammunition vehicles, capturing or killing the crews. This happened as darkness was falling and was witnessed by Lieutenant Franklin's Troop which had meanwhile worked up to the railway line on the left. The Troop Leader described the scene of burning and destruction as "a Guy Fawkes' night gone mad."

★ ★ ★

Meanwhile an important development had been taking place on the right flank which was to result in the Irish Guards capturing a vital bridge on the Meuse—Escaut Canal at the de Groote Barrier, thus effecting a breach in the enemy line which had hitherto cut straight across the Second Army's path of advance. The Household Cavalry were to play a leading role in this event, and I have borrowed from the Irish Guards History for the opening of the story.

"…The 2nd Household Cavalry had been exploring the countryside. In advance the Household Cavalry in their scout cars operated on the flanks and often well in front of the Division. They had an admirable habit of suddenly appearing out of a side road or racing straight down the road from the direction of the Germans with a fund of invaluable information and an unquenchable desire to help. If anyone wanted to know 'whether Jerry was up the road' the answer was always, 'Ask the Household Cavalry to go and see.' Above all, they could always be relied on somehow and somewhere to find a way round any obstacle, natural or unnatural. This evening the Household Cavalry found something splendid—a fine new unmapped German-built military road running due north from Exel to Overpelt and then turning due left to the Escaut Canal at de Groote Barrier."

It had come about in the following manner. During the late afternoon Lieutenant Creswell's Troop had been ordered to reconnoitre a route through Exel and if possible up to the canal bank north of Overpelt, where lay an important bridge at de Groote Barrier. "I was well aware," wrote the Troop Leader, "of the opposition which was being experienced by the Grenadier group on the main road, for several of 'A' Squadron Troops were also engaged there and I could hear their reports on the wireless. For this reason I could not bring myself to believe that the enemy would be so foolish as to leave an alternative route uncovered, and in fact I stressed in my orders to the Troop the fact that we must expect opposition. Nevertheless, although we drove tactically and with due caution, we covered a distance of twelve kilometres to within about three kilometres of the bridge at de Groote Barrier, having seen but one German standing in a field and demanding to be taken prisoner."

To attempt to reach the main road from Overpelt, where the Troop now found itself, and join up with the Grenadiers was pointless, for the general advance would gain nothing by this manoeuvre; but if Creswell could move along the canal bank and get behind the Germans, it might be possible to examine the defences of the bridge at close quarters. It was a risk well worth trying and therefore, carefully avoiding the village of Neerpelt, which was left to the east, the Troop moved north-west for a short distance, halting when nearing the canal. From this point the road ran parallel to the canal before joining the main road near the bridge, but the latter was found to be hidden from view by a large factory building; neither was it possible to see the far bank of the canal there since it was also hidden by trees. In addition, Creswell decided that if he took the Troop any farther, the cars would be heard, the alarm given, and the bridge would probably be blown. This was the opportunity for some unorthodox reconnaissance, for time was pressing and it was growing dark. A steadily growing crowd of civilians supplied the means. "I borrowed two bicycles and, leaving the Troop in command of Corporal Corton, set off for the factory with Corporal-of-Horse Cutler."

With the unthinking stupidity of crowds the world over, their departure was given a spirited ovation; and had the bystanders not been promptly silenced, the enemy must surely have been warned of the presence of the British, for already Germans had been noticed patrolling the northern bank of the canal.

The outward journey was accomplished successfully, although just before reaching the factory an enemy patrol was seen on the other side of the canal, and in moving out of sight, Corporal-of-Horse Cutler, who admitted that he was more at home in the turret of a Daimler than at the wheel of a Belgian racing bicycle, toppled off the machine, his Sten gun clattering on to the road. Fortunately, like the cheering, this mishap went unnoticed.

Leaving the bicycles outside the factory, and with a Belgian caretaker acting as look-out, Creswell and Cutler climbed to the top of the building, where the former, by dint of pushing his head through a skylight, could clearly see the bridge. As an observation post this viewpoint could hardly have been bettered. A height of one hundred feet above sea-level in those flat Campine Plains of north-east Belgium is worth at least a thousand feet in any other land. Beneath him lay the whole plan of the enemy's bridge defences, spread out as if marked up on an overprint map. Four 88-mm. guns were carefully pin-pointed, and the best lines of approach from the south studied; so were the sand-bagged positions about the bridge, as well as the personnel manning them. The enemy did not appear to be expecting immediate attack, and Lieutenant Creswell was able to complete his estimate of strength and dispositions before a burst of machine-gun fire from a post by the bridge shattered the skylight and made him duck hurriedly. However, his purpose fulfilled, he now re-joined Corporal-of-Horse Cutler on the floor below.

Before leaving the factory on the return journey, the patrol was warned by the caretaker that there were eight Germans outside the gates, "searching for them." This unwelcome news decided Creswell to abandon all thoughts of bicycling back and the machines were left behind. Clambering over an outhouse, several rubbish dumps, and a slag-heap, he and Cutler regained the road farther back and under cover of bushes. Here, to their surprise, two cars, a large black Mercedes and another staff car, lay smouldering on opposite sides of the road, and it transpired that these had crossed the bridge from the north at the time the patrol was climbing to the top of the factory. Both cars had run head-on into the rest of the Troop and had been knocked out, and the Germans reported at the factory by the caretaker were in reality the survivors of this episode.

On re-joining his Troop, Creswell wirelessed that the route was clear and urged the dispatch of an attacking force without delay, by the same route which he had taken. The Irish Guards were not slow in responding and their group covered the eight miles to the factory at top speed, where contact was made with the armoured cars. Colonel "Joe" Vandeleur, congratulating the Household Cavalrymen on their valuable work, said that the angle of approach appealed to him, adding, "I prefer an oblique approach to dead ahead; obviously boldness is the thing—we will rush the bridge."[12]

So far the Germans had given little sign that they were expecting trouble, the defenders of the bridge being no doubt lulled into a sense of security by thoughts that their battle group farther south barring the main approach road had not yet been overcome by the Grenadier Guards.

The light was failing when the Irish Guards formed up for attack as silently as possible under cover of the factory. Then, when it was practically dark, they made their dash. A green Very light described a graceful arc in the sky. Then followed a red light, and every tank machine gun south of the canal seemed to open up at once. It was too much to expect that the Germans and the bridge with its elaborate defences could be stormed without opposition, and the sappers accompanying the tanks and backed by the infantry were once again compelled to remove the fuses attached to the demolition bombs under heavy small-arms fire. But what mattered most was that the bridge did not go skywards, and, with surprise on their side, and great dash, the Irish Guards quickly overran the guns and their crews, thus establishing a small and compact bridgehead out of which was later destined to burst the spearhead of the British Second Army's advance into Holland.

Later on in the evening, when they had prevailed over the crossroad defences to the south, the Grenadiers joined up to help in the task of ensuring the safety of this most valuable prize.

The Germans had obviously intended—and their subsequent actions confirmed this—to hold on to this last safety exit of the de Groote Barrier. It was to be a bolt-hole for those of their troops remaining south of the canal, and they were not slow to react to its capture. Sadly enough,

---

12. *History of the Irish Guards in the Second World War,* p. 474. (Gale & Polden Ltd., Aldershot.)

one of the first to be killed in the ensuing series of counter-attacks was Major Peel, the Irish Guards officer in command of the Squadron of tanks which had rushed the defences.

Because of the lack of road space, Brigade Headquarters were today far behind the battle, and the Irish Guards were out of wireless touch; but just after midnight Colonel Vandeleur was with great difficulty able to report through Lieutenant Creswell's wireless straight back to 2nd Household Cavalry Headquarters, who were with Main Division farther back still, "Bridge captured intact; situation in hand, all fighting has now subsided." This was cited by General Horrocks as an outstanding example of the excellence of the Regiment's wireless communications.

Appropriately enough, the de Groote Barrier bridge was named "Joe's Bridge" in honour of Lieutenant-Colonel J. O. E. Vandeleur, commanding the Irish Guards Group.

★   ★   ★

During the late afternoon "D" Squadron had also moved up to the Escaut Canal, following the route taken by Lieutenant Creswell's Troop as far as Neerpelt. Lieutenant Jonkheer Groeninx van Zoelen's Troop found the bridge to the east of the village already blown, with the Germans entrenched on the far bank. On approaching the canal to inspect the damage and width of the gap, the cars were quite heavily mortared and had to retire slightly and take up another position of observation. Here, in the course of an interchange of small-arms fire, Trooper George Thomasson from the Support Troop was killed. Lieutenant Clark's Heavy Troop 75-mm. guns then took a hand in the proceedings and the enemy were soon quietened. However, the Germans were to remain in this area in some strength, and when the advance was eventually resumed a week later, 8 Corps experienced severe fighting before they were able to force a crossing here.

On this occasion the ever-present problem of communications in an armoured car regiment was brought out forcibly. We have heard how the Irish Guards were out of touch with Brigade Headquarters, and although the vital message regarding the bridge did eventually get through, it was very much touch and go. In the case of "D" Squadron, Major Ward was expecting important orders for the next day's advance, but he also was now out of touch with Regimental Headquarters, who had found it necessary on this occasion to remain with Division as far back as Beeringen. The Squadron Leader had therefore no alternative but to send back his Rear Link car several miles to regain contact.

Whether Regimental Headquarters should remain back with the senior formation or move up with the leading battle group was a problem continually confronting Colonel Abel Smith, and to the end of the war it was never really satisfactorily solved, for the governing factor was more one of range of the No. 19 wireless set than of unit organization.

If Regimental Headquarters were close up behind the leading Squadron of armoured cars, it was a safe bet that vital information would come through with Corps out of range and unable to decipher the message. If Regimental Headquarters were at the Headquarters of the higher formation or near it, then the reverse would hold good and Squadrons in their turn would find themselves out of touch with Regimental Headquarters. The "book" answer to the problem, which was to send out a "Step-up,"[13] was all very fine in theory, but in action reconnoitring Squadrons rarely had the officer personnel to spare. There was also a limit to the number of liaison officers available at Regimental Headquarters for such a task. Nevertheless, in spite of these difficulties, not once in all operations in which the Regiment took part in North-West Europe was there a case of a message failing to get through due to a breakdown in wireless communications.

★   ★   ★

Next morning, the 11th of September, as 11th Armoured Division had by now almost taken over responsibility for the right flank, Guards Armoured Division were able to give their undivided attention to the problem of completing the reduction of Hechtel and Bourg Leopold, both of which places were still holding out stubbornly, and to consolidate, although not enlarge, the de Groote Barrier bridgehead.[14]

Since there were still Germans on the south bank of the Escaut Canal, Major Bowes Daly was ordered to reconnoitre westwards with "A" Squadron in the direction of the village of Lommel, while Major Ward, "D" Squadron, relieved of his responsibilities in the Lille St. Hubert and Neerpelt area by the advent of 11th Armoured Division elements, concentrated to the immediate west of what was already known as "Creswell's Factory," there to await further orders.

It was a confusing morning all round. There was a dense early-morning mist and the woods west of "Joe's Bridge" were found to be sheltering enemy tanks. Several Irish Guards' tanks were reported by

---

13. A wireless car positioned between two out-of-touch stations to relay their messages.
14. The bridgehead could not be enlarged too much for fear of giving away the future intentions of operation "Market-Garden"—i.e., the drive to Nijmegen and Arnhem and the Zuider Zee.

civilians to be German, and vice versa. The unfortunate inhabitants of Lommel, after having twice been assured by the British that there was now *plus de danger*, only to be promptly shelled by the Germans, finally gave up in despair and took to their cellars, where they remained for the rest of the day, doggedly reporting everything moving, friend or foe, as being enemy.

Lieutenant Franklin's Troop pursued a 75-mm. S.P. gun after being disturbed by it at their breakfasts, but it escaped back into the trees. Corporal-of-Horse Booth's car in the same Troop pulled into a farmhouse; then someone heard a rumble, looked over a fence and saw an 88-mm. gun pulling out. Moving along the road 300 yards away were six others, led by a Mark IV tank and a S.P. with a long-barrelled 75-mm. gun. Lieutenant Creswell's Troop then came out of the mist, ran into the leader of the convoy, and had an A.P. shot put through the front wheel of one of the armoured cars, which nevertheless got away without further damage. Later in the morning Lieutenant Murray's Heavy Troop came up and his Matador engaged the S.P. gun at 1,600 yards, registering a direct hit with his 75-mm. at the first attempt and scoring four more in rapid succession, when the vehicle was seen to burst into flames and finally blow up.

"D" Squadron had a notable day. As part of the preliminary plans for the future airborne operation, General Adair was keenly concerned with the bridge at Valkenswaard, situated eleven kilometres north of the Escaut Canal and eight kilometres inside the Dutch frontier. The full significance of this bridge was of course not appreciated by the Regiment at the time, but the message which reached Major Ward at dawn on the 11th of September was that "a very senior Sunray is most anxious that you find out all about it."

The bridge lay some ten kilometres beyond the Irish Guards' bridgehead and there were no other roads except the direct main route from which it could be approached. Therefore, on receipt of his orders, the Squadron Leader decided to move his own headquarters up to the Irish Guards group immediately south of "Joe's Bridge" and from there dispatch two Reconnaissance Troops (those of Lieutenants Hanbury and Buchanan-Jardine) northwards to the perimeter defences, from whence they would await a suitable opportunity to break out.

By the time the Troops had reached their locations and Squadron Headquarters were established with the Irish Guards, the sun had already begun to dispel the early morning mists.

There was an indefinable atmosphere of uneasiness surrounding the factory area and the cross-roads immediately south of "Joe's Bridge."[15] The enemy was sniping at the factory itself, "A" Squadron kept sending warning reports of suspicious movement in the woods to the west, and the Irish Guards were suffering from harassing shell fire from guns to the north.

If one may be allowed a criticism of Guards Armoured Division as a whole, there was a tendency to establish headquarters on crossroads, a fault which as time went on, and perhaps because of the overwhelming Allied air superiority, was to become marked throughout the British Army. On this occasion, staff cars, lorries, tanks and all the paraphernalia which go to make up an armoured group headquarters were parked more or less on the cross-roads, inviting shelling. There were uncorroborated rumours that two Panthers were at large south of the bridge, but nobody worried unduly.

Suddenly the reserve troops which were harboured close to the factory (brewing up their second go of tea that morning!) were startled by a loud crash, followed by several more explosions, coming from the direction of the cross-roads. Solid shots ricochetted off the road and, throwing up a spout of small pebbles, sped past a surprised three-tonner lorry in the direction of Neerpelt. Several more bangs followed, by which time the Rear Link officer had called up Major Ward to know what was happening. Through the wireless he could hear the sounds of a machine gun firing and the distinct thud of a round being put into the breech. "In action—wait—out," answered Major Ward, followed by a succession of more crashes and the bark of a Staghound's gun. The Rear Link jumped into his car and re-joined his Squadron Leader. A gruesome sight greeted his eyes.

Several men had been killed, others lay wounded, and the remains of a Humber staff car littered the roadway. An M10 (British self-propelled gun) had been knocked out. Corporal-of-Horse Connor pointed ruefully to his Matador's gun mantlet, which had been sliced as if it had been butter, and Captain Waterhouse stood stripped to the waist, his face covered in lather, brandishing a shaving brush in one hand and a pistol in the other.

It appeared that a column of German tanks and S.P. guns had motored straight into the Irish Guards' positions, covered by the dense woods leading to Lommel. The first tank had managed to get to within a few

---

15. Not to be confused with the main cross-roads farther south, where the Grenadier Guards had knocked out the 88-mms. the previous evening.

hundred yards of the cross-roads without being seen; then it must have realized that its best chance of escape lay in firing off a few rapid rounds, skid turning and making off at speed through the trees.

No one agreed as to what exactly did happen within the next minute or so, but, piecing individual accounts together, these salient facts emerge.

The first two German shells had crashed into a Reconnaissance Troop of Honey tanks belonging to the Irish Guards, killing seven of their men and wounding others. A young gunner officer standing by an anti-tank gun had shouted to his crew to hold their fire as he thought the suspect vehicle might be British. This was his last act, for by his fatal hesitation he was killed together with his crew with the next shell. All was then confusion and for a time the only gun able to shoot back was Major Ward's 37-mm. in the Staghound. With great coolness he and his crew, Corporal-of-Horse Strowbridge and Corporals Thompson and Houghton, stood their ground, firing as hard as they could go at the German tank. There was no chance of penetrating the enemy's frontal armour, but it was hoped that by rapid fire the tank's attention might be distracted from the numerous soft vehicles at its mercy long enough to enable a heavier gun to arrive and knock it out. This was precisely what happened, and "While the Household Cavalry's pop-gun was blazing away with the greatest intrepidity," an M10 belonging to the anti-tank regiment quietly pulled into the middle of the road and with unhurried calm destroyed the German with its first shot. The muzzle flash provided the comic relief to this otherwise confused and unsatisfactory battle by burning off the eyebrows and much of the hair of the Irish Guards R.S.M.—a fine figure of a man who doubtless saw little to laugh at at the time. The wrecked car proved to have contained Colonel Vandeleur's kit, which was a total loss.

Meanwhile the other German vehicles had turned off the road and moved to a flank, knocking out two more of the Irish Guards tanks on the way. They then, backed by a company of mixed S.S. and infantry, launched a determined attack along the canal bank, threatening to recapture the bridge, but were eventually seen off by the Irishmen and, after retreating back by the way they had come, were caught by a Grenadier column moving up from the south.

★   ★   ★

While this fracas had been taking place, Lieutenant Buchanan-Jardine had been examining the possibilities of slipping out of the bridgehead and into Holland. The commander of the forward infantry positions had reported being forced to withdraw slightly that morning by shell and machine-gun fire, and from somewhere on the sand dunes to the north an enemy gun had been dropping shells into the tiny bridgehead with regularity. However, after scanning the long straight road through his glasses, and things appearing to be fairly quiet, Lieutenant Buchanan-Jardine decided to make his attempt.

He left his two armoured cars hidden up in some trees because in the circumstances they offered too large a target and would be more of a hindrance than a help. Since one of his scout cars was temporarily out of action, he borrowed a second vehicle from Lieutenant Hanbury's Troop. In this car were two tried veterans of 3 Troop, Lance-Corporal-of-Horse Brook and Trooper Bateman. Lieutenant Buchanan-Jardine decided to lead himself, with Trooper Buckley as his driver. The Irish Guards wished them luck, promised not to shoot them up *if they returned*, and the party set off.

German infantry was soon encountered and for a time the two cars were compelled to hide up in the trees. Then the Troop Leader felt that in the undergrowth there was more danger in being stalked while doing nothing and so resumed the advance at increased speed. "I felt sure that we should encounter more of these damned little men in green and that in the circumstances speed was preferable to the cautious tactical advance at this stage."

Luck was with them. By two o'clock in the afternoon they were, several miles inside the Dutch border and halted at a spot reasonably screened from observation, having run the gauntlet of three separate parties of Germans, all too surprised to fire.

The bridge over the River Dommel could be clearly seen. Immediately beyond lay the small town of Valkenswaard. A preliminary report that the bridge was still intact was wirelessed back. Doubts that it might be too fragile to hold the Shermans were soon put at rest by the sight of a German Mark IV tank which moved slowly forward out of Valkenswaard and settled like a giant toad squatting in the middle of the bridge. From enemy movement in the surrounding area, it appeared to be guarding in somewhat nervous manner the only approach into Valkenswaard from the south.

There was a small café at the side of the road close to where Lieutenant Buchanan-Jardine's party had halted, and from it now emerged a band of overjoyed Dutchmen, welcoming the first soldiers to set foot in Holland.[16] They, like the villagers on the Escaut Canal, could hardly have

---

16. The Grenadiers' historian claims that his Regiment provided the first soldier to set foot in Holland, citing a patrol which crossed the frontier on the 12th of September. Their author

done more to give away the Household Cavalrymen had they tried, but their intentions were of the best.

The Troop Leader calmed their understandable excitement and tried to find out what he could about the enemy. Then, having warned the Dutch that his appearance did not necessarily presage the immediate arrival of British forces, he bade them good-bye and good luck. They in their turn warned him that there were many "Muffen" lying in ambush on the road back. The departure was speeded by pathetic entreaties for an early return, but as events transpired, Valkenswaard was to have to wait nearly a week before being freed from enemy yoke.

There was no doubt as to tactics on the way back to the bridgehead. The Troop Leader ordered full speed ahead and the gallant little Daimler scout cars really showed what they could do. Nose to tail, with their fluid flywheels screaming defiance, they raced southwards at well over sixty miles per hour. Before the ambushing bazooka men could even raise their weapons to their shoulders the party was through. Everything on the outside of the cars was punctured and broken by small-arms fire "including the precious cooking utensils," but the bridgehead was reached safely with the occupants unscathed.

There was a sad sequel to Valkenswaard's day of rejoicing, which only came to light when Mr. A. C. Lemmens, a Dutch official working in the Burgomaster's office, wrote to me after the war. His letter, apart from the omission of a few sentences having no bearing on the history, is reproduced in its entirety.

VALKENSWAARD,
June 2nd, 1947.

DEAR SIR,

First of all I must apologize for not having written before, but I hope you will understand that it has taken quite a long time before I got some photographs.

I am very pleased I am able to give you some particulars about the two armoured cars which came to Valkenswaard on September 11th, 1944.

On Monday, September 11th, at about two o'clock in the afternoon, we saw a lot of German soldiers running along the houses holding their rifles in their hands, while their helmets and uniforms were camouflaged. They

---

cannot at the time of writing have been aware of the above Household Cavalry patrol, which was carried out a day previously and on the express orders of the Divisional Commander, Major-General Adair. Lieutenant Buchanan-Jardine was subsequently awarded, as well as the M.C., the Order of the Bronze Lion by the Royal Netherlands Government for being the first Allied soldier to set foot in Holland since the German occupation.

looked like rascals and so they went to the Belgian frontier. After those foot passengers came the "Deutsche Wehrmacht." It is impossible for me to describe all the things they went to fight with (prams, bicycles, cases on wheels which they took from the children, etc.). I must not forget to say that we also saw some tanks.

At the same time (two o'clock) the two armoured cars arrived in Valkenswaard. They did not go any farther than the first café on the road between Belgium and the first Dutch bridge they had to cross. When they arrived at the above café they left the cars and went into the café. In the twinkling of an eye the cars were surrounded by the civilians.

When the first English soldiers arrived there were standing a lot of German cars with dead bodies beside the road. I need not tell you that the civilians took the opportunity for taking everything they wanted (wheels, tyres, etc.).

At four o'clock the English soldiers went back to Belgium after having warned the Dutch people that they were not liberated yet.

Just after their return, the Germans came back. Within a few minutes all the civilians had gone. The Germans went in to the café and asked for inquiries. Of course nobody knew about the English visit. In the meantime the orange knots disappeared, but notwithstanding all this, the Germans shot three civilians (see the mark on the photograph; this is one of the killed men).

After all this we had a terrible week; we were waiting and waiting.... Day in, day out, we saw German soldiers and women going in the direction of Eindhoven. They stole bicycles and they sent the Dutch people to the frontiers to dig holes.

September the 17th, the day of our liberation.
The fight was very hard. All day long we had to hide from the rascals. At about three o'clock in the afternoon the bombardment started (English). They bombed four cigar factories and a lot of houses and shops.

After the bombardment we were liberated.

Well, this is all, and I hope that you can use these particulars. I would be very pleased if you will send the photographs back, and I would like very much to receive a book when you have finished it.

Hoping to hear from you once more,

Yours sincerely,

(Signed) A. C. LEMMENS.

★ ★ ★

Although the Germans continued to filter through from the direction of Lommel, they were mostly stragglers from farther west, where increasing pressure by 50th Division expanding the Albert Canal bridgehead at Gheel was forcing the enemy back across the Escaut Canal.

During the past few days, the battle had bid fair to become one of the "bittiest" and most involved actions ever fought by Guards Armoured Division, but gradually the general situation was clearing itself up and affairs to the south were looking much more tidy.

It was true that Hechtel was still holding out, in spite of all the efforts of the Welsh Guards group, but to everyone's relief, Bourg Leopold, with its enormous barracks now gutted by shell fire, had at last fallen. However, so impatient had the B.B.C. become at the delay that it had decided to make the place surrender on the previous day's one o'clock news, at the very moment when a message from the Brigade Commander was saying over the wireless that, "Bourg Leopold is full of Boche and I have told my chaps to sit back outside it until I can lay on a proper attack with artillery support." As far as the exhausted Foot Guards were concerned, the B.B.C. version did not go with a swing, particularly with the Goldstream group, who had incurred heavy casualties already and looked like having to face another hard day's fighting.

11th Armoured Division could now report having made firm contact with elements of 2nd U.S. Armoured Division advancing on the axis Hasselt—Asch—Sittard. During the day they reduced the village of Peer after strong resistance and then moved on to occupy Petit Brogel with relative ease. With the Inns of Court Regiment now patrolling up to the Escaut Canal from Neerpelt down to Bree, all anxiety on the score of that flank came to an end.

"B" Squadron, who had been protecting the guns of 55th Field Regiment, were relieved of their responsibilities and moved forward on to the Heath near Vlasmer, while "C" Squadron had already joined Regimental Headquarters, who, after their wireless difficulties of the previous twenty-four hours, had themselves moved up to a new location in the woods west of Hechtel.

Anticipating that at any moment the Welsh Guards might flush numbers of the enemy out of Hechtel, Colonel Abel Smith ordered Major Herbert to station some of his Troops to watch the eastern and north-eastern exits of the village, but the day closed with nothing having been seen of the enemy.

Not until a set-piece attack had been put in by the Welsh Guards group, supported by a heavy artillery barrage in which guns from 11th Armoured Division joined in on the 12th of September to pound Hechtel into a heap of rubble, did its defenders at last give in. Out of a garrison of approximately a thousand men, nearly 350 were found to have been killed and 400, including wounded, taken prisoner.

"THE BLASTED HEATH," VLASMER, BELGIUM, 15TH SEPTEMBER 1944

Officers and Corporals-of-Horse assembling to receive orders for the forthcoming battle leading up to Arnhem

The enemy, most of them paratroopers, had fought incredibly hard and bravely, and to label them "fanatics" as one broadsheet chose to do was as inexact and stupid as it would have been so to designate the valour of the Welsh Guards who had experienced such a hard battle to overcome them. The working of the "propaganda" mind was sometimes hard for the British soldier to fathom.

In the closing hours of the battle for Hechtel, "C" Squadron, which was still patrolling the north-eastern exits of the town, collected a considerable number of prisoners who had managed to evade the Welsh Guards' ring, and Lieutenant van Cutsem's Heavy Troop became so engrossed in its work that, according to Corporal-of-Horse Shepherd, "Mr. van Cutsem quite failed to notice the green trace of three 88-mm. shells whizz past over the top of his head. In addition, at the finish of the Hechtel show, about fifteen Jerries walked, or I should say ran, smack into us. Mr. van Cutsem lined them up and ordered Corporal Woods and Trooper Sloper to search them while he stood glowering over them. They were a villainous-looking bunch, and one of them, a huge hulk of a man (I believe he was a member of the Hermann Goering Division; he was dressed entirely in black with a skull and cross-bones on his chest), started protesting when his turn came to be searched—to which Mr. van Cutsem proclaimed in his rather particular tone of voice used on such occasions, 'Deal with him, Woods.' Well, Woods was a big fellow, but this German made two of him, and I cannot think that Woods's heart was entirely in his work as he stepped up to this chap. Fortunately for all concerned, the big fellow gave in first, much to Woods's relief!"

Although for a few days small pockets of Germans were to remain south of the canal, this was more due to lack of escape routes than by intent. The fall of Hechtel meant the virtual elimination of all resistance in the sector enclosed by the line of canals Escaut—Meuse—Albert.

By the 13th of September, the entire Regiment was harboured south of the Escaut Canal on a pleasant stretch of open heathland near the village of Vlasmer, and just off the main road along which trundled the supplies and reinforcements for the bridgehead. For some reason, this area came to be known to the Regiment as "The Blasted Heath" —we could have been in many worse places.

The blowing up of all the Albert Canal crossings had been a forewarning of what was to come. From now onwards advances were to be hard and slogging, with the bazooka more and more ousting the 88-mm. gun as the main eliminator of our armour.

There were other and more far-reaching causes for the slowing down of the momentum of advance, the main being the great difficulties of supply and communications. The British Army was still being fed from the Normandy beaches, and the Germans, knowing only too well what were the problems, were determined to deny to the Allies the port facilities of Antwerp for as long as possible. This they could do most effectively by holding on to the Scheldt estuary, where their guns precluded all shipping from using Europe's second largest port.

However, that which concerned us for the immediate future was the message from the Corps Commander, which read: "Top up—tidy up—tails up—and no move for several days." It was acted upon with whole-hearted alacrity. Guards Armoured Division had most certainly earned its rest and yet, welcome as were the words, we felt in our hearts that they could have but one interpretation. Official hopes that the war might be ended before the advent of the floods and snows of winter had now all but vanished.

★　★　★

The succeeding days passed rapidly. There was much work to do making good the ravages of a campaign which had taken us many hundreds of miles in the last three weeks. The weather was generally fine, although people were glad of their greatcoats when the sun went down, for night frosts had already touched up the near-by apple orchards. Brussels was but two hours' journey by road and many managed to slip in a brief semi-official twenty-four hours' leave in that delightful city, fast returning to normal. In the evenings of leisure on "The Blasted Heath," when work was done, there were the wines and the cigars from the Brussels dump and pleasant inter-squadron visits and after-dinner conversation. Speculation was rife as to what the future held in store.

Good news came through that all the members of Lieutenant Bethell's Troop, which had been knocked out in the Forêt l'Evêque in Normandy, were safe, most being prisoner in Germany; but Lieutenant Bethell, together with Lieutenant Smallwood, of "D" Squadron Heavy Troop, had been picked up by the Americans on their entry into Paris and were now back in England slowly recovering from their wounds.

By the 15th of September there grew the feeling that a renewed advance could not be long delayed, and one felt that the small bridgehead beyond "Joe's Bridge" was the clue to the likely direction of any new thrust. To add weight to this theory, a pompously worded little handbook had but recently been circulated informing all officers that the Dutch "were a very clean people." After which followed a series of rumours. Inquisitive Troop Leaders paid visits to Regimental Headquarters, but had to come away with nothing more satisfactory in answer to their questions than a wise look and a guarded, "I wouldn't know really"—which, of course, was true, but certainly not intended to be taken that way.

Then on the 16th of September Lieutenant Haskard's jeep arrived back from Divisional Headquarters loaded with a complete new set of maps covering the Low Countries up to the Zuider Zee, and the secret was out.

A warning to stand by for orders came round to every Squadron. Colonel Abel Smith would be arriving any moment. When he had finished speaking to the last Squadron and answered all questions it was late afternoon, but by then every trooper knew that the morrow would see the Household Cavalry on its way to Holland, bound northwards initially along the same road traversed by Lieutenant Buchanan-Jardine's two scout cars six days previously.

I well remember that "D" Squadron were the last to receive their orders, for they were not to be employed in the early stages, and that when Colonel Abel Smith got to the "Intention" paragraph he gave out that, "2 HCR, once beyond Arnhem, will crack about from Apeldoorn to Nunspeet and the sea beyond"; adding with infinite gusto for the benefit of those already immersed in maps and studying the fearful blue maze of rivers and other menacing-looking water obstacles, "disrupting the enemy's communications."

Lieutenant Hughes was even informed that "he might be required as temporary L.O. with the Airborne force"—had he got his parachute ready? Which question made the "D" Squadron Echelon Commander stroke his nose reflectively.

There was one rare and greatly appreciated feature about this operation—whatever might be in store for us, at least it did not presage a start at first light.

Evening came, we drank our champagne, and over "Willem Twe" cigars and coffee fortified with the last remaining dregs of calvados, discussed the prospects of the morrow. It was a dark but fine night, and not until the early hours of the morning did the last lamp go out.

Bedford 15-Cwt. Truck ("GIN PALACE")

Training in England

A recruit squad, Windsor 1941. *Front row, third from left*: Squadron Quartermaster Corporal J. Christie. (*Household Cavalry Museum*)

Squadron cookhouse on a damp evening in Yorkshire during Exercise EAGLE. March 1943. (*Household Cavalry Museum*)

HM King George VI inspecting 2nd Household Cavalry Regiment. Bridlington. 23 March 1944. *On the left*: Corporal of Horse Offen. *In background*: Humber armoured car. In beret and breeches, Lieutenant Colonel Henry Abel Smith (Commanding Officer). (*Household Cavalry Museum*)

Weymouth, December, 1943. Household Cavalry Daimler armoured car heading for the shore after waterproofing tests in a rough sea. (*War Office*)

Worth Priory, Sussex. May 1944. Donkey Race. (*Household Cavalry Museum*)

The King and Queen inspecting a composite 2 HCR troop. Gillingham Station. May 1944. (*Household Cavalry Museum*)

Normandy

First glimpse of the coast of Normandy, dusk, 13th July, 1944. (*Author*)

Men of 2 HCR assembling round their vehicles prior to being landed at Graye-sur-Mer. 13th July 1944. (*Household Cavalry Museum*)

Lieutenant Colonel Henry Abel Smith (Commanding Officer) Captain Arthur Collins (Adjutant), beside the RHQ Humber Staff Car. Normandy. 14th July, 1944. (*Household Cavalry Museum*)

Landing Ship Tanks (LSTs) grounded on the Normandy beaches. July 1944. (*Household Cavalry Museum*)

Near Graye-sur-Mer, Normandy. Seated: Surgeon–Captain Kynaston checks his medical equipment after landing. *Standing, left-to-right*: Troopers Robinson, Scowby, Healey and Lance Corporal Hilton. 14th July, 1944. (*Author*)

Graye-sur-Mer. The Regimental Echelon. *Left to right*: Regimental Quartermaster Corporal Goody; Craftsman Haines, R.E.M.E.; Corporal Briggs, the post corporal; Trooper Stinton; Sergeant Salvidge, R.E.M.E. 14th July, 1944. (*Author*)

Brécy. D Squadron Officers' Mess in farm outbuilding. *Left to right*: Lieutenants Buchanan-Jardine and Hughes, Captain Waterhouse, Lieutenant Ainsworth, Major Ward, Lieutenants Hanbury and Bethell. 15th July, 1944. (*Author*)

Normandy bridgehead before the breakout. A farmer's daughters, Paulette and Nicole, teach soldiers of 2 HCR the correct way to pronounce French phrases from the English/French phrase book issued to British troops. (*Household Cavalry Museum*)

Near Graye-sur-Mer. Line of armoured cars de-waterproofed and about to move off to the Unit Assembly Area at Brécy. Lieutenant D. B. Powle standing in foreground. 14th July, 1944. (*Author*)

North of Caen, Normandy. "Pegasus" Bridge over the Orne Canal, which was captured by British airborne troops on D Day. It was over this bridge that A and B Squadrons advanced to their first action during operation "Goodwood." 18th July, 1944. (*War Office*)

Knocked–out German Panther tank on the ill–famed road to Burcy. August, 1944. (*War Office*)

Dummy wooden tank near St. Martin des Bésaces. During the fighting on 31st July and 1st August Troop patrols encountered many similar models cleverly sited, and a dump of them was discovered by D Squadron in the village of St. Jean des Essartiers. 1st August, 1944. (*War Office*)

British armour held up on the Vire–Caen road a few miles out of Vire. This long straight stretch, dominated by enemy 88-mm. guns, was a nightmare to leading scout cars. It was first crossed when Household Cavalry cars penetrated several miles east of Le Beny Bocage and almost to Vire in the late afternoon of 1st August, 1944. (*War Office Ciné*)

Censored

Sourdevalle. General Montgomery, having visited the Regiment's infantry positions on the Burcy ridge, explains the latest situation to officers and men. *Standing, left-to-right*: Captain Ford, Lieutenant-Colonel Abel Smith, Surgeon-Captain Kynaston, Captain Collins (with head turned away from camera), General Montgomery, and Lieutenant the Hon. M. Eden. Kneeling are an officer and men from the Royal Northumberland Fusiliers (machine gunners in support). 16th August, 1944. (*War Office*)

Daimler scout car on the road to the River Seine following the breakout from Normandy. August 1944. (*Household Cavalry Museum*)

The advance to the Somme bridges. Tanks following up in the wake of the armoured cars, whose leading elements had traversed most of the way from Beauvais to the Somme during the hours of darkness. 31st August, 1944. (*War Office*)

Belgium and Holland

The liberation of Ath by A Squadron. These two photographs were brought to light by the help of Doctor Vangraefschepe, late Burgomaster of Ath, and Madame P. Delannoy, of Enghien, Belgium. They show (1) the fleeing remnants of the German rear-guard at twenty-five minutes past one, and (2) the arrival of the first British soldiers, two Household Cavalrymen in a scout car. The hands of the clock in the Grand' Place are pointing to half-past one. The Grand' Place can also be seen in the distance in top photograph. For attempting to take similar records at other points on the road several Belgian civilians were shot by the passing S.S. troops. 3rd September, 1944. (*From photographs in the possession of Madame P. Delannoy*)

'Local resistance types' with Corporal of Horse Allen. Near Brussels. 3rd September 1944. (*Household Cavalry Museum*)

Belgian civilian photograph showing the entry of Lieutenant Wordsworth and Trooper Fisher into Enghien. Note that as yet there are few people in the main street and no welcoming flags out. 3rd September, 1944. (*From photograph in the possession of Trooper Ben Fisher*)

Guards Armoured Division parade through Brussels following liberation. September 1944. Regimental HQ Matador. Captain Arthur Collins (Adjutant). Lieutenant Colonel Henry Abel Smith (Commanding Officer). (*Household Cavalry Museum*)

Humber scout car of 2nd Household Cavalry Regiment entering Brussels. September 1944. (*Household Cavalry Museum*)

Lieutenant Buchanan-Jardine's dash to Valkenswaard, Holland. This photograph was taken by a Dutch civilian and was hidden from the returning Germans, who, as part of reprisals against the population for having welcomed the Household Cavalrymen, seized hostages and shot, among others, the person marked with a cross. *Centre, with field-glasses* Lieutenant A. J. R. Buchanan-Jardine. In scout car Trooper Buckley. 11th September, 1944. (*From photograph in the possession of A. C. Lemmens, Valkenswaard*)

Trooper T. Carroll and Captain G. D. Cooper. (*Household Cavalry Museum*)

Trooper Purchase bringing up the mail to Boxmeer farm. (*Author*)

Trooper Pettit mending boots at St. Anthonis. (*Author*)

Trooper Jarvest kneading "duff" in an old petrol flimsy. The result was intended for D Squadron Rear Link crew's dinner! (*Author*)

Boxmeer, Holland. Major E. J. S. Ward and Captain C. H. Waterhouse, his second-in-command, interrogating a member of the Dutch Underground Movement who had swum over the river from the enemy side during the night. (*Author*)

Captain T. Clyde, second-in-command, C Squadron. Eindhoven, Holland. September 1944. (*Household Cavalry Museum*)

D Squadron Headquarters Staghound armoured car halted for a quick "brew up" on the way to Tiel, west of Nijmegen. (*Author*)

Nijmegen Bridge, captured by the 2nd Battalion (Armoured) Grenadier Guards and 504 Combat Team, US Army, on 20th September 1944. (*Household Cavalry Museum*)

Corporal Roy Tilney RHG, Corporal of Horse Jack Sutton RHG, Corporal Jack Guy LG. Ardennes. Winter 1944. (*Household Cavalry Museum*)

Corporal of Horse Tommy Thompson. (*Household Cavalry Museum*)

Lieutenant General Sir Brian Horrocks, GOC 30 Corps. (*Imperial War Museum*)

Corporal of Horse Smith and Corporal of Horse Bland. (*Household Cavalry Museum*)

At rest in the village of Haps. Lieutenant Jonkheer Groenix van Zoelen's Troop. *Top row, left-to-right*: Trooper Savage, Lieutenant van Zoelen, Trooper Scott, Corporal of Horse Davis, Trooper Coates. *Bottom row*: Trooper Tuckfield, Corporal Checkley, Trooper Prangnell. (*Author*)

Heavy girder bridge at Grave over River Maas. Lieutenant Colonel Henry Abel Smith (Commanding Officer) and Captain Arthur Collins (Adjutant). (*Household Cavalry Museum*)

Lieutenant David Tabor. (*Household Cavalry Museum*)

D Squadron crossing the Maas at Genap. (*Household Cavalry Museum*)

Shell-fire damage to C Squadron Support Troop vehicles. February, 1945. (*Author*)

The Reichswald, Germany

Trooper Hull emerging from hut built by Lieutenant Hughes and the author. Window frame from Goch, chair from German dug-out, corrugated iron roof from Ordnance dump, and timber from the forest. March, 1945. (*Author*)

Track laying in the forest. *Left-to-right*: Trooper Vernall. Corporal of Horse Cawte, Trooper Beadle, Corporal Meade-King, Lance Corporal Baxter, Trooper Rutland, Lance Corporal Broadrib. 20th March, 1945. (*Author*)

Lieutenants OPM Haskard and RF Oliver. (*Household Cavalry Museum*)

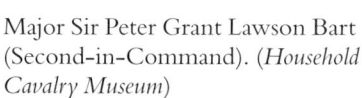

Major Sir Peter Grant Lawson Bart (Second-in-Command). (*Household Cavalry Museum*)

In the forest. Fitters at work preparing for the Rhine crossing. *Left*: Lance Corporal Broadrib and Trooper Powell, driver of a three-tonner lorry. March, 1945. (*Author*)

Briefing for the Rhine crossing. *Left-to-right*: Lieutenant Colonel H. Abel Smith, Major P. Profumo and, *between maps*, Lieutenant A. J. R. Buchanan-Jardine. *Above maps*, Lieutenant T. F. J. Hanbury. 26th March, 1945. (*Author*)

Irish Guards and D Squadron held up by enemy self-propelled gun cleverly sited on outskirts of Enschede. Typhoon plane can be seen about to dive and attack German emplacement beyond tree on right. 1st April, 1945. (*Author*)

Humber scout cars of 2 HCR and German refugees. (*Household Cavalry Museum*)

Wayside halt for a quick "brew-up" east of the Dortmund-Ems Canal. Corporal Thompson (with mug), Trooper Milner, Corporal Jenkins (kneeling), Corporal Musgrave (filling stove). Standing by car wheel, Trooper Jones. 7th April, 1945. (*Author*)

Germans of 7th Paratroop Division being doubled past D Squadron on outskirts of Haaksbergen. (*Author*)

Hitler-Jugend, some no more than ten years old. 31st March /1st April, 1945. (*War Office*)

C Squadron sign at Visselhövede, from where 2 HCR moved to Brühl. (*Household Cavalry Museum*)

Farewell to Armour

On Rotenburg aerodrome, Guards Armoured Division bade farewell to its tanks and the Foot Guards reverted to their infantry role. The Regiment provided an escort for Field-Marshal Montgomery, who took the salute at a march past of two hundred and fifty tanks. In the two Daimler armoured cars can be seen (*left-to-right*) Lieutenant Murray, Trooper Dean, Lieutenant Buchanan-Jardine and his operator. 9th June, 1945. (*Author*)

Armoured cars and scout cars of 2 HCR, parked in front of Brühl Castle. June 1945. (*Household Cavalry Museum*)

Farewell to Armour parade. 9th June 1945. (*Household Cavalry Museum*)

British Army of the Rhine

The shell of Cologne Cathedral seen through the shattered girders of the Hohenzollern bridge which spanned the River Rhine. The Regiment moved into its last billets at Brühl, near Cologne, on 14th of June, 1945. (*Author*)

Presentation of the Brussels Standard to the 2nd Household Cavalry Regiment by the Burgomaster of Brussels, Monsieur M. J. van de Meulebroeck. *Left-to-right*: Squadron Corporal Major Berrisford, Corporal of Horse Neill, Regimental Corporal Major Poupart, Corporal of Horse Jenkins. July, 1945. (*From photograph in the possession of Corporal of Horse D. G. Allen*)

The author, Major Roden Orde. (*Antonia Lloyd*)

Eric Meade–King standing next to one of his pictures of Horse Guards. (*Author*)

Roden Orde and armoured car crew. (*Author*)

Lieutenant A. F. A. Hughes, Royal Horse Guards (Blues), watches the last Life Guards' car leaving Brühl on its journey north to Goslar. 17th July, 1945. (*Author*)

The Second Household Cavalry Regiment

MONT PINCON   NEERPELT

SOULEUVRE   NEDERRIJN

NOIREAU CROSSING   NIJMEGEN

AMIENS   1944   LINGEN

BRUSSELS   BENTHEIM

NORTH WEST EUROPE 1944–1945

When the First Household Cavalry Regiment sailed for the Middle East in 1940, it left behind at Windsor the Household Cavalry Training Regiment. This unit trained all recruits and retained its horses until Sept 1940. It also formed part of a mobile reserve to be employed in the event of an enemy parachute invasion. For this task it was issued with six civilian driven buses and just six automatic weapons.

In November 1940 the training regiment was re-designated "Second Household Cavalry Motor Battalion". The "Reserve Regiment", which had been carrying out various guard duties from Hyde Park Barracks, then became the Training Regiment and moved to Windsor, while the new Motor Battalion moved to Stoney Castle, Pirbright.

In September the Motor Battalion role was changed to that of armoured car regiment in the newly formed Guards Armoured Division. 2 HCR moved to Bulford and then to Trowbridge. The whole of 1942 and 1943 was a period of intense and protracted training, based first in Norfolk then in Yorkshire.

At last, in May 1944, 2 HCR drove south to Brighton where the opening of the "second front" was eagerly awaited. They first saw action in Normandy in July during the attack towards Falaise. It was a difficult battle initiation in close wooded country around Bény Bocage, which did however result in the brilliant capture of a crossing over the River Souleuvre.

When the break-out came in August, 2 HCR advanced across Picardy to the Seine. The next four days saw an exhilarating opposed pursuit of over 120 miles and the capture of three bridges over the River Somme.

The most rapid advance of the war, however, 90 miles by lunchtime, was on 3rd Sept when 2 HCR's armoured cars entered Brussels, where they got an overwhelming reception. The next day they seized and held the bridge in Louvain, 30 miles east of Brussels.

On the 11th Sept, having advanced steadily northwards, 2 HCR were the first British troops to cross into Holland. They had already been the first into Belgium since 1940.

During the Battle of Arnhem, they were the only British troops to make actual contact with the Polish Parachute Brigade just west of Arnhem.

After a month on the Maas, the Regiment was rapidly switched at Christmas into the American sector, west of Namur. Here they provided for some days the only direct information about the German Ardennes offensive, to HQ 2nd Army.

Following the Reichswald battles, 2 HCR crossed the Rhine and again led the Guards Armoured Division northwards, parallel to the Dutch border towards Bremen. There were numerous spirited engagements and losses but also the satisfaction of liberating our own prisoners of war.

By 23 April 45, 1 HCR had joined them between the Weser and Elbe Estuaries. The two regiments fought alongside until the end of the war, when 2 HCR occupied the German naval base of Cuxhaven.

A page from the original 2HCR photo album, now in the Household Cavalry Museum.

Part Four

From the Escaut to the Ardennes

Chapter I

"The Width of One Road"

"Market-Garden"—Advance to Valkenswaard and Eindhoven; Lieutenant Palmer's Troop and Captain Balding loop west—Grenadier Guards' tanks halted by fragile wooden bridges—Link-up with 101st U.S. Airborne Division—Successful patrol to Aalst—Trooper Jones's shoot—Eindhoven—Zon bridge—"A" and "D" Squadrons on "The Blasted Heath"—Advance resumed ("B" Squadron)—Link-up with 82nd U.S. Airborne Division—Waal-Maas Canal bridge found damaged by Lieutenant Kavanagh's Troop—Another crossing at Heumen near Malden—Fighting at approaches to Nijmegen road bridge; narratives of Captain Cooper and Lieutenant Tabor—Situation during evening of 19th September— Journey of Guards Armoured Division Echelon from "The Blasted Heath" (escorted by "A" and "D" Squadrons)—Regiment concentrated in suburbs of Nijmegen.

"Market-Garden," for such was the name given to the joint Anglo-American operation in which we were about to take part, was a bold and ambitious attempt to turn the enemy's Siegfried Line defences by outflanking them to the north. If successful, not only would it cut off communications between Germany and the Low Countries, but it would throw open the entire North German Plain and the road to Berlin to the Allied Armies. We looked upon it as a final all-out effort, aiming at winning the war on the Western Front before the winter set in.

Before elaborating on the Regiment's part in the operation, it is necessary to understand fully what the task involved and to know who was to carry it out.

The essential feature of the whole plan was "the laying of a carpet of airborne troops" across five successive major water obstacles on an extremely narrow front. These were the Neder Rijn at Arnhem, the Waal at Nijmegen, the Maas at Grave, and two important canals, the Wilhelmina, north of Eindhoven, and the Zuid Willemsvaart, running parallel to the Maas and linking the towns of Helmond and s'Hertogenbosch.

For this purpose one British Airborne Division and two American Airborne Divisions, as well as, later, a Polish Parachute Brigade, were to be employed—all except the last preceding the advance of the ground forces.

The 1st British Airborne Division was to capture the road and railway bridges over the Neder Rijn at Anthem, while, later, the Polish Parachute Brigade was to land to the immediate south of the bridges.

82nd United States Airborne Division was to seize the bridges at Nijmegen and Grave, in connection with which the capture of the high ground between Groesbeek and Nijmegen was vital.

101st United States Airborne Division was to capture the bridges and defiles on 30 Corps axis between Grave and Eindhoven. These included the bridge over the canal at Zon, whence the Division was to advance south and take Eindhoven; the bridge at Veghel; and the area north of Zon, with the object of capturing the St. Oedenrode bridgehead.

The main object of all these landings was "to facilitate the passage of 30 Corps," whose intention it was to "thrust north with all possible speed from the Meuse—Escaut Canal bridgehead, linking up along the airborne carpet eventually to secure the general area Arnhem—Nunspeet."

The Guards Armoured Division was to be the spearhead of the advance "with the ultimate task of dominating the area between Apeldoorn and the Zuider Zee." 2nd Household Cavalry Regiment, once the Division had broken out of the Meuse—Escaut bridgehead, would lead the advance on one centre line which was to be not only that of Guards Armoured Division but of 30 Corps as well. This ran through Valkenswaard, Eindhoven, St. Oedenrode, Veghel, Uden, Grave, Nijmegen and on to Arnhem.

To widen what would be a dangerously narrow corridor, 8 Corps were subsequently to move up over the Escaut Canal on our right and 12 Corps on our left—the latter being the stronger of the two formations, for it was anticipated that when the larger part of the German Fifteenth Army found itself cut off in Western Holland it would react strongly, if only in a desperate attempt to regain its own lines. This, to a certain extent, was what happened, but, inconveniently for 30 Corps, some time elapsed before 12 Corps came on to the scene.

"Market Garden" appeared to possess certain unique features. In the first place, the air part of the scheme was to be the largest Allied airborne operation ever to be undertaken. In the second place, the hazarding of an entire Corps along one single narrow road[1], with no chance of deployment for over sixty miles, and inside enemy occupied territory the whole way, was an extremely bold move which had never before

---

1. "Horrocks's salient was about forty yards wide. That was all he needed—just the width of one road" (Alan Moorehead in *Eclipse* Hamish Hamilton Ltd., London).

been attempted, even in North Africa. Another aspect, about which we knew nothing at the time, was that the whole operation had only been decided upon at the last minute.[2]

One presumed at the time that the operation could only have been deemed possible because of the chaotic state of affairs within the German camp. Subsequent fighting was to prove that the enemy had in fact regained his balance to a remarkable degree and was not quite so groggy as imagined.

We were well aware that the plan was dangerously dependent on good weather for the airborne forces: that the balance between success and failure was a delicate one, closely related to the most detailed traffic control—the assembling and marshalling of forces requiring the most careful organization. It had to be so flexible that once Guards Armoured Division had broken through, the Corps Commander could call forward any body of troops he required. Thus, at no time could an order of march for over 20,000 vehicles be prescribed.

Should any of the bridges at Grave, Nijmegen or Arnhem be found destroyed, it was of paramount importance that the Regiment fan out along the banks to seek out new points suitable for crossing. Bridging "on a vast scale" had been assembled in the Bourg Leopold area and organized in columns to be held in readiness to be called forward at a moment's notice.

During the course of our regrouping, the enemy made a number of small counter-attacks against the bridgehead and, disturbing fact, it was becoming increasingly evident that he was succeeding in the organization of a co-ordinated defensive system. However, during the night of the 16th/17th September 11th Armoured Division, now forming part of 8 Corps, put in some feint attacks, and probed away steadily to our right in the area Lanklaer—Bree. We hoped that the enemy might be deceived.

Because of flying conditions in England and over the North Sea there was doubt up to the last moment as to whether operation "Market-Garden" could take place at the appointed time, but at half-past twelve (midday) on the 17th of September General Horrocks at his forward headquarters overlooking the canal received the signal he was awaiting. The airborne forces had left their bases in England and France.

Over Belgium the skies were a clear blue, and those in the Regiment not immediately concerned with the initial stages of the advance walked over to a sandy eminence, hoping to catch a glimpse of the aerial armada

---

2. The report of the First Allied Airborne Army says: "The first mention of 'Market Garden' at this Headquarters was in a phone call from Lieutenant-General Browning, just back from the Continent, to the Chief of Staff at 1430 hours, 10th September."

as it appeared over the tops of the pine trees. They had not long to wait. Far to the west the first tiny dots could already be seen. These grew rapidly in size until it was possible to distinguish numbers on the wings of the leading planes. Then with a dull roar the aerial convoy veered northwards into occupied Holland and was lost to sight. Not one enemy plane took the air to meet them.

Zero hour, the time at which the land attack was to be launched, was at twenty-five minutes to three. The Irish Guards group lined up across "Joe's Bridge," and close behind them waited Major Wignall's Squadron ("B"). "Tac" Regimental Headquarters took up their allotted station close to 5th Brigade Headquarters, while Major Herbert's Squadron ("C") moved into place to their immediate rear.

Shortly after two o'clock in the afternoon, a heavy artillery barrage (300 guns), intended to soften up the enemy defences, crept inexorably up the cobbled road towards Valkenswaard, probing and blasting both sides. Medium guns opened up close behind the two reserve squadrons, "A" and "D,"[3] adding their noise to the infernal din of hundreds of shells whistling and screeching overhead.

After twenty minutes or so the barrage lifted and the tanks of the Irish Guards began to move out of the bridgehead. Then, as the range gradually became too great for the guns, the first squadron of rocket firing Typhoons took on the task, swooping to the attack and following one another on the "cab rank" system controlled by an R.A.F. officer in a contact car with the leading tanks. To those of us who were, as yet, onlookers, the sudden dive, followed seconds later by a terrifying hiss ending in the dull roar of an explosion, was shattering enough. To the enemy, sheltering in their trenches or behind their gun shields, the effect must have been appalling.

The first wave of Irish Guards tanks bore through, the enemy having evidently gone to ground, but stunned as the Germans must have been, no sooner had the barrage ceased than they reappeared. In quick succession nine tanks were knocked out by 88-mms. and bazookas, many of the Guardsmen being killed by machine-gun fire as they left their burning turrets. Still, the attack was pressed home. Prisoners began to trickle back over the canal; they were a tough lot —one of them managed to secrete and then throw a grenade into a carrier at the side of the road, killing a sergeant. At half past three the Germans in their turn began shelling the road and several lorries went up in smoke. Then one of the Typhoons

---

3. As part of the general scheme, and in view of the exposed nature of the flanks, "A" and "D" Squadrons were to wait on "The Blasted Heath" until such time as developments allowed them to be ordered forward to escort Guards Armoured Division echelon and the R.A.S.C. columns.

unfortunately knocked out two Sherman tanks. "B" Squadron, not yet directly engaged, nevertheless lost two armoured cars belonging to Lieutenant Kavanagh's Troop. The road was being heavily mortared by the Germans after the Squadron had passed across the Dutch frontier, and there was a jam of tanks, armoured cars, lorries, and half-tracks waiting to move forward. Suddenly Corporal-of-Horse Johnson saw a half-track trying to pull across the road on to the grass verge, which was mined. "Get off that verge! " shouted Johnson in warning, but he was too late. The half-track disintegrated in a violent explosion which must have been caused by a land mine. All the crew except the officer in command, who died of wounds some hours later, were killed instantly; Johnson, standing in his turret, had both his eardrums blown in and was badly concussed, but before collapsing remembered putting his hands to his head "to see if it was still there, it felt so light." Corporal Britton, in the other Daimler car, was wounded by bomb splinters in the head, but after having been taken to a barn serving as a first aid post, insisted on getting back to his car which was, together with its companion, lying wrecked at the side of the road, with the body and suspension blown off the wheels. When it became obvious that the car would have to be abandoned, Britton found an infantry officer, got the car dragged off the main road, where it was blocking the way, and suggested that it might form a pill-box for his troops, who were at that time holding the flank with some anti-tank guns. The officer fell in with the suggestion readily and his men were given a brief demonstration on how the 2-pounder worked. Having done this, Britton's wounds took effect, and he collapsed.

★   ★   ★

Grimly the Irish Guards fought their way along the road against stiff opposition. As they put it, "The Intelligence spent the day in a state of indignant surprise: one German regiment after another appeared which had no right to be there." Already identifications had shown that two parachute battalions and two battalions of 9 S.S. Division were in the area—the latter formation a complete surprise. Valkenswaard was reached by dusk where it was decided that Major Wignall's Squadron should now take over the lead from the Irish Guards and continue the advance next day.

Double summer time had only just ended and darkness appeared to fall with unexpected suddenness. The worried German commander at Eindhoven rang up the Town Clerk at Valkenswaard, with instructions to the garrison to hold on at all costs—a message which the Town Clerk took great delight in delivering in person to the Irish Guards! On this note ended the day's fighting.

The night was bitterly cold and it was raining hard. Fires from burning houses and hayricks lit up the sky, and in the distance glowed what remained of the factory which produced those excellent "Willem Twe" cigars.

Regimental Headquarters and most of "B" and "C" Squadrons slept by the side of the road, with a long line of vehicles double-banked back into Belgium. "Thank goodness," wrote a trooper, "there was little enemy shelling and no enemy planes."

It was a decidedly bedraggled column which prepared to move off again at dawn on the 18th of September. The regimental intention was that Major Herbert's Squadron ("C") should seek out a possible alternative route to the east of Valkenswaard, carrying out patrols ahead of the Welsh Guards group, while Major Wignall's Squadron should continue reconnaissance of the centre line and, in particular, make contact with 101st U.S. Airborne Division troops, information as to the progress of which was still very vague. It was believed that they had not yet reached Eindhoven.

"C" Squadron soon ran into strong enemy opposition three miles east of Valkenswaard, and further attempts to find a way round were halted by the collapse of a small bridge at Zeelberg. Corporal John Smith's scout car was hit by a bazooka and both he and Trooper Way, whose first day out as driver this was, were seriously wounded, Smith dying of his wounds the next day. In wooded country such as this the bazooka, wielded by resolute infantry against the armoured car patrol, was proving a most formidable weapon. There was really little answer to it except the keenest observation. The Welsh Guards group came up with artillery support, but progress on this flank remained negligible although fighting continued all day.

On the main axis, the story is best opened by following the leading "B" Squadron Troop. Early morning visibility was extremely bad and Colonel "Joe" Vandeleur, commanding 3rd Irish Guards, under whom "B" Squadron were operating, rightly refused to allow Major Wignall to move off until the light had improved sufficiently to enable the scout car commander to see some way ahead. Even so Lieutenant Tabor moved off just before half past five, in no way put out by the discovery on waking that he had spent the night next to three dead Germans and an unexploded Typhoon rocket.

The plan was for the whole squadron to advance up the main road, with Lieutenant Tabor's Troop one and a half miles ahead. In the event of the latter meeting opposition, the second and third Troops were to loop to the east and west respectively and try to find an alternative way round.

Corporal Sparrow was in command of the leading scout car. The road out of Valkenswaard ran for several miles through dense pinewoods, opening out at a later stage into flat, sandy country. It was misty and visibility was down to 400 yards when, after advancing approximately two miles, Sparrow suddenly sighted a Panther tank and two self-propelled guns in a side turning. The crew of the Panther were sitting on top of their tank and he gave them a long burst from his Bren gun before retiring out of sight. Lieutenant Tabor, on reporting this opposition, was ordered to remain in observation pending the arrival of the tanks of the Irish Guards. However, the infantry arrived first and the position was explained to them. Before anything could be done about it, however, there was a rumbling sound and all three German vehicles drove out of the side turning and were off up the road towards Aalst. The two scout cars were after them like terriers, and after another mile or so one of the self-propelled guns was sighted on the outskirts of Aalst.

Meanwhile, on first receipt of the report of enemy armour, Major Wignall had ordered two more Troops to start off on their loops. The Troop to the east, like "C" Squadron farther south, soon found itself held up, in this case by impassable water obstacles. But to the west Lieutenant Palmer's Troop began to make effective if slow progress. It is with his story that we are now concerned, returning to Lieutenant Tabor's Troop later on.

★   ★   ★

Travelling with Palmer's Reconnaissance Troop was a Humber scout car commanded by Captain Balding and carrying, in addition, an American sergeant with a wireless set whose task was to try to establish contact with his airborne compatriots at the earliest opportunity. Captain Balding's aim was to liaise with 101st U.S. Airborne north of Eindhoven and then keep the Regiment informed of the developing situation.

At first the small streams spanned by fragile wooden bridges baffled all attempts to cross them. But with admirable perseverance the Troop kept pegging away. Eventually a way was found across the River de Run, and thereafter the route improved. Enemy were encountered but were soon dealt with, for clearly nobody expected the armour to attempt such a cross-country run, and shortly before midday Lieutenant Palmer linked up with the Americans to the north of Eindhoven near a village called Woensel.[4]

---

4. The Troop picked up several U.S. paratroopers who had dropped in the wrong place and took them on to re-join their comrades north of Eindhoven.

The Troop was enthusiastically greeted by Brigadier Higgins, second-in-command of 101st U.S. Airborne Division. From him it was learnt that the northern approaches to Eindhoven were not yet clear of enemy and that the Germans had blown up the bridge at Zon when the Americans were but two hundred yards from it. This was bad news, for several valuable hours would be lost in repairing it. However, Captain Balding was able to pass back over the wireless the exact measurements of the gap and other R.E. requirements, which enabled the necessary bridging material to be brought forward in the Divisional column ready for the sappers to start work the moment Zon should be reached. In addition, he was able to forward the request that a telephone call be put through to "Zon 244." This unorthodox manoeuvre straight through the German controlled telephone exchange was carried out with complete success, and an American officer was able to inform Divisional Headquarters that the airborne engineers were already hard at work preparing the approaches for them.

The information that "Stable Boys[5] have contacted our Feathered Friends" created great excitement at Divisional Headquarters. It was the first of the three vital link-ups which would be necessary before the British Airborne could be relieved in their turn at Arnhem.

In the meantime, on receipt of news of a way round to the west, the Grenadiers had sent their tanks to follow the armoured cars, but the wooden bridges proved unequal to carrying the weight of the Shermans. The leading tank came to grief at the first stream south of the village of Waalse, where the bridge collapsed and threw vehicle and crew into the water with, luckily, no more serious casualty than that of an unfortunate sergeant who swallowed so much filthy water that he was sick for days afterwards. The remainder were unable to follow and were compelled to return to the main road. More attempts were made at different places, but the result was always the same—the bridges would not take the strain.

Meanwhile, as the Irish Guards group were fighting their way up the main road from Aalst, severe fighting was also taking place north of Eindhoven for possession of the Eindhoven—Boxtel and Eindhoven —St. Oedenrode Y-roads. Without control of this important junction, further advance southwards into Eindhoven would be difficult for the Americans.

By three o'clock in the afternoon, forward patrols had advanced south to as far as the railway line north of the town, but the American

---

5. Stable Boys – one of the more polite nicknames by which the Foot Guards referred to the Household Cavalry! *Author.*

paratroopers were not too happy about their western flank, which in places was beginning to be hard pressed. Lieutenant Palmer had already met some wounded Americans who told him that they would be grateful for help in repelling German attacks on the bridge they were holding west of Zon. As further immediate patrolling by the Armoured Car Troop was now curtailed by the blown Zon bridge, Major Wignall gave permission for Lieutenant Palmer to go to the aid of the Americans, and until dusk the troop fought by their side, finally being ordered to withdraw, which they did, bringing the Americans back on top of the armoured cars to Zon.

We must now pick up the main advance which we left on the outskirts of Aalst, temporarily held up by a self-propelled gun.

The Irish Guards tanks which had been called to the support of Lieutenant Tabor took some time in arriving, having to pass through "B" Squadron as well as the transport of most of the infantry on the narrow road, and as the situation remained quiet the Troop Leader decided to probe forward himself to see what was brewing up. He soon encountered a group of German infantry, who scattered when fired on. Shortly afterwards the tanks arrived on the scene and the commander of a Firefly[6] set about dealing with a German self-propelled gun. He took five shots at it, obviously hitting it several times, but there was no reply or movement, whereupon Tabor decided to push on and discovered that the vehicle had been abandoned due to a damaged track.

At this stage, the patrol met a Dutch civilian, who supplied Tabor with valuable information about the enemy dispositions, including a sketch map of the German defences outside Eindhoven. Unfortunately, it was impossible to understand most of what he said and he was passed back with his map to the Irish Guards. It subsequently transpired that he was the manager of Philips Electrical Works at Eindhoven, and his information proved accurate even down to details of individual gun emplacements.

At the northern end of Aalst was a small bridge over a stream which, when the patrol approached it, was found to be covered by another self-propelled gun 200 yards distant to the north. This was reported and Tabor's four-man patrol dismounted and crawled into the ditch to observe. They saw a motor-cycle combination drive up to the gun from the direction of Eindhoven and halt. "We gave it a good long burst of Bren, which must have annoyed the S.P. gun as it fired three rounds of

---

6. The Firefly – Sherman tank armed with a 17-pounder gun as opposed to the smaller 75-mm. gun.

armour-piercing shot at us in quick succession." In his reports, Lieutenant Tabor, like Captain Cooper, always evinced the greatest surprise when his aggressive tactics annoyed the Germans!

After a minute or two the S.P. started up and moved off down a side road to the right, where it was joined by an armoured half-track. These could be heard driving off together, and as by this time the tanks were in Aalst, Tabor decided to move on. Keeping close to Lance-Corporal-of-Horse Sparrow to give him fire support, the two scout cars crossed the bridge about a hundred yards apart.

Rather naturally, their weather eye was on the right of the road, which was the way taken by the S.P. gun, and it was therefore a nasty surprise when two 88-mm. guns in emplacements opened fire from the opposite side at a range of no more than 200 yards. Sparrow put down smoke and reversed, but Tabor could not do the same for fear of blinding Sparrow's driver, Trooper Price. He therefore opened fire with his Bren to distract the enemy gunners. Both crews got back to cover without being hit, although the guns fired seven rounds at the retiring scout cars in rapid succession. The leading tanks were "very enthusiastic about the little drama at the bridge," and grateful that the planned German ambush had been foiled.

As it had become obvious that the scout cars would be unable to carry on the advance farther without assistance from the Irish group, Lieutenant Tabor was ordered to hand over temporarily the advance to them, so he next set about finding a suitable O.P.

> "We were successful in finding the top window of a near-by house and ran out a remote control to it.[7] Our O.P. gave us limited observation over the area occupied by the 88-mm. guns, but unfortunately we had to run the gauntlet of small-arms fire for about fifty yards. Once installed, we called for artillery fire and were given good support. We had several shoots at the 88-mms., and as the result of another shoot there was a large explosion which I believe to have been an S.P. gun destroyed by a direct hit."

It was now about midday, and as there seemed to be some delay about clearing up the opposition, Lieutenant Tabor went back along the village street to report to Major Wignall at Squadron Headquarters, which were then about half a mile away. He left his driver, Trooper C. Jones, in charge of the O.P. "Squadron Headquarters were found comfortably

---

7. A remote-control wire enabling the wireless in the scout car to be used at a distance from the vehicle. Invaluable to Troop Leaders when crawling forward to an exposed position of observation.

ensconced with some of them having a haircut in a near-by shop." The situation was explained in detail to Major Wignall, who proceeded to "hot up some action from the supporting troops, as the operation was running well behind schedule by now," due principally to the great difficulties arising from there being only one road on which to bring up the various supporting arms, each clamouring for priority of movement. On returning to his car, Tabor found that Trooper Jones had been directing a very successful artillery shoot on to the German positions. As the latter had never been taught anything about it and was not even a wireless operator but merely knew what he had picked up as driver listening to his Troop Leader, this was a most remarkable achievement.

About mid-afternoon Tabor noticed several civilians on the road about a mile away towards Eindhoven. This was a significant sign for it was unlikely that they would have been there if the German guns were still in operation, so the Troop Leader and Lance-Corporal-of-Horse Sparrow crossed the bridge on foot, silenced two or three Germans on the right of the road and found that the gun positions had been recently abandoned. "After all this delay we were most impatient and now really got the bit between our teeth. Casting caution to the winds, we moved up the main road at top speed, through Eindhoven and out on the other side before the Dutch realized what was happening. Within an hour we had reached the blown bridge at Zon, where we had to remain and settle down for the night."

★　★　★

It will be seen that the main burden of the advance along the road to Eindhoven, as far as it concerned the Regiment, had been undertaken by four men in two scout cars, and to the west, from which direction was effected the first link-up, by one Reconnaissance Troop and a liaison officer's car. Some idea of the difficulties of employing armour in such country can be gathered by the fact that at no point in the day's fighting were the British tanks ever able to use their numerical superiority, due to the impossibility of deployment off the road. Thus a few S.P. and 88-mm. guns had sufficed a disorganized enemy to slow down the advance of an entire armoured division to walking pace throughout the day.

★　★　★

As the Irish Guards entered Eindhoven with the rest of "B" Squadron and Regimental Headquarters, the joy of the population, which contained many thousands of workers from the Philips Electrical Works, was most touching to behold. It may have lacked the slightly more Latin-flavoured exuberance of the Belgians, but it was nevertheless quite as spontaneous.

Orange banners and the national flag appeared everywhere, and stolid faces broke into broad smiles as the more vociferous bellowed their welcome in the woolly gutturals of what must surely be the ugliest language in the world.

The armoured drive through seething crowds in a double-banked column, swaying mudguard to mudguard, was, as the Adjutant, Captain Collins, remarked, "a terrifying experience for drivers and car commanders alike." As in Belgium, the population seemed to possess inexhaustible supplies of chalk with which they tried to scribble their names on the cars as they sped by. By a miracle nobody was run over.

A fine night with no moon followed the eventful day and it was hoped that the blown bridge at Zon would be repaired by six o'clock next morning. It was said that the German prisoners working for the Sappers became so infected with the urgency of their task that one inquisitive Gunner officer who came to see how things were progressing was bluntly told in English to move out of the way as he was hindering operations!

★   ★   ★

Back on the Escaut Canal, 8 Corps were completing plans to force a crossing after midnight near Lille St. Hubert, while on the other flank 12 Corps had secured a lodgement across the canal near Lommel during the day and were building up on the north bank in face of considerable opposition. With the thought of what was expected of them on the morrow, Guards Armoured Division were beginning to feel rather "flank conscious."

"Joe's Bridge" and "Creswell's Factory" were both subjected to a sharp bombing attack, but neither place suffered much damage, while on "The Blasted Heath" "A" and "D" Squadrons and the regimental echelon under Major Williams had their sleep disturbed by some enemy planes dropping anti-personnel bombs, which also caused no serious casualties.[8]

---

8. In the afternoon a hostile plane had flown over "The Blasted Heath" on reconnaissance. After dusk three or four more German planes flew over and scattered anti-personnel bombs over the harbour area. Somebody started a rumour that they were "Butterfly" bombs—a delayed action type liable to explode if touched. Major Williams ordered the Squadron echelons to remain where they were until a search party had cleared and checked the grass tracks. The alarm about "Butterfly" bombs proved false, but somehow in the general excitement Lieutenant Oliver in his "Gin Palace" failed to receive the "all clear" message. What he did get was a summons to

Zon bridge was completed before schedule, and a few minutes before six o'clock in the morning on the 19th of September Lieutenant Kavanagh's Troop crossed over the canal on the next lap of the journey to Arnhem. "B" Squadron, who could not be relieved because it was not possible to bring up "C" Squadron through the traffic, were now working under command of the Grenadier Guards group, who had relieved the Irish Guards group.

The Americans had already ensured the safety of the water obstacles from Zon onwards to Veghel and the advance thereafter was rapid. Shortly after eight o'clock in the morning Kavanagh's Troop made contact with elements of 82nd U.S. Airborne Division on Grave bridge, an advance of twenty-five miles in two hours which left the tanks well behind. The Americans had captured intact this vital 250 yards steel structure spanning the Maas, a very fine performance indeed, and now the second vital link-up had been effected by the regiment. A brief halt and talk with the commander on the spot elicited the information that Nijmegen bridge, spanning the River Waal, had also been captured. This news unfortunately proved to be quite incorrect, for the Americans farther north had found the approaches to be far too strongly defended for their limited resources to be able to overcome without further aid.

Lieutenant Kavanagh's Troop, however, pressed on in high hopes until it got to within two miles of Nijmegen, where it was found that another bridge carrying the road over the Waal—Maas canal at Neerbosch had been badly damaged, having been partially blown, and it would therefore be too weak to carry the tanks.[9] However, with the help of the American paratroopers, another bridge to the east near Heumen (Malden) was soon discovered, over which the Grenadier tanks were able to cross.

In the meantime the troop at Grave bridge was forced to wait until the sappers had dealt with several other "nasty-looking bombs attached to the structure and thereabouts" before it could resume the advance up the main road. While the sappers were at work Kavanagh was unluckily injured by his own scout car reversing as he was making his report to

---

attend the Squadron Leader's orders, about 300 yards away in the direct path of where the bombs had supposedly been shed. The Troop Leader made that journey protesting volubly to himself and all who cared to listen, convinced that every step would be his last. Nor did he ever forgive Major Williams for what he considered to have been a most unwarrantable risk of a valuable M.T. officer's life!

9. This was a typical example of the value of armoured cars to an armoured formation. By warning Guards Armoured Division of the damaged bridge in good time, and by having the sappers up with the leading Troop (Lieutenant Kavanagh's), not only was the correct amount of bridging rapidly moved up the column, but General Adair was able to divert the Grenadiers' tanks east immediately after they had crossed Grave bridge, instead of their being committed farther north and then having to turn on the main road, with all consequent dislocation of traffic and delays.

Major Wignall, who had come forward to see for himself what was the situation and state of the bridge. He was knocked over and the wheel passed over his leg, breaking his ankle and several bones in the foot and leg. In consequence, Lieutenant Tabor, whose Troop had led during the previous day, was once again called upon to continue the advance as soon as the sappers had confirmed that the bridge would carry the armoured cars.

By the railway bridge on the outskirts of Nijmegen he met a German patrol, but not wishing to become involved and delayed in the town, he looped to the east, where he eventually met a Dutchman who led him to an American battalion headquarters. Shortly afterwards he was joined by Captain Cooper in his Humber scout car, and both were directed by an American colonel to his forward platoon, which was in position on a high escarpment overlooking the road to Beek.

On the way Tabor and Cooper entered a hospital bell tower, but observation was not sufficiently good to remain there and the party moved on. The hospital appeared to have been evacuated in a hurry because the disturbed beds were exactly as they had been left by the patients. The American platoon was soon reached and found to be experiencing trouble from enemy "flak," 88-mm. guns in emplacements on the low ground about 400 yards from the river. The guns were something over 2,000 yards from the escarpment and therefore out of range of the Americans' machine guns and 75-mms., which were sited too far back in the town. The escarpment gave a fine view over Nijmegen bridge except for the southern approaches, which were out of sight. The observation would also have been good towards Elst and Arnhem but was unfortunately slightly obscured by mist at the time. However, the German 88-mms. were clearly marked on the defence overlay map which had been supplied to Troops before the operation, and Tabor brought up his two Daimler armoured cars, whose 2-pounder guns had just about the range of the enemy emplacements.

This would hardly be the type of shoot for which the gunners had been trained at Linney Head, but the crews were equal to the occasion. Both cars elevated their guns for maximum range and fired salvoes of A.P. shot into the emplacements. Observation was not easy at that range and neither car had any H.E. shells available, but the shooting had the desired effect and after a few minutes the Germans evacuated their gun positions.

Shortly afterwards another 88-mm. on the north bank of the river, obviously attracted by the flashes of the 2-pounders, opened fire with air bursts, so Lieutenant Tabor retaliated by calling up an artillery shoot by wireless. This was a map reference shoot, but the gunners scored a direct hit with their first salvo which effectively silenced the Germans in that area.

The enemy next moved up four 105-mm. guns into an orchard between the village of Ressen and the Nijmegen—Arnhem railway and opened fire. This shelling was particularly severe on the Americans, but Tabor could obtain no further support from the gunners for a message had come through that ammunition was desperately short and all available shells required for a divisional attack which then was being "laid on."

Tabor's Troop was ordered to withdraw at about four o'clock in the afternoon, leaving Captain Cooper with the Americans to relay back information. The latter's account gives an excellent picture of the situation on that sector during the afternoon's fighting:

"On the outskirts of Nijmegen I was informed that there were Germans in the town. Skirted round the suburbs to the east and saw only a couple of Germans—shot at them and went on. Finally (a great relief), met a company of U.S. Airborne in the suburbs, who told me of another company of theirs farther on and nearer the bridge, from which, he said, they had been driven off. Eventually reached them on high ground overlooking the bridge and the far bank. [He has now joined up with Lieutenant Tabor's Troop.] Collected a member of Dutch Underground people, who gave me a lot of valuable information. He is staying with me indefinitely. Climbed a church tower and picked out a lot of German positions and guns and sent this information back to R.H.Q. and to the U.S. platoon which was being sniped from some houses. Hid the scout car in some trees and went forward to their trenches, where we exchanged information which I sent back. They are badly in need of supplies which have not been dropped and they were glad to see us. Wirelessed back for support. In the meantime we had a great shoot on some dug-in 88-mms. —my Bren gun dismounted from the scout car. The enemy crews eventually abandoned their gun sites, carrying off the dead and wounded. Also shot a German off his bicycle and shot up a three-tonner and shot at Germans going in and out of pill-boxes at the north end of the bridge—the best shoot I've had yet. Twenty minutes later the Germans opened up on us from the other side of the river. We could see the gun flashes—this part was hell, for a great many of the shells were air-bursts. Got into car with Towler as one burst in a tree above us which carried away the aerial for the second time today, holed the front tool box, and sent a large piece through the top of the car, missing us by inches. Decided to get into trench with the Americans and stayed there for one and a half hours, by which time completely deaf and covered with dust. Got back into car and helped to direct our artillery on to the enemy guns, which appeared to knock out at least one of them. By 4.30 in the afternoon Nijmegen was being steadily shelled, although the Grenadier tanks had not yet arrived. Every time we moved somebody shoots at us from the houses —Americans eventually mop them up. Ordered to stay in this position, as it is said to be important. I captured a German range-finder and a lot of maps and talc from the abandoned gun position."

★　★　★

In the meantime Captain Balding had made contact with both the Airborne Corps Headquarters and 82nd U.S. Airborne Division Headquarters in the forest on the high ground some five miles south of Nijmegen. From them he learnt that the situation was thought to be as follows.

The northern sector of Nijmegen was still in German hands. The road bridge over the River Waal was (as the Regiment knew already) held at both ends by the enemy, but the Americans held the high ground commanding the south-eastern approaches to the town. The perimeter of their defences ran roughly in a circle bounded by the southern portion of Nijmegen—Groesbeek—Mook—Grave, thence along the main road back to Nijmegen. They explained that so large a commitment meant that they were not strong enough to hold key points and at the same time launch an attack in sufficient strength to hope to succeed in capturing the road bridge. Moreover, owing to deteriorating flying weather, much of their force had not yet arrived.

We could not help thinking that it was curious that no troops had been dropped to the north of Nijmegen road bridge, for this country which formed an island would have been easier for airborne troops to defend, being almost impregnable to tank attack, and would have given access not only to the southern and easier approaches to Arnhem bridge but, above all, to the open and northern end of the great Nijmegen bridge, the master key to the whole enterprise.[10]

---

10. "Unfortunately, available reports concerning the terrain between the Waal and the Neder Rijn, including the opinion of Dutchmen living there, was that the area was basically unsuitable for airborne dropping or landing zones. Moreover, the flak defences of Arnhem and in the region of the Deelen airfield made it necessary to land some eight miles from Arnhem itself. These were difficulties which had to be accepted, but in the event they placed us at a great disadvantage." (Montgomery, *Normandy to the Baltic*, Hutchinson & Co. (Publishers) Ltd.)

Meanwhile little was known of what was happening to the British Airborne at Arnhem except that they were hard pressed, and this thought which hung like a gloomy cloud over us all was to persist for several more days.

The tantalizing sight of the huge road bridge, over 2,000 feet in length, whose centre span towering over the surrounding district was so vital a link, spurred on the Grenadiers. They fought on all afternoon and by seven o'clock, after bitter combat, had in conjunction with the Americans reached a traffic roundabout only 300 yards short of the bridge. But there, after a final tank attack had been beaten back by the enemy, it was realized that an assault was not possible without large-scale artillery support, and they were withdrawn at nightfall.

The forward American positions nearest the bridge were shelled heavily all through the night, and many houses were hit and caught fire. Captain Cooper and his crew were still with them.

"We had three near misses in the trench but managed to get in a few hours' dozing. This sort of shelling is perfectly bloody and gives you a splitting headache and seems to jar the whole system. Every now and again the Spandaus opened up from the other side of the river and bullets whistled over our heads. These American troops are splendid types—extremely brave, very cheerful, and indifferent to the worst. The bridge, an enormous girdered affair, has been wired for blowing, which the 'Underground' have twice cut, and is covered by every conceivable German weapon."

Not until long after midnight did the fighting in this sector die down, and meanwhile progress on the two-flank corps was, as Montgomery put it, "depressingly slow."

★   ★   ★

Before carrying the general story forward into the next day, let us return for a while to "The Blasted Heath." Here, by midday on the 19th of September, the large and unwieldy divisional echelon and R.A.S.C. supply column was assembling in preparation for its move northwards, protected by "A" and "D" Squadrons, and under the over-all command of Major Ward.

This collection of assorted transport consisted of over 800 vehicles and, in addition, a number of anti-aircraft guns, bridging equipment and various engineer units. The responsibility for so large and vulnerable a cargo was an unenviable one and the difficulties of control were soon manifest. The possibility of being able to defend the hundreds of soft vehicles from enemy flank attack was in reality non-existent, and the most that could be done was to space the armoured cars, at intervals, one to about twenty vehicles and hope for the best. It was found that on an average each Troop was responsible for about sixty vehicles, and the car commanders could never see more than a dozen of their charges at any given time.

The leading vehicle of the column moved off in the late afternoon, and not until it had almost entered Eindhoven did the last lorry follow suit from "The Blasted Heath."

From the moment of entering Dutch territory rumours of the enemy began to circulate down the column. The more they were officially denied, the more, it seemed, did they become wilder in their nature. We thought at the time that they must have been of civilian origin, but their persistency gave rise to the suspicion that some at least must have emanated from fifth column sources. In addition, the Germans really were making the first of a series of efforts to cut the centre line. Elements of 107 Panzer Brigade, described as "a small but well-equipped pocket Panzer division," coming from the area of Venlo, launched a sharp tank attack, well supported by 88-mm. guns, against Zon bridge. This was eventually repulsed before attaining its objective but resulted in a further batch of rumours.

There then occurred a curious incident. Major Ward had ordered forward his Rear Link officer in his Staghound, accompanied by Lieutenant Metcalfe in a scout car, to try to establish contact by wireless with the Regiment, by this time in Nijmegen. A temporary halt had been called just south of St. Oedenrode to pass a difficult message, when a D.R. appeared, covered in mud. Slowing down and only pausing long enough to shout "There's a pocket Panzer division on the road moving south towards you and orders are that you have got to turn round," he was off again in a flash.

Before he could be grabbed by authority he had dashed down a large part of the column, spreading his alarming message. There was no wireless with the lorries, and unfortunately a batch of R.A.S.C. vehicles took him at his word and, without more ado, turned about and made off at full speed back the way they had come. Corporal-of-Horse Booth, of "A" Squadron, who was in one of the rear blocks, said afterwards that at one moment he was in the centre of a line of some twenty lorries and the next he could see an empty space up to his Troop Leader's car. Eventually the lorries were collected together again in a field near Aalst and they re-

GRAVE BRIDGE, HOLLAND

"D" Squadron escort to Guards Armoured Division convoy being attacked, as it crosses the River Maas, by Focke-Wulf fighter, 20th September, 1944. The artist, Corporal Meade-King, is one of those depicted at the bottom of the embankment.

joined the convoy, but the mysterious D.R. was never run to earth and disappeared for ever into the unexplained pages of military history.[11]

When but half the convoy had passed through Eindhoven, it was already beginning to grow dark. Worried by the rumours and uncertainties, the officer in command of the Dutch Resistance, sole garrison in the town, ran along the streets advising the inhabitants to lock their doors and stay inside. Once the convoy had passed through, the town would be more or less defenceless until the rearward flanking formations had caught up.

All of a sudden a cluster of parachute flares lit up the sky. Then came more. The streets were illuminated as if by daylight and those within the orbit of their glare felt unbearably exposed. Immediately after the flares, the first enemy bombs began to fall. The Luftwaffe pilots, who were probably men chosen for their intimate knowledge of Eindhoven airfield and district, bombed accurately and systematically. Some of the planes dived to within 300 feet of the cars, pinpointing targets and machine gunning. The "A" Squadron armoured cars nearest the scene fired back into the inky blackness above the flares, but with little hope of hitting the enemy. It was all over rapidly. One block of Philips factory was in ruins, blazing fiercely from end to end. So were many houses silhouetted against the sky. A tragic ten minutes for happy liberated Eindhoven.

In the initial attack, half a dozen ammunition lorries received direct hits and at once the shells within them began to explode, adding their own unpleasant brand of noise and danger to the deeper detonation of the bombs. Presently a number of petrol lorries caught fire as well and their flames spread to other vehicles loaded with small arms. Bullets exploded everywhere, and it "now seemed that the city was being engulfed by every sort of explosion at once." In all, eighteen R.A.S.C. lorries were destroyed; a grievous loss at the best of times, but one to be doubly felt when the shortage of ammunition at the front had already begun to assume serious proportions.

Realizing that the immediate problem lay in getting the disrupted column on the move again, Captain Profumo, second-in-command of "A" Squadron, mustered all the available civilians together to help in

---

11. Booth relates that he was trying to halt the lorries on his own initiative when "a Major" came upon the scene and countermanded him, ordering him to turn round also. This he rightly refused to do without a direct order from Major Daly. It is now known that a Dutch traitor in the Underground Movement had warned the Germans of the proposed operation "Market-Garden," and it is reasonable to suppose that the armour which "fortuitously" found itself travelling through Arnhem at the time of the droppings, as well as the spate of rumours, were part of the enemy's attempts to disrupt the Allied plans.

clearing away the debris blocking the road—a task which he achieved "with great rapidity and calm efficiency."

But ill fortune seemed to dog this supply convoy. Shortly after the head had passed through Veghel, a commander senior in rank to Major Ward bluntly informed him that he proposed to take his unit off the road and into an adjoining field—there to rest and await daylight. He refused to admit of the urgency of getting forward without delay and stuck to his point in spite of all argument. He was left to his own devices and Major Ward pushed on with the rest of the convoy.

At Uden part of the front portion of the column took a wrong turning in the village, and could not be halted until nearing Nistelrode, which place was only two miles from Heesch, an enemy strong-point, so ran the Dutch civilian's story. Again the circumstances were peculiar, and one wondered whether fifth column work or German sympathizers might not have had a hand in the proceedings, for it was found that a divisional sign in Uden—plain and unmistakable —was pointing down the road in the wrong direction.

When the mistake was realized it was past one o'clock in the morning and pitch dark. Captain Waterhouse and I went out on foot to search for a likely spot at which to turn the lorries. Nistelrode, the likeliest place, consisted of one street and a collection of houses whose inhabitants, somewhat naturally, were all sound asleep. Eventually, after much banging on doors, two sleepy Dutchmen opened up. We asked them as best we could whether they knew if the Germans were in the next village. "Ya," said one. "Ne," muttered his companion. "Deutsch Panzers?" bawled Captain Waterhouse. "Ya," said number one. "Ne," said number two. We left them to argue it out.

In view of the somewhat meagre information which we had brought back, Major Ward decided that there could be no question of risking so many urgently required soft vehicles by taking a loop through Heesch which would have brought us back eventually on to the main road. The column was to be turned round.

Not only was the cobbled road barely wide enough to take two lines of traffic, but from both verges there was a six-foot drop into a ditch filled with water. The 3.7-inch anti-aircraft guns accompanying the column were towed and the drivers said that there was not enough room in which to turn about without going over the bank. One mistake, and we should be confronted with the unpleasant prospect of half the column facing one way and half the other, neither being able to move. At this juncture an enemy plane flew up and down the main road and then turned off to drop a flare on the very spot where it was calculated that the column should have been had it not taken the wrong turning!

The next few hours were to be an ordeal of bent wings and dented radiators and officers moving up and down the line of vehicles trying to rouse sleepy drivers who kept falling asleep at the wheel. Eventually everything was sorted out and the head of the column moved on towards Grave bridge, which was reached at dawn. From here the various unit groups dispersed to their locations. Three Focke-Wulf planes made a half-hearted attack on part of "D" Squadron Headquarters and some of the troops. Every type of weapon let fly and optimistic marksmen claimed a hit, but oddly enough no crashed German plane was ever reported. By far the best thing which came out of this episode was the sketch made on the spot by Corporal Meade-King, which figures on page 345.

During the afternoon "A" and "D" Squadrons re-joined the Regiment in the woods south of Nijmegen, and "D" Squadron learnt that they were due to operate again on the morrow.

Daimler Armoured Car Gunner

Chapter II

The Battle to Reach Arnhem

The Battle for Arnhem—A variety of tasks—Lieutenant le Poer Trench's Troop discovers Oss food dump—"Splice the Mainbrace"—Grenadier Guards capture Nijmegen road bridge—"D" Squadron's advance with Irish Guards towards Arnhem thwarted—Renewed attempt by "C" Squadron successfully reaches Polish Airborne Brigade near Dreil (Captain Wrottesley's and Lieutenant Young's Troops)—Major Herbert brings up "C" Squadron Headquarters; Captain Clyde's narrative—Death of Trooper Holmes—Desperate state of Arnhem defenders— Lieutenant Creswell's Troop finds a first-class interpreter—Centre line cut— Lieutenant Wordsworth's Troop has a field day at St. Antonis—Lieutenant Franklin's Troop at Volkel—Axis reopened to traffic on 23rd September—Activity on the Maas—A temporary lull.

The tasks allotted to the Regiment for the 20th of September were threefold. Firstly, to give support to the Americans holding on to the high ground east of Nijmegen town—these soldiers were being subjected to strong pressure by the enemy coming from the direction of the Reichswald; secondly, to reconnoitre to the west of the axis between the Rivers Waal and Maas; and thirdly, to reconnoitre east and west of the corridor south of the Maas, for we were still, as the official reports stated, "very naked on the flanks."

The country beyond the eastern suburbs of Nijmegen is thickly wooded and enclosed, a kind of coniferous Welwyn Garden City, totally unsuited for armoured cars, and any assistance which these vehicles might be able to give the hard-pressed paratroopers would be moral rather than material.

It was a different story on the other flank. Here, thousands of disorganized Germans, actually outnumbering the available 30 Corps troops which could be spared to deal with them, were trapped and divided in mind as to whether to rally and fight on in isolated groups until the situation became stabilized, or cut and run for it across the single British line of communications. As has so frequently happened before in war, the enemy did both, and at the most inconvenient times.

"Never," wrote a Divisional Staff Officer at the time, "can those who like this kind of thing have had fewer dull moments. Patrols of the Household Cavalry, dispersed to the four winds, as much as thirty miles apart, were reporting fantastic engagements. In one place, cut off entirely from us, they were directing our artillery … in another they had discovered a ferry in perfect working order, but on the far bank. They were in telephonic communication with the Dutch on the far bank, who might be persuaded to bring it across—might they use it? 'No'—they were already far enough afield."

We find Major Herbert's Squadron engaged on "defensive recces" to the east along the River Maas. These were of necessity of a rather vague order, because little was yet known about the enemy on that flank. Part of the Squadron's task was "to find out the German intentions in that area," and therefore strong efforts were made to push along both banks of the Maas. Good progress was made and many prisoners taken. Eventually, after shooting up barges found to be ferrying soldiers both ways—such was the confusion of the German command at that period— and after several brushes with infantry hidden up along the flood banks and in farms adjoining the river, the Squadron was halted decisively by well sited anti-tank guns. Nevertheless, Troop patrols had by then succeeded in penetrating upstream as far as Cuyk on the northern and Mook on the southern bank of the Maas. To the south, patrols of 8 Corps were still many miles distant and, from all accounts, finding the going extremely heavy.

Great importance had been attached by higher command to the finding of adequate aerodrome sites as close to Nijmegen as possible, because it was visualized that during the early stages of the fighting most of the Airborne's supplies would have to be flown in to relieve the already overloaded road artery. Therefore, Major Wignall's Squadron spent the first few hours of daylight probing in the area of Grave and west of the Corps centre line.

It is a countryside honeycombed with canals and intersecting drainage dykes, with few fields of sufficient length to provide runways for aeroplanes. However, by noon two good sites had been found, and the troops were then released to carry out their work of patrolling farther afield to the west.

One of these patrols, commanded by Lieutenant le Poer Trench, penetrated deep into enemy territory and up to the approaches of s'Hertogenbosch before being held up. When halted it had travelled a distance of over seventeen miles from the axis at Grave, and although it could get no farther and had in fact been ordered back to base, it was fired by rumours of a large food dump which was stated to exist in the area. Close questioning of the local and rather "cagey" peasants had produced no results worth mentioning; understandably, the Dutch were themselves hoping to benefit from such a place as soon as the Germans had cleared out. Nevertheless the search was intensified on the return journey, and on switching across to a hitherto unexplored part of the country—a melancholy low-lying district actually below river level and bounded to the north by the Maas—the Troop reached the small town of Oss, situated on a branch railway line running into Nijmegen. There appeared to be few Germans in the vicinity, and the patrol eventually came to a series of railway tracks forming part of a siding leading up to a large square-built warehouse. This proved to be the food dump in question. Its contents exceeded all expectations, and before the goggling eyes of the Household Cavalrymen lay revealed sacks of flour, tinned meat, jars of Bols gin and mountains of sugar. There was much else in the provision line, but it was the sugar and gin which caught Lieutenant Trench's eye, and his laconically drawled message announcing the discovery belied the subsequent speed of his actions. Within the hour, "B" Squadron were in possession of a heavily guarded lorry load of these estimable commodities.

The news of the discovery travelled like wildfire up to the highest levels, and before the day was out long lines of R.A.S.C. lorries were queuing up on the Grave road ready to make a quick dash into "No-man's-land." However, Regimental Headquarters' counter-move was inspired, and when the first vehicle moved off, there, waiting in almost unctuous politeness, ready to escort and *protect* the column both ways, was an entire squadron of armoured cars.[1]

It was said that there was enough food in Oss to feed the British Army for several months. This was perhaps underrating the British soldier's appetite, but it does at least denote the importance of the find, which was to prove of the utmost value when the enemy made his most serious attempt at severing communications a few days later, and for a time 30 Corps' ration situation was critical.

Oss was to remain for over a week a land of fabulous promise. It tempted the staidest into a sense of reckless plunder and adventure. Records show that even Divisional Headquarters temporarily dispensed with its protection Troop of tanks, which in a few carefree hours of freedom met the enemy head-on, fought a spirited action, and finally returned laden with drink and prisoners, the latter, we were informed, mostly bakers. When a more orderly system of pillage was eventually brought in, and buccaneering expeditions were organized on a unit

---

1. Major Herbert's "C" Squadron, plus all the three-tonners he could muster, it is hardly necessary to add. *Author.*

basis, the storehouse was nominally left in charge of a supply officer from Division detailed for the job, but he felt rather lonely at night and could be tempted to relax from the strictest interpretation of his orders by an offer of protection from the armoured cars. "D" Squadron hit upon the further original idea of turning up with troops commanded alternately by a Life Guards officer and a Blues officer. The second arrival would explain that he came from a different unit. Then a third person, using the ruse successfully employed by Captain Ward in Albert, would explain that the stars on his shoulder denoted a branch of the R.A.M.C., whose patients required a special diet. Yet a fourth attempt at obtaining illegal food and drink failed after it had been planned to pass off "D" Squadron's Jonkheer as representing Dutch forces.

In the early days following the discovery of Oss, the Germans, wise to the fact that our troops were practically non-existent on this flank, exploited the situation and also made daily food raids on the unguarded warehouse. By tacit agreement, the British drew rations in the morning while the enemy helped himself to what he wanted in the afternoon. The Dutch caretaker on the premises was therefore forced to play a somewhat tricky diplomatic role, and with Nordic earnestness insisted that both sides should sign for what they had taken in a ledger set aside for the purpose. The unwritten agreement worked smoothly, apart from one notable exception which might well have ended in tragedy. But this story belongs to succeeding pages and will be recorded in due course.

★   ★   ★

Two paramount tasks faced 30 Corps throughout the 20th of September: (1) to capture the Nijmegen road bridge intact or to force an assault crossing of the River Waal at some other place; (2) to relieve the 1st British Airborne Division. As it was then considered almost a certainty that the bridge would at any moment be blown by the Germans, "B" Squadron in its westward patrolling was to be closely concerned with the finding of a suitable jumping-off ground for a crossing in force west of Nijmegen. With this in view, Lieutenant Palmer's Troop probed along the south bank of the River Waal. Lieutenant Jonkheer Groeninx van Zoelen, from "D" Squadron, was also working with this Troop. As his Squadron had been held back in Belgium during the initial stages, he had asked for permission to take part in the battle for Nijmegen, which so intimately concerned the future of his native country. In this case his orders were to try to establish telephonic contact with Arnhem by means of the Dutch civil exchanges—there had, as yet, been no wireless contact established with the British Airborne. The telephone scheme was not as far-fetched as it might appear at first sight. There was a possibility that the Arnhem post office might still be in British hands, or if not, at least in those of the Dutch Resistance. We remembered Captain Balding's success at Eindhoven.

The route traversed a stretch of land bounded by the Waal and the Maas up to where the two rivers almost join near the village of Heeselt. It is a country with an atmosphere of its own which Groeninx van Zoelen noted with care. "The country is absolutely lovely here and the castle at Wijchen beautifully restored. It is very flat and the roads are lined with tall poplars, all bent to the prevailing wind, and here and there a clump that hides another ancient castle—all of them, alas, now in ruins or publicly owned."

After advancing many miles without encountering "anything exciting apart from some eggs and a few bewildered Germans," a halt was made at the village of Wamel when it was found that the Troop was getting out of wireless range. On the opposite side of the river lay the village of Tiel and moored alongside the far bank was a flat-bottomed ferry, of the sort worked by a hand-operated continuous chain. The Germans were crossing in small parties farther down the river, but a local inhabitant told Groeninx van Zoelen that it might be possible to manoeuvre it across, because there were quite a number of civilians on the opposite bank. Back at Regimental Headquarters this news caused a great stir. At one stage Colonel Abel Smith considered that it might even be possible for Major Wignall's entire Squadron to ferry itself over to the northern bank. Once over, the armoured cars, backed by the infantry of the Support Troop, might well have staged a diversion of considerable nuisance value, or even held and consolidated a small bridgehead pending the arrival of reinforcements. However, the prospect of staging a minor D Day in a single flat-bottomed barge of doubtful vintage was a problem demanding further careful examination. In the end the plan was vetoed by General Adair. Perhaps it was as well that the ferry in any case refused to budge from the mud bottom.

The patrol then moved off to Leuwen, which promised to provide a good observation post, and Groeninx van Zoelen, whose message had already been put through one telephone exchange before being cut off, tried to put through another call to Arnhem. Meanwhile there was a new diversion.

The look-out scout car was surprised to see a tug-boat towing three large barges approaching at a steady four to five knots. The tug was flaunting the Nazi Swastika flag at the masthead and sailing upstream towards Nijmegen—presumably out of touch with the latest situation. Rapid messages passed over the wireless. Dutch or German, "it must on no account be allowed to progress any farther." The northern bank was still entirely in enemy hands and, apart from the Regiment's armoured-car patrols, there were as yet no British troops west of Nijmegen on the south bank.

In view of the importance of the convoy, Lieutenant Palmer decided to "persuade" the Nazi tug-master to heave-to and come quietly ashore. Moreover, it was felt that the barges might be more usefully employed later on as forming part of a ferry service than they would be at the bottom of the Waal.

Corporal-of-Horse Kendrick placed himself with the two armoured cars overlooking as much of the river as possible. If the enemy refused to stop, then the tug and barges were to be sunk.

Peremptorily, the man at the wheel was hailed, but he either failed to hear or was forced at pistol point to ignore all orders to halt, and so both the 2-pounder guns opened rapid fire, aiming at the water line, while the Besas sprayed the decks. It was a one-sided if unorthodox affair from the start. The armour-piercing shots tore through the sides of the tug and fearful clanking noises came from within. Steam began to hiss from the holed deck and, with a despairing wail on its siren, the wretched vessel attempted to turn with its screw threshing wildly. The barges with full way on were unable to conform and soon became inextricably entangled with their own hawsers. In a short time, and to a chorus of cheers from a gathering Dutch audience, the tug sank, while the barges, riddled with holes, settled into the mud.

Meanwhile, to complete the scene, "on the bank, about half a mile upstream, and eating enormous bunches of grapes," both officers waited for the telephone from Arnhem to ring.

The Troop's message, "Am engaging," followed by an equally terse report of the termination of the engagement, had all the traditional brevity of the Navy, and Headquarters Guards Armoured Division, entering into the spirit of the occasion, wirelessed back, "Congratulations on a brilliant naval engagement—splice the mainbrace!"[2] It was not long before the Daimler works heard of the episode, a colourful version of which was produced as an advertisement, complete with sinking barges, explosions, spouting machine guns and flying pennants. Background to

---

2. The "Splice the Mainbrace" signal, which gained a certain amount of local notoriety at the time, actually formed part of a message passed over the air between Major the Hon. F. F. G. Hennessy, Grenadier Guards, and Captain A. J. R. Collins, 2nd Household Cavalry Regiment.

the scene was Nijmegen bridge, and over all the triumphant inscription, "It has been ascertained that the armoured cars were Daimler"!

Having witnessed the destruction of their river convoy from the far bank, the Germans decided to send over a fighting patrol at nightfall. Crossing some miles downstream, they even ferried over an anti-tank gun, and a sharp little action was fought between them and the Troop close to Wamel which resulted in the Germans beating a hasty retreat westwards, leaving their dead behind. After which, its work over for the day, the Troop returned to Squadron Headquarters, close to Grave bridge.

★   ★   ★

The tale of the day's patrolling having necessarily drawn us away from the main centre line, we must return once more to the approaches to the vital Nijmegen road bridge.

The enemy, having frustrated the Anglo-American attempt to storm the bridge on the evening of the 19th, was now fully alerted and resisting all efforts to dislodge him from its approaches. During the night of the 19th/20th September he had been reinforced from the direction of Arnhem with a strong leavening of S.S. troops to boost up the supposedly falling morale of the Wehrmacht. It was now planned to capture the bridge by another joint Anglo-American effort. All the morning of the 20th was taken up in clearing the town as far as the southern approaches, and the brunt of the fighting fell upon the Grenadier Guards and the American 504 Regimental Combat Team, already established in the area. The Regiment was not involved, but Captain Cooper was still with the forward outposts where, with Troopers Carroll and Towler, he had remained without a break for the past twenty-four hours—his task that of keeping Headquarters in touch with developments in that hotly disputed sector.

"Early on, in the half light of dawn (20th), the Germans attacked ... a half-hearted affair, but it was unpleasant all the same. They eventually cleared off, leaving behind a few dead and some prisoners. In retaliation we lobbed a few grenades into a machine-gun post." This annoyed the enemy, who started to come back and succeeded in manning an 88-mm. gun site, deserted since the previous evening because of its exposed position. "But," continues the narrator, "we fired off a good number of Bren magazines into them and now, having finished all our ammo, had only a tommy-gun left."

At about eight o'clock in the morning the guns of the Leicestershire Yeomanry came into action with telling effect and for a time were directed on to targets across the Waal by Captain Cooper. He was by then situated on top of a hospital roof and finding it "rather unpleasant because they [the Germans] immediately replied with heavy mortars and high explosive shells."

It was also noticeable that the German aircraft were more active than at any other time since the days of Caen, and from the hospital roof they could be seen attacking and shooting down the supplies being flown in to Arnhem.[3]

Captain Cooper was now joined by a Gunner officer, who arrived in a self-propelled gun "just as a hell of a battle was going on in the town and both sides were shelling each other non-stop." The noise was reaching its deafening climax when round a corner quietly appeared both Generals Horrocks and Adair. They had come up to see for themselves how their plans were progressing and were taken to the vantage point in use. "They told me," noted Cooper, "that it's one of the best O.Ps. ever and were delighted at the Regiment having found it."

The day wore on. Slowly, and not without serious casualties, the Grenadiers crept closer and closer to the river. There was much bitter hand-to-hand fighting. By mid-afternoon the Americans and Grenadiers had advanced through an ornamental garden, overrun the large roundabout, one of whose roads led to the bridge, seized a small tower which was the focal point of the German defences, and cleared the Valkhof, a heavily wooded open-air fort honeycombed with underground passages and entrenchments, from which bastion the Dutch were said to have resisted for three days in 1940. Dominating the ruined buildings of the waterfront, the huge steel framework of Nijmegen bridge still towered aloof and impersonal. Below, Germans and Allies tore into one another with renewed fury.

By late afternoon it appeared as if half the town were on fire. Thick sulphurous fumes from a burning warehouse curled upstream over the tired and dusty troops. Tracer streaked to and fro across the water, weaving fantastic patterns, while on the far bank, flashes from what seemed to be one continuous rumbling explosion lit up the darkened sky. It was a grim scene and, to those who witnessed it, one never to be forgotten. Yet, miraculously, the bridge still stood.

Darkness had fallen when Captain Cooper's party was recalled to Regimental Headquarters for further orders, but by then they had been at their post of vantage long enough to witness the final culmination of

---

3. "During the day," recorded Captain Collins in the War Diary, "as many as sixty planes were seen in the air at the same time."

the day's struggle—the storming of the road bridge by the tanks of the 2nd (Armoured) Grenadier Guards.

★   ★   ★

A regimental history has little space available in which to record the deeds of other units, but the capture of Nijmegen bridge was of such importance that brief mention must be made of this gallant exploit.

The attack was a pattern of Anglo–American co-operation. After the previous day's experience, direct frontal assault, except in the last stages, was considered out of the question. It was therefore decided that a crossing of the river should be made by the Americans during the afternoon of the 20th at some distance west of the railway bridge; the intention being that they should eventually work round to the north side of the road bridge (the objective), thus threatening it from the rear. When this had been achieved, a direct frontal assault on the road bridge would be launched by the Grenadier Guards.

Thirty-two British-built type assault boats were lent to the soldiers of 504 Regimental Combat Team. These were frail craft, and the Americans had never before held a paddle in their hands, but this did not in the least deter them from trying. The selected crossing place was about a kilometre west of the railway bridge, was over six hundred yards wide, and was dominated from the northern side by a strongly defended emplacement—an ancient moated fortification known as the Haatz van Holland, said to date back to the days of Charlemagne.

The Germans must have had suspicions that all was not well and they began to plaster the assembly area with shells. In spite of this the Americans launched themselves into the swirling current, supported by the fire of the Leicestershire Yeomanry 25-pounders and tanks of the Irish Guards. Bobbing and spinning, the frail little craft soon found themselves up against heavy interlacing small-arms fire from the far bank. An ineffective smoke-screen trailed downstream at the mercy of an adverse breeze; thus the Americans remained totally exposed the length of the crossing. Few of the first wave reached the other side, but a second wave, their boats so punctured with bullet holes that only by baling with their tin hats could the Americans keep afloat, managed to get across. Others soon followed, some of the men swimming, during the last stages, with their weapons kept above their heads. Gradually a small bridgehead, at first barely a hundred yards wide and less in depth, was gained. How bitter was the struggle is shown by the fact that within the space of sixty yards of that bloody perimeter, the corpses of 138 dead Germans were afterwards counted.

There was now another menace to face. The Germans had mounted 88-mm. guns on the Haatz van Holland and these threatened to blow the bridgehead back into the river. But the fort was surrounded by a moat filled with muddy green water, and by some instinct of preservation the pinned-down paratroopers sensed that a small zone remained free from fire, and owing to an oversight on the part of the Germans their guns were sited so that they could not be depressed far enough to cover this gap. Realizing their predicament, the Germans tried to bring up machine guns at the double, but they were too late and the Americans were on them before they could fire. A further 75 Germans were left dead in the moat alone. Thenceforward the Americans moved eastward to capture the railway bridge[4] on the northern side, and, continuing along the high embankment, they finally cut the main road to Arnhem about a mile north of the road bridge.

Now was to come the turn of the Grenadiers. A Troop of tanks had been held in readiness, but its first attempt was driven back by accurate 88-mm. fire from the opposite bank. There was in addition a self-propelled gun shooting directly across the bridge. Another of the difficulties was that the structure, itself 700 yards long, had an embankment of equal length on the far side, thus making it impossible for tracked vehicles to leave the road for a distance of nearly a mile. However, in the gathering gloom, the same Troop tried again. Firing at anything that moved, it reached the main structure and rapidly disappeared from the sight of observers on the near bank. Two Sherman tanks were quickly knocked out, but a third somehow avoided the bazookas and other missiles aimed at it by the enemy perched up in the girders of the bridge and reached the far end unscathed. It skidded broadside through a road-block and, after knocking out two anti-tank guns, finally came to a halt a mile beyond, to join up with the gallant remnants of 504 Regimental Combat Team.

In the meantime, travelling behind the fifth tank (second Troop over), Lieutenant Jones, a Sapper officer, dashed across to cut the wires, thus neutralizing the demolition charges which had been set up. He discovered that although the chambers constructed in the main buttresses

---

4. This led to a misunderstanding which might have had serious consequences. At about six o'clock in the evening the Grenadiers, waiting for the signal to attack, received a message that the Americans were already in occupation of the northern part of the road bridge. This appeared strange to the Grenadiers, who were at the time being subjected to steady enemy shelling from that quarter. In spite of this, someone persisted that the American flag could be seen flying on the far side. This subsequently turned out to have been the flag placed on the railway bridge!

NIJMEGEN BRIDGE

Scene of a famous Grenadier Guards and American Airborne joint exploit, shown being shelled by the enemy some days after Its capture.

were empty of explosives, charges had been laid with great care running the full width of the bridge under the second span from the northern end. Some idea of the size of the structure can be gained from the fact that Lieutenant Jones and his men collected over seventy prisoners while searching for charges—most coming from the chambers built into the buttresses.

The reason why the Germans failed to blow so vital a structure will perhaps forever remain a mystery. There were several theories put forward. It was stated that a member of the Dutch Underground had cut the wires, but this was said of practically every bridge captured by the Allies in North-West Europe. Had he done so, the exploit must have taken place long before the actual storming, for no civilian could have lived on the bridge (nor was seen) at the height of the battle. And why, assuming that the wires had been cut earlier, did the Germans not repair them?—their own troops were using the bridge both ways almost to the end. The blowing of a bridge under enemy pressure is at the most favourable of times a tricky operation, being almost invariably a question of being too early or too late. Perhaps it is more reasonable to assume that the Germans, in Army parlance, were "pushed," and when soldiers are "pushed" at times of crisis, mistakes occur.

Hopes were now again high that the British Airborne would be relieved within the next twenty-four hours, but these were doomed to disappointment. Guards Armoured Division was ordered to renew the advance to Arnhem at maximum speed and at all costs to make contact with the Airborne Force before it was too late. However, the country between the rivers, which came to be known as "The Island," was quite unsuitable for tanks. The main road was built on a high embankment and no tracked vehicle could hope to leave it. Drains and impassable ditches criss-crossed the land. Infantry, the correct arm to employ in such circumstances, was in short supply, and already committed to both flanks south of the bridge and in the bridgehead itself. There was therefore no alternative but to make the best of things and carry on with the available armour, pending the arrival of 43rd Division, whose 130th Brigade was then in the course of moving up the centre line from Eindhoven.

★   ★   ★

"D" Squadron spent the night of 20th/21st September by the side of a sandy track in the woods south of Nijmegen. They slept soundly, in spite of the noise of the barrage overhead, for nothing is more tiring than a long convoy drive. They were roused from their slit trenches at four o'clock in the morning, and the message was passed round that "The Grenadiers have made it." Those who had gone to sleep wondering when they would be awakened by that dull reverberation denoting yet another bridge destroyed could hardly believe their ears.

The Irish Guards were already across the river, holding the small bridgehead and preparing to move forward during the morning. "D" Squadron were to join them at once and screen their advance northwards, at the same time probing the flanks for weak spots. Now familiar with the intricacies of Nijmegen's burning streets, Captain Cooper was arriving from Malden (Regimental Headquarters) to guide the Squadron to the Waal. A detour would be necessary because some of the centre streets were still not clear of enemy.

A gulped breakfast of cold baked beans and a mug of chlorinated tea is not the best send-off at half-past four in the morning, and it lay heavy and regurgitating on the stomachs as the men climbed into their chilly turrets. Sounds of street fighting echoed between the houses as the cars circled the eastern part of the town. Towards the river bank could be heard the harsh crack of shells bursting on the cobblestones. The Squadron wheeled past the roundabout and its knocked-out guns. Poor Nijmegen—suburban and rather genteel before the war, one suspected—now looked indescribably forlorn. Broken glass and discarded equipment lay strewn about the place and a damp mist shrouded the roofless houses. In the half-light the mass of the bridge loomed up, gigantic and seemingly out of focus. There was a smell of cordite in the air, and pallid waxen corpses sprawled grotesquely across the pavements, bearing testimony to the severity of the previous day's fighting. Many Germans had also been killed on the bridge itself and lay crumpled beneath the spot whence they had been shot down from the girders. A slumped figure was still strapped aloft, shot dead as he had tried to snipe at passing traffic. One could not but admire the courage of such men, and again one felt the label "fanatic" to be a rather cheap gibe. However, warnings that others were still very much alive made every car commander peer upwards intently, ready to spray the steel framework with bullets at the slightest sign of movement.

The Irish Guards informed Major Ward that the going ahead was "extremely sticky." They had made no advance from last night's positions. The road north to Elst was firmly held and any British tank movement was promptly shelled with accuracy. Accordingly, a Troop was looped eastwards and after some time it managed to link up with the Americans fighting in the area of Bemmel. But it could advance no farther and was recalled.

It was the same story to the west. Now back again with "D" Squadron, Lieutenant Jonkheer Groeninx van Zoelen made several attempts to loop in the direction of Valburg but came up against well-sited anti-tank guns dominating the approach routes.

Further attempts along the main road fared little better, but Lieutenant Ainsworth's Troop was able to pin-point six 88-mm. guns and warn the Irish Guards. Later, these same guns were to account for several of their tanks.

The real villain of the piece, however, was the country. Dykes, low-lying swamps, waterways, and orchards which reduced visibility, all made the task of the tanks extremely difficult, and it was impossible for them to get off the road. Progress was measured in yards while the situation at Arnhem grew hourly more desperate.

Typhoon support had been promised, but for some reason this was not forthcoming. The Irish Guards lost three tanks in rapid succession, victims of a Tiger tank, and as the leading vehicle looked back at nearly fifty more Shermans silhouetted, one behind the other, on the embanked road, there seemed really no valid reason why these should not eventually all share the same fate. The only available artillery support was to come from one regiment of field guns, but it was over an hour after the call that the first shells landed.

With such a deadlock, and a target of several miles of closely packed vehicles to choose from, the enemy guns now decided to range on the bottleneck north of the bridge, and "D" Squadron Headquarters, together with Lieutenant Metcalfe's Support Troop and two Reconnaissance Troops, came in for half an hour's intensive shelling. Major Ward's Staghound was hit, had its tyres blown off and most of its outside equipment neatly stripped. Next came the turn of the Rear Link car, followed by a Daimler and the three White scout cars in succession. However, from all this unpleasantness only one person, Corporal-of-Horse Thompson, was slightly wounded.

There are few things more trying to the nerves and temper than being shelled with no immediate chance of retaliation, especially when the fall of shot coincides with every change of position with the greatest accuracy. This was no routine harassing fire on to the bridge approaches, and it was therefore with great satisfaction that we learnt that the Irish Guards had captured three civilians suspected of directing the German fire from an adjoining house. After this, as anticipated, the shelling abated.

In the early afternoon a message came through that the Polish Airborne Brigade was on its way from England.[5] The proposed drop was farther west than originally planned, but from there, close to the village of Elst, it was hoped that use might be made of the Heveadorp ferry and thus contact be made with the British Airborne opposite. All hope of capturing the Arnhem road bridge had already been abandoned, for it was now known that the town was entirely in enemy hands and that what remained of the British Airborne force was probably concentrated some miles to the west.

The first Dakota transport planes were sighted at a quarter past four and the Germans greeted them with a heavy barrage of flak which swept up to meet them from positions half a mile ahead of the leading Irish Guards tanks and "D" Squadron cars. The pilots, undeterred by the bursting shells, deviated neither right nor left, but flew straight on with extreme gallantry, intent only on dropping their human freight over the selected zone. Many planes could be seen to have been hit and crashed before attaining their objective. The others, enveloped in bursting shells and appearing to the ground onlookers to be terribly cumbersome and slow, carried on.

All at once the air seemed filled with hundreds of parachutes like so many swinging mushrooms floating slowly down to earth. One failed to open and plummeted to the ground. The rest disappeared behind the horizon and the village of Elst. Then as suddenly as it had filled, the sky was once more empty, while away to the west the drone of the homeward bound Dakotas grew fainter and fainter.

Unfortunately, the Poles had dropped nearer the village of Elst than had been intended and they were to suffer considerable casualties from the German forces which lay between them and our own leading troops.

The ground battle, which had appeared to halt momentarily to gaze skywards at the arriving Poles, was quickly jerked back to its own sphere of action by a thud, followed by the crackle of exploding bullets, as yet another Irish Guards tank was hit and burst into flames. Traffic piled up behind the stricken Sherman and although several other tanks tried

---

5. The wireless message, coined, I suspect, by the Adjutant rather than the Colonel, reached "D" Squadron thus: "Look out for Rupert's father's foreign feathered friends—they'll be arriving any moment and dropping this side of the Blue." As an example of the knots into which we were cheerfully prepared to tie ourselves in the belief that we were hoodwinking the enemy, it was to remain an all-time classic. [Translation: For "Rupert" read Lieutenant Buchanan-Jardine. His father, Sir John Buchanan-Jardine (R.H.G.), had acted as Liaison Officer with the Poles when they were stationed in Scotland. For "feathered friends" read Airborne troops. "Blue" was the current jargon for river]

every trick they knew to get off the road and continue cross-country, they only succeeded in getting themselves hopelessly bogged down.

Brigadier Norman Gwatkin arrived on the scene shortly after, resplendent in a brilliant bird's-eye silk scarf and quite imperturbable, to see what could be done to initiate further action in the long line of stationary vehicles representing so much wasted fire power. However, after a brief conference with his commanders, the difficulties of the situation were only too obvious to him. Infantry was the one hope of forcing a way up the road to Elst, and they could only achieve their object if supported by an adequate artillery barrage. Throughout the day acid comments had been passed about the feeble shelling of our own guns, quite unlike what we had been accustomed to expect from the gunners. The reason for this unusual inactivity, and which was not known to the forward troops, was that the Germans had cut the only line of communication farther back at Veghel and we were already perilously short of ammunition.

In fact, so serious were the possible consequences of this cut that General Horrocks was compelled to order the R.A.F. to groundstrafe on recognition within the bomb line. This unorthodox and necessarily risky procedure was carried out with great skill by the air arm, and the road was eventually reopened with practically no damage to our own vehicles.

Later in the day information came through that units of 43rd Division would be taking over from the Irish Guards group next morning, and "D" Squadron were ordered to withdraw over the river for the night.

★　★　★

It was dark when the last "D" Squadron Troop recrossed Nijmegen bridge on the way back to harbour. There had been no time to bury the German dead, who still lay thick on the ground. Among them, close to the water's edge, an American paratrooper with gold rings in his ears was unconcernedly rattling dice with two tough-looking companions. They stood up and grinned, shouting a greeting, before resuming their interrupted game, squatting on tin helmets which had belonged to three German corpses huddled against an anti-tank gun. These Americans, someone remarked, "are so eternally cheerful that nothing ever appears to worry them."

Meanwhile "B" Squadron, carrying on with their previous day's task, had continued to patrol to the west, particularly in the direction of s'Hertogenbosch, where extensive reconnaissances had brought troops to within a mile of the town. Along the River Waal, Lieutenant Tabor's scheme of "annoying" the Germans at every opportunity was brought to a temporary close when he was wounded near Tiel trying to blow down an enemy occupied house with his PIAT mortar.

"C" Squadron profitably continued to escort R.A.S.C. lorries from the Oss warehouse.

So ended operations for the 21st of September—a bitterly disappointing day after all the promise of the previous twenty-four hours, and the highlight of the Grenadiers' capture of Nijmegen bridge.

★   ★   ★

The story of the part played by the Regiment in the renewed attempts at relieving the British Airborne at Arnhem is best opened by Colonel Abel Smith's own narrative of the orders he originally received and the action which he took to carry them out.

"Late in the evening of the 21st [September] the following orders were received by 2 H.C.R.: 'Intelligence believes that the enemy will withdraw during the night. 43 Infantry Division will relieve the Guards Armoured Division during the night, and continue the advance next day. One Squadron of 2 H.C.R. will advance to Arnhem, covering 43 Division at first light.'

"On receipt of these orders I immediately drove off to 43rd Division Headquarters as the Intelligence appreciation of the enemy intentions seemed extraordinary. The enemy had fought most tenaciously all day, and if they could hold us a little longer, the airborne troops would be doomed.

"The G.1 was soon found. He was not yet in the picture, having only just arrived to take over. The Divisional Commander had gone to bed, giving orders that he was not to be disturbed. The following orders were therefore given by me to Major Herbert, 'C' Squadron: *'The enemy may be withdrawing. 43rd Division are to advance to Arnhem tomorrow morning. "C" Squadron will join up with the Poles immediately south of Arnhem and will advance at first light.'*

"It was appreciated that the enemy could hold all the direct routes to Arnhem; therefore patrols would in the first place move east and west along the north bank of the Waal in the hope that the enemy would not expect us in that direction. Should either patrol get through, after two or three kilometres, it would move north to the Neder Rijn."

★   ★   ★

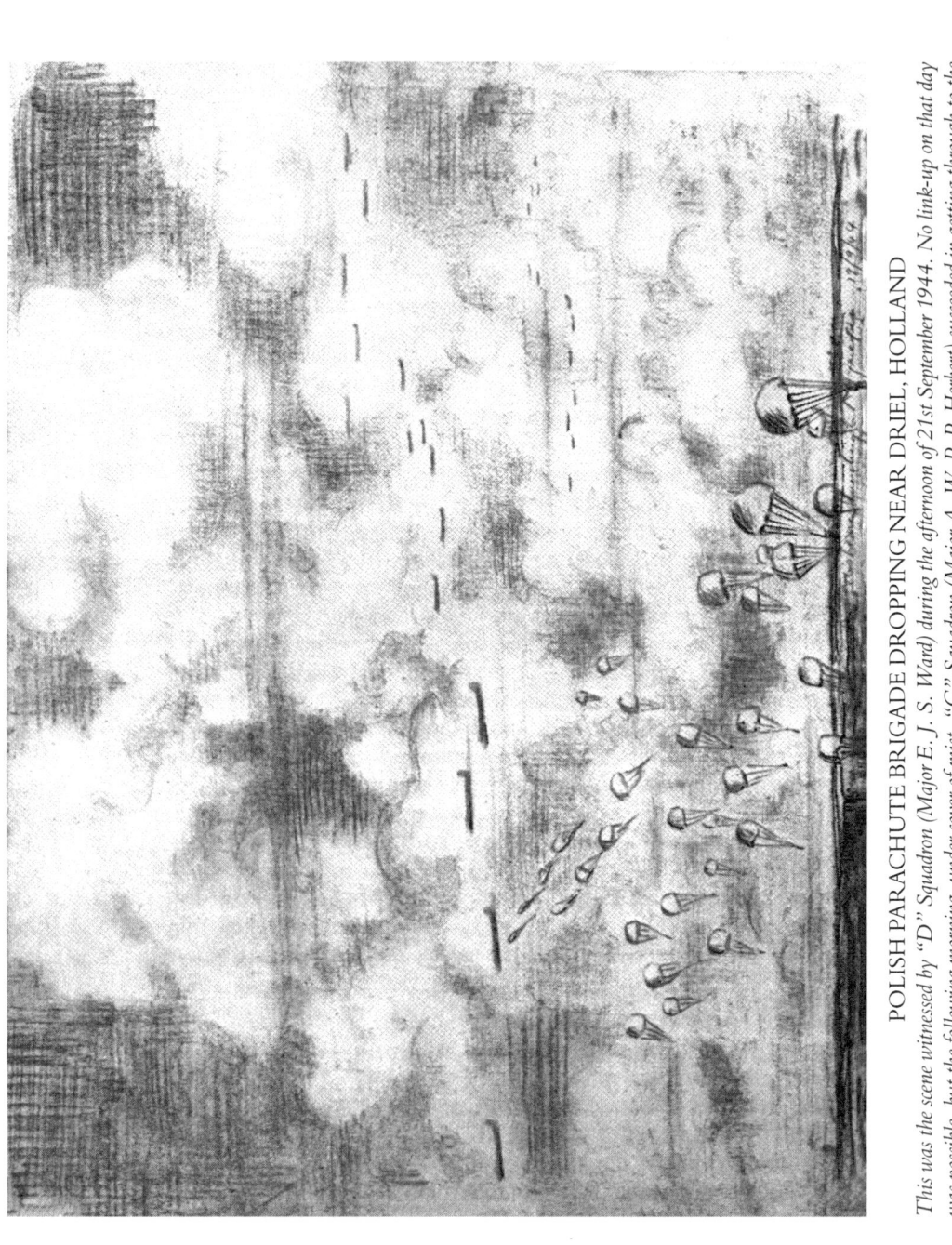

POLISH PARACHUTE BRIGADE DROPPING NEAR DRIEL, HOLLAND

This was the scene witnessed by "D" Squadron (Major E. J. S. Ward) during the afternoon of 21st September 1944. No link-up on that day was possible, but the following morning, under cover of mist, "C" Squadron (Major A. W. P. P. Herbert) succeeded in getting through to the isolated Poles on the south bank of the Neder Rijn opposite Arnhem.

Dawn came with a thick mist. From the point of view of air resupply, conditions were considered "even worse" than those prevailing in the past two days. Yet in the circumstances, for the armoured cars they could not have been bettered. After the slow and slogging progress of the last forty-eight hours, everything was to happen with a rush. "The Household Cavalry," later wrote Major Hennessy at Division, "saw their opportunity and slipped through. Perhaps this was their most brilliant action."[6]

Major Herbert, commanding "C" Squadron, fully realized that "D" Squadron had been given an almost similar role the day before and had been decisively halted on both flanks. Therefore if the Germans were to be deceived, speed of action before the fog lifted was imperative. Accordingly, two Troops, one moving east and the other west, were ordered across the Waal immediately. Squadron Headquarters and reserve troops were held in readiness to take advantage of the slightest indication that the enemy had withdrawn and were located at a suitable point on the perimeter of the bridgehead.

The original appreciation that the westerly route would offer the best chance of success was soon confirmed when Lieutenant Corbett's Troop reported itself held up by an anti-tank screen on the outskirts of Bemmel to the east of the main road, whereas 5 Troop (Captain Wrottesley) made excellent progress. His cars could see no more than fifty yards ahead of them and could hear the Germans talking on all sides, "but we reckoned that they were as blind as we were, certainly could not see enough to man their weapons, and if they heard us, probably thought that we were friendly vehicles—anyhow that was what we hoped to be the case, and the desperate situation of the Airborne warranted corresponding risks on our side." Map reading was in the circumstances difficult, and at one time one of the cars took a wrong turning but succeeded in joining up again without mishap. By eight o'clock in the morning the Troop had motored clean through the enemy defences and had linked up with the Poles. One solitary German had been met on the way, and he was allowed to disappear into the fog, that the sounds of shooting might not give the game away.

The Poles had not experienced too happy a time. They had incurred severe casualties on landing, had not been able to effect any contact with the British on the opposite bank, and were very short of anti-tank weapons and ammunition. They were delighted to see the Household Cavalry cars and greeted them with acclamation.

---

6. *From a Purely Personal Point of View*, by Major the Hon. F. F. G. Hennessy, M.B.E., Grenadier Guards.

Meanwhile, wasting no time, Major Herbert had already dispatched 2 Troop, commanded by Lieutenant Young, with orders to join Captain Wrottesley at all costs. The fog was beginning to lift very slightly—a doubtful blessing in the circumstances. He followed the same route which ran initially west along the river bank for about six miles and then struck north, arriving at Driel from the west side along the Neder Rijn bank by a road running from Heteren to Driel.

"Things were exceptionally quiet at this time," wrote Lieutenant Young, "and as for myself, we passed several Mark IVs which we liked to presume at the time had been knocked out, but these we discovered later from Peter Herbert proved to be very much alive! "

On the way several Air Force pilots and air crews were picked up. They had been shot down and were in temporary hiding. One of them, an Australian War Correspondent, subsequently wrote an article in one of the London papers describing the meeting. He was particularly impressed with the bearing of Corporal McNeil, one of the scout car commanders, whom he described as "that cool, calm and good-looking pipe-smoking Corporal!"—a designation which he was not allowed to forget in the N.C.Os.' Mess for many a day to come.

On coming on to the raised road which served as a dyke and ran parallel to the Neder Rijn, the Troop saw some Germans on the far bank. These were engaged, but as there was practically no return fire it was assumed that they were stray bodies. Of the British Airborne there was still no sign of life.

On reaching Driel, Lieutenant Young found that a full-scale battle was in progress, with the Polish soldiers hard pressed to deal with attacks coming in simultaneously from the direction of Arnhem and Elst. It was therefore arranged that Captain Wrottesley should remain with the Poles, his main task being to act as wireless link between them and 30 Corps, for his message had been the first communication received from that body since they had landed. In addition, Wrottesley's Troop was to help the Poles in stemming the German armour which was continually infiltrating into their positions from the east.

Lieutenant Young was now ordered to investigate the river bank east of Driel to try to discover a suitable crossing place for the DUKWs (amphibious craft) which it was proposed to bring up with supplies as soon as possible. In the course of this patrol contact was made with two British Airborne soldiers (who had swum the river during the night) and a Polish Airborne soldier. Battle was then joined with an enemy patrol, and eventually a large-scale map belonging to the river engineer at Driel was captured. This gave details of the river currents and bank surfaces and was to prove most useful in helping to decide on future possible crossing places for the relieving body.

Later on the patrol moved farther east with the object of attaining the area of the Arnhem railway bridge.

"I took two scout cars; in one was Trooper Holmes and myself, the other contained Corporal McNeil and Trooper Gadsden. We investigated the river bank almost as far as the railway bridge but were fired on by the enemy's anti-tank guns from the opposite bank and were compelled to retire. We then encountered one German patrol, which we subsequently discovered was part of the main attack about to be put in on Driel. We then returned to Driel, to discover from the Poles that no one had previously been along the road in daylight because of the fire from the far bank. Their supplies were scattered all along this area, and because they were without armour it was quite impossible for them to retrieve the stuff they so much wanted.

"The main attack on Driel began shortly after eleven o'clock, and at this point I had difficulty with the Polish general, who was anxious that we should use our cars as tanks, as there was still enemy armour in the area. The Polish general was charming but quite fanatical, and if he had thought it the least possible would have asked us to fly our armoured cars into battle!

"This attack, which was a particularly vicious one, lasted with little intermission until dark, and the Polish Forces were extremely grateful for the added fire power of the two Troops, for by now most of their automatics were worn out or the ammunition expended. They were also short of food and water."

The news of the link-up with the Poles, which was considered a great triumph[7] and the penultimate stage in the relief of the British Airborne, set hopes on high again. As soon as the first message arrived, 30 Corps began to organize a mixed relief column from 43rd Division aiming to force a way through the enemy opposition west of the main road to Elst, but this naturally took some time and in the meantime "C" Squadron were to be kept busy.

Major Herbert had already decided to go forward himself with his headquarters to see at first-hand how things stood. "Throughout," in the terms of the official report, "his had been the driving force and the

---

7. Thus the three link-ups in operation "Market-Garden," with 82nd U.S. Airborne Division at Eindhoven, with 101st U.S. Airborne Division at Grave, and with the Polish Brigade at Driel had all been effected by 2nd Household Cavalry Regiment.

initiative in seeing that all possible exertions be made to hasten forward the means of relieving the Airborne."

Unfortunately, the fog was already showing signs of lifting when "C" Squadron Headquarters, led by Lieutenant Hopkinson's Troop, prepared to pass through the outposts of 43rd Division. Captain Clyde, Major Herbert's second-in-command, describes the scene and what followed.

"The first mile and a half after crossing the bridge was parallel to the river and on a narrow road banked six feet high on either side. If you want to present yourself as a target there's nothing like having to get nose to tail well silhouetted against the sky line, and on a road where at no place could you begin to turn round—even a scout car, let alone the series of three-tonner lorries which we always had up with us.

"Arthur and Dickie[8] had reported no opposition and no visibility. They had mentioned one or two surprised 'Krauts' cooking breakfast, but they were swallowed up in the mist before either side could do anything much about it. For reasons of wireless touch, morale, and because we couldn't think of any good reason why we shouldn't, we followed the same route.... I followed directly behind Harry Hopkinson's Troop, leading Headquarters. In the first half mile we had to pass a lot of infantry vehicles—carriers and lorries—parked by the side of the road. They belonged to troops who had been dug in for the night on the perimeter. As a result we debouched from their forward positions very much bunched up, and at that instant the mist began to clear. In a matter of minutes visibility was normal, and as the leading scout car of Harry's Troop became level with the first village [Oosterhout] (the height of the road above ground level gave this effect to the eye), there was an unpleasant crack, a puff of smoke, and that was the scout car. I saw a figure jump clear and roll down the embankment. It was Corporal Bland. Trooper (Harold) Read, the driver, was killed on the spot. Then the chaos started.

"At this moment Peter Herbert was getting back wireless news from Dickie Wrottesley and Arthur Young that practically the whole of the civilized world was waiting to hear and God knows how big were the 'Sunrays' listening in, and chipping in, on the Rear Link set. Harry Hopkinson couldn't move back his Troop until we moved, we couldn't move until the three-tonners moved, and damned if the infantry carriers weren't coming up behind them just to make it more like Piccadilly Circus than ever. Luckily, the German shooting was erratic, but one knew full well that we were all sitting like pheasants on the bough of a

---

8. Lieutenant Young and Captain Wrottesley.

tree. Smoke seemed to be the immediate answer, and then try to back each vehicle out of trouble. Needless to say, my own smoke, tended so carefully through the length and breadth of England and across half northern Europe, went off like a damp squib at a range of five yards! Peter and Philip Armes were yelling their heads off on the wireless in their cars trying to pass back a message, and Harry had got back under cover of the embankment on his feet, and I kicked open the door and dropped to the floor of my Staghound to get out and make a plan with him. There was another nasty crack and I looked up to see that the periscope had been shot away, just at the back of where my head had been a few seconds before. I then knew that I was clearly destined for some far more unpleasant fate later in life, like living in a Socialist State!"

To recount all the individual adventures which befell people on this day would fill many more pages than possessed by this history—a few must suffice.

There proved to be more than one German tank firing down and across the dyke road, some being hidden in the buildings of Oosterhout village, and backed by about a hundred infantrymen and a self-propelled gun which kept firing into the hulk of the burning scout car. Corporal-of-Horse Brown, on seeing that he could not move back owing to the press of vehicles immediately behind him, managed to pass round the scout car and open up on what he saw was another tank hiding behind an outhouse. He had only the smoke and flash of a gun to go on and, being unable to move over the six-foot drop from the road to the field beneath, was unable to observe results. He was, however, able to smoke out the farmhouse area and blind the German vehicle while the infantry of the Wiltshires then deployed across country. Later that evening the tanks of the 4th/7th Dragoon Guards confirmed that a Mark III tank had been found knocked out and abandoned, Corporal-of-Horse Brown claiming with justification a "kill."

The Wiltshires subsequently encountered strong resistance in Oosterhout village and this was not cleared up until the arrival of the tanks, by which time Major Herbert had been ordered to withdraw his Headquarters out of range of the German armour.

The knowledge that the two armoured cars were still at Driel, both with their wirelesses in full touch, produced the inevitable result. For every one message sent back by them to Regiment, Corps sent forward two further questions to be answered.

"*Was the Arnhem railway bridge blown?*"

"Yes, it was."

"*Who is holding the northern end?*"

"By the shots that are being directed at us from that area, I presume it must be the Germans."

"What about the ferry?"

"The Heveadorp ferry has been destroyed."

"Can you see if there are any other ferry boats lying about?"

"The Gunners are interested in your information about the enemy north of the Railway Bridge—can you move up to report on the effect of their shooting?"

"What is the state of the tracks leading to the river's edge and will it carry the DUKWs without bogging?"

"The C.R.E. 43 Division wishes to know the width of the gap of the blown railway bridge—can you send back a bridging report?"[9]

The very full wireless Log Book for the day shows that at ten minutes to one in the afternoon, Lieutenant Young sends back a report that "the southern bank is now under continuous fire at the place recommended for crossing—I am about to look for a better place." A quarter of an hour later, Captain Wrottesley's Troop is off to help the Poles to repel another attack, wirelessing that "Resistance has thickened up considerably and there is concern at the state of ammunition," both for the Poles and his own armoured cars. Yet again, five minutes later, he calls up for fire on to the south bank of the river where the enemy are forming up. The medium guns[10] respond magnificently and the attack is broken up before it can get going.

Meanwhile, during the afternoon, Major-General Urquhart, commanding the British Airborne Division, judged it indispensable to send two officers across the river to acquaint his Corps Commander, Lieutenant-General F. A. M. Browning, of the now truly desperate situation at Arnhem. For this purpose he chose Lieutenant-Colonel C. B. McKenzie, G.S.O.(1), and Lieutenant-Colonel E. C. Myers, the C.R.E. These two gallantly made the crossing of the Neder Rijn under fire in a small rubber boat and eventually found the Polish Headquarters, where, in their words, "there was a battle going on and we couldn't make out which were Poles and which were Germans!"[11]

Here, using the Household Cavalry Wireless net, the G.1 spoke to the B.G.S., 30 Corps, his messages being relayed through R.H.Q. of 2 H.C.R., and for the first time the outside world had confirmation of

---

9. It was subsequently ascertained that the railway bridge had been blown by the Germans on the 17th of September in the face of the approaching British Airborne troops.

10. Initially all the observation for the guns of 64th Medium Regiment, R.A., was carried out by Lieutenant Young's Troop. These guns rendered invaluable support to the hard-pressed British Airborne throughout the day.

11. Narrative of "By Air to Battle."

what it feared must be the case. "We are short of food, ammunition and medical supplies; we cannot hold out for more than twenty-four hours; all we can do is to wait and pray."

★   ★   ★

The general plan of 43rd Division, when it had once broken out of the bridgehead, was to advance with two brigades up; 129th Brigade on the right keeping to the main Nijmegen—Arnhem road, while on the left 214th Brigade was to keep more or less to the route taken by the two "C" Squadron Troops.

Unfortunately, when the two Household Cavalry Troops had first got through, it was considered probable that the Germans had withdrawn, and the commander 43rd Division, Major-General Thomas, in order to save precious time, cancelled his fire plan. His attack therefore met with considerable opposition and it became necessary to *"reculer pour mieux sauter,"* with all the delay entailed in such a manoeuvre.

The lifting of the fog had given back to the enemy their eyes, and throughout the rest of the day progress was to be painfully slow. By last light, 129th Brigade were still short of Elst, but earlier on, however, 214th Brigade made some progress in the area of Valburg. They thereupon pushed forward a mobile column, consisting of the 5th Duke of Cornwall's Light Infantry and a Squadron of tanks belonging to the 4th/7th Dragoon Guards (8th Armoured Brigade), with DUKWs laden with supplies, through Valburg.

It was during this advance that a sergeant-major in a rear carrier of the column turned to his driver and quietly said, "Don't look now, but we are being followed by Tigers! " With commendable presence of mind, the column continued on its way, followed by the Tigers at meticulous road spacing. A message was then sent by D.R. warning an officer farther up the column of this jungle drama, and an ambush of PIATs was quickly dropped off. In due course the unsuspecting Tigers appeared round a bend in the road and the leader was knocked out at short range. A second ran into it and the remaining Tiger, followed by four Panthers, ran into the ditch in its confusion.

The mixed column made contact with the Poles by half past eight in the evening, but the link-up was marred by a most unfortunate incident which occurred in the half-light. On hearing the rumble of tanks, Lieutenant Young's Troop had moved forward cautiously to investigate, having been warned that a relieving force was on the way, but quite prepared for the noise to be caused by further German tanks. Soon the leading scout car caught a glimpse of a Sherman turret, and Lieutenant Young gave orders to the Poles nearest him to show recognition panels. The armoured cars likewise brought out their yellow strips. They then advanced down the road to welcome the British Force, carrying in addition yellow smoke cartridges which they fired off fairly liberally. However, the leading tank failed to recognize the signals and opened fire on the Troop, which was half exposed. The first shot caused superficial damage to Young's car, carrying away the tool box, a tyre, etc., but the second shot drilled a hole in the front armour plate of the scout car, killing Trooper Reginald Holmes outright.

The Troop's immediate reaction was to imagine that the Shermans were being used by the enemy, and several of the Poles who had witnessed the episode were preparing to take them on with their bazookas, but then the sound of an English voice was heard and it was realized that there had been a tragic mistake. Even so, the fiery Poles were beside themselves with rage, and it took all Lieutenant Young's powers of persuasion to stop them knocking out the first tanks to arrive. Trooper Holmes was buried the next day in Driel churchyard with full military honours.

It was a sad ending to the day's operations for a Troop which had done so well. Apparently, although fullest details of location had been sent back on the wireless, the message had never reached the relief column, which moved up not expecting to find any British armour with the Poles. The unit involved in this tragic incident made full acknowledgment in its own history, deeply regretting the mistake.

★   ★   ★

The situation of the Arnhem defenders was now very serious. Efforts during the day to fly in medical aid for the growing numbers of wounded had only been partially successful, a high percentage of packages falling into German hands. The defenders, hourly growing weaker, were reduced to drinking rain water caught in their tin helmets and waterproof capes. Moreover, the German tanks, because of the British shortage of anti-tank weapons and ammunition, were now able to close in and blast the soldiers from house to house almost without reprisal.

Assault boats had formed part of the mixed relief column and preparations were begun for a crossing of the river during the night. Well aware of this move, the Germans kept shelling and mortaring the assembly points. The swift flowing current was too strong and the rafts were swept away. In addition, the drizzling rain of the past few days had so softened the banks that the wheels of the DUKWs failed to grip.

To make matters worse, the banks themselves were steep and had to be prepared under continuous shell and small-arms fire. Only a limited amount of supplies could be ferried across on rafts during the hours of darkness, and at the first sign of dawn this had to cease.

One important factor governing the whole of 30 Corps' operations at this stage must be borne in mind. There had been a second complete cessation of forward traffic because the Germans had again succeeded in cutting the centre line between Uden and Veghel on the 22nd of September.

At first light on the 23rd of September, Colonel McKenzie, the G.1 of the Airborne Division, decided that he must see his Corps Commander at his headquarters near Nijmegen without delay, and so prepared to set off, escorted, as had been arranged, by Captain Wrottesley's Troop. The Troop Leader put Colonel McKenzie in his own seat of the first armoured car, while he himself led in a scout car.

Presently the party drew near to a windmill where a still-burning German tank blocked part of the road. Captain Wrottesley dismounted to signal the armoured car past the obstruction. Then, at the moment the armoured car was passing through the gap a Panther tank suddenly appeared out of a side road, and "with its dirty green nose," opened up on the Troop. A brief fire fight ensued, in which Colonel McKenzie with admirable coolness acted as loader to the 2-pounder and managed to get off eight rounds. History does not relate what happened to the German tank, but Colonel McKenzie eventually found himself upside down in a ditch and was forced, together with the two other members of the crew, to take to the fields. For a time it was feared that they had been captured or killed, and so it was with relief that shortly afterwards "the G.1 was recovered, after making a detour across the fields," and, in the further words of Colonel Abel Smith, "safely delivered to his Corps Commander."

★ ★ ★

In the meantime Lieutenant Corbett's cars had set off to relieve the remaining Troop (Lieutenant Young's) with the Poles but ran into several tanks and mobile guns between Elst and Driel. Corporal-of-Horse Jenkins's car got itself bogged and found itself under fire from a self-propelled 75-mm. which fired seven shots in succession, "which," said Corporal Chennel, "made us think that the German gunner must have been cross-eyed, for he kept firing at exactly the same place and always just missing us. However, as the car was completely stuck, Mr. Corbett decided that we should evacuate it, and we eventually got back to the others, including a section of the Support Troop who were farther on. I must say that the driver of our car, Trooper Gardner, was remarkably cool throughout this episode, but seemed to think that we should have stayed put with the stranded car. Personally, I think that this was because we had a large amount of food aboard and Gardner was a great lover of his food! "

Efforts to relieve the Airborne were to continue for a further two days. These were attended by much gallantry and loss of life. On the 22nd of September about 250 Poles had been ferried across the Neder Rijn. On the night of the 23rd of September a further infantry detachment crossed the river, but intense fire from the high ground on the north bank put a stop at first light to these operations. Bad weather, which had dogged the whole operation, necessitated the cancellation of a plan to fly in the 52nd (Air Portable) Division. Fighting continued violently in the vicinity of Bemmel and Elst, which meant that the ground route was never really clear for the relieving supply columns. The main axis was cut for the third time on the 24th of September and traffic was not able to resume until the following day. All these factors, coupled with the fact that on only two out of eight vital days of battle had the weather permitted "even a reasonable scale of offensive air support and air transportation," decided the 21 Army Group Commander (Montgomery) to order the withdrawal of the gallant Arnhem bridgehead.

★   ★   ★

"C" Squadron were withdrawn to south of the Waal into reserve on the 24th September. In a small but nevertheless vitally important way, the Household Cavalry Regiment had played a prominent part in the closing stages of the ground operations. To the drive and initiative of Major Herbert was due the detailed knowledge which enabled 30 Corps to plan for all the assault equipment to be sent forward with the relief column as early as it was. Only by the speedy and bold action of his two Troops could these efforts have come to fruition. The time taken by the relief column to reach the Poles is in itself an indication of what might have happened had the Troops not seized their chance before the mist rose. Although both Troop Leaders had rightly refused to allow their Troops to be embroiled in dog fights and used as tanks by the Poles, there had been no refusal to accept all enemy targets as they had presented themselves, and when the mixed column eventually arrived both Troops were down to their last few rounds of Besa ammunition, complaining bitterly that it was "rather wasteful to use up 2-pounder shots on German infantrymen!"

The Polish general, on the day following the relief, and before the departure of the two Troops, insisted on inviting both commanders for a drink in his temporary headquarters, and congratulated them on the part which they and their men had played in the operation.

★ ★ ★

Turning to other sectors of the front and south of the main battle, Major Daly had relieved Major Wignall's Squadron on the 22nd of September, to continue reconnaissance towards s'Hertogenbosch. Patrols radiating from Grave had several brushes with the enemy, but in no place could the territory be said to be held by the Germans—they were by now in a state of complete disorganization, and it became more a case of rounding up prisoners and moving from village to village, some of which were found to contain groups of infantry, while the majority were unoccupied. One Troop penetrated as far west as Rossum, fourteen kilometres due west of Oss, while another, Lieutenant Franklin's,[12] was able to watch the enemy concentrating in s'Hertogenbosch—a town which was to hold out until the last days of October.

Lieutenant Creswell set off on patrol along the south bank of the Waal to the same area, near Tiel, where Lieutenant Tabor had been wounded on the 21st. There were reports from the Dutch that enemy had been crossing in numbers. On reaching the village of Leeuwen the Troop Leader was hailed in English by a civilian. He turned out to be a Dutchman, Walter Proehl by name, who had been in hiding from the Germans in a farmhouse across the river until warned of the approach of the British cars. He had then rowed over under the noses of the enemy.

Proehl, who had married an English girl compelled to flee from Holland in 1940 on the advent of the Nazis, offered his services to the Regiment in any capacity so long as it had to do with fighting the Germans.

Interpreters had not yet been officially recognized by the Division, but here was obviously a man eminently fitted for the job. A note was therefore hastily scribbled and forwarded to the Princess Irene's Regiment (Dutch), which was in the neighbourhood of Grave, and it

---

12. Lieutenant Franklin's Troop in the course of its patrol picked up some U.S. Airborne troops who must have dropped too far west.

MAP 10
THE THREE STAGES
IN
2 HCR's LINK-UP
WITH
THE AIRBORNE FORCES

A *18 Sept.* With 101 US AIRBORNE DIVISION
North of EINDHOVEN

① Capt. Balding & Lieut. Palmer's Troop
② Main advance – Lieut. Tabor's Troop
Perimeters at first light 18th Sept

B *19 Sept.* With 82 US AIRBORNE DIVISION
at GRAVE

③ Lieut. Kavanagh's Troop
Perimeter at first light 19th Sept.

C *22 Sept* With 1 POLISH PARACHUTE BRIGADE
GROUP at DRIEL

④ Capt. Wrottesley's & Lieut. Young's Troops
Perimeters at first light 22nd Sept.

Scale of Miles
0   1   2   3   4   5

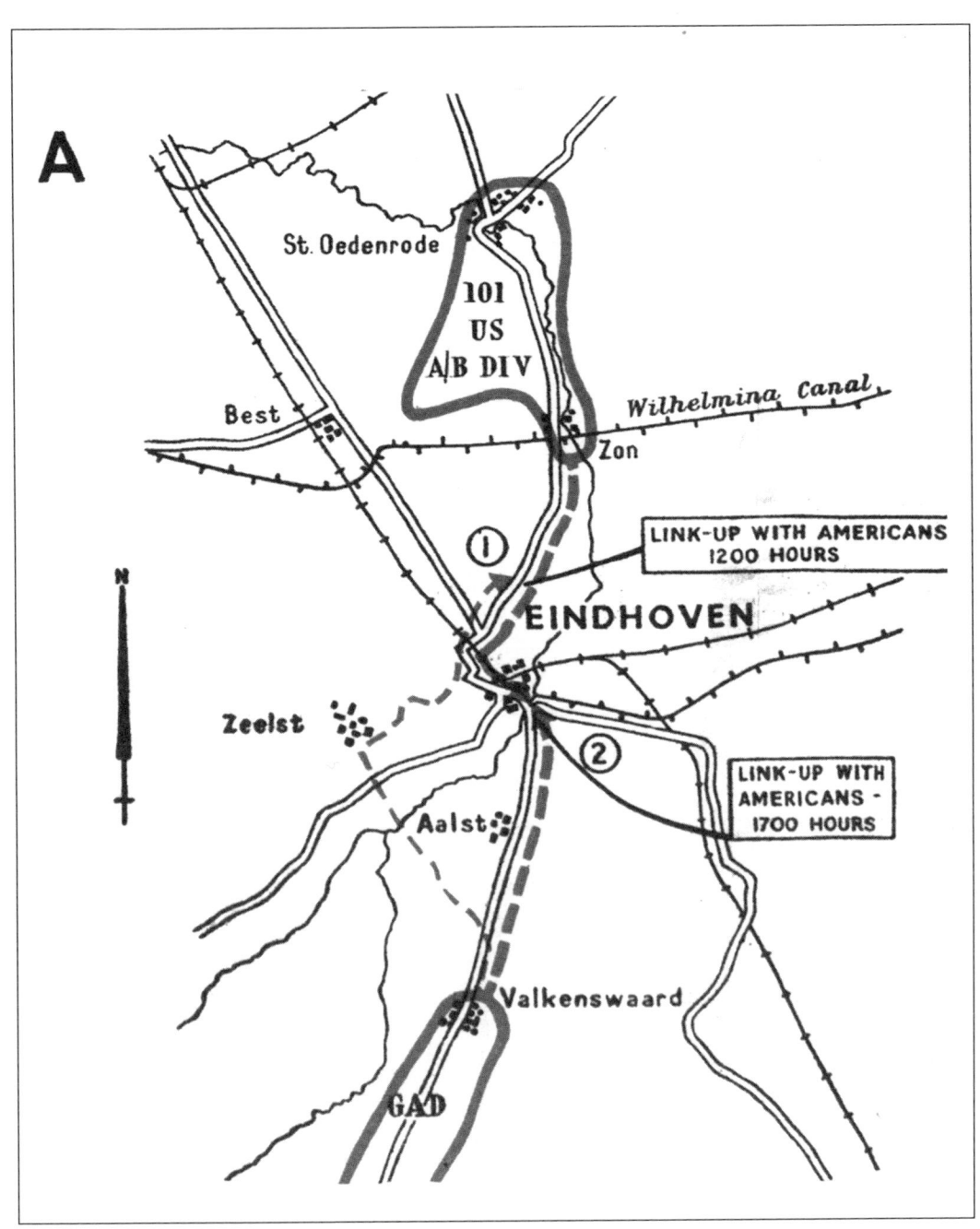

A

St. Oedenrode

101
US
A/B DIV

Best

Wilhelmina Canal

Zon

① LINK-UP WITH AMERICANS
1200 HOURS

N

EINDHOVEN

Zeelst

② LINK-UP WITH
AMERICANS -
1700 HOURS

Aalst

Valkenswaard

GAD

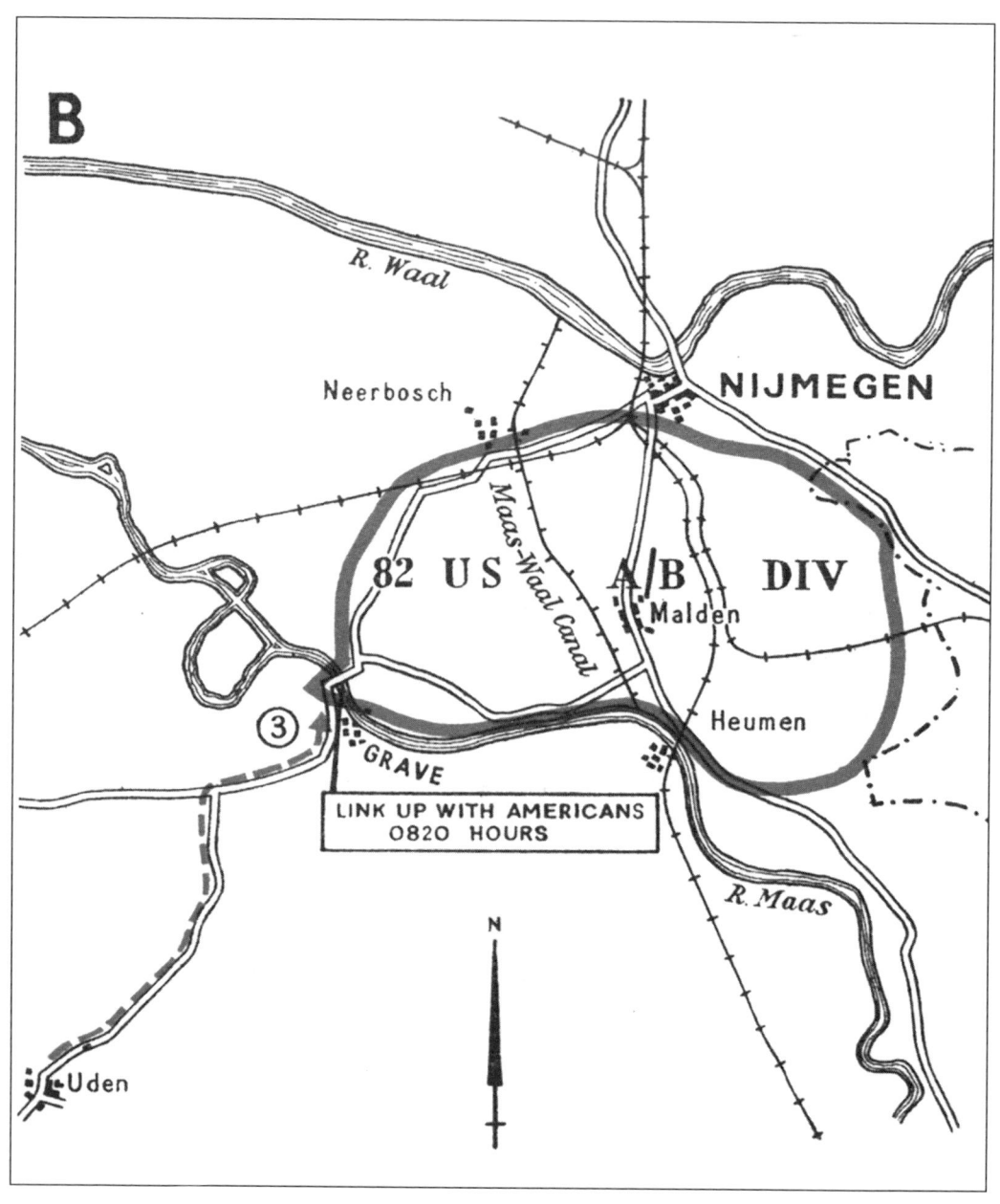

B

R. Waal

Neerbosch

NIJMEGEN

82 US

Maas-Waal Canal

A/B   DIV

Malden

Heumen

③

GRAVE

**LINK UP WITH AMERICANS
0820 HOURS**

R. Maas

N

Uden

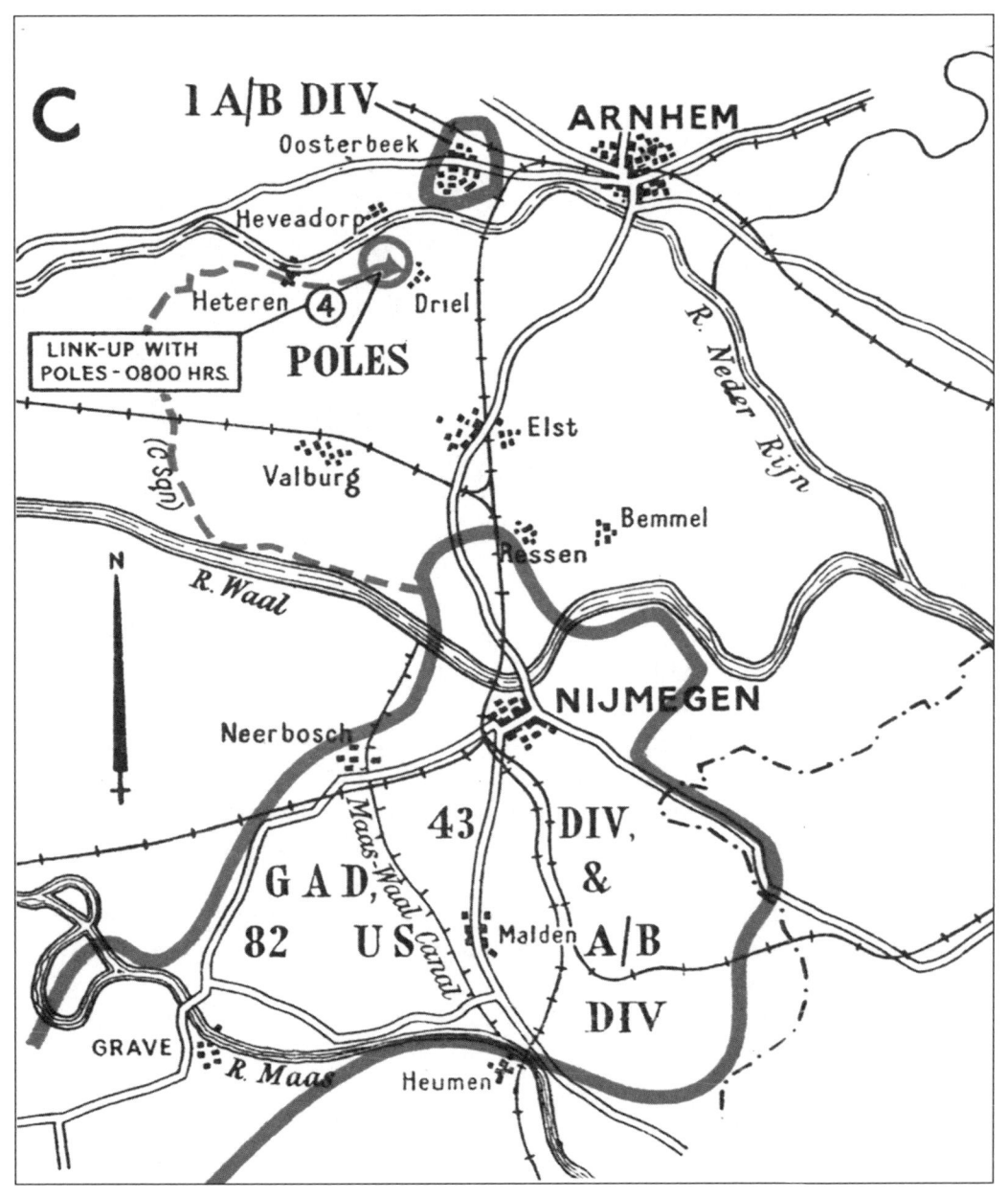

C

1 A/B DIV
Oosterbeek
ARNHEM
Heveadorp
Heteren (4) Driel
LINK-UP WITH
POLES - 0800 HRS.
POLES
(C Sqn)
R. Neder Rijn
Elst
Valburg
Bemmel
Ressen
N
R. Waal
NIJMEGEN
Neerbosch
43 DIV,
&
G A D, Maas-Waal Canal Malden A/B
82 US DIV
GRAVE R. Maas
Heumen

ON "THE ISLAND," SEPTEMBER 1944
Germans captured near Bemmel. Irish Guards tank keeps a look-out to the flank.

was pointed out that as Proehl was "illegal" with no rank and a civilian
into the bargain he might be shot if caught by the Germans.

The Dutch Regiment proved co-operative, and practically offered to
give him any rank he chose, but without pay! This didn't worry Proehl
in the least, who, to his satisfaction, joined 2 H.C.R. officially, thus
becoming one of its first interpreters. Later, interpreters were officially
recognized by the authorities and given the rank and scale of pay of
sergeant.

Proehl was seriously wounded later on in the campaign and flown
back to England, where he was reunited with his wife some days before
the end of the war in Europe.

Towards evening Major Bowes Daly received an urgent message to
recall his Troops as quickly as possible—the Squadron was required
elsewhere. It appeared that the enemy, attacking from the north-west
with tanks, lorried infantry and self-propelled guns, had breached the
centre line between Uden and Veghel. It was another thrust from our
old friends the "Pocket Panzer Division" (107 Panzer Brigade). To meet
this thrust, General Horrocks had ordered Guards Armoured Division
to release 32nd Brigade from the Nijmegen area to move down south as
soon as possible to the threatened area. "A" Squadron were being placed

in support of them in a reconnaissance role. By late evening contact had been made with the enemy, but no decisive action took place that night, and for twenty-five precious hours the supplies so urgently required to maintain the offensive were prevented from moving up the Corps life line.

The 23rd of September was to be another day of mist and intermittent rain, and while the Grenadier and Coldstream groups composing 32nd Brigade were engaging the enemy near Uden, "A" Squadron continued to operate under them on the flanks. In addition, the Squadron took part in several skirmishes of their own both near the centre line and when advancing eastwards to the River Maas. In particular, the Support Troop under Lieutenant Wordsworth had a good day and collected a substantial haul of prisoners from places as far afield as the villages of St. Antonis and Oploo.

"My Squadron," wrote the Troop Leader, "was harboured in the area of Zeeland at the time about four kilometres north-east of Uden. There had been wild civilian rumours of thirty enemy tanks roaming about at will in the vicinity and we had been ordered to find out what was happening to the east. My whole Troop was sent out in support of No. 2 Troop under Peake to St. Antonis, with Jack Creswell's Troop at hand if required, in order to prevent the Germans approaching the centre line from the east. We thought that we were in for a quiet day, but it turned out to be quite the opposite. Two largish bodies of enemy entered the village at different times during the day, and as a result of a lot of running about on their flat feet by my chaps, the bag at the end of the day was two lorries, one motor-car (a runner which eventually did several journeys to Brussels), two motor-cycles, seven killed, four wounded (one of these an officer who was prodded in the behind with a bayonet by one of my chaps because he refused to run fast enough), and fifty prisoners. We suffered one cut finger. Corporal-of-Horse Coles got a bit bored sitting with No. 5 Troop being out of the battle and decided to join in, which he did most successfully, running around with a Bren gun. This was one of our best days, for, as you know, most of October was to be spent crawling around the banks of the Maas on our tummies.

★   ★   ★

Nearer the centre line, Lieutenant Franklin's Troop was held up close to Volkel, where resistance was to take the Coldstream group some time to eliminate.

The following description, a composite effort, is based on individual recollections of the day by members of the Troop, principally Corporal-of-Horse Booth.

"On being called away from our patrolling west of the main road towards s'Hertogenbosch (evening of the 22nd), we had moved up to and passed through Heesch.[13] It was a nice little village and the inhabitants were very friendly, although naturally worried by all the alarming rumours. The next morning we found ourselves located near Volkel. Lieutenant Franklin had halted the Troop and we were all in a position to observe a line of 88-mm. guns in a row. These guns were partially concealed by an embankment a kilometre to our east at a place called Oosterens. We had brought with us a Dutchman picked up at Afferden.[14] He very bravely volunteered to go forward to find out what he could about the enemy. It was hoped that as he was dressed in civilian clothes the Germans would not pay much attention to him. After a time the Dutchman returned, and Lieutenant Franklin duly reported his findings, which proved to be remarkably accurate. The Troop was ordered to advance no farther, but to keep the enemy guns in sight and await the arrival of the Coldstreamers, who were coming forward with tanks and infantry.

"Suddenly the Troop was amazed to see what they thought must be another airborne landing.[15] American planes towing gliders were arriving and being heavily shot at by the 'flak' guns which must have been hidden on the far side of the village of Oosterens. As the result of the enemy shelling several of the planes were forced to cast off their gliders. One came down in a field beside us complete, the Dakota and the glider, and one of the engines had dropped off, setting the wheel of the plane on fire. Within a short time, fourteen paratroopers in the most spotless order, their trousers beautifully creased, came over towards us. They had breakfasted in England, and on being asked how it was looking, one of them replied, 'As sweet as a green pea!' This was about their third attempt to get to Arnhem, they said, as they had had to turn back owing to weather being so bad. One glider on this journey had been ditched in the Channel. I have never seen anything like their kit. They had jeeps, rifles, grenades hung all over them, chewing gum, and even brand-new frying pans. They even offered us a jeep which they couldn't remove from a smashed glider!

---

13. A village three kilometres south of Oss and the scene of considerable fighting two days later.
14. On the River Waal.
15. Probably part of the Glider Regiment of 82nd U.S. Airborne Division, which did land that day. *Author.*

"'Say, boys, which way is the battle?' demanded one of the Americans. We pointed in the direction of the 88-mms. and warned them that there were a number of them about. We also suggested that they should be careful about showing themselves when going forward to observe with their jeeps, and that we ourselves had been ordered to await the arrival of tank and infantry reinforcements. 'Say, Buddy,' remarked a big fellow, 'we came here to fight and that's what we're going to do.' With which remark the entire party, complete with jeeps, motored off towards the enemy guns.

"Lieutenant Franklin had arranged with their commander that if they must go they should carry a white flag on their return journey as a recognition signal to avoid being shot up in error. This they agreed to do and we saw them disappear round a bend in the road. All at once there was a tremendous burst of firing and the sound of loud explosions and much shouting. After an interval, the survivors came back waving the flag as instructed.[16]

"Shortly after this the Coldstream group arrived in force. Lieutenant Franklin supplied the commander of the first tank with all the information he had, and also told him what had happened to the Americans, but as the situation appeared to be quiet at the time, the Troop Leader (Lieutenant Franklin) formed the impression that perhaps his story was not entirely credited. Anyhow, there was a brief conference and the first tanks went in to the attack. Straightway three went up in quick succession and the attack stopped dead. There was another "O" Group [Orders Group] at the side of the road, then the column got under way once more, supported by 3-inch mortars and infantry. The Germans replied with mortars and the Coldstream casualties began to trickle back in growing numbers. Then in a further five minutes or so there was even more noise—lots of bangs, shouts and explosions as the Foot Guards got in among the Germans with their bayonets, then silence, and shortly afterwards people began to filter back along the road. An officer remarked that 'Seven Panther tanks have just got away and are hovering about,' but these were not seen again and nothing further untoward happened. Nearly all the 88-mms. were knocked out and many prisoners taken.

"As a Troop we took no part in the actual fighting, but three things I shall always remember on that day—the utter imperturbability of the Coldstream Guards as they went in to the attack; the sudden and extraordinary arrival right into the middle of the battle of their echelon lorries to disgorge hot food for the soldiers; and lastly, the sight of the commander of the group stalking about apparently unarmed and

---

16. The Americans eventually returned to Volkel and Lieutenant Franklin took them on the armoured cars to Veghel at nightfall.

accompanied by a huge Bruce Woodcock of a Guardsman, armed with a rifle with a telescopic sight, and whose other job appeared to be to feed his commanding officer on enormous bread and cheese sandwiches. This Colonel was extremely brave and between bites at his sandwich was always going into the thick of things 'to have a look for myself.' Oosterens was eventually burnt to the ground."

The axis which was eventually reopened to traffic during the afternoon of the 23rd of September was again cut south of Veghel on the 24th by elements of 6th Parachute Regiment. Therefore Major Daly's Squadron, still under command of 32nd Brigade, continued chasing rumours and enemy throughout the next day.

Much German activity was reported both from the Gennep crossing and farther north at Cuyk, close to which place Lieutenant Routledge's Troop lost a scout car to a bazooka, both members of the crew being taken prisoner. It was subsequently learnt that Trooper Albert Smith, the driver, who had been seriously wounded, died in captivity on the following day. Corporal Scambler, the car commander, kept a careful diary of his subsequent days as a prisoner of war, and part of this has been included in Appendix A.

★   ★   ★

There were now signs that the Germans were becoming worried by the impending arrival on our right flank of 8 Corps, advanced elements of which were already driving the enemy northwards and compelling them to seek flight over the Maas. This was the chance for which "A" Squadron had been waiting, and Major Daly's patrols continued to harry the hard-pressed Germans from the west until a considerable haul of prisoners had been made.

The remainder of the Regiment was now in reserve in the Nijmegen area, living off captured German rations and grumbling at having to eat the quite excellent Oss liver paste for breakfast in lieu of those revolting baked beans.

"C" Squadron moved into first-class barracks which, although badly damaged by bombing, were in the main habitable. These were up to date, light and airy, with plenty of baths, and gave us all an idea of how much better the continental neutral countries, who never expected to have to fight, looked after the comforts of their peacetime soldiery than we did in Britain.

"B" Squadron, although officially in reserve and resting, were stationed some way to the south of Nijmegen on the main axis and close to Grave bridge, for there was a possibility that they might be called upon to support "A" Squadron should the Germans choose to step up their raids on the centre line. "D" Squadron were still harboured in the woods south of Nijmegen, as were Headquarter Squadron.

There was no shortage of female collaborators in Nijmegen, and these erring women were marshalled together under the strict supervision of black uniformed Dutch officials and ordered to sweep and scrub the barracks and billets until they shone.

Humber Scout Car

Chapter III

OSS Incident

The Divisional Intelligence Summary was in excellent form with its issue of the 24th of September. It stated that it was only "remnants of a Panzer Division" which had cut the precious centre line. The morale of the German Army was to all intents and purposes "non-existent," and, in a final burst of wishful thinking, "as for the left flank, nothing but elderly river guards were manning the defences along 53 Grid Line." It may have been these reassuring thoughts which decided Major Ward, as he sat under the dripping trees in Nijmegen woods, to send his echelon commander, Lieutenant Hughes, on a journey to Oss. The Squadron had exhausted its first allocation of sugar, and besides, Oss reputedly contained some excellent apricot brandy.

Regimental Headquarters, thinking on similar lines, were preparing to send out a party under Lieutenant Winterbottom. The latter was already familiar with the food dump, having noted on a previous visit that the "Dutch factory 'Direktor' owned some good sherry, had a concealed wireless set which he turned on full blast to London (rather tactlessly in view of the proximity of the enemy), and ran the Underground telephone network from his offices."

There were in actual fact three Wehrmacht dumps in Oss—two under the control of the Schwaanenburg factory, containing tinned foods, bacon, meat and carboys of Bols gin; and one, the Philips factory, which was a sort of welfare dump for the German Army, and also contained Bols gin as well as a great quantity of maraschino and apricot brandy, cigars, sugar, etc.

The final party detailed for the journey consisted of Lieutenant Winterbottom and his driver, Trooper Bishop, in a scout car, accompanied by a three-tonner lorry and a 15-cwt. truck with crews; Lieutenant Hughes and his driver, Trooper Royle, in the "Gin Palace"; and a French interpreter named René Cournault, who, attaching himself to the Regiment when in France, had liked the job and remained on ever since. He brought his private Citroen car which he had picked up somewhere from the retreating Germans.

The Winterbottom-Hughes cavalcade eventually joined up with another large Oss-bound convoy assembled together by Guards

Armoured Division and escorted by some "A" Squadron cars under the command of Captain Profumo.

The outward journey passed off uneventfully, and the main convoy halted on the outskirts of Oss while a Troop made a cursory reconnaissance of the Schwaanenburg factory, which lay alongside a railway line. Meanwhile another party, headed by Lieutenants Hughes and Winterbottom, went off on their own half a mile farther on to the Philips factory, taking only the "Gin Palace" and Citroen, and leaving the rest of their vehicles with the main convoy.

The Philips factory consisted of a large three-storeyed red brick building also with railway lines running into it. The whole was enclosed by a high wall surmounted with villainous spikes. Proceeding with caution, the party made contact with a Dutch overseer dressed in the favoured black uniform and leggings very similar to the S.S. troops. The yard in front of the factory was seething with Resistance men wearing orange armbands and carrying rifles. Among them were also "those Charlie Chaplin cops with curious helmets." Everybody was talking at the same time.

The "Direktor," in fact one of Philips's porters, told Winterbottom that the German Quartermaster at s'Hertogenbosch had that moment telephoned saying that he was coming over immediately to replenish his stocks. Only with the greatest difficulty had he been persuaded to postpone his visit with the story that "the storekeeper was away for the day in Eindhoven." The "Direktor" was naturally concerned about his fate should the Germans discover the falsehood, but Winterbottom reassured him by saying that the British were there in "immense" strength. He also explained the rather obvious reasons for the visit but took some time in so doing. "In fact," added Hughes, "Ian Winterbottom took far too long, yobbing away in German. On my venturing to remonstrate he explained the delay as being part of his 'velvet glove policy,' but I suspect that he was in reality rather proud of his German! Much more to the point, René Cournault kept prancing around gesticulating and urging, 'vite, mais vite alors, it faut agir, it faut agir!' "

Eventually Winterbottom slipped off to bring up his R.H.Q. lorries while the remainder under Hughes went inside to examine the stores, with the "Direktor" and another man carrying a large ledger in which he jotted down details of the transactions. This ledger was already crammed with German signatures, interspersed between which were a few rather lonely-looking British names.

The yard outside was now empty, and a brooding silence descended over the building.

What followed has been gathered from Lieutenant Hughes's personal story.

"We made our selection and had started to pile up the stuff on to a hand trolley preparatory to loading up the 'Gin Palace' when something made me look up. I saw my driver, wide mouthed with surprise, silently pointing out of the doorway at the far end of the store room. As I moved across I saw to my horror four or five huge Germans purposefully moving about the yard in single file. Many more were behind, and in their tin helmets they looked extremely sinister and business-like. They had arrived in a lorry and were well armed. We only had our service revolvers. Somewhere in the back of the 'Gin Palace' was our Bren gun of doubtful vintage.

"Some of the Germans had already spotted the 'Gin Palace' and were nosing about it suspiciously. Meanwhile Cournault, the 'Direktor,' the two drivers and myself had slipped quietly out by a back door to make a plan. Of the Dutch Resistance there was now no sign—they had vanished into thin air.

"After a brief conference, conducted in hoarse whispers, it was ascertained that the 'Direktor' possessed a key to the back door of the warehouse but not to that of another gate through the wall. This wall was at least ten feet high with spikes on top. However, in spite of this formidable obstacle, we all leapt over it with ease and on to the road beyond, after which the Direktor' must have 'filed' away on his own, for we did not see him again.

"After a while I began to think that what we had taken to be Germans might conceivably have been Americans on the scrounge like us—with Airborne helmets of vaguely similar shape, a mistake in identity was perhaps possible? So the three of us moved warily into a near-by house and from a first-floor window looked down into the warehouse yard. It was overflowing with Germans. One great brute was even doing the 'Lower Star Post crouch'[1] under our very window! As clearly the enemy were about to 'seek, find and destroy,' we decided to retreat yet farther and took up a new position of observation on top of a haystack in a neighbouring farm. There we hid to await developments.

"It may have been three hours or only three-quarters of an hour that we remained there—it certainly felt a very long time. Every so often one of us would take a turn and peep over the top of the stack to see what was happening. I began to wonder whether I should have carried

---

1. 'Lower Star Post crouch' – A term coined by cadets at Sandhurst during the war to denote the bent attitude affected by them on exercises in order to satisfy Instructors and Umpires that their scheme was being taken seriously, Lower Star Post being a favourite hide-out for Umpires. Immediate adoption of the crouch was the only effective counter to the cry. "You're under fire, what are you going to do about it?". *Author.*

the battle into the enemy camp by some daring counter-stroke, but no plan appeared feasible … there were an awful lot of Germans in the yard below!

"We lay full length on the sloping side of the haystack discussing in whispers how long a letter might take to reach England from a German prisoner-of-war camp. 'In war,' I remarked to Cournault, 'nothing matters but the safety of one's kit. So long as I can keep my bedroll, all is well. If we get out of this safely, what do you most wish to find again?" 'Ah,' said the Frenchman with Gallic fervour, 'mon képi pour la défilée à Berlin.'

"Our reflections were suddenly interrupted by the sounds of foot-steps approaching, closer and closer. We gripped our revolvers, prepared for the worst. Then, to our unutterable relief, a hen ran across our front and we realized that what we had been hearing was her scratchings in the litter at the foot of the stack.

"A moment later the noise of firing and shouting and general pandemonium broke out, and to our gratification we saw the German lorry whizz past our haystack in full flight. After that, complete silence once more. We decided to 'do a recce' and crept round the wall to our right, and there to our great relief met Philip Profumo, who had arrived complete with Staghounds. It was his cars which had put the Germans to flight.

"He found that the enemy had obligingly loaded up the 'Gin Palace' for us, leaving the engine running, but the Dutch Resistance, who had reappeared as suddenly as they had vanished, were about to drive it off in their turn and we were only just in time to stop them! As for poor Cournault's Citroen, it had come off badly in the battle and lay riddled with bullets from the Staghound and all four tyres were flat. Cournault was heart-broken, but at least he did get back his blue and gold braided *képi*, which was still in the back seat intact."

Through the Burgomaster of Oss, it was possible in later years to trace what had become of the harassed "Direktor." He proved to be alive and well, having suffered no ill effects either from his high jump over the spikes or from the Germans. Alphons Hendrick Snoek (for such was his name) remembered the Oss incident vividly, and wrote me the following letter. His version is worth recording:

OSS.
15th November, 1948.
At the time of the liberation of Oss (September, 1944) I was Chief-Porter of N. V. Philip's Factories, settled at Oss. In these factories the Germans had a food store in which lots of spirits was gathered too. When Oss was

liberated for a few days an English Military truck and a civil car appeared at the entrance to the factories. This civil car belonged to a French officer who was accompanied by an English officer. After having made acquaintance we all together went to the stores, which lied on a distance of about 40 yards from the entrance. When we were a while in the stores outside was called to us, "the Germans are at the entrance." At first we would not believe this, but when there was called again we looked through the window and saw outside at the entrance on about 40 yards of our store a big truck, with a lot of German soldiers on it. I also saw that these Germans had their guns ready for firing and some of them even had a Bren gun. As we saw that we stood imponent against this superior power, the best of all for us was to remove as quick as possible. We sneaked through the store and along the wall of the building. We hastened us to the surrounding wall on the other side of the factories. In normal times it is very difficult to jump over this wall, but now it went as quick as if we were greyhounds. In this way I got on the street and went as quick as possible to my pension to expect the coming things. Later I heard that the officers after a few hours came back to the entrance, found their cars still there, and got back to their sub-division just as if nothing had happened at all.

(Signed) ALPHONS HENDRICK SNOEK.

That evening "D" Squadron were delighted to welcome back their echelon officer, but it would hardly be correct to say that he appeared "as if nothing has happened at all." He was nevertheless able to do full justice to a hearty meal of tinned goulash and apricot brandy. In addition, as most of the regiment were still in reserve, he was assured of a good night's rest, wrapped in his own bedroll and with all his kit, including his treasured set of cut-throat razors, carefully laid out by the faithful "Old Bill."[2]

Next morning early, a new Divisional Summary for the past twenty-four hours was circulated. There was only passing reference to activities on the left flank, but the relevant paragraph read as follows: "South of the Maas enemy inf. approached OSS from the WEST this afternoon and were seen off by our armoured cars. They did NOT get near the important food dump at OSS which is reported as being very large indeed." It was tactfully arranged that the echelon commander should not be shown the offending document, but be allowed to sleep on undisturbed.

---

2. Trooper G. B. Taylor, known to all the Squadron as "Old Bill".

Chapter IV

Continued Patrols to the West

Withdrawal of Arnhem bridgehead—Heesch cross-roads—Corporal Ray's action—Maas patrols—"D" Squadron at Leur—Underwater attack on Nijmegen bridge—Refitting—"D" Squadron work for 52nd Division—German raids on farms in Tiel area—Methods to combat this nuisance—Food poisoning at Leur.

On the morning of the 25th of September, Field-Marshal Montgomery reluctantly gave the order to withdraw the gallant remnants of the Airborne Division. The position had become virtually untenable owing to casualties and shortage of supplies. "Furthermore, there was little prospect of expanding the bridgehead as reinforcements could only be got over on a limited scale in assault boats under cover of darkness, across a stretch of river which was completely dominated both from north-east and north-west. Also, owing to the enemy operations against the Corps axis there was a shortage of assault boats and artillery ammunition."[1]

We had become accustomed to the comforting thunder of our own artillery whenever there had been a hold-up in the Normandy campaign. Now this support was noticeably reduced and the long silent intervals were depressing in their import.

Throughout the night of 25th/26th of September a battalion of the Dorsetshire Regiment operated to cover the withdrawal of the 1st British Airborne Division, whose remnants were now concentrated in the Oosterbeek area north of the Neder Rijn. As heavy an artillery programme as circumstances permitted was laid on in support. The Field Artillery were to fire available ammunition down to 25 rounds per gun. By the greatest courage and skill, 2,323 Airborne troops were safely brought across the river, but only at the cost of 200 men of the Dorsets, who had ensured the success of the evacuation. Thus ended the audacious but ill-fated attempt to reach the Zuider Zee.

The question of whether, as a whole, the "Market-Garden" operation was worth the results is for discussion on an altogether different plane. Opinion is still divided on the subject, certainly in the United States, where unfortunately the ill-informed verdict of Mr. Ralph Ingersoll that

---

1. *A Short History of 30 Corps in the European Campaign*, p. 38.

it gave the British another opportunity to stage a second Charge of the Light Brigade gained a certain amount of publicity.[2] At least the heroism of the British Airborne, those men whose gallant exploits have made history, will never be called into question.

The conclusion of the Arnhem operation signified the end of a definite phase, and all the *élan* of the Allied drive was now to bog down into the stagnation of winter warfare. At all headquarters consolidation and build-up diagrams replaced the maps and sweeping arrows of advance. Mobile bath units caught up, there was talk of forty-eight hours' leave to Brussels, and the local cinema opened up with an Esther Williams film whose title escapes me, though the accompanying posters exhorted us to come and journey with "six feet of thrilling torso through thrashing tropic seas." Renewed orders from Rear Base for the surrender of our finest captured cars met with the same lack of response as previously, for we knew only too well that under their new owners they would only grace the curb outside the Elysée bar in Brussels.

"B" Squadron, who had relieved "A" Squadron during the evening of the 24th September, continued routine patrolling in the protection of the centre line. This was not now an onerous task and consisted in sending out Troops radiating in a circle from Grave. However, contact was made with the enemy to the east and patrols reported a growing flow of traffic moving towards the River Maas through the village of St. Antonis. Urgent requests for Typhoon support to strafe the convoys met with the reply that these were already engaged farther north in aiding the Arnhem evacuation, and so the armoured cars continued on their own, severely mauling transport and capturing many prisoners.

8 Corps was in the process of arriving on the right flank, and during the afternoon of the 25th of September, patrols of the Inns of Court Regiment were met in the area of Gemert.

★   ★   ★

In the west, the Foot Guards, particularly the Grenadiers, were becoming involved in some heavy fighting around the cross-roads at Heesch. It was to take a full-scale attack by their tanks and infantry before the enemy was finally eradicated at the end of the month. Heesch lay on the main road, about half-way between s'Hertogenbosch and Grave. It is doubtful whether the enemy ever consciously wished to retain control of Heesch,

---

2. *Top Secret* by Ralph Ingersoll—a sensationalist piece of anti-British journalese by an American newspaper man attached to one of their Army Group Headquarters.

but lying as it did on an important route back to Germany, retreating columns continually attempted to force their way to the Maas by passing through it. In addition, 12 Corps, now approaching on the left flank, were driving the Germans before them. It was at this period that Lance-Corporal Ray, of "B" Squadron had a notable encounter with the enemy in the area. A strong force of 712 Division coming in from the west, and probably unaware of the true situation, had clashed with the Grenadier group, then holding the village. Ray had been ordered to patrol a certain exit road to give warning of the approach of any further body from the same direction. He was in a concealed position in a scout car on his own when he sighted a column of about forty Germans on bicycles and armed with bazookas, machine guns and rifles, approaching in two files—one on each side of the road.

Manoeuvring into a good position, he waited until the first file was directly in his line of vision, then opened fire with his Bren gun. With the exception of two men all were either killed or wounded as they frantically scrambled off their machines and into the ditch. Meanwhile those from the other file had managed to take cover in the ditch and behind a fence at the opposite side of the road and were in the process of stalking the scout car. But by ignoring the hastily fired bazookas, Corporal Ray was able to back his car and move across on a line with the ditch. The Germans now found themselves huddled in a straight line one behind the other, many unable to fire for fear of hitting the man in front. However, they refused his offer to accept surrender, and eventually out of forty-odd men only three lived to escape across the fields.

On the 26th of September there was a sharp bombing attack on the Nijmegen road bridge and the traffic roundabout, and S.Q.M.C. Ralph Sergeant and Trooper Stanley Graves, both of "C" Squadron, were killed. Two days later a further bombing raid hit Headquarter Squadron area during breakfast, wounding ten Household Cavalrymen, including Corporals-of-Horse Hayward and Simpson.

With heavy commitments on both flanks of the centre line, 32nd Brigade tended to employ the armoured cars in ever-widening sweeps both to the east and west. Patrols went out at the crack of dawn and continued operating until darkness. Liaison was again made with the Inns of Court Regiment, who, although firmly established on the right flank, were not yet in complete control of the Boxmeer—Gennep—Cuyk sector of the Maas. This part of the country was to remain a source of general annoyance to the British for many more days, but passed out of the regimental zone of responsibility now that 8 Corps had arrived.

To the west the Germans still continued to offer strong resistance to the Grenadier group attacking the village of Heesch. One hundred and sixty prisoners had been taken during the afternoon of the 26th and a large number killed and wounded, but in spite of these losses the Germans were still in occupation of the western half of the village on the morning of the 27th.

"D" Squadron had by now relieved "A" Squadron in this area and were still operating under command of 32nd Brigade. Lieutenant Jonkheer Groeninx van Zoelen was ordered to make contact with the Grenadier group at first light and find out their requirements for the day's patrolling. On arrival the Troop Leader was informed by the infantry that things were fairly sticky by the cross-roads and there was considerable enemy mortaring coming from the village.

The Troop advanced warily, with the eventual task of striking west towards s'Hertogenbosch and reporting on what reinforcements the enemy appeared to be sending into Heesch. After proceeding for about a mile the leading scout car encountered a party of about ten Germans, who were fired on by Corporal Hart as they came running out of a house. The next moment there was a bright flash and an explosion and the scout car became an inferno of blazing petrol. It had been hit by an A.P. shot which killed Corporal Henry Hart and travelled through the engine to set alight the petrol tank. Seeing that there was nothing he could do for his commander, whose death had been instantaneous, Trooper Gee bailed out and ran back under fire to Corporal Wilson's car, which, with Groeninx van Zoelen's Daimler, had come forward to cover him. How Gee escaped the enemy bullets at such close range will remain a mystery. After a brief rest he was back at work in another scout car, only to be knocked out again shortly afterwards. Gee was to have five scout cars knocked out under him. He remain unscathed throughout, and his nerve to the last was apparently as good as ever.

German resistance at Heesch having hardened, the rest of the Troop was unable to move farther west, and on news of the Grenadiers preparing a set-piece attack on Heesch from the north, Groeninx van Zoelen was ordered back to Squadron Headquarters. The village continued to hold out for another day, after which the remnants of the enemy withdrew, having yielded up to the Grenadiers a total of some three hundred prisoners besides many killed and wounded.

With the point of contact between 8 Corps and 30 Corps established at St. Antonis, the need for further patrolling by the Regiment east of the centre line ceased altogether. "A" Squadron's relief of "D" Squadron on the 28th was a mere formality. Only one patrol was called out and saw nothing of importance on its tour of duty. By the 29th of September, the entire Regiment was at rest.

★ ★ ★

There was a general atmosphere of settling down into winter quarters at the end of the month. The side streets of Nijmegen were lined with the cumbersome DUKWs no longer required for immediate use. More cinemas opened for the troops, and at Grave a general regimental reshuffle took place. Regimental Headquarters, still as faithful as ever to their love of fresh air, moved to Neerbosch by the banks of the Waal–Maas canal, and shivered in tents, while Sabre Squadrons made themselves snug in warm billets and barns. They were well spread out, but not too far from R.H.Q. for essential administrative purposes.

"A" Squadron were just off the main road near Grave bridge, "B" in the outskirts of Nijmegen; "C" had elected to remain on in their barracks with the female collaborators to look after their needs. "D" Squadron undoubtedly drew the best location when billeted in the village of Leur, eight miles from Nijmegen and quite unharmed by war.

Leur church was a beautiful little thirteenth-century building surrounded by trees. It boasted a small and squat belfry constructed of deep red brick of the mellowness which many Dutch churches in the district appeared to possess. Surmounting the church was a graceful and ornate weathercock whose gilded plumage seemed almost to wave in the autumnal breezes. The interior was simple yet in no way puritanical. Four ancient murals could still be faintly discerned, and against one of the walls a stone marked the high-water level of the famous flood of 1729.

Here, in this atmosphere of calm simplicity, Padre Moore conducted a regimental church service by permission of the Dutch Protestant minister. It was the first time since landing in Europe that the Regiment had been able to attend a service indoors, and Captain Ford was there once again to accompany the hymns. He was always a great stand-by on these occasions, being equally at home at the organ or piano.

★ ★ ★

During the early hours of the 29th of September an underwater attack was carried out on both the road and railway bridges at Nijmegen. It was only partially successful, and of the twelve men who took part, ten were captured and one killed. The men belonged to the German Navy and were said to have been specially trained for such a job in Venice. They were briefed and entered the water at about midnight from their own lines about six miles upstream. They were in two parties, one for each bridge, carrying two torpedoes per party. After surmounting a barbed-wire obstacle which one of the prisoners said he found on the river bed, the frogmen rode their torpedoes to their respective bridges. However, the current proved too strong for the road bridge party, which was forced to fire its torpedoes prematurely after having laid them horizontally alongside one of the stone piers.[3] The men then swam away downstream with orders to land at Ochten, thirteen miles distant, but something went wrong and they fell into British hands instead. The damage to the railway bridge was severe and was never repaired, but the road bridge, which was found to have a gap of some 90 feet, was soon spanned by Bailey bridging.

★　★　★

The first ten days in October were spent in resting and refitting and some hastily snatched twenty-four hours' leaves when transport was available to Brussels.

In turns, one Squadron at a time remained at four hours' notice in support of 52nd Reconnaissance Regiment (52nd Division), which had lately arrived and was now responsible for the defence of the western flank between the Maas and the Waal. The arrangement was that the armoured cars were not to be called upon unless an enemy attack threatened to develop into something more than a local skirmish. Only "D" Squadron Troops, who, being at Leur, were therefore closer than anyone else, had any work to do, and this was generally of a most vague and nebulous order, normally ending in the collection of vast quantities of eggs and the dispelling of rumours.

The country west of Leur was most attractive and much less populated than other parts of Holland. It was dotted with small mixed farms and villages dominated by huge churches. The weather was fine on the whole and days closed with glorious sunsets. There was a refreshing absence of military notices (except on the cross-roads in Leur, where outside the officers' mess were forty-seven unit direction posts!), and the only visible sign of war lay in the relays of Allied planes passing overhead to bomb the Ruhr. These could be seen running into German flak put up over Wesel or even far away Duisburg, the largest inland port in Europe.

Birds were migrating southwards in their thousands, and it was possible to motor miles along the river banks of a Ruisdael country of

---

3. The torpedoes were intended to be automatically armed by being stood on end.

windmills and waterways without encountering a soul apart from an occasional Keeshond dog chained to a lock gate or a few children playing by a barge.

The district, bounded by the two rivers, was only lightly held, and the Germans on the northern bank of the Waal used to row over at will by night to terrorize the inhabitants and loot the villages of pigs and poultry. Wamel, lying opposite Tiel, came in for a good deal of attention. A favourite trick of the Germans was to toss a hand grenade through the window of the last sleeping cottage before re-embarking. Any villager who had been too friendly with the British stood the risk of being carried off as hostage. In their fear of reprisals, the poor farmers naturally exaggerated the strength of the enemy marauding parties, and reports of an increasingly alarming nature kept coming through to "D" Squadron.

On the 2nd of October, the outposts of 52nd Reconnaissance Regiment reported that they had had an encounter with the enemy and had lost a carrier and a D.R. Their appreciation was that the enemy might be preparing to come over with a strong raiding party because considerable activity had been noticed in the area of Tiel. However, preliminary reconnaissance by "D" Squadron Troops failed to find any trace of enemy on the south side of the river. More as a help to civilian morale than with any hope of catching Germans, on the following day Major Ward ordered out Lieutenants Hanbury's and Buchanan-Jardine's Troops.

These found the Dutch peasants in a great state of "flap," and nothing would satisfy them until an elaborate search had been carried out. Some of the local farmers felt, not without justification, that the British patrolled their lands in daytime, pumped them for information about German-held localities across the river, strafed the enemy until he had been thoroughly irritated, and then retired to their comfortable billets for the night, leaving the defenceless Dutch to foot the bill and endure the inevitable reprisals.

However, on this occasion Lieutenant Hanbury decided that the two Troops would put on a demonstration of strength to impress the nervous farmers. Very pistols were fired across the water, mingled with tracer ammunition and smoke of all descriptions, including most of the yellow recognition smoke which our Allied Air Forces so studiously ignored. Lieutenant Buchanan-Jardine's Troop attacked a hen house suspected of harbouring Germans. This also was carried out with maximum showmanship in conjunction with 52nd Reconnaissance Regiment, everybody, including a D.R. in the lead, firing their weapons for all they were worth. The conclusion of the attack, a running commentary of which was relayed back to Squadron Headquarters by Lieutenant Hanbury, was veiled in mystery because the Troop Leader was seized by one of his uncontrollable fits of laughter and became unintelligible even to Major Ward. Operation "Henhouse," which resulted in no Germans and no casualties, was, however, a great boost to civilian morale. The general effect exceeded all expectations and no other Troop was ever needlessly called out again from the comfortable Leur billets.

★   ★   ★

On another occasion, 52nd Division outposts wirelessed that they had encountered a fairly strong raiding party near Wamel, had lost several carriers and suffered some casualties. It was thought that the enemy had crossed by using a large ferry and, as there were then no guns on call to the Division, could we help? Major Ward ordered Lieutenant Jonkheer Groeninx van Zoelen's Troop and Lieutenant Clark's Heavy Troop to the spot immediately. By the time they got there, all was quiet and the enemy had flown.

"However," wrote Groeninx van Zoelen, "by far the most terrifying thing I have ever had to do was to climb the high steeple of the village church, as the last part was up extremely small but very long ladders." From this lofty perch the river could be observed over a distance of many miles, and as an O.P. for the Heavy Troop guns it was unequalled. The suspect ferry could be seen moored to the bank, and Lieutenant Clark moved off to destroy it. He reported that:

> "After immense expenditure of shells we sunk it at its moorings on the north bank, destroyed several other boats and then returned home. On the way back I had an unpleasant experience, that of being trapped under a scout car upside down in a dyke, the result of a driving accident. I got myself into a position where I could get my nose out of the water, but my driver, Trooper Buckley, was pinned head down by the sandbags falling on top of him. Corporal-of-Horse Connor by a very prompt bit of towing pulled the scout car upright, but not before Buckley had stopped breathing. Fortunately, there was at hand a Dutchman who was expert at artificial respiration; after considerable pumping he brought a gallon or so of water and duckweed out of Buckley. The weed was followed by a spate of the worst possible barrack-room language. Thus we knew that Buckley was alive. He went back to England with a collapsed lung and double pneumonia but returned in the spring to join 'C' Squadron. I returned to the mess immediately for an enormous whisky!"

Leur witnessed a strange case of food poisoning which, with the exception of Captain Waterhouse on leave, Major Ward at R.H.Q., where he had gone to dine, and one other officer, was to knock out the entire "D" Squadron officers' mess. It was put down, although never actually proved, to some soup made from tinned kidneys from Oss. After one mouthful only, each taster in turn felt unwell, sweated profusely, and retired to sit doubled up in agony in a corner. Groeninx van Zoelen, the only person present who had not yet eaten, wirelessed for Captain Kynaston, who on arrival with that familiar pained but sympathetic expression on his face was greeted with wan smiles from his patients, still crawling about the floor. Nobody succumbed, and I was the quickest to recover, having wisely swallowed the front page of the *Daily Mirror* as an emetic.

Recovery in every case proved rapid and complete. A full official report was sent in by Captain Kynaston to the proper authorities, who felt that this might be the sinister prelude to an outbreak of mass poisoning of British soldiers by fifth column agents! But nothing came of it. Someone seemed to remember that the kidneys had had a curious white powdery appearance before they had been cooked, so it was decided to blame the kidneys and leave it at that. It may be that the Germans ousted from Oss were having the last laugh after all.

Chapter V

"SHAEF"

"Shaef" Period—The Regiment under command 8 Corps, October and November, 1944—Watch on the Maas—"Shaef" waxes stronger and stronger—Daily patrols and problems of using armoured cars at night—The Heavy Troops on their mettle— German night patrols blow up the best O.Ps., civilian collaboration suspected— Captain Wrottesley's Troop captures bogus British truckload of Germans near Beugen—Diary of a Support Troop officer—A night with "D" Squadron echelon on patrol, recollections of Corporal Meade-King—Lieutenant van Cutsem becomes one of Field-Marshal Montgomery's liaison officers—Lieutenant-General Sir Richard O'Connor's letter of appreciation to Colonel Abel Smith—Return to 30 Corps and move to Belgium

By the beginning of October it appeared probable that the Germans would aim at stabilizing the front north of the Waal, and at the same time continue to do their utmost to deny to the Allies the use of Antwerp as a port by holding on to the Scheldt estuary. For the Allies, the prize remained the Ruhr. Delays and set-backs were increasingly to cause alterations of plan, but this remained the ultimate objective.

The project of clearing the area between the Rhine and the Maas, as a preliminary to striking at the Ruhr, came to be known as "The Battle for the Rhineland," but before this could take place it was necessary to do some large-scale mopping up.

West of the Maas, occupying an area known as the Peel Marshes,[1] the enemy was in greater strength than had been anticipated, and he evidently intended to fight hard to retain the bridgehead. The country favoured defensive tactics, and the one American armoured division which had come up from as far south as Metz to deal with the enemy west of Venlo was clearly insufficient for the task. As events transpired, two Corps (8 and 12) were to become involved before the Germans were finally driven back across the river in December.

To complete the general picture, it is worth remembering that not until the last day in September did Calais fall, thus only then freeing

---

1. Peel Marshes – the full area occupied by the enemy Maas bridgehead at the beginning of October, and this included the Peel Marshes, was from Boxmeer in the north, Overloon, Deurne, roughly to west of Meijel, then along the Noorer canal to its junction with the Bois le Duc canal east of Weert, thence south to Maeseyck (see Map 12).

the Canadians for the clearance of the Scheldt. 8 Corps, by now well-established east of the axis up to the banks of the Maas to as far south as Boxmeer, was ordered to clear the Peel bridgehead by attacking southwards towards Venlo. If successful this would mean that 8 Corps would be saddled with an exposed left flank bordering on the Maas, of over forty miles in length. To help protect part of this flank, the Regiment was lent from Guards Armoured Division, and passed temporarily to under command of 11th Armoured Division, with whom we had not worked since Normandy days. We were assured that the job was to last but a few days; in fact the Regiment did not rejoin Guards Armoured Division until a month later.

The period which follows came to be known in the Regiment, and by many outside people as well, as the era of "Shaef"—a somewhat facetious if apt designation coined by 8 Corps Headquarters because of the assortment of arms and variety of units which Colonel Abel Smith was gradually able to collect under his command. It can best be dealt with in general terms with isolated actions and minor incidents taken at random to illustrate the character of the operations.

Throughout the weather remained uniformly vile, and Squadrons relieved one another in their chosen locations with a regularity bordering on the monotonous. The War Diary describes the job as being "interesting." There was certainly no shortage of hard work for the Troops, particularly the support Troops, who proved invaluable in all the night patrolling that had to be carried out.

The Regiment moved from the Nijmegen area to take over from the 3rd Reconnaissance Regiment on the Maas on the 11th of October. Regimental Headquarters set itself up in the village of Wanroij. Headquarter Squadron under Major Williams was located centrally and comfortably in the village of Haps, Major Williams sharing a house with a large quantity of Dutch children and even greater number of Friesian cows.

For two or three days minor adjustments in frontage and dispositions were made to conform with the advances of 8 Corps, but when settled the regimental area of responsibility stretched from Groeningen (inclusive) to Cuyk (inclusive), a distance of twelve miles as the crow flies, but considerably more when the bends of the river were taken into account.

The Regiment operated three Squadrons up and one in reserve. To the south, patrols radiated from Squadron Headquarters situated in a damp, evil-smelling farmhouse west of the village of Boxmeer. In the centre they worked from a disused brickyard, sinister and deserted save for one old night watchman who was suspected of being in touch with the enemy and of concealing a wireless antennae in the stump of his wooden leg. At the northern extremity the operating Squadron patrolled from a small café by a level crossing outside Cuyk, whence the Germans could undoubtedly hear every word of the wireless messages shouted back into the No. 19 Set. 8 Corps stressed the point that if the regimental sector were attacked from across the river, we were to be prepared to hold out for twenty-four hours before reinforcements could arrive.

The sector proved relatively quiet, although the Germans still had two small bridgeheads within it—one near Boxmeer and Sambeek and the other close to Gennep, where the girders of a partially blown railway bridge across the Maas afforded a good approach for the enemy to slip reinforcements into a complicated trench system on the home side. Neither bridgehead had yet been eliminated by 8 Corps because the Germans dominated the ground from the far bank and could row over at will during the night.

Broadly speaking, "Shaef" grew in relation to the southward progress of 8 Corps, and although each addition to its strength gave rise to still more facetious remarks at Corps, generally led by Captain Garnett as liaison officer, the laughter soon died when it was appreciated how useful the added manpower could be to help cover the large front at night.

Here, taken from the War Diary, is the record of "Shaef's" growth to power.

On the 14th of October it became officially known as the "2 H.C.R. Group" and was composed of the Regiment, with under command 3rd Reconnaissance Regiment and the Inns of Court Regiment (less two Squadrons). When two days later 11th Armoured Division moved south and 3rd Division became responsible for 8 Corps' flank, more troops were allotted to "Shaef." These were the 91st (Argyll and Sutherland Highlanders) Anti-Tank Regiment, two batteries of which were self-propelled guns and one battery towed. Also a carrier-borne company of four 4.2-inch mortars and another of medium machine guns, both from the Middlesex Regiment. In support was a battery of 25-pounders from the 25th Field Regiment, R.A., as well as some heavy ack-ack guns from 8 A.G.R.A.

On the 18th of October two platoons of searchlights cheerfully reported for duty, and goodness knows what night operation the "Jeepers" might not have been called upon to undertake by the aid of their artificial moonlight had they not been, as the Adjutant regretfully notes, "whisked away before they could be used."

In no way discouraged by this set-back, Colonel Abel Smith somehow managed within the next two days to lay his hands on a Flight of Air

O.Ps. from Corps! In fact, during the last days of October and well into November, "Shaef" waxed stronger and stronger. Sapper parties arrived to help the Support Troops in their work of mining, de-mining and booby-trapping roads and buildings, and the approaches to our strong-points became so labyrinthine and dangerous that a journey to Regimental Headquarters without previous consultation with "Nipper"[2] was tantamount to suicide.

The C.C.R.A. lent eighty men from the 121st L.A.A. Regiment, R.A., who performed invaluable work in helping with the night patrolling. On the 3rd of November, the Royals came under command, taking over the Inns of Court sector to the south.

"Shaef attained its apogee on the 9th of November when 450 men of the 63rd Anti-Tank Regiment (Oxfordshire Yeomanry) took their place in the line with a Dutch company. The latter were preceded by a booklet which laid down how they were equipped and armed and contained the reassuring statement that some of them had fired off their weapon "at least twice."

★ ★ ★

The Dutch are a prolific race, even under the most adverse circumstances of occupation, and initially, vacant accommodation was not easy to find. However, after some searching and squeezing, the Regiment was able to get under cover of barns and other farmhouse shelters. A house and adjoining buildings in the village of St. Hubert served as most comfortable billets for whichever Squadron was at rest.

As might be expected, the country was absolutely flat and frequently waterlogged, and most of the fields leading up to the Maas were surrounded by earthen banks topped in places by bushes. This did not aid observation and frequently resulted in vehicles bogging themselves badly while searching for enemy patrols.

Daily, as soon as light made it possible, Troops would sally forth from their headquarters and make for the Maas. Scout cars would link up with friends on the flank and the Troop Leaders, after satisfying themselves that there were no Germans in their sector, would take their cars to a suitable observation post, conceal the vehicles from view, and settle down to a steady watch of the opposite bank.

Civilians would bring in their stories of Germans roaming through the villages during the night. Sometimes it would be that a hostage had

---

2. Lieutenant Wordsworth, whose Support Troop was responsible for mining and booby-trapping.

Night Patrol. Öeffelt. Oct/44

WATCH ON THE MAAS

2nd H.C.R. night patrol at a listening post. Behind the railway embankment can be seen the beam of one of the searchlights used to produce artificial moonlight.

been taken, at other times of an enemy threat as to what they would do to them when they returned in force to drive back the British for good. The Germans were always plugging this tale, and its propaganda effect on civilians later on when the Ardennes counter-offensive started was very strong.

At night time it was only too easy for the odd German patrols to cross over the river, lie hidden up all day, and do their damage the following night, but it was impossible in the limited time and with the number of men available to search all houses over an area of fifty square miles.

Church towers, windmills, and in particular St. Agatha's, a monastery near Cuyk, all made excellent O.Ps. The Germans were well aware of this, and although they rarely shelled them during the day, soon found a much better method of neutralizing them, as we shall read later on.

Some days were full of incident, many others boring in the extreme; according to temperament, one hoped for one or the other. Seated in the top storey of a high building or church belfry, the Troop Leader would drop a long lead to his scout car below and send back his reports when anything stirred on the other side of the river. The work was a great drain on wireless batteries, for it was not always politic to risk giving away a good O.P. with the noise of running engines, but the Corps of Signals were equal to the task and the battery-charging lorries were kept hard at it.

As soon as German activity was spotted, a message would be relayed back to Regimental Headquarters, who were all pining to set the cogs of "Shaef" in motion. The 25-pounder guns would be warned to stand by for action, the Heavy Troops would energetically pound away at buildings and suspicious-looking sheds on the far bank, and even the ack-ack batteries, tired of staring into empty skies, would depress muzzles in anticipatory relish of being asked to join in the fun. "In fact," wrote a Household Cavalryman, "such was the degree of offensive activity which one solitary German soldier could unwittingly call down upon himself, that no one would have been in the least surprised to hear that Colonel Abel Smith had ordered Major Williams and Corporal Smitheram to take off from Haps on an airborne glider raid."[3]

Perhaps looking back on things and bearing in mind the preponderating weight of artillery at our disposal, the results hardly justified the number of shells of varying calibres which were hurled across the river at the

---

3. Corporal G. W. Smitheram was Headquarter Squadron clerk and stand-by to Major Williams. He was usually to be seen sheltering behind the "In," "Out" and "Pending" files, half obscured by the acrid fumes of his inseparable pipe. At Wolterton in Norfolk and Snaith in Yorkshire, he was the owner of a voracious little dog which carried on unceasing warfare against Captain Ford's trouser legs.

slightest provocation. The Anti-Aircraft Battery made no bones of the fact that they were amateurs at the art of ground strafing and indirect fire and suffered from a malignant predisposition to bounce their shots long-hop into the German lines, to the discomfort of our O.Ps. Of the part played by the Heavy Troops, Lieutenant Clark summed up:

> "I remember taking part with Piccolo Pete's[4] Troop one morning in a rather successful piece of harassing of the 'Krauts' covering a ferry just north of Boxmeer. On the other hand, the Heavy Troop fired a lot of rounds in this area with no tangible results. Mostly we fired indirectly, a process so inaccurate that on one occasion I nearly hit the windmill in which I had established my own O.P.!"

However, this should not be taken to mean that within the limits of the 75-mm. gun, marksmen were not able to achieve most creditable performances. On one direct shoot, two gunners in Lieutenant van Cutsem's Heavy Troop, Lance-Corporal Harwood and Trooper Clifford, knocked down a church steeple which the Germans were using as an O.P. at a range of nearly 3,000 yards, obtaining 27 hits out of 35 shots. Clifford likewise demolished a windmill in 16 shots, thereby costing Captain Wrottesley a "fiver" lost to Lieutenant van Cutsem, and also hit a signpost first time at over a mile range, bagging, to everyone's surprise, four Germans out of a bazooka section.

Life for the Hun was hazardous. Invariably overlooked and up to his knees in water, his daily round was made as intolerable as human ingenuity and Colonel Abel Smith's latest ideas could devise. And yet, in all his wretchedness, the German soldier remained as accurate and methodical in routine as ever. Day after day, he would pass the same spot to the minute, be duly strafed, scuttle out of his car and scramble for the ditch. Only one vehicle, supposedly an ambulance, was given the benefit of the doubt, but it was always reported. Its unfailing appearances became a stand-by for the luncheon interval, when a marked falling off in the intensity of Troop reports was to be noticed. A sample of the Wireless Log for the 17th of October is revealing. Only the explanatory remarks in brackets are mine:

1300 hours	R.H.Q. (*Adjutant*): "Anything to report?"
	"A" Squadron: "Wait—Out."
1311 hours	R.H.Q. (*sharply*): "I say again, anything to report?"
	"A" Squadron (*in pained tones, those of Lieutenant Brayne-Nicholls*): "I say again, WAIT, WAIT, Junior Sunray is on a Personal Recce."

---

4. Lieutenant Jonkheer Groeninx van Zoelen.

1322 hours "A" Squadron (*triumphantly*): "At 1318 hours, moving from figures 7847 (trench entrance) to figures 7748 (latrine), an enemy ambulance." R.H.Q.: "Roger—Out."

1345 hours R.H.Q. (*another voice, Lieutenant the Hon. M. Eden's*): "Could you, ah ... implement the message regarding the enemy ambulance with ... ah ... special reference to the second group of figures which are not clear to me."

"A" Squadron (*voice of an operator not quite "in the picture"*): "Ambulance now returning."

1345 hours R.H.Q. (*definitely Captain Collins*): "This is the SIXTH time this ambulance has been mentioned today. From now on ALL reference to it will cease—OUT."

The same Log Book shows the tempo to increase slightly during the afternoon. "Party of Germans moving about by Café—have hosed them up," is followed by a Heavy Troop report that "I am moving to a new position where I can shell the tower where there is suspected enemy O.P."; and yet another message that "Enemy D.R. shot off his machine and two lorries hit, one has burnt itself out and exploded."

The hours roll slowly by and it starts to rain. Someone calls up and reports that "Seven Germans with seven rifles have got out of seven separate slit trenches, stretched themselves and got in again! " One almost feels sorry for the boredom of the poor devils and senses that it might be a kindness to relieve their monotony by dropping a ranging shot over the river.

★   ★   ★

Daytime encounters used generally to occur at first light when patrols encountered a returning enemy night raiding party. Also, the Germans frequently laid mines on the stretches of road which they knew we had to use, and great vigilance was needed to avoid them. "A" Squadron lost two cars this way. A scout car in Lieutenant Peake's Troop ran over a mine in the Boxmeer sector, turning a complete somersault with the force of the explosion. Fortunately, both occupants, Corporal Gorton, and Trooper Court, managed to extricate themselves through the side door, but acid from the overturned batteries had run into their eyes. With presence of mind, Gorton, who was the less badly hurt, dashed some water from his water-bottle into Court's face, thereby saving his sight.

Boxmeer was a particularly bad area for mines, and on the same day, the 27th of October, Lieutenant Palmer's leading scout car met with a similar fate. The driver, Trooper Taylor, escaped with bad bruising and shock, but in Corporal Cronin (a broken arm and leg) he had lost his seventh car commander of the campaign.

Lieutenant Redfern's Troop ("A" Squadron) ran into an enemy ambush near Gennep bridge, where the Germans kept infiltrating along trenches running parallel to the river and were, it was strongly suspected, in contact with fifth column sympathizers who knew the exact movements of the armoured car Troops. A scout car was bazooka-ed and the crew, Corporal Eric Rose, and Trooper John Senior, killed.

On another occasion Lieutenant Wordsworth did good work after two friendly self-propelled guns had been knocked out by mines on the banks of the Maas. The crews got away safely, but the area in which the vehicles were stranded was swept by fire. As only the tracks had been damaged, it was decided to attempt recovery, and Lieutenant Wordsworth volunteered to go forward on foot ahead of the armoured recovery vehicle to clear the mines up to the self-propelled guns. He cleared the route, but M.G. fire was subsequently found to be too intense for recovery to take place and the vehicles were abandoned. It afterwards transpired that Wordsworth's mine detector had not been functioning at the time!

Captain Wrottesley's Troop was patrolling one day along the road to Beugen when a British 15-cwt. truck passed, moving towards the river. Thinking it strange that a British car should be motoring so casually straight towards the enemy, the Troop Leader shouted at the driver to halt. Instead of stopping, the truck speeded up. His suspicions now aroused, Wrottesley gave chase and ordered his gunner to fire a warning burst of Besa at the rapidly disappearing vehicle. The car then stopped and, after a half-hearted attempt at escaping over the fields, three "British" soldiers gave themselves up. Their story must have provided the security people with food for thought. Escaping from a prisoner-of-war camp at Bayeux four days previously, these Germans had stolen an army truck, obtained British uniforms, food and an unlimited amount of petrol, then motored across northern France and Belgium and remained unchallenged until caught by the armoured cars within a quarter of a mile of safety.

It was but natural in this frontier area that many of the local inhabitants should have family connections over the river; and it is certain that, if not actively collaborationist, a number of civilians were prepared to hunt with the hounds in daytime and run with the hare at night. They were past-masters at telling us what the Germans had done to their villages at night, but not averse to informing the enemy where we were, and what we had done, by day. In fairness, it must be added that when the German patrols came over, they frequently threatened the Dutch with reprisals if they did not feed and hide them. Quite a few inhabitants were removed as hostages.

One by one the best observation posts, which could only be manned during the day, succumbed at night. The churches were singled out for special attention. On the 18th of October, Beugen church went up with a noise which sounded like the explosion of an ammunition factory. It was followed three nights later by those of Boxmeer and Oeffelt. The loss of Boxmeer, which showed remarkable knowledge on the part of the enemy of the recent movements of our patrols, was infuriating. It removed one of the best observation posts on the front. The noise of the Boxmeer church explosion, which was even greater than that of Beugen, was explained next morning when the extent of the damage was revealed. Its medieval tower of great constructional strength had been cut clean away from its foundations and deposited in one neat but enormous pile of rubble on the exact spot where it had stood. The sappers who came to examine the damage were convinced that, by the completeness of destruction, the Germans must have prepared for its demolition over a period of days, bringing over the charges, with the connivance of collaborators, every night.

One of the destroyed churches had been founded in A.D. 1420, and with a substantial miracle to its credit was locally reputed to be indestructible. When Lieutenant Hopkinson brought up a patrol on the morning after its demolition, he found himself to be the object of a hostile demonstration, for the unfortunate Dutch could never understand why either side should use their places of worship as O.Ps.

It was not until the 7th of November that permission was granted to place a military control on all crossings of the railway line (which ran parallel to the Maas) down to the suspect villages. Arrangements were then made to move civilians from the zone, allowing only the farmers in possession of strictly controlled passes to till their fields during the day. The advantage of this control, a nuisance to enforce, was that it kept the enemy guessing, made him patrol for his information, and protected civilian life, quite a few villagers having been beaten up in the past. It is only fair to add that until that date "Shaef" had not enough troops to enforce such a control even had it been ordered.

The character of night operations on the Maas was quite different. In daytime the mobility of the Troops and their fire power generally kept the enemy to their trenches. Once it was dark, the armoured cars were quite blind, as is all armour, and the Germans grew bolder. Counter-measures fell largely on the Support Troops.

There was a prevailing idea in certain quarters that the Germans might stage a fairish sized counter-attack by crossing by pontoon on a dark night. Therefore when Lieutenant Ainsworth's Troop reported at three o'clock in the morning that he could hear "the sounds of heavy hammer blows at regular intervals coming from the area of Sambeek and the river," there was some disquiet. Ten minutes later a heavy mortar barrage landed in some empty fields behind Boxmeer and Beugen. A farm burst into flames and lit up the sky for miles around. Was this the expected attack? Patrols were alerted, but nothing further happened and the alarm died down. The hammer blows proved to have been the Germans revetting their waterlogged trenches, which they dared not do in daylight. The fire had been caused by the "D" Squadron cooks accidentally setting alight to a barn with their petrol cooker—Lieutenant Hughes receiving the resultant "rocket" on behalf of his men when he returned at daylight from a patrol inside enemy territory!

★   ★   ★

Lieutenant Wordsworth's recollections of the Support Troop in "A" Squadron and Corporal Meade-King's narrative will recall many episodes to those who guarded the river line at this period.

"Three or four minor incidents happened to my Squadron during the hours of darkness. They were not amusing then, but, looking back, they appear in a slightly different light. One night in the Oeffelt area, I was ordered by Colonel Henry to do a particularly filthy and tricky patrol. On this sort of party I always took the same two troopers, Wilson and Dearlove, and these two were with me on this occasion. I am as blind as a bat without my glasses, and on this night I very stupidly left them behind. It was pouring with rain and perfectly foul. The object of our patrol was to report if a certain wood on our side of the river bank was occupied or not. On nearing our objective we carefully picked our way over a series of enemy trip wires stretched across the path and ploughed on until I thought we were somewhere near the wood. We lay full length whilst I tried to make up my mind on how to carry out my task, when suddenly, about five yards in front of me, what I had taken to be an innocent bush moved, and it was quite obvious we were much too near the enemy for our liking. Why no one saw us I cannot imagine, because it was very short range. We then proceeded to roll for about twenty yards until we considered it safe to get up and run. As bad luck would have it, the last man tripped over the last of the trip wires and we began making an enormous noise, but luckily no one was hurt. We spent a hectic two hours being chased from field to field, and eventually returned to Oeffelt, which was then being held by one of our own Troops.

"When based at St. Agatha's Monastery, Cuyk, one night I was on the usual stroll along the river bank with a section I happened to be leading, and was just about to open a gate into a field when the enemy very kindly did it for me from the other side. The usual chaos ensued; the majority of the enemy ran away except for two blithering idiots who ran towards me. They might have got away with it because I thought for some considerable time that they were members of my own patrol, but as they proceeded to lie on the ground in spite of my yelling at them, it eventually dawned upon me that they might not be understanding what I was saying. They turned out to be a German R.S.M. and sergeant.

"Another incident happened in Boxmeer near the end of the patrolling season when the regular patrols were a bit weary, and members of the echelon suddenly found themselves taking part in these parties. I was in the café in Boxmeer and had sent out two patrols in directions which I thought it quite impossible for them ever to meet. Unfortunately, they managed to meet in a very big way, and threw about ten grenades at each other. They then came back separately to me, informing me that they had wiped out an enormous amount of Germans. The whole matter was eventually cleared up, and the remarkable part was that no one had suffered any injuries at all, in spite of each side's magnificent claims.

"On another occasion 'Field-Marshal' Peake set out on a patrol along the top of one of the dykes. It was a very dark night. He was dressed in gum-boots and gas-cape, and he carried an extremely noisy Sten gun. He could be heard miles away when he was walking normally, but when he proceeded to topple over the side of the dyke it was too much for a lot of people and immediately every small-arms weapon in the neighbourhood opened up somewhere or other. I was told that a lot of swearing came from the bottom of the dyke and very loud inquiries from the rest of his patrol, who were similarly dressed, as to how he was getting on."

★   ★   ★

Corporal Meade-King's story deals with one night when he was commander of one of the echelon sections and called in to help out the Support Troops in their night patrolling.

"When we reached the Brickyard (central sector), we found our living quarters to be a row of ovens lined with straw. This was where we were to sleep during the daytime, between our patrols. I was to take a section out that night, and as at this time there was a certain novelty attached to the job, I was told to accompany the Squadron Leader to the village during the afternoon to see the lie of the land, and to receive my orders for the night. The village of Oeffelt seemed peaceful enough when we reached it; it looked out over the River Maas, separated from the river by a stretch of flat country cut up by floodbanks. On the edge of the village,, was the row of trenches which we were to occupy that night, facing the river and the intervening country over which, I was told, I might expect enemy patrols to advance upon us to perform some outrage in the village behind. A railway embankment surmounted by drunken telegraph poles and apparently festooned with wires ran from the village to the river, and as we stood by the trenches we could see in the distance the outline of the broken bridge which carried the railway track across the river to the German lines. It was to this bridge that the Squadron Leader told me I was to lead my patrol so that I might find out what activity, if any, was going on across the river.

"By seven o'clock that night we had returned to the village, this time arrayed in all the protection we could muster against the damp chill of the night. The weight of my clothes was such that my movement was restricted to that of a diver on the bed of the sea, and as it was all bound to me by my equipment, I wondered what I should do if I was called upon to run.

"This time the village was less peaceful; there was great noise of shell fire on our left, and civilians were bolting across the open space between the houses as though they expected to be picked off like running rabbits.

"A Troop of Daimlers was already installed at a point commanding the main street; it was upon them that we were to fall back in the event of an enemy attack. Two dismounted gunners were added to my section, and one of their officers appeared to be taking charge of the proceedings. A Royal Engineers sapper, he told me, was just about to go out on to the floodbanks to lay the 'booby-traps' for the night, and it would be as well if I accompanied him so that I should know the position of the traps. Accordingly the three of us set out in solemn procession, our heads bowed low below the floodbanks, the officer in front of me, and at the head of the party the sapper who, from a large reel, began paying out lengths of gossamer-like wire. We had not gone far before I was surprised to see the officer begin to perform a fantastic dance in front of me, but I was soon following suit as the all-embracing coils of wire, infuriating in their invisibility, began entwining themselves relentlessly round my ankles and mounting slowly to my waist. They seized upon the buckles of my gaiters and twanged merrily on the butt of my Sten gun as I writhed about, trying to free myself from the phantom web. I wanted to laugh, but I was restrained by the look of piteous contempt on the face of the sapper, who, seated upon the side of the bank, was waiting impatiently for us to extricate ourselves.

"It was dusk when we returned to the trenches, and the Gunner officer began giving me my final orders. I told him of the orders I had already received from my Squadron Leader, and it was finally decided that the bridge, being now completely obscured, would be difficult to reach, and that I should compromise by taking two men out to a listening post as close to it as possible, twice during the night, and that they should remain there for half an hour at a time. This entailed my making the journey from the post back to the trenches on my own, so I came to an arrangement with the corporal in charge of the section in the next trench to mine by which I should show myself against the sky on top of the floodbank on nearing the trench (a thing which we assumed no German was likely to do), so that I might avoid being shot by his section. The first time I made the return journey I followed this plan to the letter, only to be met with a great deal of confused whispering, amongst which I was able to distinguish the words, 'Shall I let him have it, Corp?' Although the corporal was quite au fait with the plan himself he had omitted to tell it to his Bren gunner!

"My orders for the night were to take part of my section on a mobile patrol, at the end of which we were to make contact with a similar patrol from another Squadron working from a village farther down the river. After this I was to report at intervals during the night to the officer in charge of the armoured car Troop in our village. When everything was settled I took my section into the trench; we mounted the Bren gun on the parapet and with our Sten guns in our hands leaned against the back of the trench, waiting for what might happen, with the long night ahead of us.

"As the darkness descended the night became quieter; the shelling had stopped, birds and animals had become silent, and soon there was only the sighing of the breeze in the reeds in front of us, and the tiny muffled sounds and shuffling noises in our trench. It became almost uncannily quiet, so that when we tried to remove the cap of the thermos of tea we had brought with us, the noise of scraping metal was as though someone had shouted in church.

"Some time during the small hours the shelling started again, but this time it was nearer to us. You could hear the distant cough as the gun fired, followed by a pause, and then the high-pitched note of the shell, descending the scale until it was terminated abruptly by the crash of the explosion. The lower the note descended the scale, the nearer one might expect the shell to burst, so that we found ourselves sinking lower and lower in the trench in unison with the note of the oncoming shell. When one of them reached such a low pitch that we were all in a heap on the floor of the trench, there was a mighty crash right on the parapet. Earth fell into the trench and a great cloud of smoke swept over us. As we rose again I saw the top of Phil Rayner's[5] bald head—for some reason he had removed his helmet—emerging from the smoke which had settled at the bottom of the trench, like a mine surfacing at sea. After that very creditable near miss, the German gunners apparently decided to rest upon their laurels, for there was no more firing that night, and once more things relapsed into that deadly silence, punctuated at intervals by the rattle of the thermos flask.

"I tried to remember when, at this time of the year, one might expect it to begin to get lighter. A little song kept running through my head, 'All the world is waiting for the sunrise.' I liked the tune and it seemed very apt. I was almost relieved when the time arrived for me to set out on the patrol, and leaving my two gunners to man the Bren in the trench, I and the remaining men embarked on the route I had been given. I had been told to walk through the fields on the far side of the railway embankment until I struck a track; we were then to turn left down the track until we contacted the other patrol. This seemed simple enough, and, filled with courage which surprised me at the time, but which I attributed to the flask in my pocket which had contained my accumulated rum rations over a period of two or three months, we set out into the unknown, my section trailing behind me. I cannot say how much ground we covered on that patrol. A voice muttered behind me, 'No future in this, you know, Corp.' But still we plodded on—I had my patrol to contact and, as far as I knew, the whole of the plans of the Guards Armoured Division would be set at naught if I did not do so! Never before or since have I travelled over so much uninteresting and lifeless country.

"After I had reinstalled the remainder of the section in the trench, I took Rayner with me and we set off into the village to report to the armoured car Troop. We tried to walk quietly through the deserted streets, but they were full of rubble and our efforts to keep on our feet and to do it silently must have sounded like a gang of road-menders at work. At the top of the main street we could see the faint light of the wireless valves inside the armoured car shining up on to the face of the car commander as he leant in the turret. As we followed our tortuous path towards him I thought of the 2-pounder and Besas which were trained in our direction, and wondered whether we should have the good fortune to be taken for Englishmen rather than Germans—it seemed to me that the odds were about even.

"I had nothing to report and was relieved at the Troop Leader's nonchalance over the result of my patrol, and after another hectic journey through the village we reached the trench once more.

---

5. Trooper P. W. Rayner, fitter.

"As we had become more accustomed to the darkness, the prospects of any action had seemed to become more remote and one had to force oneself more and more to remain vigilant. The flood banks, which earlier had stood out as black silhouettes against the sky, had now faded into a uniform greyness with the surrounding country. From time to time a searchlight from somewhere beyond the railway line would cast a pale glow over the fields,[6] but everything seemed asleep and lifeless, and it was difficult not to sink into a sort of coma in keeping with our surroundings. Even the thermos, being now empty, had ceased to disturb the silence. There was time now to think. I began to wonder how I would react to various circumstances. Supposing a man had been hit when the shell burst near the trench, how would I have got him back to the village? What would I do if an enemy patrol loomed out of the mist in front? Would I become petrified with terror or would I coolly lob a grenade into its midst? 'All the world is waiting for the sunrise' was still running through my head; I wished I knew the rest of the words. When would the sun rise anyway? There was a faint streak of light, a very faint one, away over the river in the distance. How would I paint that? What colour was the darkness above it? It wasn't really black; it was very deep blue with some green in it. 'All the world is waiting for the sunrise.'

"If there is anything more startling than a shriek in the night, it must be an unexpected burst of machine-gun fire, and when the Besa on the armoured car roared out in the village behind us it was as though a gigantic dagger had stabbed through the darkness, shattering the silence into a thousand jagged fragments which hurtled against the houses, beat against the windows and doors, to be hurled backwards and forwards as the whole village seemed to scream in its sleep. Then silence, deeper even than before, and a pale glow as the great floodlight on top of the car swept over the houses, searching, lighting up nooks and crannies, windows and doorways; then darkness again, and more silence; and from the man beside me, two scarcely audible words crammed with meaning.

"The pale streak on the horizon grew more quickly after that; trees in the foreground began to take shape again, soft edged at first but gaining in strength, as if they were growing out of the mist which hung low over the vicinity of the river. One's courage grew with the daylight; we began to relax and to talk softly to each other. A flight of wild duck flew over our heads towards the river, and I tightened my grip instinctively on my Sten gun, imagining I was waiting for a morning flight.

"We could hear sounds from across the river now, lorry engines, a rumble which sounded like a railway train, and a surprising amount of horse-drawn transport. We imagined the enemy getting on with their daily jobs, which were no doubt so similar to the ones to which we were

---

6. See sketch by Corporal Meade-King on page 406. *Author.*

"SHAEF" PERIOD, OCTOBER 1944

Daimler armoured car and a self-propelled gun under regimental command relieving the Echelon in Oeffelt village at dawn. Every morning the Dutch girl by the doorway used to go to the round of cars and infantry posts, dispensing welcome cups of coffee.

accustomed. The corporal of the guard moving amongst the sleeping forms and shouting the German equivalent of 'wakey, wakey,' the ration lorry going out, and the duty cook dispensing his early morning brew of something probably made of acorns to cold unshaven sentries.

"When we were eventually recalled to the village, the crews of the armoured and scout cars were already drinking coffee brought out to them by a pleasant-looking Dutch girl, and were laughing and joking about the events of the night. Someone had found a printed bill pinned on some railings; it told how our wounded who had been left behind at Arnhem were all doing well, and how our doctors and the Germans were working in harmony together, and, in the words of a doctor from Birmingham, 'what a pity it was that we and the Germans were not united in fighting the Russians.' It was the man who had posted this bill who had called down the wrath of the Besa upon himself, but there had been no sign of him when daylight came. Perhaps he was back over the river by now, holding in his hand a steaming cup of acorn brew."

★ ★ ★

During this period on the Maas, Lieutenant van Cutsem left his Heavy Troop in "C" Squadron to take up a job at 21 Army Group Headquarters. He had become a liaison officer there, or, as someone put it, "one of Monty's boys." His lean, spare figure, moving purposefully about its tasks, legitimate or otherwise, was to be missed by many. Perhaps no person in the British Army could register disapproval of a scheme or some minor military tediousness better than Bernard with a disdainful shrug or shrewdly timed question. One ineradicable memory is of him at Bulford, dressed in breeches, battle-dress top, and that extraordinary tank crash-helmet with bootlaces hanging from its brim, initiating the younger and more credulous members of the mess into some intrigue of his, the subtleties of which would not have disgraced a Venetian doge. Of him the story ran that his best coup at 21 Army Group Headquarters was the secreting away of all current copies of the *Tatler* from the Senior Officers' Mess lest the Field-Marshal, reputedly a regular reader of every issue, might discover that his liaison officer, while on a mission to London, had been inadvertently caught by the photographer at Newmarket.

★ ★ ★

In October came the first details of the proposed demobilization scheme. Unlike A.B.C.A. talks, it naturally excited great interest, and the barns were filled to capacity as the troops assembled to hear unfortunate

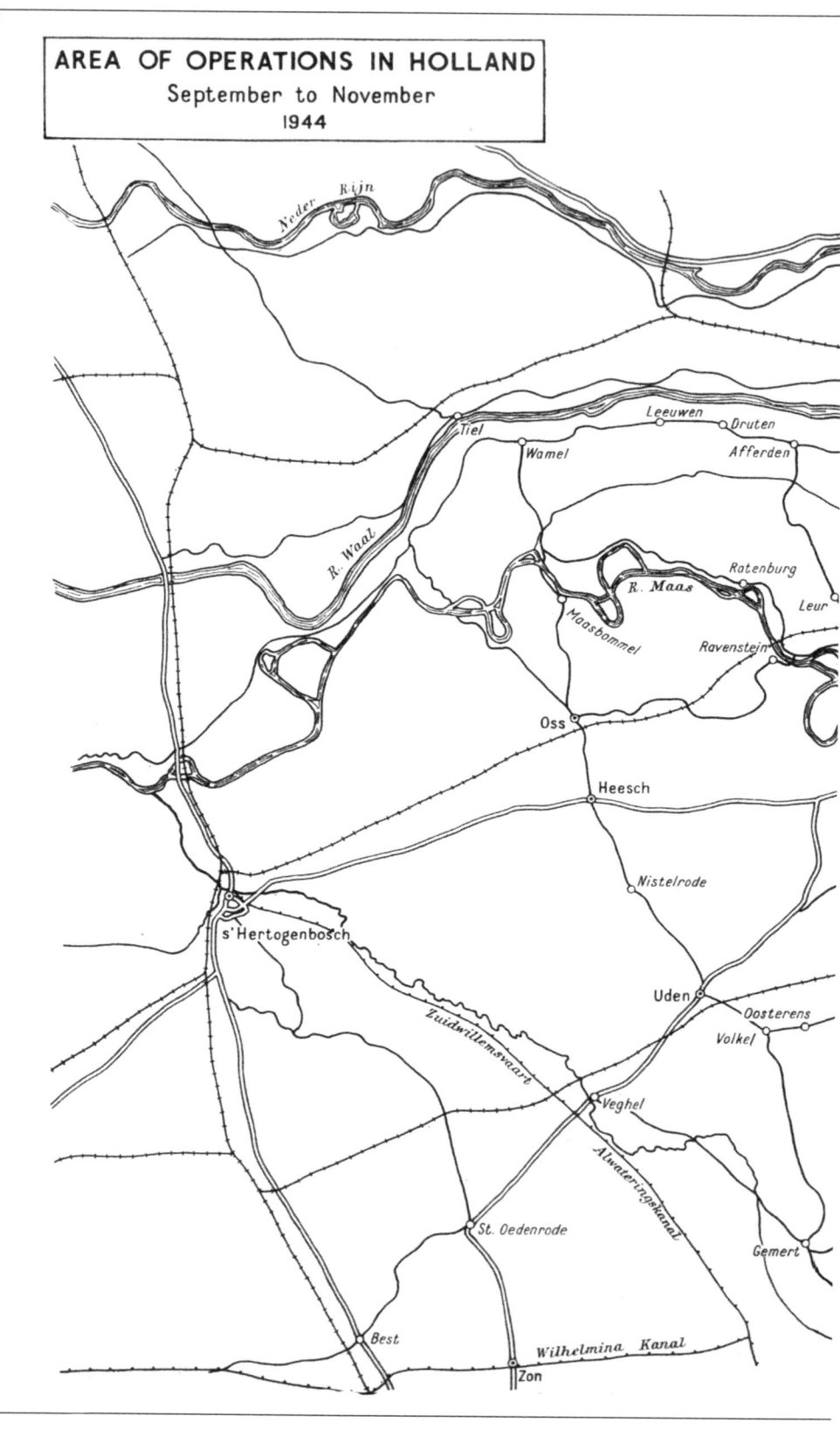

AREA OF OPERATIONS IN HOLLAND
September to November
1944

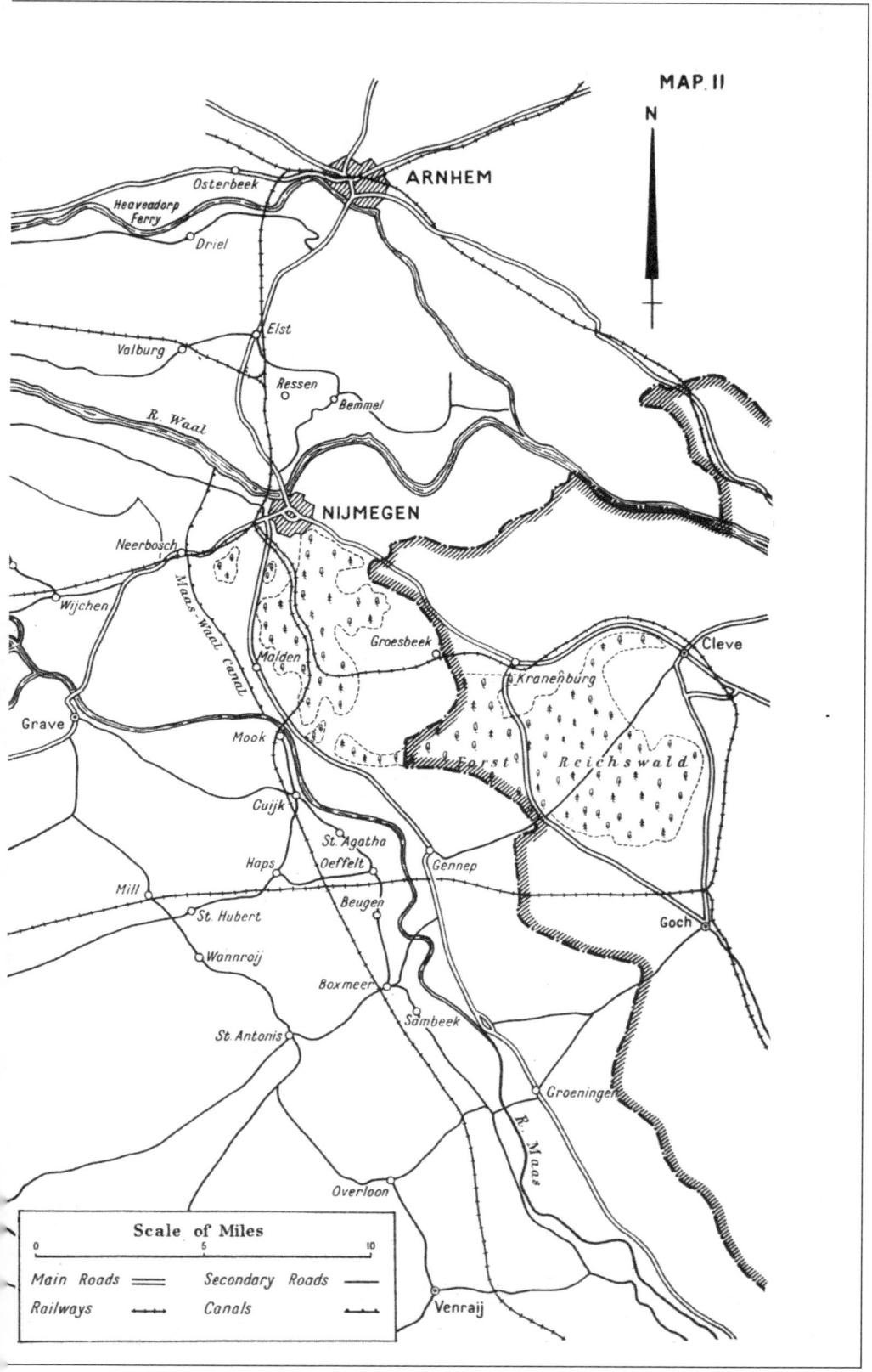

MAP. II

N

Osterbeek
ARNHEM
Heaveadorp
Ferry
Driel

Elst
Valburg
Ressen
Bemmel
R. Waal

NIJMEGEN
Neerbosch
Wijchen
Maas-Waal Canal
Malden
Groesbeek
Kranenburg
Cleve
Grave
Mook
Forst
Reichswald
Cuijk
St. Agatha
Haps
Oeffelt
Gennep
Mill
Beugen
St. Hubert
Goch
Wannroij
Boxmeer
St. Antonis
Sambeek
Groeningen
R. Maas
Overloon
Venraij

Scale of Miles
0   5   10

Main Roads ═══   Secondary Roads ───
Railways ┼┼┼┼   Canals ┴┴┴

officers detailed to explain impromptu the implications of a scheme as yet imperfectly understood in Whitehall. As the end of the war was not yet in sight, there were some who felt with good reason that this release of the news was a trifle premature. Doubtless political pressure lay behind the move.

★   ★   ★

To remind everyone that we were still fighting the Germans, a strange object was seen rising straight up into the sky on one of the few fine days of October. It soared rapidly and to such height that even the keenest eyes soon lost sight of it. A tail of what looked like smoke or condensed vapour was left in its wake. It was noticed that the object was accelerating the whole time and travelling at great speed, and observers saw that it appeared to have risen from well north of Arnhem. There were many guesses as to what it was. Some time later the first news of the existence of the V2 rocket was released to the general public.

★   ★   ★

Although the regimental task was in essence the same, by early November things had eased up considerably. 32nd Guards Brigade were situated at Grave, with orders to concentrate in Haps in a counter-attack role should the occasion demand it. In addition, 43rd Division from 30 Corps had transferred one of their battalions to the area of Cuyk. This unit was also intended for employment in immediate counter-attack in the event of the,enemy crossing the river in our sector.

Lieutenant-General Sir Richard O'Connor, commanding 8 Corps, made a tour of inspection of the "Shaef" front, and followed this up with a letter to Colonel Abel Smith at the conclusion of the period on the Maas which greatly pleased the Regiment.

HEADQUARTERS,
8 CORPS, B.L.A.
9th November, 1944.

DEAR ABEL SMITH,
Again I feel I am greatly indebted to you and your Regiment.

I can honestly say that I have never yet met a Unit which so whole-heartedly carries out the spirit of the instructions that are given to them. Whether you are chasing the enemy through France and Belgium, watching the line of the Meuse, digging trenches, or acting as infantrymen in defence, you always do it 100 per cent. You command a great Regiment and are very rightly proud of it.

In this last task you have got an organisation going which is by far the best that could be produced in the circumstances, and I hope you will do all you can when handing over to the Royals to make them realize the responsibility of it and the difficulties and that it is in fact no sinecure.

All good luck to you wherever you go. I hope to be able to come up and say good-bye to you tomorrow.

Yours ever,

R. N. O'CONNOR.

LIEUTENANT-COLONEL H. ABEL SMITH,
COMMANDING OFFICER,
2 H.C.R.

★ ★ ★

On the anniversary of Armistice Day, 11th of November, the Regiment learnt that the watch on the Maas was at an end. The job, which was to have lasted four days, had endured for over a month. Until then the efforts of General Horrocks to get us back to his Corps had been unavailing. Now that his Corps was to move over to the right flank of the British Army in Belgium and southern Holland, he was to be allowed to take his armoured car regiment with him. The Canadians became responsible for the Nijmegen bridgehead. The Royals came up to relieve us, and next day everyone concentrated in the area of Haps to prepare for a long night drive into Belgium. In a friendly gesture, the Anti-Tank Regiment, 91st Argyll and Sutherland Highlanders, who had played an important part in the functioning of "Shaef," bade farewell to Regimental Headquarters on their pipes.

It was quite dark and raining once more when the first car set off behind the tank transporters of Guards Armoured Division, bound for the colliery village of Waterschei. "Shaef" had passed from the region of reality into the realms of memory.

Scammel Recovery Vehicle

Chapter VI

Waterschei

The first part of the convoy's journey on the 11th November was down the "Club" axis. route, through Veghel, Uden, Eindhoven and Hechtel. Then right-handed past the "Royal" Tiger tank which still lay by the side of the wood where it had been knocked out by the Welsh Guards, to Bourg Leopold, over Beeringen bridge southwards, touching the outskirts of Hasselt, and thus on to Waterschei. It was an unpleasant all-night drive with side lights only. Several days' rain, followed by a change in temperature, had produced a thick fog. Beyond Hasselt the route ran through part of a vast American ammunition dump which for some reason had been allowed in places to overflow into the roadway. As the stacks of shells and cases of grenades and mortar bombs had not even been painted white at the corners, many cars collided with them, some head-on, others managing to escape with broken wings. Next morning the stranded vehicles made it appear as if there had been a sharp engagement with the enemy. However, although Captain Hudson and his R.E.M.E. staff had more repair work to do after this one-night drive than during the entire watch on the Maas period, most of the damage proved to be only superficial.

Already frayed tempers were not improved by the divisional convoy arriving at the deploying point ahead of scheduled time, causing the Regiment to overshoot Major Sir Peter Grant Lawson's harbour party. In spite of this contretemps, Squadrons had settled down into excellent billets by midday.

There was not enough room in Waterschei for everyone and so, as in Holland, the Regiment was split up. Regimental Headquarters were in Waterschei, as were "C" and "D" Squadrons, who were billeted in a large school building. "A" Squadron were in the neighbouring village of Niel-près-d'Asch and "B" Squadron close by in the village of Dorne. H.Q. Squadron were partly in Asch and partly in Winterslag.

The Regiment was some distance away from the main body of Guards Armoured Division, most of which were located farther east across the Meuse in the region of Gangelt and Sittard, holding a quiet sector of the line.

The manifest slowing down of operations at this stage was ascribed to a variety of reasons, not the least of which were the immense problems of supply still facing the Allies and the astonishing manner in which Hitler had rallied his scattered armies from being an apparently beaten rabble in France into once again manning an unbroken line from the North Sea to the Swiss frontier.

The Allied supply problem was greatly eased when the port of Antwerp was eventually opened for the handling of goods on the 26th of November, although the immediate result was a stream of V bombs directed on to its unfortunate inhabitants.

The French 2nd Armoured Division under General Leclerc entered Strasbourg, the capital of Alsace, on the 23rd of November, while formations of the American Ninth Army, a recent arrival, continued to make slow progress towards the River Roer. These were the two main advances during the month. But the temptation to forget the "Big Picture" and rely on vague snippets from the daily newspapers is very great when out of the line, and in truth most of us were rather vague as to what was happening. We were in comfortable billets, could relax in warm baths, had the certainty of a good night's rest, and dwelt with pleasurable anticipation on the thought of forty-eight hours' leave in Brussels.

This part of Belgium is flat and ugly and is situated on the top of a large coalfield. Collieries abound in the district, so do slag-heaps, football teams with an ambition to play the British, hospitable pithead officials, and hideously futuristic concrete-cum-red-brick churches. When we arrived there was still a good deal of witch-hunting going on for dubious political ends, the inevitable aftermath of German occupation. The miners in particular, who had been given the unenviable choice of either continuing to work for the Germans in the pits or else see their families starve, had now conveniently forgotten this aspect of the situation and were in many cases celebrating their new-found freedom by chasing up the unpopular colliery directors, accusing them, irrespective of guilt or otherwise, of being "sales collaborateurs," thus subscribing to the reigning myth that left-wing extremism was synonymous with patriotism. The general object of this sport appeared to be the elimination of anyone fortunate enough still to possess a large car, which was then spirited away to the Brussels *marché noir*.

There was also a large collaborators' camp in Waterschei, housing many thousand malefactors behind barbed wire.

The Regiment was to remain in the Waterschei area for nearly six weeks, and the period can be conveniently divided up into three sub-headings: (1) operational; (2) training; (3) rest and entertainments.

There was really very little operational work for the Regiment. Echoes of war on the front of the Second Army continued to reach us from across the Maas in the shape of messages from Captain Ford.

In conjunction with the American thrust directed at Cologne, it was arranged that 30 Corps should mount an attack in the Geilenkirchen sector, east of Sittard. For this purpose XIX U.S. Corps and 84 U.S. Division came under its temporary command. The attack was launched on the 18th of November and made painful headway against strong enemy resistance. Geilenkirchen itself was enveloped and captured, but after a few days, further progress was halted by heavy rains, making the ground impassable to all wheeled traffic. Captain Balding took part in the operation as personal liaison officer between General Horrocks and the American Commander of XIX Corps.

The termination of this operation resulted in the Germans being more or less presented with a salient of their own west of the River Roer. This was considered to be a foothold from which they might be able to make themselves a nuisance. In addition, more troops were required to contain this bridgehead than if the line were straightened from Geilenkirchen northwards towards Roermond, the junction of the Maas and the Roer. It was with the object of eliminating the salient that operation "Shears" was conceived at the end of the month. Guards Armoured Division were to advance towards Heinsberg and from there "B" Squadron would fan out behind the German lines towards the Maas.

The Squadron, under command of Major Wignall, had already moved on the 25th of November to the area of Nuth in Holland, coming into 30 Corps reserve under command of 8th Armoured Brigade. It formed part of a group called "Foxforce" set up as reserve against possible enemy counter-attacks from the Geilenkirchen—Wurm sector.

Over and above using "B" Squadron in a reconnaissance role, the proposed attack intended employing a number of Household Cavalry officers in a liaison capacity. After weeks of bad weather, however, when large tracts of land on both sides of the Maas were flooded to a depth of several feet, and after everyone had studied aerial photographs and overlay prints of enemy defences until they were known by heart, the operation was cancelled on the 14th of December. Other formations carried out the attack in a modified form later on.

During the middle of December the pontoon bridge at Berg which linked "B" Squadron east of the Meuse with the rest of the Regiment finally collapsed under the pressure of the swollen waters, and to reach Waterschei vehicles had to make a detour of many miles. However, "B" Squadron reported that they were quite happy in their self-contained isolation at Nuth in Holland.

Training in a foreign country during a war and in the middle of winter is somehow a difficult subject to tackle, or about which to appear enthusiastic. In addition, comfortable as it was, the Waterschei area could hardly have been less suitable for armoured training, being very much built up, and the only open ground within miles being either in use as firing ranges, such as Lommel and Beeringen, or else stocked with American ammunition and stores. Nevertheless, when the opportunity arose, a limited amount of Troop training, including driving instruction and wireless exercises for those new officers and men who had joined the Regiment on the Maas in Holland, took place. Captain Cooper also ran a small-arms course for all the Dutch interpreters. This temporarily distracted their minds from the numerous food and currency rackets then in full spate.

Needless to say, "Maintenance" proved a great stand-by and filled much of the working day. For the Squadron fitters and the L.A.D. staff there was always plenty to do. Under Captain Hudson this branch had achieved miracles of hard work and recovery, but except during the "Shaef" period the Regiment's war had been one of movement, and there was still much to be done on vehicles, some of which were now in a bad shape. These cars, so austere in outline while training in England, now bristling with home-made gadgets, forged in the light of battle experience, were an astonishing sight. Unlike training in England, the powers that be had long ceased to worry over "unauthorized modifications"; if the invention worked in practice to the advantage of the Troop in battle, then good luck to it. But there was more than a grain of truth in the remark of one officer, on inspecting a "D" Squadron Staghound, that "it only lacked the White Knight's beehive to qualify for a place in 'Through the Looking Glass.'"

By the beginning of December, Colonel Abel Smith and his escort of mechanical experts had inspected all fighting vehicles in the Regiment. Even the trooper with the shaving glass had been reinstated to his place at the rear of the inspecting party to check for dirty grease nipples.[1]

---

1. The latter was a reincarnation of Sunday Maintenance Parades at Bulford and, as far as Colonel Abel Smith was concerned, an indispensable adjunct to the ceremony. Still vivid are the memories of that inquisitorial semi-circle about the armoured car—the Commanding Officer, the Squadron Leader, the Technical Adjutant (then Captain Balding), Captain Myall, R.E.M.E., and the trooper with the shaving glass. And woe betide the Troop Commander if, when the glass had been flashed to the underside of the car, the verdict was, "Dirty nipple."

Fortunately the inspection did not cover all those German cars gathered in by Squadrons which had still escaped the general round-up in Holland. There were many "priority" claims on these cars. The Squadron seconds-in-command were convinced that they ought to be theirs as they had no staff cars under the establishment; the messing officers as firmly claimed them as means of transport for illegal merchandise and the various bartering materials so useful in Belgium; and the mechanist corporals-of-horse because, tired of having to send out breakdown crews to tow them in, they wished to blow them up for good and all. There was one other claimant, the Dutch interpreter Roos. Roos was firmly convinced that he should have been allotted a Belgian collaborator's car of his own for fighting the Germans. Throughout the campaign his refrain ran, "I tell you I gotta getta car—it is so easy in Belgium." He never succeeded in his ambition, failing to realize that the Belgian who allows a Dutchman to get away with something for nothing has not yet been born.

Shortly after settling in to Waterschei, the Regiment received a visit from General Horrocks. It was the first occasion that he had had the chance to visit us since we had come under his command in the l'Aigle days before the Seine crossing. He spoke to all Household Cavalrymen gathered together in the Casino Cinema at Waterschei. Beginning his talk with praise and following it up with a detailed account of the doings of the Regiment, he carried forward into a general résumé of 30 Corps' work from the Normandy advance up to the end of the Maas period. He concluded with the realistic and, as it turned out, remarkably accurate prophecy that the Allies would have to fight all the way to Berlin. The Regiment left the Casino Cinema greatly inspired by its first experience of one of his talks. As one trooper wrote in his diary, "Quite apart from anything else, it was a glorious chance to get off maintenance and the grease and muck for once and profit by an interesting and extremely instructive lecture on the past, present and even future, by a person of unquestionable authority."

★　★　★

With the temporary cancellation of "Shears" in mid-December, arrangements were made to move Guards Armoured Division back to the Diest—Aerschott area for intensive training, and the Regiment was allotted a rather unsatisfactory district for billeting. However, no one need have worried. Neither the training area nor the billets were ever to be sampled.

★　★　★

Household Cavalrymen will probably remember their days at Waterschei for two reasons: firstly, the amount of entertainment and absence of most of war's campaigning discomforts; and, secondly, the rude shock which uprooted them a few days before the Christmas festivities were due to take place.

The slowing down of the war permitted Field-Marshal Montgomery to hold an investiture at Headquarters Guards Armoured Division, Gangelt, where, among others, members of 2nd Household Cavalry Regiment were decorated. As the Band of the Life Guards played at the ceremony, it was quite a Household Cavalry party.

The distance from Waterschei to Brussels by road was only sixty-five miles, but forty-eight hours' leave for the men was at first slow to get going because of the great numbers involved. However, by the end of November some forty to fifty a week were being sent off by lorry to leave centres in Brussels and Antwerp. For officers, the Eye Club and other leave hotels were in full swing.[2]

The Belgians are by nature a most hospitable race and the local inhabitants were no exception, throwing open their homes without reservation to the Household Cavalrymen. When the Regiment first arrived in the streets of the colliery town it was heartening to see both the young and the old stopping soldiers to make certain that they got good billets. Settling in became one continuous "getting the feet under the table."

There were several cinemas in the neighbourhood and a large dance hall patronized with great enthusiasm by the Household Cavalry, but it was when the Life Guards Band came over from Brussels to play at a local concert that social life in Waterschei attained the heights. Then it became the ambition of every aspiring Waterschei mother to see her daughter escorted to the concert by a *cavalier* from "La Garde Royale." The eligible male population of Waterschei did not quite share this point of view which upset the "walking out" ratio of the district, but all things considered, they took it in remarkably good part. They had their revenge when Waterschei United challenged and triumphed over the Regiment in a football match played before the eyes of all the local feminine beauty.

---

2. The Eye Club, named after the Divisional sign, was for members of Guards Armoured Division only. It was sponsored by, and given the blessing of, General Adair. It was small, intimate, and excellently run with a minimum of rules and regulations. There was a first-class bar and the secretary, Captain Worrall, would always allow departing members to fill up the backs of their jeeps with crates of wine and spirits to reprovision their thirsty messes. The club was situated centrally in Brussels, in the Boulevard Anspach, half-way between the Place de Broukere and the Bourse. It has now resumed its original function in the city's life, that of a humble bed and breakfast commercial traveller's hotel, the Taverne Anspach.

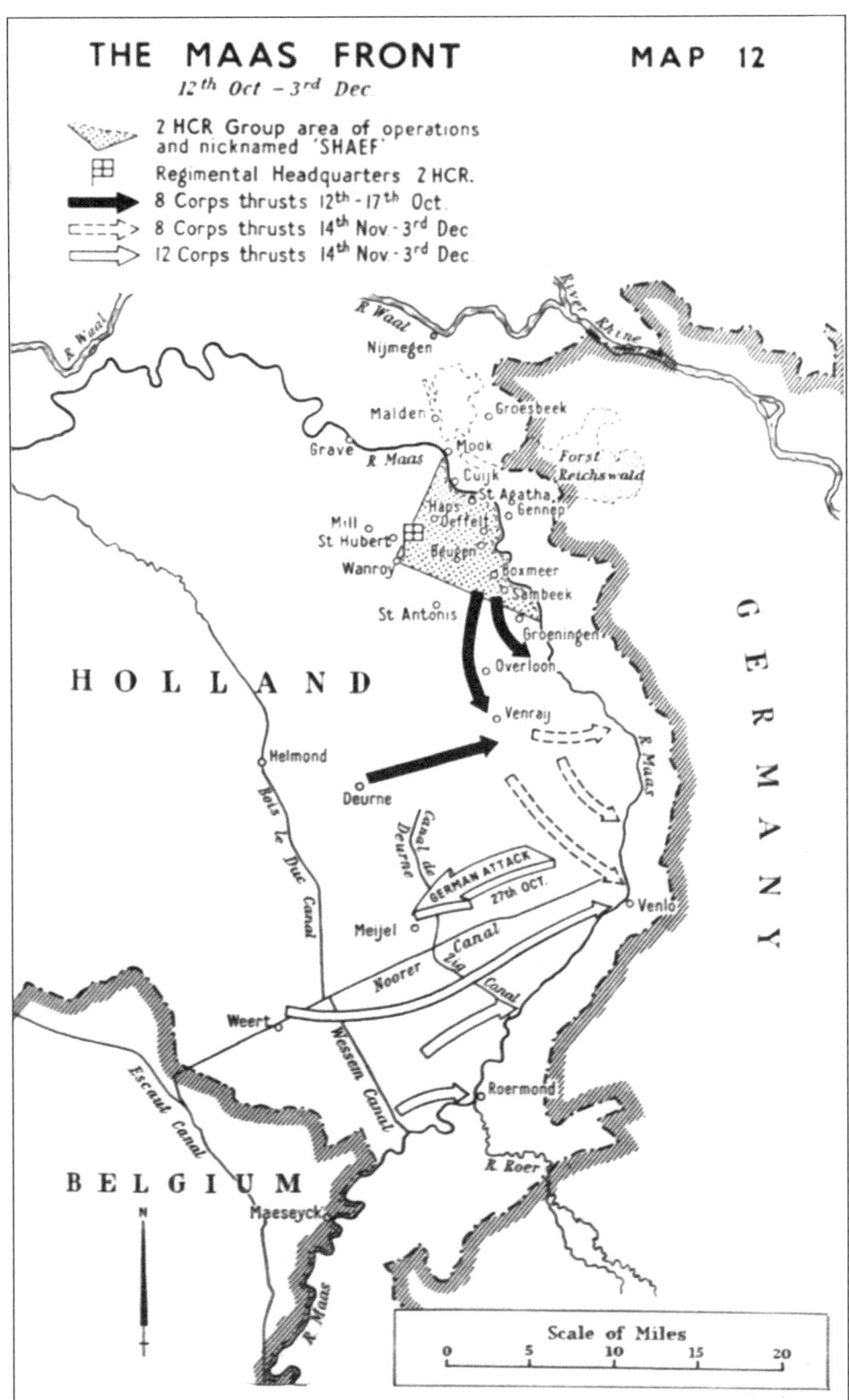

THE MAAS FRONT

12th Oct – 3rd Dec.

2 HCR Group area of operations and nicknamed 'SHAEF'

Regimental Headquarters 2 HCR.

8 Corps thrusts 12th – 17th Oct.

8 Corps thrusts 14th Nov – 3rd Dec.

12 Corps thrusts 14th Nov – 3rd Dec.

MAP 12

R Waal

Nijmegen

River Rhine

Malden

Groesbeek

Grave

R Maas

Mook

Cuijk

Forst Reichswald

St Agatha

Haps

Mill

St Hubert

Oeffelt

Gennep

Beugen

Wanroy

Boxmeer

St Antonis

Sambeek

Groeningen

Overloon

HOLLAND

Venraij

Helmond

R Maas

Deurne

Canal de Deurne

GERMAN ATTACK

27th Oct.

GERMANY

Meijel

Venlo

Bois le Duc Canal

Noorer Canal

Zig Canal

Weert

Wessem Canal

Roermond

Escaut Canal

R Roer

BELGIUM

N

Maeseyck

R Maas

Scale of Miles

0   5   10   15   20

COPYRIGHT, STANFORD, LONDON

Waterschei was visited by numerous E.N.S.A. parties, which were greatly enjoyed by the Household Cavalrymen and their Belgian friends whom they brought along as guests. For a time, the E.N.S.A. artists, some of whom were Belgian, made the Mardaga Hotel at Asch their Headquarters. The Mardaga was a pleasant little inn and restaurant close to Waterschei. It had a comfortable dining-room and a co-operative proprietor who could always be relied upon to provide a well-cooked meal at a moment's notice. The place became a favourite officers' rendezvous when the day's work was done. To the romantically inclined, cooped up in the kindly yet rather drab atmosphere of a colliery village, the presence of an E.N.S.A. troop seemed to endow the Mardaga with the glamour and vague "naughtiness" of an Edwardian back-stage door. And so it was that nightly, as the last tarpaulins were draped over the cars to close yet another maintenance parade, a curious assortment of liberated vehicles might be seen moving furtively out in the half-light towards the Asch road, bound for a world of Ruritanian assignations and cheap champagne where young and not so young officers jostled one another for the favours of a smile from "Miss" Oplabeek or the "Queen" of Liége. But it was all very harmless, if symptomatic, and soon to be interrupted by Field-Marshal von Rundstedt.

★   ★   ★

Diaries for this period are so full of dates for private parties and Squadron "At Homes" that it is really difficult to believe that there was a war on. Captain Collins notes for the period 1st to 16th December: "Things are very quiet—perhaps too much so."

By mid-December Christmas arrangements were in full swing, so was leave to Brussels. Pigs and geese, carefully hidden away in near-by villages, were living out their last days on earth, watched over with loving care. A curious-looking car reminiscent of an express delivery van might be seen travelling at high speed over the surrounding countryside, piloted by Lieutenant Oliver. It frequently crossed the Belgian-Dutch frontier at the dead of night, inviting the gravest suspicion. In fact had customs and barriers been anything but a memory, it must assuredly have been halted and a most interesting haul of goods been found beneath its old tarpaulin.

Even Regimental Headquarters had Christmas geese in training. One had become a great pet of the officers' mess, and Captain Cooper felt that the fattening-up process should be expedited by a diet of champagne. Thus one evening, to the (understandable) annoyance of the

Mess President, who had retired to bed and did not make the discovery until next morning, the bird was elected to honorary membership of Headquarters Officers' Mess. The inaugural ceremony required the beast to be lifted on to the dining-room table and given a saucer of champagne, which it drank with gusto, "eventually becoming completely swizzled, to the detriment of its table manners and the cloth." There is no record of its subsequent debauches nor any trace that it took even a passive part in Christmas celebrations, but it was suspected of having drunk itself to death in the N.C.Os.' Mess.

★　★　★

On the 16th of December, a trooper in "B" Squadron wrote: "Although this place is rather boring after a time, it is comfortable and the food is good; that after all is what matters. We understand that we may be here until after Christmas. In the meantime the Germans are doing absolutely nothing, nor are we. The enemy appear to be only too happy to leave us alone if we return the compliment." This trooper was not alone in his misjudgement of the situation.

On the 17th of December, an officer noted: "Lunch at the Mardaga —dinner also; drink or two with near-by American friends, then home to bed. For the first time for ages German bombers are over in some strength. Much ack-ack and bangs—several fires started, etc." Brussels was crowded with soldiers on forty-eight hours' leave, doing their Christmas shopping. The night clubs were in full swing; silk stockings were selling in back alleys at the equivalent of £5 a pair; while in the streets, smooth customers in padded shoulders were unloading Dutch guilders in exchange for Belgian francs, and, incredible as it may now seem, English pounds. There was a curfew of sorts to which nobody paid the slightest attention.

Far away to the south, in the hilly and wooded country beyond the Meuse known as the Ardennes, the Germans had been making what was officially labelled "a fair-sized diversionary attack with certain air support against units of the First American Army." This had met with *some* success, but nobody worried unduly; the Americans would soon deal with it.

By the 18th of December the Bruxellois were beginning to get a bit agitated. They did not agree with the officially inspired statements and, with memories of the occupation still fresh in their minds, preferred to consider the "diversionary attack" a full-scale counter-offensive and make their plans accordingly. Throughout the capital one began to sense a growing fear and anxiety. The British tried to reassure the Belgians, but the latter could not forget 1940. "Ah vous ne savez pas ce qu'ils peuvent faire, ces Boches, et ils ont toujours dit qu'ils reviendraient, les bandits."

The Eye Club was quiet and practically empty. There had been no messages—no orders for recall to unit. Back at Waterschei preparations went forward for moving into training quarters near Louvain, and, taking advantage of the lull, Colonel Abel Smith had made arrangements to fly to England to take part in a conference to discuss the future of the Household Cavalry after the war.

Even on the 19th of December Troop runs were still in progress in the environs of Waterschei and lorries were debouching their leave freight close to the Cinquantenaire Park, Brussels. But at Louvain a party of mystified British Tommies had set up a token roadblock. No one really knew what it was for, but it caused a frightful traffic jam. By then civilian cars with prams and mattresses piled high on their roofs were speeding one way only—towards Brussels. Their occupants full of stories of burnt villages and enemy armoured columns roaming at will—"just as in 1940," they reiterated.

"Then suddenly, in the evening of the 19th," noted Lieutenant the Hon. M. Eden, "as we were just sitting down to a heavy dinner in the mine manager's house, in came Arthur Collins, smacking his cheeks and looking grave, and we all had to up sticks." The news had just come through that the Regiment was to stand by, ready to move immediately. Along the road to Asch and the Dutch frontier columns of tanks and carriers and lorries crawled by, flashing their headlights on and off in that curious frenzy of anti-dazzle hysteria which periodically seemed to assail the British Army.

Colonel Abel Smith had already left for England and was on his way to the Brussels aerodrome, and Major Sir Peter Grant Lawson, the second-in-command, urgently summoned to Army Headquarters, was even then heading for the Dutch border, where he was to receive his orders direct from General Dempsey. By nine o'clock a complete fog of war had descended over news of the battle front, "and apparently the powers that be were just as much in the dark as the ordinary soldier."[3]

Until the return of Sir Peter Grant Lawson there was no choice but to contain our anxious curiosity in silence and prepare furiously for the impending move.

A regiment which has been static in billets for well over a month "with its feet under the table," and is not expecting to move in the

---

3. War Diary, 19th December, 1944.

middle of Christmas preparations, can be excused a certain degree of confusion when a snap order to *stand by to move* hits it as it did that evening. The cafés were full; many of the billets were out of the way. Key men were in Brussels or in neighbouring villages with Belgian friends. Many cars had their sumps off and vital kit was stowed away in half a dozen different places. There were no maps; these had to be collected in Holland by Captain Cooper after a hectic skidding journey at full speed through dense fog in a scout car. And yet in spite of all this, the Regiment assembled with creditable speed. Notices were flashed on to the cinema screens, the dance halls were emptied, and D.Rs. excelled themselves in routing out unwitting absentees with the ingenuity of native trackers. In the darkened corridors of the Waterschei school buildings there was a constant coming and going, loading of kit, rearranging of Troops, sorting out of ammunition, and filling up with petrol and water. All cars not fit for the road were ruthlessly left behind to their fate.

Rumours grew as the cars were loaded. Some said that perhaps the Regiment was to be used to round up German parachutists; others, that the Americans were short of armoured cars and that we were being lent to General Patton. But the most prevalent rumour was that it was really an exercise devised by Colonel Henry to keep everyone on their toes and that, due to the proximity of Christmas, it could not last long!

Whatever our likely role, it had now become abundantly clear that the Germans facing the American 1st Army had broken through in a much more serious manner than had at first been thought possible. Should they succeed in reaching the Meuse there would be a grave threat to the lines of communication of the entire northern group of armies. "At least," said a pessimist at Guards Armoured Division Headquarters, "we had Dunkirk to play with in 1940; now we haven't even got that."

★　★　★

Major Sir Peter Grant Lawson did not return with orders from General Dempsey until well after midnight. All the Squadron Leaders were fast asleep in the Orderly Room awaiting his arrival. His had been a terrible journey both to and from Neerpelt, where Second Army Tactical Headquarters was situated; the roads were slippery and a really dense fog had reduced visibility to a few feet. At one time Corporal-of-Horse Purnell, the Colonel's personal D.R., had become separated from the second-in-command's scout car, due to the pea-soup atmosphere, but by dint of much asking and great determination he had managed to reach Neerpelt in good time on his own.[4]

It appeared that nothing was known of the German whereabouts on the front of the American 1st Army, except that they were moving fast towards the River Meuse. The Regiment was therefore to reconnoitre the line of the Meuse from Namur inclusive to Visé inclusive, and to find out whether the enemy had yet succeeded in crossing at any point. Had they done so they were to be shadowed relentlessly. Also, and this it was stressed was most important, because we should be operating in the American sector and across the supply lines of the U.S. Ninth and part of the U.S. First Armies, a detailed report was to be sent in of all roads and bridges leading up to the Meuse. It is interesting to note— and a measure of the chaos ensuing when a break-through takes place between Allied Army boundaries—that the orders included a request for information about roads and bridges which had been in constant use since mid-September by the Americans!

As the river frontage to be covered was over forty miles long and Second Army Headquarters sixty miles back, it can be seen that the problem of wireless communication was of paramount importance. It was not an easy one to solve, for apart from the truly vast distances involved, an additional problem was the fact that, being in another sector of the front, our own frequencies, attuned to avoid clashes with other British units, were to be badly jammed by the American sets. However, by remembering training lessons in Yorkshire, and by sitting on top of the highest hills, of which at last there were to be some, touch was maintained throughout. Captain Garnett went to Second Army Tactical Headquarters, which had a No. 9 set tuned in to the Regimental Command Net, and at the same time "B" Squadron moved in from Nuth to Waterschei, where it was to remain for a time, acting as a wireless step-up to Army. Thus for over twenty-four hours, 2 H.C.R.'s reports were to be the only news received by Second Army Headquarters of the Americans south of the Meuse, and the feat of keeping in constant touch during the critical succeeding days marked the high-water mark of our wireless reputation, of which we were justly proud.

★   ★   ★

4. "'Know where the Second — Army is?' said the face of a D.R. looming out of the cotton wool. The 2nd Household Cavalry had also been ordered to send a representative to the conference, and here was Peter Grant Lawson's D.R. lost, it is true, but at least able to report that Peter was ahead. This was welcome news." (Major the Hon. F. F. G. Hennessy, M.B.E., Grenadier Guards. *From a Purely Personal Point of View*)

AH A

1.   Rear Link to Tac Army, including an officer.

2.   Incl VISE to incl NAMUR

          (a) Where has Hun reached river?

          (b) Is he trying to cross?

          (c) Has he succeeded in crossing?
                If so, strength, etc (normal) *(every hr.)*

3.   Incl VISE to incl NAMUR

          Complete list of bridges by classes:

                e.g. Class 40 at HUY.

4.   Main road report within the square:

                HASSELT _ MAASTRICHT _ NAMUR _ TIRLEMONT

          (a) Blown bridges

          (b) Bad traffic congestion

          (c) One-way or two-way.

5.   Frequent negative reports on para 2.

6.   You are operating in American sector.

MW

2210 hrs.

19. Dec;

Copy of written orders handed by General Dempsey to Major Sir Peter Grant Lawson on the night of 19th December at his Neerpelt Headquarters on the Dutch border.

By dint of everyone working with a will and much scrambling and pushing, the first Squadron of armoured cars moved off in the early hours (0400 hours) of the morning of the 20th of December. *Au revoirs* were sad as the Belgians, with tears in their eyes, pressed food and presents on the soldiers with the request "Please come back quickly." Wistfully they inquired, "Who is coming to take your place —are we being left without any British?" And then invariably the final cry, "Ah, you English, you do not really know him, the Boche."

The damp and drizzling fog had now descended like a suffocating blanket over the entire countryside, and in many places the leading scout car commanders had to dismount and advance part of a doubtful way on foot. There was no telling but that the next village might not contain the enemy spearhead. Rumours grew wilder and wilder. The first report of a blown bridge came from Lieutenant Buchanan-Jardine's Troop in "D" Squadron. It was on the outskirts of Genk, not more than five miles from Waterschei and on the Albert Canal. This caused a minor flap. Was it the first act of sabotage? Had parachutists landed? It died down quickly when the Troop Leader confirmed from a calm and sensible civilian that the bridge had been blown up by the British in 1940!

The Regiment was moving three Squadrons up, "A" right, "D" centre and "C" left, and as the information about the enemy was either non-existent or contradictory, no opportunity was lost of stopping American drivers and asking them the latest news. These proved either to be cheerfully unaware of anything wrong at all or else extremely suspicious of the British armoured cars, which they seemed to regard as being in league with the enemy if not downright hostile. There was good cause for this attitude because the Americans had as yet no idea that the British were moving across their lines of communication, and they also knew that German saboteurs were in the offing, but it did not make things easier for the Regiment. Yet somehow the Belgians seemed to have had word that we were coming and many had waited up all night at their doors for news, staring sleepily at the unusual night movement. And it was always, "The Boche are in the next village."

There were no other British units in the area and the familiar multi-coloured signs had given way to the dull black-and-white uniformity of the American stencilled boards. Progress continued to be wearisome and slow, caused partly by the traffic of our Allies but in the main by the thick fog. All through the hours of darkness the Squadrons sent back an unending stream of information about road surfaces and their width, traffic bottlenecks, blown bridges and, as regards the enemy, negative but vital information. By dawn the fog began to clear as a fine rain took its place.

Shortly before eight o'clock on the morning of the 20th, the first Troop looked down over the escarpment and on to the small town of Andenne and the River Meuse beyond. The inhabitants were going peacefully about their work and there was not a sign of the enemy. By ten o'clock Squadrons, with their headquarters on the high ground overlooking the river front, had established that no sizeable body of Germans had reached or had crossed the Meuse between Visé and Namur.[5] A network of roads to the rear had been reconnoitred, and Second Army supplied with the information which it required upon which to base subsequent dispositions.

The narrative has so far deliberately avoided all reference to the enemy situation south of the Meuse because what has been recorded was in fact all that was known at the time. This is a good stage at which to leave the Regiment for a while and examine the events leading up to the period which had ended our hopes of a peaceful Christmas in the Waterschei area.

Letter from General Sir Miles Dempsey regarding the German counter-offensive in the Ardennes

THE OLD VICARAGE,
GREENHAM,
NEWBURY,
BERKS.
1st December, 1949.

DEAR ORDE,

I can best answer your letter by giving you this background to the part played by 2 H.C.R. in December, 1944.

On 16 December, the Germans launched a counter-stroke on the front of the First and Third American Armies. North of the First Army was the Ninth American Army; north of the Ninth Army was Second Army, whose sector was from exclusive Maastricht northwards.

Although the German attacks were far to the south of Second Army, I realized that if they penetrated deeply and crossed the Meuse they would become a direct threat to Second Army's rear and the administrative area

---

5. It is interesting to note that documents subsequently captured from the Germans showed that von Rundstedt planned to make his first and main crossing between the old fortress town of Huy and Andenne, directly in the line of "D" Squadron and part of "A" Squadron. See also letter from General Sir Miles Dempsey.

in which all our reserves of ammunition, petrol and so on were being built up.

Accordingly I started at once to create a strong reserve freed from all other operational commitments.

My diary tells me that on

17 December I ordered 12 Corps to get Gds. Armd. Div. out of the line and assembled with 8 Armd. Bde: that on

18 December I ordered 12 Corps to move 43 Div. and 34 Armd. Bde. to the area Hasselt—Bree, and that 53 Div. were already in reserve in the Turnhout area.

This gave me a free reserve of three Divisions and two Armd. Bdes. H.Q. 30 Corps were also available.

The situation on the front of First and Third American Armies deteriorated considerably during 17-19 December, so much so that by the evening of 19 December leading elements of the enemy reached Marche and there were no American fighting formations between Marche and R. Meuse.

The situation which was a possibility on 16 December was now a distinct probability.

Although it was not within my province to send fighting formations into the American sector without previous arrangement with them, and although it was not until the night of 19/20 December that the Supreme Commander placed command of the battle "north of the break" under C.-in-C. 21 Army Group, General Montgomery telephoned me at 1700 hrs. 19 December and gave me the all clear to get positioned in rear of the American armies. He added to my reserves by placing 51 Div. (from Canadian Army) under my command.

I decided to send 2 H.C.R. to R. Meuse at once, in the true Armd. Car role, to get information whilst the reserve Divisions and Armd. Bdes, which I placed under H.Q. 30 Corps, were assembling.

Though the enemy offensive never in fact reached R. Meuse, the task given to 2 H.C.R. was exceedingly well carried out, and there is this remark in my diary: "... Despite the fog, the Regt. was disposed on the river line shortly after first light 20 December..."

How well placed the Regt. would have been to provide information if the enemy offensive had continued!

As regards your other point—the issue of written orders. Any operation orders or instructions that a senior commander writes in war are the brief résumé of the verbal directions he has personally given to a subordinate commander—probably just the two of them in a caravan.

The enclosed order,[6] which I gave to Peter Grant Lawson after our talk in my caravan, is a typical example. I wrote a great many similar notes during the campaign.

---

6. See page 436.

In two and a half years of fighting I received only one written order from General Montgomery without a previous talk, and I believe I issued one myself.

The full written order covering all the operational details is the job of the Chief of Staff, and no commander should ever become involved in this.

Yours sincerely,

MILES DEMPSEY.

Chapter VII

On the Meuse and Beyond

Events leading up to von Rundstedt's Ardennes counter-offensive—Americans take shock of first impact—2 H.C.R. patrols along the river front—"C" Squadron cross river in search of information—The Fog of War—Changes in regimental responsibility—Bastogne—Christmas Day—Corporal-of-Horse Jenkins and Trooper Beckett in Rochefort fighting—Captain Clyde's narrative—Much work for liaison officers—Captain Cooper's diary—Andenne Bridge—Summary of the Ardennes battle

While the Allied armies were building up and planning for the next offensive deep into the Rhineland which was to finish the war—when advances were limited to platoon and company objectives and whole divisions were being moved back into winter training quarters—the German High Command was planning a last desperate gamble. How near it came to success few at the time realized, but for days the fate of Brussels and Antwerp, and consequently the British and Canadian armies' lifeline, was to tremble in the balance.

All through November the Germans had been building up their depleted armies. The German equivalent to the Home Guard—the Volkssturm—had been formed. Men formerly considered unfit were drafted to the quiet sectors of the front to take their place with youths of sixteen and seventeen. At the same time, the garrisons of Norway and Denmark, the Baltic States and even the Balkans were combed for men who were then withdrawn to help reconstitute a German army equal in size if not in quality to that which had started the war.

Our Intelligence was aware that von Rundstedt, able planner, and victor of the German break-through in the Ardennes in 1940, had been reinstated by Hitler as Commander-in-Chief, Western Front. It was also known that a complete new army, the Sixth S.S. Panzer Army, fed from the best S.S. troops and Panzer Grenadiers, had completed its re-equipping, and had moved west over the Rhine. These two facts, viewed in the light of after events, must have pointed to the strong possibility of a counter-offensive. But what was not known to Allied Intelligence was that under the pine trees of the Eiffel Forest, greatly assisted by the bad weather nullifying aerial reconnaissance, three armies, the new Sixth S.S. Panzer, the Fifth Panzer and the rehabilitated Seventh, had been assembled in secrecy and with consummate skill, ready for the strike.

There is a nice story of American origin (which is probably as true as any other concerned with Hitler) that after the abortive attempt on the Fuehrer's life in July, he had amused himself when recovering in bed from his injuries by working out the details of the new offensive. He was, they said, literally blown into bed to hatch the von Rundstedt surprise.

The plan towards which von Rundstedt had directed his energies was not so fantastic or desperate as it has since been made out. His information was excellent. Agents left behind in France and the Low Countries were supplying him with a constant stream of news. By December he knew where every Allied division was placed, and it was obvious that, braced as they were for the offensive, the Americans had the bulk of their forces in the line. Almost everything was in the shop window, and the last thing that any British or American commander expected was an enemy counter-offensive.

Von Rundstedt had selected for his operation a thinly held sector of the First United States Army front, knowing full well that from Trier to Monschau, a distance of seventy-five miles, no more than four divisions were in the line—a disposition which, in Eisenhower's words, was "a calculated risk," based on the probability that the enemy would not in his present desperate state take a risk in winter which if it failed would ultimately be of disastrous consequence to Germany.

Throughout history the Ardennes has been the gateway in and out of Germany. Three times within living memory the French and Belgians have been rolled back by the disciplined hordes emerging through it from the east. Doubtless, as a young Staff Officer, von Rundstedt had studied and restudied the terrain until he was familiar with every road and stream and forest ride within it.

The Luftwaffe, which had been little in evidence, was regrouped and it was planned to put up thousands of aircraft in support of the ground forces. A brigade of Germans dressed in American uniform and travelling in American tanks and jeeps was to be used to create confusion and alarm. Sabotaging parachutists were held in readiness to be dropped behind the line, with lists of Allied commanders to be liquidated. The flying bomb barrage was to be stepped up and directed principally at Liége and Antwerp. Never before had eight Panzer divisions—a total of over a thousand tanks—been engaged on so narrow a front. No less than seventeen Infantry, Panzer Grenadier and Parachute divisions were to back up the armoured spearhead.

On the 14th and 15th of December the Fifth Panzer Army slipped quietly off through the forests to group itself around the town of Prum.

Equally silent and undetected, the Sixth Army took its place. On the 16th of December, preceded by the heaviest barrage fired by the enemy during the entire war, von Rundstedt struck simultaneously between Monschau and Echternach and dropped parachute parties along the projected route.

The shock was chaotic and the thin American line simply disappeared. An American division newly landed took the first blow and was rolled up. Another armoured division was caught on its flank and thrown completely off balance. Headquarters after headquarters were encircled or overrun, and a stream of flying bombs intensified the savage onslaught. The roads filled with fleeing civilians, hampering friend, and unconsciously aiding the foe. Then, to spread the confusion, ostensibly friendly tanks appeared, only to open fire when within range.

The first German prisoners captured had all the confidence of 1940 and arrogantly predicted victory for the Reich in a matter of months.

When Stavelot fell, the Americans lost one of their key points of communication. Now no one—least of all S.H.A.E.F.—had any clear idea of what was happening, but it was obvious that since the first vague message on the 16th stating that "some penetrations of the American line have been made, using tanks,[1] "things had deteriorated alarmingly. With incredible speed the Germans appeared in one village after another. It would appear that all through the 17th of December the battle was out of control. On the 18th a thick fog had descended over the battlefield. What has been described as "the major imponderable of war," the question of why and when will a soldier fight over and above a certain accepted standard of courage and devotion to duty, was being decided among the wooded heights east of the Meuse. We now know that it was only the desperate resistance of isolated American units, fighting often without orders or information from above, which saved the day for the Allies. In the midst of utter confusion and bloodshed, the Americans held on when by all normal standards hope should have been abandoned. It was this early resistance—this and nothing else—which saved Belgium and Holland from being overrun once more.

When by the 19th of December it became apparent that the German counter-offensive was a direct threat to Liége and Antwerp likely to cut off the British and nearly half the American forces from their supply bases, General Eisenhower made an important decision. He ordered Field-Marshal Montgomery to assume temporary operational command

---

1. First message to reach 12 Army Group Headquarters on the 16th of December. See General Eisenhower's "Report by Supreme Commander to the Combined Chiefs of Staff" (H.M. Stationery Office).

of the U.S. troops north of the penetration, for, because of the split, it was obviously impracticable for General Bradley to retain control of the Ninth and half the First U.S. Armies isolated as they were from his 12 Army Group Headquarters, located far to the south. Concentrations for the forthcoming Rhineland battle were therefore stopped immediately, while preparations were made to regroup in such a manner as, firstly, to seal the German bulge and, secondly, to collect an adequate counter-attack force on the northern flank. Meanwhile instructions were issued for the Seventh U.S. Army to side-step northwards from Alsace to the limits of safety, thus releasing as much of the Third U.S. Army as possible to counterattack the southern flank of the penetration.

Meanwhile, in the words of Montgomery, "the situation remained unpleasantly vague, and I undertook emergency measures to get reconnaissance troops down to the line of the Meuse and to assist in forming effective cover parties for the Meuse bridges between Liége and Givet. Detachments of S.A.S. Troops and Tank Replacement Centre Personnel were sent to the river in the Namur—Givet sector while armoured cars of Second Army established patrol links between Liége and Namur."[2]

This then was the general situation (as known) when the Regiment arrived on the Meuse early on the morning of the 20th of December.

★   ★   ★

One of the first Troops to arrive on the scene was Lieutenant Franklin's, feeling not unnaturally that it might at any moment encounter the full might of von Rundstedt's Panzer elite. But everything was quiet and peaceful. "As dawn broke I came over the last ridge of hills and looked down on to the little village of Andenne, just over the river, and a few houses shattered at each end of the concrete and steel bridge. I breathed a sigh of relief and ordered breakfast. In the road, Trooper Lees dug a hole, poured petrol into it, and a match completed the cooking arrangements. I had been asked for a report on the blown bridge and reminded them that it had been blown up for the last four years and over, but they still seemed inquisitive, so off I went to a little hut and told the foreman there

---

2. *Normandy to the Baltic* by Field-Marshal the Viscount Montgomery of Alamein (page 176), Hutchinson & Co (Publishers) Ltd., London. The armoured cars referred to are those of 2 H.C.R. Patrol links were from Visé to Namur and not as stated, Liége to Namur. In actual fact 29th Armoured Brigade did not arrive on the line of the Meuse until the 21st of December, nor did the S.A.S., who were Belgian troops. This is made clear in the privately printed "History of 11th Armoured Division," page 2 of the section devoted to 29th Armoured Brigade.

that I was going to build a new bridge and wanted the full particulars of the old one. I little guessed for what I had asked. Plans were unrolled before my gaze and the width, depth, and speed of current, soil at banks and everything about the river was noted down by me in metres, centimetres, and millimetres. I think that he almost expected me, like the devil, to build another bridge overnight. I am not sure that I did not give such assurances!"

As to what was happening south and east of the Meuse, we knew as yet very little, for Major Sir Peter Grant Lawson had not been allowed to send his patrols beyond the river bridges. There was good reason for this veto because we were still the only British troops in the area, and it was General Dempsey's intention that, should the enemy arrive on the Meuse and effect a crossing, our armoured cars were to shadow their armour unremittingly until an effective British counterattack force could be assembled.

We had been warned that the Germans had dropped parachutists behind the lines and that they were employing numbers of trained saboteurs, both as civilians and in Allied uniform. For this reason patrols were soon halting Americans and checking their identity papers. They reciprocated with enthusiasm, and as nobody had been told what to look for, there were some tense incidents requiring tact to complete formalities without bloodshed to either party.

Our Allies appeared to be unconversant with what was happening farther east in the battle zone, and until we were permitted to cross the river we had to fall back largely on information gathered from refugees. This was either unreliable and hours out of date or else downright alarmist. But it appeared fairly certain that the Germans had reached Marche—a surmise which proved correct to within a few miles.

Meanwhile the hours sped by as an orgy of spy fever spread over the countryside, and long convoys of Negro-driven transport continued to swirl over the Liége bridges into the darkening gloom, blissfully unaware of the thunder of arms to the east. We wondered what the maximum speed of the Panther tank would be in the thick fog which still enveloped the countryside. Much appeared to depend on the answer to this question, for on the entire river line Dinant—Namur there was still no sizeable body of defensive armour should the enemy choose to drive due west. This latter move was in fact taking place—for the stiff American resistance on both flanks of the bulge was beginning to canalize the German drive away from Liége and Huy and on towards Dinant.

Colonel Abel Smith, who had got no farther than Brussels before being recalled, arrived back at three o'clock in the afternoon. By dusk the situation had taken on a slightly more reassuring aspect. 30 Corps was in the process of establishing a strong striking force behind the regimental reconnaissance screen and preparing to bar the roads to Brussels. The intention was to strike at the right flank of the German thrust should the enemy succeed in crossing the river. News later came through that Guards Armoured Division would be moving into position to our north within the triangle Diest—St. Trond—Tirlemont. But having first to disengage from the Gangelt sector near Sittard, its units would not be arriving until the morrow. Darkness came with still no sign of enemy, but refugees pouring back in ever-growing numbers.

At two o'clock on the morning of the 21st of December the Regiment reverted to under command of 30 Corps, whose Headquarters had moved down to Hasselt. Regimental responsibility now became the line Charleroi—Namur—Huy (inclusive); Namur town being held by a scratch force, including some Royal Engineers on the bridges disguised under the mysterious name of "R" Force. "A" Squadron was on the right, "B" centre, and "D" on the left.

Permission was at last given for the Regiment to cross the Meuse, and Colonel Abel Smith ordered Major Herbert to send out patrols at first light to make contact with as many American formation headquarters as possible in the extensive area of Ouffet—Marche —Rochefort. Major Herbert's Troops soon found out that, contrary to civilian rumours, the Americans had been grimly hanging on to the important road communication centres of Vielsam, Marche and Bastogne, thus denying to the enemy the unimpeded progress which his supply columns urgently required if he was to reach the Meuse. Except to the west, where the German 2nd Panzer Division was thrusting hard towards Givet, it was found that a line was definitely forming on both sides of the bulge.

This information had not been too easy to come by because, like the British, the Americans had been deluged with spy stories and were rightly security minded. In addition, they had suffered from numerous enemy outrages behind their lines and had also got wind of a story that a certain Hungarian cut-throat named Otto Skorzeny, in the pay of the Germans, was at large and bent on assassinating General Eisenhower.

As our patrols had been given no American passwords they were frequently detained and in one case even arrested, when a patrol was placed in custody for the night in spite of the most vehement protests from its commander that he was not Otto Skorzeny. Fortunately, the Americans forgot the wireless set, and the Troop Leader was able to relay back a stream of information, including lists of U.S. headquarters locations taken off the map in the detaining formation's own operations room!

From now on the Regiment maintained one Squadron patrolling daily south of the Meuse along the westerly limits of the German break-through, while the remaining three Squadrons manned the river line in anticipation of a role which, thanks to the tenacity of the Americans, never materialized. In fact, for those north of the Meuse it became another "Shaef" period, with the added advantage of there being no enemy to deal with.

At ten o'clock on the morning of the 21st the Regiment reverted to under command Guards Armoured Division, whose units were now beginning to arrive.

That the repeated emphasis on the fog of war which the Adjutant makes in the War Diary is in no way exaggerated can be seen by a glance back to the following account written from a divisional standpoint by Major the Hon. F. F. G. Hennessy. The time is nine o'clock on the morning of the 20th. The scene is Second Army Headquarters, which the narrator had just reached ahead of General Horrocks.

> "'This is splendid,' said the General; 'if we keep our heads and don't do anything silly this may shorten the war by months.'
>
> "It was now 9 a.m. and already, by some brilliant driving through the night, the Household Cavalry had reported Liége and Namur clear of enemy. This was wonderful and invaluable news. It left, in the Corps Commander's words, three courses open. One, to try to hold the Meuse, possibly arriving too late and too weak in the vital spot. Two, to hold on to the 1940 Dyle positions, thereby abandoning a vast amount of equipment and stores. Three, to stand back in the Tirlemont—St. Trond area waiting until he [the enemy] crossed the river and then go in with a whoop and cut him to pieces. The latter course he decided was not only the most attractive but the soundest. Could the Guards Armoured Division be formed up with one battalion group in Tirlemont and the other in St. Trond ready to strike at first light next morning?
>
> "The Grenadiers have their own traditional formula for meeting every contingency. It consists of the straightforward reply, 'Sir.' Just as the Chinese economize in words and obtain their meaning and expressions entirely by inflection of the voice, so the Grenadier can, by skilful employment of this single monosyllable, imply everything from immediate co-operation to abject insubordination. On this occasion my Grenadier training stood in good stead. I played a 'Sir' and went away to think it out.
>
> "I was out of wireless range with Divisional Headquarters; the orders to move and concentrate in the Diest—Louvain area had already reached the Troops and in fact some had already started; they would be

arriving through what promised to be another foggy night—to change the destination of the whole division to new concentration areas under such conditions and without previous reconnaissance was a risky task, especially when one considers that at least five divisions were on the move at the same time. And the vital American supply route which passed through our area had also to be kept clear at all costs.

"But it was a risk-taking season. And we had always been rather proud of our march discipline. Now was the time to put it to the supreme test.

"'Sir,' I repeated in a quite different tone of voice. By now it was midday and the Household Cavalry had just reported back to Army, under whose direct command they were now working, that the whole river line was clear of the enemy as far as Givet.

"The fog was now less thick, but their task had not been an easy one and they had carried it out with outstanding skill and alacrity. Furthermore, their commander had organized five scout car patrols with orders to make a wide sweep of the Ardennes itself. It must be realized that at this time no one at all at any Headquarters, either British or American, knew how far the spearhead of the German advance had penetrated. It was, however, confidently reported from every quarter that they had passed through Marche, an important centre of communications only some twenty miles from Liége and Namur.

"The five patrols were given five objectives, each with a code name, *Rugby*, *Leicester*, etc. Marche was *London*. At 4 p.m. the news came through, 'London clear of enemy.'[3] 'That's something, anyhow,' commented the General, with a grin.[4] He had heard it on his own wireless set but had not yet received the code-names. Here was authentic definite news spoken by someone who was actually standing in the main street. Things were beginning to look much better.

"Back in the divisional sector there was much speculation during the day as to whether we should ever succeed in extracting ourselves from the line. The enemy were showing themselves very restive to our front. Should they attack, as was confidently expected, any chance of relief was out of the question.

"In fact the attack never came in and, as dusk fell, the Division started pulling back over our Affreuse Old Meuse and on through a cold and misty night to a dispersal point which we had set up at Hasselt. Here, through one of the longest nights I can ever remember, harassed officers and M.Ps. strove to convince doubting drivers that they were not fifth columnists endeavouring to turn the column straight into the enemy lines, but that there had in fact been a change of plan.

---

3. Message from "C" Squadron, 2 H.C.R.
4. Major-General Adair, commanding Guards Armoured Division.

"'Who are you? First Grenadiers—straight on down the road to St. Trond—halt with your head short of the main Louvain—Namur road and get off into the fields as fast as you can at first light. Above all keep that main road clear—it's the American supply route and I reckon they are going to need it.'

"'But Diest is my destination.'

"'I know, but the hotels are terrible, and, my dear, the drains! Please try St. Trond. They say that they make some wonderful brandy out of army petrol there.'

"'First Coldstream, are you? Turn right and carry on to Tirlemont. Yes, I did tell him St. Trond, but you've changed brigades now. You'll find yourself under 32nd Guards Brigade tomorrow morning.'

"'How's it going?' I said to Pat at about 3 a.m.

"'Well, it's going—only the grey light of dawn will reveal how,' he replied."

The grey light of dawn (21st December) did reveal, as we have seen, that Guards Armoured Division were arriving safely, and within a few hours the roads were clear, each unit having neatly fitted itself into its allotted area.

★   ★   ★

The frontage of river for which the Regiment was now responsible was still considerable. It had merely been shifted farther west, the distance from Charleroi to Huy along the Rivers Sambre and Meuse being over fifty miles. The method of operating which was adopted was for a Troop to be responsible for a bridge or ferry, with cars placed in a tactical position near the site being watched. Permanent guards were placed at the site. This procedure was not always possible because there were many more bridges and likely crossing points than Troops; in which case Troops were split, and even then sometimes no more than a patrolling scout car could be spared for a long stretch of river. It was a busy time, for numbers of refugees, including Luxemburgers who spoke suspiciously Germanic French, kept crossing the Meuse and had to be screened.

On one occasion civilians reported that there was a German parachutist examining the banks of the Meuse near Huy. A scout car was dispatched immediately to the scene. One miserable little man with his clothes in tatters was found lurking in the reeds, almost frozen to death. He looked remarkably inoffensive and as unlike one of Skorzeny's cut-throats as can be imagined, but the Belgians explained his ragged clothes and poor physique as another example of the Hun's cunning. There was nothing for it but to take him back to Squadron Headquarters for further questioning. On arrival the little man, who only spoke German, burst into tears, and explained that he was a baker from the town of Luxemburg. He had fled on the approach of the Germans, somehow travelled straight through the enemy bulge, and emerged on the Meuse, to his intense surprise, near Namur. His car had run out of petrol and he was hoping to obtain further supplies, offering his services as a baker in exchange. While making a preliminary investigation he had been horrified to see what he imagined to be "the black berets of the German Panzer Corps d'Elite." It turned out to be the crew of one Household Cavalry 3-tonner on the opposite bank. He was eventually sent back to Lieutenant Haskard in the shameless way that Sabre Squadrons used to rid themselves of border-line Social Welfare cases by dumping them on to the Intelligence Officer.

On another occasion Lieutenant Buchanan-Jardine was patrolling along the road to Namur near the village of Hingeon. It was about eight o'clock at night and bitingly cold. A routine roadblock had been set up and vehicles made to halt for examination of identity papers. Suddenly an American six-wheeled lorry appeared round a corner and only just managed to stop on the icy road in time. The elements had caused the heavily muffled crew to put up a celluloid sidescreen which was opaque. The contents of the lorry were draped with a black tarpaulin tightly tied down. A request for identification papers was answered from the depths of the frost-encrusted cab by a non-committal mumble. The order was repeated peremptorily and accompanied by a threatening gesture from the covering tommy-gun. In answer, the sidescreen on the driver's side burst open and a grinning coal-black face wrapped in a balaclava popped out, "Say, boss, has you ever seen a black German?"

The main line from Liége to Namur and Brussels ran alongside the river and German prisoners would sometimes try to escape by leaping out of a passing cattle truck. Most would be picked up immediately, but a few escaped the vigilance of the guards. It happened that one morning "A" Squadron received an urgent message from the Belgians that the local countryside was in a panic. "Fourteen Germans, led by a ruffianly looking type, wearing half British, half civilian uniform and old boots with holes in them, are ravaging the district." It turned out to be nothing more harmless than Lieutenant Hopkinson and his Support Troop on a routine patrol.

★ ★ ★

The question of tie-ups with the various units which were now beginning to arrive was a problem for the Commanding Officer. There were meetings to be arranged at every level, both British and American. To take but a few examples, there were the U.S. anti-sabotage guards, the U.S. Engineers on the bridges at Huy and Andenne, our own Sappers, Field Security Sections, and even the Belgian Gendarmes. All took a deal of time and patience.

It will be remembered that originally there was talk of the 30 Corps plan being to allow the Germans to cross the Meuse and then to crack at them on their flank. But had this been permitted to happen (assuming that the Germans had broken clean through the Americans) the battle must have taken place in the middle of the U.S. Supply Dumps for the northern group of armies. Accordingly, Field-Marshal Montgomery, who since the 20th of December, it will be remembered, had been in command of part of First U.S. Army and the Ninth U.S. Army north of the bulge as well as his own 21 Army Group, altered the plan to one of holding the line of the Meuse.[5]

Encouraging news now came through that at Bastogne, an important road centre urgently required by the Germans for the continuance of their advance, the isolated 101st U.S. Airborne Division[6] was making a magnificent stand against great odds. This body of men, which we had met at Eindhoven, had been flown to the battle area from Rheims, arriving at a critical phase on the 18th of December just in time to be surrounded and cut off in Bastogne. In no way dismayed by the turn of events, the American commander, Major-General MacAuliffe, fought back with determination and successfully repelled attack after attack. He was able to strafe the German lines of communication (which were compelled to pass within gun range of the Bastogne garrison) to such good effect that the enemy was forced to divert troops urgently required elsewhere to contain the Americans. On the 22nd of December, the German commander of the investing troops sent forth an order to surrender. "The fortunes of war are changing. This time it is you who are completely surrounded by strong German armoured forces. We have captured Marche—your position is hopeless—honourable surrender will be accorded," etc. etc. Back went the unusual but lucid reply, "Nuts."

5. As Montgomery saw it, "Clearly the first problem before us was to halt the enemy advance and oppose it with a firm front in conjunction with 12 Army Group to the south; this demanded certain regrouping, behind which we had 30 Corps ready to hold the line of the Meuse" (*Normandy to the Baltic*, page 176; Hutchinson & Co.)

6. The commitment of this Division removed the last reserve available in the European theatre of operations. Other Divisions were hurriedly ordered out from England, ahead of training schedule. (See Eisenhower's report to the Combined Chiefs of Staff, page 94.)

Meanwhile, although the momentum of the German offensive appeared to be slowing down, the threat to Liége and Dinant remained serious.

"C" Squadron continued their patrols in search of information, while Captain Balding, now installed at First U.S. Army Headquarters, sent back much information which 30 Corps and Second Army lapped up with avidity. His was a delicate mission to carry out at this stage, for Anglo-American feelings in certain headquarters were a trifle tense, to say the least. Insinuations about faulty American Intelligence in the Eiffel still rankled, and the fact of "Monty" taking over command of all their fighting troops north of the break-through, and tactless remarks in certain sections of the British Press to the effect that "Monty will show them how it should be done" did not improve matters. Nor must it be forgotten that the Americans were doing ninety-nine per cent. of the fighting while the British, through circumstances outside their control, could only sit back on the Meuse and await events in comparative comfort and security.

The 22nd December must have been an anxious day for the British Commander-in-Chief, for as fast as he assembled his American Corps defensively in the path of the German thrust on Liége, its units were sucked into immensely heavy fighting. A second American Corps was formed and drawn into battle before it had the chance to act offensively, and so for the third time in twenty-four hours yet another Corps was re-formed in front of Liége.

The next day, the 23rd of December, opened with promise of an improved situation because it was apparent from captured documents that the enemy was behind schedule, and at no place had he yet reached the Meuse. I well remember sitting in the little parlour of a farmhouse overlooking the river from the heights above Andenne. Messages from "C" Squadron kept coming through continually. Moving over the Meuse at dawn, the Squadron drove up to the château at Sorée, and from there half-Troops would probe forward along the northern sector of the Panzer spearhead from Rochefort to Marche and up to as far as Grandmesnil.

Back on the River Meuse things remained very quiet and there was little for Troops to do but to keep maps up to date, mark up the enemy situation, motor up and down the banks of the river, check suspicious civilians and rumours, and allay the fears of the Belgians, who were still convinced that the Germans would be arriving at any moment. When General Dempsey arrived on a tour of the river front in his jeep, it was to find "D" Squadron Headquarters in a little café at Hingeon, comfortably ensconced in the bar, eating Zeeland oysters from a large barrel which Groeninx van Zoelen had newly brought back with him from a Brussels forty-eight hours' leave.

Those troops off duty lived and slept in houses close to their posts. The inhabitants were delighted to accommodate their guests and reposed

Despatch rider and Staghound armoured car on the Meuse.

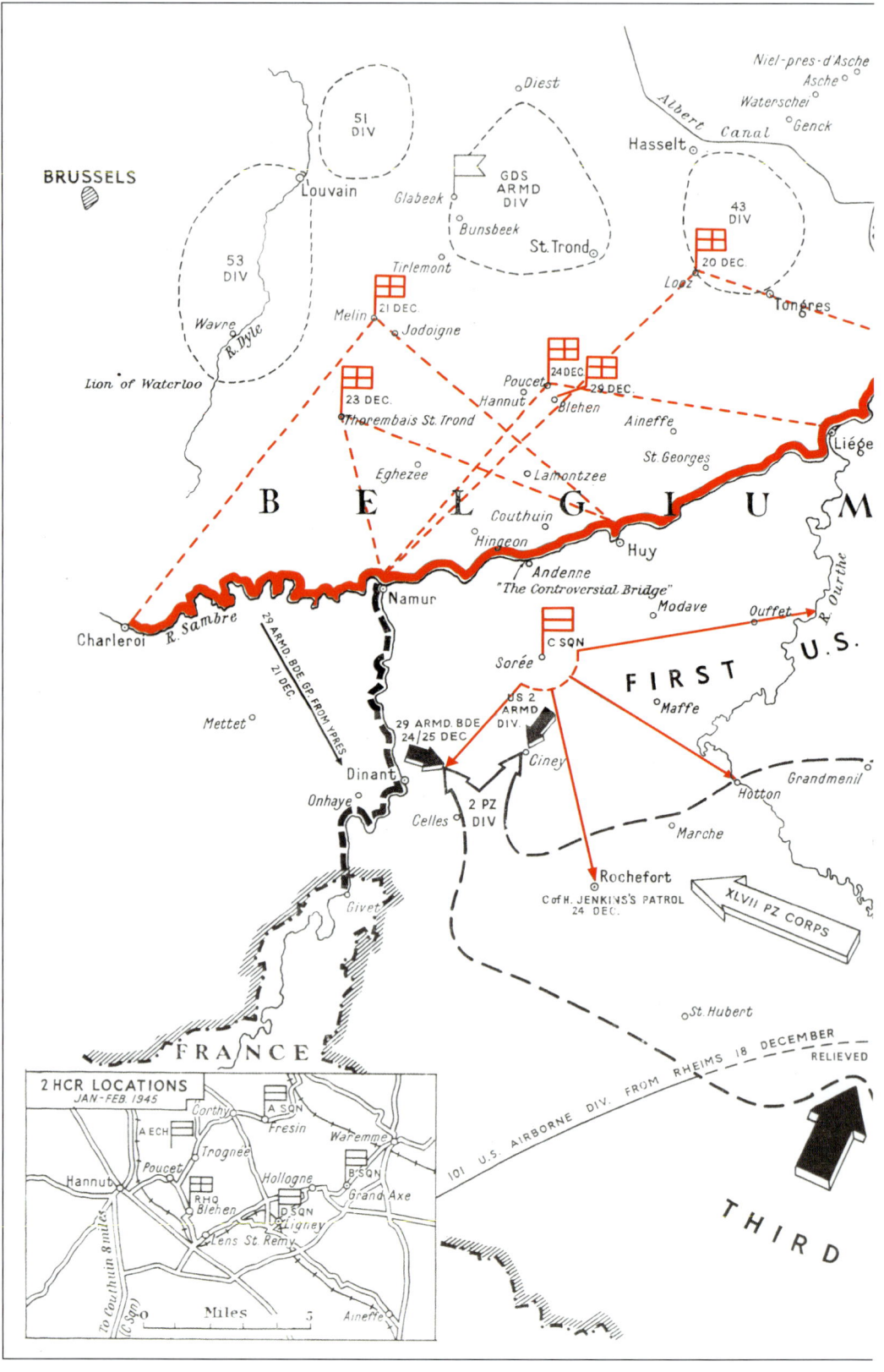

Niel-pres-d'Asche
Asche
Waterschei
Genck

BRUSSELS

Albert Canal

Hasselt

51 DIV

Diest

Louvain

GDS ARMD DIV

43 DIV
20 DEC.

Glabeek

Bunsbeek

St. Trond

Looz

Tongres

53 DIV

Tirlemont

Melin
21 DEC.
Jodoigne

24 DEC.
Poucet
Hannut
Blehen
29 DEC.

Aineffe

Liége

Wavre

R. Dyle

Lion of Waterloo

23 DEC.
Thorembais St. Trond

St. Georges

B   E   L   G   I   U   M

Eghezee

Lamontzee

Couthuin

Hingeon

Huy

Andenne
"The Controversial Bridge"

Modave

Ouffet

R. Ourthe

Namur

C SQN

Sorée

FIRST   U.S.

Charleroi

R. Sambre

29 ARMD. BDE. GP. FROM YPRES

Maffe

Mettet

21 DEC.

29 ARMD. BDE.
24/25 DEC.

US 2 ARMD. DIV.

Ciney

Grandmenil

Dinant

Celles

2 PZ DIV

Hotton

Onhaye

Marche

Givet

Rochefort
C of H. JENKINS'S PATROL
24 DEC.

XLVII PZ CORPS

St. Hubert

F   R   A   N   C   E

2 HCR LOCATIONS
JAN.-FEB. 1945

A SQN

Corthy

Fresin

Waremme

A ECH

Trognee

Poucet

Hollogne

B SQN

101 U.S. AIRBORNE DIV. FROM RHEIMS 18 DECEMBER

RELIEVED

Hannut

RHQ
Blehen

Ligney

Grand Axe

Lens St. Remy

T   H   I   R   D

To Couthuin 8 miles

(C Sqn)

Aineffe

Miles   5

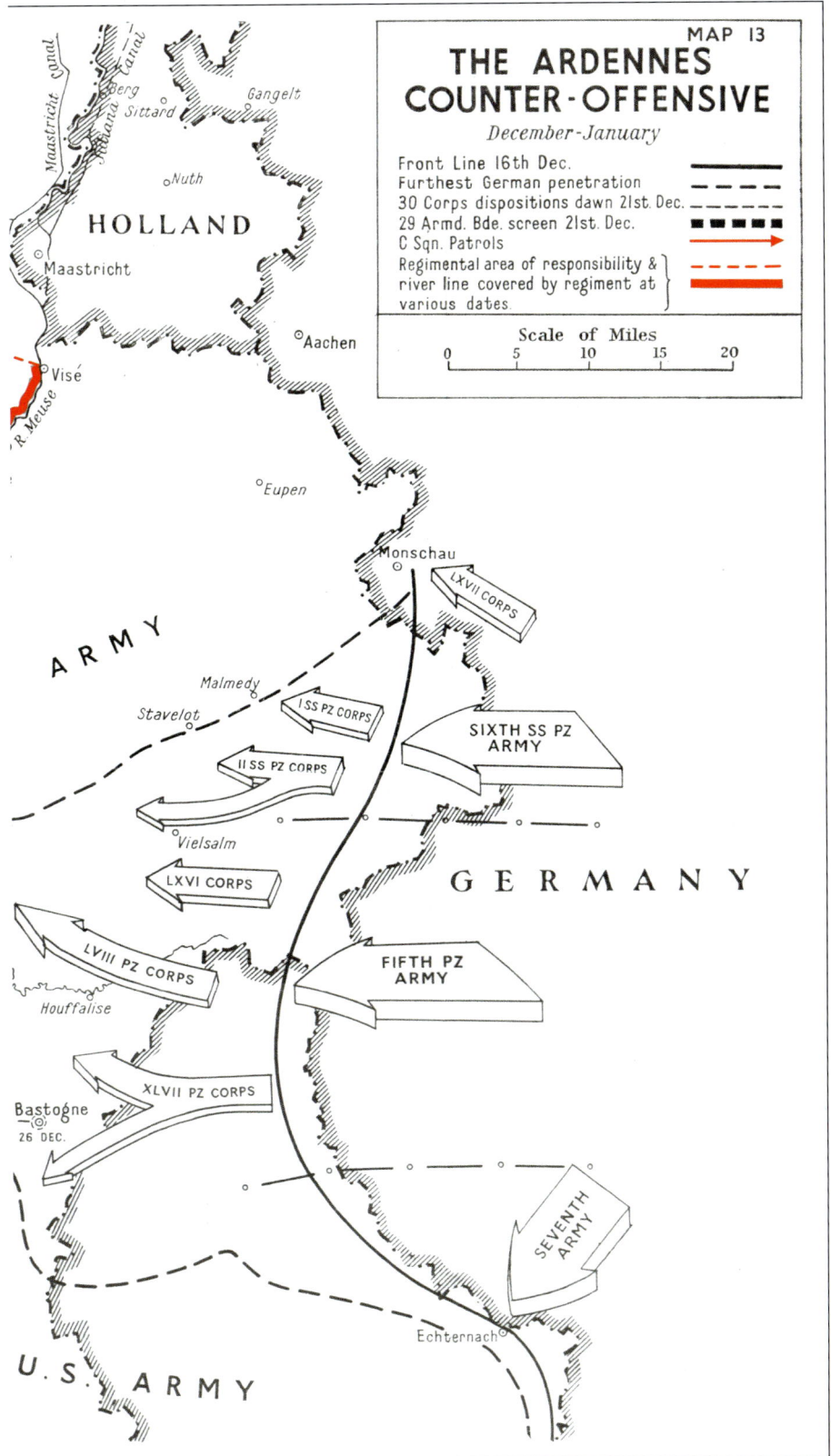

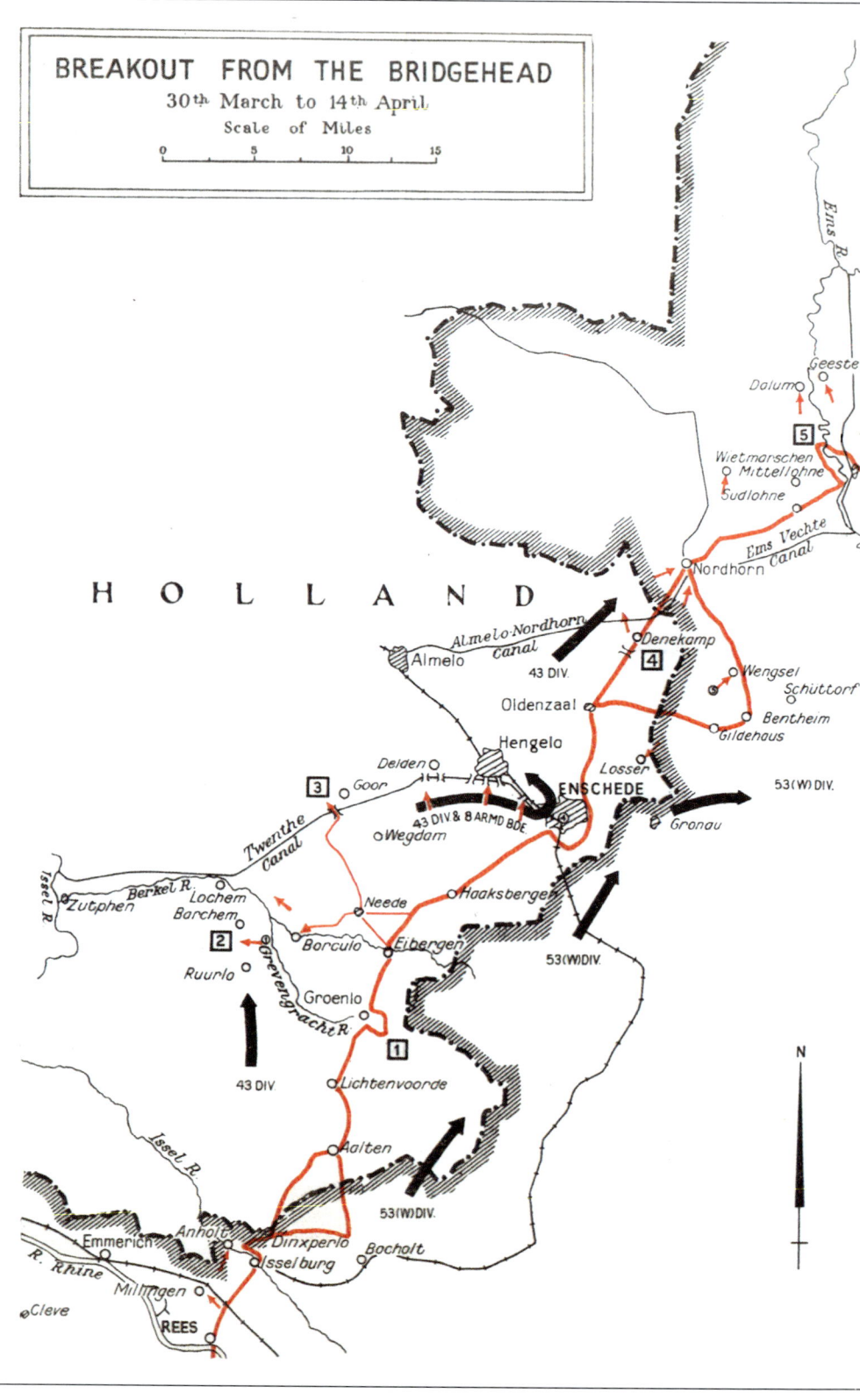

BREAKOUT FROM THE BRIDGEHEAD
30th March to 14th April
Scale of Miles

0 — 5 — 10 — 15

H O L L A N D

Ems R.

Geeste
Dalum
5
Wietmarschen
Mittellohne
Südlohne
Ems Vechte Canal
Nordhorn
Almelo-Nordhorn Canal
Almelo
Denekamp
43 DIV.
4
Wengsel
Schüttorf
Oldenzaal
Bentheim
Hengelo
Gildehaus
Losser
Delden
ENSCHEDE
53(W)DIV.
3 Goor
43 DIV & 8 ARMD BDE
Gronau
Twenthe Canal
Wegdam
Zutphen
Berkel R.
Lochem
Barchem
Neede
Haaksbergen
Issel R.
Grevengracht R.
2
Borculo
Eibergen
53(W)DIV.
Ruurlo
Groenlo
1
N
Lichtenvoorde
43 DIV
Issel R.
Aalten
53(W)DIV.
Anholt
Emmerich
Dinxperlo
R. Rhine
Millingen
Isselburg
Bocholt
Cleve
REES

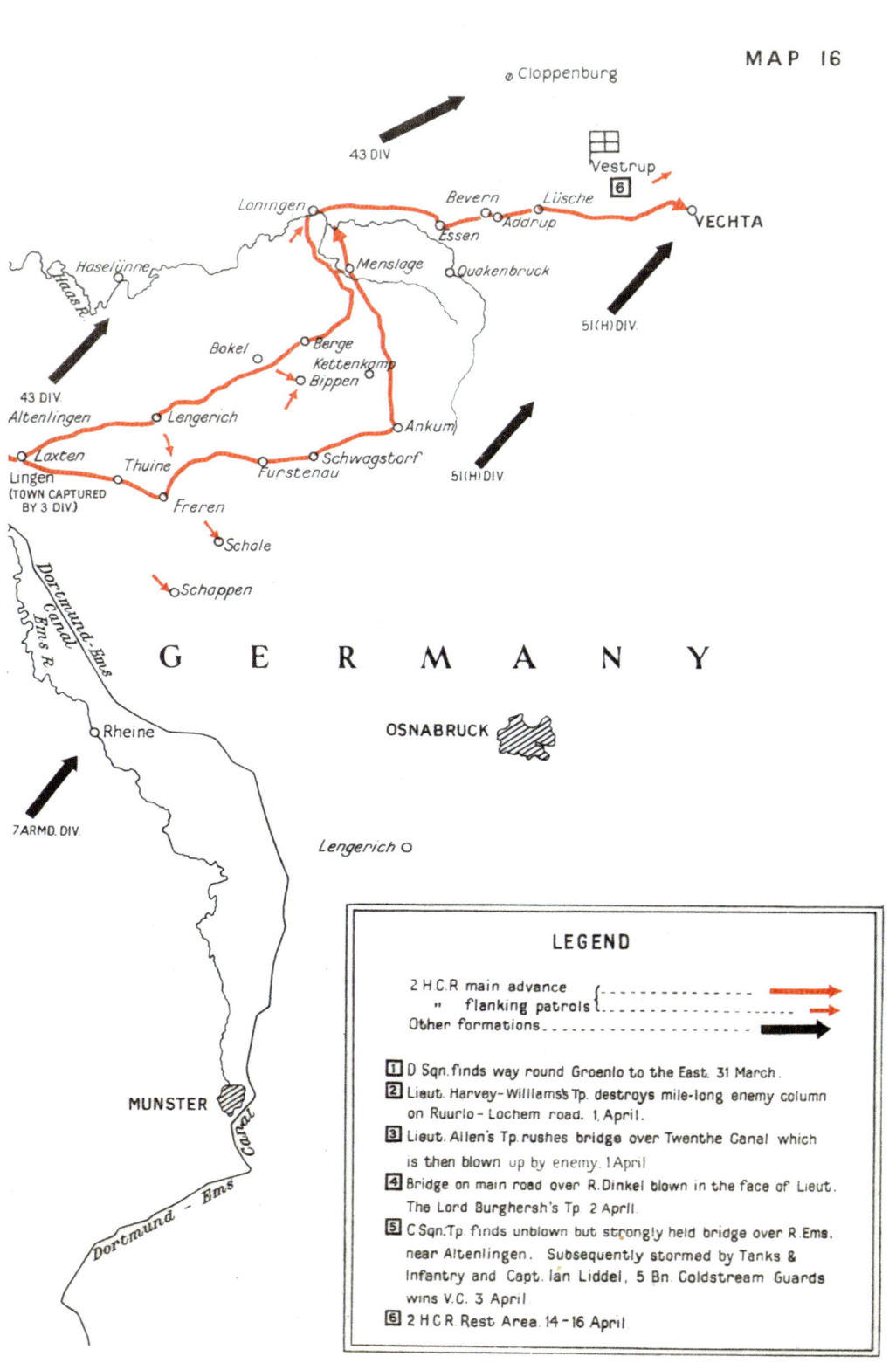

MAP 16

Cloppenburg

43 DIV

Vestrup
6

Loningen   Bevern   Lüsche
           Essen   Addrup   VECHTA
Menslage   Quakenbruck
                          51 (H) DIV.
Haselünne

Bokel   Berge
         Kettenkamp
         Bippen
43 DIV.
Altenlingen
Lengerich   Ankum
Laxten   Thuine   Schwagstorf
Lingen   Furstenau
(TOWN CAPTURED   51 (H) DIV.
BY 3 DIV)   Freren

Schale

Schappen

G E R M A N Y

OSNABRUCK

Rheine

7 ARMD. DIV.

Lengerich

MUNSTER

LEGEND

2 H.C.R. main advance
       „   flanking patrols
Other formations

[1] D Sqn. finds way round Groenlo to the East. 31 March.
[2] Lieut. Harvey-Williams's Tp. destroys mile-long enemy column
    on Ruurlo – Lochem road. 1 April.
[3] Lieut. Allen's Tp. rushes bridge over Twenthe Canal which
    is then blown up by enemy. 1 April
[4] Bridge on main road over R. Dinkel blown in the face of Lieut.
    The Lord Burghersh's Tp. 2 April.
[5] C Sqn. Tp. finds unblown but strongly held bridge over R. Ems.
    near Altenlingen. Subsequently stormed by Tanks &
    Infantry and Capt. Ian Liddel, 5 Bn. Coldstream Guards
    wins V.C. 3 April.
[6] 2 H.C.R. Rest Area. 14 – 16 April.

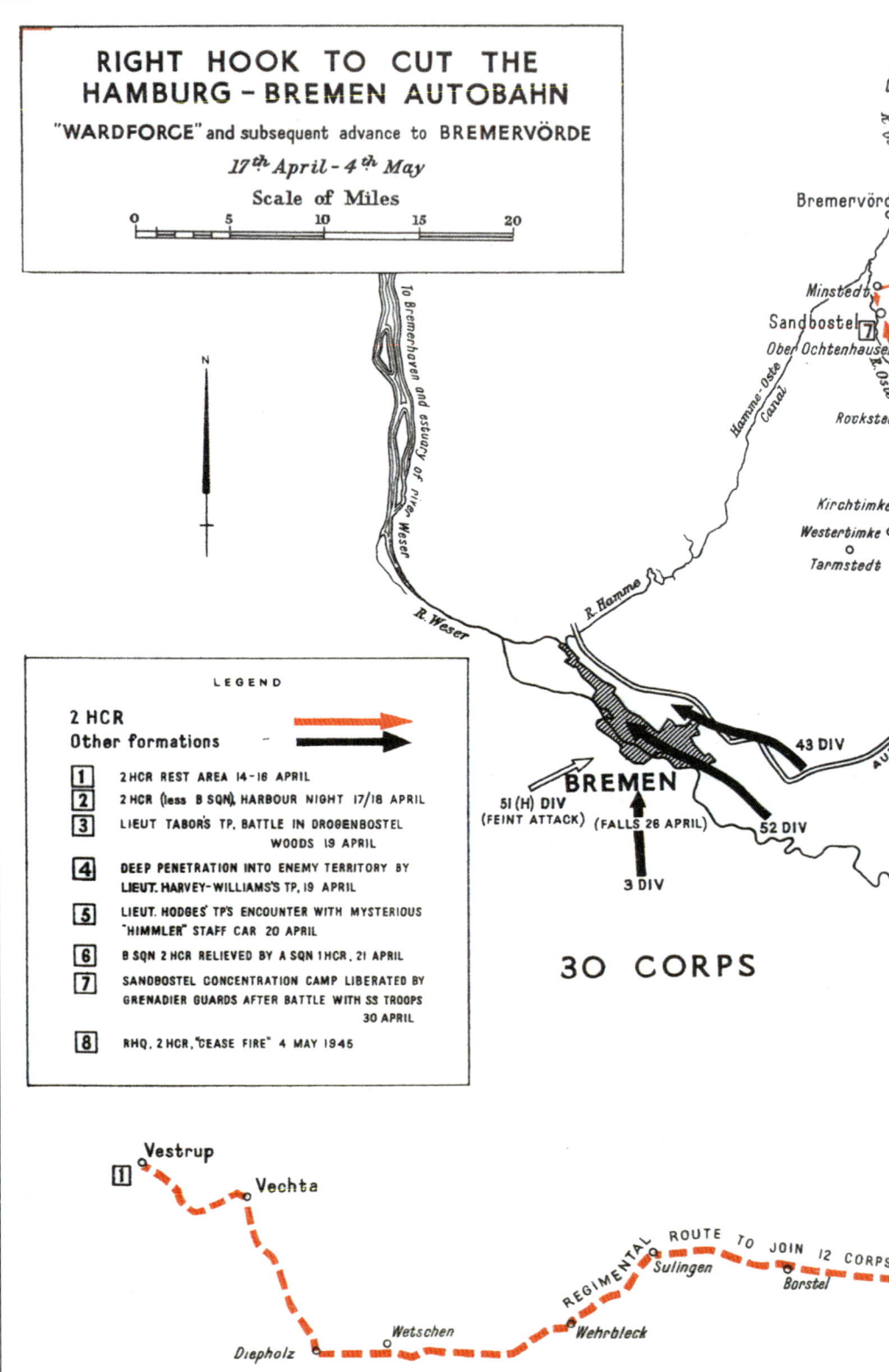

RIGHT HOOK TO CUT THE HAMBURG – BREMEN AUTOBAHN

"WARDFORCE" and subsequent advance to BREMERVÖRDE

17ᵗʰ April – 4ᵗʰ May

Scale of Miles

0   5   10   15   20

N

To Bremerhaven and estuary of river Weser

Bremervörde

Minstedt

Sandbostel

Ober Ochtenhausen

Rockstedt

Kirchtimke

Westertimke

Tarmstedt

Hamme-Oste Canal

R. Oste

R. Weser

R. Hamme

43 DIV

BREMEN

51 (H) DIV
(FEINT ATTACK)   (FALLS 26 APRIL)

52 DIV

3 DIV

AUT

30 CORPS

LEGEND

2 HCR
Other formations

1 2 HCR REST AREA 14-18 APRIL

2 2 HCR (less B SQN) HARBOUR NIGHT 17/18 APRIL

3 LIEUT. TABOR'S TP, BATTLE IN DROGENBOSTEL
   WOODS 19 APRIL

4 DEEP PENETRATION INTO ENEMY TERRITORY BY
   LIEUT. HARVEY-WILLIAMS'S TP, 19 APRIL

5 LIEUT. HODGES' TP'S ENCOUNTER WITH MYSTERIOUS
   "HIMMLER" STAFF CAR 20 APRIL

6 B SQN 2 HCR RELIEVED BY A SQN 1 HCR, 21 APRIL

7 SANDBOSTEL CONCENTRATION CAMP LIBERATED BY
   GRENADIER GUARDS AFTER BATTLE WITH SS TROOPS
   30 APRIL

8 RHQ, 2 HCR, "CEASE FIRE" 4 MAY 1945

Vestrup

1

Vechta

REGIMENTAL ROUTE TO JOIN 12 CORPS

Sulingen

Borstel

Wetschen

Wehrbleck

Diepholz

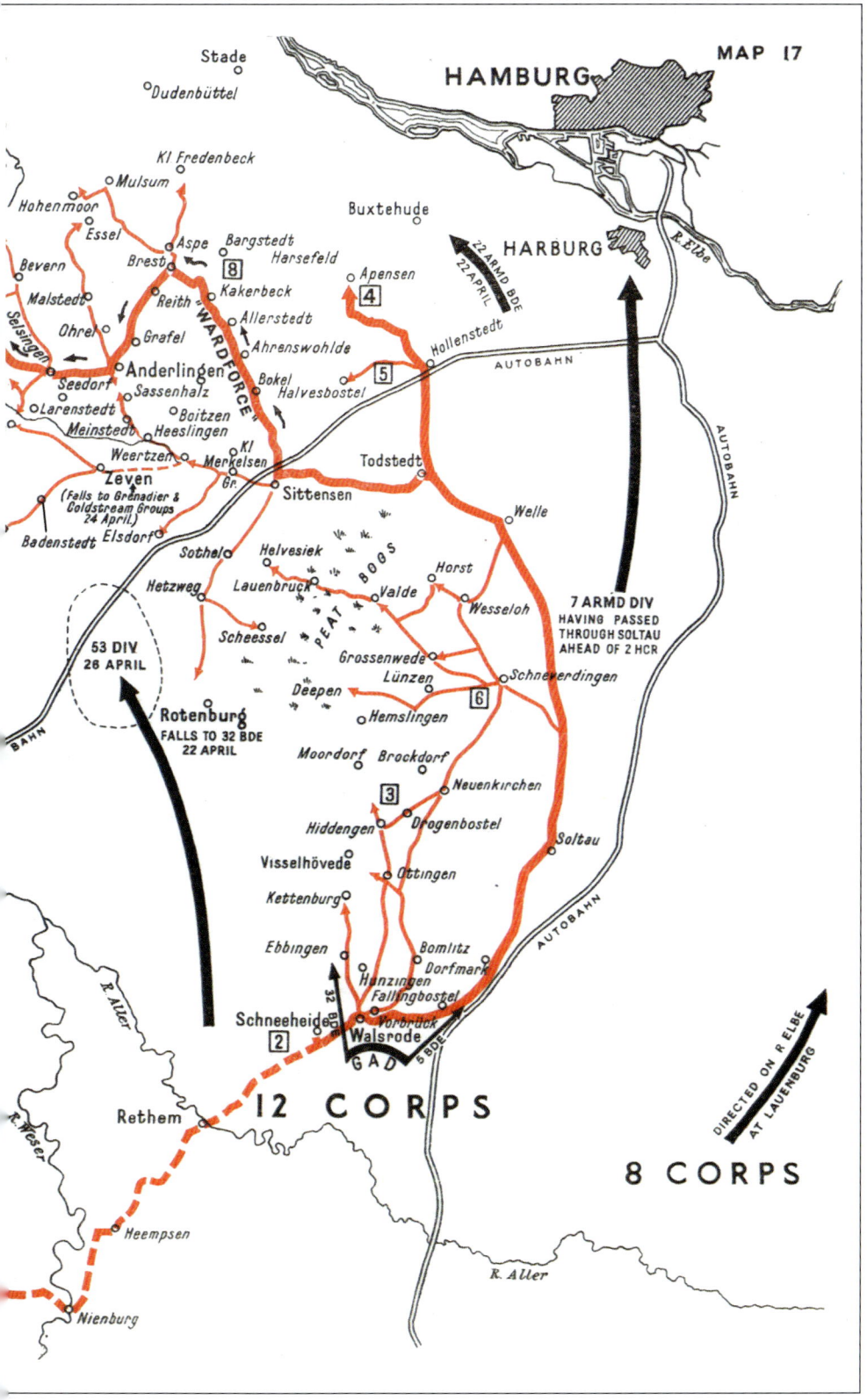

MAP 17

HAMBURG

Stade
Dudenbüttel

KI Fredenbeck
Mulsum
Hohenmoor
Essel
Aspe
Bevern
Bresth
Malstedt
Reith
Ohrel
Grafel
Anderlingen
Seedorf
Sassenhalz
Larenstedt
Boitzen
Meinstedt
Heeslingen
Weertzen
KI
Merkelsen
Zeven
(Falls to Grenadier &
Coldstream Groups
24 April.)
Badenstedt
Elsdorf
Gr.
Sittensen

WARDFORCE

8

Bargstedt
Harsefeld
Buxtehude

Apensen
4

Kakerbeck
Allerstedt
Ahrenswohlde
Bokel
Halvesbostel
5
Hollenstedt

AUTOBAHN

HARBURG
R. Elbe

22 ARMD BDE
22 APRIL

Todstedt
Welle

7 ARMD DIV
HAVING PASSED
THROUGH SOLTAU
AHEAD OF 2 HCR

AUTOBAHN

Sothel
Hetzweg

Helvesiek
Lauenbruck

PEAT BOGS

Valde
Horst
Wesseloh

Scheessel

Grossenwede
Lünzen
Deepen
Hemslingen

Schneverdingen
6

53 DIV
28 APRIL

Rotenburg
FALLS TO 32 BDE
22 APRIL

BAHN

Moordorf
Brockdorf

Hiddengen

3

Neuenkirchen

Drogenbostel

Visselhövede
Ottingen
Soltau

Kettenburg

AUTOBAHN

Ebbingen
Bomlitz
Dorfmark

32 BD

Hanzingen
Fallingbostel

DIRECTED ON R. ELBE
AT LAUENBURG

Schneeheide
Vorbrück
Walsrode

2

5 BDE

R. Aller

GAD

12 CORPS

Rethem

8 CORPS

R. Weser

Heempsen

Nienburg

R. Aller

COPYRIGHT, STANFORD, LONDON

THE BRUSSELS STANDARD

Presented to the 2nd Household
Cavalry Regiment by the inhabitants of
Brussels in commemoration of the
part played by the Regiment in
the liberation of the Belgian
capital on 3rd September 1944.
(*Vivian of Hereford*)

an abiding faith in the efficacy of the armoured cars to stop the worst that von Rundstedt could launch against them.

During the day, the regimental role changed again. As it had been decided to hold the line of the Meuse, and as 29th Armoured Brigade had now arrived and was firmly established on the river between Namur and Givet, the regimental line was reduced in length. New responsibility was for the sector Namur exclusive to Huy inclusive—a great reduction in mileage. This rearrangement, with "A" Squadron on the right and "D" Squadron on the left, allowed "B" Squadron to be swung back into reserve, where they remained in an anti-parachute role centred on the village of Lamontzee. In the meantime, because of problems of wireless communication, Regimental Headquarters moved forward first of all to Melin near Jodoigne (21st December) and then to Thorembais St. Trond.

The day was marred by an unfortunate accident, caused by the hard frost which had ushered in the beginning of a cold spell which was to last without a break until February. In the morning, Lieutenant Halliday, of "C" Squadron, was ordered to reconnoitre a route and subsequently to escort General Horrocks from Huy bridge to the Headquarters of VII U.S. Corps, located south of the Meuse at Maffe. The road leading to this village twists through wooded slopes and in parts deep gorges for about six miles, until it reaches, after a series of turns, the road junction at Modave. The roads were icy and treacherous, and Halliday's scout car skidded straight off the slippery surface and over a high embankment, overturning several times before pinning him and his driver beneath it. Halliday received serious injuries which sent him back to England and out of the war for good, but his driver had a miraculous escape, suffering no more than a bad shaking.

There are better ways of spending Christmas Eve than having to enter enemy country in search of information and be compelled to stay there for the night, but this was the role which Corporal-of-Horse Jenkins and his driver, Trooper Beckett, of "C" Squadron, were destined to play, and did so with some distinction. They formed part of No. 4 Troop, "C" Squadron, commanded by Lieutenant Corbett. In order to increase the range of action, the Troop had been split into two halves, the second part under command of Corporal-of-Horse Jenkins. He had with him in the armoured car Corporal Chennel and Trooper Gardner, and in the scout car Corporal Mansell and Trooper Beckett. Jenkins's orders were to find out whether the town of Rochefort, which was then the apex of the German thrust, was still in American hands.

On reaching a small hamlet about a mile from Rochefort it was apparent that heavy fighting was in progress, but it was impossible to see whether the troops in occupation of the town were Americans or Germans. Leaving the armoured car in charge of Corporal Mansell with orders to wait unless summoned forward by wireless, Jenkins and Beckett drove into Rochefort from the west, but in the meantime the Germans converged towards the Meuse from two sides and Mansell was eventually ordered to retire, shadowing the enemy.

On reaching Rochefort, Corporal-of-Horse Jenkins found that the Americans were in the process of beating back a German attack led by Tiger tanks and supported by infantry and a heavy artillery barrage. There was further determined fighting until dusk, by which time the Americans had been reduced to about a company strong. These troops and the two Household Cavalrymen now found themselves gradually driven back until finally surrounded in the grounds of the local hotel. Throughout the night of Christmas Eve the Germans put in repeated attacks with tanks and infantry, but they were all repelled. In the course of the fighting the Americans lost all their transport and Corporal-of-Horse Jenkins had his scout car knocked out.

When dawn came the American commander decided that it would be courting disaster and serve no useful purpose to remain on in Rochefort, as his company was greatly reduced through casualties and almost all ammunition had been expended. He accordingly decided to cut his way through the enemy cordon and withdraw if possible to the British lines.

Corporal-of-Horse Jenkins had gained a certain amount of local knowledge during his previous day's reconnaissance, and in view of this the American commander decided to entrust half of what remained of his company to him. Jenkins thereupon reconnoitred under heavy fire the proposed line of retreat, and in so doing discovered a railway line not yet covered by enemy machine guns.

Using this information to good purpose, he was eventually able to lead his Americans right through the German lines without the loss of a single man and rejoin the British outposts at Givet, twelve miles away. It was a fine performance on the part of this N.C.O. and the Americans "were most impressed by his map reading and field craft!" Rochefort remained in enemy hands until the 29th of December, when it was recaptured by the Americans.

After five days of fog, the weather suddenly broke, clear, sunny, and bitterly cold. This was by far the best Christmas present which could have been granted to the Allies. At last their bombers and fighters could take to the air again and, sweeping in from aerodromes all over France, Belgium, and England (they even came over enemy-held territory from Italy), five thousand aircraft pounded and strafed the German bulge.

The battle ground began to resemble what we had seen in Normandy and assumed in places the proportions of the Mortain debacle. The carnage in vehicles was appalling. In addition, nearly every one of von

Rundstedt's supply roads was now under cross fire from the stranded American garrisons that refused to give in, and the effect was to wither up the German supplies until only a thin trickle of petrol and ammunition was reaching their spearhead to the west.[7]

"C" Squadron's patrols continued to report heavy fighting on the line Ciney—Celles, at one place less than five miles from Dinant. 29th Armoured Brigade were now in action side by side with a combat team from our old friends the 2nd U.S. Armoured Division pressing down from the north. All through Christmas Day and into Boxing Day the German spearhead, led by the battered 2 S.S. Panzer Division, pushed and struggled to gain the Meuse, ignoring the ominous signs of their comrades digging in on both flanks. On the hard icebound roads, tanks locked in deadly combat waltzed and skidded from village to village. Even the petrol in the carburettors solidified when, engines were stopped, and men froze to death in their foxholes during the night. We thought of the hardships being endured by the American infantry on the exposed ridges of the Ardennes and blessed our good fortune and relative comfort behind the Meuse.

Meanwhile, although everyone was resigned to the thought that Christmas celebrations had been indefinitely postponed, efforts were made to make the day a special one, as far as operational commitments would allow.

Captain Clyde wrote of "C" Squadron:

> "Ours was really a very comfortable set-up, consisting of more or less snooping on the Americans in daylight and retiring to safety and comfort behind the Meuse at night. The immediate result was a new variety in rations: every third trooper started to chew gum, suddenly acquired an automatic rifle, rubber over-shoes, and mackintosh jackets. There was a sudden and mysterious increase in the losses of complete ration boxes, bedrolls, and pistols!
>
> "Squadron Headquarters spent Christmas Day in a château south of the river. I will always remember the bright clear sky which was creased from dawn to dusk with the vapour trails of the endless flow of American bombers. The château had an excellent cellar and a most accommodating host. Strangely enough, by midday, traffic on the forward net was fitful; by three o'clock all touch was lost, but the air miraculously cleared in time for the 'return home' order".

---

7. Von Rundstedt had aimed at capturing enough petrol west of the Meuse to take his Panzers on to Antwerp. Failure to cross on the second day of the counteroffensive and now the Allied air blow finally sealed the fate of his effort.

Somewhat similar effects had been noted in "A" Squadron, situated in the Namur region, and Major Bowes Daly decided that energetic military operations of a local nature would be advantageous during the afternoon; the result was that Lieutenant Wordsworth's Support Troop spent several hours on the slopes of the north side of the Meuse close to where the late King Albert of the Belgians lost his life in a climbing accident. He wrote:

> "Christmas Day was spent at a village called Marche-les-Dames on the river between Namur and Huy. On Christmas Day itself my whole Troop was most royally entertained by the local inhabitants. A large meal was provided, and also largish quantities of Pernod, which was certainly a new one on most of my chaps, were consumed. By the middle of the afternoon their visibility was about five yards, so you can imagine my horror when some expert came over and told us that parachutists were reputed to have dropped on an extremely high hill overlooking the village. How we got to the top I have not much idea, except that I can remember pulling a Bren gun up most of the way. We took one look at the top, said we couldn't see a thing, and returned absolutely furious at what had proved to be a false alarm!"

★   ★   ★

Perhaps the liaison officers spent the hardest-worked Christmas of all, scouring the countryside for information and at the mercy of their wireless sets and "Higher Sunrays." Captain Ford, who had temporarily forgotten the war on forty-eight hours' leave, arrived back from Paris late in the evening of the 23rd, expecting to find the Regiment fighting a stern rear-guard action. He was told to make for Aerschott, to which place 30 Corps had moved back, and there he relieved Captain Cooper. Captain Garnett was with Guards Armoured Division in a filthy little village called Glabeek, and Captain Balding, who had started with First U.S. Army Headquarters south of the river, was now with 43rd Division on the left flank of the Regiment. Captain Cooper, no sooner back from 30 Corps, was in turn ordered to relieve Major Seely.[8]

> "Christmas Day. Flying bombs arriving overhead very often. A hard-white frost and up by six o'clock—breakfast with Regiment at Poucet, then left

---

8. Major Seely, who had been second-in-command of the Sherwood Foresters Armoured Car Regiment, which had been disbanded, had managed by devious military manoeuvres to get himself attached to 2 H.C.R. as an additional liaison officer. He joined the Regiment on the Maas and remained with it until the end of the war.

for 29th Armoured Brigade to relieve Jim Seely as L.O. Intensely cold even in tank suit and sheepskin coat. Thousands of planes going over all day in a clear blue sky. Their Tactical H.Q. at Onhaye over the river; German tanks are filtering through, but the Americans seem to have the situation in hand (more or less). Met General Horrocks at Onhaye and picked up Corporal-of-Horse Jenkins and driver. They were cut off at Rochefort and fought their way out... Got billets in a downstairs parlour of a café, with my wireless going with a lead through the window as usual. Christmas dinner with Towler consisting of tea, captured German pork and biscuits—perfectly bloody! Met Brigadier Roscoe Harvey and one or two others I know—freezing hard all the time. The German tanks got almost into Dinant. Supper with Brigadier Harvey in next-door house. Locals came in and we all drank a toast in champagne. Wireless touch with the Regiment good—they are over forty miles away.

"December 26th. Still freezing hard. Breakfast cooked by Towler on the Belgian kitchen stove—bully, beans, and biscuits. Got a lot of information back. The S.S. and Panzer Grenadier Regiments opposite us have advanced a little during the night—quite a few of their prisoners coming in. Got some Typhoon rocket targets for the air! Twenty German tanks and soft vehicles hit.... 'C' Squadron's patrols as usual down to the fighting round Marche, etc. German planes attacked us during the night, machine gunning the road. They flew in very low and also dropped a few bombs. The civilians are still very frightened about the German advance and hundreds of refugees are still coming back. We lost two sappers killed on the road this morning. Wireless not so easy today; the American interference is very bad."

★   ★   ★

Meanwhile those of us not on duty soon found excuses to borrow a vehicle and pay calls on neighbours along the river bank. On the road from Tirlemont to Diest, Major Williams's Headquarter Squadron was billeted in the village of Bunsbeek, as were most of the Squadron echelons. The houses were most adequate and the people, as usual, extremely hospitable. Lieutenants Oliver (when he was not in Brussels) and Hughes were unearthed, living quietly and comfortably with the village priest and his old housekeeper. The priest was a dear old man with sound and philosophical ideas on the *marché noir*, which he insisted should in many of its "beneficial" activities merely be labelled "Le Marché parallel." He possessed some excellent brandy, and his Household Cavalry guests drank, between Christmas services, to the successful outcome of the Battle of the Bulge. I seem to recall that one session was interrupted by a ring on the doorbell and a parishioner came in with a "marché parallel" boiling fowl, which the old priest promptly secreted under his cassock with a gentle smile.

In their turn, the echelons repaid calls, bringing adequate allocations of cigarettes, gin and whisky and other N.A.A.F.I. supplies collected by Captain Firth and his staff. R.Q.M.S. Goody and the storeman, Corporal Wincombe, could always be relied upon to get that something extra from the supply point, and this time they had excelled themselves.

There was champagne, and the men soon found how to obtain sacks of freshly baked American white bread. We bought bottles of sickly-sweet beer which tasted like bad Guinness and treacle, and discovered some "Burgundy" in Huy, purchased at an outrageous price and fortified with chips of sandalwood and colouring matter. We exchanged bully beef for eggs and cigarettes for cheese, and a Belgian barber in Andenne offered free haircuts and shampoos to the men. One Household Cavalryman, a road-mender in civilian life, came back in some confusion, reeking of scent and having had his eyebrows plucked. With a nice feeling for foreign habits, he explained: "I didn't dare stop the barber because I felt that this might be a Belgian custom at Christmas time."

The Guards Armoured Division Newssheet, the *News Guardian*, came out with a special Christmas number in colour, and was full of appropriately festive jokes and poems. Inevitably there was reference to Oss and a rhyming alphabet where, under "W for Walter," Colonel Sale's fiery pre-luncheon unapproachability was duly satirized.

Unaffected by this seasonal levity, the Divisional Intelligence Newssheet continued on its way, earnest and solemn, contenting itself with a psychological study of German soldiers' letters to their girlfriends, thus again proving to its satisfaction that an enemy break in morale was imminent. And while "C" Squadron remained on their task south of the Meuse, the rest of the Regiment, except R.H.Q.,[9] found ample time to enjoy the hospitality of the kindly Belgians in château and cottage, all of whom tried to make the men feel something of the home atmosphere which they were missing. In short, 2nd Household Cavalry Regiment spent Christmas, 1944, like most other British units in North-West Europe, in circumstances infinitely better than had appeared possible less than a week ago.

★　★　★

---

9. Regimental Headquarters had made four moves in the last four days, all caused by changes in the wireless situation. Then again, on Christmas Eve, R.H.Q. had to move to Poucet, near Hannut, because great difficulty was being experienced in keeping in touch with 43rd Reconnaissance Regiment on the left flank. There was another move shortly to Blehen, which had better billets.

On the 27th of December, the Regiment was once again ordered to change its dispositions. This time its screen was to be extended to a line from Namur (exclusive) to Visé (inclusive) but excluding Liége city. However, resulting from a further conference at Headquarters, Guards Armoured Division—at which place incidentally there was still a considerable fog as to what bridges did or did not exist on the front, for many had been destroyed in 1940, while other pontoons had been put up in the meantime—the responsibility was again reduced to that of holding a line Namur (exclusive) to Liége (exclusive).

The 3rd Irish Guards were to be responsible for the road bridge at Huy and the bridges in Liége, for each of which tasks they used one company. This adjustment in the line necessitated several changes, and the Regiment was now located as follows: "A" Squadron on the right, based on Namur; "D" Squadron, who apart from minor moves had stayed put the whole time, located above Andenne and "B" Squadron, relieved of their anti-parachute role, on the left, with new headquarters at the village of St. Georges, half-way between Huy and Liége.

The 24th, 25th and 27th of December had been wonderful days for the air, as we have seen. One message from Captain Cooper reported that on a small stretch of road leading from Celles to Ciney he had counted over seventy smashed up enemy tanks and vehicles. Many others had been abandoned for lack of petrol, and every hillside lane contained its quota of derelict Tigers, half-tracks, and saloon cars minus their wheels.

On the 28th of December, 30 Corps sappers took over the task of close protection of the Huy and Liége bridges. At the same time the Americans completed a new pontoon bridge at Andenne and for the time being were made responsible for both its protection and demolition, if the need arose. "D" Squadron were to keep in close touch the whole time. This arrangement started a chain of events which might well be entitled "The Saga of the Bridges".

Briefly, this is the story. For the first day things were relatively quiet. Then, on the 30th of the month, 51st (Highland) Division, which had been in Army Group Reserve to the south of Liége, moved a brigade west and took over the protection of Huy bridge and the river to the east of Huy. Elements of 6th Airborne Division, which had been recently flown over from England in the emergency, then took over the town of Namur, and the Regiment (less both "C" Squadron, withdrawn from their patrol duties, and "B" Squadron, no longer required, in reserve) therefore became responsible for the River Meuse line exclusive Namur to exclusive Huy, but—and here was the snag—including the American bridge at Andenne.

The Americans already had a strong detachment with anti-tank guns in position, and the small force of infantry which the Regiment could provide, mostly of attached R.E. personnel from 11th Field Company, could not be of much use in the circumstances. Therefore Colonel Abel Smith set off on an energetic round of visits, determined to get the matter "buttoned up." When he reached 30 Corps it was arranged that the Chief of Staff, Second Army, be rung up, and through him it was decided that "although the responsibility was British, the U.S. forces would look after the close protection of the bridge." A somewhat unsatisfactory state of affairs, as the British on the spot had no jurisdiction over the Americans. Well might the Adjutant write on the last day of the year that "the question of the protection of Andenne bridge is most difficult."

However, the Regiment was ordered to "maintain the closest contact with the Americans by liaison officer at all times." Back came the Colonel, and to and fro went Major Ward from his farmhouse headquarters above the river to the American strong-points guarding the pontoon commanded by a Major from Minnesota who, although most co-operative, hadn't a clue as to the meaning of this sudden frantic British interest in a bridge which he had defended adequately and without interference when the general situation had been far worse. Eventually Captain Balding arrived on the scene to speak his language, and after a further spate of conferences between the Americans, regimental representatives and even the Belgian gendarmerie, the problem appeared to have been settled.

Then came an urgent message summoning Major Ward to the bridge at three o'clock in the morning. It appeared that the acting Corps Commander, Major-General Thomas, had decided to come and take a hand in the proceedings and had motored unannounced up to the structure without a single American sentry challenging him. "Gee!" said a G.I. apologetically to me, in explanation, "if we'd known that that little guy of yours was a general we'd have shot off all our guns at him to welcome him to the river." For all this, it was decided that a British detachment must defend the bridge as well as the Americans, an arrangement which, as no high-level ruling as to how it was to be done could be obtained, gave promise of further interesting arguments at lower levels. Not until daybreak was the problem finally settled to everybody's satisfaction, up to and including the acting Corps Commander's.

★   ★   ★

On the 2nd of January 1945, when it was clear that the German counter-offensive had come completely adrift, the Regiment was relieved of all further responsibility and ordered to concentrate north of the Meuse in the area of Hannut. So ended our part in the Ardennes battle. Only "C" Squadron had seen any actual fighting, and theirs had been the relatively enviable role of phantom work on a large scale. Nevertheless, we were left in no doubt as to the value of our information, which in the early days was the only accurate information available to Corps, and even Army. From the 19th of December to the date of their withdrawal on the 30th, eleven days in all, "C" Squadron fighting vehicles had each averaged over seventy miles per day. "Thank you all," wrote General Dempsey from Second Army, "for your most efficient work, in trying conditions, and at a rather delicate time."

The crisis of the Ardennes struggle could be said to have passed when Patton, driving up from the south, relieved the beleaguered 101st Airborne at Bastogne on Boxing Day. Thus in the New Year the Allies passed over to the offensive. From the north and from the south, immense pressure directed on Houffalise came down on the German salient. In order to enable the First U.S. Army to operate with the maximum pressure on a narrow front, 30 Corps took over the sector Hotton—Rochefort; that which had been the head of the salient now became the scene of a stubborn enemy rearguard. Two British divisions, 53rd and 6th Airborne, with 29th Armoured Brigade under command, took part, and were to be involved in heavy fighting in appalling weather conditions.[10] On the 16th of January the First and Third American Armies joined hands at Houffalise, exactly one month to the day after the offensive had been launched.

Captain Balding took part in this latter operation as a liaison officer for 30 Corps.

The estimated enemy casualties in the month's fighting were placed at some 120,000 men, together with over 600 tanks and assault guns destroyed. Moreover, Hitler's last attempt to check the Allied Air Force had so depleted the Luftwaffe that he was never again able to make good his losses.

---

10. 53rd Division was subsequently relieved by 51st Division.

Chapter VIII

Farewell to Belgium

2 H.C.R. concentrates in Blehen area—Wintry conditions—Changes in regimental command—Departure of R.C.M. Jobson—Preview of "Veritable"—Farewell to Belgium

Snow had settled deep over the land when Squadrons sat down to enjoy their postponed traditional Christmas dinners. The weather was to remain thus for over a month, one of the severest winters within living memory.

Regimental Headquarters who had made yet another move from their château at Poucet on the 29th of December, were now established in more comfortable billets in the village of Blehen, close to Hannut. "A" Squadron had elected to stay on in Namur for their Christmas dinner and then moved up to Lens St. Servais, two days afterwards moving again to the appropriately named village of Fresin. "B" Squadron, having eaten their dinner at their Headquarters at St. Georges and taken somewhat longer to recover, travelled up to Grand Axhe four days later. "C" Squadron found their operational Headquarters in the Château de Couthuin by the Meuse to be so comfortable that they finally persuaded Colonel Abel Smith to allow them to remain on. When the weather, which was worsening daily, eventually rendered the roads impassable to all but jeeps, this was to prove a disadvantage (in the opinion of R.H.Q., at least!), but the Squadron was agreed that the advantages of the château and the hospitality of the Count and Countess d'Envos far outweighed the inconveniences of supply problems, which they were quite prepared to risk. "D" Squadron, having exercised restraint, waited until they had been installed in billets in Ligney, and then, in fifteen degrees of frost, made up for lost time with a huge spread in the village café. The echelon remained at Trognée, whence it had moved some time previously from Bunsbeek.

The Belgian countryside around Hannut is in distinct contrast to the hills of the Ardennes. It is in the nature of a flattish plateau rising very gradually but evenly from a height of 150 feet above sea-level on the line Hasselt—Tirlemont to 500 feet and more when it drops abruptly to the River Meuse. Apart from the city of Liége, it is essentially an agricultural district, growing among other things much sugar beet. Although flat, it is without the dreary dykes and slagheaps of northern Belgium and lacks that atmosphere of cramped suburbia associated with the Dutch frontier lands. The people speak French and also a curious patois, a mixture of French and old Burgundian dialect. Unlike Flemish, this language has, alas, no newspapers or literature to keep it alive, and is inevitably doomed to extinction.

Many of the villages are linked by little narrow-gauge trains or trams (we never could decide which they were) with their tooting horns which the drivers use incessantly. They appeared with startling suddenness from out of the middle of beet fields, round street corners, and even in one Squadron area through somebody's back-yard. The inhabitants, whose traditions belong more to Liége than to Brussels, were just as eager to welcome their British soldiers as had been the capital, and spared no pains to make the men comfortable.

The severe cold created a difficult fuel problem, for with each Squadron split up into many different billets, the token allocation of coal, when it did occasionally arrive, was quite inadequate for needs. However, there were some unofficial visits with lorries on driving instruction to the Liége collieries, and even back to far away Waterschei.

Because of the weather, little recreational sport could be indulged in, and not a football match was played during the entire period. The officers in "D" Squadron were fortunate in making the acquaintance of a kind and most generous host, in the person of Monsieur Alexandre Naveau, whose home was close at hand in the village of Hollogne. Monsieur Naveau senior possessed a magnificent cellar which had survived the German occupation by being carefully bricked up; there were also several partridge drives, and warm baths whenever required. In addition, the Squadron benefited by the gift of many tons of extra coal, normally intended to fire the boilers of the Naveau sugar refining plants. So what with one expedient and another, the rigours of January were survived in reasonable warmth.

For those who had the leisure to observe, a trip to the other side of the Meuse and into the heart of the Ardennes hills was well worth the visit. It was an attractive country which increased in beauty the farther towards Germany one travelled. There the pine forests had a stillness and snowy solitude which belied the battles still raging ahead. On the slopes and clearings it was possible to ski, particularly for "C" Squadron, who were nearer this little Switzerland.

How completely is the Ardennes period in January 1945, recaptured by a visiting war correspondent's description! "... all round Brussels and Liége it was milky fog. But when you drove past the frozen canals and the tobogganing children up to the heights of the Ardennes, the sun broke through and it was like a spot-lighted stage, mile upon mile of untrodden snowfields under the clear and frosty lamp of the winter sun. If you turned your back to the ruined villages and forgot the war for a moment, then very easily you could fancy yourself to be alone in this radiant world where everything was reduced to primary whites and blues; a strident sparkling white among the frosted trees, the deep blue shadows in the valley and then the flawless ice-blue of the sky. Flying Fortresses went by, immensely high, spinning out their vapour trails half-way across Belgium.

> "All this was an uplifting thing to see, and it triumphed for a little in the mind until one came upon a stranded tank threshing madly in a ditch or saw a line of infantry passing over the hill. And then in the villages one met a recurring tragedy as sharp as any in this war. These Belgians had had their outbursts of joy at the liberation, only to see the Germans come back again. Then the shells of the Allies returned a second time. As the Germans retired they took with them the men of the villages to work in Germany. No wonder that the women stood at their doorways asking over and over again, 'Are you sure they have really gone for good?'"[1]

★ ★ ★

On the 9th of January, a further heavy fall of snow effectively completed the road chaos, and except on the main arteries, where American bulldozers cleared the way, practically all traffic came to a standstill. On the main Hannut road, Negro convoys, undeterred by the conditions, skidded and slithered their way through to the Meuse bridges, and we marvelled at the Americans' casualty figures in vehicles which by the end of the month lay piled up in dumps all over the countryside.

Training, except a day's practice shoot on the field firing ranges at Bourg Leopold and two days' use of the anti-tank range at Lommel on the Dutch frontier, was cancelled. The accident rates on the icebound roads would have been out of all proportion to any benefit derived. As it was, on the journey to Lommel, Corporal-of-Horse Royston's Daimler car charged into the middle of a large dump of high explosives, burying itself beneath an avalanche of shells and phosphorous bombs which fortunately failed to go off. Half an hour later, eleven cars in the space of a minute played follow-my-leader into a snowdrift. Only the drivers will know how the journey to Lommel was ever accomplished, nevertheless

---

1. *Eclipse* by Alan Moorehead. (Messrs. Hamish Hamilton Ltd., London.)

apart from the turrets freezing up during firing and having to be thawed out at intervals, all crews managed to fire off the requisite number of practice rounds. With what benefit to their numbed senses in the arctic conditions is another question.

★   ★   ★

Towards the end of January, several changes in command took place within the Regiment, some of which had necessarily been postponed because of the Ardennes counter-offensive. Major Sir Peter Grant Lawson, who had been second-in-command of the Regiment throughout the campaign, left to take up a Staff appointment in England. He had commanded the combined "A" and "B" Squadron group in the Regiment's first action in Normandy, operation "Goodwood," and by a coincidence, owing to Colonel Abel Smith's absence, was also in command when the Regiment was ordered to the Meuse during the Ardennes battle. Of all who took part, Sir Peter Grant Lawson is the least likely to forget those hectic hours of darkness when, during the night of the 19th/20th December, the literal and metaphorical fog of war had descended over Allied Headquarters. Not only had he to carry out against the clock the appalling solo journey to the Dutch border, but on his return frame rapid orders which allowed of there being some hope of reassembling four widely dispersed Squadrons to reach the threatened river crossings before it was too late. How successfully he achieved this task we have already read. Major Sir Peter Grant Lawson was succeeded by Major Ward from "D" Squadron. The vacancy thus formed was filled by Captain Profumo, who moved up from having been second-in-command to Major Bowes Daly in "A" Squadron. In turn, Captain Profumo was succeeded by Captain Hall, who had been A.D.C. to Lieutenant-General Sir Richard O'Connor at 8 Corps since Captain Garnett had re-joined the Regiment.

Further changes were necessitated by Major Wignall leaving to become second-in-command to 1 H.C.R., who, after a long spell in the Middle East and on Italian fronts, had returned to England. The 1st Regiment was shortly to come out to play its part in the North-West European theatre of operations. Captain Clyde, second-in-command of "C" Squadron to date, thereupon became "B" Squadron leader in place of Major Wignall, and the vacancy in "C" Squadron was filled by Captain Cooper, who in returning to "C" Squadron was renewing old acquaintanceships, for he had been the Squadron's Rear Link officer in training days in England.

Finally—and this was to be a great wrench for the Regiment—
Mr. Jobson, who had been Regimental Corporal-Major since the
formation of 2 H.C.R., sailed for the United Kingdom after prolonged
and sad good-byes. He was returning to Windsor to become Regimental
Corporal-Major to the Household Cavalry Training Regiment. Breaks
within any unit are somehow always more of a wrench after the shared
adventures and discomforts of campaigns, and we had all hoped that Mr.
Jobson might have remained with us until the end of the war, but it
was not to be. His skill and tact in dealing with and training N.C.Os.
was unsurpassed, and he had rightly built up a position and reputation
second to none. He was succeeded by Corporal-Major Poupart from
"B" Squadron.

The history of this period would hardly be complete without
mention of what was destined to be the Regiment's last "scheme" of
the war. This was an exercise designed by Colonel Abel Smith to polish
up the wireless technique of some of the echelon commanders, who
were officially presumed to be spending too much time "shopping" in
Brussels and not paying enough attention to the No. 19 set in the back
of the "Gin Palace"!

The exercise ran true to the form of all such skeleton wireless schemes.
Everything started off with a rush and torrent of messages. Thereafter,
when Troops had learnt that, however many mythical German Army
Corps they destroyed, there was still no hope of being allowed to chase the
foe into Brussels or up to the heights of La Vieille Barrière, enthusiasm
waned.[2] The end came dramatically when Lieutenant Oliver (for whose
benefit the scheme had allegedly been produced in the first place), was
asked to "check your net!" "Check MY net! " came the astounded
rejoinder. "My —'s perfectly all right; you check your —." A form of
procedure which considerably startled the Monitoring Divisional Signals
Officer, to say the least of it.

★   ★   ★

On the 1st of February deep snowdrifts again blocked all side roads,
and General Horrocks, who had planned to lunch at Regimental
Headquarters, did not arrive until eight o'clock in the evening, in time
for dinner. Even the main roads were temporarily blocked, although the
bulldozers worked day and night to clear them for urgent traffic.

---

2. La Vieille Barrière, Montaigu. A restaurant near Diest very popular with Guards Armoured
   Division and much patronized by Major Bowes Daly. The food and cooking were up to the best
   Brussels standard.

On the 3rd of February, Colonel Abel Smith took Squadron and Troop Leaders to 30 Corps Headquarters at Boxtel. For the past few weeks there had been rumours that 30 Corps Staff were back in Holland, planning their part in the destruction of the enemy still remaining between the Maas and the Rhine, and now we were to see for ourselves on an elaborate relief model what was to be the future regimental role in operation "Veritable." Days of leisure in Belgium were numbered.

As was normal, we learnt the date of our departure from the local inhabitants long before the official release of news from Orderly Room, and the Belgians collected from far and wide to make their 7th Feb. adieus. We had experienced the good-byes under stress at Waterschei, but never were such scenes as were witnessed on the 7th of February in the little villages which had housed our men for over a month. Every crew was inundated by presents of food and drink and hand-knitted comforts. Then, as the order to start up was given over the air and the cars throbbed into life, all restraint broke down and the vehicles were besieged by almost as many people as on that September Sunday in Brussels. Numerous were the lingering handclasps and exchanged addresses and tears. One Belgian stood in the middle of the street at Ligney and wept openly. "I fail to understand this extreme emotion", wrote Corporal-of-Horse Royston, a phlegmatic Yorkshireman, "but it does show that we must have left a good name behind." One little girl who had managed to crawl into the turret of a Daimler cried bitterly when she was gently lifted down by a trooper and told that she could not come to Holland, and indeed some of her older sisters looking as if they, too, would not have been averse to making the journey, appeared to share her feelings.

After the war had ended, I happened to be passing through the district on a Mess wine-purchasing expedition to Beaune in Burgundy. The 2nd Household Cavalry Regiment had ceased to exist and we were now split up again into Life Guards and Blues, but the car in which I was travelling still carried the 44-serial number of an armoured car regiment. Deciding to loop via Blehen for old time's sake, I halted for a moment in Trognée by the curious little open-air grotto with its altar and rows of stone benches, next to the house where Major Williams used to live his life of quiet seclusion. A young Belgian girl glanced inquiringly at the now rare sight of a British Army car; then she noticed the serial number and gave a shout of recognition, running off to rouse the entire village with her cry of "Le quarante-quatre … le quarante-quatre." In a matter of moments the car was surrounded. Where was Trooper Jones, and Trooper White who did the clog dance at Christmas? How was that tall corporal with a moustache? Did the pale-faced Major who commanded the "Trognée garrison" finally manage to transport all his luggage safely through Germany, and was Monsieur Slater still attending to his needs? Questions poured in and I was not able to leave these friendly people until I had been made to wait for letters and pencilled messages addressed to countless Household Cavalrymen both in Brühl and Wolfenbüttel. They seemed to take it very much to heart that 2 H.C.R. had been disbanded, and as a village elder muttered, shaking his head, "it would never have happened if you'd have stayed on here." Most assuredly, the Regiment had left its mark in this tiny corner of Belgium.

Humber Staff Car

Part Five

"Veritable" and Across the Rhine

Chapter I

Return to Nijmegen

Operation "Veritable"—Return to Nijmegen—Regiment under command of 15th (S.) Division—Bad weather for the assault—No role for armour—"D" Squadron and Tactical R.H.Q. in Germany—Bad weather continues—Traffic control points—Lieutenant the Lord Burghersh's Troop escorts Mr. Churchill on visit to front—Proposed changes in equipment—Departure of Major Collins to Second Army Headquarters—Lieutenant Creswell succeeds him as Adjutant

The battle of the Ardennes had set back Allied plans for the conquest of Germany by many weeks. It will be remembered that early in December an operation to clear what was known as the Roermond triangle, and in which "B" Squadron was to have been engaged, had been cancelled because of the bad weather. The task had been undertaken by other formations in January, and by the 26th had been completed. Thus, by the elimination of this last enemy salient, the stage was set for the battle of the Rhineland.

The plan for the advance to the Rhine was as follows. The Canadians and British were to wheel south-east from Nijmegen between the Maas and the Rhine, clearing out in the process the Reichswald forest, through which ran the Siegfried Line. The ultimate aim was to attain the general line Geldern—Xanten and then swing left-handed to reach the Rhine opposite Wesel. This operation was called "Veritable." Then, in conformation and a week later, General Simpson's Ninth U.S. Army, from a jumping-off ground north of Aachen, would attack in a north-easterly direction across the River Roer. The two armies were to join hands somewhere opposite the Ruhr, thus overrunning all territory west of the lower Rhine.

Between these two forces a considerably depleted British Second Army was committed to hold the line of the Maas from approximately Roermond to Cuijk, minus 30 Corps, which would move up to come under command of First Canadian Army for "Veritable."[1]

---

1. This switch-over was to give rise, on the home front, to considerable misunderstanding of the true situation. The Press and the B.B.C. naturally continued to refer to the "Canadian Army" in their communiqués, and people began to wonder where was the British Army. It is worth noting that 30 Corps under Canadian command comprised the largest concentration of troops yet assembled by 21 Army Group under one Corps—namely, one armoured division, six infantry divisions, three armoured brigades, eleven regiments of 79th Armoured Division, and five A.Gs.R.A.; a total of just over 200,000 all ranks.

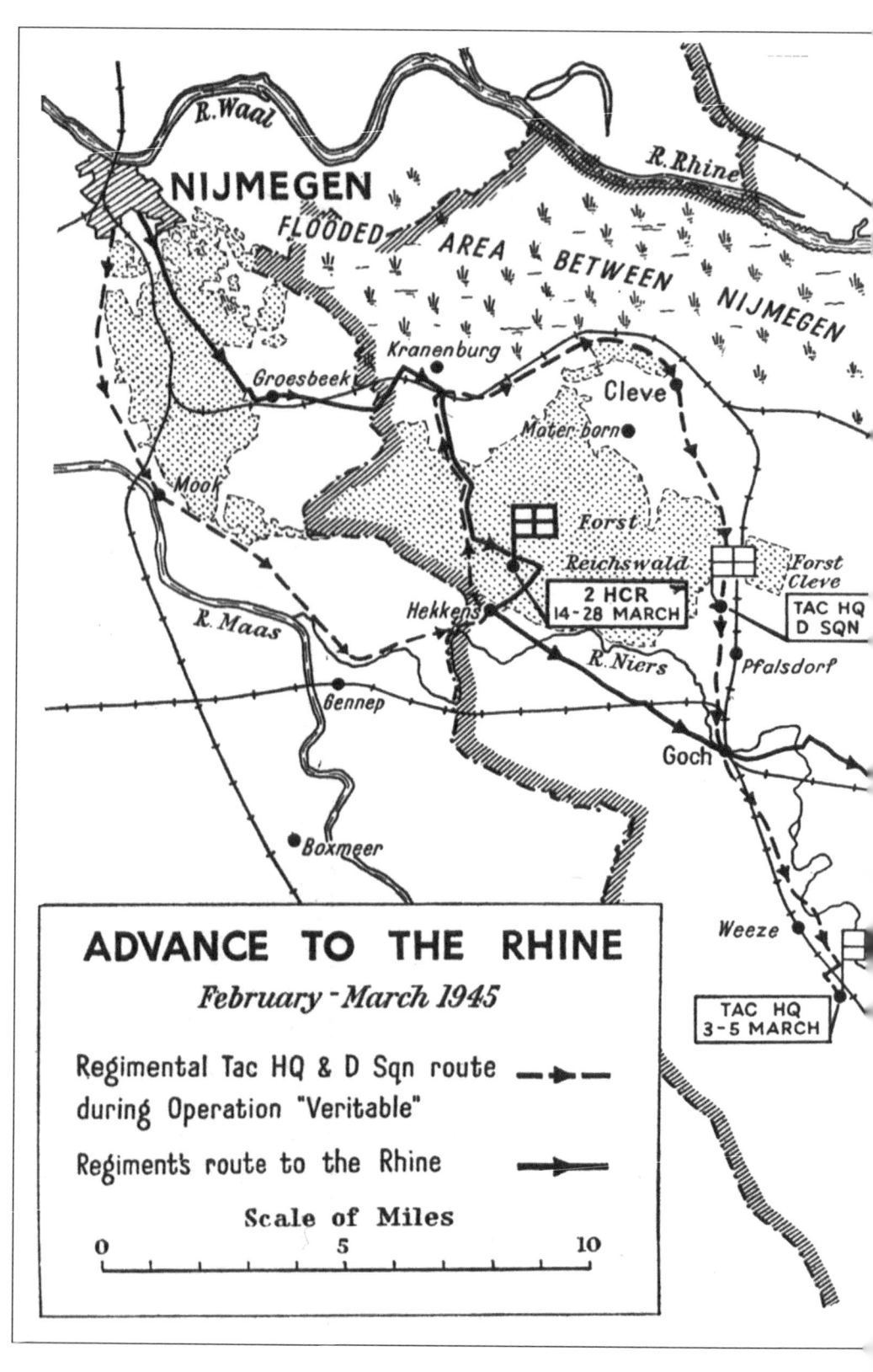

ADVANCE TO THE RHINE

February - March 1945

Regimental Tac HQ & D Sqn route ---▶--
during Operation "Veritable"

Regiment's route to the Rhine ━━▶

Scale of Miles

0   5   10

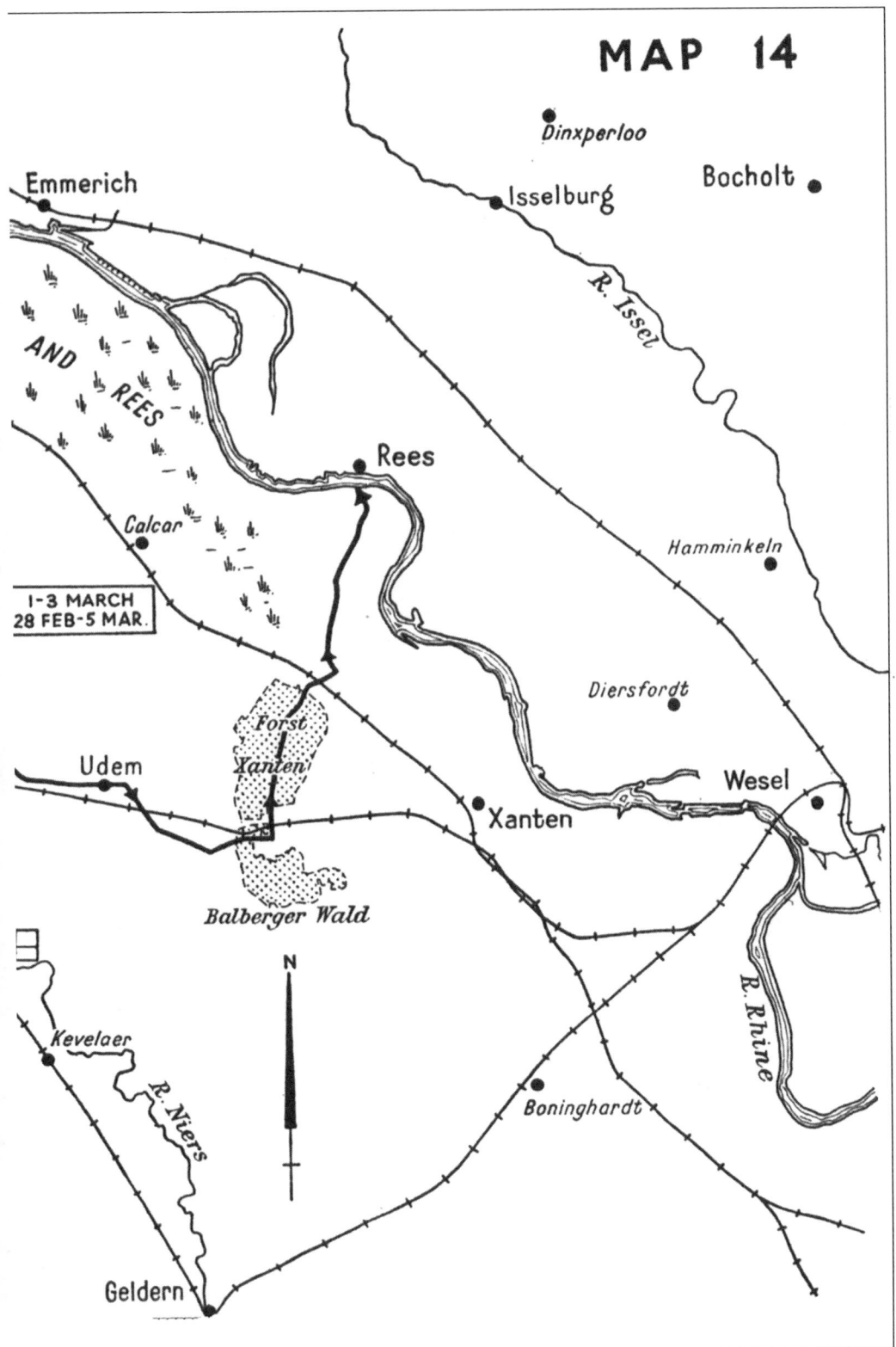

MAP 14

Dinxperloo

Bocholt

Emmerich

Isselburg

R. Issel

AND REES

Rees

Calcar

Hamminkeln

1-3 MARCH
28 FEB-5 MAR.

Forst
Xanten

Diersfordt

Udem

Xanten

Wesel

Balberger Wald

N

R. Rhine

Kevelaer

R. Niers

Boninghardt

Geldern

The nature of the battle due to begin in the early hours of the 8th of February was forecast by Field-Marshal Montgomery in the following extract from a personal message to his troops: "In 21 Army Group we stand ready for the last round.... The rules of the last round will be that we continue fighting till the final count: there is no time limit. We know our enemy well; we must expect him to fight hard to stave off defeat, possibly in the vain hope that we may crack before he does. But we shall not crack; we shall see this thing through to the end. The last round may be long and difficult, and the fighting hard; but we now fight on German soil; we have got our opponent where we want him; and he is going to receive the knock-out blow: a somewhat unusual one, delivered from more than one direction."

RETURN TO NIJMEGEN, FEBRUARY 1945
For the Floods caused by the rapid thaw, heavy rains, and German defensive inundations of the River Waal.

For the attack to be successful much depended on the cold weather continuing, but by the 7th of February a thaw had set in and 2 H.C.R. moved off in pouring rain. Before reaching St. Trond, the weight of the leading vehicles in "B" Squadron proved too much for the main road surface, which after successive weeks of frost and snow now collapsed entirely. All save a few armoured cars had to turn round and find another route. However, from then onwards the road stood up well, and after a good run through Hasselt and Eindhoven to Vught, thence via s'Hertogenbosch to Grave bridge, the Regiment halted for a few hours' sleep on a heath near Wijchen. The last thirty miles of the run had been accomplished in total darkness without even side lights permitted because of the need of hiding the great concentration of troops assembling for "Veritable." After a dawn breakfast, the Regiment moved into billets in Nijmegen.

I do not quite know what we expected to see there, but so proprietary did we feel about Nijmegen and district, with all its memories of September and October, 1944, that we were almost surprised to notice the predominating maple leaf signs of the Canadians instead of the rampant boar of 30 Corps and the eye of Guards Armoured Division.

On arrival, 2 H.C.R. was placed under command of 15th (S.) Division. The plan was that if 15th (S.) Division should obtain a breakthrough on to the high ground west of Cleve, known as the Materborn feature, the Regiment was to pass through, exploiting in the direction of the Hochwald forest. However, owing to circumstances, principally the floods and the terrible state of the roads, the opportunity for the employment of armour never arose, and the Regiment could only wait about in Nijmegen at gradually lengthening periods of notice to move. By the 10th of February it was clear that we were not to be used in the original role, and the Regiment reverted to under command Guards Armoured Division on the 13th of February.

★   ★   ★

The town of Nijmegen was packed with soldiers of every description and most of the billets had been snapped up by the first arrivals. I can remember seeing Captains Waterhouse and Cooper of the harbour parties spinning a coin for the privilege of their Squadron occupying an empty girls' school, without roof or windows.

The main infantry attack was preceded at five o'clock in the morning (8th February) by an overwhelming barrage of one thousand field, medium and heavy guns, backed by all the resources of Bomber Command and the U.S. "Heavies" (U.S. 9th Bombardment Division). To the sound of this infernal din, we knocked from door to door requesting overflow accommodation, while on a grass plot in the middle of one of Nijmegen's once smart residential squares, Corporal-Major Ring supervised the erection of his meticulously carpentered green latrines.[2]

---

2. The latrines were the pride of "D" Squadron, there being nothing quite like them in the British Army. They were built to Corporal-Major Ring's own specifications by a Belgian carpenter in Ligney and were painted bright green. Severe in style, they were claimed to be windproof, collapse-proof, and relatively rainproof. They perished, riddled by splinters, when a shell burst in the middle of the Nijmegen square at the end of February.

Late that evening a message came through that the Regiment was to be prepared to move towards the Reichswald at first light, but after a disturbed night, caused by the uproar of the guns and some desultory German counter-battery work, we arose, only to have to wait about all morning again wondering when we were going to move and whither.

Colonel Abel Smith informed Squadrons during the afternoon that the Regiment would now be at three hours' notice and that the men could go off into the town for two hours if they so wished. Thereafter, day by day, as the infantry slogged their way forward by slow degrees in a war in which platoons and companies went sailing into battle in their armoured amphibious craft, we sat and waited. Gradually as the advance made headway and the pressure of troops in Nijmegen relaxed we improved our billets. The water supply, which had been cut off, was restored, and public baths provided adequate showers and a swimming bath, but the lack of adequate space under cover and the need for dispersal prevented anything but vehicle cooking. This was an embarrassing procedure, and not liked by the men because they found themselves surrounded by throngs of wistfully hungry little faces, as the Dutch children watched them eat. Holland, being only part liberated and still disorganized, was desperately short of the necessaries of life, and in spite of the most careful watch, equipment kept disappearing from the cars at night.

On the 10th of February a trooper wrote: "We are still waiting but there is a change in the original plan (whatever that was), and we are to be attached to Guards Armoured Division once more," adding with insight, "we have a shrewd idea that they are still back at Tilburg and consider that we can prepare to spend more days in Nijmegen." On the same day, the Regiment was called upon to provide ten traffic control points on the main 30 Corps axis to the Reichswald. Each post consisted of one officer and three other ranks, travelling in two scout cars, and was welcomed as a relief from the monotony of life in gloomy Nijmegen. The state of the flooded roads was very bad and the axis of 53rd (W.) Division, which formation had been entrusted with the clearance of the northern side of the Reichswald Forest, gave way completely and had to be closed for repair. Farther north, the Canadians floundered in even deeper waters caused by the thaw and the still rising Rhine.

Destruction of houses and other property was perhaps more complete than anything we had yet witnessed. After two days of this, their first experience of Germany, the detachments were relieved and returned to Nijmegen.

Although the enemy must have been aware by now that most of the British Army was packed into the Nijmegen area while awaiting deployment, there was, surprisingly enough, little shelling. One gun, however, probably self-propelled or moving on a railway mounting, used to shell the town at frequent intervals throughout the day and night and the British gunners were never able to locate it. It caused a number of civilian and military casualties and a fair amount of damage including, on the 24th of February, the destruction of two of "C" Squadron's White scout cars. Nine troopers helping to move lorries away from the blazing wreckage were wounded, two, Troopers Scaife and Workman, seriously.

The gun, which continued to evade all efforts to locate it, scored another direct hit some days later, this time on "B" Squadron's cookhouse, causing several more casualties. Of these, one of the less seriously wounded men, Trooper Sharpe, walked over to the Regimental Aid Post with a gash in his arm. After preliminary treatment Captain Kynaston sent him back to collect his small kit before evacuating him to hospital. No sooner had Sharpe reached the spot where he had been wounded than another shell exploded in the crater caused by the first one, a splinter hitting him in the leg. He informed Captain Kynaston quite firmly when brought in a second time that he did not think he'd bother about the small kit after all.

Meanwhile the battle had progressed slowly, and on the 27th of February 2 H.C.R. once again came under two hours' notice to move, for employment under Guards Armoured Division, whose 32nd Brigade[3] had been engaged for some days in the battle for Goch.

Although up to this stage the Regiment, in common with most of the armour, had taken no part in the battle, a short review of what had been taking place will help the reader to grasp the meaning of future developments.

Operations had been hampered throughout by the bad weather and consequent flooding. Furthermore, the "hedgehog" policy of the enemy had reinforced the main Siegfried defences with a series of self-contained "boxes," transforming many of the towns and villages into formidable strong-points. Mines abounded, especially in the Reichswald Forest itself.

By the 10th of February, the spearhead of the advance had reached the middle of the Reichswald and was echeloned back on the flanks to the Maas and the Rhine. The forest was cleared after three further days of severe fighting, where in places the infantry had to struggle knee-deep in water among the splintered trees and dug outs. Cleve fell to 15th (S.) Division at the same time, and it was from this area that the Regiment

---

3. Under command of 51st (Highland) Division.

was to have been passed through, to exploit in the direction of Calcar and Emmerich. On the west bank of the Rhine the Canadians were fighting opposite Emmerich.

In the meantime the Germans were rushing up reserves to plug the gap in the Reichswald. These troops, which included some of the best Panzer Grenadier and Parachute units, had only been made available by the enemy thinning out their line opposite the American Ninth Army, which it will be remembered was to be launched over the Roer as the southern part of the Allied pincer movement. Thus in order to protect themselves in this sector the Germans broke the dams on the Roer river, hoping to hold up the Americans by floods if not by manpower. As a temporary measure it was a great success, and a fortnight of unrewarding battle for the British and Canadians passed before General Simpson was able to move. Then, on the 23rd of February, the Americans surged across the subsiding waters. By the 27th of the month they were on the outskirts of Mönchengladbach; meanwhile, on our front Goch had fallen and to the north the Canadians still struggled for possession of the vital Uden—Calcar ridge.

With the capture of Goch, and the progress made on both flanks, two of the three main defensive belts which the Germans had organized between the two rivers had been pierced and overrun. It now remained to break through the last system, known as the Hochwald "lay-back," running along the high ground from Geldern to Rees. 30 Corps was therefore directed from the Goch area on a line Weeze, Kevelaer and Geldern. There were now hopes that the armour might at last find a role, but it was not to be.

★ ★ ★

Colonel Abel Smith was anxious to get his Regiment well forward for the possible break-through because of the inevitable lack of road space available once things started to happen, but General Horrocks ruled that only one Squadron of armoured cars should be moved forward to join Guards Armoured Division in the area of Pfalzdorf on the south-east corner of the Reichswald Forest. "D" Squadron, under command of Major Profumo, were therefore ordered to advance on the 28th of February, and were joined by Regimental Tactical Headquarters the next day. Apart from the traffic control posts, this was the Regiment's first experience of Germany.

★ ★ ★

"D" Squadron spent the first night in some swampy fields, and subsequently found shelter in a derelict house and adjoining barns. Tactical Headquarters were lucky to find "a reasonably unbattered house in an area where almost every building had been demolished."

Here the devastation far surpassed that encountered at Caen and Vire, and it was a gruesome experience to live in it. Where we had been led to believe that there would be resentment and treachery, we met the blank, dull despair of peasants too stupefied to weep. For the Germans, the catastrophe which their leaders had so needlessly brought upon them had gone far beyond the point of personal grief. It seemed that, burdened as he was by the non-fraternization problem, the British soldier was for a time at a loss to know what to do. One sensed the beginning of an immensely complicated problem of relationship between victor and vanquished, to which no one yet knew the answer. We had arrived in Germany profoundly ignorant and with a mass of preconceived notions, and where we had been expecting to find a deep sense of guilt, we encountered nothing but a numbed sense of defeat and hopelessness.

The district we were in was not a rich one. There were no silk stockings and leather goods in shops or well-stocked cellars of looted wines and sides of bacon; if there ever had been, then preceding troops had performed a remarkably efficient clean-up. All that we found left were a few battered pieces of cheap furniture, some sacks of potatoes, and a quantity of bottled fruit.

Cleve, like Cassino in Italy, was one of the places where it could with truth be said that every house and building had been utterly destroyed. The other villages we passed through were not much better. Incongruous sights greeted the eye at every turn. One would find a soldier walking about the ruins in a top hat—I don't know why this essentially agricultural part of the country possessed so many top hats. Outside Krannenburg, at the entrance to what had once been the church, two soldiers from a Scottish regiment were eating their dinners under an enormous coloured parasol, while a third was trying to work a treadle sewing machine in the pouring rain.

Everywhere one saw those signs of hurried civilian flight—a pair of spectacles left on the shop counter, a half-finished meal, a child's toy train lying crushed in the road. I remember picking up Winston Churchill's "The World Crisis, 1911-1918," which, covered in mud, was rescued from the floor of a demolished schoolroom. One pondered over its prophetic words written in the early twenties. "So strange indeed is the present international situation that it passes the wit of man to say what portent will have appeared in the European sky by the time these words see light. Armed to the teeth and feverishly adding to their armaments, the nations of Europe are asking themselves, 'Is this the peace for which we fought?'"

★　★　★

It continued to rain throughout the first days of March and the cars sank lower and lower into the quagmire. There was nothing to do but to wait, for Guards Armoured Division were still held up while the infantry of 53rd (W.) Division strove to enter Weeze, still tenaciously defended by paratroops.

The continual bogging of the vehicles compelled "D" Squadron to line up on a relatively dry stretch of farm-track close to the forest of Cleve. The men had got hold of stoves and coal briquettes from the ruined houses, and so managed to keep fairly dry and warm. The Squadron echelon spread itself around a farm, whose terrified owners and equally frightened Polish labourers had barricaded themselves into a back room. At first nobody would come out, but eventually the farmer sent a Polish woman to parley. She was a tough-looking customer, with the thick neck and high cheek bones of the Slav peasant, but she worked herself into a state of complete hysteria before it could be explained that no one wished to harm her. At last the farmer himself ventured forth, waving a protective document in front of him and shouting "Eisenhower, gut Eisenhower." It transpired that he was holding the deeds to his farmhouse and that one of its past owners named Eisenhower had sailed for the United States over a hundred and twenty years before. The name is a common one in Germany, but the farmer obviously considered it a safe-conduct and it was not long before the story was flying round the Regiment that the Supreme Commander's cousin was locked up next door to "D" Squadron, and what was going to be done about it?

Meanwhile, after twenty-four hours' fighting, the infantry captured Weeze, and quickly went on to take Kevelaar and Geldern, where it then linked up with American forces from the south. The Germans now realized that their efforts to hold on to the west bank of the Rhine had failed and they started to plan for the evacuation of their remaining troops through the only bridgehead still left in their possession at Wesel. All British and Canadian forces were therefore swung in this direction.

On the 3rd of March, after another day of orders to move and counter-orders to remain *in situ*, Tactical Headquarters got off to a good start, while "D" Squadron, still not permitted to move, ironically cheered the cavalcade of command vehicles, dominated by the elephantine bulk of the A.C.V., as it joined the southbound convoys for Weeze and beyond. But this was definitely not the Regiment's day, and it was halted on orders some two miles south of Weeze by the River Niers, where it remained, in the words of Lieutenant Turnbull, the Signals Officer, "with Colonel Henry champing at the bit."

For the next two days, the 4th and 5th, it continued to pour with rain, and "D" Squadron waited in depressing conditions for news that they might be used. The time was passed in trying to keep dry by lighting fires, stoked by rafters from the ruined houses, and in discussing non-fraternization in all its aspects. Even at this stage there was a distinct uneasiness that the order was bound to give the Germans more laughs than the Allies righteous satisfaction.

On the 5th of March, Tactical Headquarters and "D" Squadron returned to Nijmegen. It was noticed that, in spite of strict orders about the looting of china and crockery, Regimental Headquarters Mess had acquired a fine collection of assorted cups and saucers. Captain Balding's ingenious explanation was that they were about to be bulldozered into the side of the road when he had rescued them from the rubble.

Although in the south the Americans[4] had made startling advances, there had never been any break in the front of the First Canadian Army, and the German forces, which contained a large proportion of paratroops, had fought hard and skilfully throughout. Only at the very end were Guards Armoured Division to be given a role, when they were pushed through the infantry on the 4th of March, the day before the Regiment's return to Nijmegen. They were successful in capturing Bonninghardt.

Back in Nijmegen, while waiting for the reduction of the Wesel bridgehead, the Regiment turned once more to inspections and normal training. Formations were moving forward in preparation for the assault on the Rhine. The Regiment was fully up to strength and no troops were detached.

On the night of the 9th/10th of March the Germans evacuated the bridgehead completely, blowing the last available bridge across the Rhine.

While Tactical Headquarters and "D" Squadron had been employed in Germany waiting for the break-through which never materialized, more traffic control points had gone out from Nijmegen. An officer's diary gives a good picture of the front as it then was:

---

4. On the 5th of March First U.S. Army entered the western outskirts of Cologne, the city falling two days later. To the south the same army captured Remagen bridge, when a spearhead seized the Luddendorf railway bridge over the Rhine. Full advantage of this exploit could not be taken because the structure had been so damaged by enemy shell fire that it finally collapsed into the river some days after capture.

FIRST NIGHT IN GERMANY

28th February 1945: Fitters' jeep and armoured cars preparing to spend the night in a field near Bedberg. The projection at the end of the 2-pdr. gun is the "Littlejohn" apparatus, which, acting as a squeeze-gun, increased the muzzle velocity of the projectile

"*March 2*. The floods have gone down a little, exposing large numbers of dead cattle and horses. Groesbeek utterly destroyed. Still hundreds of broken gliders where U.S. Airborne originally landed.

"*March 3*. Move to 30 Corps Headquarters on the Reichswald via Mook, Gennep, Hekkens; complete shambles all the way. Got all my troops on traffic duties. Lunch in Mess there with Neville Ford. G.A.D. are moving up and David Burghersh has arrived. He is escorting Churchill tomorrow. Very cold and wet and slept with all clothes on in a tent which leaked badly. A few German planes over and heavy A.A. fire.

"*March 4*. Rained all through the night, up early. Move to new area postponed until eleven o'clock. Saw Churchill, Montgomery, Eisenhower and Crerar going round the front. Four o'clock, have new orders to move and have been given three new control points, Goch, Weeze and Kevellaer. Set off in Staghound, terrible traffic jam all the way, so eventually went on on back of motorcycle. Dark night and it is still raining but lit by the searchlights (artificial moonlight). Countryside all the way is completely laid waste by our shelling. No animals living; dead horses, cows, and pigs everywhere. Not a single home intact; even the trees are all blasted. Got into a row of semi-detached German houses— no roofs, downstairs floors not too bad. Chucked out all debris and broken furniture and moved in. Shambles of broken personal belongings everywhere. Up all night with the telephone ringing continually. 32nd Brigade were moving by throughout the night.

"*March 5*.—Got half an hour's sleep at 7.30 while Trooper Prangnell took over the telephone, then interrupted when an officer came in to know why his brigade could not go through. Have only seen two German women in the area. Clothes, furniture, valuables, are scattered everywhere. No animals except dead ones, not even a chicken. We have got a stove going and cooked a lunch of German food, bottled fruit, etc., and are eating off good German china plates! The roads are crammed with our stuff going towards the Rhine. Civilians are slowly beginning to come back to find nothing but ruins, ruins and yet more ruins." (Diary of Captain G. D. Cooper.)

Pending developments farther afield, Colonel Abel Smith decided to organize a series of troop runs in the area of Druten, that canal-intersected part of Holland where months previously "D" Squadron had conducted operations under the command of 52nd Division. It was still as deserted as ever. An improvised field firing range was set up where troops could fire across the Waal and incidentally annoy a few stray Germans. These were not amused and replied by wreaking vengeance on the local farmers who, having supplied the Regiment with many dozen eggs in the past, now saw all their chicken houses blown to bits and their neighbours terrorized.

THIS IS GERMANY, MARCH 1945

Two proposed changes in equipment might have affected us had the war gone on longer than it did; as it was, they never got beyond the stage of discussion. One was the replacement of the Heavy Troops' Matadors by the Alecto, a tracked self-propelled gun of 95-mm. calibre. It was decided not to apply for this vehicle because of the admittedly poor anti-tank performance of its gun. Secondly, it was proposed to replace the White scout cars used by the Support Troops, and as Medical vehicles, by the White scout car half-track. The White scout car, a very hard riding vehicle and a brute to turn in narrow roads, was obsolescent, and in any case half-tracks were due to be issued to the Squadron fitters. Staghounds and Daimler armoured cars and the Daimler scout car were to continue unaltered and unchallenged in their particular sphere until the cessation of hostilities.

It was learnt on the 11th of March that the Regiment was to be prepared to move into the Reichswald to concentrate for the forthcoming crossing of the Rhine. Just before this took place, Captain (by now Honorary Major) A. J. R. Collins, the Adjutant, left to take up a staff appointment at Second Army Headquarters. His departure left a gap not easy to fill. Arthur Collins, whose four and three-quarter years as Adjutant must surely have broken all records for length of service, could have gone far on the Staff had he chosen to move on, but he preferred to remain with the Regiment, to whose cause he was utterly devoted.

His Adjutancy spanned the period during which the Regiment had transferred from being a cavalry unit to that of a motor battalion, and later again to an armoured car regiment, in which last role it was to do all its fighting. That these changes, fraught with pitfalls of training and adaptability, were always carried to a successful conclusion, and at the same time the separate traditions of both Life Guards and Blues maintained throughout, was in no small measure due to him.

It would be but the bare bones of the story to add that on him as Adjutant fell the main burden of upholding the standards of discipline and *esprit de corps* which under all conditions never faltered. But there was more to it than that. Arthur Collins was one of those persons gifted with the rare double attribute of a tireless constitution and an exceptionally retentive memory. In the years of training and subsequently during operations he would be seen working long after others had retired to their beds for the night. At a conference, to hear him place every Household Cavalryman not only by name and present job, but also by Squadron and Troop and courses passed or failed, was a tour de force at which one never ceased to marvel. Nor is it in any way a slight on his successor to say that the 2nd Household Cavalry Regiment was never again quite the same without him. Perhaps, according to our temperaments, we sometimes tend to build up a picture of a friend at variance with facts or events, but to me Arthur Collins will always represent a deep voice "over the air" which could always be heard, whatever the distance which separated us, and which, whatever the crisis during action, always made sense.

Lieutenant J. N. Creswell, who commanded Lieutenant-General Sir Richard O'Connor's H.Q. Protection Troop in Normandy and had subsequently re-joined the Regiment in Brussels as Troop Leader in "A" Squadron, succeeded Major Collins. He was to remain in this post until the disbandment of 2 H.C.R. in Germany in the summer of 1945—a most successful Adjutant. He also goes down to history (according to himself!) as the first person to have been allowed by Colonel Abel Smith to light a cigarette in the A.C.V. during a battle.

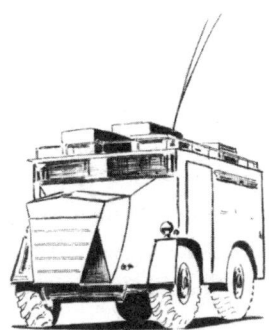

A.E.C. Armoured Command Vehicle

Chapter II

From the Reichswald to the Dortmund—
Ems Canal

Move to the Reichswald—Leave to U.K.—Medical organization within the Regiment—The 2 H.C.R. "Planning Room"—Colonel Abel Smith briefs his Regiment for Operation "Plunder"—Mr. Churchill watches Airborne arrival from a hill near Xanten—Crossing the Rhine at Rees —"B" and "D" Squadrons pass through the infantry bridgehead to exploit—Harbour for the night at Anholt and Aalten in Holland—Slogging advance belies optimistic first appreciations—Groenlo bypassed—Corporal Bugby's narrative—Lieutenant Harvey-Williams's Troop creates havoc behind enemy lines—Lieutenant Franklin's recollections—"D" Squadron push on to outskirts of Eibergen—Trooper Gee loses his third scout car—Trouble at Enschede—A disturbed night with the Irish Guards—Lieutenant Allen's Troop in gallant action west of Enschede—"B" Squadron push on to outskirts of Oldenzaal—The Almelo-Nordhorn Canal—Discovery of "a wooden bridge of doubtful strength" results in Welsh Guards' brilliant night dash to Ems Canal—Another vital bridge north of Altenlingen—Coldstream storm across Ems river—185 Brigade (3rd Division) follow suit with assault crossing of Ems Canal—"A" and "D" Squadrons at Bentheim—Sudlohne—The larger picture

The wretched cold and rain which had prevailed during the first half of the month gave way to beautiful spring-like weather as we moved off into the Reichswald on the 14th of March, there to prepare for the Rhine crossing. As we crossed the frontier we passed a large warning notice put up by the Canadians, "This is Germany—you are warned." Far from referring to the stunned civilians or potential "werewolves," it might well have been to warn us of the frightful track over which we were about to travel before reaching our destination at the south-eastern corner of the forest. The Canadian sappers, working like beavers, had repaired the ravages of shelling and floods by placing logs cemented together with earth across the road. Without this form of repair, no traffic could have moved, but the method took little heed of people's backs, and the effect on those who rode in armoured cars was crippling. Well aware of this, the Canadians had sardonically christened an extra bad stretch the "Livercure Mile."

Entering the forest proper was a relief from the depressing contemplation of devastated villages, but even here signs of the bitterness of the fighting were much in evidence. A new type of shell fitted with what was known as a proximity fuse[1] had been employed for the first time, and the trees were splintered in a manner reminiscent of pictures of the First World War. Little imagination was required to realize what must have been the crippling effect of the shelling on the morale of the Germans sheltering below.

By the sides of the road and deep into the forest rides, the Canadians had built themselves the neatest of log cabins—complete backwoods affairs with smoking chimneys and washing hanging out on lines to dry. So tidy and shipshape, they almost reminded one of a Hollywood set.

No sooner had the armoured cars been parked amidst the slanting rays of sunshine and clean smell of pines than every man in the Regiment evinced the greatest determination to emulate what he had seen. The forest rang to cries of "timber" as tree after tree crashed to the ground, felled by the Staghound matchets, which were now at a premium. Huts sprang up like mushrooms. The men lacked the professional touch of the Canadian lumberjack, nor was anyone able to find out the secret of making earth and brushwood waterproof, but tarpaulins and groundsheets served as well, and the huts, besides being most ingenious, were very comfortable to live in.

There was no question of wandering off the beaten track into the forest, because mines were still about in quantities and taped paths had to be strictly adhered to. Everywhere lay great dumps of German equipment. There were baskets of 88-mm. shells by the thousand, mountains of hand grenades and belts of machine-gun ammunition, and gas masks and their containers in numbers sufficient to re-equip the British Army.

As if the sun were making amends for the preceding months, day succeeded day in brightest sunshine. The air was laden with the smell of resin, and the men were fit and happy in this sort of Boy Scout atmosphere, which for all its drawbacks was infinitely preferable to the drabness and misery of Nijmegen.

The Germans had abandoned, mostly in fair condition, a number of well-constructed dug-outs with timber-revetted sides. These were soon cleaned out and the larger ones filled with "bulldozered" curtains, tables, and chairs, to become comfortable messes. Nor were bricks in short supply; one had only to send a lorry to the nearest village to gather up what had once been a house, and "D" Squadron Officers' Mess built

---

1. Proximity fuse – a tiny radio valve fitted into the head of the shell caused it to explode on nearing a solid obstacle. These shells were deadly if fired at a wood, for they went off tree-top high.

itself a fireplace worthy of a Loire château which kept every subaltern arguing into the small hours as to why it smoked so foully.

The Reichswald period was notable for the quantities of whitebait (alas, without "deep" fat to cook them in) consumed, and barrels of oysters bought in Nijmegen. Nobody could explain, least of all the Dutch fishmonger, how these managed to run the gauntlet of enemy-occupied Holland and cross the Scheldt, but the matter was not probed too deeply.

Forty-eight hours' leave had started up again three days after reaching the forest, and it was evident that the lorries were now going back to Blehen and Ligney and Trognée as frequently as to Brussels.

Leave to the United Kingdom had begun some time back and, considering the difficulties of transport and accommodation, the system was working very smoothly. In a little over two days it was possible to be home in England. Some members of the Regiment managed to make the journey part of the way by road and via Brussels. This frequently meant a night at the Metropole, where Captain Garnett, who had recently left the Regiment and was now running an other ranks' leave hotel, would dispense hospitality. The hotel was well worth a visit, if only to be greeted by Garnett, elegantly gracing, like some slim Mogul of industry, a palatial office which would not have disgraced the chairman of the Coal Board. Here he conducted the day's business while Belgian Baronesses from "Le Welfare" dutifully flitted through the swing doors in obedience to his wishes.

★ ★ ★

One aspect of war which so frequently gets overlooked, and yet is of such vital importance to regimental well-being and morale, is the Medical organization. In the case of an armoured car regiment this is doubly important because, normally working on a much wider front than an infantry or tank battalion, the medical officer is always confronted with the problem of mobility and being at the right place at the right time. Surgeon-Captain Kynaston worked his regimental aid post as follows.

There was one White scout car per Sabre Squadron, fitted with stretcher and manned by two orderlies apiece, trained by the medical officer and under the command of the Squadron Leader at all times.

For himself at Regimental Headquarters there was also a White scout car with a driver, Trooper Turner and, later in the campaign, Trooper Quantrill; his officer's servant, Trooper Scowby, a wireless operator, Trooper Evans, and an orderly, Corporal Hilton. All the crew were trained orderlies. There was an ambulance car attached, and for specific operations further ambulances were often attached from the Field Ambulance.

A comparison between the regimental aid post in training and what it was visualized might happen, and the regimental aid post in action, is interesting. In training, the entire regiment was put through a first-aid course as far as was possible. The collection of casualties was a problem which continued to worry Surgeon-Captain Kynaston, for he could not see how it would be possible to cover two and sometimes three centre lines at the same time during an advance. "I was very apprehensive of this, for I felt it to be bad for morale if men knew that medical aid would be difficult to obtain. The official plan was to dump casualties beside the road, to be picked up later. (This in action was never resorted to.) I was apprehensive, too, because by the nature of the regimental role of pushing out in front I thought that casualties would be very high, and chances of me crossing from one centre line to the other in response to calls would mean that I was never where I was wanted most."

In fact, casualties in action, in spite of the nature of the work, were to prove relatively light. Help for serious cases was almost always near at hand because Field Ambulance advanced posts were very mobile and often not far behind Squadron Headquarters. In major advances, such as up to Brussels, Arnhem, etc., Captain Kynaston was always up with the leading squadron, usually behind the Second-in-Command's Staghound, and with his wireless netted to the Squadron command net. "We very soon worked out an efficient drill with the men in my own car. On receipt of news of a casualty, the driver stayed with my car, Trooper Scowby got ready the stretcher and blankets, Hilton the dressings, and Evans the Field Medical Card, while I did the treatment.[2] Thus my misgivings in the training period were happily not realized."

★   ★   ★

As the days lengthened, so the steady rumble of traffic increased in volume as it moved up to the assembly areas preparatory to the Rhine assault. Then suddenly we awoke one sunny morning to find that, in a clearing between R.H.Q. and the road, a large marquee had appeared. It was surrounded by a double apron of Dannert wire, in front of which a trooper mounted solemn guard. This was the "2 H.C.R. Planning

2. According to Captain Kynaston, the routine broke down only once, this on the run to Brussels. There were several minor skirmishes in which, wrote Kynaston, "my Corporal Hilton insisted on dashing off, rifle in hand, to take part in the sport, and I had to push on without him on one occasion, which taught him a lesson!"

Room," and those who remembered "Shaef" smiled tolerantly as they surveyed the billowing pavilion which housed the secrets of our future destiny. The fame of the planning room soon spread beyond the confines of the Reichswald, and representatives from neighbouring units, including the officers commanding the 1st and 2nd Grenadiers and Colonel Black of the Manitoba Dragoons, the Canadian armoured car regiment which was to be on our left flank when operations commenced, visited the tent. Here they studied the planner's arrows which led to Bremen and Hamburg and the still-distant Baltic.

The 1st Household Cavalry Regiment, which had recently come over from England, was not far away, having relieved the 11th Hussars on the Maas, and we had several visits from their officers, including on successive days one from Colonel Eric Gooch and another from Major Wignall.

On the 23rd of March, accompanied by his Intelligence Officer burdened with the largest map we had seen since General Sir Oliver Leese's divisional lectures at Warminster, Colonel Abel Smith briefed each of his Squadrons in turn, explaining the plan of the assault and what the likely role was to be. As usual, he exuded optimism, and as the monstrous map with its arrows and bounds and report lines rippled in a gentle breeze, he told the assembled men that the Regiment would be in Hamburg within forty-eight hours after the crossing of the Rhine—a forecast made by others at the time, but belied by events.

★ ★ ★

The plan of operation "Plunder," the great assault across the River Rhine north of the Ruhr, involved the use of three Allied armies. Under the command of Field-Marshal Montgomery, the U.S. Ninth Army on the right and the British Second Army on the left were to attack over the river between Rheinberg and Rees. They would capture the communication centre of Wesel and then expand the bridgehead sufficiently to secure the roads through Wesel from enemy action, thus enabling the river to be bridged at Emmerich. The Second Army was to assault north of Wesel and concentrate first on the capture of that town. It was also to bridge at Xanten and Rees. To assist the Second Army, the First Allied Airborne Army was timed to drop XVIII Airborne Corps[3] after the commencement of the ground assault and to seize the key terrain north and northwest of Wesel. The Canadians on the left flank

---

3. Comprising U.S. 17th and British 6th Airborne Divisions.

would take no active part in the assault, but were to hold firmly to the line of the Rhine and Maas from Emmerich westward, thus ensuring the safety of the bridgehead and guarding the Scheldt estuary and the port of Antwerp from enemy interference behind our lines.

The Regiment was again to operate under command of Guards Armoured Division in 30 Corps.

★   ★   ★

That same evening, in our dug-outs and log cabins, we drank to the success of the infantry—the 51st (Highland) Division—who, with a Canadian brigade under command, were to start crossing the Rhine opposite Rees. At four minutes past nine Lieutenant-General Horrocks, the Corps Commander, received a signal at his O.P. that the first British troops were across—men of the Black Watch—and had landed safely on the enemy bank. All night long the artillery thundered, and by morning we knew that along the river a series of almost bloodless landings had taken place.

As the ground troops were pushing forward in the early hours of the 24th the airborne forces were forming up in bases in France and England, from there to fly in to drop ahead of the advance in the area of Hamminkeln and Diersfordt on the right flank of the British bridgehead. We saw the first waves of Dakotas and attendant gliders fly past just before ten o'clock, and they continued for nearly three hours.

It was an inspiring sight as with their wings glinting in the sunshine they flew inexorably forward to deliver over fourteen thousand troops into battle.

Meanwhile, standing on a hill-top near Xanten, Mr. Churchill was determined not to miss an event which he more than any other living person had been responsible for bringing to successful fruition. He was looking across the morning mists towards the place where the troops were still crossing. The story is told by a witnessing correspondent that the gallant old warrior could contain his feelings no longer.

"I should have liked," he said, "to have deployed my men in red coats on the plain down there and ordered them to charge." Then he added with gusto, "But now my armies are too vast." With these words the Prime Minister sprang to his feet and went coursing wildly for a few steps down the hill. "They're coming," he shouted, "they're coming!" as the first planes of the airborne armada hove into sight. Two days later General Dempsey's senior intelligence officer stood before a roomful of correspondents and said: "This is the collapse. The German line is

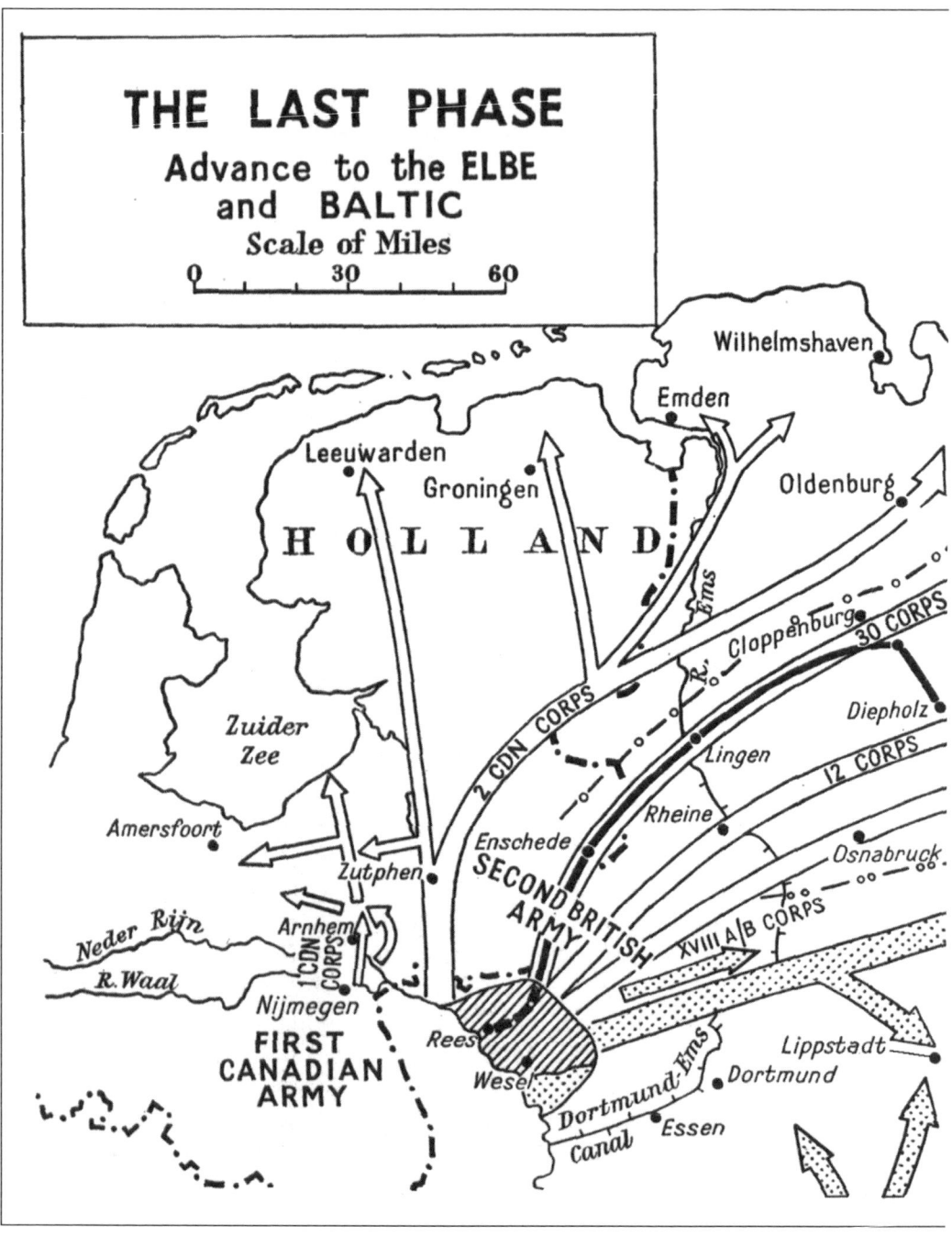

THE LAST PHASE

Advance to the ELBE
and BALTIC

Scale of Miles

0   30   60

Wilhelmshaven

Emden

Oldenburg

Leeuwarden

Groningen

HOLLAND

R. Ems

Cloppenburg

30 CORPS

Diepholz

Zuider Zee

2 CDN CORPS

Lingen

12 CORPS

Amersfoort

Rheine

Enschede

Osnabruck

Zutphen

SECOND BRITISH ARMY

Neder Rijn

Arnhem

1 CDN CORPS

XVIII A/B CORPS

R. Waal

Nijmegen

Lippstadt

Rees

Dortmund-Ems

Dortmund

FIRST CANADIAN ARMY

Wesel

Essen

Dortmund Canal

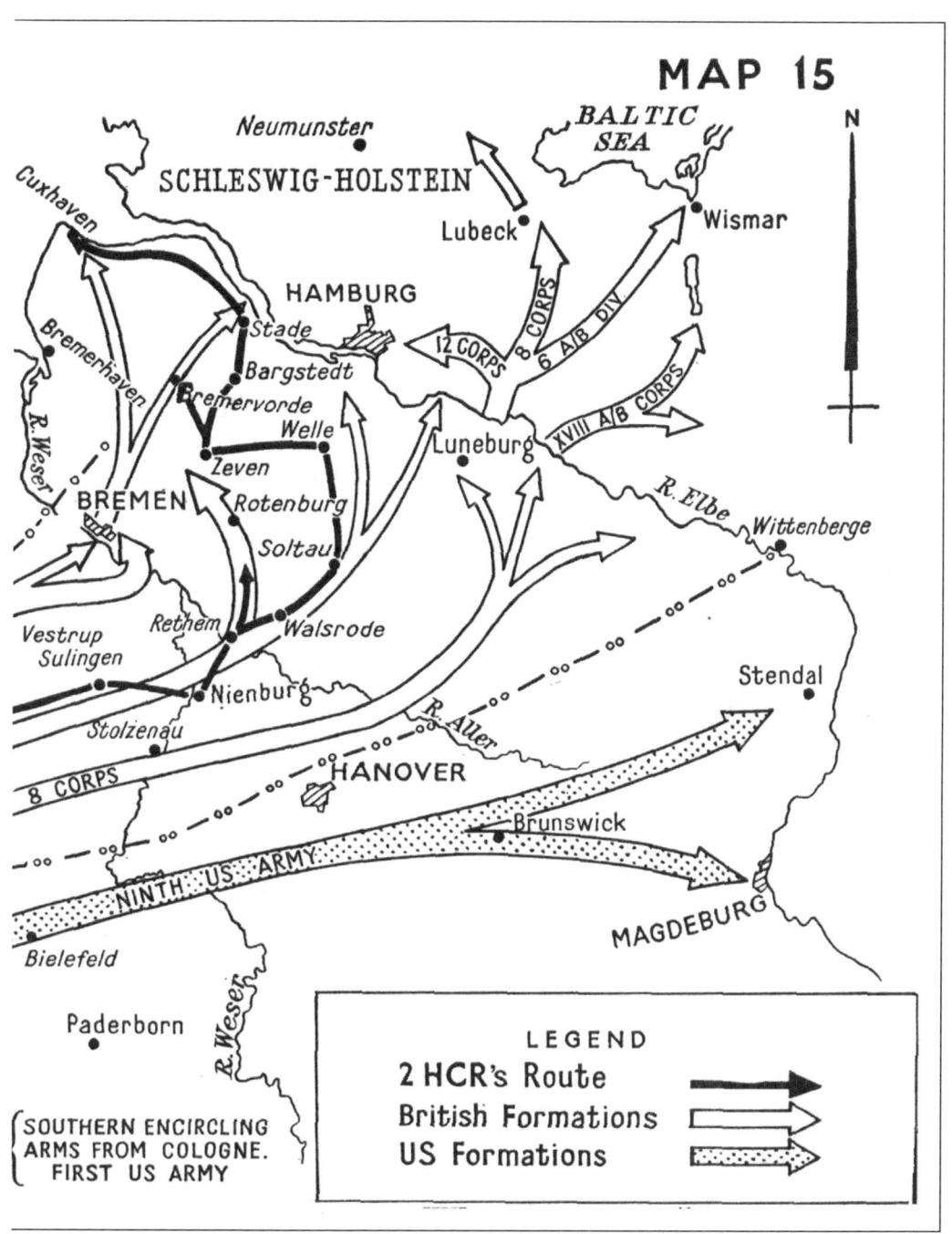

MAP 15

BALTIC SEA

N

Neumunster

SCHLESWIG-HOLSTEIN

Lubeck

Wismar

Cuxhaven

HAMBURG

Stade

12 CORPS · 8 CORPS · 6 A/B DIV

Bremerhaven

Bargstedt

Bremervorde

Welle

XVIII A/B CORPS

R. Weser

Zeven

Luneburg

Rotenburg

BREMEN

Soltau

R. Elbe

Wittenberge

Vestrup
Sulingen

Rethem

Walsrode

Stendal

Nienburg

R. Aller

Stolzenau

8 CORPS

HANOVER

Brunswick

NINTH US ARMY

MAGDEBURG

Bielefeld

R. Weser

Paderborn

LEGEND

2 HCR's Route

British Formations

US Formations

SOUTHERN ENCIRCLING
ARMS FROM COLOGNE.
FIRST US ARMY

broken. The enemy no longer has a coherent system of defence between the Rhine and the Elbe. It is difficult to see what there is to stop us now." There was a spirit of boundless optimism in the air.

We waited, and knew that the task of Guards Armoured Division, once across the Rhine, had already been defined as being the spearhead of 30 Corps whose object was "to advance deep into Germany, protecting the left flank of Second Army." The Canadians to the west were to open up a supply route through Arnhem and then to advance northwards into Holland, and would certainly for some time be echeloned back.

On the 28th of March orders came through that the Regiment was to concentrate at Uden, preparatory to crossing the Rhine at Rees. I see that my personal diary records the day thus: "Visited Leur and Tiel farmhouses in search of yet more eggs (how much of the British Army's spare time is devoted to this recreation). Arrived back at 1500 hours to find that we are moving at 2300 hours. Good-bye to dug-out and shack built with such loving care, in spite of all the chaffing that Tony Hughes and I should never complete it. Philip Profumo decided on 'high' tea in the Reichswald as a final send-off.

Two dozen oysters and three eggs each, and champagne! Depart on the dot, completely blown out—the men likewise! It's raining and the roads are very skiddy—shall miss Jarvest's wonderful driving.

"Arrive 0100 hours in the morning. Raining. Uden shattered ruins. Reveille six o'clock in a swamped field. Slept on a shattered shop counter. Tony Hughes and his echelon forgot to bring up the remaining eggs in the morning. They were looking well fed and dry, and Hugo and I were practically speechless with rage! On a somewhat broader front the news is wonderful. 6th Guards Tank Brigade are miles into Germany with the American Airborne on their backs. Colonel Henry may be right about Hamburg after all, although we shall have to get a move on to keep up to his schedule."

★   ★   ★

We stood about for most of the day, adjusting maps, reading the Intelligence reports, and drinking tea. Then, during the late afternoon, Colonel Abel Smith issued his orders. Guards Armoured Division were to cross the river during the night of the 29th/30th of March and pass through 51st (Highland) Division. The Regiment already knew its objective—Hamburg. "B" and "D" Squadrons were to lead on two centre lines and they therefore moved up to the Hochwald, where 5th Guards Brigade were already harbouring preparatory to the crossing.

It was still raining hard when at three o'clock in the morning of the 30th of March the leading elements of Guards Armoured Division began to cross the Rhine at Rees. Even though the Regiment had taken no part in the storming of this almost legendary waterway, the event was significant enough to jolt all but the sleepiest trooper into a state of wakefulness. How many dozen pontoon bridges had we crossed since that first rickety affair in Wiltshire where General Sir Oliver Leese waited to greet us with his brisk dawn "good morning"? We knew it all so well by now. The depressingly cold feelings of that uncivilized hour before sunrise. The lingering taste of tepid tea gulped from a greasy tin mug. The pencil rolling to the bottom of the turret floor at the critical moment of a message, and the damp smears of condensation nullifying all attempts to peer through the map talc to check the route. Then, as the bridge is neared, a quick test of the "intercom" —"Driver, can you hear me?" The strange gripping feeling as the car dips to the water's edge. The Military Police signalling frantically to close up and, if by chance this has already been anticipated, the equally urgent signs to open out. The musical, almost mesmeric, sound of the rumbling sleepers as they take the weight of the wheels and the pontoon boats bob and dance as the current strains against the anchoring ropes. The sudden draught of cold air mid-stream; the agony of mind as the driver ahead stalls his engine and the self-starter grinds through an eternity before the engine responds once more.

The Rhine, studied from mid-stream, was a mighty river, and there was a sense of deep exhilaration in crossing it which we all felt deeply.

Once on the other bank, there came the mad scramble to catch up with the car ahead, followed by the violent application of brakes as the entire column as far as the eye could see came to an abrupt halt in a long line of tanks and lorries and armoured cars. Then for no visible reason everyone was off again at breakneck speed.

As we sped through what little remained of Rees, the Highlanders were resting at the side of the road, weary and mud-stained from their exertions. They spotted the divisional sign and chaffingly shouted "Mind the paint."

The immediate task of the Regiment was to pass through the forward elements of 51st (Highland) Division, then holding the perimeter of the bridgehead, and push on into Holland on the general line Rees—Anholt—Dinxperlo—Aalten—Groenlo. "D" Squadron were to lead on the right and "B" Squadron on the left.

"D" Squadron's route led through Isselburg. It then swung east behind the front line of 51st Division and turned north again at a cross-roads north-west of Bocholt, which was still being fiercely contested. All went well up to this point, but subsequently the story was one of demolitions and mines in greater quantities than had been encountered since Normandy, and progress was painfully slow.

★　★　★

"B" Squadron on the left had a more eventful day, for much of "D" Squadron's area had already been cleared by 12 Corps troops who were operating on the right. All forward troops travelled west of the main road, and initially advanced with speed, after having passed through the forward infantry positions in the Millingen area. Here, several tanks belonging to 8th Armoured Brigade had been hit by bazookas and lay smoking on the roadside.

Lieutenant Tabor's Troop ran into opposition about a mile north of Millingen, but as this consisted only of infantry in comparatively open country, the enemy withdrew when fired upon. A German light armoured car took one look at the Daimlers and scuttled off as fast as it could go. Farther on, at a crossing of a stream two miles north of Millingen, the bridge was blown up in the Troop's face, but an alternative way round was found and a truckload of Germans retiring from the blown bridge were shot up. At that moment some of our own tanks appeared and, mistaking the Troop for Germans, opened fire, fortunately with no damage resulting. "B" Squadron then advanced towards Anholt but were unable to find a way across the River Issel south of the town. However, Lieutenant Palmer's Troop and some Grenadier tanks eventually effected penetration, and after considerable casualties had been inflicted on the enemy the column moved on, finally harbouring for the night outside Anholt. "D" Squadron in the meantime were harbouring south of Aalten. In the course of the day's fighting, seven lorry-loads of infantry were shot up, three of them without a single man escaping.

Meanwhile, Regimental Headquarters and the two reserve Squadrons had moved up to Bocholt with 5th Guards Brigade Headquarters and were thus in a good position to resume the advance at dawn.

As far as hopes of emulating the startling advances taking place on the right flank were concerned it had been a bitterly disappointing day, and this state of affairs was to continue all through Germany. We noticed with concern that prisoner identifications included a growing proportion of men from 2nd Parachute Corps, and this highly efficient formation was to continue to exercise a high degree of control until the final surrender. Its demolition of both roads and bridges was most thorough. In addition, the enemy had added another trick to their repertoire—the sowing of mines amidst the debris of their own cratering and at places where troops were likely to by-pass the obstruction. Lieutenant Jonkheer Groeninx van Zoelen was thus wounded as he was guiding a lorry past the last crater before reaching harbour for the night.

After the non-fraternization and glum looks of the Reichswald period, it was a strange experience by a twist of the frontier to leave the fluttering white handkerchiefs and sheets of Germany and encounter once again the Union Jacks, the Stars and Stripes, and the orange favours of the welcoming Dutch. For them, the worst part of the war was at last over.

In the hope that the front might reveal a weak spot which the armour could exploit, Colonel Abel Smith decided to work three Squadrons up. Accordingly, at about nine o'clock in the evening (30th March), "A" and "C" Squadrons were ordered to join "D" Squadron at Aalten. "B" Squadron remained in reserve and spent the day moving slowly forward by fits and starts, a process almost as tiring as actual fighting.

"C" Squadron were having their evening brew up when orders came through that they must move forward at once.

"Many prisoners were still coming down the road from the two forward Squadrons as we pulled into a ploughed field not far from Isselburg, where we were hoping to spend the night. Then at about nine o'clock at night when we were about to get down to it, orders came through to move up to join the Irish Guards group and 'D' Squadron at Aalten. I went off with a harbour party—it was pitch dark. Eventually located the Irish Guards group by the burning haystacks and houses (they always light their way into harbour), where I saw Denis Fitzgerald[4] and decided to park Squadron alongside a concrete road for the night. The Squadron arrived in at 2.15 in the morning, followed by Claudie Hamilton's echelon.[5] Peter Herbert arrived shortly afterwards with orders for the morrow's advance. We are in Holland again." (Diary of "C" Squadron officer.)

It was still dark when the advance towards Groenlo was resumed next morning. Little opposition was encountered at first. The Germans had withdrawn behind their barricades of roadblocks and blown bridges, and the grinding business of circumventing these obstacles under sporadic sniping and mines was to begin all over again. "As far as the eye can see," wirelessed back one car, "the road is blocked by felled trees; it's just like Normandy." By nine o'clock "D" Squadron were approaching the

---

4. Major D. R. S. Fitzgerald, Irish Guards.
5. Captain the Lord Claud Hamilton, Irish Guards.

medieval town of Groenlo, working in close liaison with the Grenadier tanks. To the left, "C" Squadron had been ordered to try to infiltrate behind the Germans holding up 43rd Division, and they had already experienced several clashes with the enemy.

★ ★ ★

"D" Squadron found the outskirts of Groenlo held by a light force of enemy, mostly clustered in the thick woods on the southern edge of the town. A moat surrounded the place and most of the bridges were found to have been blown. Major Profumo was therefore ordered to by-pass Groenlo and to find an alternative way round, leaving the town itself to be reduced by the Grenadier group. This was a good move as it happened, because the Grenadiers, having overcome the German opposition in the southern half, found themselves held up after fighting their way across a bridge in the northern suburbs. "But even this did not cause a bottleneck in Groenlo because the Household Cavalry had explored the by-roads to the east and the whole battalion (Grenadiers) was able to slip past the guns and follow the Household Cavalry round to rejoin the main road two miles north of the town."[6]

This successful manoeuvre was mainly the result of a good piece of work by Lieutenant Harris's armoured cars in "D" Squadron, the same Troop which had encountered the first roadblock barring the way into Groenlo on the main road.

Lance-Corporal-of-Horse Bugby had led off in his scout car and had not gone very far when he made contact with enemy infantry who fired off their bazookas at him from flanking positions; luckily, all shots missed. At this stage, the road lay beneath high banks with only the turret tops of the cars showing. This meant that very little fire could be directed on to the German emplacements, so Lieutenant Harris decided to speed on, after warning the remainder of the Squadron of the ambush. "On coming up to a cross-roads," wrote Bugby, "another group of infantry were caught with their pants down, some in more senses than one, and we let them have it good and proper." Fortunately for the enemy, a Dutch priest came out of a cottage and, ignoring the machine-gun fire, ran to tend the wounded Germans. "It was an extremely brave and disinterested act of devotion, but it put a stop to our battle for fear of hitting him, so we again pushed on."

---

6. *The Grenadier Guards in the War of 1939-1945*, p. 228. (Gale & Polden Ltd.)

"LONDON BRIDGE", GERMANY

2nd Household Cavalry Regiment crossing the River Rhine by pontoon bridge at Rees, 30th March 1945.

The next incident took place when a solitary German cyclist was seen bicycling for all he was worth towards the advancing Troop. He was waving a stick grenade in one hand, "and looked as if he was out to break all records both for speed and novel form of suicide." Corporal Bugby, being a humane person, decided to give this lunatic a chance, so he stood up in the scout car, aimed the Bren at him, and waited. At about twenty yards' range, when there appeared no alternative but to give him a burst of fire, the German suddenly thought discretion to be the better part of valour. He threw up his hands, wobbled violently from side to side and described a neat somersault into the ditch with his bicycle wrapped about his ears. British soldiers being basically good-natured, Bugby merely roared with laughter, picked him up by, the scruff of the neck and bundled him back to the rear scout car before resuming his journey northwards.

The country now opened out somewhat, and Trooper Rose, driver of Bugby's car, caught sight of more movement ahead. This proved to be a half-company of infantry, who took refuge in a large farmhouse. Lieutenant Harris decided that they were in too great number to be ignored by the Troop and so the buildings were surrounded and riddled with the fire from three vehicles. Soon the white flag was hoisted and fifty-three Germans surrendered. They admitted that they had been ordered to hold a bridge east of Groenlo, the one subsequently used by the Grenadier group, and had been surprised by the Troop before getting into position. In their equipment were found mines, demolition material and enough bazookas to halt an armoured brigade. Corporal-of-Horse Royston then "spent a busy half-hour smashing up their rifles and Spandaus with the thoroughness of a Yorkshire opening batsman piling up a Test century."

★   ★   ★

On the left flank of the advance "C" Squadron's attempt at cutting in behind the enemy met with equal success. Lieutenant Young's Troop took thirty-two prisoners, nearly all from 8 Parachute Division, and shot up twelve vehicles, "most of which caught fire immediately and were burnt out, including unfortunately a beautiful green Mercedes touring car filled with wooden mallets, corkscrews and black silk stockings!" The psychological aspect of the German looting mind is strange indeed.

"C" Squadron kept up the pressure until nightfall with continued success. Lieutenant Harvey-Williams's Troop passed through the Irish Guards positions (they were now in reserve) with orders to aim for Ruurlo, which lay well to the north-west of Groenlo. The Troop accounted for a number of enemy on the way, reporting that they "somehow did not think that the Germans were expecting them, for they were mostly travelling the wrong way." Back on the centre line Captain Cooper noted that "endless prisoners came doubling back, thoroughly frightened, to Squadron Headquarters, where they were packed off to the nearest café, where the ever-present 'Résistance' took good care of them."

When still short of Ruurlo, revised divisional orders to "concentrate upon creating as much dislocation and disturbance in the German rear as possible" entailed the Troop striking northwards, towards the Twenthe Canal and Lochem. For this raid, and as the enemy had thickened up on the ground, Lieutenant Harvey-Williams decided to lead with the two armoured cars—this gave him more fire power immediately available in front.

Corporal-of-Horse Brown was in the second armoured car and describes what followed:

> "We had had a sticky patch of map reading, perhaps not quite up to our usual standard, but the side roads were very difficult, and there were quite a few enemy about. We soon made contact with them again but pushed on rapidly. We were meeting odd vehicles, horses and carts, Jerries on push bikes, and almost all manner of strange things. As we got towards Ruurlo the Germans became thicker on the ground, and I was busy shooting some up in a farmyard just as we neared the place proper when I received an urgent message from my Troop Leader saying he was having trouble on the level crossing in the centre of the village. So I went off to join him. Here the place certainly did appear to be full of Jerries, and I found him with a dead horse lying across the road. He succeeded in charging it and got over without belly-ing the car, and as it was obvious that we had caught the enemy napping, we decided to continue on through the village."

On reaching a T-road with the intention of turning right-handed towards Lochem, Lieutenant Harvey-Williams found that he had cut right through the middle of a large enemy convoy of guns, half-tracks, and lorries. These were facing north, and the Troop Leader, although having no means of finding out its length, decided to drive past it in the same direction, doing as much damage as possible in the resultant confusion.

In the lead was Lieutenant Harvey-Williams's armoured car, driven by Trooper Clarke, the gunner being Trooper Marshall. Backing him up close behind was the scout car, commanded by Corporal Ray and driven by Trooper Parsons. Next came the second armoured car with Corporal-of-Horse Brown and Troopers Hopper and Holman forming the crew, and behind the armoured car a section of Lieutenant Hopkinson's Support Troop, commanded by Corporal-of-Horse Parker. Bringing up the rear were Corporal Bland and Trooper Bishop in another scout car.

Most of the German vehicles were halted at the side of the road with crews dismounted when the armoured cars descended on them like a tornado, all guns firing. It was impossible to miss at such close range and lorries burst into flames and exploded as men, ammunition and petrol were scattered in every direction. The Troop had traversed over a third of the way down the column before the enemy thought of returning the fire. The others still in front, warned by the yells and curses from the rear, either leapt into their lorries and speeded forward or else dived for the ditch and fired off their bazookas. The faster drove the enemy along the road, the faster sped the pursuing armoured cars after them. Both armoured car turrets were kept trained half right and all that the gunners had to do was to keep their fingers pressed on the trigger mechanism until the belt of ammunition ran out. At this stage "a large German sergeant" lobbed a bazooka at the White scout car which missed and exploded against another German vehicle. Corporal-of-Horse Parker's Support Section returned the compliment with interest by hurling grenades into all the open lorries they were able to overtake. In the confusion a German officer's saloon car was sandwiched between the Support Troop scout car and Corporal Bland's vehicle and drove on, powerless to do anything about it, until a "Jeeper" emptied a Bren-gun magazine into its petrol tank, causing it to swerve sharply to the right, blocking Bland's road. Thereupon Trooper Bishop, the driver, put his foot hard down on the accelerator pedal and barged the flaming car into the ditch.

By this time, the Germans in front had formed some sort of a defensive position and were lining the ditches with their bazooka men and 37-mm. anti-tank guns. "This made things rather more tricky," added Brown, "because we were forced to look at both sides of the road at the same time. However, they kept on missing us, and I think hit quite a few of their own cars, which only increased their confusion, as they swore at one another. Then Corporal Camidge, who was standing up in the White scout car, firing his Bren gun, was hit in the lung by a rifle bullet and as he was in a serious plight we laid him down on the floor of the car, while the others resumed firing standing with their legs straddled across him."

The next moment Lieutenant Harvey-Williams's car was hit in the wheel by a bazooka which blew off a tyre, wrecked the steering mechanism and sent it crashing into the ditch. The Troop Leader and his operator scrambled out, ran up to Corporal-of-Horse Brown's car as it passed, and jumped on to the back. Trooper Clarke followed suit by leaping on to the front tool box of Corporal Bland's scout car and lay flat on his face while the vehicle accelerated fast out of this rather hot spot.

Five hundred yards farther on they came to the end of the German column, and the now badly battered Troop, once clear of the firing, decided to take shelter in a small wood to reorganize and see what could be done for Corporal Camidge, who was in a bad way. The three armoured vehicles were placed in an all-round defensive position and the Support Troop dismounted to prevent stalking. But the Germans had rightly appreciated that the Troop must now be short of ammunition and they decided to put in an attack from the road and across country. Corporal-of-Horse Brown was down to his last two belts of Besa and nine rounds of armour-piercing shot, the latter ammunition "a rather wasteful method of dealing with individual infantrymen." However, Corporal-of-Horse Parker's section still had some Bren ammunition left, "so in strictly controlled bursts we prepared to give the Jerry as good as he intended to give us."

To everyone's surprise, the next German move was to call off the projected attack and a Red Cross party advanced up the road in charge of a German doctor carrying a large white flag. He asked Lieutenant Harvey-Williams for a truce, requesting that firing stop until the wounded, who were lying scattered along the road to Ruurlo, had been attended to. This was granted after the doctor had been asked to look at Corporal Camidge. He said he would survive if taken to a German hospital without delay and suggested that his party should carry him off. However, as a message had come through that No. 3 Troop under Lieutenant Bruce-Lockhart was on its way, the offer was refused and the German party withdrew.

Careful watch was kept for any German ruse as they gathered in their casualties. They could be seen three hundred yards away building a roadblock which effectively put an end to any hope of regaining Ruurlo that way. To the west was a large belt of trees, through which no car could pass, and running eastwards was a narrow track which appeared from the map to end in nothing but fields. As the Troop Leader was deciding on his next course of action a column of about twenty-five Germans came marching down the road from the north towards Ruurlo, led by an officer on a bicycle, the men all carrying "their bazookas at the slope and in immaculate formation." In view of the ammunition shortage, Lieutenant Harvey-Williams hoped to make them surrender, and two

German prisoners were doubled at the point of the gun to go and tell them to give up. But they refused. "On they came," said Corporal-of-Horse Brown, "and just as they were deploying we laid on the Bren, my Besa, and a .300 Browning which we had on one of the cars and let them have it in controlled bursts. Talk about shooting sitting birds! "

However, mainly because of the limited firing, a number of survivors were able to run for cover to a farmhouse about 400 yards away, and then started to snipe at the Troop from outbuildings and haystacks. They were also able to seal off the road to the north by placing bazooka men in the ditches where they could not be seen or shot at.

With less than a belt of ammunition left between the cars, Harvey-Williams decided to make a dash for it, and, led by Corporal Bland along a previously reconnoitred track, the Troop slipped away at dusk to make contact with Lieutenant Bruce-Lockhart's Troop on the outskirts of Ruurlo without encountering further trouble.

Two days later a follow-up party reported that on a sector of the road measuring one and three-quarter miles long, sixty-eight vehicles, ranging from carts to light armoured cars and half-tracks, had been counted knocked out. A member of the Troop wrote later: "We have become accustomed to having most of our bridges and liberated towns claimed by other units, from the Somme bridges onwards, but what did rather get us was the six o'clock news, maybe two days after the episode. It reported our long burnt out German convoy north of Ruurlo as having been shot up by a Typhoon patrol! "

★   ★   ★

Meanwhile "A" Squadron had also been making progress in their "disrupting" role to the east of Groenlo, and by midday had reached a small stream named the Grevenracht, where there was a more or less general halt to await the arrival of the tanks. The partnership of tanks-cum-infantry and armoured cars was working very smoothly, and it was only this close co-operation which enabled an over-all if slow advance to be maintained at all over the countless small bridges and streams which were now being met at every turn.

Lieutenant Franklin describes what troops were having to contend with:

> "It had taken a day and a night drive for 'A' Squadron to be brought within striking distance of the front, and I was pleased to note that when we stopped I found three Teller mines which on closer inspection turned out

to be nothing more than slats of wood. I had had my Troop harboured for the previous night in a little cottage on the border, and in the morning we were to take over the advance.

"The other Squadron ('C' Squadron) that was to work on our flank pulled out in the dim half-light, and the few Sherman tanks accompanying it as a battle group followed them out of the field where they had spent the night; I tagged on behind, and struck off on my own route in the village of Aalten. I was to pass through our forward line of troops, the position of whom I had been given the night before. Arriving there I found nobody and going down the hill on the road to Lichtenvoorde I was indeed surprised to find my leading car held up by a tree felled across the road. I halted with the Squadron some little way behind where they were, giving me breathing space to fight the coming battle in my own way and not become involved.

"I reported this road-block, and was told it was absurd, as our own troops would be bound to have had some patrols in the area ahead! At that time I was not prepared to argue, as I thought I might be wrong, but my attention on telling the leading car to loop round the obstacle if he possibly could was drawn to some movement on my right, and about 200 yards or less away from me across a ploughed field. This was in fact a section of Germans crawling towards three 20-mm. anti-tank guns in emplacements, pointing one in my direction and the others up the road down which I had come! My gunner quickly engaged the one pointing in my direction with the machine gun, although it seemed an eternity to me while the turret traversed on to that barrel that looked as if it was aiming straight at my head. He got the first shot in, and hit it low with a burst, then fired some armour-piercing shot at its brown shield which was distinctly showing over the diggings.

"By now my corporal in the scout car had opened things up, and it was a free for all party, and I was engaging the men who were crawling to the guns. I remember one sublime Jerry who was sitting with his back next to a haystack eating something; and I looked in wonder at him, for he seemed completely indifferent to the shooting. It only occurred to me afterwards that perhaps he was dead!

"The crawling Jerries were definitely discomfited by the fire, for they withdrew at speed to a farmhouse, and I saw that many of them had not even got their trousers on. They had been caught in the proverbial state.

"While we were all shooting at anything that moved, I ducked down into the turret to report on the wireless what was happening. My Squadron Leader still seemed a little incredulous that the enemy should so depart from the rules of the book in that they had retaken up the positions from which they had been driven the previous day. However, he told me that the other Squadron had had exactly the same experience but had somehow managed to overcome it. That I took to be an obvious hint to me to do the same, so I sent off the leading scout car to find a hole in the obstacle on the road and he disappeared down a track to the right of the felled tree. I then looked back at the guns and saw to my horror that one of them had swung round and was again pointing in my direction, just when we had thought that the Jerries were finished. I loosed off at him, my operator getting a good bead on the target and spattering it with mud if nothing else.

"By now, too, the Heavy Troop (Lieutenant George Murray), with its Matador's 75-mms., had opened up on the map reference I had given for the target and the shells were actually falling slap on the farmhouse about fifty yards from it. I remarked to my corporal that he was firing too high and was beginning to enjoy the battle, which now obviously had so much in our favour! What he was indeed engaging was an object I had not even seen, a concrete gun turret supporting a large gun, which he reported afterwards was probably a 105-mm.—enough to penetrate about a dozen of our cars lined up behind one another.

"By this time, my corporal had found a way out of the trouble, which was via a small cart-track round the fallen tree and coming out behind a farm building on the road we had left. It was just wide enough to get along, and we took it while a hail of shells began coming out of one of the haystacks that we had set alight in the shindy. This was the normal custom of the Germans to hide their ammunition in haystacks as cover from air. As often as not they were then hit in the ground fighting.

"We then left the remainder of the Squadron to puzzle out the battle, and on the way round our loop met a crowd of frightened civilians who indicated that there were no Germans on their side of the road, however many there might be on the other. I therefore sent back my rear scout car to bring up the rest of the Squadron and awaited his return. On the other side of the road I watched what was obviously an order group of a German company arguing as to the position behind the farmhouse. They had no idea that we had got round their amateur roadblock and I was determined not to give away my position until I was ready to continue the advance. The enemy sections were now withdrawing in the fields on either side of the road and leaving the road itself, as far as I could tell, unoccupied for our renewed advance.

"I must have been a little too clever, for as we advanced again we were greeted by a volley of shots, some of them exploding close enough to pierce my bed-roll, which has leaked ever since! I decided to go flat out and ducked down into the turret. The leading scout car, seeing me in such a hurry, itself put on a burst of speed, and we were round the corner before I looked up again.

"We had by now got parallel with the enemy troops in the fields, who got down where they were in a ditch, and we exchanged a few parting shots, with the Germans not worrying overmuch by now, for they felt themselves obviously overrun and in other ways *hors de combat*. I just caught a glimpse of one of the armoured White scout cars in the distance opposite me, probably belonging to the Royals who were operating on the left. We then went on to the next town, which we found to be practically deserted of German soldiers. Actually there were a lot of bangs going on, and a monk in his brown robes came across and told me that there were only two Germans left, who were blowing up something or other.... We resumed the advance, for by now our chaps at the back were beginning to ask questions again, and I now turned off on my separate reconnaissance, allowing the main Squadron body to continue down the road in their own time.

"As we were now leading the brigade (in this sector), I could take my time, which means a lot to the average Troop Leader, who hates being hustled in any way. I found that we could not get up the track which had originally been given me, so after getting some farm horses to pull out the cars which had got stuck, I chose another route. We had found two good little 'sports cars' with their German crews who had not had the time to get away, and so took the prisoners along on our own cars. They were an amusing lot, one of them quite a humourist to judge from his looks, and we eventually bundled them off down the centre line to make their way back to the prisoner-of-war cages.

"On starting up the next track we came upon another section of infantry armed with a Spandau machine gun, and as they were busy eating their lunch (or rather their breakfast; it was still only eight o'clock in the morning), they stood up with their hands in the air without any attempt at fighting....

"The reconnaissance had by now fanned out into a 'five Troops up Swan,' and we were not now on a very important centre line. We were ordered to report on a subsidiary bridge, which we found to be neither blown nor held, and we were then ordered to hold on to it ourselves. We also captured another lorry and in it found two wireless sets, one civilian and one army. We were not ordered to rejoin the Squadron until nightfall, and when night did come I made a mistake which I might have had cause to regret, but it must have been one of our lucky days....

"We were ordered to rejoin our Squadron headquarters at a certain place along the centre line. I took this to be the old centre line that we had been given in our orders—not realizing that in the battle the centre line had been altered to a very minor road to loop round the main enemy opposition. I therefore set off in the dark to rejoin a route which I thought the best part of a brigade had taken. On coming to a village in the by now complete blackness, we halted and checked up on how far we had to go. My corporal shone a torch on to a signpost, and as he did so a small vehicle drew up opposite and a man walked across to talk to him. 'Is this the road to—?' said my chap, and then to my horror and everyone else's, it dawned that something was wrong. The man answered in what the Corporal thought to be Dutch but I realized was German. I could see that his car was a Volkswagen. By this time, the corporal had twigged what had happened and calmly walked back to his car, putting out his torch and car lights. We moved on and then saw what was a roadblock in front and coming up to it was a German soldier leading a horse and cart. We passed him and, as luck would have it, found a place in which to turn the cars round, where some other German vehicles were already parked. We turned those cars round with their reverse steering quicker than they had ever been turned round before. As we went we saw further sections of German infantry marching up to their outposts, but this time we gave them no chance to take us for their own cars and we passed without exchanging a shot in that eerie patrol. Later we found out that there were several self-propelled guns in the village, which was the headquarters of the 8th Parachute Division which had got left behind on the flank of our advance. It was to take quite a large tank attack the next day to clear the place—Ruurlo, it was called.... We got back to our Squadron the next day, after finding a Sherman tank which had fallen through one of the bridges on our route, and where we had to wait for a new one to be built."

★   ★   ★

During the late afternoon, after the Foot Guards had encountered stubborn resistance in several places, there occurred something of a break-through on the centre line, and "D" Squadron were able to push on to the outskirts of Eibergen. But this village was found to be firmly held by paratroops protecting the crossings of the River Berkel. The Grenadiers, who had been fighting all day, were thereupon passed through at nightfall, and soon ran into serious opposition on the southern outskirts. The enemy could plainly see them from whatever angle they approached and there were many casualties from mortar fire before the village finally fell during the night.

It had been a trying day; every important bridge had been blown, every culvert cratered, and every roadblock at least lightly held. The promised armoured dash whose momentum was to carry us to the gates of Hamburg and Bremen was becoming a struggle to beat the enemy to his own demolitions, and we realized with growing conviction that in a country ideally suited to delaying tactics, the German was a master at this game.

After dark, the armoured cars and tanks withdrew to harbour in the general area some miles south of Eibergen. There was to be little sleep and much bogging of cars; a very early start next morning was the best that could be hoped for. All through the night houses burnt, while flares from the slowly retreating enemy arched across the skies.

★   ★   ★

The orders for the next day's advance, the 1st of April, could not have been simpler. Neither was there need, at this stage, for them to be otherwise. Since crossing the Rhine, the objective had really been the limit of the day's advance, and once the time of starting was known (which not infrequently came through in the middle of the night) there was really nothing for the car commander to do but to mark up his map and prepare to keep going until first contact was made with the enemy. There was neither the opportunity to make careful reconnaissance nor the guarantee that the positions encountered in the evening would be there in the morning. All this was a nerve-racking strain, especially for the crews of the leading scout cars.

Cars moved forward at dawn. There were again three Squadrons up, "D" Squadron on the right working with the Irish Guards group and heading for Enschede, "B" Squadron on the left with 32nd Brigade and aiming for the Twenthe Canal crossings west of Enschede. Initially "A" Squadron were to have remained in reserve with "C" Squadron but were soon drawn into the fighting to the west on a rather extended front. It was correctly anticipated that the Twenthe Canal would prove to be the next serious obstacle. This waterway links the important manufacturing towns of Enschede and Hengelo with the River Ijssel north of Zutphen, and so to the Rhine.

Progress on both flanks was at first rapid until "D" Squadron, after having looped right at Eibergen, ran into trouble on approaching Haaksbergen. Two scout cars were lost, the first one, commanded by Corporal Goodyear, making it the third time that Trooper Gee as driver had been knocked out in a scout car without himself being hit. He described the incident later:

"This 'brew up' was when with Lieutenant Hanbury's Troop. I had been transferred to them from No. 1 Troop in the Reichswald. We were moving up with Corporal Brook leading, Corporal Goodyear and myself second. Our orders were to advance and take a bridge before it could be blown up. The bridge was O.K. and we pushed on. As we came out of a wood, Corporal Brook saw a German in a hole at the side of the road with his hands up. While he was talking to him and taking him prisoner an 88 fired at us, going over the top of Corporal Brook's car and knocking down a house. We laid down smoke and started to reverse, but while in reverse the Germans hit our car—I think it must have been another anti-tank gun. Anyway, we bailed out and into a ditch on the roadside, Corporal Brook carrying on back to where we were in the ditch. He shouted at us to jump in, as the Germans were now having the odd pot at us in the meantime. Corporal Goodyear jumped in and I followed, head first, as all the time the car had to keep moving! This caused Corporal Brook's car to swerve into the ditch at the other side of the road and we had once again to bail out and crawl out of range along the ditch, which was filled with muddy water. So back to the Troop, where we drank the best part of a bottle of Lieutenant Hanbury's whisky before being fitted up with another scout car."

The Irish Guards' tanks were close at hand when this hold-up occurred, but they could make no headway at first against what proved to be an extremely cleverly sited series of gun emplacements to the flanks, backed by bazooka men in the ditches. The main road was also covered by several other 88s. However, an R.A.F. liaison officer had been attached to the Irish group headquarters (with the name "Hank" written in large capitals, American style, on the back of his flying jacket!), and he called up the rocket-firing Typhoons, who proceeded to attack the guns under the very noses of the armoured cars. As "Hank" was himself underneath his own aeroplanes, the rest of us felt greater confidence than was normally the case. The Typhoons came so low and fired with such accuracy that a Household Cavalryman was able to photograph one of the rockets leaving a plane before hitting the enemy gun emplacements.

As a general engagement became imminent, the Dutch civilians in Enschede warned "D" Squadron that the Germans were still in the town in some strength. We had been told this story before only to find that the enemy had flown, but this time it proved to be correct. Major Profumo was therefore ordered to advance his Troops in close contact with the Irish Guards group from the south while Major Clyde, of whose Squadron more later, attempted to probe into the town from the west.

Lieutenant A. B. Murray, who had recently taken over Lieutenant Jonkheer Groeninx van Zoelen's Troop in "D" Squadron, made a determined attempt to reach the railway bridge with his Troop from the south, but all to no avail. It was well covered by anti-tank guns and an 88 knocked out his scout car, killing the commander, Corporal Thomas

Checkley, and driver, Trooper Alfred Plank. Some moments later the Germans blew the railway bridge, seriously damaging the roadway as well, and the entire group was forced to make a detour to the right, several more guns having been located in the meantime covering the Enschede approaches both from the west and east.

This time "D" Squadron followed the Irish Guards, who had their infantry up with them ready to deal with expected trouble on re-joining the main road north. The detour was enlivened by the presence of a single quick-firing 20-mm. gun which no one bothered to silence as it darted in and out of side turnings with great skill and adherence to the principles of fire and movement, taking pot shots at each car as it moved over the main eastern cross-roads of the town.

Enschede was somewhat precariously occupied that night by Guards Armoured Division, and Divisional Headquarters, with total indifference to their safety, established themselves on a large airfield beyond. The Irish Guards group and "D" Squadron agreed to harbour together to the east of the town. It was raining, blowing half a gale, two tanks had been knocked out at dusk, and there were lots of Germans straggling in the rear. In spite of these disadvantages, some sleep might have been possible had not Headquarters, 8th German Parachute Division, unknown to us, been established some four thousand yards behind our leading body of troops. This militant headquarters seemed to be making a habit of fighting the rear-guard action and being left behind at night.

Its personnel decided to battle their way out with the assistance of a scratch force of S.S. soldiers from a neighbouring N.C.Os.' training school. By coincidence, they chose to cut their way to freedom through the Irish Guards group next to "D" Squadron's leaguer.

It had become almost axiomatic within the Regiment that whenever operating with "the Micks" something quite out of the ordinary in the run of battles was bound to occur. There are many versions of what actually did happen in the early hours of the 2nd of April, but my notes, written at the time, are probably no more inaccurate than any others.

"April 2nd—an awful night. Poured with rain and all the cars bogged themselves in a field of peat. 'D' Squadron eventually sank quietly in one field while the Irish Guards' tanks conformed on the other side of the road. As there were quite a few Germans in the offing we made a tight leaguer. Dug ourselves shallow slit trenches (which filled with water) and squelched into them. Philip, Hugo, Tom and self bundled into the staff car and comforted ourselves with a tot of whisky. Loud bangs from the direction of Enschede town centre. At about two o'clock in the morning all hell let loose. It started with several loud bangs, then much swearing in German, followed by machine-gun fire. It was pitch dark, some of us had got into our bedrolls, but I happened to be fully dressed and staggered across to Philip's staff car with a torch. I shan't forget seeing Tom Hanbury emerging from his sleeping bag, swaying about on one leg in his silk pants, murmuring sleepily, 'What's up?' He was far more concerned with the state of his trouser creases than anything else. Bumped into Hugo and said I thought this must be a counter-attack. Corporal Bugby had been firing a Bren gun, a trifle optimistically I felt, through my legs, and I told him to desist, however good his aim in the dark. How blind and vulnerable is armour at night—if the infantry only realized this! Colonel Henry's dictum, 'It is always wrong to do nothing in war,' ran through my mind, but I felt that this of all occasions was the time to remain still and do absolutely nothing, which was in fact all anyone could and did do. The odds were too much in favour of hitting friends in the next field. Eventually the cursing and the shouting died down. The sentries had seen and reported nothing. The nearest Irish Guards' sentries were none the wiser. Soon the Squadron had settled down again to snatch a few hours of damp, troubled sleep.

"As we all went off to operate at crack of dawn, the true cause of the rumpus was to remain a mystery until the following night, when Paddy Pole-Carew, in charge of the Irish Guards echelon, told us their story.

"It appeared that about a hundred and fifty yards to our right, and straight towards the Irish Guards leaguer, had come a force of Germans, probably up to a company in strength. Their leading man was challenged by the sentry, but the remainder scattered after being fired on by one of the guard tanks. The alarm being given, a large body of the enemy made off towards the shelter of a small shed, where a platoon of Guardsmen were sleeping. The surprise was complete and mutual. The tanks dare not fire for fear of wounding their own comrades, and the fight which developed in the inky blackness with fists, teeth, and butt ends of rifles was in the best tradition, though of short duration. Some of the shouts had come from poor fellows wounded and entangled in a roll of protective Dannert wire. In the morning, a dead German was picked up a few yards from Battalion Headquarters, but who had finished him off or how he had got so far nobody knew. The German casualties, Pole-Carew described as being 'most satisfactory.' The Irish Guards had also sustained casualties."[7]

★   ★   ★

---

7. According to *The History of the Irish Guards in the Second World War*, the Germans left behind 15 dead, 17 wounded, and 25 prisoners. The Irish Guards lost 3 men killed and 13 wounded.

Farther west, "A" Squadron had been called forward to support "B" Squadron, whose commitments on the left flank had become more than could be tackled by their available troops. Lieutenant Murray had the unpleasant experience of bogging his Matador car within a hundred yards of the Twenthe Canal near the village of Debden, while the enemy took shots at him from the far bank. However, although the car, which was being stalked by bazooka men, had temporarily to be abandoned, it was subsequently recovered. "By far the worst of the affair," wrote a brother officer, "was that George Murray, always a great one for his kit, lost everything, and we were not allowed to forget his vanished comforts."

★ ★ ★

"B" Squadron's day, made notable by an extremely gallant action on the part of Lieutenant Allen's Troop, begins with their story as related by Major Clyde.

"On the 31st of March 'B' Squadron had been placed in reserve by Colonel Henry on the brigade centre line, to move behind Divisional Headquarters. We'd had a moderate twenty-four hours one way and another, and this was called a rest. We'd have much preferred to operate! We stopped and started, moving a hundred yards in half an hour, and it was no rest at all. By evening, tempers were frayed and we were very tired. Suddenly I was called to move up to Regimental Headquarters and warned that we would probably be on the move all night. It started to pour with rain and it took me two hours to fight through the traffic to get to R.H.Q. There I found Colonel Henry. Everyone was very tired for they had been on the move for three days and nights without a break. The Colonel was tapping his leg, a nervous habit of his when deep in thought. A quite unmoved Oliver Haskard told me that the Colonel had just had a wireless talk with Bowes Daly and that my Squadron, which should have been in reserve, would have to operate instead of 'A' Squadron because Bowes could not come to Regimental Headquarters in time. (The Division was then working on two widely separated centre lines with 32nd Brigade on the left and 5th Brigade on the right. The country in between was stiff with enemy, and it would not be possible to make the journey cross-country in the dark in anything like the time, let alone the enemy obstacles.) This, then, is the background for what was to follow.

"'B' Squadron was therefore ordered to switch centre lines in the dark and be up to 32nd Brigade leading troops to operate at dawn next day, the 1st of April. It was now raining like hell, pitch dark, and we had, of course, all the wrong maps set. There is no point in listing everything that went wrong that night, except to say that every vehicle in the Squadron was stuck at one time or another, and that I ended up by sitting on the leading scout car reading the map because I felt that if anyone went wrong (and there was good reason to) it had better be myself.

"We arrived at Brigade Headquarters an hour before we were due to cross the start line. We got up to the start line with ten minutes to spare. We passed through the tanks, who looked rested, well breakfasted, and were looking at their watches expectantly, and I had to give out the most hurried and, I expect, inadequate orders of all time! Bill Allen was to lead and he was to reconnoitre the main bridge over the canal west of Enschede and seize it and hold it for the armour if possible. The troops had had no sleep, were soaked to the skin, and had had nothing to eat. Morale should have been very low, but in some extraordinary way it wasn't. Bill's Troop in particular went like smoke, and nothing would stop them. He reported that he had got to the bridge, said it was hard to tell whether it was held or not without getting too close and giving any chance of surprise away. Then he wirelessed that he was going to rush it … and that was the last I heard…."

★   ★   ★

The capture of the bridge over the Twenthe Canal was considered to be of the utmost importance, and when Major Clyde arrived at his rendezvous near Neede, some miles north-west of Eibergen, the Brigade Commander was there to have a word with the Squadron. He came over and spoke personally to several of the Troops, including Lieutenant Allen's. The time was twenty past five in the morning.

As we have heard, it had been a terrible scramble to get everyone away on time, but no one was late. Major Clyde decided to move four Troops up. No. 2 Troop, commanded by Lieutenant the Lord Burghersh, was on the right, directed on to the crossing between Enschede and Hengelo; next came Lieutenant Tabor's Troop aiming for the bridges in Hengelo itself; Lieutenant Palmer's Troop to a bridge immediately west of Hengelo; and finally Lieutenant Allen's Troop, well out to the west, bound for the bridge which crossed the canal south-west of the village of Goor. The tanks and infantry of the Coldstream group were to follow, prepared to exploit with the utmost vigour as soon as the armoured cars had found a likely crossing spot or had seized a bridge.

Lieutenant Allen's Troop first encountered opposition in the shape of a heavy gun and other weapons of smaller calibre. These held up progress for a time. Later on "about 120 Germans impeded the advance. They lay flat on their faces in the ditches with bazookas, whilst their pals on the flanks fired machine guns at the Troop. Eventually we had to wait for the tanks and infantry, who came up at great speed and soon sorted them out." At this stage Lieutenant Cavendish's Heavy Troop arrived on the scene to add its quota of shell fire to the battle. The combined effort proved too much for the enemy, who fled eastwards, leaving many prisoners behind.

About a mile from the canal bridge there was another hold-up when some more bazooka men in a house fought obstinately until driven out into the open after one of the tanks had shelled the outer walls, setting fire to the building, which was gutted.

The noise of battle must have warned the Germans on the far bank of the canal that the Troop was approaching because, on reaching another house close to the waterway, Corporal Beaven's scout car was engaged by heavy small-arms fire to its front. Lieutenant Allen thereupon withdrew his cars slightly, hoping to conserve as much element of surprise as possible for the proposed dash to the bridge. Meanwhile a dismounted patrol revealed that, whereas the map indicated a bridge to be in existence at the proposed crossing point, there was in fact nothing more than a track leading up to the canal bank. This was a great disappointment. Further search showed that there was not even a ferry or small boat in sight and that the width of the obstacle was about forty yards.

To the left there was a dead straight road running parallel to the canal and about five yards from the bank the whole way. At the far end, five hundred yards away, the road turned sharply to the right and over a large single-span structure not marked on the map. This was obviously the canal bridge to aim at.

Unfortunately, the country, apart from being quite flat, which was to be expected, was also devoid of trees. The bridge was therefore in full view of the enemy, as were its approaches. The Germans had positioned their infantry in emplacements, with guns on both sides of the canal covering the bridge from three directions, able to fire down the straight part of the road parallel to the canal. Scanning the countryside through his glasses, Lieutenant Allen noted that two 88s and another gun of smaller calibre were pointing in the direction of the concealed Troop. On the bridge were two 500-lb. bombs wired up for blowing, while on the northern bank two more 88s could be seen to be manned and dug in to emplacements. What he had already noted was enough to convince the Troop Leader that an unobserved approach was out of the question and that any plans avoiding that issue were a waste of time. He recorded that:

"Some heavy fire was now coming over our heads from the immediate
vicinity of the bridge, and it appeared that if the bridge could be taken it
would have to be done quickly or not at all. I told Tommy Clyde this and
he answered in words to the effect that he left the matter to my judgment
on the spot—that I could try to rush the bridge if I thought it possible,
but 'for —— sake, watch out for yourselves!'"

By this time there were three tanks close at hand, but after a brief
conference between respective Troop Leaders, it was decided that as
tanks were, firstly, considerably slower and, secondly, noisier than the
armoured cars, Allen's Troop should lead the dash. As obviously the
opposition would be heavy, there was no point in initially hazarding the
lightly armed scout cars, and these were left behind in an archway sheltered
from sight of the bridge. This was a great disappointment to Corporal
Beaven, who was left in charge of the remainder of the Troop (two
scout cars and their crews, Troopers Webb, Fisher and Fleetwood) with
orders to rejoin the first part of the Troop should it succeed in capturing
the bridge. "This N.C.O. had carried out consistently excellent work,
but particularly on this day, where his map reading, quick thinking and
personal bravery were up to the highest standards, confirming me in my
opinion," wrote his officer, "that the hardest position in an armoured car
Troop to fill successfully, because it demands so many qualities, is that of
leading scout car commander."

The first armoured car to advance was commanded by Lieutenant
Allen, who had transferred from a scout car. With him rode Corporal-
of-Horse Knight and Trooper Karop as driver. The object of this unusual
combination is explained by the fact that Lieutenant Allen had decided
that when things began to hot up everything would take place so rapidly
that it would be easier to keep his second-in-command in the picture by
having him in the same car. Allen would then also be able to make a dash
for the bomb wires and fuses on the bridge, leaving Knight in command
of the Troop Leader's car and on the wireless to the Squadron Leader.
In the second Daimler were Lance-Corporal Mellish-Smith, Trooper
McNinley, gunner-operator, and Corporal Payne, driver.

Immediately on coming out of cover of the house and turning left
along the canal road, the cars were subjected to intense fire. The small
calibre stuff, machine-gun, and rifle fire, came from a road and some
houses which ran parallel to the canal, but on the other side of the water.
Mortars were registering on the road immediately ahead of the armoured
cars with the evident intention of slowing them down by cratering the
road. Firing straight down the road and obliquely from a number of

emplacements north-west of the bridge were the heavy guns. "From the bridge area itself the fire was necessarily of heavier calibre and judging from the blobs made in the road it was probably the 88s and something like a 40-mm. gun."

The Germans appeared to have been put off their aim by the sudden bursts of machine-gun fire from the front armoured car, and shells from their heavy guns were narrowly missing the two vehicles which were now travelling very fast and zigzagging as far as the width of the road would allow. "Ever since rounding the bend," noted Allen, "the enemy must have had a good view of us but judging from their indifferent shooting at a few hundred yards, we hoped that we might just make it."

The two cars took the right-angled turn on to the bridge travelling at a good thirty-five miles per hour and passed slap between the bombs with a foot to spare. Shells were now exploding all-round the cars and actually hitting the bombs with their splinters. Once over the bridge, "a good many things happened rather quickly, as they have a habit of doing in war."

It had been the intention of the first car to turn right-handed again as soon as the bridge had been crossed, but it was going too fast for the driver, Trooper Karop, and he was unable to wrench the heavy wheel round sufficiently, with the result that the vehicle finally came to a halt fifteen yards beyond the turning, which was itself north of the bridge by some hundred yards. Realizing what had happened, Corporal Mellish-Smith in the second car ordered his driver to slow down and he himself took up the position originally intended for his Troop Leader.

Meanwhile, Lieutenant Allen had jumped out of Corporal-of-Horse Knight's car and run towards the bridge to pull out the fuse wires which he could see dangling over the side. He had almost reached his objective when the bridge blew up in his face. During this time Corporal-of-Horse Knight, whose last orders from Allen had been to rejoin the other car, had been engaging two enemy guns which were firing on him from a position to the west and half-way to the bridge from where he was halted. Firing and loading his Besa by himself, he knocked out the nearest gun, and had actually silenced the second with a shot from the 2-pounder when the car received a direct hit on the turret and he was killed instantly. The enemy continued to pump high explosive into the now burning hull, but Trooper Karop, the driver, managed to crawl out and into a ditch, from where he prepared to make his way back to the surviving car. He shot two Germans coming to search for him and then found his withdrawal cut off by another body of enemy, compelling him to hide up again.

While this action was in progress, Lieutenant Allen had been crawling back to Corporal Mellish-Smith's car to wireless the news of the bridge, and at the same time aid his crew in driving back a further threat in the shape of a body of about fifty infantry advancing along the canal road from the east. He was hit in the leg but managed to clamber on to the back of the Daimler, from where he tried to get a message through to the Squadron. But the next moment a shell fired from the south bank of the canal burst against the car and he was thrown into the ditch, where he lay, badly wounded in the left calf and thigh, and in considerable agony. Seeing him lying helpless, Corporal Mellish-Smith, with complete disregard for his own safety, leapt out of the turret and ran across with some morphia and bandages. He was riddled with shots before he could get to his Troop Leader and died almost at once. This left two men in the Daimler, Trooper McNinley and Corporal Payne, the driver. Unaware then of Corporal-of-Horse Knight's fate, these two decided to reverse their damaged car and rejoin the other vehicle, taking aboard their wounded Troop Leader in passing. But in reversing on the narrow road, the Daimler was badly ditched, with its back wheels at the bottom of an embankment and the front wheels on the road. It then became impossible to depress the machine guns low enough to cover the road from where the German infantry had by now crept up to within grenade distance of the car. The first wave of Germans rushed the car, jumped on to the front, and were promptly shot up, but others swarmed on to the back, capturing Payne and McNinley and Lieutenant Allen, who was still lying, unable to move, in the ditch.

Their subsequent experiences as prisoners of war are related in Appendix A, p.597. Lieutenant Allen, after being carried some distance by his men, where his wounds were dressed, was taken to "some apparently high-level formation headquarters" in Enschede, where, although in considerable pain and weakened by loss of blood, he was rigorously questioned (to no avail) "by an S.S. Major with a perfect English accent, steely blue eyes and distinctly sadistic tendencies." Later in the day he was taken to a hospital some twenty miles away which fortunately turned out to be on "B" Squadron's future centre line. After being operated on that night, he awoke the next day to find Major Clyde, Lieutenant Seyfried and Captain Kynaston by his bedside.[8] He was moved to a Canadian hospital in Ghent via Venlo. Gangrene had set

---

8. The German hospital was overrun on the 2nd of April during the advance towards Nordhorn by Lieutenant the Lord Burghersh's Troop.

in rather badly, but after two more operations and great kindness from the Canadians he was back in England within six weeks.

Trooper Karop, after a series of adventures in dodging the Germans, swam the Twenthe Canal at night and was able to regain his Squadron the next day. The bodies of Corporal-of-Horse Percy Knight and Corporal Ian Mellish-Smith had been left by the enemy where they had fallen and were recovered before the advance was resumed on the 2nd of April, by Captain Julian Ward.

★   ★   ★

Of the other "B" Squadron troops engaged on the 1st of April, Lieutenant the Lord Burghersh's Troop soon found itself embroiled with the same enemy rear-guards responsible for having held up "D" Squadron and the Irish Guards group south of Enschede, but Lieutenant Tabor's Troop had better luck. They made good progress and the only enemy encountered were in the form of scattered and withdrawing bodies of infantry and "soft" vehicles, which were easily brewed up or by-passed. The bridges at Hengelo were reached shortly before ten o'clock in the morning, but they had all been blown at the sound of the Troop's approach when it was still half a mile from the nearest of them.

Lieutenant Tabor then spoke on the telephone to the Dutch Resistance in Hengelo, who told him that the aerodrome outside the town was strongly defended by 88-mm. flak guns. As crossings to the immediate west were also blown, Major Clyde ordered the Troop to move east and try to pass through Enschede, where tanks from the 1st Coldstream were fighting a stiff battle in the western suburbs. The Troop managed to find a way through some side streets before the Germans awoke to the fact, and thus out on to the main road to the north-west. Here the armoured cars had a sharp engagement with an enemy self-propelled gun which fired five shots at them, but only succeeded in demolishing a house before being forced to withdraw. The Troop eventually moved on and harboured in the woods east of the main road Enschede—Oldenzaal. This marked the limit of Guards Armoured Division's advance for the day.

★   ★   ★

Information about the enemy available to the Regiment before it resumed its advance on the 2nd of April was largely based on civilian reports. It amounted to this. Units of 8th Parachute Division were withdrawing

towards Lingen, which lay on the proposed line of advance to the north-
east. Three airfields on the route, although without airworthy craft, were
full of G.A.F.[9] personnel. In addition, aerial reconnaissance indicated a
line of deep anti-tank ditches on the line Bentheim—Nordhorn, and
these appeared to be defended. It was proposed to push on to Oldenzaal,
and from there the advance would fork, one battle group, 5th Brigade,
being directed towards the old castle town of Bentheim, the other, 32nd
Brigade, to Nordhorn. "A" and "B" Squadrons continued to operate.
Little opposition was encountered up to Oldenzaal, the last town in
Holland, which was passed amidst scenes of greatest enthusiasm. On
re-entering Germany our vaguely self-conscious expression of the
conquering hero gave way once more to what a trooper was heard to call
"the stern Cromwellian stuff with the non-frat blinkers up." Coincident
with the hardening of expressions so did the German resistance stiffen.
Especially was this the case on the right centre line.

The first obstacle proved to be a large crater in the middle of the road
on the way to Bentheim, which the Irish Guards filled in with a house
specially blown down for the purpose. Original as was this form of road
repair, nearly four hours were to elapse before the column could resume
its advance. Soon afterwards, Lance-Corporal Bennett and Trooper
Pickles of "A" Squadron were wounded by an anti-tank gun which
knocked out their scout car. When the Irish Guards tried to make further
progress, they were halted by infantry and bazookas at Gilderhaus, and
the German paratroops constituting its defence were not finally evicted
until the following morning.

★   ★   ★

To the left, "B" Squadron were able to make better progress. Lieutenant
the Lord Burghersh's Troop encountered only scattered opposition
until reaching the east side of the village of Denekamp, where the
bridge over the River Dinkel was blown as the leading car reached it.
Major Clyde thereupon dispatched Lieutenant Tabor's Troop to find
an alternative route for the brigade, and they were able to capture two
rather flimsy bridges to the north. Just across the Almelo—Nordhorn
Canal the same Troop discovered a large German hospital in the process
of being evacuated and where Lieutenant Allen was discovered later on
in the day. Lieutenant Tabor pushed on and soon re-joined the main

---

9. G.A.F. (German Air Force) personnel were run on similar lines to our Air Force Regiment. They
   were responsible for the defence of aerodromes. They were frequently encountered manning the
   dual-purpose 88-mm. guns.

road about halfway between Denekamp and Nordhorn. This road was found to be covered by a self-propelled gun which let fly every time the Troop showed its nose, so the cars again looped west and eventually, by travelling cross-country, reached the outskirts of Nordhorn from the south-west. Yet another self-propelled gun and some Volkssturm with bazookas then caused a certain amount of delay, and the running was again taken up by Lieutenant the Lord Burghersh's Troop which in the meantime, after having successfully knocked out an 88-mm., had discovered a way round to the south and set up an excellent O.P. watching Nordhorn itself and the Bentheim—Nordhorn road. Over 1,500 Germans withdrawing from Bentheim were counted, and several trainloads of troops being evacuated from the town. But having nothing but scout cars on his patrol, Lord Burghersh could do little to interfere apart from shooting up laggards with the Bren guns. The Welsh Guards were unable to give any help because they had been delayed by the small bridges which could not carry their tanks. Had they been able to come up in time great havoc might have been wreaked.

★   ★   ★

Lieutenant Palmer's Troop also succeeded in reaching the outskirts of Nordhorn. It then became engaged in a fierce street battle in its attempts to approach within range of a withdrawing trainload of Germans. At one time Major Clyde was reporting back to Regiment that his patrols could "see and count clearly over 250 mixed enemy vehicles, including self-propelled guns, lorries, carts and bicyclists, and in addition about 2,000 infantry scrambling away as fast as they can go."[10] But try as they would, the Troops could not find a way over the Sud–Nord Kanaal to get within range of this inviting target.

Later in the evening the whole of "B" Squadron met up in Nordhorn. The population of the town appeared to be friendly, and white flags and sheets fluttered in token of surrender from every window.

★   ★   ★

While this was taking place, 32nd Brigade, with the Scots-Welsh group in the lead, entered Nordhorn, and a sharp battle ensued before the centre of the town was cleared. Meanwhile the bridges over the Sud-Nord Kanaal were blown in their faces. However, "B" Squadron patrols were

---

10. Regimental Battle Log, 2nd April, 1945.

ordered to continue exploiting to the north-west, and by nightfall the Regiment was able to inform Brigade that a Troop had found "a wooden bridge of doubtful strength about three miles north of Nordhorn."

The importance of this discovery was soon appreciated at Divisional Headquarters, and General Adair made the bold decision to hazard an armoured group in a dash through the night in the hope of seizing one or possibly both bridges at Lingen over the next two obstacles, the River Ems and the Dortmund—Ems Canal. The Welsh Guards tanks and the Scots Guards infantry riding on the back of them were chosen to carry out the task. It was nearly midnight when this drive started off. Two Squadrons of tanks and half the next had crept carefully over the flimsy structure north of Nordhorn before it collapsed. Then started what must have been one of the boldest and most spectacular dashes of the campaign. Shooting at everything that moved, the tanks drove at full speed down the main road.

Approaching the first bridge over the Ems, the infantry dismounted and two platoons rushed across the river. But no sooner had they reached the far bank than the enemy blew the bridge and so frustrated a gallant exploit which deserved greater success.

★   ★   ★

By the 3rd of April the advance had taken on a somewhat lopsided appearance, for whereas 5th Brigade group were still halted before Bentheim, 32nd Brigade group were moving well ahead, to concentrate in the vicinity of Sudlohne, but were denied further progress by the Ems and its defenders.

As both "A" and "D" Squadrons were to remain on the Bentheim front for several more days in a relatively static role, it is best to continue with the story on the left flank, which directly concerns "B" and "C" Squadrons.

Following the failure of the Welsh-Scots group to bounce the Lingen bridges, it was obvious that the Germans would try to hold up the advance on the double line of waterways, and so 32nd Brigade were ordered to remain in the area Sudlohne—Mittelohne, while 3rd (Br.) Division, which had been following up for just such a purpose, prepared to make an assault crossing south of Lingen town. It was felt that there was small likelihood of the enemy having left any bridges intact to the north, but, remembering recent experiences and forlorn hopes which had come off in the past, the Regiment was ordered to carry out patrols downstream (northwards).

Not long afterwards, in the words of a divisional report, "the Household Cavalry Regiment ["C" Squadron] with their eyes as usual looking in sixteen different directions at once," discovered a bridge, some three miles north of Lingen, at a place called Altenlingen.

It was unblown, and from a small escarpment about four hundred yards away from the river it was possible to obtain a perfect view of the German dispositions on the far bank. A small sandy track ran up an incline to the bridge itself, and on the far side there was a roadblock consisting of trees stacked on top of one another. The bridge itself was a modern concrete structure and placed along the roadway were several large aerial bombs. Immediately beside the far end there was an ack-ack post, and inside the post were three 88-mm. guns. It was impossible to estimate the number of entrenched troops guarding this strong point, but it was obvious that they were numerous. In addition, several 20-mm. quick-firing guns were seen to be manned.

A message giving location and all that could be seen of the bridge dispositions was immediately sent back to Divisional Headquarters. The task of assaulting this formidable obstacle fell to the Coldstream Guards group, and the full story of how it was successfully carried out belongs to the annals of that Regiment. Suffice to say here that it was accomplished with great gallantry, and for his part in the action Captain Ian Liddell, of the 5th Battalion Coldstream Guards, was awarded the Victoria Cross. It was a tragedy that he did not live to receive this supreme award, for he was killed in battle near Rotenburg a few days before the end of the war.

As soon as the news was received that the bridge had been captured intact, 185th Brigade (3rd Division), who had been reconnoitring south of Lingen for a suitable place for an assault crossing during the night, were halted and switched over. The Brigade crossed the Coldstream bridge and during the hours of darkness successfully stormed the canal beyond. Then followed forty-eight hours' stiff fighting with 3rd (Br.) Division opposed to a parachute division and the Grossdeutschland Training Brigade before Lingen was finally captured, and Guards Armoured Division were able to resume the advance.

★   ★   ★

Returning to the right flank, we find the battle for Bentheim in full swing, with the brunt of the fighting in this relatively static action shared by the Irish and Grenadier Guards groups. Both "A" and "D" Squadrons in turn shared the flanking patrols searching out the weak spots in the enemy's defences. But little progress was made, due principally to the marshy nature of the ground, the numerous streams and the flimsy bridges crossing them. Whenever a bridge was found to offer a way round Bentheim, the tanks invariably broke it down with their weight.

The immediate objective on the right flank was the River Ems via Schuttorf, but east of Gilderhaus the Irish Guards lost three tanks, all knocked out by self-propelled guns, "and the commanders had to cope with the problem of two vehicle-bound battalions strung out like a snake for several miles to the rear."

Major Profumo, commanding "D" Squadron, made determined efforts to find a way out of the impasse and sent his patrols to loop to the north and south, but all to no avail. They bogged down badly and the tanks fared no better.

The 4th of April was another day of slow progress, but "A" Squadron, who had taken over from "D" Squadron, eventually found a way round on foot to the left on to the Bentheim—Nordhorn road by using Lieutenant Wordsworth's Support Troop. This was an excellent patrol which in fact cut off German communications with the north. But the Troop encountered bad luck, and "A" Squadron's Dutch interpreter, Sergeant Walter Proehl, and Trooper Digges were badly wounded. Proehl was accompanying Lieutenant Wordsworth on a foot patrol through the thick woods to the north of Bentheim when the party came upon a roadblock consisting of a tree felled across the road. "I ran round this obstacle," related the Troop Leader, "as my objective could be seen through my glasses to be on the other side. The two others, Trooper Digges and Proehl, followed, and had the misfortune each to tread on a Schu mine. Luckily, some Grenadiers were about two miles down the road and their two stretcher-bearers and myself managed to get them out, but unfortunately both lost a foot." Walter Proehl, who, it will be remembered, had joined "A" Squadron on the Maas in late September, was a great loss to the Regiment. Under no circumstances could his duties of interpreter have been taken to mean that he should form part of a fighting patrol, but that he should do so, and by no means for the first time, was typical of the man. "He was," wrote Lieutenant Wordsworth, "not only extremely good at his job, but was always game to go out on any armoured or foot patrol that was going." Proehl's argument was that the information which he could obtain from civilians might often save a Troop much unnecessary fighting, and that the best place from which this could be done was on the back of an armoured car. Nothing would daunt him, and time and again he would come under fire clinging to his precarious perch on top of the engine cover. His well-merited Military Medal was one of the most popular awards in the Regiment.

By midday (4th April) the whole of Bentheim was in British hands, and from the summit of the impregnable-looking old castle it was possible to see the white flags of surrender fluttering damply from the windows of Schuttorf, the next village ahead.

★   ★   ★

Both right-hand Squadrons were now withdrawn to rest, "D" Squadron in a farmhouse off the main road between Bentheim and Gilderhaus and "A" Squadron in Bentheim itself. The former place appeared to have served as a repository for loot from occupied countries and there was a large warehouse filled with bales of parachute silk, many yards of which eventually found their way back to England via "D" Squadron. The packing of parcels suitably disguised to pass the postal censors was in full swing when a message of some urgency came through to say that the enemy had been reported in strength in the villages of Losser and Gronau to the south. This area had not yet been cleared, for the country lay between two prongs of advance, that of Guards Armoured Division on the left and a 12 Corps formation on the right. However, after three Troops had searched the countryside in a driving rainstorm for half a day and with nothing to show other than one broken-down Czech motor-cycle combination and two Polish deserters, patrols were withdrawn to harbour.

By the time that the Lingen bridgehead was firmly established on the 5th of April, Guards Armoured Division were due to pass through 3rd (Br.) Division and resume the advance eastwards. A resumption of operations on the right centre line was therefore a wasteful dissipation of effort, and 5th Brigade were accordingly switched over to the north with the intention of concentrating the divisional drive on one centre line until such time as the two brigade groups could once more be deployed.

The Regiment was therefore concentrated near Sudlohne. "C" Squadron and part of "B" Squadron were called upon to carry out occasional sweeps to the north, and their patrols collected a number of prisoners trying to work eastwards across the River Ems. This work ceased during the afternoon when the Royals took over the area.

"B" Squadron thereupon moved into Lingen, which was by then mostly in the hands of 3rd (Br.) Division. Heavy fighting was still going on in the outskirts, and the night of 5th/6th April was spent by Major Clyde's Troops in the northern suburbs, which were made most uncomfortable by a local counter-attack carried out by a few self-propelled guns and infantry.

The purlieus of Sudlohne had taken on a very cosmopolitan appearance. "C" Squadron, in the course of their sweep, had collected numbers of Allied prisoners of war and escaping concentration camp inmates. North of Lingen 1,800 Poles and Russians had only just been halted in the act of massacring their guard of twenty German soldiers who, on the advent of the armoured cars, had thrown away their arms a trifle prematurely. A Household Cavalryman noted that "the civilians here could not be more correct; they keep offering us butter and milk, and we have captured a dump of thousands of eggs and so had scrambled eggs for tea and supper."

Sudlohne was noteworthy for the number of false alarms, half-hearted enemy attacks, and stray shots continually disturbing the equanimity of Headquarters. On one such occasion Trooper Vernall, a "D" Squadron fitter, was busy changing a wheel when a volley of bullets, overthrows from the Lingen battle, spattered into a duck-pond close to where he was working. An officer from a neighbouring unit chanced to be passing. "Good gracious! " he exclaimed, "these must be bullets." Vernall, a gamekeeper in civilian life, walked over to the pond, whose surface was whipped up at his feet by yet another fusillade. He turned to the officer slowly. "Well, sir, they ain't bloody trout rising! "

But the picture which sticks in my mind more vividly than any other at this period is of Captain Balding, then commanding Headquarter Squadron while Major Williams was on U.K. leave, riding past the tanks and flails and other modern engines of war to pay "C" Squadron a visit, mounted on a powerful chestnut charger which he had captured the previous day complete with saddle and bridle.

★ ★ ★

Although the story of the Regiment's advance on 30 Corps' front had so far been one of demolitions, roadblocks, and bazookas, this was not the case elsewhere. Advances to the south had been startling and the picture was one of utter and absolute collapse on the enemy front.

So completely had the Germans relied on their vaunted Siegfried Line that apart from a few hastily improvised field defence works there were no barriers of any consequence east of the Rhine. Nor was it now possible for them to re-establish a line capable of stemming the Allies' momentum. Their only hope of prolonging the struggle for any length of time lay in retreating into the so-called "National Redoubt" deep in the heart of the Bavarian Alps. Daily we heard tales of yet more devastation caused by Allied bombing, factories at a standstill, and increasing numbers of troops on the march to prison camps. If ever despair gripped at the heart of the German soldier, it must surely have been now. Yet, obedient to Hitler's orders, he fought on.

To the south, the largest double envelopment in the history of war was taking place. The Ninth U.S. Army, advancing at speed towards the Elbe, had detached one of its Corps to swing south round the back of the industrial Ruhr, and the First U.S. Army had likewise swung one of its Corps from south of Cologne to form the southern arm of the encirclement. The two arms joined hands at Lippstadt on the 1st of April, thus trapping three hundred and twenty-five thousand German troops, including the picked men massed in March to meet the threat which the Germans had erroneously thought would come from the surprise Remagen bridgehead. Among the captured were over thirty general officers.

In this vast and now grossly overcrowded industrial area were millions of civilians, already short of food. Hundreds of bombed locomotives littered the railway sidings, their boilers pierced and useless. Transport finally collapsed as drivers of the remaining engines dimmed their fires and went home in sullen despair. Ammunition, which to date had been plentiful, ceased to flow from the assembly lines. At last Hitler's peasant-like obstinacy in fighting for every inch of terrain in preference to organized withdrawal had ended in unparalleled hardship and disaster.[11]

It is a curious reflection that the immediate effects of this disaster to German arms might have been even worse had their communications allowed them to learn the full extent of what was happening, but statements from prisoners taken on our front at this stage showed clearly that they were quite out of touch with the situation and had simply been fighting on in obedience to their local commander's instincts.

Meanwhile, with the aim of Second Army the line of the River Elbe from Wittenberge to the Cuxhaven peninsula, armoured spearheads probed north-eastwards with varying results. On the right, where resistance was lightest, 8 Corps were already well ahead, and by the 5th of April had established troops on the line of the River Weser between Minden and Stolzenau. On our immediate right flank, 12 Corps were engaged in bitter fighting in the Rheine area, where troops from a near-by officer cadet training school held up the advance for several days. But this was cleared on the 6th of April and rapid progress made thereafter to the Weser.

---

11. The encircled Ruhr armies finally surrendered on the 18th of April.

On our left the Canadians, entrusted with the capture of Arnhem and the opening up of north Holland, were still some way back.

Bremen and Hamburg, the two principal cities of the north-west German plains, remained the objective of 30 Corps, and this then was the direction towards which we headed our cars on the morning of the 6th of April.[12]

Ford 3-Ton Lorry

12. Due to the resistance subsequently encountered on 30 Corps front, this was later modified, and 12 Corps troops finally captured Hamburg.

Chapter III

From Lingen to Vestrup

Onwards from Lingen—Freren and Lengerich—The River Hase—2 H.C.R. concentrates at Vestrup

Hopes that the regimental front would at last conform to what was happening in the south were soon to fade in the wooded country east of Lingen. The plan to advance on one centre line was abandoned almost immediately by Guards Armoured Division, and 5th Brigade were therefore directed towards Furstenau while 32nd Brigade advanced towards the village of Lengerich (not to be confused with the larger place of the same name farther south in 12 Corps area).

There would be little point in recounting the story of the Regiment's advance during the next few days in terms of villages captured and burnt, Squadrons employed, and distances travelled. It was hard going all the way, especially for the leading scout cars and the tanks with whom we were working in closest liaison all the time. Much of the difficulty of advance was caused by the skilful delaying tactics of the enemy, but as two and frequently three Squadrons were engaged each day, some indication of its nature must be given. I therefore propose to let two diaries, Captain Cooper's and my own, carry on the story until the Regiment halts to rest in the village of Vestrup on the 14th of April.

On the 6th of April, with the clearance of Lingen, Guards Armoured Division resumed their advance to the east on the 6th of April. "B" Squadron were now in the lead carrying out reconnaissance for 32nd Brigade group. During the day, 43rd Division, who had been brought forward, followed through, and were directed north-east towards Haselunne. "D" Squadron, now in reserve, prepared to take over from "B" Squadron the next day, and so they too crossed the Dortmund—Ems Canal at Lingen.

> "We crossed the pontoon bridge over the Ems Canal in the early morning after a long, bumping ride across country. A land of heath and birch. 'B' Squadron are in front, but from reports on the air, progress is very slow. On the way into Lingen, a small pig emerged from a burning house and walked unconcernedly down our line of temporarily halted cars, followed by many hungry-looking troopers' eyes. I had my doubts whether it

would get very far, and my fears were confirmed when a shot rang out shortly afterwards. A Besa had gone off by mistake and 'accidentally' hit the porker. Amazing scenes in Lingen. A large butter store had been raided by civilians—soldiers had joined in to help them; everyone was helping himself, walking away with armfuls of the stuff. Our cars did not fail to get their share. This looting business is a tricky affair—the store had been blown apart by shell fire and the butter was lying about all over the place; it's asking a lot of soldiers to let the stuff go rancid or else be picked up for the asking by 'Mil. Gov. Det.' . ." (Lieutenant R. P. G. Orde.)

When during the day it became clear that the advance was not going as had been hoped, 5th Brigade group took the right-hand route towards Freren and 32nd Brigade group the left towards Lengerich. The Division was once more on two centre lines. "D" Squadron moved up to take over the reconnaissance role on the left. Late at night they harboured near the Lingen cross-roads and Regimental Tac. Headquarters also were now over the river.

"'B' Squadron on the right have hardly moved today. They immediately came up against mines and 88-mms., and by evening had only got three miles. We have now taken over on the left advance. Hugo [Captain C. H. Waterhouse)] went up to forward tank Squadron, but they are held up, too; he stayed up there as liaison in his Staghound, but there was never any chance of us being loosed. Regimental Tac. Headquarters have also come over the canal and are harboured just behind us. We harboured bang on the Lingen cross-roads and paid for it by a disturbed night, 6th/7th April. Either an 88-mm. or a S.P. had got our spot taped and decided to drop firstly H.E. and then, when that had been exhausted, high trajectory armour-piercing stuff, which kept coming over regularly at five-minute intervals. The H.E. damaged quite a few three-tonner lorries and blew off some tyres; luckily, no personnel casualties. The effect of the armour-piercing shot was rather like someone dropping lumps of lead on to one from the top of St. Paul's Cathedral. Extremely accurate they were and most unpleasant, rocking the ground as they landed, but did no damage. 'C' Squadron, whose role seems to have been irrevocably bound up with the northern flank, had to send out two Troops on a Tiger hunt scare. Went as far as Geeste, but found nothing. Bailey and Corbett had to stay out all night though. The alarm was probably caused by the Canadians, who are advancing on our left flank but still some way back. They probably flushed some Germans towards us." (Lieutenant R. P. G. Orde.)

By the 7th of April forward armoured car Troops on the right had reached the outskirts of Freren, with 5th Brigade group about to attack it. On the left, 32nd Brigade group with "D" Squadron were still some miles short of Lengerich.

"So near the end of the war, these slogging matches are very trying, especially for the scout car crews. At crack of dawn Troops set off in front of tanks, but are soon held up and make way for the tanks and infantry. Nor can the tanks do very much about it and the unfortunate infantry are much overworked and in short supply as usual. Hugo again liaising with the forward tanks. The idea is that if the front shows signs of loosening, Philip Profumo can soon send up the armoured cars, but there is no point in cluttering up the already congested roads with unwanted traffic. The tanks are having by far the worst time now; G.A.D. have lost over ninety since crossing the Rhine. Midday we had a shoot up. The entire Squadron was lined up along the road in rather wooded country. All of a sudden there was a burst of Spandau fire from the trees which swept rather too close to our heads for our peace of mind. Everybody leapt into their cars as quickly as they could and opened up on the wood. Pandemonium for a few minutes. It was a rather fine sight to see all the cars firing at the same time. Milner, my gunner, caused a greenhouse to disintegrate with a round of H.E. and set alight to a farmhouse, which was soon a blazing inferno. It is terrible that war makes one so impersonal, and it's only afterwards that there is time to think of the tragedy of that little farm with its smoking remains and dead cattle. When the gun traversed, poor Hull got caught up in the front of my Staghound, on which he was cooking dinners in case we moved off quickly, and so nearly got his eardrums blown in by the blast of the 37-mm. when it went off. He and the dinners were swept off into the road. Net result of all the noise and firing—no visible enemy casualties, a few frightened villagers, and a staggering expenditure of ammunition. Later on, talking to a Grenadier officer, we came to the conclusion that we had all been firing at one another through the wood, and not at the enemy. Such things happen in war. Corporal Wright and Trooper Aspinall wounded by 'Moaning Minnies'; it was bad luck for they were well behind in our convoy, halted, and in their cars at the time." (Lieutenant R. P. G. Orde.)

Meanwhile "C" Squadron, who were due to take over the advance on the left centre line on the morrow, and "A" Squadron on the right had both crossed the River Ems during the day.

"Up at six o'clock—glorious day after heavy shelling at night by our own batteries. Slow progress in column all day. We went through Lingen about 11.30 in the morning and were parked in the town for the rest of the day. The town has not been completely destroyed this time, but a good deal of fighting has been taking place. All the shops, etc., are abandoned and looting is in full swing among the remaining civilians. We picked up a good deal of stuff lying about the place. A big milliner's and tobacconist's has been utterly ransacked. The Cockney sense of humour again, I suppose: all shop-window dummies out in the streets dressed in a variety of clothes. In one big shop a soldier playing the piano in the broken display window, while everybody help themselves. There are wireless sets and typewriters here, and I found a 16-bore shot gun. While looking for a place to spend the night, found a great many cheeses in the station; they are good but smelt rather like the dead horses lying about. Every house, every room is ransacked. Many weeping civilians—no resistance, just lots of white flags and pathetic scenes. 5.30 p.m. ordered to push on out of the town and pass the Coldstream group. For a change, the dust is now awful. Took Squadron forward while Peter [Major A. W. P. P. Herbert, "C" Squadron] went to Headquarters for orders. Burnt-out and burning German cars all the way. Although dust on the roads, the fields are too soft for the armoured cars, and two scout cars bogged themselves. Went on to find somewhere else for harbour. One farm still burning—all cows (about fifty) burnt in stalls. Farmer just standing dazed outside, his children beside him crying. Germans or not, one is sorry. No wash, early move tomorrow, shelled all night, little sleep...." (Captain G. D. Cooper.)

From the 8th of April the advance continued slowly for the next three days, with "A" and "B" Squadrons still on the right, with 5th Brigade group and "C" and "D" Squadrons with 32nd Brigade group on the left. By the evening of the 10th, Bippen and Menslage were reached. There was to be a good deal of shelling by retreating guns and multiple rocket mortars ("Moaning Minnies"). Among the seriously wounded was Corporal-of-Horse Brown, hit in the thigh when trying to clear up an enemy roadblock of trees and mines.

"We move up through Lengerich, which is still burning, but the going is very slow. Harvey-Williams's Troop held up by roadblocks and bazooka men. Rory Corbett's Heavy Troop fires a few rounds of H.E. into their midst, and the Coldstream-Welsh group move round to outflank them, and the Germans start shelling our column. Later we capture three civilians directing fire with a wireless set in a cellar. A lot of prisoners, mostly paratroops. Reached wood near Bokel by dusk. A three-tonner goes up behind us; there is a lot of shelling. Three Germans, dead officer and two privates, lying in road; they held on until the last and until overrun. Pryer, my gunner, has caught a pig which is kicking up a hell of a noise. Woods near Bokel still full of Germans. The Brigade harbour party coming up behind us has been shot up by a party of Germans; one officer killed, and Tony Leatham came in for assistance. We sent out two armoured cars and a party on foot to shoot them up. Mail came up as usual—how the devil it ever gets up I wouldn't know! ..." (Captain G. D. Cooper.)

The 9th of April—Regimental Headquarters and "D" Squadron are harboured by the side of the road outside Lengerich, while "B" and "C" Squadrons are some way ahead operating.

"Rather warm day. 'B' and 'C' Squadrons are on the job. It is the first time we have been with R.H.Q. *in toto* for some time. We are all parked by the side of the road under some trees. Lengerich is just round the corner. The men are writing letters and the Padre has come round to arrange for a service here tomorrow morning. After the rain there is a rather beautiful light and one can see miles to the north across open fields. Behind the harbour, three German soldiers have just been buried with their helmets surmounting three rough wooden crosses. They were killed at the first bend in the road by their gun. It is still there, so cleverly camouflaged that it is impossible to see it unless one looks very closely. It is a 37-mm. anti-tank gun, but with a sort of large bazooka affair with fins which is fired from the barrel instead of an ordinary A.P. round. There was quite a battle here, and a sergeant in the Scots Guards did very well before being shot dead (some say a possibility of a V.C. here). General Alan and Aylmer Tryon[1] came up to see the scene of the action. One of the Germans manning the gun must have been rather an artist, for I picked up a most attractive sketch of the view down the road which he had done while awaiting the inevitable arrival of the British. He must also have been a composer of sorts, for I discovered a bloodstained edition of Goethe's poems and several sheets of music paper, half used, on which he had been setting verses from 'Hermann and Dorothea' to music...." (Lieutenant R. P. G. Orde.)

Out beyond, in the area of Berge, the going was still extremely slow, and the absence of passable side roads was a great handicap to the leading armoured cars. But to the south, 51st (Highland) Division were beginning to make better progress. Between the two axes of Guards Armoured

---

1. Major-General Alan Adair, Commanding Guards Armoured Division and Captain the Hon. Aylmer Tryon, Grenadier Guards, his A.D.C.

Division's advance there was strong resistance to the Grenadier group at Kettenkamp.

> "Going extremely sticky this morning. Bazooka ambush hit the leading scout car and Corporal Hopper and Trooper Wilkinson both killed— the car brewed up. The Coldstream group are doing a set-piece attack just north of Berge. Have captured quite a lot of cigars and fourteen pairs of scissors, endless cigarette lighters, and 100 Dutch cheeses. The Germans have apparently everything. Philip Profumo came up today, as 'D' Squadron relieve us tomorrow. Fair amount of shelling. Refused an old farmer permission to go into village as he might get the German artillery on to us...."
>
> "*April 10th* German guerrillas pretty active today; 2 i/c Scots Guards wounded while going into wood. Also sergeant never came back. Heard a noise underneath house today and found entrance to cellar. Went down with pistol and discovered three children and three women absolutely terrified. They had been told that they would be shot by the British and had been there three days with no light, air, or food. Got them into open and gave the children sweets...." (Captain G. D. Cooper.)

The Division continues to be held up, mostly by blown bridges along the River Hase. Meanwhile, awaiting the construction of a bridge south of Loningen, there is much mopping-up to do. "A" and "D" Squadrons operating.

> "We are well astride the Ankum—Loningen road, and the encouraging advances on our flanks make one feel that things should get moving, once the bridge is built. One of our prisoners today said that he had come straight from Norway and was pitchforked into battle and told to go and hold a place which fell ten days ago. We feel certain that if only the German communications were not so chaotic, they would realize what has happened to the south, and to avoid encirclement would retreat. As it is, these damned parachutists are fighting every inch of the way. Glorious weather and we are located by a rather nice farmhouse close to the River Hase and just south of Menslage, dated 1685 (a barn) and built of dark red bricks and timbered. All Troops operating are held up by blown bridges and/or roadblocks. Same with 'A' Squadron to the south.
>
> "The infantry (British) on both flanks, advancing across wood and heath, are driving a lot of Germans out into the open. Very great danger of shooting one another up. Tony Hughes sent to keep 43 Division 'in the picture' regarding movement of our armoured cars. He was most thorough in letting both us and 43 Division know what was happening all

the time, but one infantry patrol, after warning us that they were coming down the north side of a railway embankment, suddenly appeared from another direction, and were shot up by Murray's Troop. One subaltern winged. He couldn't have been nicer, and said it was his own fault entirely. They were crawling through some grass and there were also enemy there at the same time. Turned out to be friend of Murray's; they were at the same O.C.T.U. together! Thought that with luck his wound might get him back to England in time for the peace celebrations! Tony Hughes had some explaining to do to Major-General Thomas ('Von Thoma') (43rd Division), who took the incident as a personal affront. Tony's description of the scene extremely amusing and Thomas got little change out of him. The countless times 2 H.C.R. patrols shot up by own planes, tanks and infantry during the campaign would make interesting reading.

"At noon, an Italian officer came into Squadron Headquarters, dressed in a Ruritanian outfit complete with puffy breeches, light brown boots, and spurs. Gold braid and ribbon everywhere. He carried a Revelation suitcase, was smiling broadly, and smelt of scent and garlic. Gave a half bow, half salute to Philip and announced with a sweeping flourish that he wished to fight for the British on condition that we fetched his luggage, which was in the next village, still in enemy hands. He was told that as far as fighting for us he was a trifle 'pushed' and was bundled off in a lorry loaded with morose-looking Hun prisoners. Last sight of him, he was still grinning broadly at the joke of it all. The men greatly amused at this unexpected burlesque." (Lieutenant R. P. G. Orde.) On the 12th of April the Regiment continued to carry out careful liaison with 51st (Highland) Division on the right and 43rd Division on the left. The bridge across the River Hase now ready and 2 H.C.R. crossed at first light., Emsteck was reached on the 13th of April, and with units of 51st (Highland) Division swinging northwards across and ahead of Guards Armoured Division, the Regiment's task was complete. The armoured cars concentrated on the 14th of April at Vestrup for a well-earned breather.

13th April. "The Irish group have taken Essen. We push on beyond but are held up by bazookas and infantry, the usual thing. Bill Pooley's Troop is held up. I went up with Heavy Troop and jeepers and we put in an attack from the right with heavy covering fire from our 75 mms. and our Staghounds. Enemy cleared off. Captured one wounded left behind (leg half blown off); gave morphia and took back on the back of a scout car. Collected a lot of bazookas.... Blew up five farmhouses where Germans were digging in and they cleared off. Dead Germans, mostly very young, boosted up by sprinkling of S.S., all over the place. Mostly killed by our shelling, for they have the most appalling wounds. Shot an old sow who had one leg blown off and used all the sucking pigs for eating…." (Captain. G. D. Cooper.)

"We are working with the Coldstream group—Bevern and Addrup both being taken after some initial opposition. Roadblocks all the way. All farms on fire with civilians trying to put them out. Further on Lusche is blazing from end to end; the flames being across the road, we had to dash quickly through them. The Germans have now no artillery and the racket of our own guns is infernal. Some civilians actually cheer us in a sort of hysteria of relief that it is over for them, but others, a great many, stand weeping by their burning homes. It grew dark before we could harbour and the dust and traffic moving forward was very great. Everywhere lit up by blazing homesteads—odd sniping, dead Germans, and everybody on both sides very tired indeed. This country looks so cut out for peace and quiet; the farms are well built (or rather were!) and the early blossom and young green add contrast to the continual scene of desolation and human misery. The roads are now filled with hordes of displaced persons of every nationality, whole families together, roaming about the countryside in an orgy of happiness-cum-looting. One Slav shouted 'Viva Tito!' as he passed us in a chugging farm tractor. I hate this Communist clenched fist salute greeting, for all this 'gallant Russian steamroller' stuff to the east; I ignore them and have ordered my crew to do the same…."

"*April 14th*. At long last we are in Vestrup, with three days' complete rest." (Lieutenant R. P. G. Orde.)

Bedford Water Truck

Chapter IV

Move to 12 Corps

Vestrup was a little village of dark red brick and timbered houses, and, due to the fact that the Germans had decided to evacuate it during the night, almost unharmed. By midday on the 14th of April, everyone had settled down into farms and houses, looking forward, perhaps more than at any other stage of the campaign, to the prospect of three or four days' rest.

The general front, and Hamburg in particular, faded from mind, and we lived in the present. "The civilians," wrote a trooper, "are most courteous, and do all our washing and mending. We are in a lovely house, the sun is shining, and I rested all afternoon, consuming large quantities of wine! " There was a curfew for all civilians, and one or two drives to round up enemy believed to be hiding in the adjoining woods. One such drive beat out ten square miles of country, combed all isolated houses and cellars, and brought back "One German boy in S.S. uniform, aged fifteen (very frightened), two grinning Italians (very funny), two deer (dead), three eggs (fresh), five discarded German uniforms and a naughty picture postcard contained therein." Outside "C" Squadron's mess, Captain Cooper and Lieutenant Corbett bathed in a tub set out on the grass, to the amusement of the local frauleins, while the usual Gestapo villain discovered masquerading in civilian clothes was frog-marched down the road to be grilled by Lieutenant Haskard.

The clean and well-fed appearance of the villagers was striking—there was no shortage of food here. Nor, in fairness to this farming community, did the displaced persons look hungry. In most cases working on the farms, they had been well fed and cared for, and indeed several of them made a point of bringing us signed slips of paper vouching for the humane treatment meted out to them by Herr "that" or Frau "this." There were a number of tearful farewell scenes where a prisoner of war had become one of the family, sometimes, we suspected, in more senses than one.

When the Germans had got over their initial fright they showed great interest in the armoured cars. I watched one little schoolboy, with his flaxen hair plastered down in a sort of Nazi version of the "Brylcreem boy" go the rounds of the vehicles, carefully examining everything. I called him over and asked sternly, "What are you looking at?" and he replied unhesitatingly, "The guns." The following conversation then took place:

"How old are you?"

"Nine."

"Where did you learn your English?"

"At home from my sister, sir."

"How old is she?"

"Twelve."

"Where is she?"

"In Hamburg, at school."

"How did she learn such good English that she could teach you so well?"

"We all learn English at school, sir."

"In order to sail over to England as the Master Race and conquer us?"

To this last rather unfair question the boy did not reply, but he made no sign that such had not been his future intention! He was next asked what was the present state of Hamburg, and was it badly damaged by bombs? He was about to answer but checked himself in time, realizing that the Allies had not yet captured the place and might be wanting to know military secrets. Instead he replied: "I do not know anything about Hamburg."

"Is it like London ? " inquired a trooper.

"I have not been to London, so cannot know," countered the youth.

"London has been badly damaged by your Luftwaffe and so has Hamburg been hit by the Royal Air Force."

To which the German boy replied, "London did not give in."

This last remark ended the conversation, and he was told to run along and not come near the armoured cars again. He clicked his heels, gave a quick little bow, and marched off.

"Well, can you beat that, sir?" said Corporal-of-Horse Copus. "You've got to hand it to them sometimes."

Thus in a land which at times could look so innocent and gay, a country of gabled hamlets and winding streams, and quaint old houses with facades of twisted stone and timber, where the repose of centuries pervades the churches and their Hanoverian coats of arms, one passed the hours pondering on the enigmas and contradictions of this strange people. Abruptly our reverie was jerked into reality—on the evening of the 16th we heard that the rest was at an end; an urgent order to move had just come through to Regimental Headquarters.

★   ★   ★

By 16th April, paralysis of the entire German administrative machine had begun to grip the land as the American armies swept through the centre of the country. It seemed that what little remained of the German plan to fight to the bitter end, centred on the Bavarian Redoubt and holding on to the ports of Bremen and Hamburg. But already British troops were pouring over the Weser and swinging northwards towards Hamburg. If Bremen could be outflanked from the east and the autobahn cut, communication between the two great ports would be severed. This was to be the new task for Guards Armoured Division, who had therefore been ordered to join 12 Corps in the area of Rethem bridgehead. We were sorry to leave 30 Corps at this stage of the war.

Under the command of Major Ward the harbour party set off at half past five on the morning of the 17th of April—the Regiment was to follow on later in the day. Because of traffic congestion, the temporarily successful bombing of a bridge, and some bad road diversions, the journey entailed the party making a wide sweep by way of Vechta, Diepholz, Sulingen and Nienburg on the River Weser. Here the other Guards Armoured Division representatives were met, and it was learnt that the Regiment was to harbour at Stocken, which was some ten miles farther on to the south of Rethem and be prepared to operate at first light.

The country from Vechta onwards had been practically untouched and, as the day was warm and sunny, the fourteen hours' non-stop convoy run proved almost enjoyable. On arrival at Stocken it was found that due to the rapid progress made by 12 Corps during the day the Regiment was to move farther on and harbour for the night on the open heath near Schneeheide, ten miles away.

Rethem, where 53rd Division had encountered strong resistance from S.S. elements, was still burning when the first armoured cars arrived. The Germans had made a stand by the railway station, where a train unit had fought fiercely to the last man and gun: seven mounted 88-mm. guns and two 105-mm. guns lay knocked out with their barrels pointing skywards. We counted thirty-eight dead Germans among the debris, and as we turned towards the centre of the town, a backward glance revealed the nine gun silhouettes thrown up against a vivid sunset and the ruins of the station—an unearthly combination of beauty and desolation which many still remember. "B" Squadron were the first to arrive in harbour, for they had been given early road priority in the hope that there would be a few spare hours of daylight left for reconnaissance that evening; but it was already dark, there came a sudden violent thunderstorm, cars bogged in the heathland, two hundred S.S. were reported in the vicinity, and little headway could be made against the spate of orders and harbouring instructions which flowed in. Not until past midnight was the last vehicle in the convoy parked, very much on the alert.

"Squadron Leaders then went for orders and returned with forty-nine maps per Troop and twelve large-scale sheets per car, as well as ten extra quarter-inch maps for the Troop Leaders. It was raining hard and we had to sort them all out on our knees in the pitch dark, while odd shots rang out from a near-by house which was set alight by tracer to quieten it. Tempers ran extremely high!" Thus wrote a member of "C" Squadron.

★ ★ ★

At this stage, the considerable redisposition of Troops tended to make it difficult to know exactly what was happening, but if the following salient points are borne in mind, the movements of the Regiment during the next few days will be easier to follow.

The capture of Bremen by 30 Corps had been given top priority, but it was anticipated that this would entail several days' close infantry fighting. Opposition to the west of the town was organized and effective. This was the reason why, with the object of carrying out a wide right hook and cutting the autobahn, Guards Armoured Division had come under command of 12 Corps. The primary task of 12 Corps remained the capture of Hamburg, but to begin with the Regiment would be operating in their area.

In effect, Guards Armoured Division, with the Regiment screening their advance, were to carry out a wide pincer movement directed on Zeven, "but," said the directive, "the farther north they go towards Hamburg before they swing left the better, but they may have to capture Rotenburg."[1]

Initially the axis of advance was to have been Walsrode—Visselhovede—Schneverdingen, with the Regiment fanning out widely to the east. But 32nd Brigade's thrust towards Visselhovede came up

---

1. Extract from General Sir Miles Dempsey's directive on the 16th of April 1945 to the commanders of 12 and 30 Corps.

against most determined resistance outside the village. So an ambitious and somewhat unusual plan was devised.

5th Brigade was launched on an even wider easterly hook to strike at Zeven from the east, thus outflanking the opposition coming from a Marine division at Visselhovede—a formation, to use an Irish-ism, all at sea in mobile land warfare, but still capable of stubborn and effective resistance in a defensive role.

It was a bold move, for if unsuccessful, Guards Armoured Division would be seriously split and its brigades over fifty miles apart. It also meant that, initially, the right-hand advance would be in the wake of 7th Armoured Division, who by the morning of the 18th had captured Soltau and were well beyond to the north.[2] The move succeeded beyond expectations.

Colonel Abel Smith decided to work three Squadrons up—"D" on the right, "C" in the centre and "B" on the left.

"B" Squadron had been called forward on the night of 17th/18th April and ordered to operate immediately. Priority flags had got the cars through the traffic to Walsrode in record time, and Major Clyde started his Troops up the Visselhovede road as the light began to fade. They soon encountered roadblocks, although one Troop found a way round the obstacle to the west and made contact with a patrol of 11th Hussars which reported enemy in strength at Ebbingen, five miles north of Walsrode. Darkness then halted further attempts at penetration northwards.

By ten o'clock on the morning of the 18th, the Regiment had made excellent progress in the centre, where "C" Squadron had already passed through Schneverdingen, after making further contact with the armoured cars of 11th Hussars. On the right, "D" Squadron were held up for some time by blown bridges east of Fallingbostel and were eventually ordered to follow up "C" Squadron's route and to deploy farther north.

"B" Squadron experienced a most difficult day, as considerable opposition was encountered in the woods between Ebbingen and Kettenburg. The Welsh Guards group could make but slow headway against mines and demolitions, and the Coldstream group to their right became involved with the enemy east of Visselhovede.

As "C" Squadron continued to press rapidly northwards—they were through Todstedt before midday—a large gap soon formed between them and "B" Squadron on their left. This was filled by "D" Squadron,

---

2. It should be understood that during the 18th and 19th of April the armoured cars of Guards Armoured Division (ourselves) and those of 7th Armoured Division (11th Hussars) were both working on a narrow but deep front. Where 2 H.C.R. patrols are mentioned as entering a certain village or locality, it does not necessarily follow that they were the first British troops to do so.

who now found themselves facing north-west and involved in the peat bogs separating them from the Hamburg—Bremen autobahn.

Last light saw "C" Squadron harboured half-way between Todstedt and Welle, with "D" Squadron bivouacking among the pine trees on high ground some six miles north of Soltau. Neunkirchen, a village some nine miles to the north-east of Visselhovede, had been by-passed by the Regiment and its capture late in the day by the Coldstream group allowed this formation to move south-west to aid the Welsh Guards in the capture of Visselhovede, which was still holding out and was not to fall until the following morning after a combined attack by the Scots-Welsh and Coldstream groups of 32nd Brigade.

It had been a day of glorious weather and many prisoners, but apart from the fighting on the left there had been only scattered opposition as far as the Regiment was concerned. Forest fires, in spite of the previous night's thunderstorm, were burning everywhere. One Troop alone, Lieutenant Bruce-Lockhart's, had started three, and the resultant batch of prisoners, not to mention civilians in hiding, who were driven into the open by the flames was most satisfactory.

★   ★   ★

The next day, the 19th of April, was marked by further deep penetrations northwards by the Regiment, although the main advance on the left with "B" Squadron continued to be slow, occasioned by the delay imposed on the Foot Guards by the defenders of Visselhovede and subsequent resistance at Rotenburg. 5th Brigade now turned west to continue its drive towards Zeven, and throughout the day our armoured cars operated with the Irish Guards group, who had attached a liaison officer to the right-hand Squadron, "C."

★   ★   ★

Lieutenant Tabor's narrative illustrates the type of reconnaissance which "B" Squadron were having to undertake, and also the reason why delay on the left flank was so considerable. Several scout cars and armoured cars were lost on mines.

"… My Troop was ordered to continue northwards via Hiddingen and Hemslingen. We duly started north off the main road at first light but had not gone a hundred yards before we met German infantry coming south. We fired at them and they withdrew through the thick pine woods on each side of the road. Progress was very slow as a self-propelled gun was firing just to the north, and numerous infantry had been observed.

"We eventually made good a Y-roads about two miles north of the main road. We tried both roads to the north, but in each case we were fired on by bazookas and machine guns within five hundred yards of starting. I therefore disposed the Troop round the Y-roads and started off to the west to try to find a way through the woods, accompanied by my driver. All went well to start with, and for about a mile we found a decent track. After this, however, it petered out in an area intersected by small watercourses over which we could find no way. Reluctantly, we started off to rejoin the Troop. About half-way back we saw a section of infantry moving through the trees towards the main road. When we were in a good position we opened fire and they moved off fast to the south.

"We re-joined the Troop on the main road. I was unhappy to remain there because the country was very close and we could easily be stalked. To add to this uncomfortable feeling, two bazooka bombs suddenly came lobbing over and landed close to my scout car. We immediately turned the vehicles round, using two to give covering fire while the other two turned. Then when all was ready we set off down the road, flat out, myself leading. We found that approximately a platoon of infantry had infiltrated behind us and were lining the road. As we drove past they let us have everything they had got, including about eight bazooka bombs. Luckily, we were only hit by small arms, which did no damage.

"We then withdrew to Hiddingen and took up a position covering some cultivated land west of our centre line. Here we were again attacked. In the ensuing battle most of the houses in the village 'brewed up.' After some time I saw a file of infantry crossing the open ground and going into a copse. We drove over, surrounded the copse, and fired everything we had into it. After a few minutes, thirty-two Germans surrendered, several of them wounded. We had some difficulty in transporting them to Squadron Headquarters, which was located in Neunkirchen."

★　★　★

In "D" Squadron, Corporal-of-Horse Thompson, who was commanding Lieutenant Hanbury's Troop during his absence on leave, had an equally eventful day, stalking and being stalked by an enemy self-propelled gun. Thompson had been ordered to find a way across the peat bogs to the west and was moving up a narrow track when the scout car, commanded by Corporal Wilson and driven by Trooper Gee, was fired at by a gun which had been cleverly camouflaged in the undergrowth. The shot skimmed over the top of the car, sliced off a tree at its base and ricochetted past Corporal-of-Horse Thompson's armoured car. Unfortunately, the tree fell across the engine cover of the scout car, making it impossible for Gee to reverse. Both men, however, managed to extricate themselves from the branches before the next shot finished off the vehicle. The Troop eventually got past the self-propelled gun by passing through a wood and so out of range on the other side.

★   ★   ★

Another Troop in the same Squadron, Lieutenant A. Murray's, had the unpleasant experience of being fired at by an anti-tank gun while badly bogged down in a lane. The cars were eventually hauled out and resumed the advance, only to sink again, this time up to the axles, while around the stranded cars the Germans could be seen making their preparations to stalk them from several different directions. But the enemy morale cannot have been very good in this sector, for after about half an hour Major Profumo, the Squadron Leader, was relieved to hear his Troop Leader's imperturbable voice announce that the Germans had thought better of their proposed attack after one good burst of Besa machine-gun fire. It eventually took four recovery tanks and two Scammels to extricate the Troop, for the rescuers bogged themselves in their turn. Perhaps the busiest men in the Regiment on this day were Captain Hudson and his Scammel crew. They trundled from one bogging crisis to another, and in between hauling out cars from the morasses succeeded in collecting an impressive total of prisoners, treating both their journeys into the unknown and the enemy sniping with cheerful equanimity.

★   ★   ★

Faced with the problem of yet more extended communications, Colonel Abel Smith moved up "A" Squadron, who had been in reserve north of Fallingbostel, to take their place on the left of "D" Squadron. The regimental line now faced almost due west and ran from north of Todstedt down to Schneverdingen, with patrols extending on both flanks, to a total distance exceeding thirty miles. In order to maintain touch with Divisional Headquarters, Regimental Headquarters moved to a more central position half-way between the villages of Dorfmark and Visselhovede.

Although both "A" and "D" Squadrons continued to encounter very boggy ground and were eventually reduced to an almost static role for the rest of the day, "C" Squadron, co-operating with the Irish Guards group, succeeded in pushing out long feelers towards the autobahn and north towards the River Elbe.

Their first Troops had left harbour at half past five in the morning and shortly afterwards were reporting that they had cut the Hamburg — Bremen autobahn in several places in the area of Hollenstedt—Sittensen. As all the fly-overs across the autobahn had been blown by the Germans, considerable cross-country work had to be put in before Troops could penetrate farther west, and at the end of the day the armoured cars and tanks were still some miles short of Weertzen on the road to Zeven.

Midday saw "C" Squadron Headquarters preparing to move off from the vicinity of Sittensen to catch up with their forward Troops. Captain Cooper was in the act of walking across a field to talk to his driver when he ran head-on into a six-foot-five German sergeant standing in a slit trench and aiming a bazooka at his head. Cooper was about to fire his revolver when he realized that he was facing a dead man. A piece of shell splinter had gone through the German's helmet without so much as disturbing his equilibrium. Even his eyes were wide open, fixed in steady aim to the front. "As he had been dead some time and it was rather hot into the bargain, I found a German civilian to bury the corpse."

Meanwhile, the Troop making the best headway to the north had been that commanded by Lieutenant Harvey-Williams. Wireless messages showed that it was working towards Stade, but, having been held up, was trying to find another route. This new route also proved to be blocked by the enemy, and a last message stating that the Troop was trying yet another way and had got to within a few miles of Buxtehude was followed by silence. No further news was received until Corporal Bland reached Squadron Headquarters late at night with the bad news that half the Troop had been lost after a battle with the enemy on the outskirts of the village of Appensen.

The details were as follows. Having been ordered to probe boldly towards Stade, which was (at that time) the eventual objective of Guards Armoured Division, and having twice been engaged by the enemy, Lieutenant Harvey-Williams decided to try to fight his way through the next village should it prove to be held. He hoped that once through the village, with the enemy in their present parlous state, he might then be able to advance rapidly without further hindrance to Stade. A further important task, which could only be carried out satisfactorily by advancing to within visible distance of the Stade—Buxtehude road, was that of reporting on enemy transport moving into Hamburg from the west.

The Troop's composition was as follows. In the two scout cars were Corporal Bland and his driver and Corporal Ray and his driver, Trooper Parsons. The Troop Leader's armoured car crew consisted of, as well as himself, Trooper Oakley, the driver, and Trooper Marshall, gunner-operator. Corporal-of-Horse Jarvis commanded the other Daimler, with Trooper Mitchell as driver and Trooper Jones as gunner-operator. Of the men who had formed part of this Troop (originally Lieutenant Powle's) when it had made its famous run to the Souleuvre bridge, only Corporals Bland and Ray and Trooper Parsons remained.

The Troop reached the outskirts of the village of Appensen during the late afternoon. Isolated parties of Germans had been encountered in the latter stages, but these had offered little resistance. Two small villages had been left burning in the rear as a result of skirmishes.

Appensen lay at the end of a dead straight road about half a mile long, and Lieutenant Harvey-Williams pulled the Troop into cover to take stock of the situation. Just before the road entered the village proper it was heavily lined with bushes and trees. A small church and the first houses lay immediately beyond.

While thus observing, one of the Troop suddenly spotted a large convoy of lorries hurriedly moving off to the north-west in the direction of Buxtehude. Guns were traversed on to them and eight were destroyed before they could escape out of range.

By this time more movement could be seen in the village itself and it was noticed that the Germans were moving into slit trenches on either side of the road. The Troop Leader immediately gave orders to traverse guns on to this activity and once again opened fire. After the firing had ceased and things appeared to have quietened down, Lieutenant Harvey-Williams decided that he would take the armoured cars into the village and out through the other side, leaving Corporal Bland with the two scout cars and a section of the Support Troop in a White scout car to join him later, should the enemy opposition not be too strong.

The two armoured cars moved off at fair speed, the Troop Leader's some forty yards ahead on the right of the road, while Corporal-of-Horse Jarvis kept to the left. They could thus both fire to their front.

But it is probable that, unobserved, the enemy had infiltrated into other trenches under cover of the trees, and as soon as the houses were reached by the first car, heavy fire opened up from both sides of the road on to the two Daimlers. A bazooka hit the turret of Lieutenant Harvey-Williams's vehicle, killing him instantly, and the car burst into flames. Trooper Oakley made for the ditch, badly wounded, and Trooper Marshall tried to run towards Corporal-of-Horse Jarvis's car, which had closed up to give what aid it could to the survivors. As he clambered up the front of the car a burst from a Schmeizer automatic caught him, and he died immediately.

By now bazookas were sailing through the air from all sides, for the Germans had got in behind the second armoured car, and it was hit several times, finally collapsing on its side with a wheel and suspension blown off. Corporal-of-Horse Jarvis, badly wounded in the face and head, baled out, blinded by blood, followed by Troopers Jones and Mitchell. Jones tried to make a dash for freedom, but all three were eventually captured.

The village was apparently defended by a detachment of Marines embodied into what was called a "Panzer Commando," and formed part of the hedgehog defences hastily set up to bar further advance towards Buxtehude, an important naval arsenal.

When Corporal Bland in the rear had ascertained what had happened and realized that he could be of no further help, he rightly decided to withdraw the remainder of the Troop. He had no time to lose, for the enemy had already sent a cycle patrol with bazookas to cut off his line of retreat. To the front Germans could be seen surrounding the survivors, but Bland dare not open fire for fear of hitting his own side. Nor at this stage could it be ascertained what was the exact fate of those in the Troop Leader's car.

As Bland gave the order to retire, the enemy started firing at the two scout cars, and it was decided to go "hell for leather, for besides the bazooka men in the ditches waiting for us it was now getting dark." They had gone barely a mile when they were confronted by a further substantial force of infantry with machine guns and bazookas —it seemed at this stage of the campaign as if every other German soldier was armed with this deadly instrument. The cars halted, although they felt that they had been spotted, and decided to get past using an old trick which Bland had learnt from long campaigning experience. The Germans could be seen forming up on both sides of the road under cover. They had posted their machine gunners some way from the roadside with the object of keeping down the heads of the scout car crews while their bazooka men crept close unobserved. The leading scout car moved off again very slowly, as if hesitating what to do; then at a given signal all three vehicles, which included the White scout car, accelerated as hard as they could go, firing everything they had at the ditches to put off the bazooka men. The Germans were taken completely by surprise and eventually all three cars got safely back to harbour.

The subsequent experiences of the wounded and prisoners from this Troop are worthy of mention. They were taken into the village of Appensen, where some of the inhabitants brought out water and bandages and themselves dressed the wounds. "I thought," wrote Corporal-of-Horse Jarvis, "that this was a pretty decent gesture, as we had been shelling their homes hard only half an hour before."

The men were then put into a farm cart and driven into Buxtehude, to the Marine barracks, which they gathered at the time was the Headquarters of the German North Sea Command. Wounds were again dressed by a German doctor, and Jarvis and Oakley were put into the Garrison hospital together with a batch of Germans wounded in the battle with the Troop. "We were treated very well, and in fact," continues Jarvis, "the German Admiral commanding visited us and lent us some English books from his own library. I forget his name, but he spoke perfect English, and seemed quite reconciled to becoming a prisoner of war in the next few days."[3]

On the following day both the wounded and unwounded prisoners were allowed to attend the funeral of the two Household Cavalrymen, Lieutenant David Harvey-Williams and Trooper James Marshall. They were buried together with four German soldiers who had been killed in the same action, in the cemetery of Freidhof am Muhlenweg, Buxtehude, and were accorded full naval honours by a Marine colour party. The service was conducted by a German Lutheran minister. "We noticed," said Trooper Jones, "that during the playing of the 'Last Post,' the salute given by the officers and ratings of the escort was not the 'Heil Hitler,' but the pre-war German naval salute."

"The next day the troops in Buxtehude barracks were in a great state of 'flap' over the approach of 7th Armoured Division, who were swooping in from the east, and most of them started packing their kit in readiness for the prisoner-of-war cages."

On the morning of the 21st of April, "as nobody seemed to be worrying over us, we took some pistols from the armoury, broke open a garage in the officers' block, and got ready to drive back to our own lines. A couple of Jerry mechanics helped us to get the car to start. By this time, the first patrols of the 'Cherry Pickers' had reached the barracks. The garrison were now in a great panic and 500 German Wrens prepared to sell their honour dearly! They barricaded themselves into their quarters, and Alan Moorehead in his book *Eclipse* mentions that they were still there when he reached Buxtehude a couple of days later."

This was Corporal-of-Horse Jarvis's last sight of Germany and the war, for having made contact with the 11th Hussars, both he and Oakley were flown back to an English hospital via Brussels. Jones and Mitchell

---

3. This German Admiral also interviewed Troopers Jones and Mitchell. He asked them routine questions and "merely laughed when we refused to say where we were heading to." The Admiral turned out to be Konteradmiral a. D. Siegfried Engel, whose official appointment in December, 1944, was "Second Admiral, North Sea." As such he was responsible under the Admiral at Wilhelmshaven for the drafting of all naval personnel in the area of the North Sea coast of Germany.

soon re-joined the Regiment, which was then nearing Zeven, but this is anticipating by several days.

★   ★   ★

With 5th Brigade group (Grenadiers and Irish) now concentrated west of the autobahn in the area of Grosse Meckelsen, and 32nd Brigade group (Scots-Welsh and Coldstream) closing in on Rotenburg, Regimental Headquarters moved up on the 20th of April to the village of Sittensen, where they were to remain for several days. The plan was that the Regiment, with three Squadrons up, was to push out patrols in all directions west of the autobahn. However, the Germans had brought up reinforcements during the night, and from prisoners captured, 15th Panzer Division was identified. This formation was believed to have been moved up from Bremen with the idea of blocking the British advance towards Zeven, the latter being almost the only communications centre of any importance left to the enemy in the Cuxhaven peninsula.

In spite of this opposition, an "A" Squadron patrol almost reached Elsdorff by early afternoon before being forced to retire by heavy and accurate shell fire. Subsequently the Irish Guards group, "who had been enjoying themselves enormously down at Elsdorf taking pot shots at unsuspecting German Staff officers, now met the full force of this counter-attack, which was strongly supported by artillery, mortars, and even a close support bombing attack—an astounding feat considering the state of the enemy's communications at this stage."[4]

Farther north it was the same story, and after first "C" Squadron and then "D" Squadron had failed to penetrate a screen of infantry and the usual bazookas, the Grenadier group encountered stubborn opposition before finally capturing the villages of Heeslingen and Wiersdorf, two miles east of Zeven. Close to the former place, at Boitzen, Lieutenant Bruce-Lockhart's Troop called in the Typhoons to the aid of the Grenadiers, but except to burn down the village it was of no avail—the enemy simply went to ground and popped up again as soon as the planes had left. For the next three days the Grenadiers were to remain held up in this area, while the Regiment's armoured cars probed away to the north-west and south-west.

There was little doubt that with the countryside teeming with displaced persons, German civilians, and escaping prisoners of war, much information regarding our movements was both deliberately and

---

4. *History of the Irish Guards in the Second World War"*. (Gale & Polden Ltd.)

unwittingly being passed back to enemy headquarters. Troops were accordingly ordered wherever possible to cut down telephone wires and aerials, search cellars for hidden soldiers, and generally scare the civilians into a state of co-operative obedience. The immediate result of the scaring was a flood of pistols and shot guns, as well as a selection of vintage rifles dating back to the Boer War, but information about our movements continued unabated.

"C" Squadron took their job most seriously—in fact, so conscientiously did Major Herbert carry out the spirit of the order that "he even shot the lock off a large safe in Sittensen railway yard, finding no weapons inside, however, and unfortunately nothing else of value either!"

The day's great excitement and subsequent mystery was the action in which Lieutenant Hodges' Troop in "C" Squadron was engaged. This patrol (as well as two others commanded by Lieutenants Bruce-Lockhart and Bailey) was on the morning of the 20th of April out on reconnaissance in the area where Lieutenant Harvey-Williams's Troop had last been heard of.

The territory east of the autobahn was now, broadly speaking, in British hands, while that to the west was still held by the Germans. Having ascertained from the Irish Guards outposts who were protecting the autobahn north of Sittensen that they had made no contact with the enemy during the night, Lieutenant Hodges decided to push on northwards and then off the autobahn to the west. Accompanying the Troop was a section of the Support Troop and the "C" Squadron interpreter, Sergeant Wansink, a Dutchman.

After a short distance, a roadblock of felled trees held up the advance. It was not covered by the enemy but took some time to move. A mile farther on another roadblock was encountered which the Support Troop section was in the process of clearing when surprised by a column of German armoured cars, and in the ensuing battle the White scout car was captured, together with Sergeant Wansink.

The rest of the Troop had been disposed some way ahead at the time but realizing that the German formation was somewhat larger than normally encountered, Hodges decided to move eastwards immediately to find out more about it.

In the meantime the German commander of the column, also uncertain of the strength of the British opposition, had withdrawn slightly, hidden up, and was trying to prise a few facts out of Sergeant Wansink. The Dutchman played up well. He became dumb and, in his own words, "exceeding stupid." He pretended to be one of a British party detailed to bring up rations to another operating armoured car patrol and that he had lost his way. Accompanying him, he added, there had been, apart from the White scout car, only a single lorry which he presumed had moved on and was trying to escape back to the British lines.

After heated argument and abusive threats, the German commander appeared to be moderately satisfied with the story. Wansink was then searched, but no identifications were found on him, nor did the Germans think to look into the White scout car, which could not have failed to yield clues. Then, after further shoutings and discussion among themselves, the Germans decided to move on to see what could be discovered of the British.

Poor Wansink, seeing that his plan to lead the enemy away from the Troop had misfired, now saw in addition that there was more than a fair chance that he would be blown to bits by his own side, for he was ordered to ride in the captured British vehicle. He related afterwards: "We went for about three or four miles when the Germans stopped at a side track which showed the marks of quite a few tyres of heavy vehicles. I was brusquely asked if I could explain this, but I maintained my statement that just one lorry had been with us. The German officer then decided to go down the track, put guards at each side of the road to watch this, left some cars behind, and made me stand aside between two guards."

This advance party consisted of the White scout car in the lead, filled with infantry armed with bazookas and machine guns, then a large black Mercedes car mounting twin machine guns on its front and also filled with infantry, a motor-cycle combination and some motor-cycle outriders, a small car, and finally two armoured trucks and more infantry. The main part of the column which remained behind consisted of four armoured cars and more armoured trucks—a not inconsiderable force to be at large.

"I was very anxious to know what was going to happen," continues Wansink, "for it was obvious to me that it had been our Troop that had turned off the road. After about a quarter of an hour I heard a terrific explosion, followed by heavy gun fire. This firing lasted for about a quarter of an hour, then it quietened down. Not much later the German patrol—or rather what little was left of it—returned, and the commanding officer began to tell his second-in-command, who had stayed behind, what had happened, not realizing that I could understand the whole story."

It transpired that the first thing which Hodges' Troop saw was the White scout car approaching at a good speed. Thinking that this might perhaps contain Wansink, the vehicle was allowed to approach to within fifty yards, when it was seen to be filled with Germans crouching down on the floor of the body, who suddenly sprang up and started firing machine guns and bazookas as the driver accelerated forward.

This brave though desperate form of attack could have but one ending against a Troop in a position of its own choosing among farm buildings. Corporal-of-Horse Jenkins's car immediately returned the fire, killing or wounding every German standing in the vehicle, including two bazooka men who fell back in the act of launching their bombs which exploded against a wall next to Corporal Chennel's scout car. Then Trooper Jameson, gunner in the armoured car, scored a direct hit with his 2-pounder gun on the White scout car. There was a blinding flash as with a tremendous explosion all the mines and demolition equipment normally carried in the vehicle disintegrated, killing off the remaining Germans. This was the explosion which Wansink had heard in the distance.

Meanwhile the large black Mercedes car appeared on the scene, closely followed by the motor-cycle combination and one of the armoured trucks, which let fly with a quick-firing anti-tank gun, and a second hectic battle flared up. Hodges's car took on the Mercedes, Corporal-of-Horse Jenkins's the armoured truck, while the dismounted section of the Support Troop picked off the bazooka men, aided by Corporal Hersant and Trooper Dennis in the second scout car, whose Bren gun took heavy toll on the enemy who kept dismounting from the armoured truck to try to get within bazooka range. In a short time the roadway was littered with dead and dying Germans, and the black Mercedes and all other vehicles with the exception of the rearmost truck, which withdrew, lay burning on the roadside.

Presuming that the retreating truck might give warning to the main body of Germans farther back, Hodges now decided to move off cross-country by a new route to see if these could be ambushed from another direction. Nothing further was seen of the enemy column, however, and after two more brushes with infantry patrols the Troop reached Squadron harbour at dusk, minus Sergeant Wansink and Trooper Clarkson, who had been missing since the second engagement but was subsequently to turn up safe and sound two days later.

Intense interest was caused at Divisional Intelligence Headquarters by news of the action. The I.O. had been struck by the "black Mercedes" part of the story and the report that several of the German motor-cycle outriders had been dressed in black and wore "highly polished black helmets." It was known that Himmler had been seen in the neighbourhood during the preceding week visiting the Bremen and Hamburg garrisons. Division smelt a military "scoop" which, if nothing better, might at least provide good copy for the next edition of the *News*

Guardian. Major Herbert was therefore ordered to send out further patrols at crack of dawn next day, and newspaper reporters descended on his headquarters, avid for news. They were not disappointed. Mr. Edward Gilling, Exchange Telegraph War Correspondent, immediately wrote a column entitled "HIMMLER BURNED TO DEATH?" and the newspaper publishing it had record sales within "C" Squadron.

The morning after the encounter Hodges and Bruce-Lockhart—the latter spoke German—returned to the scene of the action. The area was now in British hands. All that remained was the burnt-out parts of the White scout car, three motorcycles, and the light car. Close at hand were seven charred bodies, unrecognizable and covered with a sheet. Of the Mercedes and all its dead occupants there was not a trace. On questioning the villagers it was ascertained that German soldiers had returned after the battle and towed away the car and its gruesome contents, several other bodies also being removed. Great care appeared to have been taken that no trace of their belongings was left lying about. The mystery, if there was indeed one, was never solved, but from his suicide some weeks later at Field-Marshal Montgomery's Headquarters on Luneburg Heath we know that Himmler cannot have been one of the victims.

Wansink's subsequent experiences were interesting. He was held responsible by the Germans for having deliberately led them into a trap and he underwent an anxious half-hour's grilling, wondering whether he was going to be shot out of hand. However, the German commander decided to take him with him, and the vehicles headed northwards for some ten miles.

"We came to the middle of a wood which seemed to be a sort of headquarters. Motorcycles and cars kept coming and going in great numbers. I was made to stand outside the camp facing the other side so that I could not see what was going on, with one man on either side of me. This lasted for roughly four hours, when the cars were again ready to move, and we went on until we reached Stade. The German Major took me to the new headquarters, where the C.O., who it appeared afterwards was in command of the defence area north of the line Bremen—Hamburg, started to ask me a lot of questions which I could not (did not want) to answer. The only information I gave him was what I had told the German C.O. that morning.

"At last he gave up trying to get news out of me, and said, to my great surprise, 'I do not need any of your information about the English troops; I know exactly what your spearheads are aiming for.' And he produced an English map on which several routes were marked. He continued: 'Yesterday a complete Troop was trapped by our men. The armoured cars and scout cars were hit by our bazookas and the officer in command was killed. The others were taken prisoner. This map was found in his car.' Thus I heard from this very man the information we had set out that morning to obtain!"

★ ★ ★

The principal task for Guards Armoured Division on the 21st April remained the capture of Rotenburg, after which Zeven was to be attacked. For this reason, 5th Brigade were ordered to contain the defenders of Zeven while the main weight of the thrust was directed at Rotenburg. But, due to further counter-attacks during the night on the Irish Guards group, the Regiment was ordered to continue its patrolling, with particular emphasis on the protection of the southern flank. Accordingly, "D" Squadron carried out reconnaissance southwards but west of the autobahn while "C" Squadron undertook a similar role to the east of the autobahn.

Meanwhile "B" Squadron, based on Schneverdingen, remained separated from the main regimental body by many miles and, working on its own, patrolled north-west towards the same autobahn and across the peat bogs while the main attack on Rotenburg was being mounted. Troops encountered a good deal of scattered resistance and mines in quantity. At Grossenwede a large haul of prisoners was made. Thereafter progress was excellent through the villages of Valde and Lavenbruck and on to Helvesiek, with one of the Troops reaching the Hamburg—Bremen road before being ordered to withdraw for the night.

It had been a miserable day of incessant rain and, unusual at this stage, several German planes had taken to the air, carrying out half-hearted attacks on Troops without doing much damage.

★ ★ ★

"D" Squadron reached the Zeven—Elsdorf road at Elsdorf, but then Lieutenant Murray's Troop ran into infantry and a self-propelled gun when dealing with a roadblock.

Corporal Thompson in a scout car had just opened up with his Bren gun on to some enemy infantry when the self-propelled gun fired into the middle of the Troop from a range too great for the 2-pounder gun's return fire to be effective. The first shell hit Lieutenant Murray's car amidships, wounding him in the face, concussing Trooper Scott, the gunner-operator, and seriously wounding the driver, Trooper Prangnell, whose leg was practically severed. Seeing that the German vehicle was out of range of his own 2-pounder, Corporal-of-Horse Davis backed his Daimler armoured car off the road and ran to the assistance of the occupants of the other car who were helpless in the middle of the road. In the meantime the scout car commanded by Corporal Thompson had also been able to reach cover of some trees, but its companion vehicle was hit by another shell which blinded Corporal Styles in one eye and severed most of the fingers of his right hand. Trooper Powell, the driver, was also badly hit, but managed to shout to Corporal-of-Horse Davis, "I'm all right." He then crawled across to drag a Bren gun from the knocked-out car to deal with further firing which had started up from a near-by wood. He was later found collapsed from loss of blood still by his gun.

The task of extricating Prangnell—a tall, finely built man—through the narrow side door of the Daimler was not easy, but, as recounted by Davis later, "as soon as the crew of the German gun saw what we were doing, I must in fairness say that they did not fire a single other shot, otherwise, completely at their mercy, we must surely have had it. Captain Waterhouse was soon on the spot, and I must say he always was there when there was any trouble. Nor did he forget to congratulate Trooper Bone, who throughout had remained calmly operating his wireless back to Squadron Headquarters."

Trooper Stanley Prangnell died on the way to hospital in spite of all that could be done for him—a most likeable and efficient member of his Troop, and the news cast a gloom over his comrades in the Squadron which was not easily dispelled.

★ ★ ★

"This has been a bad day for 'D' Squadron," wrote an officer, "for in addition to Murray's bad luck, Harris's 4 Troop ran into trouble, Corporal-of-Horse Bugby and Trooper Rose being blown up on a German box mine not far from Sittensen. These two had led 4 Troop since landing in Normandy and are the last of the original scout car crews in the Squadron. Fortunately, neither are seriously hurt, although they have said good-bye to this front and, let's hope for them, the war. Bugby had the eyes of a hawk, and Rose is one of those rare characters who really do not know the meaning of fear. Trooper Scott assures me that Rose reads Wild West thrillers during pauses in action, and he certainly wears his revolver cowboy fashion strapped to his leg! He is forty-three years of age, twenty years above the average for such a job—some going for a scout car commander, and goodness knows how he 'wangled in.'"

★ ★ ★

On the other side of the autobahn (east), the Coldstream group, attacking Rotenburg from the north-east and with whom "C" Squadron were working, came in for some heavy shelling and mortaring from guns located on the aerodrome. A passage from a contemporary diary thus records the day:

"Raining hard, and we had to go off early after all to operate southwards, where the 'Micks' were counter-attacked during the night. Two of our Troops out straightaway to recce all villages around Scheesel on the outskirts of Rotenburg. Prisoners start pouring back, mostly from Bremen and Hamburg. They are really hopelessly cut off and come out of every house and village, but Rotenburg holds out with the Marine Division. Went to Brigade Headquarters and saw Brigadier Norman (Gwatkin), Tom Blackwell, and others. We are to form a strong point at Sothel for the night. Collected sixty-two prisoners and a captured lorry, all bagged by Bruce-Lockhart's Troop. Then, after having sent them back to P.W. cage, on to Scheessel. Past the last Coldstream tank and up the road to Hetzweg—very lonely! Crawled up the road to within 200 yards of 'D' Squadron's knocked-out Daimler. Germans all round it saw us. Managed to get back to car, reversed round bend and fired H.E. at them—also Browning. The S.P. returned our fire, missing us, but we had to pull back. Three more prisoners gave themselves up—two wounded—one fifteen years old. They seemed to be quite disorganized, but with odd stray pockets holding out. I think women are influencing them to chuck it. In one farm there was a young girl aged seventeen (unmarried). She has already had two children, by order of the State, and gets paid by the State for it! Many say it would have been all over two years ago but for the S.S. The young girl speaks good English. Rain and hail continues all day. Papers seem to think that the bloody war is over!". (Captain G. D. Cooper)

WHITE SCOUT CAR
Used for carrying Infantry Sections of the Support
Troop and (Modified Vehicle) as an Ambulance

Chapter V

"Wardforce", Sandbostel and "Cease Fire"

Desultory engagements pending fall of Rotenburg—Preparation for battle of Zeven—"Wardforce"—"A" Squadron at Brest—Germans blow most bridges to the north—Many prisoners—"D" Squadron push on to Anderlingen—Too late to save the Selsingen bridges ("D" Squadron)—"B" Squadron join up with "Wardforce"—Sappers short of bridging equipment—Bad news of Sandbostel Concentration Camp—Dash by Lieutenant Younghusband's Troop nearly reaches camp—Lieutenant Harris's Troop comes to his support—"B" Squadron patrol west of Selsingen—Tough fighting for the Welsh Guards—Westertimke— Major Collins in charge of prisoner-of-war evacuation from Westertimke Camp— Sandbostel Camp liberated by Grenadier Guards—Mines everywhere—1 H.C.R. on the right flank—Fighting dies down—Burgo-masters in great demand—"Cease Fire"

On the 22nd of April, pending the fall of Rotenburg, the order was to consolidate on the Zeven front. The Regiment had therefore few advances to record. "C" Squadron lost a scout car on a mine near Elsdorf, close to the spot where a patrol had halted on the previous day and where Lieutenant Murray's Troop had encountered the self-propelled gun. It was clear that the enemy were infiltrating by night back towards villages previously reported clear, laying mines, and then retiring again for the day. This last loss meant that yet another scout car partnership of long standing had finished its war, Corporal Chennel and Trooper Beckett, whose third knocked-out vehicle this was, both being wounded.

Lieutenant Corbett's Heavy Troop engaged Germans who had re-entered the village of Sothel, thus threatening the autobahn. After an hour's shelling, over fifty of the enemy gave themselves up, one Marine, aged fifty-six, saying disgustedly that he had fought for seven years, including the Spanish Civil War campaign, and, like his country, was finished for ever!

There was a slight stir at Headquarters concerning a series of wireless masts which "D" Squadron had sighted north of Heeslingen in the village of Meinstedt. Authority stated that these might have something to do with the control of the half-hearted attempts by enemy planes to strafe ground troops. But after investigation, Lieutenant Buchanan-Jardine's Troop returned to say that the so-called aerials were only the lightning conductors with which the thatched farms in the district were so plentifully provided.

By midday came the good news that Rotenburg had fallen. This permitted 32nd Brigade, which had been relieved by 71st Brigade (53rd Division), to concentrate south of the autobahn in the Sittensen area.

The 23rd of April was a day of preparation, and by nightfall all was set for the assault on Zeven. The main attack was to be carried out by 5th Brigade from the east, one battle group operating from the village of Wiersdorf and a second group from the area of Heeslingen.

"B" Squadron, who had been relieved in Schneverdingen by the arrival of "A" Squadron, 1 H.C.R., on the night of 22nd/23rd April, had moved up under Major Clyde to join the main body of the Regiment and were harboured with the Grenadiers near Weertzen. Their Troops were held available to patrol for the attacking brigade.

In addition, and this was to be the main effort as far as the Regiment was concerned, a mixed column under the command of Major Ward was to advance northwards from Sittensen by a circuitous route before swinging west with the object of cutting the main Bremervorde—Zeven road and capturing two important bridges at Selsingen. To facilitate the advance of this mixed column, Major Bowes Daly, "A" Squadron, would move out at first light and advance to the village of Brest, from which place he was to send out patrols to the north, acting as protective screen for the right flank of Major Ward's force as it swung west.

"C" Squadron were in reserve and available, like "B" Squadron, for work in co-operation with the brigade preparing to assault Zeven. As events transpired, "B" Squadron found themselves called upon to patrol to the line of the River Oste, and thus eventually became more a part of Major Ward's operation than of the main attack. As no armoured cars were to be involved in the attack on Zeven proper, it is with "Wardforce," as the column was soon nicknamed, that we are now concerned. This mixed column consisted of:

"D" Squadron, 2 H.C.R. (Major Profumo)—armoured cars.
No. 2 Squadron, Grenadier Guards (Captain Neville)—Sherman tanks.
One battery 21st Anti-Tank Regiment R.A.—dismounted as infantry and
　with a few carriers.
Some R.Es.
Liaison officer from the Leicestershire Yeomanry to act as F.O.O. for the
　25-pounders which were in support.

Credit for the conception of "Wardforce" was largely due to Colonel Abel Smith's eternally restless military mind. He believed that a threat to the German communications from a totally unexpected direction might cause them to loosen their hold on Zeven and ease the task of those entrusted with the main Guards Armoured Division attack. To further his scheme he finally persuaded General Adair to let him have a squadron of tanks and some extra infantry. This having been granted, the Divisional Provost staff entered into the spirit of the enterprise with enthusiasm, and insisted on sign-posting the route almost before the first Troop had passed the start line with neat little arrows in regimental colours marked "Wardforce Route UP." Before the conclusion of the operation, even the smallest bridges were dignified by smart painted boards marked "Cavalry Bridge."

The "Wardforce" plan worked admirably. The armoured cars found a way round, the Grenadiers' tanks formed the striking force whenever opposition was encountered, and the dismounted gunners could not have proved keener infantry, vying with the Support Troop under the command of Corporal-of-Horse Clark in winkling out bunches of enemy from woods and copses, where some had lain hidden and shivering in the damp for days. In addition, the tanks, commanded by Captain Neville, in the absence of Major Gregory-Hood on U.K. leave, proved a great help in hauling out the armoured cars when they bogged themselves with remarkable regularity in the marshy terrain.

Before the start of the operation a blown bridge spanning a stream north of Bokel had to be repaired, and Lieutenant Wordsworth and two sections of his Support Troop ("A" Squadron) went out on the night of the 23rd/24th to consolidate the site while the sappers made good the damage.

By ten o'clock on the morning of the 24th, Major Bowes Daly had attained the village of Brest with "A" Squadron. Here he established headquarters and pushed out Troops to beyond the railway line to the north. The enemy were found to be holding the villages of Harsefeld, Bargstedt and Aspe, but soon withdrew northwards on being shelled by the combined guns of two Heavy Troops, those of Lieutenant Murray, "A" Squadron, and Lieutenant Cavendish, who had been lent from "B" Squadron for the operation.

Meanwhile "Wardforce" proper arrived on the scene, to be informed as it passed through Brest that the Germans had blown all the bridges to the north during the previous night. This was, if anything, an advantage, for there could now be small chance of enemy infantry operating from that direction on to "Wardforce's" right flank.

Once beyond Brest, the going became extremely bad for the mixed column, and routes which looked feasible on the map proved in practice to be no more than boggy grass ruts. Each Troop in turn bogged itself up to the axles, only to be extricated with unfailing regularity and patience by the tanks.

There were desultory engagements with the enemy all day, but the main bar to progress was the terrain: German prisoners expressed the greatest surprise that armour had dared to move through such country, and volunteered the information that the arrival of British armour from this quarter was totally unexpected.

As each village was entered, the bag of prisoners grew. Lieutenant Buchanan-Jardine, a good German scholar, hit upon the idea of telephoning ahead to the Burgomasters, announcing the impending arrival of the British in "overwhelming strength." Nearly all talked willingly, betrayed gun positions and troop movements without a qualm, and promised to collect stragglers and prisoners. It was a rather illuminating aspect of the beaten German.

By the time the column reached the village of Grafel in the early afternoon, the problem of dealing with the growing numbers of displaced persons had become acute. Russians and Poles now began to block the roads, wandering as interested spectators between the cars and the German soldiers still concealed in the woods. They were also raiding the farms for food and drink and other sports, and what with hysterical German hausfrauen, looting D.Ps., garrulous Burgomasters, and the continual bogging of cars, the advance progressed somewhat jerkily until dusk.

Fifty prisoners were collected in Grafel without a shot being fired. These walked in, stating miserably that they had bicycled through the night from Bremen with vague orders to "blow things up—bazooka the English panzers—and generally make a nuisance of yourselves on behalf of the Fatherland." Having had nothing to eat for the last twenty-four hours they almost welcomed the advent of Corporal-of-Horse Copus's three-tonner lorry which, turned into a non-stop "Black Maria" service, bundled them off like sardines to the P.O.W. cage.

The first real check came in the late afternoon at Anderlingen, which Major Profumo's cars found to be held in some strength by a detachment of Germans hastily moved up from Bremervorde. As Anderlingen barred the way to the Bremervorde—Zeven road and as both the villages of Malstedt and Ohrel (possible loops to the north) had also been found to be held, Major Ward decided after reconnaissance to put in a set-piece attack.

Infantry, composed of "D" Squadron Support Troop and the dismounted anti-tank gunners all under the command of Corporal-of-Horse Clark, attacked from the east, while the Grenadiers in their tanks drove in from the north. A carrier soon went up on a mine, killing the commander and seriously wounding the driver, but both prongs of the attack made good progress, and by half past five in the evening the eastern side of the village was in British hands. Between sixty and seventy more enemy were captured, making a total haul for "Wardforce" for the day of nearly two hundred prisoners.

Soon the sound of horse-drawn transport and motor vehicles could be heard leaving the western part of the village, but further advances met with stiffened resistance, and elements of Gross Deutschland Division and a Panzer Grenadier Regiment were identified. Principally due to lack of infantry and shortage of ammunition for the tanks, which had already expended most of their high explosive shells, Major Ward called a halt to regroup. By this time it was getting dark and orders were received from Division to withdraw slightly and harbour for the night near Grafel.

It transpired that the enemy at Anderlingen had had enough, and, although a half-hearted attempt to attack the harbour leaguer with bazookas took place during the night, it was easily driven off with no damage to vehicles or casualties to personnel. In the morning, a bazooka bomb was discovered perilously resting on one of the tank crew's bivouacs, having failed to go off, a foot from the turret.

Meanwhile news of the main attack on Zeven was encouraging, and it was learnt that by nightfall enemy resistance in that sector had to all intents and purposes ceased to exist.

With the intention that "Wardforce" should resume its advance on the following morning, Colonel Abel Smith ordered Major Clyde ("B" Squadron) to be prepared to advance north and west from the area of Weertzen at first light. The northward part of the thrust would constitute a threat designed to loosen the enemy hold on Anderlingen by coming into it from the rear. As events turned out this was to prove unnecessary.

The morning of the 25th of April saw "Wardforce" awaiting the order to advance in the wake of a 25-pounder concentration directed on to hapless little Anderlingen. This was soon called off, ground mist making observation impossible. At the same time Lieutenant Palmer ("B" Squadron) reported that he was held up to the south at Sassenholz, where the enemy, mindful of their rear, had blown a small bridge. But neither of these contretemps made an appreciable difference. When Lieutenant Harris's Troop, "D" Squadron, approached Anderlingen through the mist, the enemy had flown and the inhabitants were already back, searching amidst the smoking ruins for signs of their belongings. They waved white handkerchiefs in token of surrender. Most of their cattle had perished in the blazing stalls, and horses lay with their heads still in charred halter ropes, a grim and horrible sight.

When Lieutenant Harris's Troop finally reached Selsingen, after having been compelled by yet another blown bridge to retrace its steps part of the way, it was to find 3 Troop under Corporal-of-Horse Thompson already in possession of the place, collecting weapons and cameras from civilians. The bridges which had been "Ward-force's" main objective had unfortunately been destroyed by the enemy before retiring some hours previously.

Nevertheless, it was learnt from a captured Staff officer that the advance of "Wardforce" had created alarm and despondency at Zeven headquarters. An advance by armour from this quarter had been considered out of the question, and when first reports arrived that tanks and armoured cars had been seen approaching from the north-east the Zeven commander, over-estimating the strength of the threat, had heavily reinforced Anderlingen. It was also later ascertained that when attacked by "Wardforce" the village was held by nearly two battalions of infantry, many drawn off from Zeven at the last moment. Thus in no small part due to "Wardforce," the enemy had been compelled to release his hold on Zeven and withdraw towards Bremen during the night.

Because of the extensive destruction of bridges, there was now a great shortage of bridging equipment, and some time elapsed before a scissors bridge could be brought up to span the gaps both at Sassenholz and on the main road separating Guards Armoured Division and "Wardforce" at Selsingen. Thus while waiting for the sappers to restore communications with 5th Brigade, Major Profumo's armoured cars continued their patrolling to the north-west, where the Germans entrenched on the high ground overlooking Selsingen were effectively mortaring the main road.

Late in the afternoon two escaped Allied prisoners of war came into "Wardforce" Headquarters, established in an old windmill half a mile north of the village of Seedorf. They brought with them the first authentic and shocking news of the Sandbostel concentration camp. After being fed and rested they were taken to Divisional Headquarters. They unfolded a terrible story.

Sandbostel had originally been an ordinary prisoner-of-war camp, but in the last few months had been used for political prisoners as well when these were being transferred from a concentration camp near Bremen. It was situated some six miles north-west of Selsingen.

No good purpose can be served here in retailing all the horrors and iniquities which these two, a Frenchman and a Belgian, revealed. It is enough to say that Sandbostel, although small as such German charnel houses went, contained over 8,000 souls in a state of the utmost degradation and filth. Typhus was rife, 400 famished political prisoners had been shot only on the previous day for raiding the food stores, and between sixty to eighty were dying on a daily average from wasting diseases.

These two prisoners had brought with them a note from the senior prisoner of war, a French Colonel, which was an urgent appeal for our immediate help. However, although the German guards of the camp had already fled, S.S. troops in a last vindictive gesture decided to occupy positions along the River Oste, which ran to within a quarter of a mile of the camp, and effectively barred further advance. As soon as "Wardforce" tried to penetrate through the woods north of Selsingen, they were brought to a halt for want of infantry.

It was not found possible for Division to allow the emissaries to return to Sandbostel, for had they been caught their fate might have been a terrible one. Moreover, another tantalizing aspect of the situation was that Guards Armoured Division as a whole was still involved with two aggressive formations to the west and not yet in a position to go for this diversionary objective, however compelling from the humanitarian point of view. But while the medical staff began to organize a relief column which could be rushed through at the first opportunity, a note of hope and encouragement was dropped over the camp by a Spitfire.

Meanwhile a gallant dash by Lieutenant Younghusband's Troop and the Support Troop commanded by Corporal-of-Horse Clark was very nearly successful in reaching the concentration camp on its own. On hearing this news, Major Ward dispatched Lieutenant Harris's Troop in support, for messages had stated that enemy had been cutting in behind Lieutenant Younghusband. This proved correct and two sharp engagements took place before twenty-four prisoners surrendered and Lieutenant Harris's Troop was able to move forward again. No sooner had he resumed his advance than Lieutenant Younghusband wirelessed that he was in serious trouble two kilometres farther on by the River Oste at a bridge where a half-company of S.S. had surrounded their vehicles. The enemy succeeded in knocking out a scout car and wounding Corporal Griffiths and Trooper Breakell, who lay helpless under fire. Corporal-of-Horse Clark, seeing their danger, crawled up to the scout car with two other troopers and managed to bring them back under cover, but was himself shot through the chest, dying within a few minutes. Both Troops were ordered back to harbour in the late evening, after having tried several more routes to Sandbostel. This proved to be the farthest advance attained until the 29th, because the Germans now brought up infantry and anti-tank guns to cover the crossing.

"A" Squadron had meanwhile been patrolling northwards from Brest and gathered in a good haul of prisoners at the cost of two casualties, Trooper Gilmore with a superficial scalp wound and Lieutenant Peake slightly wounded when his scout car blew up on a mine near Kakerbeek bridge, which had been destroyed during the night. Kakerbeek bridge, lying on "Wardforce's" supply route, was another example of the bridging problem facing the sappers, who not only had to keep communications going to the rear but were being constantly faced with urgent demands to help span craters and waterways at the front.

Captain Crewdson, the Technical Adjutant, arriving to investigate damage half an hour after Peake's car had gone up, promptly followed suit in the Scammel, victim of another set of Teller mines. He escaped with a bad shaking. When the sappers later arrived on the scene they cleared up seventeen other Teller mines from the bridge approaches alone, all set to explode by foot pressure. "I went hot and cold all over," said Lieutenant Peake, "when thinking how many times my men and I had walked up and down that stretch of road getting off the kit from the damaged car."

By last light, the bridge over the stream at Sassenholz had been repaired and "Wardforce" was in contact with the remainder of Guards Armoured Division by the shorter route.

★   ★   ★

Guards Armoured Division's objective now became the high ground five miles west of Zeven, with the armoured cars fanning out to the north and north-west towards Sandbostel; but after the narrow failure to reach the village on the 25th, it was to take a full-scale Battalion attack, supported by the guns of the Leicestershire Yeomanry, before Sandbostel finally fell on the 30th of April.

During these intervening days, and in spite of all that could be done, nobody got nearer than sighting distance of those bleak weather-beaten wooden huts with their fencing and barbed wire entanglements. Only the appalling stench of the camp could be smelt downwind as far back as Selsingen.

Yet those inmates who could still walk to the limits of the compound realized that their hour of deliverance was at hand and made frantic efforts to escape. Numbers succeeded, and, diving off into the surrounding countryside, lived there for days, tearing poultry and sheep apart like wild beasts to ease their craving for food. Many succumbed to the sudden overloading of their weakened stomachs.

When morning came on the 26th of April, it was found that the Grenadiers had lost two of their "Wardforce" tanks to bazookas fired at them during the night. There had been similar losses within other units, and it was suspected that villagers were sheltering German soldiers in their cellars during the daytime, who then emerged at night to bazooka vehicles. Reluctantly Major Ward decided that the inhabitants, who had already been warned, must be taught a salutary lesson. There was no means of finding out the guilty ones, and so two cottages in Seedorf had to be picked out at random. It was a scene which most had hoped the war might spare them. The weeping villagers were given time to fetch out their belongings, petrol and incendiary did the rest. The scorching flames of these two little cottages, the grief of their late occupants, and the looks on the faces of the rest of the inhabitants, haunted the rest of that otherwise beautiful spring day. Outside Seedorf windmill, and squatting cross-legged in the sun, sat a stocky little Mongolian—ex-inmate of Sandbostel Camp who had managed to escape. He spoke no known language and all that could be ascertained was that he came from "Kazak". With his blue vest and torn cotton trousers held up with string he sat smiling uncomprehendingly at the scene. On his lap was a plateful of bully beef which the men had given him, while his pockets bulged with stubbed cigarette ends. One was glad somehow not to be able to speak his language and have to explain the meaning of the burning cottages.

★　★　★

"B" Squadron now took over from "D" Squadron and for the next two days carried out patrols to the west. On the 26th of April crossings over the River Oste were reconnoitred on a broad front. There was much enemy mortaring and infiltrating batches of infantry requiring careful watching. On the high ground west of the river several German half-tracks were seen and engaged by the Heavy Troop at a range of two thousand yards, but results were difficult to observe. On one armoured car patrol, Lance-Corporal McCallum, in dismounting from his scout car to approach an enemy outpost on foot, was sniped at and killed.

Next morning, the 27th of April, when the "B" Squadron O.Ps. were reoccupied, Troops came under heavy and accurate shell fire and had to keep on the move continually. Lieutenant Beale thereupon took a small dismounted patrol to a village from where it was suspected the shelling was being directed. But he ran into a body of infantry lying in wait and was wounded in the hand, and Trooper Benjamin Osbourne was killed at the same time by a burst of machine-gun fire.

Later, Lieutenant Tabor was able to call down the fire of some medium guns on to the village and then lead another patrol which eventually recovered the body of Osbourne. He noted that the enemy had lost several of their men through the shelling and had retired westwards.

★   ★   ★

Meanwhile, as part of the drive towards Bremen from the east, 32nd Brigade (Scots-Welsh group) was launched in the direction of the high ground between Zeven and Tarmstedt. "C" Squadron joined the column at first light on the 26th and moved on through Wiersdorf. Five Sherman tanks belonging to the Welsh Guards were knocked out on mines in a short distance, and the entire village which lay west of Zeven was destroyed in the fighting.

The going was very slow and only two Troops were employed in reconnaissance at a time. The Panzer Grenadiers opposing the advance were well entrenched and could command the roads with their mortars and guns. At every turn, the Troops were baulked by demolitions and shelled into the bargain. Lieutenant Bruce-Lockhart's Troop was held up at Badenstedt by mines over a railway crossing and, having eventually removed these, found that a bridge farther on had been blown up. So it went on. But at last a Troop of Welsh Guards tanks working with the Scots Guards infantry found a way round and the advance was resumed. Ostertimke fell, but it was not until mid-morning on the 27th that Kirchtimke, the next village, was captured.

There was particular urgency that the advance in this sector should progress as fast as possible because on the morning of the 26th two blindfolded German officers had been escorted in to Brigade Headquarters, bringing with them terms of a local truce. One of them was the Commandant of a prisoner-of-war camp at Westertimke, which lay but two miles beyond Kirchtimke on the line of advance. Although the terms of the truce had to be refused, every effort was made to reach the place as quickly as possible, for it was now known that over 8,000 prisoners, including many Allied soldiers, seamen and airmen, were incarcerated there. However, in spite of all that could be done, it was not until the early hours of the 28th of April that the camp was finally liberated by the Welsh Guards, and in the course of the short advance many more vehicles were lost on mines. In the latter stages, due to the close nature of the fighting, "C" Squadron were ordered to withdraw and therefore suffered no casualties, but the Welsh Guards lost ten Cromwell tanks, all blown up on mines. The Germans were now making use of double-strength mines by the simple process of placing either two box or Teller mines on top of one another and burying them extra deeply. A twofold purpose was thus achieved. The resultant explosion was much more deadly and only after several vehicles had passed over the spot where a mine lay buried was there sufficient soil pressure to set off the trap. To complicate matters these mines were very difficult to detect, and for a time the sappers were puzzled by a series of mysterious explosions occurring over ground which they had previously declared clear. When the cause was eventually discovered, and a revised method of location adopted, it still took several hours before a stretch of road could be declared safe; and even then no guarantee could be given.

Although the Regiment took no part in the final stages of the liberation of Westertimke Camp, Captain Cooper, who had a relative imprisoned there and was to miss him by a few days, as he had already escaped, has left on record his impressions when forming part of the Divisional relief party.

"I left for Westertimke at 5.30 in the afternoon of the 27th, determined to get to the place as soon as possible. In my charge was a party of Naval and Air Force representatives, dozens of War Correspondents and the German commandant. It was mines all the way—we passed two half-tracks blown up, and no less than ten Welsh Guards tanks. The R.Es. were doing their best to clear the road ahead. The shelling was fairly severe and several 'Moaning Minnies' sited around the camp were paying us some considerable attention. In fact it was the worst shelling since Nijmegen days. Welsh and Scots casualties were coming back all the time. We pushed on slowly, leaving jeeps and other soft vehicles in the rear to come on later. At Kirchtimke found Colonel Jim Windsor Lewis in what remained of a house. He did not hope to reach the camp until early morning as the Germans were defending the high ground round it. An attack was about to go in that evening.

"By next morning [28th April] the camp was in our hands, and the shelling had stopped. The inmates, over 8,000 of them, Fleet Air Arm, R.A.F., some Irish Guards recently captured, Indians, Commandos, Merchant Navy, etc. etc. All mad with excitement as they had witnessed the battle from the camp. They were full of admiration for the way that our gunners had shelled the German guns and hit nobody in the camp. Had breakfast with dozens of overjoyed officers. Their food was good and they said that they had been well treated and would not have anything said against the German guard and commander—all except one officer, who was a brute of the worst type and had shot several of them earlier on. After breakfast, the White and Red Ensigns were run up, Red Cross food parcels distributed, and dozens of photographs taken. Left the camp at 3.30, by which time Generals Adair and Ritchie [Commanding 12 Corps] had arrived on the scene."

★ ★ ★

Major Collins, who was now the Staff Officer at Second Army Headquarters responsible for the immediate flying back to England and France of released prisoners, was also at Westertimke Camp that morning. He records that he had breakfast with Major Stewart Brown, the Welsh Guards Squadron Leader, and then was able to move into the camp. The chief difficulty from his point of view was to keep the released prisoners at the camp until R.A.S.C. transport could be shuttled forward from Army sources along mined roads to evacuate the prisoners to the nearest airfield. Everyone was naturally so impatient that it was not a question of laid-down drills but of quick improvisation. Staging camps, rations, clothes, etc., all had to be provided, but never, he records, was a job more worthwhile or work done more gratefully received than by the released prisoners.

★ ★ ★

By the 29th of April only two Squadrons remained in operation, "A" Squadron to the north-east beyond the railway line north of Brest and "D" Squadron, who had relieved "B" Squadron and were working north-west of Selsingen and towards Bevern and Bremervorde. Having been to the outskirts of Sandbostel previously, Lieutenant Harris's Troop ("D" Squadron) was ordered to co-operate with the Grenadiers, whose battle group of tanks and infantry was about to attack Sandbostel village and the enemy emplacements beyond.

The Troop reached its O.P. without incident, and while the men were cooking breakfasts they could observe clearly the Germans changing their sentries and the wretched inmates staggering about the camp. Two hours later a party of Grenadier officers arrived on the scene and after a brief consultation with Harris they retired to make their plan of attack.

Minutes later, Trooper White, a Daimler armoured car driver on look-out, saw a party of enemy patrolling stealthily towards him. He gave warning and it was then seen that two other parties were in the process of surrounding the Troop, one moving in from the left flank, the other on the right having already crossed the road behind the cars, and being in the course of erecting a road-block, while bazooka men had been posted clearly to await the main body of the Grenadiers. Harris wasted no time in ordering the Troop to turn about, and aiming all guns on to the road-block and ditches, the four vehicles charged down the partially completed obstruction at full speed.

Wisely, no halt was made to pick up wounded or prisoners. On hearing this news, the commander of the Grenadier group decided to move his force forward at once before the enemy could repeat their tactics and ambush the tanks. This time the Shermans took the lead and on approaching the battered road-block opened fire at some enemy stragglers and a party of Germans taking up a position by what looked like the beginning of another road-block. The Grenadiers' commander, who had at first been rather sceptical of Harris's estimate of enemy strength, now decided to share his O.P., from where he could watch the progress of his tanks. As time went on and the Shermans kept reporting rolling on without incident, he turned with a grin to the Troop Leader, saying, "How now for your estimate—my tanks are almost at the camp gates." The crack was not lost on Corporal-of-Horse Royston, who was standing next to his Troop Leader. "Had this been the signal for the enemy to act," he noted, "it could not have been better timed, for as I looked at Mr. Harris, the Grenadier Commander's wireless crackled out, 'Hullo Dog-Charlie-Fox--Sunray's leading tank shot up by enemy S.P. gun, strong infantry attack coming in from the left.' So," added Royston, "started his headache."

The Troop was then recalled for other duties, but returned next morning, 30th April. "We were anxious to see how our Grenadier friends had fared. They were now in a much worse plight than we had anticipated.

The enemy had blown up the bridge behind their King's Company, thus cutting them off completely, and an infantry battle was in progress between the S.S. and the Grenadier Guards. Many were battling to get back to our side of the bridge. Every five minutes or so two or three would come swimming or wading across the river as they fought a small rear-guard. The commander was a very worried person by now, but in spite of all his cares he very nicely came across to apologize to us for his unbelieving words of the previous day. I wish that there had been something that we armoured cars on the near side of the river could have done to help, but neither we nor the tanks could be of much use until the bridge was repaired."[1]

* * *

The Grenadiers were to be engaged in severe fighting throughout the morning of the 30th, and did not finally liberate Sandbostel until the evening of the same day, after what their history describes as being "of all the many battles which the Grenadier group fought in the campaign ... without doubt the most unorthodox." As the infantry companies worked their way under fire across the river, the inmates of Sandbostel stood on the roofs of the huts and cheered themselves hoarse. "The Grenadiers," concludes their historian, "might have been the players and the internees the spectators on Cup Final day at Wembley."

* * *

After the fall of Westertimke and Sandbostel, the Regiment's only remaining task was to continue patrolling northwards towards Bremervorde and north-east across the Harsefeld—Bremervorde railway line towards Stade. It proved a thankless job with mines and craters halting the Troops at every turn. Lieutenant Younghusband's Troop carried out an exacting patrol in which he lost a Daimler armoured car, Corporal-of-Horse Wilson being wounded by bazooka fragments. Bevern bridge was eventually reached and the Grenadiers then took over on the 30th of April.

* * *

On the right, "A" Squadron advanced to well beyond the railway line against scattered resistance which in no place was sufficient to hold up Troops. As at Westertimke, the greatest delay was caused by the enemy's widespread use of mines—in this case they were employing sea mines fused to permit of several vehicles passing over them before they blew up. On such a mine 1 H.C.R., who were now operating in the same area, lost an armoured car crew commanded by Lieutenant Tudsbery; nothing but a small part of a wheel spring, a shoulder star, and a pair of battledress trousers was ever found again, and these articles over a quarter of a mile from the scene of the explosion. Corporal-of-Horse Booth

---

1. 4 Troop, "D" Squadron, diary.

(2 H.C.R.), commanding Lieutenant Franklin's Troop at the time, the latter being on U.K. leave, saw the explosion from a few yards away. The 1 H.C.R. car "simply disappeared," leaving a huge crater which completely swallowed up one of the 2 H.C.R. scout cars which had to be extricated later by the Scammel.

★　★　★

On the 30th of April, Guards Armoured Division reverted to under command of 30 Corps and were relieved by 51st (Highland) Division, who assumed responsibility for Bremervorde. Guards Armoured Division then swung over to isolate Stade. Now only "A" Squadron remained out on patrol, and advanced almost to Düdenbüttel beyond the Stade—Bremervorde road before being ordered to halt. There was not an enemy soldier to be seen.

★　★　★

Regimental Headquarters and remaining Squadrons now moved into rest areas: Regimental Headquarters at Bargstedt, "B" Squadron at Ohrel, "C" Squadron in Sassenholz and "D" Squadron in Grafel. At Sassenholz "the photographs of Hitler in the village school were ceremoniously torn down, to the great amusement of two sweet little German girls with blonde pigtails who stood watching." (Captain G. D. Cooper's diary)

Firing gradually died down on all fronts and at last we felt that the end must be near. At ten thirty-five at night an "All Stations" call announced that Hitler had been reported dead and that Admiral Dönitz had taken over. The fight, so he said, would go on. But it is doubtful if more than a sprinkling of German soldiers ever heard the appeal, let alone were prepared to act on it.

Bremen had already fallen, Hamburg was to surrender on the 3rd of May, and the British then streamed across the Elbe. Wedged tightly into the Cuxhaven peninsula as a last refuge were large numbers of those German paratroops we had fought from the Rhine onwards. With them were stragglers and refugees from every satellite nation, renegade police, saboteurs, civilians, and displaced persons of all categories—everyone awaiting the cease fire. Almost it seemed without orders, a general halt along the line was taking place. German plenipotentiaries were already on their way to Field-Marshal Montgomery's tent on Luneburg Heath to surrender, and the news spread like wildfire.

Realizing that they were neither going to be shot nor tortured, the inhabitants began to emerge from their hide-outs with peace offerings. An unofficial market in cameras, butter, eggs, and cigarettes sprang up overnight. Burgomasters became the most harassed and sought-after people in Germany; not because of what might be their wartime guilt— we were not directly concerned with this aspect—but because of what they could produce in the way of peace-time commodities, which had suddenly become of paramount importance. Initially these burgomasters were a frightened and exceedingly cooperative bunch of officials, only too anxious to please. One even went so far as to test personally the strength of small bridges over which "D" Squadron were due to pass on the way to harbour, affixing to one doubtful structure the notice:

"ATTENTION! This bridge is not sure of itself—BY ORDER— The Lord Mayor."

★   ★   ★

At twenty minutes to three on the morning of the 5th of May 1945, the long-expected cease fire was announced. It was to take effect as from eight o'clock. Sticklers for correct military procedure looked at the pencilled signal and noted with academic interest that for the time being it was "exclusive Dunkirk," which still held out.

Regimental locations at the time of the cease fire were as follows:

Regimental Headquarters	Bargstedt
"A" Squadron	Essel
"B" Squadron	Essel
"C" Squadron	Harsefeld
"D" Squadron	Harsefeld
Headquarter Squadron	Aspe

There were no wild scenes of rejoicing, only an abiding sense of relief, and at the back of the mind the uneasy thought that there was still Japan to account for. The Divisional Gunners decided to fire a *feu de joie* at ten minutes to seven, which, as they had carefully selected a map square in the middle of the Elbe estuary and were good shots, seemed reasonable enough. But the full weight of the opening salvo was taken amidships by a six-thousand-ton German cargo vessel anchored in mid-stream on orders from the British Navy and certainly not expecting so rapid a renewal of hostilities.

"Within the Regiment," wrote Captain Creswell, the Adjutant, "mild celebrations were held in all the Messes."

Chapter VI

Last Days Before Disbandment

Cuxhaven—Visselhovede—Brühl

The enemy surrender on the British front included North and North-West Germany, Holland, Denmark, and the Frisian Islands. Pending the carrying out of Field-Marshal Montgomery's orders by the German commanders, all British units were to stand fast in their locations. There were good reasons for this because, due to the chaotic state of German communications, some time would elapse before orders could be transmitted down to lower formations. In addition, the German sappers could not yet declare roads to be free from mines.

Time passed quickly and pleasantly. Billets in the villages were generally clean and comfortable and the weather spring like. The cherry trees lining the cobbled country roads were in full blossom. Stade, the nearest town, had been some sort of central food depot and was found to be bulging with sugar and wine. Transport in the shape of captured cars, ranging from the Volkswagen to the 12-cylinder Mercedes, was abundant, and many took advantage of this fact to visit the ruins of Hamburg. Here Gestapo Headquarters yielded up an astonishing variety of pistols and revolvers—these "souvenirs" (particularly the 9-mm. Luger) were much in demand by American line of communication troops, and such a weapon brought out at the right time, with a bottle of whisky thrown in, would produce a jeep in exchange.

On the 7th of May the Regiment learnt that it was to move northwards into the surrendered area of the Cuxhaven peninsula, where, among other formations, the redoubtable 7th Parachute Division were waiting to be disarmed. There was doubt in some quarters as to how these tough fighters would react to this treatment, but all turned out well.

The sensation of motoring in carefree spirit through thousands of armed soldiers, who, it was estimated, outnumbered Guards Armoured Division troops by at least five to one, was an unusual experience. To begin with, the armoured column passed through a medley of disbanded and leaderless men looking for someone to whom they might hand over their personal weapons. Staff cars loaded with Wehrmacht and naval officers respectfully threaded their way through the regimental column, their occupants carefully scrutinizing each armoured car and its equipment as if in preparation for the next war.

Some of the civilians, curious to see the British for the first time, emerged from their cottages to stare, but the majority were quite apathetic and went about their business, thankful that for them at least the war had finished while they still had a roof over their heads.

On nearing the port of Cuxhaven it was noticeable that the German naval and military personnel looked far less tired and battle-weary than those farther inland. Officers and men saluted their conquerors with a punctiliousness that obviously came of strict orders to carry on with a dignified bearing in defeat, although the Women Naval Units, equivalent to the Wrens, and particularly well turned out, affected (at the outset) a total disregard of 2 H.C.R. by grimly staring to their front!

Regimental Headquarters and "A" and "D" Squadrons reached the port itself by seven o'clock in the evening. It was found to be practically undamaged and overflowing with soldiers and sailors, mostly line of communication troops and ratings. The civilians, in the course of being turned out of their houses to make way for the British, were in a state of tearful self-pity. "B" Squadron, under command of 32nd Brigade, had already branched off to Altonvalde, a few miles south, while "C" Squadron, under 5th Brigade, had dropped off *en route* in the area of Ottendorf.

There was one unusual incident. On leading his travel-stained Troop down to the docks, Lieutenant Buchanan-Jardine found himself confronted by an immaculately attired German naval commander who, with equally spotless crew lined up on parade, proceeded to surrender his destroyer with great ceremony. He explained with much heel clicking that, as fate had ordained that a German naval officer should be compelled to surrender to the British Army, it was at least some compensation that it should be to the Household Cavalry, and he was honoured to be their guest. Buchanan-Jardine, equal to the occasion, twirled his moustache in silence, but remained otherwise aloofly indifferent to the compliment.

Household Cavalrymen cooked their evening meals in the streets by the side of the cars. There was some time to wait for billets because the German Navy were still busy moving out of their barracks. Part of 7th Parachute Division Headquarters was likewise vacating earmarked billets, having been given three hours' grace to clear out, and German officers could be heard shouting at the top of their voices to their men and civilians alike, ordering them to sweep the dirt from corners before handing over. The state of the enemy transport was bad, and after the last German soldiers had completed their fatigues and packed up they drove off in enormous Diesel lorries which snorted and banged their way down the road with as many as four or five trailers hooked on behind.

Eventually all was quiet, and the fears expressed that the paratroopers, who were now assembling on the near-by aerodrome, might be troublesome proved groundless.

Walking towards the quayside in the cool of the evening, it was still difficult to realize that war in Europe was indeed over. A lighthouse was busy flashing messages across the estuary of the Elbe, and below, in the harbour with its crowded craft, German sailors were singing what were obviously rude Teutonic songs. Spotlights played on the bridges of the ships, while on decks below ratings would in turn get up to sing or strum on a guitar or banjo. As one passed they would spring smartly to attention and salute, and while the smoke from the funnels coiled up in the beams of the searchlights overhead there came the thought, "How long will these people remain oppressed (if at all) with a sense of total defeat?"

That night the complete surrender of Germany on all fronts was announced on the wireless, and the 8th of May (the morrow) declared to be the official VE Day.

At three in the afternoon Mr. Churchill confirmed the news of Germany's unconditional surrender. In characteristic fashion he ended his announcement, "Advance, Britannia! Long live the cause of Freedom! God Save The King! "

At nine o'clock in the evening His Majesty the King spoke to the 8th May British Empire from London, "our capital city, battered but never daunted or dismayed." Both broadcasts were heard by the entire Regiment.

With daily increasing numbers of officially inspired prophecies about what the "werewolves" were preparing for us in the way of reprisals, some asked themselves, "Will the Jerries really give us any trouble?" No one need have lost any sleep, and as far as 2 H.C.R. was concerned, the only proved case of sabotage arose when a small boy aged seven cut up a firehose outside the police station with a penknife given to him as a birthday present.

Those of the Wehrmacht still awaiting removal to prisoner-of-war camps watched the Regiment at its daily maintenance and frequently offered to help pull through the guns or else top up a back axle. When at last they departed to their barbed-wire encampments it was under the firm impression that they would be civilians again in six months or else fighting on the Allied side against Japan, and one Squadron office had already turned down five volunteers for the Household Cavalry.

THE END OF THE JOURNEY

Cuxhaven, 7th May 1945: Here on the water front took place, among many other curious incidents, the surrender of a German destroyer and its entire crew to Lieutenant Buchanan-Jardine's Troop of armoured cars.

"A" and "D" Squadrons were now billeted on the sea front, and with the weather continuing fine, many hours were spent sailing commandeered yachts and motorboats with varying degrees of skill, or else sunbathing on the sands. Because of "non-fraternization" orders, the Germans were forbidden to use the same beach as the Regiment. They duly removed themselves a few hundred yards to another site but continued to disport themselves with their sunburnt frauleins under the not entirely disinterested gaze of hundreds of Household Cavalrymen and Foot Guards. I had the uneasy feeling that the first post-war laugh was on the Germans.

★   ★   ★

Redisposition of British occupation forces on a broader front soon produced another change. On the 20th of May, when leave to the United Kingdom and Brussels was well under way, the Regiment moved southwards through Bremen and the American enclave to Visselhovede.[1] The destruction wreaked on Bremen by the Allied Air Forces had been terrible, all but the main street still being impassable to wheeled traffic. Half-way through the journey the Headquarter Squadron trailer loaded with wine from Stade ran into a tree, blocking the road with broken glass and causing a stream of champagne, burgundy and hock to flow into the gutter.

"Headquarter officers," wrote Groeninx van Zoelen, newly returned from hospital, "did not take this news very well."

Visselhovede was an attractive village lying east of and equidistant from Rotenburg and the ancient town of Verden. There were thousands of displaced persons and Russian ex-prisoners of war still at large in the district, many of the latter evincing marked disinclination to renew acquaintance with the "Worker's Paradise" farther east and preferring to live a semi-wild life in the woods. For this reason both Lieutenants Haskard and Eden were kept hard at work in a little draper's shop which served as Orderly Room, checking and issuing passes and calming hysterical hausfrauen whose farms were being raided nightly by hungry aliens in search of loot and provender.

"C" Squadron were also located in Visselhovede with R.H.Q., but the remaining Squadrons were billeted in outlying villages, "A" and "D" Squadrons in near-by Wittorf and "B" Squadron at Schitchen.

---

1. Although the port of Bremen was strictly speaking within the British zone of occupation, it had been allotted to the Americans as the port of supply for their northern group of armies.

Soon it was learnt that Guards Armoured Division, its task accomplished, was to be disbanded. The Foot Guards were returning to their true role of infantry, and of all the units forming the division only the 2nd Household Cavalry Regiment was to retain its armour. This was a sad parting, for although the Regiment had begun its campaign in North-West Europe under 8 Corps, most of its fighting had been done under command of Guards Armoured Division forming part of 30 Corps.

General Adair was determined that his division's farewell to armour should in every way be worthy of the occasion, and Rotenburg aerodrome was an obvious choice of site for the last parade. Field-Marshal Montgomery was to be present, as well as General Dempsey, the Army Commander, and his Corps Commanders, including, of course, "our own General Horrocks," as the *News Guardian* put it. Everyone prepared to bring the armoured cars taking part in the ceremony up to the highest standard of spit and polish.

The weather could not have behaved itself better on the chosen day, Saturday, the 9th of June, and as the Commander-in-Chief appeared on the saluting base, General Adair gave the general salute. Part of the Grenadiers and Coldstream were already parading as infantry, and their arms drill after a long sojourn in the world of armour was watched with critical but approving eyes.

Next, the Field-Marshal, escorted by Household Cavalry Troops, shining and glinting in the sun, drove slowly round the aerodrome in a half-track, inspecting the two hundred tanks of the division, some of which were Normandy veterans.

Then came a moving moment. At the order "Mount," the crews sprang up on to their tanks. The engines started with a thunderous roar, and a few seconds later the Shermans and Cromwells had started on their last drive. Travelling across the aerodrome at perfect spacing, they approached the Commander-in-Chief, swung their turrets towards him, the commanders saluting, and then almost before one had realized it the vehicles were away over the crest of a hill and out of sight. At the same moment, on the horizon but from the opposite side, five columns of Foot Guards came marching towards the saluting base to halt thirty yards in front of the stand. General Adair marched out and for the first time, spectators heard the new order, "Guards Division, 'Shun."

After "God Save the King," troops were ordered to concentrate round the saluting base. Field-Marshal Montgomery was in his best form. His amplifiers failed him, but he spoke in so clear and ringing a tone that they were hardly necessary.

"In this realm of armoured warfare," he said, "you have set a standard that will be difficult for those who follow after you to attain. You have achieved great results. When the Guards do a thing, they do it properly— they give a lead to everyone else. You will long be remembered for your prowess in armoured warfare. The return to the infantry is necessary for three reasons:

(1) His Majesty the King wishes it.
(2) Most, in fact probably all, senior officers in the Brigade of Guards think it is right.
(3) We need the Guards in the infantry."

Field-Marshal Montgomery concluded with a warm tribute to Guards Armoured Division's commander, Major-General Allan Adair.

"Throughout a very difficult time he never failed you. He never failed me. The Brigade of Guards were lucky to have available such a man as General Allan. I would like to congratulate him before you all."

★   ★   ★

Four days later, as part of yet another reshuffle of troops in the British zone of occupation, the 2nd Household Cavalry Regiment moved to Brühl, situated a few miles south of Cologne.[2] The long journey took two days and in its latter stages passed through part of the devastated Ruhr. The civilians in Wuppertal, which place had been bombed as heavily as most towns, stood amidst the rubble and desolation, and cheered themselves hoarse as the column sped through —a strange and, in a way, unnerving experience.

And now came to pass what many had feared would happen at the end of hostilities. Both 1 H.C.R. at Goslar in northern Germany and 2 H.C.R. in Brühl were to be re-formed and plans to this end were put afoot immediately. The Life Guards in both regiments were to form a new 1 H.C.R., under the command of Lieutenant-Colonel Wignall, and the Blues a new 2 H.C.R. under the command of Lieutenant-Colonel Abel Smith. This change, inevitable though it was, and entailing a partial return to peace-time basis, was a sad wrench for all, and especially so for the "amateurs" who had hoped that they might be permitted to spend their last days in khaki with their war-time comrades. Now for the first time in years, and in 2 H.C.R. in particular, Household Cavalrymen

---

2. Route was as follows: Visselhovede, Verden, Nienburg, Neustadt, Kamen, Unna, Wetter, Witten, Hasslinghausen, Wuppertal, Vohwinkel, Hilden, Leverkusen, Cologne, Brühl.

became aware of who was a Life Guard and who a Blue in the sense of realizing which friend would accompany him on the journey north and who would remain behind.

The change-over was scheduled to take place on the 17th of July and everyone settled down to make the most of the last few weeks together. Already the first release groups were being called up for demobilization. There were innumerable farewell parties. There were fishing expeditions to the River Ahr and the tributaries of the Moselle, and trips along the banks of the Rhine (the river was still in the main unnavigable because of sunken craft), past its romantic castles and the Lorelei and the vineyards of the Palatinate.

In spite of the heat, football still shared the honours with cricket, as recreation and inter-squadron games were played almost every day. Major Herbert was elected captain of the British Army riding team which competed in the International Tournament at Marseilles on the 3rd of July.

Lieutenant Hughes collected together the surviving members of the Städtisches Orchester Köln and organized a concert, which took place in the beautiful Bishop's Palace at Brühl. It was the first time that Mendelssohn had been played in public in Germany since Hitler's accession to power twelve years before.

Work, apart from the inevitable routine parades, consisted, as at Visselhovede, in the collection and checking of enemy ammunition dumps, and night patrols covering an extensive area, for there was still much civilian banditry. This lawlessness was inevitably, although not always accurately, put down to the displaced persons.

The Regiment became responsible for the control and supervision of a large Italian camp at Brauweiller, a task which engaged the attention of two or three subalterns at a time and half a dozen men. The acting commandant, Lieutenant the Hon. M. Eden, soon discovered that his duties amidst the good-natured but hot-blooded Latins made a startling change from normal R.H.Q. routine. He enjoyed himself enormously as "il feroce commandante." His departure, when the Regiment disbanded, was later followed by a scene which surely could only arise where Italians are concerned. The camp was notified that owing to unforeseen shortage of transport, repatriation would be delayed. Only those inmates whose homes lay north of a line of the River Po could be dealt with initially. The impatient and disappointed southerners immediately organized a demonstration which when it had reached fair proportions was swelled by the northerners afraid of missing the fun. The demonstrators, with no ill-feelings against the British, paraded outside the commandant's office to the shouts of "a morte Bruno Dina" (their own appointed liaison officer and who had nothing to do with the order in any case), and waving banners inscribed, "a basso il Po"!

Representative groups of Household Cavalrymen now started to drill daily for a parade due to take place in Brussels at the end of July, when Guards Armoured Division troops as liberators of the capital were to receive the numerous tokens of gratitude which the Belgian people were insisting on offering. But the parade did not take place until after the disbandment of 2 H.C.R., which day arrived all too soon.

Crews which had trained and campaigned together now prepared themselves to form new Troops, new Squadrons, and with regard to the Life Guards to move to new surroundings. The Blues part of 1 H.C.R., preceded by their advance party, descended upon and took over old billets. The Life Guards from 2 H.C.R. paraded for a last address by Colonel Abel Smith and then, with heavy hearts, bundled into lorries and headed south for Bonn, where they spent the night on the floors of gloomy bombed houses on the first stage of the northward journey to Goslar and Wolfenbüttel.[3]

By half past ten next morning (17th July) the last Life Guards lorry rumbled across the Rhine by way of the Cologne pontoon bridge and 2nd Household Cavalry Regiment had ceased to exist as an entity within the British Army.

Daimler Scout Car Driver

---

3. Part of the new I H.C.R. ("C" Squadron) was stationed in Wolfenbüttel, under command of Major Profumo. The remainder of Regiment at Goslar.

Epilogue

The Presentation of the Brussels Standards

On the 28th of July 1945, in glorious weather, the inhabitants of Brussels turned out to pay tribute to the men who formed part of Guards Armoured Division when their city had been liberated eleven months previously. Since that memorable day, numerous ties of affection had linked the people of Belgium with the men of the division and the demonstration which followed more than confirmed them.

Several hours before the parade was due to begin, large crowds had assembled along the route and especially around the shell of the Palais de Justice, where the main ceremony was to take place —the presentation of Standards to the 2nd Household Cavalry Regiment and the Grenadier, Coldstream, Irish and Welsh Guards.

On this day Guards Armoured Division was composed of representative parties from every regiment and numbered 3,500 strong. The parade formed up for the ceremony by the Royal Park. The Household Cavalry contingent, numbering 11 officers and 252 other ranks, was under the command of Major E. J. S. Ward. In addition there was a Household Cavalry dais party of 2 officers and 50 other ranks, commanded by Major R. Wrottesley, and a Colour party composed of Regimental Corporal-Major T. Poupart, Squadron Corporal-Major I. C. Berrisford, Corporal-of-Horse J. Neill, and Corporal-of-Horse J. Jenkins. Traditionally, in the Household Cavalry, the Standard is carried by the Regimental Corporal-Major.

At a quarter past one in the afternoon, Major-General Allan Adair, G.O.C. Guards Armoured Division, attended by a small group from each regiment and led by the Pipes of the Scots and Irish Guards and the Drums and Fifes of the Coldstream Guards, laid a wreath on the tomb of Belgium's Unknown Warrior. The Household Cavalry party for this ceremony was led by Lieutenants the Lord Burghersh and P. L. Peake. Then at two o'clock the entire Guards Armoured Division column, preceded by a massed band, marched down the Rue Royale and along the Rue de la Régence towards the Palais de Justice. Thronging the rows of steps leading up to this vast building were hundreds of spectators facing the parade ground, and in front of them was the dais where, among others, stood the Archbishop of Malines, Cardinal van Roey, the Grand Duke of Luxembourg, Lieutenant-General Sir Charles Loyd, G.O.C. London District, Brigadier N. W. Gwatkin and Lieutenant-Colonel H. Abel Smith. Lying on the drums in front of the dais were the Standards later to be presented.

The *News Guardian* reporting the ceremony wrote:

"A spontaneous burst of cheering and clapping marked the progress of the parade down the length of the Rue de la Régence; then the bands came into view, followed by the Household Cavalry contingent who led the parade. They were commanded by Major E. J. S. Ward, M.C. The remainder of the parade stretched far up the broad road, eight straight columns of marching men, with row upon row of arms swinging in time. The whole parade seemed to be split up with khaki and black blocks as the armoured and infantry units swung into view. At one time it seemed as if the parade would never fit in the tremendous open square, but with the precision that is attached to the Brigade of Guards the world over the parade was formed up facing the dais, with the Household Cavalry, being the senior regiment on parade, taking the right of the line.... Drawn up on the left of the Guards Division were men of the 1st Belgian Brigade, looking extremely smart in their battledress, and commanded by Major P. Poncelot.... They received a tremendous ovation from their countrymen as they marched to their allotted position on the parade ground."

The G.O.C. then took his place at the head of the parade and the division awaited the arrival of the principal guests. The trumpeters of the Household Cavalry sounded a fanfare, which signalled the arrival of the Burgomaster of Brussels (Monsieur M. J. van de Meulebroeck), followed shortly by the British Ambassador, Sir Hughe Knatchbull-Hugesson.

There followed a pause while the arrival of Her Majesty Queen Elizabeth of the Belgians was awaited. The Pipes of the Irish and Sots Guards played two marches, the sound of which had hardly died away before the Royal car appeared, and the Queen Mother alighted to the strains of the Belgian National Anthem.

The G.O.C. then gave the order "Troop", and the massed bands marched in slow time across the square to the martial melody of "Les Huguenots." Then, to the beat of rolling drums, the recipients of plaques came forward for the first presentations.

By this time, the Colour parties had formed up at the head of their respective regiments and marched forward to the dais, where the Burgomaster made the presentations in a graceful little speech in halting English. After which, to orders given by the G.O.C., the Colour parties "about turned" and faced the parade. "Present Arms" was given and the Belgian Anthem again played. Then, with their rifles at the slope once more, the Colour parties slow marched across the square and re-joined their regiments. Once more the order was given for the "Present," and the strains of "God Save the King" swelled across the parade ground.

Major-General Adair then took his place at the head of his old Guards Armoured Division for the last time and gave the order "Guards Division and Belgian Brigade will march past in quick time."

This order was taken up by Major Ward, commanding the Household Cavalry detachment, and the parade moved forward, wheeling to march past the saluting base and on through the crowded streets, where multitudes who had witnessed the ceremony raced through the back streets in an endeavour to see the marching men once again. In the Royal Park the G.O.C. took the salute and, after the Colours had been shown to the men, the division received the order "Dismiss" with ears still ringing with the cheers of the Brussels multitude.

In the evening an other ranks' dance was held at the 21 Club. The band of the Guards Division was in attendance, and Major-General Adair, accompanied by Mrs. Adair, visited the Club, and watched a cabaret. There was also an officers' dance and a Quartermaster's dinner.

On the following evening, the 29th, Colonel Abel Smith gave a cocktail party at the Metropole Hotel for Belgian friends and his past and present officers who had formed part of 2 H.C.R. Next day everyone departed on his respective way.

Thus for a fleeting forty-eight hours the Regiment within its own Division had lived again. Henceforth allegiance would belong either to the Life Guards or to the Blues. Yet the memories of those stirring war years, the entry into Brussels, and countless other episodes, would for all time remain an indissoluble bond in common. And even if in the passing of years the recollections of those exploits, now so vivid and seemingly unforgettable, fade slightly in detail, they will surely, as in every other British Regiment, be revived, possibly even slightly enhanced, at the Annual Reunion Dinner "for all who have served with 2 H.C.R."

Appendices

Appendix A

Prisoners-of-War Experiences

To avoid interrupting the continuity of the narrative, experiences of Household Cavalrymen captured by the enemy in battle have had to be omitted from the general narrative. Some of them are included here.

CORPORAL-OF-HORSE SOPER

Corporal-of-Horse Soper was taken prisoner during the fighting around St. Martin des Bésaces on the 31st of July, 1944, when Lieutenant Bethell's Troop was ambushed and incurred severe casualties (see page 111).

"Thinking that Mr. Bethell might still be in the car (which was burning fiercely by now), Corporal Sharp and myself dismounted and went towards the blazing car, but we found Mr. Bethell on the road alongside the vehicle. How he got out I do not know. He was in a bad way. His leg had been shot away from the knee and his foot was hanging on by two strings of flesh. His boot and sock had been blown away. We managed to get him back to my car and there I cut away the foot with a jack-knife and treated the wound as best I could. While we were attending to the wounded, the Germans moved in on us from all sides. They were infantry and must have got our cars with their PIATs. They treated us quite well. We moved through the German lines under escort until we came to a German field hospital. How Mr. Bethell, and Troopers Cable and Ramsey stuck this trip I do not know. They must have been in great pain from their wounds, for the roads were not too good, but they never murmured or complained. At the hospital our wounded were handed over to a German doctor who had once had a practice in London.

"We left Mr. Bethell and Troopers Allen and Cable at the hospital. The rest of us were taken in a lorry to a large house some miles away and it was dark when we arrived there. We were then given some black bread that I thought we should never be able to eat and then pushed into some outbuildings. We stumbled and fell over some bundles on the floor as there were no lights. When our eyes grew accustomed to the dark we were able to make out a number of other fellows there. They were all Americans, mostly air crews who had been shot down, and there were about fifty of them. We could not do anything so we lay down and went to sleep. In the morning the Germans gave us some food; then we were told to get ready to move out. At about 9.30 we were formed up and marched off under a strong guard. We must have marched about fifteen miles that day, and it was a boiling hot day. The French treated us very well, giving us food and wine as we passed through the villages. I shall never forget a Frenchwoman who brought us food. When the Germans were not looking she lifted up the apron she was wearing and underneath she had a British and American flag.

"In the evening we were put on some lorries and travelled on through the night till we came to a camp. It was still dark when we arrived. We were put into some huts. There were no lights, so we just lay on the floor again and waited for the morning. In the morning we discovered we were in a P.o.W. camp near Alencon.

"August 2nd. What a place! just a few old huts packed with men, mostly Americans. The food was terrible; I never realized that I could live on so little food. There were no cigarettes to be had, so those that wanted to smoke took some dried apple leaves from the trees in the camp and rolled them in some thin paper which the Germans were using for bandages. It's surprising what some people will do for a smoke. I have seen fellows smoke dried tea. Here the Troop was split; Corporal-of-Horse Watkins and myself were kept in the camp, while the rest were taken away.

"We stayed in this camp till August 11th. Our troops were advancing fast and the Germans had to move us. We were packed into gas-driven lorries and moved out. On the way we were strafed by our own planes. Out of the sun they came, two Mustangs. We never saw them till their cannons opened up. We lost twelve of our fellows and our lorry was put out of action. For the remainder of the journey we had to be towed, and our eyes were directed to the sky for the rest of the time.

"Towards the evening we arrived at our destination, Chartres, an old P.o.W. camp. There were all nationalities there. Here we had our first Red Cross parcel. What a godsend that was! It was just like receiving your first Christmas parcel, and everyone sat down on the straw in the big barn where we were and opened them to see the contents, like a Sunday-school treat and a lot of young children.

"August 12th, at 6a.m., we were once more ordered into the lorry. On through the countryside once more, but this time our destination Paris. The people cheered us as we passed through and some gave us the V sign. Here we were transferred from the lorries to railway box cars. We were packed into these cars just like cattle, only cattle get more room than we had; we were 42 in one car.

"August 15th. We started to move away from Paris. The train would not move very fast as the engines would not get up too much steam in case our fighters came over. The only food we had off the Germans was a loaf of bread and a tin of meat to last us three days, but the French Red Cross brought us food whenever we stopped. The railways were littered with the wrecks of trains that our fighters had shot up. It was not very pleasant for us to see these things; being locked up in the box cars, we could not have got out if our fighters had come over to strafe us. When we heard a plane overhead we wondered if our hour had come; it was a relief when one of the fellows reported it was a German plane.

"August 18th. We arrived at Chalons. This was a little better than the last camp; it was an old French barracks. Here we were interrogated. The Germans seemed to know more about us than we knew ourselves. They could even tell us our Colonel's name! We stayed here for three days, then once more into the box cars.

"Another few days and nights of sweating in these cars. The weather was very hot indeed, and this time we passed into Germany.

"August 27th. Arrived at Limburg. This was our first Stalag, 12A; it was a terrible place. The food was awful. We had a special treat twice a week—potatoes! For the rest of the week, red cabbage, boiled. Here we met Trooper Cable and Trooper Low, they had arrived a few days before us. We also met Corporal Collins from B Squadron. We were about a hundred British and 500 Americans in our compound. There were all nationalities in the camp.

"September 24th. We left Limburg. Believe me, we were not sorry to see the last of it. Into the box cars once more.

"September 29th. Arrived at Mulburg on the Elbe, Stalag 4B. This was much better. Things were organized here. They had a camp show every week and all sorts of sports. Corporal-of-Horse Watkins and myself were the only two of our Troop left here; the others were sent out on working parties.

"April 21st, 1945. The Germans informed us that the Russians were nearing the camp. At 7 a.m. the next morning they arrived. What a surprise we had! We expected to see a lot of tanks, but what we saw was a patrol of mounted cavalry on rough ponies just like our mountain ponies. Anyway we were free once more. From there we marched to Resa (?) where we stayed for about a week; then the Americans sent lorries for us and took us to Halle. From there we were flown back to England. After a few weeks' leave I rejoined the Regiment." *(Extract from letter.)*

LIEUTENANT SMALLWOOD

Lieutenant Smallwood was wounded and together with Corporal Noakes taken prisoner near Le Brien, Normandy on 3rd of August, 1944, when reconnoitring a route through the enemy lines for "D" Squadron (see page 144).

"… I went through Vire in a half-track and remember seeing Tigers there. I remember being in another half-track and fainting off and coming to. Every time I was conscious we seemed to be lost—the German commander would be looking at his map and asking the way and we kept on turning round. I suppose we were then working out of the Falaise Gap.

"I remember being in an Opel car with some Field Security bloke who spent two-thirds of the time halted, listening for aircraft. Eventually I ended up in a convent—I have a strong impression that it was at Chartres. I am quite likely wrong. I just have that impression. I was in a big hall on a rough bed. The place was absolutely full of beds—jammed in side by side and head to tail, with no space between—and was full of German and Allied wounded. My paper bandage was taken off and replaced by another one by a couple of nuns. I don't know how long I was there—possibly 72 hours. At the end of it I was able to hop about again and was feeling much better.

"From there I went in an open and antiquated old lorry to Paris. I was lying next to a poor devil of a Canadian in a bad way—the remainder of the load were German. It wasn't a pleasant ride. The sun was blazing down and the driver was very jittery about aircraft and carried out a modified sort of 'tactical driving' which wasn't very comfortable. The stretches between the villages weren't so bad. In the villages it was not nice. The cobbles jolted one badly and the Germans screamed and moaned and groaned without any restraint at all. (I wasn't too bad, but the Canadian was having hell and keeping dead quiet through it all.)

"The French leaned out of their upper windows and I don't want to be looked at again in that way. There was no exaggerated expression on their faces, but one didn't have to be very imaginative to see the hatred and triumph there. The knowledge that it was not directed against oneself did little to soften it. Sometimes they spat almost impersonally. It was a sort of vicious circle. The more the wounded screamed, the more intense was the French reaction; the windier the driver became, the faster he drove; the more the truck jolted, the more the wounded screamed. There was absolutely no doubt that, as far as France was concerned, the Germans were completely beaten.

"As the traffic increased on the outskirts of Paris you could see that ninety per cent. of the vehicles were plastered with Red Crosses; whether legitimate or not I don't know, but they were badly scared of the air. On the whole way back from Vire the only Military vehicles I saw were one Panther and three Mark IV tanks.

"In Paris I was taken straight to the hospital, where I met Tony Bethell. Somewhere on the way, in a lucid interval, I had come upon an officer from the Derbyshire Yeomanry (I keep on writing Derbyshire, but do I mean Northants?) You no doubt can check. They had just been next door to 'D' Squadron. He had told an alarming story of a night attack by paratroops which had completely cleaned them up and, he seemed to think, 'D' Squadron as well.[1] It was mainly on the strength of this, no doubt, that I gave Tony Bethell the impression that 'D' Squadron had been written off.

"... Tony Bethell has obviously given you the form as far as Paris, but as regards treatment and medical supplies I can add my further experiences. I went by train from Paris to Chalons-sur-Marne; 40 Hommes-8 Chevaux type of wagons, with the ventilators boarded up. I forget how many there were in a wagon. All of us wounded—food for three days—and again, I think, the journey took eight days. You may remember the heat; we normally only moved at night and were in the full sun in a siding by day. There was an American doctor on the train, but he was not allowed to visit us after the first two or three days. I won't go into details. We were attacked by aircraft once—the guards (their coach was marked P.o.W.; ours of course had no markings!) ran for it. When we moved off again the wagon I was in fell in half. I don't know what the casualties were, but we certainly seemed less crowded after that. Stephen Cody's driver, Austin, was in the same wagon, though I did not realize it until two years later.

"A German ambulance train stopped near us once and a Medical Officer came over. He took one smell inside our wagon and went away quickly; that was all the care we had.

"There was a bloody little N.C.O. in charge who sometimes explained with great care that he wasn't going to give us any water as he couldn't be sure that the water was pure and he wouldn't think of us losing our precious lives. When we were let out, as we were once a day, to relieve ourselves, the escort used to bring their girls along to have a look. Twenty-three and a half hours a day isn't so funny, especially when some of you have dysentery. When we detrained at Chalons some went to hospital,

---

1. Almost certainly Northants Yeomanry, who formed part of 11th Armoured Division. The officer referred to was probably the one who had spoken to me outside "D" Squadron's leaguer and whose tank we found burnt out next morning. *Author*

some to the ordinary P.o.W. camp. Those, like myself, whose wounds were covered by their clothes did not go to hospital.

"About forty-eight hours afterwards I finally passed out again—by this time one leg was infected right up to the groin. I think they were going to take it off in the end, but they pulled out and left the worse wounded behind for the Yanks to pick up.

"The treatment got steadily worse the farther back we went; there were what the troops called 'some proper bastards' behind Paris. Medical facilities were virtually non-existent. What there were were presumably reserved for their own people. A typical example of the set-up in the camp was the Red Cross parcel ramp. We never had any as the Germans said they weren't arriving. A talkative sentry complained that he wasn't getting a fair share of them as they were all going to the German officers' and N.C.Os.' messes!

"When they finally pulled out they put their surplus ammo in the building next to ours and set fire to it. We were locked in—charming chaps!" *(Extract from letter.)*

CORPORAL SCAMBLER

Corporal Scambler was captured on the River Maas in Holland, when his scout car was ambushed near St. Agatha on the 23rd of September, 1944. His driver, Trooper Smith, died of wounds in captivity in Germany two days later (see page 386).

"....... my car was bazooka-ed and my driver shot in the spine. The car crashed into a house and my machine gun was thereby smashed and we were unable to move or fire. At once 'Jerries' popped out plus a 'Schmeiser' automatic and said 'Komm aus! ' ... I helped Smith out and was bandaging his wounds when I was hauled away by the gang over the river to their Headquarters. Here I was questioned, searched and given a good meal much to my surprise. Then they told me I might be shot, and my feelings were anything but comfortable. However, I was spared and driven away to —— in Germany ... finally arriving in Emmerich by tram, where I was put in a company with eight Americans. I was hungry and we had a hunk of bread between us. Three Paratroopers arrived wounded; they were so wet we broke beds to make a fire and tried to sleep on hard boards with nothing to cover us. Two more arrived that night.

"September 24th. Hungry and stiff. Moved off in afternoon to train, place had been nicely bombed. Started off, made notes of towns as we passed. Reached Ruhr, Duisberg, and were given tea by Red Cross. Saw five Tigers on way to front. Reached Cologne that night and were given tea and soup—excellent!

"September 25th. Cadged tobacco and papers off guards for a smoke—guards were 'cushy'. Reached Koblenz and mucked around trying to find a train. Air raid siren sounded, everything stopped. Yanks bombed well through clouds. Went into cliff shelter, feeling was very high against us.

"September 26th. Reached Limburg, Stalag XIIA, at 9 p.m. in rain. Were searched. Garters, tin hat, and 1st field dressing taken from me. Put in large stone building, concrete floor. Ten minutes later 200 Paratroops (British) arrived all in the dark. They were starving, gave them the last of my bread. Slept huddled on floor—'orrible!

"September 27th. Deloused, given mess tins, weak soup at 2 p.m. and put in tents, approx. 500 per tent. Conditions disgusting. One blanket. Latrines disgusting, food wicked, all overcrowded. Very, very hungry, we searched the dustbins.

"October 7th. Got on train, 25 packed on one-third of truck, plus three guards.

"October 8th. Moved early morning after very cramped night.

"October 9th/10th/11th. Journeyed on, stopping and starting, changing engines and being locked in during air raids—had three raids. Saw Kassel well bombed. Bought bread for soap. Saw Berlin well bombed, too!

"October 12th. Reached Neubrandenburg early morning and marched to IIA very hungry and dirty. Deloused, waited for food. Soup at 2.30, lousy but had potatoes. Had one blanket only, one-sixth of loaf, small pat butter and bowl soup for day's rations. We were hungry and refused to work. Other nationalities very good to us, feeding and giving smokes. They had plenty—we were feeling pretty weak. Chased all over the shop by Jerry and bed-bugs. "October 30th. Jerry had heard that Protective Power people were coming, so they gave us pants and vests. This was stopped owing to lads pinching cotton, etc.[2]

"October 31st. First shower for three months, very inadequate, no towel or soap. Moved into next enclosure—not allowed out! Wired in!

"November 4th. Lads selling watches for bread like wildfire.

"November 6th. Debate: 'Is there a future for Airborne troops?' 'Yes.'

"November 11th. Parade, British only, for Armistice Day.

"November 16th. Went woodcutting in snow—found three mushrooms and some spuds. Driscoll put in '25' (prison) for being outside compound. . . .

---

2. The Germans feared cotton would be stolen for escape reasons. It was actually used, according to Scambler, for mending clothes. *Author*

"November 20th. Issued with half an American Red Cross parcel, plus 50 'sub' cigarettes (cigarettes hollow but for bare 1 inches). Everyone happy!

"December 2nd. New Camp Commandant!

"December 3rd. Rumours of parcels.

"December 4th. Parcels at station ... they are for Yanks. We are now trading their clothes for them at vast profits!

"December 22nd. Eleven degrees of frost. Deloused.

"December 25th (Christmas). Filthy soup. High spirits. Beer issue. Christmas tree brought in decorated by Paratroops.

"December 26th. Russians came in to entertain us for cigarettes. "December 31st. Half a Red Cross parcel. French and Serbs came in with band at midnight. Jerry came to search for extra blankets.

1945

"January 10th. Snowing hard.

"January 11th. Still snowing.

"January 16th. Very cold. Four lads escaped from 1st Kommando (work party). All recaptured. Yanks are spoiling all trading by giving ridiculous prices-40 cigarettes for one loaf!

"January 25th. Good news of Russian offensive. Four British arrive from Polish Stalag.

"January 27th. Hard snow, but Russians nearer.

"February 1st. Alert.

"February 2nd. Another air raid alert.

"February 3rd. Morning alert.

"February 6th. Lights and water cut down. Russians nearer.

"February 10th. Party sent to fetch in baled-out R.A.F. man.

"February 12th. Half Red Cross parcel. Sixty-two lads arrived in from Stalag 20A. Terrible tales of treatment and snow. Marched 500 kilometres, but grand spirits compared with Yanks. On 14th more lads— 90 of them in very bad shape.

"February 17th. One British died of dysentery and exposure.

"February 19th. Three hundred Yanks off to Hamburg.

"March 12th-26th. Bread cut to ten persons to a loaf, just a slice each. Two more British die, saw them in morgue, nothing more than skeletons and left uncovered.

"March 25th. Heard good news that Paratroop landings over Rhine successful.

"April 3rd-23rd. Had first football match, British v. Rest. Very good game, draw 2-2. Weather improves again, and the news is terrific.

President Roosevelt dies, and two minutes silence on the 13th. Raid alerts day and night now. Played French at football, and were leading 4-0 when Frenchman fouled. Fight started, and French African drew a knife!

"April 27th. Orders to move, but everyone refused. The Russians are near and we can hear the guns, saw flashes, etc., on hill of Stargardt.

"April 29th. Quite a bit of fun, patrol in camp, resistance at top of hill. Town shelled and on fire, also the submarine base. Jerries committing suicide everywhere. Looting rife everywhere.

"April 30th. Russians arrived. Showed us a film, fine propaganda for them! Two men filmed rushing to meet Russians, etc. Heard first news from B.B.C. today.

"KRIEG FERTIG" 0001 hrs. 7.5.45.

"Conditions in camp now getting worse, refugees are pouring in, and the place is filthy, sanitation now non-existent and food scarce. Met two Dutch officers and talk of modern war over tea and coffee! British and Dutch are very close to each other, and we are playing soccer, etc., with them.

"Many men have now started to make their way to our lines, and all have a good excuse to do so, the place stinks and there is a case of hydrophobia and one of typhoid. Am thinking of leaving on May 9th. A new order came Wednesday evening advising us all to stay put. That's O.K. for the Americans, who have moved to the Panzer barracks, good quarters, but we are still in our compound with the terrific stink! We were told that an officer to represent us was going to our lines to fetch help, but nothing has been done—we appear to be the forgotten '200.' An American Colonel has just arrived to help the Yanks.

"May 9th. Only Jim and I start out at 8.30 a.m. The others decided to stay put. We have heard all sorts of rumours and quite expect to be stopped. However, anywhere better than Stalag IIA.

"Started heavily laden to Stargardt, thence through country lanes to Karpin, where we stay the night in a deserted house. Hundreds of Poles and Russians are heading east, and we had a 4 km. lift by Russians, then met some French going in our direction. Reached Karpin, my feet absolutely burning, and spent twenty minutes breaking blisters!

"The village is full of Russians and Poles, and there are only a few women here. It's queer how these women all come to the British for protection. They have good reason to come, too. Rape, etc., is only too common, and they think we are above it.

"May 10th. Started late—feet bad from the start, so we rested pretty often. It was very hot ... met four Jerries, who took us on a very unnecessary 4 kms. detour—we were mad! ... by evening we were pleased to rest, feet very bad. Country around Wisemburg is beautiful, but destruction is everywhere—houses, horses, tanks and cars, etc.

"May 11th. Arose late. Apparently we need a permit. The Russians tried to grab me for work, but I managed to slip away and found that the others had been chased out with rifles. Had to run a good km. to catch them up. The state of the refugees, and especially the women and children, is awful. We are now under escort and in convoy. Hell! Travelled on north west and finished up at Russling for the night. Hope that we can get to our own lines somehow. Met two Yanks who joined us, they were chased out of their village by Russians.

"May 12th. Started early with another useless convoy. There are about 50 Jerries, too, who have to walk. Three were shot later by Russians, and we saw others who had been shot on the way. Our best horse was switched by the Russians during the night—nice people. However, the four of us were well received and fed by them tonight, which was pleasant surprise.

"May 13th. Another Jerry was shot for trying to dodge the column. A slow journey to P—, where we were well received. Taken to Kommandatur, where we met four more of our lads. Four Polish girls cooked for us, and we made a grand party."

Originally Scambler and his companions, who were making for Wittenberge on the Elbe, took the already described route through an area dotted with many lakes, large and small. Russians controlled the party for approximately half the journey to the Allied lines. They were at first very surly, but improved as they approached the British zone. On the last lap they transported the, by now, weary party by lorry, arriving eventually at a British hospital unit on Tuesday, 15th of May. Incidentally, records Scambler, he found himself quite incapable of dealing with the double rations now issued to him; his stomach had shrunk.

"Taken on the whole," he concludes, "there was nothing very exciting, but it was all very interesting now that I am home. There was plenty of bullying and threatening with rifles, however, and a few odd thumpings. The rations were poor, a slice of bread, a pint of so-called 'soup' and four potatoes a day. This apart from food we won or bartered for our own belongings. I am afraid that we cheated our American companions in certain ways, offering to exchange their clothes, etc., for one loaf, visiting other huts outside our compound, getting two or three loaves for the article and keeping the odd loaf ourselves!

"In conclusion, I almost forgot the wonderful show by the R.A.F. during the last days. At about 1p.m. one night there was an air raid warning. We heard the planes coming nearer and nearer, then our Stalag was lit up from end to end by two rows of flares. We thought we'd had it! Instead of bombs, however, cannisters, about 200 of them, were dropped by parachute from two or three Lancaster bombers. Every one fell into the camp, each containing medical equipment and a note of warning to the Germans: TOR THE BRITISH AND ALLIED PRISONERS OF WAR ONLY—HANDS OFF!' or words to that effect. The following day we sent all the parcels to the hospital for our men in there.

"It was truly a wonderful raid, though a pity it came so late—we had buried 30 of them already."

(Extracts from letters and diaries)

TROOPER PAYNE

Corporal Payne was one of the survivors in Lieutenant Allen's troop. He was taken prisoner on the Twenthe Canal near Enschede, Holland, on 1st of April, 1945 (see page 518).

"… On getting out of our car the Germans escorted us up the road to Lieutenant Allen. We never saw the other car or our troop again. We carried Lieutenant Allen up the road, a distance of 150 yards, to a house, where his wounds were dressed. Shortly afterwards we moved again, still carrying our Troop leader. We then awaited the arrival of a vehicle to act as ambulance to Lieutenant Allen from there to what we believed to be a hospital, and here we left him. We went on to another building and were asked for names and home addresses and, more particularly, the place from which we had started that morning. During this time the Germans seemed to be on edge and very uncertain as to the time it would take for our troops to arrive, as they were packing and clearing out generally. From here on the places we passed through and stayed at I cannot name at all, as we were driven by a high-ranking German officer in his car. He even offered us a drink of Schnapps. This night we spent in barracks, and the following morning we were paraded on the square with approximately seventy other British troops and all started to march for what seemed miles, only stopping in a building for a few hours before moving on again. Occasionally on our route we were joined by a few other prisoners of war. Next we were put on a train, where I cannot recall, but during the journey where the line ran parallel with the road we noticed German transport making its way in the opposite direction, and this convoy was attacked by Spitfires. The train immediately stopped and we had to disperse in the woods until the attack was over, a lot of damage having been done to the transport but none to the train. Here a Frenchman who was said to have escaped from several camps did not reboard the train and we believed he was shot. We continued our journey by train to what I think was Bremerhaven, and from here by barge, which was very cramped for room. After a day or two we arrived at PoW camp XB. Here we were given a Red Cross parcel each on arrival. The food provided at the camp was chiefly soup containing swede and potatoes, with a small portion of black bread and well-watered coffee. A few days later a number of political prisoners were brought in, all very emaciated. They were heavily guarded and later shot. Other prisoners told me they saw the bodies in a wagon ready to be taken away.

"We were liberated by the Grenadier Guards on, as far as I can remember, the 3rd of May, 1945." (*Extract from letter*)

SERGEANT WANSINK, DUTCH INTERPRETER

Sergeant Wansink, one of the Regiment's Dutch interpreters, was captured by the Germans north of Sittensen, in Germany, on 20th of April, 1945 (see page 550).

"… That night I spent in a cell under the town hall as it was too late to get me somewhere else. The next morning I was taken to a cell at the aerodrome barracks just outside the town, from which I concluded that they could not get me to a proper prisoners' camp. In this cell I spent about a week, sleeping on a low table without any blankets, eating some poor soup and black bread. But this did not matter, I only hoped that I could stay in Stade as it could not possibly last long before our troops should arrive. Anxiously I was waiting for the sound of our guns, but when I heard it at last in the distance, my hope disappeared, for I was told that the same night I would be taken somewhere else. It was already dark when I was put in an armoured car and we went to the harbour, where a boat should take us to the other side of the River Elbe. As you will see on the map, the Elbe north of Hamburg gets wider the more it reaches the sea, and it took quite a long time to get across. I was sitting on the deck, still wearing my tank suit, which was a good thing, too, as an icy wind was blowing across the water. Planes searching for targets were coming over, but our boat was not attacked. When we reached the other side at last I was taken to another barracks to spend the rest of the night in a cell

again. Next morning the journey was continued until we arrived at P——
aerodrome. In the guard-room I was registered and after that taken to a
kind of yard behind one of the buildings, where I found to my surprise
about twenty-five R.A.F. men.

"It did me a world of good that I could bring these men some news
about the advance of our troops, as they had no chance of getting
information whatsoever. The senior officer, a Squadron Leader shot
down in 1942, was in charge of all those Ps.o.W. and responsible for their
behaviour. I was the only British Army prisoner.

"The treatment was not bad. Our accommodation was in an attic
room. Here we received Red Cross parcels, so at last I got some good
food again.

"After a few days we were moved down to the ground floor and got
a separate room for each two of us. We even got sheets on our beds, so
there must have been something very much wrong! And indeed there
was something wrong, for the Germans, anyway. The Hamburg area
had unconditionally surrendered, and now it was just waiting for the
English troops to come up to occupy the district. That was the reason
why we received better treatment; the Germans were afraid for reprisals.
Of course, we were very anxious when the day of the liberation would
come. And yes, one afternoon we saw scout cars coming through the gate,
forming part of the 11th Hussars. We assisted our liberators in disarming
the German personnel and we were guarding the Germans now instead
of them guarding us. The pilots, mechanics, etc., organized their return
to England in concert with the English C.O. I arranged for re-joining
my Squadron again, went the next day to Hamburg to find the location
at Divisional H.Q., and arrived the same day at 'C' Squadron harbour.
Everyone was greatly surprised; of course, I had to tell the complete story,
and also learnt that on the day of the German attack when afterwards the
German patrol followed the track with our White scout car in front, the
officer in charge of our troop (Lieutenant Hodges) thought that I must
have been on the car and therefore delayed the attack until there was no
other choice. When the car was blown up everybody thought me killed,
and after a week missing I was reported to the Dutch H.Q. in London,
'Missing, presumably killed in action.'" (*Extract from letter*)

Appendix B

Decorations, Awards, Etc.

ORDER OF THE BRITISH EMPIRE
OFFICER

Lieutenant-Colonel W. M. Sale   R.H.G. (while serving with Guards Armoured Division H.Q.

DISTINGUISHED SERVICE ORDER

Lieutenant-Colonel H. Abel Smith   R.H.G.

MILITARY CROSS

Lieutenant A. R. J. Buchanan-Jardine	R.H.G.
Major D. Bowes Daly	R.H.G
Major A. W. P. P. Herbert	L.G.
Lieutenant T. F. J. Hanbury	L.G.
Lieutenant D. P. Powle	L.G.
Lieutenant D. J. St. M. Tabor	R.H.G.
Major E. J. S. Ward	R.H.G.
Captain. R. Wrottesley	R.H.G.
Lieutenant A. V. Young	R.H.G.
Lieutenant C. N. Younghusband	R.H.G.
Lieutenant Jonkheer F. W. E. Groeninx van Zoelen	R.H.G.

DISTINGUISHED CONDUCT MEDAL

Corporal-of-Horse W. L. Thompson   L.G.

MILITARY MEDAL

L./Corporal-of-Horse J. B. Brook	L.G.
Corporal G. Bland	R.H.G.
Corporal-of-Horse E. S. Johnson	R.H.G.
L./Corporal-of-Horse J. Loving	R.H.G.
Trooper L. W. Price	R.H.G.
Sergeant E. W. P. H. Proehl	Dutch Interpreter, attached 2 H.C.R.
L./Corporal-of-Horse C. A. Sparrow	R.H.G.

CROIX DE GUERRE WITH GILT STAR (FRANCE)

Captain C. H. Waterhouse   L.G.

CROIX DE GUERRE WITH BRONZE STAR (FRANCE)

Corporal-of-Horse J. Kendrick	L.G.

CHEVALIER OF ORDER OF LEOPOLD II WITH PALM (BELGIUM)

Major F. E. B. Wignall	L.G
Lieutenant N. D. Paget	R.H.G.

CROIX DE GUERRE, 1940, WITH PALM (BELGIUM)

Major F. E. B. Wignall	L.G
Lieutenant N. D. Paget	R.H.G.

SILVER STAR (UNITED STATES OF AMERICA)

Captain G. Balding	L.G.

MENTIONED IN DESPATCHES

Lieutenant F. B. Clarke	R.H.G.
Major A. J. R. Collins	R.H.G.
Captain D. Crewdson	R.H.G.
Captain R. L. G. Crosfield	L.G. (while serving with 1 H.C.R.)
Major A. W. P. P. Herbert	L.G. (while serving with 1 H.C.R.)
Lieutenant D. G. Hodges	L.G.
Lieutenant M. J. Hodgson	R.H.G.
Lieutenant C. A. Metcalfe	R.H.G.
Lieutenant R. M. A. Palmer	L.G.
Lieutenant-Colonel W. M. Sale	R.H.G. (while serving with 1 H.C.R.)
Captain J. H. D. Ward	R.H.G.
Captain C. H. Waterhouse	L.G.
Lieutenant F. R. B. Wordsworth	L.G.
L./Corporal-of-Horse W. F. Beaven	R.H.G.
Corporal-of-Horse W. A. Bradbury	L.G.
Corporal-of-Horse L. H. T. Brown	L.G.
Trooper D. J. Burt	R.H.G.
Corporal-of-Horse J. Jenkins	L.G.
Corporal-of-Horse J. Kendrick	L.G.
L./Corporal-of-Horse S. R. Wilson	L.G.

Appendix C

Orders of Battle

NORMANDY (13TH JULY, 1944)

Regimental Headquarters

Lieutenant-Colonel H. Abel Smith	Commanding Officer
Major Sir Peter Grant Lawson, Bart.	Second-in-Command
Captain A. J. R. Collins	Adjutant
Captain N. M. Ford	Liaison Officer
Lieutenant O. P. M. Haskard	Intelligence Officer
Lieutenant E. M. Turnbull	Signals Officer
Lieutenant N. A. Winterbottom	R.H.Q. Troop Leader
R.C.M. A. Jobson	Regimental Corporal-Major

Headquarter Squadron

Major B. R. Williams	Squadron Leader
Captain G. Balding	Second-in-Command
Captain D. Crewdson	Technical Adjutant
Surgeon-Captain R. U. F. Kynaston	Medical Officer
Lieutenant L. H. A. Smith	Transport Officer
Lieutenant C. E. Firth	Quartermaster
Captain T. R. Hudson (R.E.M.E.)	Light Aid Detachment
Captain S. F. Moore (R.A.Ch.D.)	Padre
R.Q.M.C. G. Goody	Regimental Quartermaster-Corporal
S.C.M. L. T. George	Squadron Corporal-Major
S.Q.M.C. J. Christie	Squadron Quartermaster-Corporal

Sabre Squadrons

"A" Squadron

Major D. Bowes Daly	Squadron Leader
Captain P. Profumo	Second-in-Command
Lieutenant R. G. Brayne-Nicholls	Rear Link Officer
Vacant (1 Troop)[1]	Reconnaissance Troop Leader
Lieutenant P. L. Peake (2 Troop)	Reconnaissance Troop Leader
Lieutenant F. G. Clarke (3 Troop)	Reconnaissance Troop Leader
Lieutenant M. Franklin (4 Troop)	Reconnaissance Troop Leader
Lieutenant H. R. Hoare (5 Troop)	Reconnaissance Troop Leader

---

1. Lieutenant J. N. Creswell's Troop was acting as Corps Commander's Protection Troop.

Lieutenant G. L. M. Murray	Reconnaissance Troop Leader
Lieutenant F. R. B. Wordsworth	Reconnaissance Troop Leader
Lieutenant J. Machin	Transport Officer
S.C.M. J. C. Berrisford	Squadron Corporal-Major
S.Q.M.C. Z. A. Goodacre Corporal	Squadron Quartermaster-

B Squadron

Major F. E. B. Wignall	Squadron Leader
Captain J. H. D. Ward	Second-in-Command
Lieutenant J. B. Seyfried	Rear Link Officer
Lieutenant S. J. Cody (1 Troop)	Reconnaissance Troop Leader
Lieutenant the Lord Burghersh (2 Troop)	Reconnaissance Troop Leader
Lieutenant D. J. St. M. Tabor (3 Troop)	Reconnaissance Troop Leader
Lieutenant M. G. Kavanagh (4 Troop	Reconnaissance Troop Leader
Lieutenant P. A. W. B. Everard (5 Troop)	Reconnaissance Troop Leader
Lieutenant A. C. N. Medlen	Heavy Troop Leader
Lieutenant R. M. A. Palmer	Support Troop Leader
Lieutenant R. F. Oliver	Transport Officer
S.C.M. T. Poupart	Squadron Corporal-Major
S.Q.M.C. W. J. Hills	Squadron Quartermaster- Corporal

"C" Squadron

Major A. W. P. P. Herbert	Squadron Leader
Captain T. Clyde	Second-in-Command
Lieutenant P. A. H. Armes	Rear Link Officer
Lieutenant D. B. Powle (1 Troop)	Reconnaissance Troop Leader
Lieutenant A. D. Potter (2 Troop)	Reconnaissance Troop Leader
Lieutenant R. M. Halliday (3 Troop)	Reconnaissance Troop Leader
Lieutenant D. A. Corbett (4 Troop)	Reconnaissance Troop Leader
Lieutenant C. Petherick (5 Troop)	Reconnaissance Troop Leader
Lieutenant B. M. van Cutsem	Heavy Troop Leader
Lieutenant H. S. Hopkinson	Support Troop Leader
Lieutenant J. A. R. Grice	Transport Officer
S.C.M. H. A. Turner	Squadron Corporal-Major
S.Q.M.C. R. R. Sargeant	Squadron Quartermaster- Corporal

"D" Squadron

Major E. J. S. Ward	Squadron Leader
Captain C. H. Waterhouse	Second-in-Command
Lieutenant R. P. G. Orde	Rear Link Officer
Lieutenant Jonkheer F. W. E. Groeninx van Zoelen (1 Troop)	Reconnaissance Troop Leader
Lieutenant A. R. J. Buchanan-Jardine (2 Troop)	Reconnaissance Troop Leader
Lieutenant T. F. J. Hanbury (3 Troop)	Reconnaissance Troop Leader
Lieutenant W. A. Ainsworth (4 Troop)	Reconnaissance Troop Leader
Lieutenant R. A. Bethell (5 Troop)	Reconnaissance Troop Leader

Vacant[2]	Heavy Troop Leader
Lieutenant C. A. Metcalfe	Support Troop Leader
Lieutenant A. F. A. Hughes	Transport Officer
S.C.M. A. H. Ring	Squadron Corporal-Major
S.Q.M.C. T. Ruff	Squadron Quartermaster-Corporal

General Note.—Captain H. C. L. Garnett was at the time A.D.C. to Lieutenant-General Sir Richard O'Connor, Commanding 8 Corps. He re-joined the Regiment after entry into Brussels, 5th September, 1944. Captains G. D. Cooper, R. Wrottesley and R. A. St. J. Mercer, and Lieutenants D. le Poer Trench, A. V. Young, B. C. Routledge, and I. M. Clark, landed in Normandy on 11th July with Corps Delivery Squadron. Lieutenants C. N. Younghusband and N. D. Paget were marking maps at 8 Corps Headquarters until 6th and 7th August respectively. Lieutenant the Hon. M. F. Eden re-joined the Regiment from sick leave on 10th August.

ENTRY INTO BRUSSELS (3RD SEPTEMBER, 1944)

Regimental Headquarters

Lieutenant-Colonel H. Abel Smith	Commanding Officer
Major Sir Peter Grant Lawson, Bart	Second-in-Command
Captain A. J. R. Collins	Adjutant
Captain N. M. Ford	Liaison Officer
Captain G. D. Cooper	Liaison Officer
Lieutenant N. A. Winterbottom	Liaison Officer
Lieutenant O. P. M. Haskard	Intelligence Officer
Lieutenant E. M. Turnbull	Signals Officer
Lieutenant the Hon. M. F. Eden	R.H.Q. Troop Leader
R.C.M. A. Jobson	Regimental Corporal-Major

Headquarter Squadron

Major B. R. Williams	Squadron Leader
Captain G. Balding	Second-in-Command
Captain D. Crewdson	Technical Adjutant
Surgeon-Captain R. U. F. Kynaston	Medical Officer
Captain C. E. Firth	Transport Officer
Lieutenant L. H. A. Smith	Quartermaster
Captain T. R. Hudson (R.E.M.E.)	Light Aid Detachment
Captain S. F. Moore (R.A.Ch.D.)	Padre
R.Q.M.C. G. Goody	Regimental Quartermaster-Corporal
S.C.M. L. T. George	Squadron Corporal-Major
S.Q.M.C. J. Christie	Squadron Quartermaster-Corporal

---

2. Lieutenant M. A. J. Smallwood did not rejoin "D" Squadron in Normandy until 19th July owing to breakdown of his car on journey to Gosport.

Sabre Squadrons

"A" Squadron

Major D. Bowes Daly	Squadron Leader
Captain P. Profumo	Second-in-Command
Lieutenant R. G. Brayne-Nicholls	Rear Link Officer
Lieutenant B. C. Routledge (1 Troop)	Reconnaissance Troop Leader
Lieutenant P. L. Peake (2 Troop)	Reconnaissance Troop Leader
Lieutenant F. G. Clarke (3 Troop)	Reconnaissance Troop Leader
Lieutenant M. Franklin (4 Troop)	Reconnaissance Troop Leader
Corporal-of-Horse A. E. Wileman (5 Troop)(acting)[3]	Reconnaissance Troop Leader
Lieutenant G. L. M. Murray	Heavy Troop Leader
Lieutenant F. R. B. Wordsworth	Support Troop Leader
Lieutenant J. Machin	Transport Officer
S.C.M. J. C. Berrisford	Squadron Corporal-Major
S.Q.M.C. Z. A. Goodacre	Squadron Quartermaster-Corporal

"B" Squadron

Major F. E. B. Wignall	Squadron Leader
Captain J. H. D. Ward	Second-in-Command
Lieutenant J. B. Seyfreid	Rear Link Officer
Lieutenant D. le Poer Trench (1 Troop)	Reconnaissance Troop Leader
Lieutenant W. G. Allen (2 Troop)	Reconnaissance Troop Leader
Lieutenant D. J. St. M. Tabor (3 Troop)	Reconnaissance Troop Leader
Lieutenant M. G. Kavanagh (4 Troop)	Reconnaissance Troop Leader
Lieutenant R. M. A. Palmer (5 Troop)	Reconnaissance Troop Leader
Lieutenant A. C. N. Medlen	Heavy Troop Leader
Lieutenant I. M. Corah	Support Troop Leader
Lieutenant R. F. Oliver	Transport Officer
S.C.M. T. Poupart	Squadron Corporal-Major
S.Q.M.C. W. J. Hills	Squadron Quartermaster-Corporal

"C" Squadron

Major A. W. P. P. Herbert	Squadron Leader
Captain T. Clyde	Second-in-Command
Lieutenant P. A. H. Armes	Rear Link Officer
Lieutenant N. D. Paget (1 Troop)[4]	Reconnaissance Troop Leaderder
Lieutenant A. V. Young (2 Troop)	Reconnaissance Troop Leader
Lieutenant R. M. Halliday (3 Troop)	Reconnaissance Troop Leader
Lieutenant D. A. Corbett (4 Troop)	Reconnaissance Troop Leader
Captain R. Wrottesley (5 Troop)	Reconnaissance Troop Leader
Lieutenant B. M. van Cutsem	Heavy Troop Leader
Lieutenant H. S. Hopkinson[5]	Support Troop Leader

---

3. Lieutenant H. R. Hoare had been wounded on the Somme three days' previously.

4. Wounded on 3rd September some hours before entering Brussels.

5. Took over Lieutenant Paget's Troop after latter had been wounded, but was himself captured by enemy when car knocked out in outskirts of Brussels, 3rd September.

Lieutenant J. A. R. Grice   Transport Officer
S.C.M. H. A. Turner   Squadron Corporal-Major
S.Q.M.C. R. R. Sargeant   Squadron Quartermaster-
                                              Corporal

"D" Squadron
Major E. J. S. Ward   Squadron Leader
Captain C. H. Waterhouse   Second-in-Command
Lieutenant R. P. G. Orde   Rear Link Officer
Lieutenant Jonkheer F. W. E. Groeninx van Zoelen
   (1 Troop)   Reconnaissance Troop Leader
Lieutenant A.R.J.J. Buchanan-Jardine (2 Troop)   Reconnaissance Troop Leader
Lieutenant T. F. J. Hanbury (3 Troop)   Reconnaissance Troop Leader
Lieutenant W. A. Ainsworth (4 Troop)   Reconnaissance Troop Leader
Lieutenant C. N. Younghusband (5 Troop)   Reconnaissance Troop Leader
Lieutenant I. M. Clark   Heavy Troop Leader
Lieutenant C. A. Metcalfe   Support Troop Leader
Lieutenant A. F. A. Hughes   Transport Officer
S.C.M. A. H. Ring   Squadron Corporal-Major
S.Q.M.C. T. Ruff   Squadron Quartermaster-
                                              Corporal

THE RHINE CROSSING (30TH MARCH, 1945)

Regimental Headquarters
Lieutenant-Colonel H. Abel Smith   Commanding Officer
Major E. J. S. Ward   Second-in-Command
Captain J. N. Creswell   Adjutant
Captain N. M. Ford   Liaison Officer
Captain R. Wrottesley   Liaison Officer
Lieutenant O. P. M. Haskard   Intelligence Officer
Lieutenant E. M. Turnbull   Signals Officer
Lieutenant N. A. Winterbottom   R.H.Q. Troop Leader
R.C.M. T. Poupart   Regimental Corporal-Major

Headquarter Squadron
Major B. R. Williams   Squadron Leader
Captain G. Balding   Second-in-Command
Captain D. Crewdson   Technical Adjutant
Surgeon-Captain R. U. F. Kynaston   Medical Officer
Captain C. E. Firth   Transport Officer
Lieutenant L. H. A. Smith   Quartermaster
Captain T. R. Hudson (R.E.M.E.)   Light Aid Detachment
Captain S. F. Moore (R.A.Ch.D.)   Padre
R.Q.M.C. G. Goody   Regimental Quartermaster-
                                              Corporal

S.C.M. H. A. Turner   Squadron Corporal-Major
S.Q.M.C. J. Christie   Squadron Quartermaster-
                                              Corporal

Sabre Squadrons

"A" Squadron

Major D. Bowes Daly	Squadron Leader
Captain R. W. Hall	Second-in-Command
Lieutenant R, G. Brayne-Nicholls	Rear Link Officer
Lieutenant B. C. Routledge (1 Troop)	Reconnaissance Troop Leader
Lieutenant P. L. Peake (2 Troop)	Reconnaissance Troop Leader
Lieutenant M. R. Redfern (3 Troop)	Reconnaissance Troop Leader
Lieutenant M. Franklin (4 Troop)	Reconnaissance Troop Leader
Lieutenant R. Murray (5 Troop)	Reconnaissance Troop Leader
Lieutenant G. L. M. Murray	Heavy Troop Leader
Lieutenant F. R. B. Wordsworth	Support Troop Leader
Lieutenant A. C. N. Medlen	Transport Officer
S.C.M. J. C. Berrisford	Squadron Corporal-Major
S.Q.M.C. Z. A. Goodacre	Squadron Quartermaster-Corporal

"B" Squadron

Major T. Clyde	Squadron Leader
Captain J. H. D. Ward	Second-in-Command
Lieutenant J. B. Seyfried	Rear Link Officer
Lieutenant D. le Poer Trench (1 Troop)	Reconnaissance Troop Leader
Lieutenant the Lord Burghersh (2 Troop)	Reconnaissance Troop Leader
Lieutenant D. J. St. M. Tabor (3 Troop)...	Reconnaissance Troop Leader
Lieutenant W. G. Allen (4 Troop)	Reconnaissance Troop Leader
Lieutenant R. M. A. Palmer (5 Troop)	Reconnaissance Troop Leader
Lieutenant R. E. O. Cavendish	Heavy Troop Leader
Lieutenant R.St.J. A. Beale	Support Troop Leader
Lieutenant R. F. Oliver	Transport Officer
S.C.M. T. Ruff	Squadron Corporal-Major
S.Q.M.C. W. J. Hills	Squadron Quartermaster-Corporal

"C" Squadron

Major A. W. P. P. Herbert	Squadron Leader
Captain G. D. Cooper	Second-in-Command
Lieutenant P. A. H. Armes	Rear Link Officer
Lieutenant D. H. Harvey-Williams (1 Troop)	Reconnaissance Troop Leader
Lieutenant A. V. Young (2 Troop)	Reconnaissance Troop Leader
Lieutenant L. Bruce-Lockhart (3 Troop)	Reconnaissance Troop Leader
Lieutenant D. G. Hodges (4 Troop)	Reconnaissance Troop Leader
Lieutenant F. G. Bailey (5 Troop)	Reconnaissance Troop Leader
Lieutenant D. A. Corbett	Heavy Troop Leader
Lieutenant H. S. Hopkinson	Support Troop Leader
Lieutenant W. B. Pooley	Transport Officer
S.C.M. L. T. George	Squadron Corporal-Major
S.Q.M.C. W. D. Flaxman	Squadron Quartermaster-Corporal

"D" Squadron

Major P. Profumo	Squadron Leader
Captain C. H. Waterhouse	Second-in-Command
Lieutenant R. P. G. Orde	Rear Link Officer
Lieutenant Jonkheer F. W. E. Groeninx van Zoelen (1 Troop)	Reconnaissance Troop Leader
Lieutenant A. R. J. Buchanan-Jardine (2 Troop)	Reconnaissance Troop Leader
Lieutenant T. F. J. Hanbury (3 Troop)	Reconnaissance Troop Leader
Lieutenant T. L. C. Harris (4 Troop)	Reconnaissance Troop Leader
Lieutenant C. N. Younghusband (5 Troop)	Reconnaissance Troop Leader
Lieutenant I. M. Clark	Heavy Troop Leader
Lieutenant C. A. Metcalfe.	Support Troop Leader
Lieutenant A. F. A. Hughes	Transport Officer
S.C.M. A. H. Ring	Squadron Corporal-Major
S.Q.M.C. J. H. Ledger	Squadron Quartermaster-Corporal

General Note. Lieutenant the Lord Rupert Nevill was posted to 2 H.C.R. on 24th January, 1945, but was A.D.C. to Lieutenant-General Sir Brian Horrocks, commanding 30 Corps, until the end of hostilities.

END OF HOSTILITIES (GERMANY, 8TH MAY, 1945)

Regimental Headquarters

Lieutenant-Colonel H. Abel Smith	Commanding Officer
Major E. J. Ward	Second-in-Command
Captain J. N. Cresswell	Adjutant
Captain N. M. Ford	Liaison Officer
Captain R. Wrottesley	Liaison Officer
Lieutenant O. P. M. Haskard	Intelligence Officer
Lieutenant E. M. Turnbull	Signals Officer
Lieutenant N. A. Winterbottom	R.H.Q. Troop Leader
R.C.M. T. Poupart	Regimental Corporal-Major

Headquarter Squadron

Major B. R. Williams	Squadron Leader
Captain G. Balding	Second-in-Command
Captain D. Crewdson	Technical Adjutant
Surgeon-Captain R. U. F. Kynaston	Medical Officer
Lieutenant C. E. Firth	Quartermaster
Captain T. R. Hudson (R.E.M.E.)	Light Aid Detachment
Captain S. F. Moore (R.A.Ch.D.)	Padre
R.Q.M.C. G. Goody	Regimental Quartermaster-Corporal
S.C.M. J. Jenkins	Squadron Corporal-Major
S.Q.M.C. J. Christie	Squadron Quartermaster-Corporal

Sabre Squadrons

"A" Squadron

Major D. Bowes Daly	Squadron Leader
Captain R. W. Hall	Second-in-Command
Lieutenant R. G. Brayne-Nicholls	Rear Link Officer
Lieutenant B. C. Routledge (1 Troop)	Reconnaissance Troop Leader
Lieutenant P. L. Peake (2 Troop)	Reconnaissance Troop Leader
Lieutenant M. R. Redfern (3 Troop)	Reconnaissance Troop Leader
Corporal-of-Horse A. C. Booth (acting) (4 Troop)[6]	Reconnaissance Troop Leader
Lieutenant R. Murray (5 Troop)	Reconnaissance Troop Leader
Lieutenant G. L. M. Murray	Heavy Troop Leader
Lieutenant F. R. B. Wordsworth	Support Troop Leader
Lieutenant A. C. N. Medlen	Transport Officer
S.C.M. J. C. Berrisford	Squadron Corporal-Major
S.Q.M.C. Z. A. Goodacre	Squadron Quartermaster-Corporal

"B" Squadron

Major T. Clyde	Squadron Leader
Captain J. H. D. Ward	Second-in-Command
Lieutenant J. B. Seyfreid	Rear Link Officer
Lieutenant D. le Poer Trench (1 Troop)	Reconnaissance Troop Leader
Lieutenant the Lord Burghersh (2 Troop)	Reconnaissance Troop Leader
Lieutenant D. J. St. M. Tabor (3 Troop)	Reconnaissance Troop Leader
Lieutenant T. D. Llewellyn (4 Troop)	Reconnaissance Troop Leader
Lieutenant R. M. A. Palmer (5 Troop)	Reconnaissance Troop Leader
Lieutenant R. E. O. Cavendish	Heavy Troop Leader
Lieutenant J. S. Porter[7]	Support Troop Leader
Lieutenant R. F. Oliver	Transport Officer
S.C.M. T. Ruff	Squadron Corporal-Major
S.Q.M.C. W. J. Hills	Squadron Quartermaster-Corporal

"C" Squadron

Major A. W. P. P. Herbert	Squadron Leader
Captain G. D. Cooper	Second-in-Command
Lieutenant P. A. H. Armes	Rear Link Officer
Vacant (1 Troop)[8]	Reconnaissance Troop Leader
Lieutenant W. B. Pooley (2 Troop)	Reconnaissance Troop Leader
Lieutenant L. Bruce-Lockhart (3 Troop)	Reconnaissance Troop Leader
Lieutenant D. G. Hodges (4 Troop)	Reconnaissance Troop Leader
Captain F. G. Bailey (5 Troop)	Reconnaissance Troop Leader
Lieutenant D. A. Corbett	Heavy Troop Leader
Lieutenant R. D. C. Bentley[9]	Support Troop Leader

---

6. Lieutenant M. Franklin was on U.K. leave.
7. Lieutenant R. St. J. A. Beale was wounded a few days before the "Cease Fire".
8. After Lieutenant Harvey-Williams was killed and Corporal-of-Horse Jarvis was wounded and taken prisoner, 1 Troop was not re-formed.
9. Lieutenant Hopkinson was wounded a few days before the "Cease Fire".

Lieutenant A. V. Young	Transport Officer
S.C.M. L. T. George	Squadron Corporal-Major
S.Q.M.C. P. Lacey	Squadron Quartermaster-Corporal

"D" Squadron

Major P. Profumo	Squadron Leader
Captain C. H. Waterhouse	Second-in-Command
Lieutenant R. P. G. Orde	Rear Link Officer
Vacant (1 Troop)[10]	Reconnaissance Troop Leader
Lieutenant A.R.J.J. Buchanan-Jardine (2 Troop)	Reconnaissance Troop Leader
Corporal-of-Horse W. L. Thompson (3 Troop)[11]	Reconnaissance Troop Leader
Lieutenant T. L. C. Harris (4 Troop)	Reconnaissance Troop Leader
Lieutenant C. N. Younghusband (5 Troop)	Reconnaissance Troop Leader
Lieutenant I. M. Clark	Heavy Troop Leader
Vacant[12]	Support Troop Leader
Vacant[13]	Transport Officer
S.C.M. A. H. Ring	Squadron Corporal-Major
S.Q.M.C. J. H. Ledger	Squadron Quartermaster-Corporal

---

10. Lieutenant A. B. Murray wounded in last few days of hostilities and Troop not re-formed because of other casualties.
11. Lieutenant T. F. J. Hanbury on U.K. sick leave.
12. Lieutenant C. A. Metcalfe absent sick and Corporal-of-Horse P. F. Clark killed in action a few days before "Cease fire."
13. Lieutenant A. F. A. Hughes on U.K. leave.

Appendix D

List of Fatal Casualties, Officers and Other Ranks

Including: killed in action, died of wounds, killed on active service, died on active service, died of wounds while prisoner of war

Name	Number	Regiment	Date of Death	Circumstances and Place
Ainsworth, Walton Arthur, Lieutenant		L.G.	6.12.44	Died in U.K. Troop Leader, "D" Squadron.
Alexander, George A., Second-Lieutenant		L.G.	7.11.43	Accidentally killed in jeep accident while on training. Troop Leader in "A" Squadron at Selby, Yorks.
Allenby, Frank Lawrence, Corporal-of-Horse	305020	R.H.G.	2.8.44	Killed in action, Normandy, in the village of Étouvy. Member of Lieutenant Metcalfe's Support Troop, "D" Squadron.
Ariss, Edward John George, Trooper	305650	R.H.G.	18.7.44	Died of wounds, Normandy, Biéville. Officer's servant to Captain Balding, Second-in-Command Headquarter Squadron.
Barnes, Kenneth, Lance-Corporal	305583	R.H.G.	19.7.44	Killed in action. Normandy, Orne bridgehead. Despatch rider in "A" Squadron.
Barnes, Robert Oxley, L./Corporal-of-Horse	305253	L.G.	15.6.44	Accidentally killed in motor-cycling accident on journey from Brighton to Worth. Despatch rider, R.H.Q
Brooks, David George, Trooper	5507543	L.G.	28.6.44	Died on active service, U.K.
Browning, Maurice, Trooper	295516	L.G.	18.8.44	Killed during enemy bombing raid, Trowbridge, Wiltshire. Member of "D" Squadron.

Name	Number	Regiment	Date of Death	Circumstances and Place
Checkley, Thomas Howard, Corporal	295764	L.G.	1.4.45	Killed in action, Holland, on outskirts of Enschede. Scout car commander in Lieutenant Murray's Troop, "D" Squadron.
Clark, Percy Frederick, Corporal-of-Horse	305249	R.H.G.	25.4.45	Killed in action, Germany, near Sandbostel Concentration Camp while acting in support of Lieutenant Younghusband's Troop, "D" Squadron. Member of Lieutenant Metcalfe's Support Troop
Dooley, Richard Henry, Lance-Corporal	328674	L.G.	18.7.44	Died of wounds sustained in Normandy, near Biéville. Member of "C" Squadron.
Drane, Reginald, Lance-Corporal	295435	L.G.	8.1.44	Accidentally killed by overturning armoured car near Pollington, Yorks, while on training. Member of "C" Squadron.
Dufferin and Ava, Captain, the Marquis of		R.H.G.	23.3.45	Killed in action, Burma, while serving with Field Broadcasting Unit.
Ebbage, Gordon Alfred, Trooper	305950	R.H.G.	1.9.44	Killed in action, Northern France, on outskirts of Albert. Gunner-operator in Lieutenant Tabor's Troop, "B" Squadron.
Evans, Lewis William, L./Corporal-of-Horse	2982567	L.G.	3.8.44	Died in Normandy of wounds sustained in action in Le Reculey during the afternoon of 1st August. Member of Lieutenant Wordsworth's Support Troop.
Gamble, Robert Stewart, Trooper	306204	R.H.G.	10.8.44	Died of wounds, Normandy, near le Pont de Vaudry. Member of Lieutenant Cody's Troop, "B" Squadron.
Gilmour, John McNichol, Trooper	2765141	L.G.	26.7.43	Died as the result of an accident at Billington Mortar Range, Pocklington, Yorks. Member of "D" Squadron.

Name	Number	Regiment	Date of Death	Circumstances and Place
Gower, Warwick David, Trooper	71374	L.G.	3.1.43	Killed as the result of accident to armoured car during training in U.K. near Trowbridge, Wiltshire. Member of "B" Squadron.
Graves, Stanley, Trooper	306031	R.H.G.	26.9.44	Killed in action, Holland, near Nijmegen bridge by a bomb. Member of "C" Squadron.
Greasley, Charles, Corporal	305532	R.H.G.	1.9.44	Killed in action, Northern France, near Albert. "B" Squadron electrician.
Hammond, Richard Edward, Trooper	305620	R.H.G.	14.10.42	Died in U.K. Range accident at Linney Head, Pembrokeshire. Member of Lieutenant Wood-Hill's Troop, "B" Squadron.
Hart, Henry Robert, Corporal	305970	R.H.G.	27.9.44	Killed in action, Holland, near Heesch cross-roads. Scout car commander in Lieutenant Jonkheer Groeninx van Zoelen's Troop, "D" Squadron.
Hay, Martin, Second-Lieutenant		L.G.	9.10.41	Died in U.K. Signals Officer.
Hibbert, Jack, Trooper	329215	L.G.	15.10.42	Accidentally killed as the result of armoured car overturning during training in U.K. near Trowbridge, Wiltshire. Member of "D" Squadron.
Higham, Clifford, Trooper	305635	R.H.G.	7.9.44	Killed in action, Belgium, on outskirts of Beeringen. Member of Lieutenant Corah's Support Troop, "B" Squadron.
Hill, Wilfred Owen, Trooper	329227	L.G.	14.8.44	Died in hospital, St. Martin des Bésaces, Normandy, as the result of wounds sustained south-east of Viessoix. "D" Squadron staff car driver, but was driving scout car at the time.

Name	Number	Regiment	Date of Death	Circumstances and Place
Hoddinott, Alistar Stuart, Corporal	305736	R.H.G.	30.8.44	Killed in action, Northern France, on outskirts of Auneuil near Beauvais. Scout car commander in Lieutenant Routledge's Troop, "A" Squadron.
Holmes, Reginald Alfred, Trooper	3299689	L.G.	22.9.44	Killed in action, Holland, Driel, opposite Arnhem. Scout car driver in Lieutenant Young's Troop, "C" Squadron.
Hopper, Herbert, Lance-Corporal	295477	L.G.	9.4.45	Killed in action, Germany, near Berge, east of the Dortmund-Ems canal. Scout car commander in "C" Squadron.
Housden, Raymond Thomas, Trooper	305554	R.H.G.	5.3.45	Died of wounds, Holland, in 6th Canadian C.C.S. as the result of injuries sustained in Nijmegen. Member of "B" Squadron.
Ives, Ernest Edward, Corporal-of-Horse	305554	R.H.G.	14.10.42	Died in U.K. Range accident at Linney Head, Pembrokeshire. Member of Lieutenant Wood-Hill's Troop, "B" Squadron.
Jackson, Philip Bennett, Driver	14538795	R.C. of Signals	18.7.44	Died of wounds, Normandy, Biéville
Jones, Albert Ernest, Trooper	306039	R.H.G.	12.8.44	Died of wounds, from injuries sustained in Normandy near Burcy. Member of "D" Squadron.
Joynt, Harold, Lance-Corporal	294907	L.G.	3.8.44	Died in York Military Hospital as the result of injuries sustained on 26th July in mortar range accident at Billington, near Pocklington. Member of "D" Squadron.
Kendall, Frank, Trooper	4206597	L.G.	25.2.43	Died in U.K., St. Martin's Hospital, Bath, Somerset, as the result of a training accident.

Name	Number	Regiment	Date of Death	Circumstances and Place
Knight, Percy Frank, Corporal-of-Horse	305068	R.H.G.	1.4.45	Killed in action, Holland, on Twenthe Canal west of Enschede. Member of Lieutenant Allen's Troop, "B" Squadron.
Knight, Raymond Frederick, Corporal	5958525	R.H.G.	1.5.45	Killed in Germany, east of Bremervorde, as the result of a battle accident. Member of Lieutenant Peake's Troop, "A" Squadron.
Lindsell, Francis William, Trooper	295420	L.G.	4.2.44	U.K. Killed in road accident on Goole to Snaith road, Yorkshire. Member of Headquarter Squadron.
Little, Malcolm A. A., Major		R.H.G.	5.10.44	Killed in action, Italy, while serving with 44 Recce Regiment.
Littler, Ronald George, Trooper	5733873	R.H.G.	30.8.44	Killed in action, Northern France, near Auneuil, Beauvais. Scout car driver in Lieutenant Routledge's Troop, "A" Squadron.
Mackay, Donald Percival, L./ Corporal-of-Horse	4916716	L.G.	26.7.43	Killed as the result of accident on mortar range, Billington, near Pocklington, Yorks. Member of "D" Squadron.
Maitland, Lord Ivor, Captain		R.H.G.	1943	Killed in action, Western Desert, serving with Lothians and Border Horse.
Marshall, James Frederick, Trooper	306345	R.H.G.	19.4.45	Killed in action, Germany, near Buxtehude. Gunner-operator in Lieutenant Harvey-William's Troop, "C" Squadron.
McCallum, James Yemon, Lance-Corporal	328826	R.H.G.	25.4.45	Killed in action, Germany, west of Selsingen. Member of "B" Squadron.
McGuiness, John, Trooper	305932	R.H.G.	21.7.44	Killed in action, Normandy, Orne bridgehead. Member of "A" Squadron.
Mellish-Smith, Ian Dare, Lance-Corporal	305879	R.H.G.	1.4.45	Killed in action, Holland, on Twenthe Canal west of Enschede. Member of Lieutenant Allen's Troop, "B" Squadron.

Name	Number	Regiment	Date of Death	Circumstances and Place
Myers, James Kenneth, Lance-Corporal	295116	L.G.	7.8.44	Killed in Scout car accident, Normandy, Carville, near Le Bény Bocage.
Needham, Reginald David, Trooper	296163	L.G.	31.12.44	Killed in battle accident, Belgium, near Couthuin above River Meuse. Member of "C" Squadron.
Ogbourn, Benjamin, Trooper	306290	R.H.G.	26.4.45	Killed in action, Germany, west of Selsingen. Member of Lieutenant Beale's Support Troop, "B" Squadron.
Pateman, James John, Trooper	305598	R.H.G.	21.4.43	Killed during training in motor-car accident near Aylsham, Norfolk. Member of "A" Squadron.
Plank, Alfred Ian, Trooper	296191	L.G.	1.4.45	Killed in action, Holland, outskirts of Enschede. Scout car driver m Lieutenant Murray'sTroop, "D" Squadron
Pope, Albert George, Trooper	295577	L.G.	24.4.42	Accidentally killed when scout car overturned, Bulford, Wiltshire. Member of "C" Squadron.
Porter, Eric Mayger, Corporal	305674	R.H.G.	11.5.43	Died in Norwich Hospital, Norfolk, as the result of gunshot wounds. Member of "D" Squadron.
Potter, Anthony David, Lieutenant		L.G.	18.7.44	Killed in action, Normandy, Biéville. Troop Leader, "C" Squadron.
Prangnell, Stanley Percival, Trooper	295449	L.G.	21.4.45	Killed in action, Germany, near Elsdorf. Armoured car driver in Lieutenant Murray's Troop, "D" Squadron.
Rawlence, Roger Donnithorns, Trooper	305676	R.H.G.	1.9.44	Killed in action, Northern France, outskirts of Albert. Armoured car driver, Lieutenant Tabor's Troop, "B" Squadron.

Name	Number	Regiment	Date of Death	Circumstances and Place
Read, Harold George Patrick, Trooper	4536039	L.G.	22.9.44	Killed in action, Holland, outskirts of Driel. Scout car driver, Lieutenant Hopkinson's Troop, "C" Squadron.
Reynolds, Francis Arthur, Corporal	305430	R.H.G.	21.7.44	Died of wounds, Normandy, Orne bridgehead. Member of "A" Squadron.
Reynolds, Geoffrey Arthur Cecil, L./ Corporal-of-Horse	295401	L.G.	4.8.44	Died in England as the result of wounds sustained in Normandy, Orne bridgehead, 18th July. Member of "C" Squadron.
Robins, William Douglas, Trooper	329259	L.G.	4.9.44	Killed in action. Belgium, Louvain. Driver of "D" Squadron TT Headquarters, armoured car (S.C.M. Ring's).
Rose, Eric Charles, Corporal	305973	R.H.G.	30.10.44	Killed in action, Holland, near Gennep bridge, River Maas. Scout car commander, Lieutenant Redfem's Troop, "A" Squadron.
Sargeant, Ralph Reginald, S.Q.M.C.	299518		26.9.44	Killed in action, Holland, Nijmegen. Member of "C" Squadron.
Senior, John, Trooper	305972	R.H.G.	30.10.44	Killed in action, Holland, near Gennep bridge, River Maas. Driver of Scout car in Lieutenant Redfern's Troop, "A" Squadron.
Smith, Albert Thomas, Trooper	305252	R.H.G.	25.9.44	Died in captivity in Germany as the result of wounds sustained in action in Holland, near St. Agatha's Monastery, on 23rd September. Scout car driver, Lieutenant Routledge's Troop.
Smith, George William, Corporal	305538	R.H.G.	1.9.44	Killed in action, Northern France, outskirts of Albert. Scout car commander, "B" Squadron.

Name	Number	Regiment	Date of Death	Circumstances and Place
Smith, John Richard, Corporal	328852	L.G.	19.9.44	Died in hospital, Belgium, as result of wounds sustained on 18th September east of Valkenswaard, Holland. Scout car commander, "C" Squadron.
Stainton, Edward Stewardson, Trooper	328634	R.H.G.	8.9.44	Killed as result of battle accident, Belgium, Albert Canal near Beeringen. Despatch rider in "A" Squadron.
Sutton, Raymond Dudley, Trooper	5347386	L.G.	2.8.44	Killed in action, Normandy, outskirts of Étouvy. Member of Lieutenant Metcalfe's Support Troop, "D" Squadron.
Taberner, Tom, Trooper	295690	L.G.	26.10.43	Killed as result of motor-cycle accident on training, Askham, Yorkshire. Member of "C" Squadron.
Taylor, Gordon, Lieutenant		Attached 2 H.C.R.	4.1.43	Killed as result of accident to armoured car while on training near Trowbridge, Wiltshire. "B" Squadron (attached).
Thomasson, George, Trooper	6103487	L.G.	10.9.44	Killed in action, Belgium, on Escaut Canal near Neerpelt. Member of Lieutenant Metcalfe's Support Troop, "D" Squadron.
Tudsbery, R. F. S., Lieutenant		R.H.G.	3.4.45	Killed in action, Germany. Serving with 1 H.C.R.
Walsh, Louis, Trooper	295493	L.G.	4.1.43	Killed as result of accident to armoured car on training, Trowbridge, Wiltshire. Member of "D" Squadron.
Weatherston, Harry Alexander, Trooper	305901	R.H.G.	6.7.42	Died as result of motor-cycling accident while on training, Trowbridge, Wiltshire. Member of "A" Squadron.
Wileman, Albert Eglon, Corporal-of-Horse	305037	R.H.G.	7.9.44	Killed in action, Belgium, near Beeringen bridge on Albert Canal. Member of Lieutenant Creswell's Troop, "A" Squadron.

Name	Number	Regiment	Date of Death	Circumstances and Place
Wilkinson, Jack, Trooper	4234286	L.G.	9.4.45	Killed in action, Germany, near Berge, east of the Dortmund—Ems Canal. Scout car driver in "C" Squadron.
Williams, David Hubert Harvey-, Lieutenant		R.H.G.	19.4.45	Killed in action, Germany, outskirts of Buxtehude. Troop Leader in "C" Squadron.
Wilmore, John Edgar, Trooper	328449	L.G.	2.10.44	Killed in action, Holland, Neerbosch. Driver to Captain Crewdson, Technical Adjutant. Member of Headquarter Squadron.

Appendix E

List of Wounded

Number	Name and Rank	Squadron	Date	Details
295360	Allen, B. M., Tpr.	D	31.7.44	Normandy, Forêt l'Évêque, south of St Martin des Bésaces
306006	Allen, L. E., Tpr.	—	—	—
	Allen, W. G., Lieut.	B	1.4.45	Holland on Twenthe Canal west of Enschede
601540	Andrew, F., L/C-of-H.	—	—	—
295354	Aspinall, J., Tpr.	D	7.4.45	Germany east of Lingen
305399	Austin, G. J., Tpr.	B	31.7.44	Normandy, south of St Martin des Bésaces
305906	Baird, J. S., Tpr.	A	21.7.44	Normandy, Orne bridgehead
305145	Barnes, H. R., Tpr.	—	—	—
329659	Bateman, E., Tpr.	D	24.2.45	Holland, Nijmegen
	Beale, R. A., Lieut.	B	26.4.45	Germany, west of Selsingen
305461	Beales. E. A., L/Cpl.	H.Q.	28.9.44	Holland, Nijmegen woods
328681	Beckett. G. H., Tpr.	C	21.4.45	Germany, near Rotenburg
5248696	Bennett, T. B., L/Cpl.	A	2.4.45	Holland, north of Enschede
	Bethell, R. A., Lieut.	D	31.7.44	Normandy Forêt l'Évêque, south of St Martin des Bésaces
305564	Bettam, S., Tpr.	—	—	—
327997	Birnie, W. D., Tpr.	C	13.4.45	Germany
295869	Bolden, A., Tpr.	B	1.9.44	Northern France, Albert
305527	Bradburn, J, L/Cpl.	B	27.10.44	Holland
295703	Braybrook, A. C., L/C-of-H.	—	—	—
296262	Breakell, B. N., Tpr.	D	25.4.45	Germany, near Sandbostel Concentration Camp
305217	Britton, D. A., Cpl.	B	17.9.44	Holland, on Belgian-Dutch frontier south of Valkenswaard

Number	Name and Rank	Squadron	Date	Details
295739	Brooks, R. T., Tpr.	C	24.2.45	Holland, Nijmegen
295036	Brown, L. H. J., C-of-H.	C	8.4.45	Germany, near Berge
295750	Bugby, C. R., L/C-of-H.	D	21.4.45	Germany, near Rotenburg
	Burghersh, the Lord, Lieut.	B	4.8.44	Normandy, near Burcy
295906	Cable, W. J., Tpr.	D	31.7.44	Normandy, Forêt l'Évêque, south of St Martin des Bésaces
295554	Camidge, J. W., L/Cpl.	C	31.3.45	Holland, near Ruurlo
295872	Carriage, W. G. P., Tpr.	R.H.Q.	8.4.45	Germany
305559	Champion, B, Tpr.	H.Q.	28.9.44	Holland, near Nijmegen
305981	Chennel, W. B., L/Cpl.	C	21.4.45	Germany, near Rotenburg
306087	Churchman, C. B.,. Tpr.	—	—	—
	Clark, I. M., Lieut.	D	13.8.44	Normandy, Burcy
3064894	Clark, W., Tpr.	H.Q.	19.9.44	Holland
294568	Clarke, K. W., C-of-H. (Twice)	D	1.8.44 2.9.44	Normandy, near Le Bény Bocage and Northern France in Henin-Liétard
305049	Coles, C. J., C-of-H.	A	—	—
295507	Conry-Candler, J. F., Tpr.	C	3.9.44	Belgium, Brussels outskirts
295074	Conway, F. F., L/Cpl.	D	12.8.44	Normandy, Vire-Vassy road
305838	Coots, D. C., Tpr.	B	—	Holland, near Nijmegen
305687	Coppage, G. R., Tpr.	A	1.8.44	Normandy, near Le Reculey crossroads
	Corah, I. M., Lieut.	B	7.9.44	Belgium, east of Beeringen bridge
14234875	Cottrell, A. J., Tpr.	A	21.7.44	Normandy, Orne bridgehead
305465	Court, S. H., Tpr.	A	25.10.44	Holland, near St Antonis
395345	Cridland, R. H., C-of-H.	C	—	—
305945	Cronin, E. R., Cpl.	B	25.10.44	Holland, banks of River Maas near Boxmeer
295112	Dennis, S. H., Tpr.	C	8.4.45	Germany
305845	Digges, A., Tpr.	A	4.4.45	Germany, near Bentheim
2330984	Emery, A. F., Cpl.	R.C. of S.	18.7.44	Normandy, Orne bridgehead
305090	Evans, T. G., Cpl.	A	3.9.44	Belgium, Brussels

Number	Name and Rank	Squadron	Date	Details
	Everard, P. A. W. B., Lieut.	B	4.8.44	Normandy, near Burcy
295441	Fentham, G. E., Tpr.		—	—
6098685	Flood, J., Tpr.	A	5.8.44	Normandy, outskirts of Vire
6099315	Foster,C. H., Tpr.	B	10.8.44	Normandy, outskirts of Vire
2764237	Frost,G. J., Tpr.	A	14.10.44	Holland
295770	Gilmore, A. J., Tpr.	A	24.4.45	Germany, near Brest
296083	Goff, A. G., Tpr.	H.Q.	28.9.44	Holland, Nijmegen
373985	Gorton, B. C., Cpl.	A	25.10.44	Holland, banks of Maas near St Antonis
329167	Green, S. A., Tpr.	D	4.8.44	Normandy, Near Le Bény Bocage
305851	Greenhill, G. R., Tpr.	A	3.9.44	Belgium, outskirts of Brussels
295763	Gregory, A., Tpr.	R.H.Q.	1.9.44	France, near Albert
328756	Griffiths, R. D., Cpl.	D	25.4.45	Germany, near Sandbostel Concentration Camp
4863740	Guy, J. R., L/Cpl.	H.Q.	18.7.44	Normandy, Orne bridgehead
305631	Harris, D. J., Tpr.	—	—	—
295673	Hastings, W. C., Tpr,	B	—	Holland
305728	Hawkins, W. T., Tpr.	—	—	—
305124	Hayward, D. E., C-of-H.	H.Q.	28.9.44	Holland, Nijmegen
305958	Henry, L. H. N., Tpr.	B	4.8.44	Normandy, near Burcy
295824	High, L. G., Tpr.	C	31.7.44	Normandy, near St Martin des Bésaces
295433	Hindle, J. S., Cpl.	C	24.2.45	Holland, Nijmegen
	Hoare, H. R., Lieut. (Twice)	A	5.8.44 31.8.44	Normandy, near Vire and approaches to River Somme, south of Amiens
6408745	Holder, L. T., Tpr.	A	5.8.44	Normandy, near Vire
3603574	Hollick, A. L., Tpr.	A	23.8.44	Normandy
305872	Hollick, C. J., Tpr.	A	10.8.44	Normandy
329618	Holman, R. F., Tpr. (Twice)	C	28.44 24.8.44	Normandy, near Le Bény Bocage and Beaumesnil north of L'Aigle
305144	Homer, H. H., Tpr.	H.Q.	28.9.44	Holland, Nijmegen
	Hopkinson H S, Lieut	C	23.4.45	Germany, near Selsingen
305554	Housden, R. T., Tpr.	B	31.7.44	Normandy, near St Martin des Bésaces

Number	Name and Rank	Squadron	Date	Details
305335	Hunt, J. W. T., Tpr.	B	1.9.44	Northern France, Albert
306305	Huxton, A., Tpr.	H.Q.	28.9.44	Holland, Nijmegen
306111	Illsley, W. G., Tpr.	—	—	—
2764741	Jameison, W, L/Cpl.	D	2.9.44	Northern France, in Henin-Liétard
328345	Jarvis, A, C-of-H.	C	19.4.45	Germany, near Buxtehude
306186	Jeffrey, W. F., Tpr.	—	—	—
304740	Johnson, E. S., C-of-H.	B	17.9.44	Holland, on Belgian Dutch frontier on way to Valkenswaard
306302	Joll, M. Y., Tpr.	C	3.4.45	Germany
305646	Jones, F. V., Tpr.	B	1.11.44	Holland, near River Maas
6349621	Jones, H. J., L/Cpl.	D	2.8.44	Normandy, south of Le Reculey
	Kavanagh. M. G., Lieut.	B	19.9.44	Holland, near Grave Bridge
305068	Knight, P. F., C-of-H.	B	2.8.44	Normandy, near Le Bény Bocage
823767	Lee, S. J., Tpr.	D	2.8.44	Normandy, south of Le Reculey
305472	Loving, J., L/C-of-H.	B	4.8.44	Normandy, near the Vire-Vassy road
305423	Marshall, J. F., Tpr.	A	28.4.45	Germany
295955	Martin, G. A., Tpr.	D	27.3.45	Germany, in Reichswald
305612	Martindale, W. H., Tpr.	H.Q.	28.9.44	Holland, Nijmegen
6291090	Minter, D. A., Tpr.	B	27.10.44	Holland
305922	Mitchell, R. M. ,Tpr.	B	3.9.44	Belgium, outskirts of Brussels
6102809	Moody, R. A., Cfm. (REME)	H.Q.	28.9.44	Holland, Nijmegen
14514378	Morton, D. F., Tpr.	B	31.7.44	Normandy, near St Martin des Bésaces and east of Vire-Caen road
304896	Munn, L. J., C-of-H. (Twice)	B	31.7.44 10.8.44	Normandy, near St Martin des Bésaces and east of Vire-Caen road
	Murray, A. B., Lieut.	D	21.4.45	Germany, near Elsdorf
	Murray, G. L. M., Lieut.	A	21.7.44	Normandy, Orne bridgehead
305766	Newman, C. R., Tpr.	B	1.9.44	Northern France, Albert
305934	O'Connor, J., Tpr.	—	—	—

Number	Name and Rank	Squadron	Date	Details
296132	Oakley, G. R., Tpr.	C	19.4.45	Germany, near Buxtehude
	Paget, N. D., Lieut.	C	3.9.44	Belgium, outskirts of Brussels
328299	Palmer, W. L., Cpl.	D	13.8.44	Normandy, east of Le Reculey
296196	Parker, D. W., Tpr.	R.H.Q.	4.4.45	Germany, near Lingen
	Peake, P. L., Lieut.	A	25.4.45	Germany, near Kakerbeek bridge
	Petherick, C., Lieut.	C	31.7.44	Normandy, near St Martin des Bésaces
3606152	Pickles, W., Tpr. (Twice)	A	3.9.44 2.4.45	Belgium, near Brussels and Holland north of Enschede
305735	Pitt, E. J., Tpr.	—	—	—
6292849	Playle, F. H., Tpr.	—	—	—
328582	Powell, W., Tpr.	D	21.4.45	Germany, near Elsdorf
	Powle, D. B., Lieut.	C	2.8.44	Normandy, near Burcy
5780082	Price, O. M., Tpr.	B	16.8.44	Normandy, near Tinchebray
	Proehl, E. W. P. H., Sergt.	Dutch Interpreter in A Squadron	4.4.45	Germany, near Bentheim
4980935	Riley, G. W., Cpl.	B	30.3.45	Germany, crossing River Rhine
295721	Rogers, H. W., Cpl.	—	—	—
328525	Rose, C. H., Cpl.	D	21.4.45	Germany, near Rotenburg
305454	Rudd, C. R., Cpl.	B	7.9.44	Belgium, east of Beeringen bridge
296031	Scaife, J., Tpr.	D	24.2.45	Holland, Nijmegen
295582	Shanley, E. J., Tpr.	C	24.8.44	Normandy, near Beaumesnil
5958753	Sharpe, E., Tpr.	B	24.2.45	Holland, Nijmegen
305462	Shaw, E. J., Tpr.	R.H.Q.	21.7.44	Normandy, Orne bridgehead
304756	Simpson, B., C-of-H.	H.Q.	28.9.44	Holland, Nijmegen
	Smallwood, M. A. J., Lieut.	D	4.8.44	Normandy, near le Brien
295374	Smith, F. C., L/C-of-H.	—	—	—
296158	Sparks, W. J., Tpr.	B	24.2.45	Holland, Nijmegen

Number	Name and Rank	Squadron	Date	Details
295891	Stevenson, J., Tpr.	C	18.8.44	Normandy
1945528	Styles, W. G., L/Cpl.	D	21.3.45	Germany, near Elsdorf
	Tabor, D. J. St.M., Lieut.	B	21.9.44	Holland, near Wamel
294997	Thompson, W. L., C-of H.	D	21.9.44	Holland, north of Nijmegen bridge
305556	Trinder, J., Tpr.	—	—	—
295893	Tutt, G. R., Cpl.	B	16.8.44	Normandy, near Tinchebray
305688	Tyrer, G. W., Tpr.	B	31.7.44	Normandy, near St Martin des Bésaces
45130	Ward, E. J. S., Major	D	14.8.44	Normandy, near Viessoix
306271	Way, J. L., Tpr.	C	18.9.44	Holland, east of Valkenswaard
2991561	Wilson, R., Tpr.	—	—	—
295569	Wilson, S. R., L/C-of-H.	D	28.4.45	Germany, near Bremervorde
295390	Workman, R. A., Tpr.	D	24.2.45	Holland, Nijmegen
295075	Wright, W., L/Cpl.	D	7.4.45	Germany, east of Dortmund–Ems canal
328586	Young, W., Tpr.	D	13.8.44	Normandy, east of Le Reculey
	Zoelen, Jonkheer, F. W. E. Groeninx van, Lieut.	D	30.3.45	Holland, just after crossing Rhine

Appendix F

Prisoners of War

Number	Name and Rank	Sqn	Date	Details
	Allen, Lieut. W. G.	B	1.4.45	Holland, on Twenthe canal
295360	Allen, Tpr. B. M.	D	31.7.44	Normandy, Forêt l'Évêque
	Austin, Tpr. (Lieut. Cody's Troop)	B	31.7.44	Normandy, Forêt l'Évêque
305638	Bambrough, Tpr. J.	B	31.7.44	Normandy, near St. Martin des Bésaces
	Bethell, Lieut. R. A.	D	31.7.44	Normandy, Forêt l'Évêque
305659	Blowers, Cpl. A. J.	B	31.7.44	Normandy, near St. Martin des Bésaces
295906	Cable, Tpr. W. J	B	31.7.44	Normandy, Forêt l'Évêque
	Cody, Lieut. S. J.	B	15.8.44	Near Conde-sur-Noireau, Normandy
305545	Collins, Cpl. N. W.	B	15.7.44	Near Conde-sur-Noireau, Normandy
305732	Ford-Nairn, Cpl. J. C.	A	10.9.44	Belgium near Escaut canal
295947	Gooch, Tpr. P. D.	D	31.7.44	Normandy, Forêt l'Évêque
328345	Jarvis, C.-of-H. A.	C	19.4.45	Germany near Buxtehude
4695984	Jones, Tpr. A.	C	19.4.45	Germany near Buxtehude
3062143	Lothian, Tpr. T. L.	D	4.9.44	Belgium, Louvain
306412	Low, Tpr. A.	D	31.7.44	Normandy, Forêt l'Évêque
305415	McNinley, Tpr. T.	B	1.4.45	Holland, on Twenthe canal
305991	Mitchell, Tpr. R. C.	C	19.4.45	Germany near Buxtehude
294892	Noakes, Cpl. J. P.	D	4.8.44	Normandy near le Brien
296132	Oakley, Tpr. G.R	C	19.4.45	Germany near Buxtehude
305588	Payne, Cpl. J. R.	B	1.4.45	Holland, on Twenthe canal
295905	Ramsey, Tpr. M	D	31.7.44	Normandy, Forêt l'Évêque
	Scambler, Cpl. K. C.	A	23.9.44	Holland on Maas
295583	Sharpe, Cpl. F. C.	D	31.7.44	Normandy, Forêt l'Évêque
	Smallwood, Lieut. M. A. J.	D	4.8.44	Normandy near le Brien

Number	Name and Rank	Sqn	Date	Details
305252	Smith, Tpr. A. T.	A	23.9.44	Holland on Maas (died from wounds in captivity)
305457	Soper, C.-of-H. C. K.	D	31.7.44	Normandy, Forêt l'Évêque
	Wansink, Sergt. J. A. M. (Interpreter)	C	20.4.45	Germany near Sittensen
295339	Watkins, L./C.-of-H. A. E.	D	31.7.44	Normandy, Forêt l'Évêque
	Williams, Tpr. (Lieut. Peake's Troop)	A	10.9.44	Belgium, near Escaut canal

Index

Names already appearing in their alphabetical order under Appendices "B," "C," "D" and "E" are not included in this Index. Individual Troops and Squadrons will be found under the names of the respective Troop or Squadron Leaders.

NORTH

POCKLINGTON
SELBY
POLLINGTON
HULL
R.Humber

WOLTERTON
NORWICH

E N G L A N D

BRISTOL
LONDON
WINDSOR
R.Thames
TROWBRIDGE
BULFORD
PADDOCKHURST WOODS
CALAIS
GOSPORT
PORTSMOUTH
BRIGHTON

E N G L I S H   C H A N N E L

CHERBOURG
R.Somme
ALBERT
CORBIE
AMIENS

GRAYE-SUR-MER
AMBLIE
BRÉCY
BAYEUX
LE HAVRE
BEAUVAIS
ELBEUF
CAEN
CAGNY
VERNON
R.Seine
LE BENY BOCAGE
VIRE
ARGENTAN
L'AIGLE
PARIS

F   R   A